希腊罗马神话文学选读

李明强 编注

Compiled by Li Mingqiang

Composita a Li Mingqiang

重庆大学出版社

内容提要

本书由"希腊罗马神话故事选读"和"希腊罗马神话文学作品选读"两大部分及注释构成,书后附有专有名词读音表和主要参考书目。第 1 部分"希腊罗马神话故事选读"共 33 章,选自布尔芬奇的《神话时代》,包括希腊罗马神话中的主要故事。第 2 部分"希腊罗马神话文学作品选读"包含 28 个选段,是从最具代表性的 7 位古希腊和古罗马作家的 9 部作品中选取出来的,是对本书第 1 部分的有力补充。本书对选文中的专有名词、语言难点、地理知识、历史知识、天文知识等阅读难点作了详尽的注释,填补了学习者在阅读英文版希腊罗马神话文学时的知识空白,降低了学习者学习这门课程的难度。

图书在版编目(CIP)数据

希腊罗马神话文学选读:英文/李明强编注.--
重庆:重庆大学出版社,2019.10
ISBN 978-7-5689-1665-3

Ⅰ.①希… Ⅱ.①李… Ⅲ.①英语—语言读物②神话
—作品集—古希腊③神话—作品集—古罗马 Ⅳ.
①H319.4:Ⅰ

中国版本图书馆 CIP 数据核字(2019)第 140923 号

希腊罗马神话文学选读
XILA LUOMA SHENHUA WENXUE XUANDU

李明强 编注
责任编辑:杨 琪 版式设计:杨 琪
责任校对:关德强 责任印制:赵 晟

*

重庆大学出版社出版发行
出版人:饶帮华
社址:重庆市沙坪坝区大学城西路 21 号
邮编:401331
电话:(023)88617190 88617185(中小学)
传真:(023)88617186 88617166
网址:http://www.cqup.com.cn
邮箱:fxk@cqup.com.cn(营销中心)
全国新华书店经销
重庆升光电力印务有限公司印刷

*

开本:787mm×1092mm 1/16 印张:24.25 字数:866 千
2019 年 10 月第 1 版 2019 年 10 月第 1 次印刷
ISBN 978-7-5689-1665-3 定价:79.00 元

序言 PREFACE

翻开西方语言的词典，我们可以看到不少词汇和成语都与希腊罗马神话有关。"地图册"一词在英语中是 atlas，在法语中是 atlas，在西班牙语中是 atlas，在俄语中是 атлас，在德语中是 Atlas，这是因为希腊神话人物阿特拉斯（Atlas）被印在德国地图学家和地理学家吉拉都斯·麦卡托尔（Gerardus Mercator）1595 年出版的地图册的标题页上。欧洲（欧罗巴洲）在拉丁语中叫 Europa，在英语中叫 Europe，在法语中叫 Europe，在西班牙语中叫 Europa，在俄语中叫 Европа，因为地中海东岸古国腓尼基（Phoenicia）的公主 Europa（Εὐρώπη）被变为公牛的天神宙斯虏到了克里特岛，所以该岛及以北和以西的岛屿和大陆用她的名字来命名，即欧罗巴洲。阿喀琉斯是特洛伊战争中希腊的大英雄，他全身上下只有脚后跟是致命之处，所以英语中有了成语 the heel of Achilles，意思是"致命的弱点"，相同的成语在法语中是 le talon d'Achille，在西班牙语中是 el talón de Aquiles，在俄语中是 Ахиллесова пята。

打开西方的文学作品，我们可以看到来自希腊罗马神话的典故被大量使用在诗歌、戏剧和小说中。神话题材是诗人和剧作家们钟爱的题材，从古希腊的史诗诗人荷马到 20 世纪的爱尔兰诗人叶芝，许多诗人和剧作家使用神话题材创作了大量优秀的作品。意大利的彼特拉克、薄伽丘和但丁，英国的乔叟、莎士比亚和弥尔顿，法国的拉辛，德国的歌德，都是世界文学史上的巨人，都深受希腊罗马神话的影响。

走进西方各国的博物馆和美术馆，我们可以看到众多希腊罗马神话题材的雕塑作品和绘画作品。陈列在法国巴黎卢浮宫中的雕塑作品《米洛的维纳斯》、陈列在梵蒂冈城梵蒂冈博物馆的雕塑作品《拉奥孔和两个儿子》、陈列在意大利罗马博尔盖塞美术馆的雕塑作品《阿波罗和达芙妮》、陈列在意大利佛罗伦萨乌菲兹美术馆的绘画作品《维纳斯的诞生》等都是世界美术史上的杰作，都以希腊罗马神话为题材。在古希腊和古罗马，除了以神话为题材的大型雕塑作品外，神话故事还被绘制或雕刻在罐子、盘子、酒杯等日常生活用品上，与人们的日常生活息息相关。在文艺复兴时期，希腊罗马神话与基督教的《圣经》一样，成为艺术家灵感的源泉，波提切利、拉斐尔、提香等人创作了许多神话题材作品。鲁本斯是 17 世纪巴洛克绘画大师，其以希腊罗马神话为题材创作的绘画作品多达上千幅。在 18、19 和 20 世纪，艺术家们仍然不断地从希腊罗马神话中汲取营养进行创作，只是风格不断变化和创新而已。

当我们在夜晚仰望星空之时,我们应该知道,大熊星座、小熊星座、双子星座、射手星座、猎户星座、北冕星座以及其他许多星座都得名于希腊神话。古代的希腊人通过想象力丰富的故事让它们变得鲜活起来,具有了生命力。

由此可见,希腊罗马神话对西方文化的影响巨大而深远,因此对于学习和研究西方语言、文学、艺术、历史、哲学等诸多方面的人而言,希腊罗马神话的知识是必不可少的。同时,希腊罗马神话中的许多富有想象力的故事不仅能够带给我们愉悦和美的享受,对我们的人生也颇具启迪作用。

希腊罗马神话的众多故事是分散在古希腊和古罗马神话文学作品中的。这些神话文学作品不但是古希腊和古罗马文学中的杰作,也是世界文学中的珍宝。在这些文学作品中,荷马的史诗《伊利亚特》和《奥德赛》是最古老的,多数学者认为它们创作于公元前 9 世纪和公元前 8 世纪之间。紧随其后的是《荷马式的赞歌》。赫西奥德的《工作与日子》和《神谱》创作于公元前 700 年前后。公元前 6 世纪末的抒情诗人品达写了很多首颂歌来歌颂古希腊各大运动会中的获胜者,每首颂歌中都会讲述或提到神话故事。埃斯库罗斯、索福克勒斯和欧里庇得斯是古希腊的三大悲剧诗人,他们现存的悲剧作品都以神话为题材。阿波罗尼奥斯的史诗《阿尔戈船英雄纪》讲述的是希腊英雄们寻找金羊毛的故事。在古罗马,最重要的神话文学作品当数维吉尔的拉丁语史诗《埃尼阿斯纪》。

神话故事是分散在上述神话文学作品中的,有两位作者在研究这些文学作品和相关文献的基础上,把故事汇编起来,一位是古希腊的学者阿波罗多鲁斯,另一位是古罗马的大诗人奥维德。阿波罗多鲁斯把故事汇编起来,用古希腊语进行改写,书名叫《图书馆》。汇编在《图书馆》中的神话故事叙事是清楚的,但生动性较为欠缺。跟阿波罗多鲁斯一样,奥维德也研究了古代的文学作品和文献资料,把故事汇编起来,然后用拉丁语诗歌进行改写,成果便是《变形记》——古罗马最伟大的文学作品之一。《变形记》收录的故事是最全面的,所以它成为西方各国神话学者用母语改写希腊罗马神话时参考的主要依据。

从 18 世纪开始,古希腊语和拉丁语的学习在西方国家日渐式微,掌握它们的人越来越少,所以各国学者和作家开始使用本民族语言改写希腊罗马神话故事,以满足本国人民的阅读需要。在德国,古斯塔夫·施瓦布(Gustav Schwab)1838 年至 1840 年出版了 *Sagen des klassischen Altertums*(《希腊古典神话》),在学校中广泛使用,影响深远。在美国,托马斯·布尔芬奇 1855 年出版了以希腊罗马神话为主要内容的 *The Age of Fable*(《神话时代》)。在法国,保罗·德夏尔姆(Paul Decharme)1886 年出版了神话理论兼故事叙述的著作 *Mythologie de la Grèce Antique*(《古希腊神话》)。进入 20 世纪,欧美各国出版的希腊罗马神话著作种类很多,其中最为知名的是出生于德国德累斯顿的美国作家、古典学者艾迪斯·汉密尔顿(Edith Hamilton)1942 年出版的 *Mythology*(《神话》)。

在英语国家中,布尔芬奇的《神话时代》和汉密尔顿的《神话》多年来一直是希腊罗马神话方面最经典、最权威的著作,深受学者推崇和读者喜爱。

我是从 2008 年秋季学期开始在云南大学给英语专业本科三年级学生开设"希腊罗马神话选读"这门课程的,到 2019 年已经是第 11 轮。课程伊始,由于没有合适的教材可以选用,我采用复印国外资料发给学生的方式进行教学。复印的资料不易于携带和保存,这是个问题。但更大的问题是这些原版资料有一定的阅读难度,学生在学习的过程中遇到了一些困难,比如说专有名词的发音问题等。为了降低学生的学习难度和减少他们在学习过程中可能会遇到的困难,我萌生了编写一部教材的想法。教材的编写始于 2011 年,2014 年暑假完成。从 2014 年秋季学期起到 2017 年秋季学期结束,教材一直在教学中试用。在教材试用的过程中,通过分析、总结实际教学过程遇到的各种问题和听取学生的反馈意见,我又对教材进行补充、修改和完善,直到 2018 年暑假定稿。

从大的结构上讲,本教材分为两个部分,第一部分是"希腊罗马神话故事选读",第二部分是"希腊罗马神话文学作品选读",两个部分篇幅大致相当。第一部分的 33 章选自美国作家、古典学者托马斯·布尔芬奇的《神话时代》,包括了希腊罗马神话中的主要故事。通过阅读和学习这个部分,学习者可以了解、掌握希腊罗马神话的基本知识和主要内容。如前所述,希腊罗马神话故事都是分散在古希腊和古罗马神话文学作品中的,诸如《神话时代》这样的著作是后世作家在研究和整理古希腊和古罗马神话文学作品之后改写的,所以为了让学习者能够学习和欣赏部分故事的原貌,本教材设计了"希腊罗马神话文学作品选读"这个部分——这是本教材的亮点之一,也是本教材有别于国内外同类教材的地方。"希腊罗马神话文学作品选读"部分包含长短不一的 28 个选段,是从最具代表性的 7 位古希腊和古罗马作家的 9 部作品中选取出来的,是对第一个部分强有力的补充。通过阅读和学习这个部分,学习者可以欣赏到未经改写的、原汁原味的神话作品。

我认为英语专业的学生学习希腊罗马神话课程应该达到两个主要目的,其一是掌握和积累神话知识,其二是提高英语水平。为了帮助学生到达这两个目的,选取阅读材料时,我设定了严苛的标准,尽可能选取最好的语料。布尔芬奇的《神话时代》出版于 1855 年,160 多年来不断再版重印,一直是英语世界众多希腊罗马神话故事集中的佼佼者,以收录故事全面、叙事清楚、语言典雅而著称于世。因为《神话时代》的这些优点,加之它的语言难度和词汇量适合我国英语专业高年级的学生,所以我把它的前 33 章(即希腊罗马神话部分)选入本教材第一部分。选入第二部分"希腊罗马神话文学作品选读"中的作家不但是古希腊和古罗马文学中的知名作家,同时也是享誉世界文坛的作家,他们的作品,如荷马史诗、《埃尼阿斯纪》《变形记》等,几千年来一直蜚声世界。古希腊文学和古罗马文学是西方文学的源头,所以每部重要作品一般都有多个英语译本,如荷马史诗就有 100 多种英译本。被我选入"希腊罗马神话文学作品选读"部分的英译本,译文清新、流畅,译者中的德莱顿、巴特勒和弗雷泽都是英国著名的作家、诗人或学者。所选选段也都是各部作品中的精彩部分,如在史诗《伊利亚特》的选段"The Shield of Achilles"中,通过描写阿喀琉斯盾牌上的图案,荷马把古希腊生活的多个场面栩栩如生地展现在了读者的面前。

本教材的注释近五万字,是我在查阅了国内外(主要是国外)大量资料后完成的。注释包括专有名词读音、词汇、语言难点、地理知识、历史知识、天文知识、背景知识等诸多方面。有些疑问在英文参考书中找不到答案,好在 *A Greek-English Lexicon* 和 *Oxford Latin Dictionary* 这样的大型古希腊语和拉丁语工具书为我提供了及时的帮助。希腊罗马神话中有大量来自希腊语和拉丁语的专有名词,这些专有名词的读音是学习者们面临的一个巨大挑战。本教材的专有名词读音注释非常广泛,只有极少数不太重要的、出现频率低的专有名词没有提供读音注释。教材后面还提供了"专有名词读音表",供学习者随时查阅。希腊罗马神话中的许多地名今天仍然是存在的,学习者只要手里有地图册,通过注释中的说明便能轻易地找到它们。对于那些今天已经不存在了的地名(如 Carthage),通过注释中的说明,学习者依然能够确定它们的大体位置。

英语专业高年级的"希腊罗马神话"课程通常只是每周两个学时的学期课程,想要一个学期内在课堂上学完教材中的全部内容是不容易的。教师可以根据学生总体英语水平、课时多少等实际情况制订教学计划,选择部分内容在课堂上学习和讨论,其余内容可要求学生自学。

本教材也可供本科阶段没有学习过希腊罗马神话的英语专业研究生自学使用。法语、德语、俄语、西班牙语等欧洲语言专业的本科生和研究生在进入大学前通常已经学过多年英语,有良好的英语基础,本科和研究生阶段的第二外语又通常是英语。对于这些学生而言,如果找不到用所学语言编写的恰当的希腊罗马神话教材,本教材也是他们学习希腊罗马神话的一个选择,毕竟故事都是相同的,只是在不同语言中神话人物名字的拼写方式略有不同罢了。当然了,对于广大想要提高英语水平的英语学习者来讲,本教材是难得的学习读本,因为有趣的故事能让英语学习变得更加有趣。

希腊罗马神话的内容非常丰富,涉及的知识面也十分广泛,纵然我在编写的过程中已经尽心尽力了,本教材中肯定还存在着这样或那样的缺点和不足。恳请本教材的使用者们提出宝贵的意见和建议,以便日后对它进行完善。

李明强

2019 年 3 月 昆明

目录 CONTENTS

第二部分　希腊罗马神话文学作品选读

第一部分

希腊罗马神话故事选读

Thomas Bulfinch

(1796—1867)

美国作家托马斯·布尔芬奇（Thomas Bulfinch）出生于马萨诸塞州（Massachusetts），其父查尔斯·布尔芬奇（Charles Bulfinch）是美国第一位职业建筑师。托马斯·布尔芬奇长期在波士顿商人银行（the Boston Merchants' Bank）工作，是该银行的会计。布尔芬奇的著作主要有《神话时代》（*The Age of Fable*）、《骑士时代》（*The Age of Chivalry*）、《查理曼的传奇》（*Legends of Charlemagne*），分别出版于 1855 年、1858 年和 1863 年。1881 年，这 3 部作品被合编在一起出版，书名是《布尔芬奇的神话》（*Bulfinch's Mythology*）。

1855 年出版的《神话时代》一共有 42 章，包含希腊罗马神话、埃及神话、印度神话、北欧神话和盎格鲁-撒克逊神话。从该书初版至今已 160 多年，然而它现在仍然被多家出版社出版，其影响之深远由此可见一斑。

在本读本中，编注者只选取了《神话时代》中的希腊罗马神话部分，即从第 1 章到第 33 章。在《神话时代》中，布尔芬奇从英美诗歌中选取了很多段落来说明希腊罗马神话在诗歌中的应用，但由于本读本的侧重点是神话故事，所以在这里编注者没有保留这些诗歌选段。

The Age of Fable

Chapter Ⅰ
Introduction

The religions of ancient Greece and Rome are extinct[①]. The so-called divinities[②] of Olympus[③] have not a single worshipper among living men. They belong now not to the department

---

① extinct /ɪkˈstɪŋkt/：不再存在的，不复存在的

② divinity /dɪˈvɪnəti/：神，神祇

③ Olympus /əˈlɪmpəs/：奥林匹斯山，位于今希腊东北部中马其顿大区皮埃里亚州（Pieria）南部和色萨利大区（Thessaly 或 Thessalia）拉里萨州（Larisa）北部，最高峰 2917 米，在古希腊神话中是神的住所。

of theology①, but to those② of literature and taste③. There they still hold their place④, and will continue to hold it, for they are too closely connected with the finest productions of poetry and art, both ancient and modern, to pass into oblivion⑤.

We propose to tell the stories relating to them which have come down to us from the ancients⑥, and which are alluded⑦ to by modern poets, essayists⑧, and orators⑨. Our readers may thus at the same time be entertained by the most charming fictions⑩ which fancy⑪ has ever created, and put in possession of information indispensable⑫ to every one who would read with intelligence⑬ the elegant literature of his own day.

In order to understand these stories, it will be necessary to acquaint ourselves with the ideas of the structure of the universe which prevailed⑭ among the Greeks—the people from whom the Romans, and other nations through them, received their science and religion⑮.

The Greeks believed the earth to be flat and circular, their own country occupying the middle of it, the central point being either Mount Olympus, the abode⑯ of the gods, or Delphi⑰, so famous for its oracle⑱.

The circular disk of the earth was crossed from west to east and divided into two equal parts by the Sea, as they called the Mediterranean⑲, and its continuation the Euxine⑳, the only seas with which they were acquainted.

Around the earth flowed the River Ocean, its course being from south to north on the western side of the earth, and in a contrary direction on the eastern side. It flowed in a steady, equable current, unvexed㉑ by storm or tempest. The sea, and all the rivers on earth, received their waters from it.

---

① theology /θiˈɒlədʒi/：神学
② those：departments
③ taste：审美
④ hold their place：占有一席之地
⑤ oblivion /əˈblɪvɪən/：忘记，遗忘；pass into oblivion：被遗忘
⑥ the ancients：古人，指古希腊、罗马人，也指其他古代文明民族。
⑦ allude /əˈluːd/ to：提到
⑧ essayist /ˈeseɪɪst/：论说文作者，随笔作者，小品文作者
⑨ orator /ˈɒrətə/：演说者，演说家
⑩ fiction /ˈfɪkʃn/：虚构的故事
⑪ fancy：(具有创造性的)想象力
⑫ indispensable /ˌɪndɪˈspensəbl/：绝对必要的，非常重要的，不可缺少的
⑬ intelligence /ɪnˈtelɪdʒəns/：理解，理解力；read with intelligence：读懂
⑭ prevail /prɪˈveɪl/：广为流传，盛行
⑮ 罗马人接受了希腊人的科学和宗教，其他民族通过罗马人接受希腊人的科学和宗教。them：the Romans
⑯ abode /əˈbəʊd/：住处
⑰ Delphi /ˈdelfaɪ/：希腊古镇名，古希腊最重要的神庙和太阳神阿波罗（Apollo）神示所的所在地，位于今希腊中希腊大区福基斯州（Phocis /Fokis）东部。由于其遗址保存完好，1987 年被列入联合国教科文组织的"世界遗产名录"。
⑱ oracle /ˈɒrəkl/：神谕，神示所
⑲ the Mediterranean /ˌmedɪtəˈreɪnɪən/：即 the Mediterranean Sea，地中海，位于欧洲、亚洲和非洲之间，在东南部通过苏伊士运河与红海连接，在西部通过直布罗陀海峡与大西洋连接。希腊靠近地中海东北部。
⑳ the Euxine /ˈjuːksaɪn/：黑海（the Black Sea）
㉑ unvex /ˈʌnˈveks/：不受影响

The northern portion of the earth was supposed to be inhabited by a happy race named the Hyperboreans①, dwelling in everlasting bliss and spring beyond the lofty② mountains whose caverns were supposed to send forth the piercing③ blasts of the north wind, which chilled the people of Hellas④(Greece). Their country was inaccessible⑤ by land or sea. They lived exempt⑥ from disease or old age, from toils and warfare.

On the south side of the earth, close to the stream of Ocean, dwelt a people happy and virtuous as the Hyperboreans. They were named the Æthiopians⑦. The gods favored them so highly that they were wont to leave at times their Olympian⑧ abodes and go to share their sacrifices⑨ and banquets.

On the western margin of the earth, by the stream of Ocean, lay a happy place named the Elysian Plain⑩, whither⑪ mortals⑫ favored by the gods were transported without tasting of death, to enjoy an immortality of bliss⑬. This happy region was also called the "Fortunate Fields," and the "Isles of the Blessed."

We thus see that the Greeks of the early ages knew little of any real people except those to the east and south of their own country, or near the coast of the Mediterranean. Their imagination meantime peopled the western portion of this sea with giants, monsters, and enchantresses⑭; while they placed around the disk of the earth, which they probably regarded as of no great width, nations enjoying the peculiar favor of the gods, and blessed with happiness and longevity⑮.

The Dawn, the Sun, and the Moon⑯ were supposed to rise out of the Ocean, on the eastern side, and to drive through the air, giving light to gods and men. The stars, also, except those forming the Wain⑰ or Bear⑱, and others near them, rose out of and sank into the stream of Ocean. There the sun-god embarked in a winged boat, which conveyed him round by the northern part of the earth, back to his place of rising in the east.

_____

① Hyperborean：/ˌhaɪpɜːbɔːˈriən/

② lofty /ˈlɒfti/：（山、树、建筑物等）高耸的

③ piercing /ˈpɪəsɪŋ/：刺骨的

④ Hellas /ˈhelæs/：古希腊，"希腊"这一国名从该词翻译而来。现代希腊也可叫作 Hellas 或 Ellas /ˈelæs /。

⑤ inaccessible /ˌɪnækˈsesəbl/：无法到达的,无法进入的

⑥ exempt /ɪgˈzempt/：不受危险、疾病等影响的,免于危险、疾病等的

⑦ Æthiopian /iːθɪˈəʊpɪən/：也可拼写为 Ethiopian,这里指的不是今天非洲的按国别划分的埃塞俄比亚人,而是泛指黑人。Æ 是字母 A 和 E 的连字（ligature /ˈlɪɡətʃə/）,小写形式是 æ, 在现代印刷术中分开来写为 ae, 如 archæology 写为 archaeology; 有时 æ 也可简写为 e,如 encyclopædia 可拼写为 encyclopedia。

⑧ Olympian /əˈlɪmpiən/：奥林匹斯山的

⑨ sacrifice /ˈsækrɪfaɪs/：祭品,供品

⑩ the Elysian /ɪˈlɪʒən / Plain：即 Elysium / ɪˈlɪʒɪəm /或 the Elysian fields,古希腊神话中英雄和好人死后居住的乐土。

⑪ whither /ˈwɪθə/：定语从句引导词,相当于 to which 或 to which place。

⑫ mortal /ˈmɔːtl/：凡人,与 mortal 相反的是 immortal（神）。

⑬ an immortality /ˌɪmɔːˈtæləti / of bliss：永恒的快乐

⑭ 在他们的想象中,地中海的西部居住着巨人、怪兽和巫婆。to people a place with sb.：让某人居住在某个地方；enchantress /ɪnˈtʃɑːntrəs/：女巫,巫婆

⑮ longevity /lɒnˈdʒevəti/：长寿

⑯ the Dawn, the Sun, and the Moon：黎明女神、太阳神和月亮女神

⑰ the Wain /weɪn/：北斗七星

⑱ the Bear：熊星座,参见 *The Age of Fable* 第 4 章 Callisto 的故事。

The abode of the gods was on the summit of Mount Olympus, in Thessaly①. A gate of clouds, kept by the goddesses named the Seasons, opened to permit the passage of the Celestials to earth②, and to receive them on their return. The gods had their separate dwellings; but all, when summoned, repaired to③ the palace of Jupiter④, as did also those deities⑤ whose usual abode was the earth, the waters, or the underworld⑥. It was also in the great hall of the palace of the Olympian king⑦ that the gods feasted each day on ambrosia and nectar⑧, their food and drink, the latter being handed round by the lovely goddess Hebe⑨. Here they conversed of⑩ the affairs of heaven and earth; and as they quaffed⑪ their nectar, Apollo⑫, the god of music, delighted them with the tones⑬ of his lyre, to which the Muses⑭ sang in responsive strains⑮. When the sun was set, the gods retired to sleep in their respective dwellings.

The robes and other parts of the dress of the goddesses were woven by Minerva⑯ and the Graces⑰ and everything of a more solid nature was formed of the various metals. Vulcan⑱ was architect, smith, armorer⑲, chariot⑳ builder, and artist of all work in Olympus. He built of brass㉑ the houses of the gods; he made for them the golden shoes with which they trod㉒ the air or the water, and moved from place to place with the speed of the wind, or even of thought㉓. He also shod㉔ with brass the celestial steeds㉕, which whirled the chariots of the gods through the air, or along the surface of the sea. He was able to bestow on his workmanship self-motion㉖, so that the

---

① Thessaly /ˈθesəli/：色萨利，希腊地区名，位于希腊北部。古代希腊的色萨利地区的范围和今希腊的色萨利大区的范围大致是一致的。

② 由季节女神把守的云门开启，以便让诸神通过，前往人间。passage：通过；Celestial /səˈlestiəl/：神，居住在天上的居民

③ repair to：go to

④ Jupiter：/ˈdʒuːpɪtə/

⑤ deity /ˈdiːəti/：神，神祇

⑥ underworld /ˈʌndəwɜːld/：阴间，阴曹地府，地狱

⑦ the Olympian king：Jupiter

⑧ ambrosia /æmˈbrəʊziə/ and nectar /ˈnektə/：希腊神话中神的食物和饮料

⑨ Hebe /ˈhiːbi/：参见 The Age of Fable 第 19 章 Hebe 的故事。

⑩ converse /kənˈvɜːs/ of：talk about

⑪ quaff /kwɒf/：（大口大地）喝，痛饮

⑫ Apollo：/əˈpɒləʊ/

⑬ tone：乐器发出的声音

⑭ the Muses /ˈmjuːziz/：掌管诗歌、音乐、艺术等方面的女神，总共 9 个。

⑮ strain：乐曲，旋律

⑯ Minerva：/mɪˈnɜːvə/

⑰ the Graces /ˈɡreɪsiz/：象征优雅与美丽的女神，总共 3 个。

⑱ Vulcan：/ˈvʌlkən/

⑲ armorer /ˈɑːmərə/：盔甲制作者，盔甲修理者

⑳ chariot /ˈtʃæriət/：用于战争或比赛的双轮马车

㉑ of brass：用铜

㉒ trod：动词 tread（行走）的过去式

㉓ 以风的速度，甚至是以思想的速度，从一地到另一地。

㉔ shod /ʃɒd/：动词 shoe（给马等钉蹄铁）的过去式

㉕ steed /stiːd/：骏马

㉖ 他能够让他制作的物品自己移动。workmanship /ˈwɜːkmənʃɪp/：工匠制作的物品，工艺品

tripods①(chairs and tables) could move of themselves② in and out of the celestial hall. He even endowed with intelligence the golden handmaidens whom he made to wait on himself.

Jupiter, or Jove③ (Zeus④), though called the father of gods and men, had himself a beginning. Saturn (Cronos)⑤ was his father, and Rhea⑥(Ops⑦) his mother. Saturn and Rhea were of the race of Titans⑧, who were the children of Earth and Heaven, which sprang from Chaos⑨, of which we shall give a further account in our next chapter.

There is another cosmogony⑩, or account of the creation, according to which Earth, Erebus⑪, and Love were the first of beings⑫. Love (Eros⑬) issued⑭ from the egg of Night, which floated on Chaos. By his arrows and torch he pierced and vivified⑮ all things, producing life and joy.

Saturn and Rhea were not the only Titans. There were others, whose names were Oceanus, Hyperion, Iapetus, and Ophion, males; and Themis, Mnemosyne, Eurynome, females. They are spoken of as the elder gods, whose dominion⑯ was afterwards transferred to others. Saturn yielded to Jupiter, Oceanus to Neptune, Hyperion to Apollo. Hyperion was the father of the Sun, Moon, and Dawn. He is therefore the original sun-god, and is painted with the splendor and beauty which were afterwards bestowed on Apollo.

Ophion and Eurynome ruled over Olympus till they were dethroned⑰ by Saturn and Rhea.

The representations given of Saturn⑱ are not very consistent; for on the one hand his reign is said to have been the golden age of innocence and purity⑲, and on the other he is described as a monster who devoured his children.⑳ Jupiter, however, escaped this fate, and when grown up

---

① tripod /ˈtraɪpɒd/：三只脚的凳子、椅子、桌子等
② move of themselves：自己移动
③ Jove：/dʒəʊv/
④ （原作者注）The names included in parentheses are the Greek, the other being the Roman or Latin names. （括号里的是希腊语名字,括号前的是罗马或拉丁语名字。）Zeus：/zjuːs/
⑤ Saturn：/ˈsætɜːn /；Cronos：/ˈkrəʊnəs/
⑥ Rhea：/ˈriːə/
⑦ Ops：/ɒps/
⑧ Titan /ˈtaɪtn/：希腊神话中的巨人
⑨ Chaos：/ˈkeɪɒs/
⑩ cosmogony /kɒzˈmɒɡəni/：宇宙的创造,宇宙创造学,宇宙创造的理论或叙述
⑪ Erebus：/ˈerɪbəs/
⑫ being：生物,人
⑬ Eros：/ˈɪərɒs/
⑭ issue：诞生
⑮ vivify /ˈvɪvəˌfaɪ/：赋予……生命
⑯ dominion /dəˈmɪnɪən/：统治权
⑰ dethrone /ˌdiːˈθrəʊn/：推翻
⑱ 对 Saturn 的描绘。representation /ˌreprɪzenˈteɪʃn/：描绘,表述
⑲ 参见 The Age of Fable 第 2 章关于 the Golden Age 的叙述。
⑳ （原作者注）This inconsistency arises from considering the Saturn of the Romans the same with the Grecian deity Cronos (Time), which, as it brings an end to all things which have had a beginning, may be said to devour its own offspring. （这种不一致是把罗马人的 Saturn 与希腊人的时间之神 Cronos 等同起来造成的。时间吞噬一切,所以可以说时间之神 Cronos 吞噬自己的孩子。）

espoused Metis (Prudence), who administered a draught to Saturn① which caused him to disgorge② his children. Jupiter, with his brothers and sisters, now rebelled against their father Saturn and his brothers the Titans; vanquished them, and imprisoned some of them in Tartarus③, inflicting other penalties on others. Atlas④ was condemned to bear up the heavens on his shoulders.

On the dethronement of Saturn⑤, Jupiter with his brothers Neptune (Poseidon)⑥ and Pluto (Dis)⑦ divided his dominions. Jupiter's portion was the heavens, Neptune's the ocean, and Pluto's the realms of the dead. Earth and Olympus were common property. Jupiter was king of gods and men. The thunder was his weapon, and he bore a shield called Ægis⑧, made for him by Vulcan. The eagle was his favorite bird, and bore his thunderbolts⑨.

Juno (Hera)⑩ was the wife of Jupiter, and queen of the gods. Iris⑪, the goddess of the rainbow, was her attendant⑫ and messenger. The peacock was her favorite bird.

Vulcan (Hephæstos⑬), the celestial artist, was the son of Jupiter and Juno. He was born lame, and his mother was so displeased at the sight of him that she flung him out of heaven. Other accounts say that Jupiter kicked him out for taking part with his mother in a quarrel which occurred between them. Vulcan's lameness, according to this account, was the consequence of his fall. He was a whole day falling, and at last alighted in the island of Lemnos⑭, which was thenceforth sacred to him.

Mars (Ares)⑮, the god of war, was the son of Jupiter and Juno.

Phœbus⑯ Apollo, the god of archery⑰, prophecy, and music, was the son of Jupiter and Latona, and brother of Diana (Artemis)⑱. He was god of the sun, as Diana, his sister, was the goddess of the moon.

Venus (Aphrodite)⑲, the goddess of love and beauty, was the daughter of Jupiter and Dione⑳. Others say that Venus sprang from the foam of the sea. The Zephyr㉑ wafted her along the waves to

---

① 让 Saturn 喝了一服药水。
② disgorge /dɪsˈɡɔːdʒ/: 吐出
③ Tartarus /ˈtɑːtərəs/: 位于阴间下方的深渊,被推翻的提坦众巨神(the Titans)被关押在这里。
④ Atlas: /ˈætləs/
⑤ On the dethronement of Saturn: Saturn 一被推翻
⑥ Neptune: /ˈneptjuːn/; Poseidon: /pɒˈsaɪdən/
⑦ Pluto: /ˈpluːtəʊ/; Dis: /dɪs/
⑧ Ægis: /ˈiːdʒɪs/
⑨ thunderbolt /ˈθʌndəbəʊlt/: 雷电,霹雳
⑩ Juno: /ˈdʒuːnəʊ/; Hera: /ˈhɪərə/
⑪ Iris: /ˈaɪərɪs/
⑫ attendant /əˈtendənt/: 侍从,随从,侍者
⑬ Hephæstos: /hɪˈfiːstəs/
⑭ Lemnos /ˈlemnɒs/: 希腊岛名,位于爱琴海北部,属于今希腊北爱琴大区莱斯沃斯州。
⑮ Mars: /mɑːz/; Ares: /ˈeəriːz/
⑯ Phœbus: /ˈfiːbəs/; œ 是字母 o 和 e 的连字,其大写形式是 Œ,在现代印刷术中,œ 被写为 oe,有时 o 被去掉。
⑰ archery /ˈɑːtʃəri/: 射箭术
⑱ Diana: /daɪˈænə/; Artemis: /ˈɑːtɪmɪs/
⑲ Venus: /ˈviːnəs/; Aphrodite: /ˌæfrəˈdaɪti/
⑳ Dione: /daɪˈəʊni/
㉑ Zephyr /ˈzefə/: 西风

the Isle of Cyprus①, where she was received and attired② by the Seasons, and then led to the assembly of the gods. All were charmed with her beauty, and each one demanded her for his wife. Jupiter gave her to Vulcan, in gratitude for the service he had rendered in forging thunderbolts. So the most beautiful of the goddesses became the wife of the most ill-favored③ of gods. Venus possessed an embroidered girdle called Cestus④, which had the power of inspiring love. Her favorite birds were swans and doves, and the plants sacred to her were the rose and the myrtle.

Cupid (Eros)⑤, the god of love, was the son of Venus. He was her constant companion; and, armed with bow and arrows, he shot the darts of desire into the bosoms of both gods and men. There was a deity named Anteros⑥, who was sometimes represented as the avenger of slighted⑦ love, and sometimes as the symbol of reciprocal⑧ affection⑨. The following legend is told of him:

Venus, complaining to Themis that her son Eros continued always a child, was told by her that it was because he was solitary, and that if he had a brother he would grow apace⑩. Anteros was soon afterwards born, and Eros immediately was seen to increase rapidly in size and strength.

Minerva (Pallas, Athene)⑪, the goddess of wisdom, was the offspring of Jupiter, without a mother. She sprang forth from his head completely armed. Her favorite bird was the owl, and the plant sacred to her the olive.

Mercury (Hermes)⑫ was the son of Jupiter and Maia. He presided over commerce, wrestling, and other gymnastic exercises, even over thieving, and everything, in short, which required skill and dexterity⑬. He was the messenger of Jupiter, and wore a winged cap and winged shoes. He bore in his hand a rod entwined with two serpents, called the caduceus⑭.

Mercury is said to have invented the lyre. He found, one day, a tortoise⑮, of which he took the shell, made holes in the opposite edges of it, and drew cords of linen through them, and the instrument was complete. The cords were nine, in honor of the nine Muses. Mercury gave the lyre⑯ to Apollo, and received from him in exchange the caduceus.⑰

---

① the Isle of Cyprus /ˈsaɪprəs/：塞浦路斯岛,位于地中海东部,地中海中的第 3 大岛。

② attire /əˈtaɪə/：给……穿上衣服

③ ill-favored：丑陋的

④ Cestus：/ˈsestəs/

⑤ Cupid：/ˈkjuːpɪd /；Eros：/ˈɪərɒs/

⑥ Anteros：/ænˈtɪərɒs/

⑦ slighted：被忽视的,被怠慢的

⑧ reciprocal /rɪˈsɪprəkl/：相互的

⑨ affection /əˈfekʃn/：爱慕

⑩ apace /əˈpeɪs/：快速地,迅速地

⑪ Pallas：/ˈpæləs /；Athene：/əˈθiːni/

⑫ Mercury：/ˈmɜːkjəri /；Hermes：/ˈhɜːmiːz/

⑬ dexterity /dekˈsterəti/：灵巧,熟练,机敏

⑭ caduceus /kəˈdjuːsɪəs/：双蛇节杖

⑮ tortoise /ˈtɔːtəs/：龟

⑯ lyre /ˈlaɪə/：古希腊人唱歌或朗诵诗歌时用于伴奏的一种弦乐器。

⑰ (原作者注) From this origin of the instrument, the word "shell" is often used as synonymous with "lyre," and figuratively for music and poetry.

Ceres（Demeter）① was the daughter of Saturn and Rhea. She had a daughter named Proserpine（Persephone）②, who became the wife of Pluto, and queen of the realms of the dead.③ Ceres presided over agriculture.

Bacchus（Dionysus）④, the god of wine, was the son of Jupiter and Semele.⑤ He represents not only the intoxicating power of wine, but its social and beneficent influences likewise, so that he is viewed as the promoter of civilization, and a lawgiver and lover of peace.

The Muses were the daughters of Jupiter and Mnemosyne（Memory）. They presided over song, and prompted the memory. They were nine in number, to each of whom was assigned the presidence⑥ over some particular department of literature, art, or science. Calliope was the muse of epic poetry, Clio of history, Euterpe of lyric poetry, Melpomene of tragedy, Terpsichore of choral dance and song, Erato of love poetry, Polyhymnia of sacred poetry, Urania of astronomy, Thalia of comedy.

The Graces were goddesses presiding over the banquet, the dance, and all social enjoyments and elegant arts. They were three in number. Their names were Euphrosyne, Aglaia, and Thalia.

The Fates were also three—Clotho, Lachesis, and Atropos. Their office⑦ was to spin the thread of human destiny, and they were armed with shears, with which they cut it off when they pleased. They were the daughters of Themis（Law）, who sits by Jove on his throne to give him counsel.

The Erinyes⑧, or Furies, were three goddesses who punished by their secret stings the crimes of those who escaped or defied public justice. The heads of the Furies were wreathed with serpents, and their whole appearance was terrific and appalling. Their names were Alecto, Tisiphone, and Megæra. They were also called Eumenides⑨.

Nemesis⑩ was also an avenging goddess. She represents the righteous anger of the gods, particularly towards the proud and insolent⑪.

Pan⑫ was the god of flocks and shepherds. His favorite residence was in Arcadia⑬.

The Satyrs⑭ were deities of the woods and fields. They were conceived to be covered with

---

① Ceres：/'sɪəriːz /；Demeter：/dɪ'miːtə/
② Proserpine：/'prɒsəpaɪn /；Persephone：/pɜː'sefəni/
③ 参见 *The Age of Fable* 第 7 章。
④ Bacchus：/'bækəs /；Dionysus：/ˌdaɪə'naɪsəs/
⑤ 参见 *The Age of Fable* 第 21 章。
⑥ presidence /'prezɪdəns/：主持，掌管
⑦ office：职责
⑧ Erinyes：/ɪ'rɪnɪiːz/
⑨ Eumenides：/juː'menɪdiːz/
⑩ Nemesis：/'neməsɪs/
⑪ insolent /'ɪnsələnt/：傲慢的，无礼的
⑫ Pan：/pæn/
⑬ Arcadia /ɑː'keɪdɪə/：希腊地区名，位于伯罗奔尼撒半岛中部，高原，多山。在今天的希腊，阿卡迪亚（Arcadia）是伯罗奔尼撒大区的一个州。
⑭ Satyr：/'sætə/

bristly① hair, their heads decorated with short, sprouting horns, and their feet like goats' feet.

Momus② was the god of laughter, and Plutus③ the god of wealth.

Roman Divinities

The preceding are Grecian④ divinities, though received also by the Romans. Those which follow are peculiar to Roman mythology:

Saturn was an ancient Italian deity. It was attempted to identify him with the Grecian god Cronos, and fabled that after his dethronement by Jupiter he fled to Italy, where he reigned during what was called the Golden Age. In memory of his beneficent dominion, the feast of Saturnalia⑤ was held every year in the winter season. Then all public business was suspended⑥, declarations of war and criminal executions⑦ were postponed, friends made presents to one another, and the slaves were indulged with great liberties. A feast was given them at which they sat at table, while their masters served them, to show the natural equality of men, and that all things belonged equally to all, in the reign of Saturn.

Faunus⑧, the grandson of Saturn, was worshipped as the god of fields and shepherds, and also as a prophetic god. His name in the plural⑨, Fauns, expressed a class of gamesome⑩ deities, like the Satyrs of the Greeks.

Quirinus was a war god, said to be no other than Romulus, the founder of Rome, exalted after his death to a place among the gods.

Bellona, a war goddess.

Terminus, the god of landmarks. His statue was a rude stone or post, set in the ground to mark the boundaries of fields.

Pales, the goddess presiding over cattle and pastures.

Pomona presided over fruit trees.

Flora, the goddess of flowers.

Lucina, the goddess of childbirth.

Vesta (the Hestia of the Greeks) was a deity presiding over the public and private hearth. A sacred fire, tended by six virgin priestesses called Vestals⑪, flamed in her temple. As the safety of the city was held to be connected with its conservation, the neglect of the virgins, if they let it go out, was severely punished, and the fire was rekindled from the rays of the sun.

---

① bristly /'brɪsli/：猪鬃一样的

② Momus：/'məuməs/

③ Plutus：/'pluːtəs/

④ Grecian /'griːʃn/：希腊的，希腊人的。该词不常用，现多用来指建筑风格或面部轮廓。

⑤ Saturnalia /ˌsætə'neɪlɪə/：古罗马的农神节，从 12 月 17 日开始，持续 7 天，其间人们可无拘无束地行乐。

⑥ suspend /sə'spend/：暂时停止

⑦ execution /ˌeksɪ'kjuːʃn/：处决

⑧ （原作者注）There was also a goddess called Fauna, or Bona Dea.

⑨ plural：(名词的)复数形式

⑩ gamesome /'geɪmsəm/：快活的

⑪ Vestal：/'vestl/

Liber is the Latin name of Bacchus; and Mulciber of Vulcan.

Janus[1] was the porter of heaven. He opens the year, the first month being named after him[2]. He is the guardian deity[3] of gates, on which account he is commonly represented with two heads, because every door looks two ways. His temples at Rome were numerous. In war time the gates of the principal one were always open. In peace they were closed; but they were shut only once between the reign of Numa[4] and that of Augustus[5].

The Penates[6] were the gods who were supposed to attend to the welfare and prosperity of the family. Their name is derived from Penus[7], the pantry[8], which was sacred to them. Every master of a family was the priest to the Penates of his own house.

The Lares[9], or Lars, were also household gods, but differed from the Penates in being regarded as the deified spirits of mortals. The family Lars were held to be the souls of the ancestors, who watched over and protected their descendants. The words Lemur[10] and Larva[11] more nearly correspond to our word Ghost.

The Romans believed that every man had his Genius[12], and every woman her Juno[13]: that is, a spirit who had given them being, and was regarded as their protector through life. On their birthdays men made offerings to their Genius, women to their Juno.

Chapter II
Prometheus and Pandora

The creation of the world is a problem naturally fitted to excite the liveliest interest of man, its inhabitant. The ancient pagans[14], not having the information on the subject which we derive from the pages of Scripture[15], had their own way of telling the story, which is as follows:

---

① Janus：/ˈdʒeɪnəs/

② 即 January

③ the guardian deity：守护神

④ Numa /ˈnjuːmə/：罗马国王，公元前 715 年至公元前 673 年在位。

⑤ Augustus /ɔːˈɡʌstəs/：第一位罗马皇帝，生于公元前 63 年，卒于公元 14 年。

⑥ Penates /pɪˈnɑːtiːz/：护神

⑦ Penus：（拉丁语）食物

⑧ pantry：家中存放面包和食物的房间

⑨ Lares /ˈlɑːriːz/：家神

⑩ Lemur /ˈliːmə/：亡魂

⑪ Larva /ˈlɑːvə/：游魂

⑫ Genius /ˈdʒiːniəs/：男人的护身神

⑬ Juno：天后，她也是保护妇女的女神。罗马神话中还有一个神叫 Junones，是罗马的妇女护身神。

⑭ pagan /ˈpeɪɡən/：不信仰基督教的人，异教徒

⑮ Scripture：基督教的《圣经》。《圣经》《旧约全书》第 1 卷《创世记》记载有基督教的上帝创造日月星辰和天地万物的故事。

Before earth and sea and heaven were created, all things wore one aspect①, to which we give the name of Chaos②—a confused and shapeless mass, nothing but dead weight, in which, however, slumbered the seeds of things. Earth, sea, and air were all mixed up together; so the earth was not solid③, the sea was not fluid④, and the air was not transparent. God and Nature at last interposed⑤, and put an end to this discord⑥, separating earth from sea, and heaven from both. The fiery part, being the lightest, sprang up, and formed the skies; the air was next in weight and place. The earth, being heavier, sank below; and the water took the lowest place, and buoyed up⑦ the earth.

Here some god—it is not known which—gave his good offices in arranging and disposing⑧ the earth. He appointed rivers and bays their places, raised mountains, scooped out valleys, distributed woods, fountains, fertile fields, and stony plains. The air being cleared, the stars began to appear, fishes took possession of the sea, birds of the air, and four-footed beasts of the land.⑨

But a nobler animal was wanted⑩, and Man was made. It is not known whether the creator made him of⑪ divine materials, or whether in the earth, so lately separated from heaven, there lurked still some heavenly seeds. Prometheus⑫ took some of this earth, and kneading it up with water, made man in the image of the gods⑬. He gave him an upright⑭ stature, so that while all other animals turn their faces downward, and look to the earth, he raises his to heaven, and gazes on the stars.

Prometheus was one of the Titans, a gigantic race, who inhabited the earth before the creation of man. To him and his brother Epimetheus⑮ was committed the office of making man, and providing him and all other animals with the faculties necessary for their preservation⑯. Epimetheus undertook to do this, and Prometheus was to overlook his work, when it was done.

---

① aspect /ˈæspekt/：样子，外表

② Chaos：/ˈkeɪɒs/

③ solid /ˈsɒlɪd/：坚实的

④ fluid /ˈfluːɪd/：能流动的

⑤ interpose /ˌɪntəˈpəʊz/：插入，干预

⑥ discord /ˈdɪskɔːd/：混乱状态

⑦ buoy /bɔɪ / up：使浮起

⑧ dispose /dɪˈspəʊz/：(用一种特别的方式)安排

⑨ birds of the air, and four-footed beasts of the land：birds took possession of the air, and four-footed beasts took possession of the land.

⑩ want：缺少

⑪ of：用（某种材料）

⑫ Prometheus /prəˈmiːθjuːs/：该词在希腊语中的意思是"先觉者"。

⑬ in the image of the gods：按照神的模样

⑭ upright /ˈʌpraɪt/：直立的

⑮ Epimetheus /ˌepɪˈmiːθjuːs/：该词在希腊语中的意思是"后觉者"。

⑯ The office of making man, and providing... was committed to him and his brother Epimetheus. office：任务；commit... to... ：把……交给……；faculties necessary for their preservation：生存下来所需要的能力；faculty /ˈfækəltɪ/：能力

Epimetheus accordingly① proceeded to bestow upon the different animals the various gifts of courage, strength, swiftness, sagacity②; wings to one, claws to another, a shelly covering to a third, etc. But when man came to be provided for, who was to be superior to all other animals, Epimetheus had been so prodigal③ of his resources that he had nothing left to bestow upon him. In his perplexity④ he resorted to⑤ his brother Prometheus, who, with the aid of Minerva, went up to heaven, and lighted his torch at the chariot of the sun, and brought down fire to man. With this gift man was more than a match for all other animals⑥. It enabled him to make weapons wherewith⑦ to subdue them; tools with which to cultivate the earth; to warm his dwelling, so as to be comparatively independent of climate; and finally to introduce the arts and to coin money, the means of trade and commerce.

Woman was not yet made. The story (absurd enough!) is that Jupiter made her, and sent her to Prometheus and his brother, to punish them for their presumption⑧ in stealing fire from heaven; and man, for accepting the gift⑨. The first woman was named Pandora⑩. She was made in heaven, every god contributing something to perfect her. Venus gave her beauty, Mercury persuasion⑪, Apollo music, etc. Thus equipped, she was conveyed to earth, and presented to Epimetheus, who gladly accepted her, though cautioned⑫ by his brother to beware of Jupiter and his gifts. Epimetheus had in his house a jar, in which were kept certain noxious⑬ articles⑭, for which, in fitting man for his new abode, he had had no occasion⑮. Pandora was seized with an eager curiosity to know what this jar contained; and one day she slipped off the cover and looked in. Forthwith⑯ there escaped a multitude of plagues for hapless⑰ man,—such as gout⑱, rheumatism⑲, and colic⑳ for his body, and envy, spite㉑, and revenge for his mind,—and scattered themselves far and wide. Pandora hastened to replace the lid! but, alas! the whole

---

① accordingly /əˈkɔːdɪŋli/: 于是,因此

② sagacity /səˈɡæsɪti/: 睿智

③ prodigal /ˈprɒdɪɡl/: 浪费的,挥霍的

④ perplexity /pəˈpleksəti/: 困惑

⑤ resort /rɪˈzɔːt / to: 求助于

⑥ 人类得到这份礼物后,其他所有动物就远远不是人类的对手了。

⑦ wherewith /weəˈwɪð/: with which

⑧ presumption /prɪˈzʌmpʃn/: 胆敢,胆大妄为

⑨ and to punish man for accepting the gift (fire)

⑩ Pandora: /pænˈdɔːrə/

⑪ persuasion: 能说会道, 巧言善辩

⑫ caution /ˈkɔːʃn/: 警告,建议

⑬ noxious /ˈnɒkʃəs/: 有害的

⑭ article: 物品

⑮ occasion /əˈkeɪʒn/: 需要

⑯ forthwith /fɔːˈθwɪð/: 立刻,马上

⑰ hapless /ˈhæpləs/: 运气不好的,倒霉的

⑱ gout /ɡaʊt/: 痛风

⑲ rheumatism /ˈruːmətɪzəm/: 风湿

⑳ colic /ˈkɒlɪk/: 腹痛

㉑ spite: 怨恨、恶意

contents of the jar had escaped, one thing only excepted, which lay at the bottom, and that was hope. So we see at this day, whatever evils are abroad①, hope never entirely leaves us; and while we have that, no amount of other ills can make us completely wretched.

Another story is that Pandora was sent in good faith②, by Jupiter, to bless man; that she was furnished with a box, containing her marriage presents, into which every god had put some blessing. She opened the box incautiously, and the blessings all escaped, hope only excepted. This story seems more probable than the former; for how could hope, so precious a jewel as it is, have been kept in a jar full of all manner of evils, as in the former statement?

The world being thus furnished with inhabitants, the first age was an age of innocence and happiness, called the Golden Age. Truth and right prevailed, though not enforced by law, nor was there any magistrate③ to threaten or punish. The forest had not yet been robbed of its trees to furnish timbers for vessels, nor had men built fortifications④ round their towns. There were no such things as swords, spears, or helmets. The earth brought forth all things necessary for man, without his labor in ploughing or sowing. Perpetual spring reigned, flowers sprang up without seed, the rivers flowed with milk and wine, and yellow honey distilled from the oaks.

Then succeeded the Silver Age, inferior to the golden, but better than that of brass. Jupiter shortened the spring, and divided the year into seasons. Then, first, men had to endure the extremes of heat and cold, and houses became necessary. Caves were the first dwellings, and leafy coverts of the woods, and huts woven of twigs. Crops would no longer grow without planting. The farmer was obliged to sow the seed and the toiling ox to draw the plough.

Next came the Brazen Age, more savage of temper⑤, and readier to the strife of arms, yet not altogether wicked. The hardest and worst was the Iron Age. Crime burst in like a flood; modesty, truth, and honor fled. In their places came fraud and cunning, violence, and the wicked love of gain⑥. Then seamen spread sails to the wind, and the trees were torn from the mountains to serve for keels⑦ to ships, and vex the face of ocean. The earth, which till now had been cultivated⑧ in common⑨, began to be divided off into possessions. Men were not satisfied with what the surface produced, but must dig into its bowels⑩, and draw forth from thence⑪ the ores⑫ of metals. Mischievous iron, and more mischievous gold, were produced. War sprang up, using both as weapons; the guest was not safe in his friend's house; and sons-in-law and fathers-in-law,

① abroad：流行，盛行
② good faith：真诚，诚意
③ magistrate /ˈmædʒɪstreɪt/：执法官，地方法官，治安官
④ fortification /ˌfɔːtɪfɪˈkeɪʃn/：防御工事，堡垒，要塞
⑤ temper：特点，品质
⑥ gain：战利品，财富的获取，利益
⑦ keel /kiːl/：（船的）龙骨
⑧ cultivate /ˈkʌltɪveɪt/：耕种
⑨ in common：共同地
⑩ bowel /ˈbaʊəl/：内部，深处
⑪ from thence：from that place
⑫ ore /ɔː/：矿石，矿砂

brothers and sisters, husbands and wives, could not trust one another. Sons wished their fathers dead, that① they might come to the inheritance②; family love lay prostrate. The earth was wet with slaughter, and the gods abandoned it, one by one, till Astræa③ alone was left, and finally she also took her departure.

　　Jupiter, seeing this state of things, burned with anger④. He summoned the gods to council. They obeyed the call, and took the road to the palace of heaven. The road, which any one may see in a clear night, stretches across the face of the sky, and is called the Milky Way⑤. Along the road stand the palaces of the illustrious gods; the common people of the skies live apart, on either side. Jupiter addressed the assembly. He set forth⑥ the frightful condition of things on the earth, and closed by announcing his intention to destroy the whole of its inhabitants, and provide a new race, unlike the first, who would be more worthy of life, and much better worshippers of the gods. So saying he took a thunderbolt, and was about to launch it at the world, and destroy it by burning; but recollecting the danger that such a conflagration⑦ might set heaven itself on fire, he changed his plan, and resolved to drown it. The north wind, which scatters the clouds, was chained up; the south⑧ was sent out, and soon covered all the face of heaven with a cloak of pitchy⑨ darkness. The clouds, driven together, resound with a crash; torrents of rain fall; the crops are laid low; the year's labor of the husbandman⑩ perishes in an hour. Jupiter, not satisfied with his own waters, calls on his brother Neptune to aid him with his. He lets loose the rivers, and pours them over the land. At the same time, he heaves the land with an earthquake, and brings in the reflux⑪ of the ocean over the shores. Flocks, herds, men, and houses are swept away, and temples, with their sacred enclosures, profaned. If any edifice remained standing, it was overwhelmed, and its turrets lay hid beneath the waves. Now all was sea, sea without shore. Here and there an individual remained on a projecting hilltop, and a few, in boats, pulled the oar where they had lately driven the plough. The fishes swim among the tree-tops; the anchor is let down into a garden. Where the graceful lambs played but now⑫, unwieldy sea calves gambol⑬. The wolf swims among the sheep, the yellow lions and tigers struggle in the water. The strength of the wild boar serves him not, nor his swiftness the stag. The birds fall with weary wing into the

---

① 　that：以便

② 　come to the inheritance：继承遗产

③ 　(作者原注)The goddess of innocence and purity. After leaving earth, she was placed among the stars, where she became the constellation Virgo—the Virgin. Themis (Justice) was the mother of Astræa. (Astræa 是天真和纯洁女神,离开地球后,她被安置在星星中间,成为室女座。公正女神 Themis 是 Astræa 的母亲。)

④ 　burn with anger：怒火中烧

⑤ 　the Milky Way：银河

⑥ 　set forth：叙述,陈述,讲述

⑦ 　conflagration /ˌkɒnfləˈɡreɪʃn/：大火

⑧ 　the south：the south wind

⑨ 　pitchy /ˈpɪtʃɪ/：和沥青一样黑的

⑩ 　husbandman /ˈhʌzbəndmən/：农夫,庄稼汉

⑪ 　reflux /ˈriːflʌks/：回流,倒流

⑫ 　but now：就在刚才

⑬ 　unwieldy /ʌnˈwiːldɪ/：笨拙的;gambol /ˈɡæmbəl/：跳跃,嬉戏

water, having found no land for a resting-place. Those living beings whom the water spared fell a prey to① hunger.

Parnassus② alone, of all the mountains, overtopped③ the waves; and there Deucalion④, and his wife Pyrrha⑤, of the race⑥ of Prometheus, found refuge⑦—he a just⑧ man, and she a faithful worshipper of the gods. Jupiter, when he saw none left alive but this pair, and remembered their harmless lives and pious demeanor⑨, ordered the north winds to drive away the clouds, and disclose the skies to earth, and earth to the skies. Neptune also directed Triton⑩ to blow on his shell, and sound a retreat to the waters. The waters obeyed, and the sea returned to its shores, and the rivers to their channels⑪. Then Deucalion thus addressed Pyrrha: "O wife, only surviving woman, joined to me first by the ties of kindred and marriage, and now by a common danger, would⑫ that we possessed the power of our ancestor Prometheus, and could renew the race as he at first made it! But as we cannot, let us seek⑬ yonder temple, and inquire of the gods⑭ what remains for us to do." They entered the temple, deformed as it was with slime⑮, and approached the altar⑯, where no fire burned. There they fell prostrate⑰ on the earth, and prayed the goddess to inform them how they might retrieve their miserable affairs. The oracle answered, "Depart from the temple with head veiled and garments unbound, and cast behind you the bones of your mother." They heard the words with astonishment. Pyrrha first broke silence: "We cannot obey; we dare not profane the remains⑱ of our parents." They sought the thickest shades of the wood, and revolved⑲ the oracle in their minds. At length Deucalion spoke: "Either my sagacity deceives me, or the command is one we may obey without impiety. The earth is the great parent of all; the stones are her bones; these we may cast behind us⑳; and I think this is what the oracle means. At least, it will do no harm to try." They veiled their faces, unbound their garments, and picked up stones, and cast them behind them. The stones (wonderful to relate) began to grow soft, and

---

① fall a prey to: 成为……的牺牲品
② Parnassus /pɑːˈnæsəs/: 山名,位于今希腊中希腊大区福基斯州,Delphi 以北不远处,海拔约 2 460 米。
③ overtop /ˌəʊvəˈtɒp/: 比……高
④ Deucalion: /djuːˈkeɪljən/
⑤ Pyrrha: /ˈpɪrə/
⑥ race: 血统
⑦ refuge /ˈrefjuːdʒ/: 避难处
⑧ just: 正直的
⑨ demeanor /dɪˈmiːnə/: 行为,举止
⑩ Triton /ˈtraɪtn/: Neptune 之子;参见 *The Age of Fable* 第 22 章关于 Triton 的叙述。
⑪ channel /ˈtʃænl/: 河床
⑫ would: 但愿
⑬ seek: 前往
⑭ inquire of the gods: 向神打听
⑮ deformed /dɪˈfɔːmd / as it was with slime: 因为泥浆而变得面目全非的
⑯ altar /ˈɔːltə/: 祭坛
⑰ prostrate /ˈprɒstreɪt/: 拜倒在地的
⑱ remains: 遗骨,遗骸,遗体
⑲ revolve /rɪˈvɒlv/: 反复思考,仔细揣酌
⑳ we may cast these (the stones) behind us

assume shape①. By degrees, they put on a rude resemblance to the human form, like a block half-finished in the hands of the sculptor. The moisture and slime that were about them became flesh; the stony part became bones; the veins② remained veins, retaining their name, only changing their use. Those thrown by the hand of the man became men, and those by the woman became women. It was a hard③ race, and well adapted to labor, as we find ourselves to be at this day, giving plain indications of our origin.

Prometheus has been a favorite subject with the poets. He is represented as the friend of mankind, who interposed in their behalf when Jove was incensed④ against them, and who taught them civilization and the arts. But as, in so doing, he transgressed⑤ the will of Jupiter, he drew down on himself the anger of the ruler of gods and men⑥. Jupiter had him chained to a rock on Mount Caucasus⑦, where a vulture preyed on his liver, which was renewed as fast as devoured. This state of torment might have been brought to an end at any time by Prometheus, if he had been willing to submit to⑧ his oppressor; for he possessed a secret which involved the stability of Jove's throne, and if he would have revealed it, he might have been at once taken into favor. But that he disdained to do⑨. He has therefore become the symbol of magnanimous⑩ endurance of unmerited suffering, and strength of will resisting oppression.

Chapter Ⅲ
Apollo and Daphne—Pyramus and Thisbe—Cephalus and Procris

The slime with which the earth was covered by the waters of the flood produced an excessive fertility, which called forth⑪ every variety of production, both bad and good. Among the rest, Python⑫, an enormous serpent, crept forth, the terror of the people, and lurked in the caves of Mount Parnassus. Apollo slew him with his arrows—weapons which he had not before used against any but feeble animals, hares, wild goats, and such game⑬. In commemoration⑭ of this illustrious

① assume shape：呈现出形状
② vein：(石头上的)纹理,条纹,纹路；(人体中的)血管。注意前后两词的意义。
③ hard：双关语,可表示：(像石头一样)坚硬的；(人)能吃苦耐劳的。
④ incensed /ɪnˈsenst/：生气的,发怒的
⑤ transgress /trænzˈgres/：违背,违反
⑥ the ruler of gods and men：Jupiter
⑦ Mount Caucasus /ˈkɔːkəsəs/：高加索山,西面是黑海,东面是里海,在俄罗斯、格鲁吉亚、阿塞拜疆和亚美尼亚四国境内。
⑧ submit to：屈服于
⑨ But he disdained to do that.
⑩ magnanimous /mæɡˈnænɪməs/：有巨大勇气的,勇敢的
⑪ call forth：使产生,引起
⑫ Python：/ˈpaɪθən/
⑬ game：猎物
⑭ commemoration /kəˌmeməˈreɪʃn/：纪念

conquest he instituted① the Pythian games②, in which the victor in feats of strength, swiftness of foot, or in the chariot race was crowned with a wreath of beech leaves; for the laurel③ was not yet adopted by Apollo as his own tree.

Apollo and Daphne

Daphne④ was Apollo's first love. It was not brought about by accident, but by the malice⑤ of Cupid. Apollo saw the boy playing with his bow and arrows; and being himself elated with his recent victory over Python, he said to him, "What have you to do with warlike⑥ weapons, saucy boy? Leave them for hands worthy of them. Behold⑦ the conquest I have won by means of them over the vast serpent who stretched his poisonous body over acres⑧ of the plain! Be content with your torch, child, and kindle up your flames, as you call them, where you will, but presume⑨ not to meddle with my weapons." Venus's boy heard these words, and rejoined⑩, "Your arrows may strike all things else, Apollo, but mine shall strike you." So saying, he took his stand on a rock of Parnassus, and drew from his quiver⑪ two arrows of different workmanship⑫, one to excite love, the other to repel it. The former was of gold and sharp pointed, the latter blunt and tipped with lead⑬. With the leaden shaft he struck the nymph Daphne, the daughter of the river god Peneus⑭, and with the golden one Apollo, through the heart. Forthwith the god was seized with love for the maiden, and she abhorred the thought of loving. Her delight was in woodland sports and in the spoils of the chase⑮. Many lovers sought her, but she spurned them all, ranging the woods, and taking no thought of Cupid nor of Hymen⑯. Her father often said to her, "Daughter, you owe me a son-in-law; you owe me grandchildren." She, hating the thought of marriage as a crime, with her beautiful face tinged all over with blushes, threw her arms around her father's neck, and said, "Dearest father, grant me this favor, that I may always remain unmarried, like Diana." He consented, but at the same time said, "Your own face will forbid it."

---

① institute /ˈɪnstɪtjuːt/：建立
② Pythian /ˈpɪθɪən/ games：古希腊重要性仅次于奥林匹克运动会的运动会,每四年举行一届。关于古希腊的运动会,参见 The Age of Fable 第 20 章。
③ laurel /ˈlɒrəl/：月桂树
④ Daphne：/ˈdæfniː/
⑤ malice /ˈmælɪs/：恶意,怨恨
⑥ warlike /ˈwɔːlaɪk/：战争的,用于战争的
⑦ behold /bɪˈhəʊld/：看
⑧ acre /ˈeɪkə/：(复数)土地
⑨ presume /prɪˈzjuːm/：放肆,冒昧
⑩ rejoin：回答
⑪ quiver /ˈkwɪvə/：箭筒,箭囊
⑫ workmanship /ˈwɜːkmənʃɪp/：(产品的)做工,工艺
⑬ lead /led/：铅
⑭ Peneus：/ˈpiːnjuːs/
⑮ the spoils of the chase：打猎的成果,打猎的战利品;the chase：打猎
⑯ taking no thought of Cupid nor of Hymen：既不想恋爱,也不想结婚。Hymen /ˈhaɪmən/：古希腊、罗马神话中的婚姻之神,艺术作品中表现为一手持火炬和婚纱的年轻男子。此处指婚姻。

Apollo loved her, and longed to obtain her; and he who gives oracles to all the world was not wise enough to look into his own fortunes. He saw her hair flung loose over her shoulders, and said, "If so charming in disorder, what would it be if arranged?" He saw her eyes bright as stars; he saw her lips, and was not satisfied with only seeing them. He admired her hands and arms, naked to the shoulder, and whatever was hidden from view he imagined more beautiful still. He followed her; she fled, swifter than the wind, and delayed not a moment at his entreaties①. "Stay," said he, "daughter of Peneus; I am not a foe. Do not fly② me as a lamb flies the wolf, or a dove the hawk. It is for love I pursue you. You make me miserable, for fear you should fall and hurt yourself on these stones, and I should be the cause. Pray③ run slower, and I will follow slower. I am no clown④, no rude peasant. Jupiter is my father, and I am lord⑤ of Delphos⑥ and Tenedos⑦, and know all things, present and future. I am the god of song and the lyre. My arrows fly true to the mark⑧; but, alas! An arrow more fatal than mine has pierced my heart! I am the god of medicine, and know the virtues⑨ of all healing plants. Alas! I suffer a malady⑩ that no balm can cure!"

The nymph continued her flight, and left his plea half uttered. And even as she fled she charmed him. The wind blew her garments, and her unbound hair streamed loose behind her. The god grew impatient to find his wooings thrown away, and, sped by Cupid, gained upon her in the race. It was like a hound pursuing a hare, with open jaws ready to seize, while the feebler animal darts forward, slipping from the very grasp. So flew the god and the virgin—he on the wings of love, and she on those of fear. The pursuer is the more rapid, however, and gains upon her, and his panting breath blows upon her hair. Her strength begins to fail, and, ready to sink, she calls upon her father, the river god: "Help me, Peneus! open the earth to enclose me, or change my form, which has brought me into this danger!" Scarcely had she spoken, when a stiffness seized all her limbs; her bosom began to be enclosed in a tender bark⑪; her hair became leaves; her arms became branches; her foot stuck fast in the ground, as a root; her face became a tree-top, retaining nothing of its former self but its beauty. Apollo stood amazed. He touched the stem, and felt the flesh tremble under the new bark. He embraced the branches, and lavished kisses on the wood. The branches shrank from his lips. "Since you cannot be my wife," said he, "you shall assuredly be my tree. I will wear you for my crown; I will decorate with you my harp and my

---

① entreaty /ɪnˈtriːti/：祈求,恳请

② fly：逃离

③ pray：please

④ clown：乡巴佬

⑤ lord：主人

⑥ Delphos /ˈdelfəs/：希腊岛屿 Delos 的古名,Apollo 的出生地。参见 *The Age of Fable* 第 4 章 Latona 的故事。

⑦ Tenedos /ˈtenədɒs/：岛屿名,位于爱琴海北部。该岛今天叫 Bozcaada,属于土耳其。在 Delphos 岛和 Tenedos 岛都有 Apollo 的神庙,所以他说他是这两个岛的主人。

⑧ 我射箭百发百中。

⑨ virtue：巨大的价值

⑩ malady /ˈmælədi/：疾病

⑪ bark：树皮

quiver; and when the great Roman conquerors lead up the triumphal pomp to the Capitol①, you shall be woven into wreaths for their brows. And, as eternal youth is mine, you also shall be always green, and your leaf know no decay." The nymph, now changed into a Laurel tree, bowed its head in grateful acknowledgement.

Pyramus and Thisbe

Pyramus② was the handsomest youth, and Thisbe③ the fairest maiden, in all Babylonia④, where Semiramis⑤ reigned. Their parents occupied adjoining houses; and neighborhood brought the young people together, and acquaintance ripened into love. They would gladly have married, but their parents forbade. One thing, however, they could not forbid—that love should glow with equal ardor in the bosoms of both. They conversed by signs and glances, and the fire burned more intensely for being covered up. In the wall that parted the two houses there was a crack⑥, caused by some fault in the structure⑦. No one had remarked⑧ it before, but the lovers discovered it. What will not love discover! It afforded a passage to the voice; and tender messages used to pass backward and forward through the gap. As they stood, Pyramus on this side, Thisbe on that, their breaths would mingle. "Cruel wall," they said, "why do you keep two lovers apart? But we will not be ungrateful. We owe you, we confess, the privilege of transmitting loving words to willing ears." Such words they uttered on different sides of the wall; and when night came and they must say farewell, they pressed their lips upon the wall, she on her side, he on his, as they could come no nearer.

Next morning, when Aurora⑨ had put out the stars, and the sun had melted the frost from the grass, they met at the accustomed spot. Then, after lamenting their hard fate, they agreed that next night, when all was still, they would slip away from watchful eyes, leave their dwellings and walk out into the fields; and to insure a meeting, repair to a well-known edifice standing without⑩ the city's bounds, called the Tomb of Ninus⑪, and that the one who came first should await the other at the foot of a certain tree. It was a white mulberry tree, and stood near a cool spring. All was agreed on, and they waited impatiently for the sun to go down beneath the waters and night to rise up from them. Then cautiously Thisbe stole forth, unobserved by the family, her head covered with a

---

① Capitol /ˈkæpɪtəl/: 罗马的 Jupiter 神庙
② Pyramus: /ˈpɪrəməs/
③ Thisbe: /ˈθɪzbi/
④ Babylonia /ˌbæbɪˈləʊnɪə/: 巴比伦，位于美索不达米亚东南部，底格里斯河和幼发拉底河之间，相当于现代伊拉克南部地区，即从伊拉克首都巴格达到波斯湾的地区。
⑤ Semiramis /seˈmɪrəmɪs/: 亚述（Assyria /əˈsɪrɪə/）国王 Ninus 的王后 Sammu-ramat 在希腊语中叫 Semiramis，Ninus 死后，Semiramis 执政多年。
⑥ crack: 裂缝
⑦ structure /ˈstrʌktʃə/: 建造过程
⑧ remark /rɪˈmɑːk/: 注意到
⑨ Aurora /ɔːˈrɔːrə/: 黎明女神
⑩ without: outside
⑪ Ninus /ˈnaɪnəs/: 亚述国王，Semiramis 的丈夫。

veil, made her way to the monument and sat down under the tree. As she sat alone in the dim light of the evening she descried a lioness, her jaws reeking with recent slaughter, approaching the fountain to slake① her thirst. Thisbe fled at the sight, and sought refuge in the hollow of a rock. As she fled she dropped her veil. The lioness after drinking at the spring turned to retreat to the woods, and seeing the veil on the ground, tossed and rent it with her bloody mouth.

Pyramus, having been delayed, now approached the place of meeting. He saw in the sand the footsteps of the lion, and the color fled from his cheeks at the sight. Presently he found the veil all rent and bloody. "O hapless girl," said he, "I have been the cause of thy death! Thou, more worthy of life than I, hast fallen the first victim②. I will follow. I am the guilty cause, in tempting thee forth to a place of such peril, and not being myself on the spot to guard thee③. Come forth, ye lions, from the rocks, and tear this guilty body with your teeth." He took up the veil, carried it with him to the appointed tree, and covered it with kisses and with tears. "My blood also shall stain your texture," said he, and drawing his sword plunged it into his heart. The blood spurted from the wound, and tinged the white mulberries of the tree all red; and sinking into the earth reached the roots, so that the red color mounted through the trunk to the fruit.

By this time Thisbe, still trembling with fear, yet wishing not to disappoint her lover, stepped cautiously forth, looking anxiously for the youth, eager to tell him the danger she had escaped. When she came to the spot and saw the changed color of the mulberries she doubted whether it was the same place. While she hesitated she saw the form of one struggling in the agonies of death. She started back, a shudder ran through her frame④ as a ripple on the face of the still water when a sudden breeze sweeps over it. But as soon as she recognized her lover, she screamed and beat her breast, embracing the lifeless body, pouring tears into its wounds, and imprinting kisses on the cold lips. "O Pyramus," she cried, "what has done this? Answer me, Pyramus; it is your own Thisbe that speaks. Hear me, dearest, and lift that drooping head!" At the name of Thisbe Pyramus opened his eyes, then closed them again. She saw her veil stained with blood and the scabbard⑤ empty of its sword. "Thy own hand has slain thee, and for my sake," she said. "I too can be brave for once, and my love is as strong as thine⑥. I will follow thee in death, for I have been the cause; and death which alone could part us shall not prevent my joining thee. And ye, unhappy parents of us both, deny us not our united request. As love and death have joined us, let one tomb contain us. And thou, tree, retain the marks of slaughter. Let thy berries still serve for memorials of our blood." So saying she plunged the sword into her breast. Her parents ratified her wish, the gods also ratified it. The two bodies were buried in one sepulchre⑦, and the tree ever after brought forth purple berries, as it does to this day.

---

① slake: 解（渴）

② thy /ðaɪ/: your; thou /ðaʊ/: （主格）you; hast: 主语为 thou 时, have 的屈折变化形式。

③ thee /ðiː/: （宾格）you

④ frame: 身体

⑤ scabbard /ˈskæbəd/: 剑鞘

⑥ thine /ðaɪn/: your, 用在以元音开头的名词前, 如: thine eyes; （名词性物主代词）yours

⑦ sepulchre /ˈseplkə/: 坟墓

Cephalus and Procris

Cephalus[1] was a beautiful youth and fond of manly sports. He would rise before the dawn to pursue the chase[2]. Aurora saw him when she first looked forth, fell in love with him, and stole him away. But Cephalus was just married to a charming wife whom he devotedly loved. Her name was Procris[3]. She was a favorite of Diana, the goddess of hunting, who had given her a dog which could outrun every rival, and a javelin which would never fail of its mark[4]; and Procris gave these presents to her husband. Cephalus was so happy in his wife that he resisted all the entreaties of Aurora, and she finally dismissed him in displeasure, saying, "Go, ungrateful mortal, keep your wife, whom, if I am not much mistaken, you will one day be very sorry you ever saw again."

Cephalus returned, and was as happy as ever in his wife and his woodland sports. Now it happened some angry deity had sent a ravenous[5] fox to annoy the country; and the hunters turned out in great strength to capture it. Their efforts were all in vain; no dog could run it down; and at last they came to Cephalus to borrow his famous dog, whose name was Lelaps. No sooner was the dog let loose than he darted off, quicker than their eye could follow him. If they had not seen his footprints in the sand they would have thought he flew. Cephalus and others stood on a hill and saw the race. The fox tried every art; he ran in a circle and turned on his track, the dog close upon him, with open jaws, snapping at his heels, but biting only the air. Cephalus was about to use his javelin, when suddenly he saw both dog and game stop instantly. The heavenly powers who had given both were not willing that either should conquer. In the very attitude[6] of life and action they were turned into stone. So lifelike and natural did they look, you would have thought, as you looked at them, that one was going to bark, the other to leap forward.

Cephalus, though he had lost his dog, still continued to take delight in the chase. He would go out at early morning, ranging the woods and hills unaccompanied by any one, needing no help, for his javelin was a sure[7] weapon in all cases. Fatigued with hunting, when the sun got high he would seek a shady nook[8] where a cool stream flowed, and, stretched on the grass, with his garments thrown aside, would enjoy the breeze. Sometimes he would say aloud, "Come, sweet breeze, come and fan my breast, come and allay the heat that burns me." Some one passing by one day heard him talking in this way to the air, and, foolishly believing that he was talking to some maiden, went and told the secret to Procris, Cephalus's wife. Love is credulous. Procris, at the sudden shock, fainted away. Presently recovering, she said, "It cannot be true; I will not believe it unless I myself am a witness to it." So she waited, with anxious heart, till the next

---

① Cephalus：/ˈsefələs/
② the chase：被追赶的对象，猎物
③ Procris：/ˈprɒkrɪs/
④ fail of its mark：击不中目标；mark：目标，靶子
⑤ ravenous /ˈrævənəs/：极度饥饿的，掠夺成性的
⑥ attitude：姿态
⑦ sure：靠得住的
⑧ nook：隐蔽的地方

morning, when Cephalus went to hunt as usual. Then she stole out after him, and concealed herself in the place where the informer① directed her. Cephalus came as he was wont when tired with sport, and stretched himself on the green bank, saying, "Come, sweet breeze, come and fan me; you know how I love you! you make the groves and my solitary rambles delightful." He was running on in this way when he heard, or thought he heard, a sound as of a sob in the bushes. Supposing it some wild animal, he threw his javelin at the spot. A cry from his beloved Procris told him that the weapon had too surely met its mark. He rushed to the place, and found her bleeding, and with sinking strength endeavoring to draw forth from the wound the javelin, her own gift. Cephalus raised her from the earth, strove to stanch the blood, and called her to revive and not to leave him miserable, to reproach himself with her death. She opened her feeble eyes, and forced herself to utter these few words: "I implore you, if you have ever loved me, if I have ever deserved kindness at your hands, my husband, grant me this last request; do not marry that odious Breeze!"② This disclosed the whole mystery: but alas! what advantage to disclose it now! She died; but her face wore a calm expression, and she looked pityingly and forgivingly on her husband when he made her understand the truth.

Chapter Ⅳ
Juno and Her Rivals, Io and Callisto—Diana and Actæon—Latona and the Rustics

Io

Juno one day perceived it suddenly grow dark, and immediately suspected that her husband had raised a cloud to hide some of his doings that would not bear the light. She brushed away the cloud, and saw her husband on the banks of a glassy river, with a beautiful heifer③ standing near him. Juno suspected the heifer's form concealed some fair nymph of mortal mould—as was, indeed, the case; for it was Io④, the daughter of the river god Inachus⑤, whom Jupiter had been flirting with, and, when he became aware of the approach of his wife, had changed into that form.

Juno joined her husband, and noticing the heifer praised its beauty, and asked whose it was, and of what herd⑥. Jupiter, to stop questions, replied that it was a fresh creation from the earth⑦.

① informer /ɪnˈfɔːmə/：通报者，告密者
② 如果有人把英语中的 breeze 误认为是一个女孩的名字当然是很可笑的，但在古希腊语中，αὔρα（breeze）是一个阴性名词，所以把它误解成一个女孩的名字是说得通的。
③ heifer /ˈhefə/：小母牛
④ Io：/ˈaɪəʊ/
⑤ Inachus：/ˈaɪnəkəs/
⑥ of what herd：属于哪个牛群
⑦ 它（小母牛）是刚从地里长出来的。

Juno asked to have it as a gift. What could Jupiter do? He was loath to give his mistress to his wife; yet how refuse so trifling① a present as a simple heifer? He could not, without exciting suspicion; so he consented. The goddess was not yet relieved of her suspicions; so she delivered the heifer to Argus②, to be strictly watched.

Now Argus had a hundred eyes in his head, and never went to sleep with more than two at a time, so that he kept watch of Io constantly. He suffered③ her to feed through the day, and at night tied her up with a vile rope round her neck. She would have stretched out her arms to implore freedom of Argus④, but she had no arms to stretch out, and her voice was a bellow⑤ that frightened even herself. She saw her father and her sisters, went near them, and suffered them to pat her back, and heard them admire her beauty. Her father reached her a tuft of grass, and she licked the outstretched hand. She longed to make herself known to him, and would have uttered her wish; but, alas! words were wanting. At length⑥ she bethought⑦ herself of writing, and inscribed her name—it was a short one—with her hoof on the sand. Inachus recognized it, and discovering that his daughter, whom he had long sought in vain, was hidden under this disguise, mourned over her, and, embracing her white neck, exclaimed, "Alas! my daughter, it would have been a less grief to have lost you altogether⑧!" While he thus lamented, Argus, observing, came and drove her away, and took his seat on a high bank, from whence he could see all around in every direction.

Jupiter was troubled at beholding the sufferings of his mistress, and calling Mercury told him to go and despatch⑨ Argus. Mercury made haste, put his winged slippers on his feet, and cap on his head, took his sleep-producing⑩ wand, and leaped down from the heavenly towers to the earth. There he laid aside his wings, and kept only his wand, with which he presented himself as a shepherd driving his flock. As he strolled on he blew upon his pipes. These were what are called the Syrinx⑪ or Pandean⑫ pipes. Argus listened with delight, for he had never seen the instrument before. "Young man," said he, "come and take a seat by me on this stone. There is no better place for your flocks to graze in than hereabouts⑬, and here is a pleasant shade such as shepherds love⑭." Mercury sat down, talked, and told stories till it grew late, and played upon his pipes his

---

① trifling /ˈtraɪflɪŋ/：微不足道的
② Argus：/ˈɑːɡəs/
③ suffer：同意，允许
④ of Argus：from Argus
⑤ bellow：哞（hǒu）哞，牛鸣声
⑥ at length：in the end
⑦ bethink oneself：想起，想到
⑧ altogether：完全
⑨ despatch（dispatch）/dɪˈspætʃ/：处决，杀死
⑩ sleep-producing：催眠的
⑪ syrinx /ˈsɪrɪŋks/：排箫
⑫ Pandean /pænˈdiːən/：of Pan
⑬ hereabouts /ˌhɪərəˈbaʊts/：在这附近
⑭ a pleasant shade such as shepherds love：牧羊人喜欢的那种舒服的阴凉处

most soothing strains, hoping to lull the watchful eyes to sleep, but all in vain; for Argus still contrived to keep some of his eyes open though he shut the rest.

Among other stories, Mercury told him how the instrument on which he played was invented. "There was a certain nymph, whose name was Syrinx, who was much beloved by the satyrs[①] and spirits[②] of the wood; but she would have none of them, but was a faithful worshipper of Diana, and followed the chase. You would have thought it was Diana herself, had you seen her in her hunting dress, only that her bow was of horn and Diana's of silver[③]. One day, as she was returning from the chase, Pan met her, told her just this, and added more of the same sort[④]. She ran away, without stopping to hear his compliments[⑤], and he pursued till she came to the bank of the river, where he overtook her, and she had only time to call for help on her friends the water nymphs. They heard and consented. Pan threw his arms around what he supposed to be the form of the nymph, and found he embraced only a tuft of reeds[⑥]! As he breathed a sigh, the air sounded through the reeds, and produced a plaintive[⑦] melody. The god, charmed with the novelty and with the sweetness of the music, said, 'Thus, then, at least, you shall be mine.' And he took some of the reeds, and placing them together, of unequal lengths, side by side, made an instrument which he called Syrinx, in honor of the nymph." Before Mercury had finished his story he saw Argus's eyes all asleep. As his head nodded forward on his breast, Mercury with one stroke cut his neck through, and tumbled his head down the rocks. O hapless Argus! the light of your hundred eyes is quenched at once! Juno took them and put them as ornaments on the tail of her peacock, where they remain to this day.

But the vengeance of Juno was not yet satiated. She sent a gadfly[⑧] to torment Io, who fled over the whole world from its pursuit. She swam through the Ionian sea[⑨], which derived its name from her, then roamed over the plains of Illyria[⑩], ascended Mount Hæmus[⑪], and crossed the Thracian strait[⑫], thence named the Bosphorus[⑬](cowford), rambled on through Scythia[⑭], and the

---

① satyr /'sætə/：森林之神，在早期的希腊艺术品中被表现为长着马耳朵和马尾巴的人，在后来的罗马艺术品中被表现为长着山羊耳朵、尾巴、腿和角的人，其性好色。

② spirit：神灵，鬼怪

③ only that her bow was of horn and Diana's of silver：唯一的区别是她的弓是动物的角做成的，而 Diana 的弓是银子做的。

④ told her just this, and added more of the same sort：告诉她她像 Diana，还添加了一些诸如此类的话。

⑤ compliment /'kɔmplimənt/：恭维话

⑥ a tuft of reeds：一丛芦苇

⑦ plaintive /'pleintiv/：忧伤的

⑧ gadfly /'gædflai/：牛虻

⑨ the Ionian /ai'əuniən/ sea：地中海的一部分，东边是希腊，北边是亚得里亚海（Adriatic Sea）海口，西边是意大利。

⑩ Illyria /i'liriə/：古代地区名，位于巴尔干半岛（Balkan Peninsula）西北部，包括今天的阿尔巴尼亚（Albania）北部、门的内哥罗（Montenegro）、克罗地亚（Croatia）靠近亚得里亚海的部分地区。

⑪ Mount Hæmus /'hiːməs/：位于今巴尔干半岛和保加利亚（Bulgaria）的巴尔干山脉（Balkan Mountains），巴尔干山脉在保加利亚语中叫 Stara Planina，在拉丁语中叫 Hæmus。

⑫ Thracian /'θreiʃn/ strait：即今天的博斯普鲁斯海峡（the Bosphorus）。

⑬ Bosphorus /'bɔsfərəs/（Bosporus /'bɔspərəs/）：博斯普鲁斯海峡，位于土耳其，连接黑海（the Black Sea）和马尔马拉海（the Sea of Marmara）。Bosphorus（Bosporus）一词的字面意思是"牛涉水而过之处"。

⑭ Scythia /'siðiə/：古代地区名，包括今天的欧洲东南部和黑海附近的亚洲地区。

country of the Cimmerians①, and arrived at last on the banks of the Nile②. At length Jupiter interceded③ for her, and upon his promising not to pay her any more attentions Juno consented to restore her to her form. It was curious to see her gradually recover her former self. The coarse hairs fell from her body, her horns shrank up, her eyes grew narrower, her mouth shorter; hands and fingers came instead of hoofs to her forefeet; in fine④ there was nothing left of the heifer, except her beauty. At first she was afraid to speak, for fear she should low⑤, but gradually she recovered her confidence and was restored to her father and sisters.

Callisto

Callisto⑥ was another maiden who excited the jealousy of Juno, and the goddess changed her into a bear. "I will take away," said she, "that beauty with which you have captivated my husband." Down fell Callisto on her hands and knees; she tried to stretch out her arms in supplication⑦—they were already beginning to be covered with black hair. Her hands grew rounded, became armed with crooked claws, and served for feet; her mouth, which Jove used to praise for its beauty, became a horrid pair of jaws; her voice, which if unchanged would have moved the heart to pity, became a growl, more fit to inspire terror. Yet her former disposition⑧ remained, and with continual groaning, she bemoaned her fate, and stood upright as well as she could, lifting up her paws to beg for mercy, and felt that Jove was unkind, though she could not tell him so. Ah, how often, afraid to stay in the woods all night alone, she wandered about the neighborhood of her former haunts⑨; how often, frightened by the dogs, did she, so lately a huntress, fly in terror from the hunters! Often she fled from the wild beasts, forgetting that she was now a wild beast herself; and, bear as she was, was afraid of the bears.

One day a youth espied her as he was hunting. She saw him and recognized him as her own son, now grown a young man. She stopped and felt inclined to embrace him. As she was about to approach, he, alarmed, raised his hunting spear, and was on the point of⑩ transfixing⑪ her, when Jupiter, beholding, arrested⑫ the crime, and snatching away both of them, placed them in

---

① Cimmerian /sɪˈmɪərɪən/：古代游牧民族，最初住在克里米亚（Crimea），公元前 8 世纪末被赶到小亚细亚（Asia Minor）。[小亚细亚又叫安纳托利亚（Anatolia /ˌænəˈtəʊlɪə /），是亚洲最西边的一个半岛，北临黑海，西临爱琴海，南临地中海，是今土耳其国土的主体部分。]

② the Nile /naɪl/：尼罗河，位于东非，世界最长的河流（约 6 670 千米），发源于非洲中东部的维多利亚湖（Lake Victoria）附近，向北流经乌干达（Uganda）、南苏丹（South Sudan）、苏丹（Sudan）和埃及（Egypt），注入地中海。

③ intercede /ˌɪntəˈsiːd/：说情，求情

④ in fine：in the end, at last

⑤ low：吽，牛鸣叫

⑥ Callisto：/kəˈlɪstəʊ/

⑦ supplication /ˌsʌplɪˈkeɪʃn/：哀求，祈求

⑧ disposition /ˌdɪspəˈzɪʃn/：气质

⑨ haunt /hɔːnt/：经常去的地方

⑩ be on the point of：正要……

⑪ transfix /trænsˈfɪks/：刺穿

⑫ arrest：使停止

the heavens as the Great and Little Bear①.

Juno was in a rage to see her rival so set in honor, and hastened to ancient Tethys and Oceanus②, the powers③ of ocean, and in answer to their inquiries thus told the cause of her coming: "Do you ask why I, the queen of the gods, have left the heavenly plains and sought your depths? Learn that I am supplanted④ in heaven—my place is given to another. You will hardly believe me; but look when night darkens the world, and you shall see the two of whom I have so much reason to complain exalted⑤ to the heavens, in that part where the circle is the smallest, in the neighborhood of the pole. Why should any one hereafter tremble at the thought of offending Juno, when such rewards are the consequence of my displeasure? See what I have been able to effect! I forbade her to wear the human form—she is placed among the stars! So do my punishments result—such is the extent of my power! Better that she should have resumed her former shape, as I permitted Io to do. Perhaps he means to marry her, and put me away! But you, my foster-parents⑥, if you feel for me, and see with displeasure this unworthy treatment of me, show it, I beseech you, by forbidding this guilty couple from coming into your waters." The powers of the ocean assented, and consequently the two constellations⑦ of the Great and Little Bear move round and round in heaven, but never sink, as the other stars do, beneath the ocean.

Diana and Actæon

Thus in two instances we have seen Juno's severity⑧ to her rivals; now let us learn how a virgin goddess punished an invader of her privacy⑨.

It was midday, and the sun stood equally distant from either goal, when young Actæon⑩, son of King Cadmus⑪, thus addressed the youths who with him were hunting the stag in the mountains:

"Friends, our nets and our weapons are wet with the blood of our victims; we have had sport enough for one day, and tomorrow we can renew our labors. Now, while Phœbus⑫ parches the earth, let us put by our implements⑬ and indulge ourselves with rest."

There was a valley thick enclosed with cypresses and pines, sacred to the huntress queen,

---

① the Great and Little Bear：大熊星座和小熊星座，又叫 Ursa /ˈɜːsə / Major 和 Ursa Minor.

② Tethys /ˈteθɪs/：sister and wife of Oceanus；Oceanus：/əʊˈsɪənəs /. 参见 *The Age of Fable* 第 22 章关于 Oceanus 和 Tethys 的叙述。

③ power：（异教的）神

④ supplant /səˈplɑːnt/：取代

⑤ exalt /ɪɡˈzɔːlt/：提升

⑥ my foster-parents：Juno 是 Saturn 和 Rhea 的女儿，Jupiter 的妹妹；由于在 Jupiter 与其父 Saturn 的战争中 Rhea 把 Juno 交给 Tethys 和 Oceanus 抚养，所以 Tethys 和 Oceanus 是 Juno 的养父母。

⑦ constellation /ˌkɒnstəˈleɪʃn/：星座

⑧ severity /sɪˈverɪti/：严厉

⑨ privacy /ˈprɪvəsi/：秘密，隐私

⑩ Actæon：/ækˈtiːɒn/

⑪ Cadmus /ˈkædməs/：关于 Cadmus 的故事，参见 *The Age of Fable* 第 12 章。

⑫ Phœbus：太阳神 Apollo 的称号，在希腊语中的意思是"纯洁的""明亮的""光彩夺目的"。此处指太阳。

⑬ implement /ˈɪmplɪment/：武器，工具

Diana. In the extremity① of the valley was a cave, not adorned with art, but nature had counterfeited art in its construction, for she had turned the arch of its roof with stones as delicately fitted as if by the hand of man. A fountain burst out from one side, whose open basin was bounded by a grassy rim. Here the goddess of the woods② used to come when weary with hunting and lave③ her virgin limbs in the sparkling water.

One day, having repaired thither④ with her nymphs, she handed her javelin, her quiver, and her bow to one, her robe to another, while a third unbound the sandals from her feet. Then Crocale, the most skilful of them, arranged her hair, and Nephele, Hyale, and the rest drew water in capacious⑤ urns. While the goddess was thus employed in the labors of the toilet⑥, behold Actæon, having quitted his companions, and rambling without any especial object, came to the place, led thither by his destiny. As he presented himself at the entrance of the cave, the nymphs, seeing a man, screamed and rushed towards the goddess to hide her with their bodies. But she was taller than the rest and overtopped them all by a head. Such a color as tinges the clouds at sunset or at dawn⑦ came over the countenance⑧ of Diana thus taken by surprise⑨. Surrounded as she was by her nymphs, she yet turned half away, and sought with a sudden impulse for her arrows. As they were not at hand, she dashed the water into the face of the intruder⑩, adding these words: "Now go and tell, if you can, that you have seen Diana unapparelled⑪." Immediately a pair of branching stag's horns grew out of his head, his neck gained in length, his ears grew sharp-pointed, his hands became feet, his arms long legs, his body was covered with a hairy spotted⑫ hide⑬. Fear took the place of his former boldness, and the hero fled. He could not but admire his own speed; but when he saw his horns in the water, "Ah, wretched me!" he would have said, but no sound followed the effort. He groaned, and tears flowed down the face which had taken the place of his own. Yet his consciousness remained. What shall he do? —go home to seek the palace, or lie hid in the woods? The latter he was afraid, the former he was ashamed, to do. While he hesitated the dogs saw him. First Melampus, a Spartan dog, gave the signal with his bark, then Pamphagus, Dorceus, Lelaps, Theron, Nape, Tigris, and all the rest, rushed after him swifter than the wind. Over rocks and cliffs, through mountain

---

① extremity /ɪkˈstremətɪ/：尽头

② the goddess of the woods：Diana

③ lave：wash

④ thither /ˈðɪðə/：to that place

⑤ capacious /kəˈpeɪʃəs/：容量大的

⑥ toilet：梳洗

⑦ Such a color as tinges the clouds at sunset or at dawn：blush

⑧ countenance /ˈkaʊtənəns/：面部

⑨ 措手不及的 Diana

⑩ intruder /ɪnˈtruːdə/：入侵者，闯入者

⑪ unapparelled /ˈʌnəˈpærəld/：没有穿衣服的，裸体的

⑫ spotted /ˈspɒtɪd/：有斑点的

⑬ hide：兽皮

gorges that seemed impracticable①, he fled and they followed. Where he had often chased the stag and cheered on② his pack③, his pack now chased him, cheered on by his huntsmen. He longed to cry out, "I am Actæon; recognize your master!" but the words came not at his will. The air resounded with the bark of the dogs. Presently one fastened on his back, another seized his shoulder. While they held their master, the rest of the pack came up and buried their teeth in his flesh. He groaned,—not in a human voice, yet certainly not in a stag's,—and falling on his knees, raised his eyes, and would have raised his arms in supplication, if he had had them. His friends and fellow-huntsmen cheered on the dogs, and looked everywhere for Actæon, calling on him to join the sport. At the sound of his name he turned his head, and heard them regret that he should be away. He earnestly wished he was. He would have been well pleased to see the exploits④ of his dogs, but to feel them was too much. They were all around him, rending and tearing; and it was not till they had torn his life out that the anger of Diana was satisfied.

Latona and the Rustics

Some thought the goddess in this instance more severe than was just, while others praised her conduct as strictly consistent with her virgin dignity. As usual, the recent event brought older ones to mind, and one of the bystanders⑤ told this story: "Some countrymen⑥ of Lycia⑦ once insulted the goddess Latona⑧, but not with impunity⑨. When I was young, my father, who had grown too old for active labors, sent me to Lycia to drive thence⑩ some choice⑪ oxen, and there I saw the very pond and marsh where the wonder happened. Near by stood an ancient altar, black with the smoke of sacrifice and almost buried among the reeds. I inquired whose altar it might be, whether of Faunus⑫ or the Naiads⑬, or some god of the neighboring mountain, and one of the country people replied, 'No mountain or river god possesses this altar, but she whom royal Juno in her jealousy drove from land to land, denying her any spot of earth whereon to rear her twins⑭. Bearing in her arms the infant deities⑮, Latona reached this land, weary with her burden and parched with thirst. By chance she espied in the bottom of the valley this pond of clear water,

---

① impracticable /ɪmˈpræktɪkəbl/: (道路等)无法通过的

② cheer on: 嗾(sǒu)使,怂恿做坏事

③ pack: (猎狗、野兽等的)一群

④ exploit /ˈeksplɔɪt/: 业绩,功绩

⑤ bystander /ˈbaɪstændə/: 旁观者

⑥ countryman /ˈkʌntrimən/: 乡下人

⑦ Lycia /ˈlisiə/: 古代地区名,位于小亚细亚西南部海岸。

⑧ Latona: /ləˈtəʊnə/

⑨ impunity /ɪmˈpjuːnəti/: 免受惩罚

⑩ thence /ðens/: 从那里

⑪ choice: 优质的,上等的

⑫ Faunus /ˈfɔːnəs/: 参见 *The Age of Fable* 第 1 章关于 Faunus 的叙述。

⑬ Naiad /ˈnaɪæd/: 住在河流、湖泊中的仙女

⑭ her twins: Latona 是双胞胎兄妹 Apollo 和 Diana 的母亲。

⑮ the infant deities: Apollo 和 Diana

where the country people were at work gathering willows and osiers①. The goddess approached, and kneeling on the bank would have slaked her thirst in the cool stream, but the rustics② forbade her. 'Why do you refuse me water?' said she; 'water is free to all. Nature allows no one to claim as property the sunshine, the air, or the water. I come to take my share of the common blessing. Yet I ask it of you③ as a favor. I have no intention of washing my limbs in it, weary though they be, but only to quench my thirst. My mouth is so dry that I can hardly speak. A draught of water would be nectar to me; it would revive me, and I would own myself indebted to you for life itself. Let these infants move your pity, who stretch out their little arms as if to plead for me;' and the children, as it happened, were stretching out their arms.

"Who would not have been moved with these gentle words of the goddess? But these clowns④ persisted in their rudeness; they even added jeers and threats of violence if she did not leave the place. Nor was this all. They waded into the pond and stirred up the mud with their feet, so as to make the water unfit to drink. Latona was so angry that she ceased to mind her thirst. She no longer supplicated the clowns, but lifting her hands to heaven exclaimed, "May they never quit that pool, but pass their lives there!" And it came to pass accordingly. They now live in the water, sometimes totally submerged, then raising their heads above the surface or swimming upon it. Sometimes they come out upon the bank, but soon leap back again into the water. They still use their base voices in railing⑤, and though they have the water all to themselves, are not ashamed to croak⑥ in the midst⑦ of it. Their voices are harsh, their throats bloated, their mouths have become stretched by constant railing, their necks have shrunk up and disappeared, and their heads are joined to their bodies. Their backs are green, their disproportioned⑧ bellies white, and in short they are now frogs, and dwell in the slimy pool."

The persecution which Latona experienced from Juno is alluded to in the story. The tradition was that the future mother of Apollo and Diana, flying from the wrath⑨ of Juno, besought all the islands of the Ægean⑩ to afford her a place of rest, but all feared too much the potent⑪ queen of heaven⑫ to assist her rival. Delos⑬ alone consented to become the birthplace of the future deities. Delos was then a floating island; but when Latona arrived there, Jupiter fastened it with

---

① osier /ˈəʊziə/: 柳条
② rustic /ˈrʌstɪk/: 乡下人
③ of you: from you
④ clown: 乡下人
⑤ rail: 责骂
⑥ croak: (青蛙、乌鸦)呱呱叫,发出低沉、沙哑的声音
⑦ midst: middle
⑧ disproportioned /ˌdɪsprəˈpɔːʃnd/: 不成比例的
⑨ wrath /rɒθ/: 愤怒,(因愤怒而进行的)报复和惩罚
⑩ the Ægean /iːˈdʒiːən/: 爱琴海,地中海的一部分,位于土耳其和希腊之间。
⑪ potent /ˈpəʊtnt/: 强大的,权力大的
⑫ queen of heaven: Juno
⑬ Delos /ˈdiːlɒs/: 希腊岛屿名,属于今希腊南爱琴大区基克拉泽斯州。

adamantine① chains to the bottom of the sea, that it might be a secure resting-place for his beloved.

Chapter V
Phaëton

Phaëton② was the son of Apollo and the nymph Clymene③. One day a schoolfellow laughed at the idea of his being the son of the god, and Phaëton went in rage and shame and reported it to his mother. "If," said he, "I am indeed of heavenly birth, give me, mother, some proof of it, and establish④ my claim to the honor." Clymene stretched forth her hands towards the skies, and said, "I call to witness the Sun which looks down upon us, that I have told you the truth. If I speak falsely, let this be the last time I behold his light. But it needs not much labor to go and inquire for yourself; the land whence⑤ the Sun rises lies next to ours. Go and demand of him⑥ whether he will own⑦ you as a son." Phaëton heard with delight. He travelled to India⑧, which lies directly in the regions of sunrise; and, full of hope and pride, approached the goal whence his parent begins his course.

The palace of the Sun stood reared aloft on columns, glittering with gold and precious stones, while polished ivory formed the ceilings, and silver the doors. The workmanship surpassed the material; for upon the walls Vulcan had represented earth, sea, and skies, with their inhabitants. In the sea were the nymphs, some sporting in the waves, some riding on the backs of fishes, while others sat upon the rocks and dried their sea-green hair. Their faces were not all alike, nor yet unlike,—but such as sisters' ought to be. The earth had its towns and forests and rivers and rustic divinities. Over all was carved the likeness of the glorious heaven; and on the silver doors the twelve signs of the zodiac⑨, six on each side.

Clymene's son advanced up the steep ascent, and entered the halls of his disputed⑩ father.

---

① adamantine /ˌædəˈmæntaɪn/：坚固的，牢不可摧的

② Phaëton：/ˈfeɪtn/

③ Clymene：/ˈklɪmɪni/

④ establish：证实，证明

⑤ whence /wens/：from which

⑥ demand of him：问他，向他打听

⑦ own：承认

⑧ India /ˈɪndɪə/：印度，位于南亚次大陆，是中国的邻国之一。印度位于希腊以东非常遥远的地方，位于希腊与印度之间的国家从西向东分别是土耳其、叙利亚、伊拉克、伊朗、阿富汗和巴基斯坦。

⑨ the twelve signs of the zodiac：黄道带的十二宫。黄道带分为相等的 12 个部分，称为黄道带十二宫。黄道带十二宫以十二星座来命名，分别是：白羊宫（Aries /ˈeəriːz/）、金牛宫（Taurus /ˈtɔːrəs/）、双子宫（Gemini /ˈdʒemɪnaɪ/）、巨蟹宫（Cancer /ˈkænsə/）、狮子宫（Leo /ˈliːəʊ/）、室女宫（Virgo /ˈvɜːgəʊ/）、天秤宫（Libra /ˈlaɪbrə/）、天蝎宫（Scorpio /ˈskɔːpiəʊ/）、人马宫（Sagittarius /ˌsædʒɪˈteəriəs/）、摩羯宫（Capricorn /ˈkæprɪkɔːn/）、宝瓶宫（Aquarius /əˈkweəriəs/）和双鱼宫（Pisces /ˈpaɪsiːz/）。zodiac /ˈzəʊdiæk/：黄道带（天上向黄道两侧延伸 9 度的区域），也就是地球围绕太阳公转的轨道。

⑩ disputed /dɪspˈjuːtɪd/：有争议的

He approached the paternal① presence, but stopped at a distance, for the light was more than he could bear. Phœbus, arrayed in a purple vesture, sat on a throne, which glittered as with diamonds. On his right hand and his left stood the Day, the Month, and the Year, and, at regular intervals, the Hours. Spring stood with her head crowned with flowers, and Summer, with garment cast aside, and a garland formed of spears of ripened grain, and Autumn, with his feet stained with grape-juice, and icy Winter, with his hair stiffened with hoar② frost. Surrounded by these attendants, the Sun, with the eye that sees everything, beheld the youth dazzled with the novelty③ and splendor of the scene, and inquired the purpose of his errand④. The youth replied, "O light of the boundless world, Phœbus, my father,—if you permit me to use that name,—give me some proof, I beseech you, by which I may be known as yours⑤." He ceased; and his father, laying aside the beams that shone all around his head, bade him approach, and embracing him, said, "My son, you deserve not to be disowned⑥, and I confirm what your mother has told you. To put an end to your doubts, ask what you will, the gift shall be yours. I call to witness that dreadful lake⑦, which I never saw, but which we gods swear by in our most solemn engagements⑧." Phaëton immediately asked to be permitted for one day to drive the chariot of the sun. The father repented of his promise; thrice and four times he shook his radiant head in warning. "I have spoken rashly," said he; "this only request I would fain⑨ deny. I beg you to withdraw it. It is not a safe boon⑩, nor one, my Phaëton, suited to your youth and strength. Your lot is mortal, and you ask what is beyond a mortal's power. In your ignorance you aspire to do that which not even the gods themselves may do. None but myself may drive the flaming car of day. Not even Jupiter, whose terrible right arm hurls the thunderbolts. The first part of the way is steep, and such as the horses when fresh in the morning can hardly climb; the middle is high up in the heavens, whence I myself can scarcely, without alarm, look down and behold the earth and sea stretched beneath me. The last part of the road descends rapidly, and requires most careful driving. Tethys, who is waiting to receive me, often trembles for me lest I should fall headlong. Add to all this, the heaven is all the time turning round and carrying the stars with it. I have to be perpetually on my guard lest that movement, which sweeps everything else along, should hurry me also away. Suppose I should lend you the chariot, what would you do? Could you keep your course while the sphere was revolving under you? Perhaps you think that there are forests and cities, the abodes of gods, and palaces and temples on the way. On the contrary, the road is through the midst of frightful

---

① paternal /pəˈtɜːnl/：父亲的

② hoar /hɔː/：灰白的

③ novelty /ˈnɒvlti/：新奇

④ inquired the purpose of his errand：询问他的来意

⑤ yours：your son

⑥ disown /dɪsˈəʊn/：否认

⑦ that dreadful lake：即阴间的河流 Styx,众神发誓时都请该河作证。lake：溪流

⑧ engagement /ɪnˈɡeɪdʒmənt/：正式的承诺

⑨ would fain：宁愿

⑩ boon：请求

monsters. You pass by the horns of the Bull①, in front of the Archer②, and near the Lion's③ jaws, and where the Scorpion④ stretches its arms in one direction and the Crab⑤ in another. Nor will you find it easy to guide those horses, with their breasts full of fire that they breathe forth from their mouths and nostrils⑥. I can scarcely govern them myself, when they are unruly⑦ and resist the reins. Beware, my son, lest I be the donor⑧ of a fatal gift; recall⑨ your request while yet you may. Do you ask me for a proof that you are sprung from my blood? I give you a proof in my fears for you. Look at my face—I would that you could look into my breast, you would there see all a father's anxiety. Finally," he continued, "look round the world and choose whatever you will of what earth or sea contains most precious—ask it and fear no refusal. This only I pray you not to urge. It is not honor, but destruction you seek. Why do you hang round my neck and still entreat me? You shall have it if you persist;—the oath is sworn and must be kept,—but I beg you to choose more wisely."

He ended; but the youth rejected all admonition⑩ and held to his demand. So, having resisted as long as he could, Phœbus at last led the way to where stood the lofty chariot.

It was of gold, the gift of Vulcan; the axle was of gold, the pole and wheels of gold, the spokes of silver⑪. Along the seat were rows of chrysolites⑫ and diamonds which reflected all around the brightness of the sun. While the daring youth gazed in admiration, the early Dawn threw open the purple doors of the east, and showed the pathway strewn with roses. The stars withdrew, marshalled⑬ by the Day-star⑭, which last of all retired⑮ also. The father, when he saw the earth beginning to glow, and the Moon preparing to retire, ordered the Hours to harness up the horses. They obeyed, and led forth from the lofty stalls the steeds full fed with ambrosia, and attached the reins. Then the father bathed the face of his son with a powerful unguent⑯, and made him capable of enduring the brightness of the flame. He set the rays on his head, and, with a foreboding sigh, said, "If, my son, you will in this at least heed my advice, spare the whip and

---

① Bull：金牛座，金牛宫，即 Taurus。这里使用的是星座的英文名称，在关于"黄道带的十二宫"的注释中使用的是星座的拉丁语名称。

② Archer /ˈɑːtʃə/：人马座，人马宫，即 Sagittarius。

③ Lion：狮子座，狮子宫，即 Leo。

④ Scorpion：天蝎座，天蝎宫，即 Scorpio。

⑤ Crab：巨蟹座，巨蟹宫，即 Cancer。

⑥ nostril /ˈnɒstrəl/：鼻孔

⑦ unruly /ʌnˈruːli/：难驾驭的

⑧ donor /ˈdəʊnə/：给与人

⑨ recall：收回

⑩ admonition /ˌædməˈnɪʃn/：警告

⑪ axle /ˈæksl/：车轴；pole：车辕；spoke：轮辐

⑫ chrysolite /ˈkrɪsəlaɪt/：贵橄榄石

⑬ marshal /ˈmɑːʃl/：引领

⑭ Day-star：晨星

⑮ retire：退出

⑯ unguent /ˈʌŋgwənt/：药膏

hold tight the reins. They go fast enough of their own accord①; the labor is to hold them in. You are not to take the straight road directly between the five circles, but turn off to the left. Keep within the limit of the middle zone, and avoid the northern and the southern alike. You will see the marks of the wheels, and they will serve to guide you. And, that the skies and the earth may each receive their due share of heat, go not too high, or you will burn the heavenly dwellings, nor too low, or you will set the earth on fire; the middle course is safest and best. And now I leave you to your chance, which I hope will plan better for you than you have done for yourself. Night is passing out of the western gates and we can delay no longer. Take the reins; but if at last your heart fails you, and you will benefit by my advice, stay where you are in safety, and suffer me to light and warm the earth." The agile youth sprang into the chariot, stood erect, and grasped the reins with delight, pouring out thanks to his reluctant parent.

Meanwhile the horses fill the air with their snortings and fiery breath, and stamp the ground impatient. Now the bars are let down, and the boundless plain of the universe lies open before them. They dart forward and cleave the opposing clouds, and outrun the morning breezes which started from the same eastern goal②. The steeds soon perceived that the load they drew was lighter than usual; and as a ship without ballast③ is tossed hither and thither④ on the sea, so the chariot, without its accustomed weight, was dashed about as if empty. They rush headlong and leave the travelled⑤ road. He is alarmed, and knows not how to guide them; nor, if he knew, has he the power. Then, for the first time, the Great and Little Bear were scorched with heat, and would fain, if it were possible, have plunged into the water⑥; and the Serpent⑦ which lies coiled up round the north pole, torpid⑧ and harmless, grew warm, and with warmth felt its rage revive. Boötes⑨, they say, fled away, though encumbered with his plough, and all unused to rapid motion.

When hapless Phaëton looked down upon the earth, now spreading in vast extent beneath him, he grew pale and his knees shook with terror. In spite of the glare all around him, the sight of his eyes grew dim. He wished he had never touched his father's horses, never learned his parentage, never prevailed in his request. He is borne along like a vessel⑩ that flies before a tempest, when the pilot can do no more and betakes himself to his prayers. What shall he do? Much of the heavenly road is left behind, but more remains before. He turns his eyes from one direction to the other; now to the goal whence he began his course, now to the realms of sunset

---

① of one's own accord: 主动地,自动地,自愿地
② goal:（赛跑等的）起点
③ ballast /'bæləst/：压舱物,即放置在轮船底舱中让其保持稳定的重物,如沙、铁、铅等。
④ hither and thither: here and there
⑤ travelled:（行人、车辆）常走的
⑥ 参见 *The Age of Fable* 第 4 章 Callisto 的故事。
⑦ Serpent：巨蛇座,拉丁语名称是 Serpens。
⑧ torpid /'tɔːpɪd/：（动物）蛰伏的
⑨ Boötes /bəʊˈəʊtiːz/：牧夫座
⑩ vessel：船

which he is not destined to reach. He loses his self-command, and knows not what to do,—whether to draw tight the reins or throw them loose; he forgets the names of the horses. He sees with terror the monstrous forms scattered over the surface of heaven. Here the Scorpion extended his two great arms, with his tail and crooked claws stretching over two signs of the zodiac. When the boy beheld him, reeking with poison and menacing with his fangs, his courage failed, and the reins fell from his hands. The horses, when they felt them loose on their backs, dashed headlong, and unrestrained went off into unknown regions of the sky, in among the stars, hurling the chariot over pathless places, now up in high heaven, now down almost to the earth. The moon saw with astonishment her brother's chariot running beneath her own. The clouds begin to smoke, and the mountain tops take fire; the fields are parched with heat, the plants wither, the trees with their leafy branches burn, the harvest is ablaze! But these are small things. Great cities perished, with their walls and towers; whole nations with their people were consumed to ashes! The forest-clad mountains burned, Athos and Taurus and Tmolus and Œte①; Ida②, once celebrated for fountains, but now all dry; the Muses' mountain Helicon③, and Hæmus; Ætna④, with fires within and without⑤, and Parnassus, with his two peaks, and Rhodope⑥, forced at last to part with his snowy crown⑦. Her cold climate was no protection to Scythia, Caucasus burned, and Ossa and Pindus⑧, and, greater than both, Olympus; the Alps⑨ high in air, and the Apennines⑩ crowned with clouds.

Then Phaëton beheld the world on fire, and felt the heat intolerable. The air he breathed was like the air of a furnace and full of burning ashes, and the smoke was of a pitchy darkness. He dashed forward he knew not whither. Then, it is believed, the people of Æthiopia⑪ became black by the blood being forced so suddenly to the surface, and the Libyan desert was dried up to the condition in which it remains to this day. The Nymphs of the fountains, with dishevelled⑫ hair, mourned their waters, nor were the rivers safe beneath their banks: Tanais smoked, and Caicus,

---

① Athos /ˈæθɒs/：山名,位于希腊北部圣山僧侣自治共和国;Taurus：山名,位于土耳其地中海沿岸;Tmolus：山名,位于土耳其境内;Œte：又叫 Œta /ˈiːtə/,希腊山名,位于中希腊大区,是品都斯山脉 (the Pindus) 的一个东南走向的分支。

② Ida /ˈaɪdə/：希腊神话中有两座叫 Ida 的山。一座位于小亚细亚西北部,即位于今天的土耳其境内,特洛伊战争中,诸神就是在这座山上观看希腊和特洛伊的鏖战。另外一座位于希腊的克里特岛 (Crete)。

③ Helicon /ˈhelɪkən/：希腊山名,位于中希腊大区维奥蒂亚州 (Boeotia 或 Voiotia)。

④ Ætna (Etna) /ˈetnə/：欧洲最高的活火山,海拔 3 323 米,位于意大利西西里岛 (Sicily) 的东部。

⑤ with fires within and without：里面外面都有火;without：在外面

⑥ Rhodope /ˈrɒdəpi/：欧洲巴尔干半岛山名,主要位于保加利亚,少部分位于希腊北部东马其顿和色雷斯大区。

⑦ crown：顶峰

⑧ Ossa /ˈɒsə/：山名,位于希腊色萨利大区 (Thessaly) 拉里萨州(Larisa) 东部;Pindus /ˈpɪndəs/：希腊大陆的主要山脉,从阿尔巴尼亚延伸到希腊中部地区。

⑨ Alps /ælps/：阿尔卑斯山脉,欧洲最高的山脉,位于欧洲南部。

⑩ Apennines /ˈæpənaɪnz/：亚平宁山脉,从西北向南贯穿意大利。

⑪ Æthiopia：/ˌiːθɪˈəʊpɪə/

⑫ dishevelled /dɪˈʃevld/：(头发)凌乱的

Xanthus, and Meander①; Babylonian Euphrates② and Ganges, Tagus③ with golden sands, and Cayster④ where the swans resort. Nile fled away and hid his head in the desert, and there it still remains concealed. Where he⑤ used to discharge his waters through seven mouths into the sea, there seven dry channels alone remained. The earth cracked open, and through the chinks light broke into Tartarus, and frightened the king of shadows⑥ and his queen⑦. The sea shrank up. Where before was water, it became a dry plain; and the mountains that lie beneath the waves lifted up their heads and became islands. The fishes sought the lowest depths, and the dolphins no longer ventured as usual to sport on the surface. Even Nereus⑧, and his wife Doris, with the Nereids⑨, their daughters, sought the deepest caves for refuge. Thrice Neptune essayed⑩ to raise his head above the surface, and thrice was driven back by the heat. Earth, surrounded as she was by waters, yet with head and shoulders bare, screening⑪ her face with her hand, looked up to heaven, and with a husky voice called on Jupiter:

"O ruler of the gods, if I have deserved this treatment, and it is your will that I perish with fire, why withhold your thunderbolts? Let me at least fall by your hand. Is this the reward of my fertility, of my obedient service? Is it for this that I have supplied herbage for cattle, and fruits for men, and frankincense⑫ for your altars? But if I am unworthy of regard⑬, what has my brother Ocean done to deserve such a fate? If neither of us can excite your pity, think, I pray you, of your own heaven, and behold how both the poles are smoking which sustain your palace, which must fall if they be destroyed. Atlas faints, and scarce holds up his burden. If sea, earth, and heaven perish, we fall into ancient Chaos. Save what yet remains to us from the devouring flame. O, take thought for our deliverance⑭ in this awful moment!"

Thus spoke Earth, and overcome with heat and thirst, could say no more. Then Jupiter omnipotent⑮, calling to witness all the gods, including him who had lent the chariot⑯, and showing them that all was lost unless speedy remedy were applied, mounted the lofty tower from whence he diffuses clouds over the earth, and hurls the forked lightnings. But at that time not a cloud was to be found to interpose for a screen to earth, nor was a shower remaining unexhausted.

---

① Tanais：即今天位于俄罗斯境内的顿河（the Don River）；Caicus, Xanthus, and Meander：河流名,在今天土耳其境内。

② Euphrates /juːˈfreɪtiːz/ 幼发拉底河

③ Tagus /ˈteɪɡəs/：伊比利亚半岛最长的河流,流经西班牙和葡萄牙,在里斯本附近注入大西洋。

④ Cayster /ˈkeɪstə/：河流名,在今天土耳其境内。

⑤ he：the Nile

⑥ the king of shadows：Pluto；shadow：鬼

⑦ his queen：Proserpine；关于 Proserpine 的故事,参见 The Age of Fable 第 7 章。

⑧ Nereus：/ˈnɪərjuːs/

⑨ Nereid：/ˈnɪəriːɪd/

⑩ essay：try

⑪ screen：遮挡

⑫ frankincense /ˈfræŋkɪnsens/：乳香

⑬ regard：尊重

⑭ deliverance /dɪˈlɪvərəns/：解救,拯救

⑮ omnipotent /ɒmˈnɪpətənt/：全能的

⑯ him who had lent the chariot：Apollo, father of Phaëton

He thundered, and brandishing a lightning bolt in his right hand launched it against the charioteer[1], and struck him at the same moment from his seat and from existence! Phaëton, with his hair on fire, fell headlong, like a shooting star which marks the heavens with its brightness as it falls, and Eridanus[2], the great river, received him and cooled his burning frame. The Italian Naiads reared a tomb for him, and inscribed these words upon the stone[3]:

"Driver of Phœbus' chariot, Phaëton,

Struck by Jove's thunder, rests beneath this stone.

He could not rule his father's car[4] of fire,

Yet was it much so nobly to aspire."

His sisters, the Heliades[5], as they lamented his fate, were turned into poplar trees, on the banks of the river, and their tears, which continued to flow, became amber[6] as they dropped into the stream.

Chapter VI
Midas—Baucis and Philemon

Midas

Bacchus[7], on a certain occasion, found his old schoolmaster and foster-father, Silenus[8], missing. The old man had been drinking, and in that state wandered away, and was found by some peasants, who carried him to their king, Midas[9]. Midas recognized him, and treated him hospitably, entertaining[10] him for ten days and nights with an unceasing round of jollity. On the eleventh day he brought Silenus back, and restored[11] him in safety to his pupil. Whereupon Bacchus offered Midas his choice of a reward, whatever he might wish. He asked that whatever he might touch should be changed into gold. Bacchus consented, though sorry that he had not made a better choice. Midas went his way, rejoicing in his new-acquired power, which he hastened to put to the test. He could scarce believe his eyes when he found a twig of an oak, which he plucked

---

① charioteer /ˌtʃærɪəˈtɪə/：驾车者

② Eridanus /ɪˈrɪdənəs/：即 the Po /pəʊ/ River，意大利最长的河流，发源于意大利和法国交界处的阿尔卑斯山，注入亚得里亚海。

③ stone：墓碑

④ car：chariot

⑤ Heliades：/heˈlaɪədiːz/

⑥ amber /ˈæmbə/：琥珀

⑦ 关于酒神 Bacchus 的故事，参见 *The Age of Fable* 第 21 章及 *The Homeric Hymns* 中的选段 "To Dionysus"。

⑧ Silenus：/saɪˈliːnəs/

⑨ Midas：/ˈmaɪdəs/

⑩ entertain /ˌentəˈteɪn/：招待，款待

⑪ restore：归还

from the branch, become gold in his hand. He took up a stone; it changed to gold. He touched a sod; it did the same. He took an apple from the tree; you would have thought he had robbed the garden of the Hesperides①. His joy knew no bounds, and as soon as he got home, he ordered the servants to set a splendid repast on the table. Then he found to his dismay② that whether he touched bread, it hardened in his hand; or put a morsel to his lips, it defied his teeth. He took a glass of wine, but it flowed down his throat like melted gold.

In consternation③ at the unprecedented④ affliction⑤, he strove to divest⑥ himself of his power; he hated the gift he had lately coveted⑦. But all in vain; starvation seemed to await him. He raised his arms, all shining with gold, in prayer to Bacchus, begging to be delivered from his glittering destruction. Bacchus, merciful deity, heard and consented. "Go," said he, "to the River Pactolus⑧, trace the stream to its fountain-head⑨, there plunge your head and body in, and wash away your fault and its punishment." He did so, and scarce had he touched the waters before the gold-creating power passed into them, and the river-sands became changed into gold, as they remain to this day.

Thenceforth⑩ Midas, hating wealth and splendor, dwelt in the country, and became a worshipper of Pan, the god of the fields. On a certain occasion Pan had the temerity⑪ to compare his music with that of Apollo, and to challenge the god of the lyre⑫ to a trial of skill. The challenge was accepted, and Tmolus⑬, the mountain god, was chosen umpire⑭. The senior⑮ took his seat, and cleared away the trees from his ears to listen. At a given signal Pan blew on his pipes⑯, and with his rustic melody gave great satisfaction to himself and his faithful follower Midas, who happened to be present. Then Tmolus turned his head toward the Sun-god, and all his trees turned with him. Apollo rose, his brow wreathed with Parnassian⑰ laurel, while his robe of Tyrian⑱ purple swept the ground. In his left hand he held the lyre, and with his right hand struck the strings. Ravished with the harmony, Tmolus at once awarded the victory to the god of the lyre,

---

① Hesperides /heˈsperɪdiːz/: Atlas 的女儿们，居住在最西边，看守金苹果果园。

② dismay: 强烈的失望

③ consternation /ˌkɒnstəˈneɪʃn/: 惊恐

④ unprecedented /ʌnˈpresɪdentɪd/: 没有先例的，前所未有的

⑤ affliction: 痛苦

⑥ divest /daɪˈvest/: 摆脱

⑦ covet /ˈkʌvɪt/: 渴望

⑧ Pactolus /pækˈtəʊləs/: 河流名，在今土耳其西部，注入盖迪兹河 (the Gediz River)。该河的泥沙中曾含有银金矿。

⑨ fountain-head: （河流的）源头

⑩ thenceforth /ˈðensˈfɔːθ/: 从那时起

⑪ temerity /təˈmerəti/: 胆量

⑫ the god of the lyre: Apollo

⑬ Tmolus: /ˈtmɒləs/

⑭ umpire /ˈʌmpaɪə/: 裁判

⑮ The senior: 长者，指 Tmolus.

⑯ his pipes: 即 the Syrinx 或 Pandean pines，参见 The Age of Fable 第 4 章 Io 的故事中 Mercury 给 Argus 讲的故事。

⑰ Parnassian /pɑːˈnæsɪən/: of Mount Parnassus

⑱ Tyrian /ˈtɪrɪən/: of Tyre, made in Tyre; Tyre /ˈtaɪə/: 古代腓尼基 (Phoenicia /fəˈnɪʃə/) 港口、商贸中心；古代腓尼基大至相当于现代的黎巴嫩。Tyre 以生产深红色或紫色的染料而闻名。

and all but Midas acquiesced① in the judgment. He dissented, and questioned the justice of the award. Apollo would not suffer such a depraved pair of ears any longer to wear the human form, but caused them to increase in length, grow hairy, within and without②, and movable on their roots; in short, to be on the perfect pattern of those of an ass.

Mortified③ enough was King Midas at this mishap④; but he consoled himself with the thought that it was possible to hide his misfortune, which he attempted to do by means of an ample turban⑤ or head-dress. But his hair-dresser⑥ of course knew the secret. He was charged not to mention it, and threatened with dire punishment if he presumed⑦ to disobey. But he found it too much for his discretion to keep such a secret; so he went out into the meadow, dug a hole in the ground, and stooping down, whispered the story, and covered it up. Before long a thick bed of reeds sprang up in the meadow, and as soon as it had gained its growth, began whispering the story, and has continued to do so, from that day to this, every time a breeze passes over the place.

Midas was king of Phrygia⑧. He was the son of Gordius⑨, a poor countryman, who was taken by the people and made king, in obedience to the command of the oracle, which had said that their future king should come in a wagon. While the people were deliberating⑩, Gordius with his wife and son came driving his wagon into the public square.

Gordius, being made king, dedicated his wagon to the deity of the oracle, and tied it up in its place with a fast⑪ knot. This was the celebrated Gordian knot, which, in after times it was said, whoever should untie should become lord of all Asia. Many tried to untie it, but none succeeded, till Alexander the Great⑫, in his career of conquest, came to Phrygia. He tried his skill with as ill success as others, till growing impatient he drew his sword and cut the knot. When he afterwards succeeded in subjecting all Asia to his sway⑬, people began to think that he had complied with the terms of the oracle according to its true meaning.

Baucis and Philemon

On a certain hill in Phrygia stands a linden tree⑭ and an oak, enclosed by a low wall. Not far

---

① acquiesce /ˌækwɪˈes/：赞同,同意
② within and without：不论里面还是外面
③ mortified /ˈmɔːtɪfaɪd/：深感受辱的
④ mishap /ˈmɪshæp/：厄运,灾祸
⑤ turban /ˈtɜːbən/：包头巾
⑥ hair-dresser：理发师
⑦ presume /prɪˈzjuːm/：胆敢
⑧ Phrygia /ˈfrɪdʒɪə/：古代地区名,位于小亚细亚中西部。
⑨ Gordius：/ˈɡɔːdɪəs/
⑩ deliberate /dɪˈlɪbərət/：商议
⑪ fast：牢固的,紧的
⑫ Alexander /ˌælɪɡˈzɑːndə/ the Great：亚历山大大帝,生于公元前356年,卒于公元前323年,希腊著名哲学家亚里士多德（Aristotle）的学生,马其顿（Macedonia /ˌmæsiˈdəʊnjə/）国王。亚历山大大帝一生征服了许多地方,最东到今印度的旁遮普邦（Punjab /pʌnˈdʒɑːb/）。他的帝国在他死后迅速瓦解。
⑬ sway：统治
⑭ linden tree：椴树

from the spot is a marsh, formerly good habitable① land, but now indented with pools, the resort② of fen-birds and cormorants③. Once on a time Jupiter, in human shape, visited this country, and with him his son Mercury (he of the caduceus), without his wings. They presented themselves, as weary travellers, at many a door, seeking rest and shelter, but found all closed, for it was late, and the inhospitable inhabitants would not rouse themselves to open for their reception. At last a humble mansion received them, a small thatched cottage, where Baucis④, a pious old dame, and her husband Philemon⑤, united when young, had grown old together. Not ashamed of their poverty, they made it endurable by moderate desires and kind dispositions. One need not look there for master or for servant; they two were the whole household, master and servant alike. When the two heavenly guests crossed the humble threshold, and bowed their heads to pass under the low door, the old man placed a seat, on which Baucis, bustling⑥ and attentive⑦, spread a cloth, and begged them to sit down. Then she raked out the coals from the ashes, and kindled up a fire, fed it with leaves and dry bark, and with her scanty⑧ breath blew it into a flame. She brought out of a corner split sticks and dry branches, broke them up, and placed them under the small kettle. Her husband collected some pot-herbs in the garden, and she shred them from the stalks, and prepared them for the pot. He reached down with a forked stick a flitch of bacon⑨ hanging in the chimney, cut a small piece, and put it in the pot to boil with the herbs, setting away the rest for another time. A beechen bowl was filled with warm water, that⑩ their guests might wash. While all was doing, they beguiled the time with conversation.

On the bench designed for the guests was laid a cushion stuffed with sea-weed; and a cloth, only produced⑪ on great occasions, but ancient and coarse enough, was spread over that. The old lady, with her apron on, with trembling hand set the table. One leg was shorter than the rest, but a piece of slate⑫ put under restored the level. When fixed, she rubbed the table down with some sweet-smelling herbs. Upon it she set some of chaste Minerva's olives⑬, some cornel berries preserved in vinegar, and added radishes and cheese, with eggs lightly cooked in the ashes. All were served in earthen dishes, and an earthenware pitcher, with wooden cups, stood beside them. When all was ready, the stew, smoking hot, was set on the table. Some wine, not of the oldest, was added; and for dessert, apples and wild honey; and over and above all, friendly faces, and

---

① habitable /ˈhæbɪtəbl/：适合居住的

② resort /rɪˈzɔːt/：常去之地

③ cormorant /ˈkɔːmərənt/：鸬鹚

④ Baucis：/ˈbɔːsɪs/

⑤ Philemon：/fɪˈliːmɒn/

⑥ bustling /ˈbʌslɪŋ/：忙乱的

⑦ attentive /əˈtentɪv/：有礼貌的，殷勤的

⑧ scanty /ˈskænti/：不充足的

⑨ bacon：腊肉，熏咸肉

⑩ that：so that

⑪ produce：拿出来

⑫ slate：石板

⑬ Minerva's olives：参见 *The Age of Fable* 第 14 章 Minerva 的故事。

simple but hearty welcome.

Now while the repast proceeded, the old folks were astonished to see that the wine, as fast as it was poured out, renewed itself in the pitcher, of its own accord. Struck with terror, Baucis and Philemon recognized their heavenly guests, fell on their knees, and with clasped hands implored forgiveness for their poor entertainment①. There was an old goose, which they kept as the guardian of their humble cottage; and they bethought them to make this a sacrifice in honor of their guests. But the goose, too nimble, with the aid of feet and wings, for the old folks, eluded their pursuit, and at last took shelter between the gods themselves. They forbade it to be slain; and spoke in these words: "We are gods. This inhospitable village shall pay the penalty of its impiety; you alone shall go free from the chastisement②. Quit your house, and come with us to the top of yonder hill." They hastened to obey, and, staff in hand, labored up the steep ascent③. They had reached to within an arrow's flight of the top, when turning their eyes below, they beheld all the country sunk in a lake, only their own house left standing. While they gazed with wonder at the sight, and lamented the fate of their neighbors, that old house of theirs was changed into a temple. Columns took the place of the corner posts, the thatch④ grew yellow and appeared a gilded roof, the floors became marble, the doors were enriched with carving and ornaments of gold. Then spoke Jupiter in benignant⑤ accents⑥: "Excellent old man, and woman worthy of such a husband, speak, tell us your wishes; what favor have you to ask of us?" Philemon took counsel with Baucis a few moments; then declared to the gods their united wish. "We ask to be priests and guardians of this your temple; and since here we have passed our lives in love and concord⑦, we wish that one and the same hour may take us both from life, that I may not live to see her grave, nor be laid in my own by her." Their prayer was granted. They were the keepers of the temple as long as they lived. When grown very old, as they stood one day before the steps of the sacred edifice⑧, and were telling the story of the place, Baucis saw Philemon begin to put forth leaves, and old Philemon saw Baucis changing in like manner. And now a leafy crown had grown over their heads, while exchanging parting words, as long as they could speak. "Farewell, dear spouse⑨," they said, together, and at the same moment the bark closed over their mouths. The Tyanean⑩ shepherd still shows the two trees, standing side by side, made out of the two good old people.

---

① entertainment /ˌentə'teɪnmənt/：招待
② chastisement /'tʃæstɪzmənt/：惩罚
③ ascent /ə'sent/：上坡路
④ thatch：茅草屋顶
⑤ benignant /bɪ'nɪgnənt/：随和的
⑥ accent：口气
⑦ concord /'kɒnkɔːd/：和谐
⑧ edifice /'edɪfɪs/：（巨大而宏伟的）建筑
⑨ spouse /spaʊz/：夫,妻,配偶
⑩ Tyanean /ˌtaɪə'niːən/：of Tyana；Tyana /'taɪənə/：城镇名,位于小亚细亚。

Chapter Ⅶ
Proserpine—Glaucus and Scylla

Proserpine

When Jupiter and his brothers had defeated the Titans and banished them to Tartarus, a new enemy rose up against the gods. They were the giants Typhon, Briareus, Enceladus①, and others. Some of them had a hundred arms, others breathed out fire. They were finally subdued and buried alive under Mount Ætna, where they still sometimes struggle to get loose, and shake the whole island② with earthquakes. Their breath comes up through the mountain, and is what men call the eruption③ of the volcano④.

The fall of these monsters shook the earth, so that Pluto was alarmed, and feared that his kingdom would be laid open to the light of day. Under this apprehension⑤, he mounted his chariot, drawn by black horses, and took a circuit of inspection to satisfy himself of the extent of the damage. While he was thus engaged, Venus, who was sitting on Mount Eryx⑥ playing with her boy Cupid, espied him, and said, "My son, take your darts with which you conquer all, even Jove himself, and send one into the breast of yonder dark monarch, who rules the realm of Tartarus. Why should he alone escape? Seize the opportunity to extend your empire and mine. Do you not see that even in heaven some despise our power? Minerva the wise, and Diana the huntress, defy us⑦; and there is that daughter of Ceres⑧, who threatens to follow their example⑨. Now do you, if you have any regard for your own interest or mine, join these two in one." The boy unbound his quiver, and selected his sharpest and truest arrow; then straining the bow against his knee, he attached the string, and, having made ready, shot the arrow with its barbed point right into the heart of Pluto.

In the vale of Enna⑩ there is a lake⑪ embowered in woods, which screen it from the fervid⑫ rays of the sun, while the moist ground is covered with flowers, and Spring reigns perpetual. Here Proserpine⑬ was playing with her companions, gathering lilies and violets, and filling her basket

---

① Typhon：/ˈtaɪfɒn /；Briareus：/braɪˈeərɪəs /；Enceladus：/enˈseladəs/
② the whole island：西西里岛（Sicily）
③ eruption /ɪˈrʌpʃn/：爆发
④ volcano /vɒlˈkeɪnəʊ/：火山
⑤ apprehension /ˌæprɪˈhenʃn/：焦虑,不安
⑥ Eryx /ˈerɪks/：山名,位于意大利西西里岛西北部。
⑦ 智慧女神 Minerva 是一位处女女神。月亮女神 Diana 也是一位处女女神,喜欢打猎。
⑧ daughter of Ceres：Proserpine
⑨ follow their example：像 Minerva 和 Diana 一样,不恋爱,不结婚,一直做处女。
⑩ Enna /ˈenə/：城市名,位于意大利西西里岛中部。
⑪ 这个湖叫 The Lago（lake）di Pergusa,在 Enna 以南大约 6 公里处。
⑫ fervid /ˈfɜːvɪd/：炽热的
⑬ Proserpine /ˈprɒsəpaɪn/：也可拼写为 Proserpina /prəˈsɜːpɪnə /。

and her apron with them, when Pluto saw her, loved her, and carried her off. She screamed for help to her mother and companions; and when in her fright she dropped the corners of her apron and let the flowers fall, childlike she felt the loss of them as an addition to her grief. The ravisher① urged on his steeds, calling them each by name, and throwing loose over their heads and necks his iron-colored reins. When he reached the River Cyane②, and it opposed his passage, he struck the river-bank with his trident③, and the earth opened and gave him a passage to Tartarus.

Ceres sought her daughter all the world over. Bright-haired Aurora④, when she came forth in the morning, and Hesperus⑤ when he led out the stars in the evening, found her still busy in the search. But it was all unavailing⑥. At length, weary and sad, she sat down upon a stone, and continued sitting nine days and nights, in the open air, under the sunlight and moonlight and falling showers. It was where now stands the city of Eleusis⑦, then the home of an old man named Celeus⑧. He was out in the field, gathering acorns and black-berries, and sticks for his fire. His little girl was driving home their two goats, and as she passed the goddess, who appeared in the guise of an old woman, she said to her, "Mother⑨,"—and the name was sweet to the ears of Ceres,—"why do you sit here alone upon the rocks?" The old man also stopped, though his load was heavy, and begged her to come into his cottage, such as it was. She declined⑩, and he urged her. "Go in peace," she replied, "and be happy in your daughter; I have lost mine." As she spoke, tears—or something like tears, for the gods never weep—fell down her cheeks upon her bosom. The compassionate⑪ old man and his child wept with her. Then said he, "Come with us, and despise not our humble roof; so may your daughter be restored to you in safety." "Lead on," said she, "I cannot resist that appeal⑫!" So she rose from the stone and went with them. As they walked he told her that his only son, a little boy, lay very sick, feverish, and sleepless. She stooped and gathered some poppies⑬. As they entered the cottage, they found all in great distress, for the boy seemed past hope of recovery. Metanim⑭, his mother, received her kindly, and the goddess stooped and kissed the lips of the sick child. Instantly the paleness left his face, and healthy vigor returned to his body. The whole family were delighted—that is, the father, mother, and little girl, for they were all; they had no servants. They spread the table, and put upon it

---

① ravisher /ˈrævɪʃə/：劫掠者，强奸犯
② the River Cyane /sɪˈæni/：该河在西西里岛锡拉库萨（Syracuse 或 Siracusa）附近。
③ trident /ˈtraɪdənt/：三叉戟
④ 黎明时，明亮的光线像头发一样，所以这里用复合形容词 bright-haired 来描写黎明女神 Aurora。
⑤ Hesperus /ˈhespərəs/：the evening star, 汉语翻译为"昏星"。
⑥ unavailing /ˌʌnəˈveɪlɪŋ/：无用的
⑦ Eleusis /ɪˈljuːsɪs/：城市名，位于阿提卡（Attica 或 Attiki）。
⑧ Celeus：/ˈsiːlɪəs/
⑨ Mother 一词可用于称呼年长的女性。
⑩ decline /dɪˈklaɪn/：婉言谢绝
⑪ compassionate /kəmˈpæʃənət/：有同情心的
⑫ appeal /əˈpiːl/：请求
⑬ poppy：罂粟
⑭ Metanim：/mɪˈtænɪm/

curds and cream, apples, and honey in the comb①. While they ate, Ceres mingled poppy juice in the milk of the boy. When night came and all was still, she arose, and taking the sleeping boy, moulded his limbs with her hands, and uttered over him three times a solemn charm②, then went and laid him in the ashes. His mother, who had been watching what her guest was doing, sprang forward with a cry and snatched the child from the fire. Then Ceres assumed her own form, and a divine splendor shone all around. While they were overcome with astonishment, she said, "Mother, you have been cruel in your fondness to your son. I would have made him immortal, but you have frustrated③ my attempt. Nevertheless, he shall be great and useful. He shall teach men the use of the plough, and the rewards which labor can win from the cultivated soil." So saying, she wrapped a cloud about her, and mounting her chariot rode away.

Ceres continued her search for her daughter, passing from land to land, and across seas and rivers, till at length she returned to Sicily④, whence she at first set out, and stood by the banks of the River Cyane, where Pluto made himself a passage with his prize⑤ to his own dominions. The river nymph would have told the goddess all she had witnessed, but dared not, for fear of Pluto; so she only ventured to take up the girdle which Proserpine had dropped in her flight, and waft it to the feet of the mother. Ceres, seeing this, was no longer in doubt of her loss, but she did not yet know the cause, and laid the blame on the innocent land. "Ungrateful soil," said she, "which I have endowed with fertility and clothed with herbage and nourishing grain, no more shall you enjoy my favors." Then the cattle died, the plough broke in the furrow, the seed failed to come up; there was too much sun, there was too much rain; the birds stole the seeds—thistles⑥ and brambles⑦ were the only growth. Seeing this, the fountain Arethusa⑧ interceded for the land. "Goddess," said she, "blame not the land; it opened unwillingly to yield a passage to your daughter. I can tell you of her fate, for I have seen her. This is not my native country; I came hither from Elis⑨. I was a woodland nymph, and delighted in the chase. They praised my beauty, but I cared nothing for it, and rather boasted of my hunting exploits. One day I was returning from the wood, heated with exercise, when I came to a stream silently flowing, so clear that you might count the pebbles on the bottom. The willows shaded it, and the grassy bank sloped down to the water's edge. I approached, I touched the water with my foot. I stepped in knee-deep, and not content with that, I laid my garments on the willows and went in. While I sported in the water, I heard an indistinct murmur coming up as out of the depths of the stream; and made haste to escape

---

① comb：蜂巢

② charm：咒语

③ frustrate /frʌˈstreɪt/：阻挠

④ Sicily /ˈsɪsɪli/：西西里岛，现在是意大利的一个区。

⑤ prize：掠夺来的东西，战利品

⑥ thistle /ˈθɪsl/：一种叶子和茎都长刺的植物

⑦ bramble：一种长刺的灌木，枝条长得很长。

⑧ Arethusa：/ˌærɪˈθjuːzə/

⑨ Elis /ˈiːlɪs/：古希腊地区名，位于伯罗奔尼撒半岛西北部，相当于今西希腊大区的伊利亚州（Ilia）。

to the nearest bank. The voice said, 'Why do you fly, Arethusa? I am Alpheus①, the god of this stream.' I ran, he pursued; he was not more swift than I, but he was stronger, and gained upon me, as my strength failed. At last, exhausted, I cried for help to Diana. 'Help me, goddess! help your votary②!' The goddess heard, and wrapped me suddenly in a thick cloud. The river god looked now this way and now that, and twice came close to me, but could not find me. 'Arethusa! Arethusa!' he cried. Oh, how I trembled,—like a lamb that hears the wolf growling outside the fold. A cold sweat came over me, my hair flowed down in streams; where my foot stood there was a pool. In short, in less time than it takes to tell it I became a fountain. But in this form Alpheus knew me and attempted to mingle his stream with mine. Diana cleft the ground, and I, endeavoring to escape him, plunged into the cavern, and through the bowels of the earth came out here in Sicily. While I passed through the lower parts of the earth, I saw your Proserpine. She was sad, but no longer showing alarm in her countenance. Her look was such as became③ a queen— the queen of Erebus④; the powerful bride of the monarch of the realms of the dead."

When Ceres heard this, she stood for a while like one stupefied⑤; then turned her chariot towards heaven, and hastened to present herself before the throne of Jove. She told the story of her bereavement⑥, and implored Jupiter to interfere to procure the restitution⑦ of her daughter. Jupiter consented on one condition, namely, that Proserpine should not during her stay in the lower world have taken any food; otherwise, the Fates forbade her release. Accordingly, Mercury was sent, accompanied by Spring, to demand Proserpine of Pluto⑧. The wily monarch consented; but, alas! The maiden had taken a pomegranate⑨ which Pluto offered her, and had sucked the sweet pulp⑩ from a few of the seeds. This was enough to prevent her complete release; but a compromise⑪ was made, by which she was to pass half the time with her mother, and the rest with her husband Pluto.

Ceres allowed herself to be pacified with this arrangement, and restored the earth to her favor. Now she remembered Celeus and his family, and her promise to his infant son Triptolemus⑫. When the boy grew up, she taught him the use of the plough, and how to sow the seed. She took him in her chariot, drawn by winged dragons, through all the countries of the earth, imparting to mankind valuable grains, and the knowledge of agriculture. After his return, Triptolemus built a magnificent temple to Ceres in Eleusis, and established the worship of the goddess, under the

---

① Alpheus：/æl'fiːəs/

② votary /'vəʊtəri/：忠实的追随者，信徒

③ become：适合

④ Erebus /'erɪbəs/：位于阳间和阴间之间的黑暗之地，神话中该词常用来指阴间。

⑤ stupefied /'stjuːpɪfaɪd/：茫然的，发呆的

⑥ bereavement /bɪ'riːvmənt/：失去亲人

⑦ restitution /ˌrestɪ'tjuːʃn/：归还，物归原主

⑧ of Pluto：from Pluto

⑨ pomegranate /'pɒmɪɡrænɪt/：石榴

⑩ pulp：（水果的）果肉

⑪ compromise /'kɒmprəmaɪz/：折中方案

⑫ Triptolemus：/trɪp'tɒlɪməs/

name of the Eleusinian① mysteries②, which, in the splendor and solemnity of their observance, surpassed all other religious celebrations among the Greeks.

There can be little doubt of this story of Ceres and Proserpine being an allegory③. Proserpine signifies the seed-corn④ which when cast into the ground lies there concealed—that is, she is carried off by the god of the underworld. It reappears—that is, Proserpine is restored to her mother. Spring leads her back to the light of day.

Glaucus and Scylla

Glaucus⑤ was a fisherman. One day he had drawn his nets to land, and had taken a great many fishes of various kinds. So he emptied his net, and proceeded to sort⑥ the fishes on the grass. The place where he stood was a beautiful island in the river, a solitary spot, uninhabited, and not used for pasturage⑦ of cattle, nor ever visited by any but himself. On a sudden, the fishes, which had been laid on the grass, began to revive and move their fins⑧ as if they were in the water; and while he looked on astonished, they one and all moved off to the water, plunged in, and swam away. He did not know what to make of this, whether some god had done it or some secret power in the herbage. "What herb has such a power?" he exclaimed; and gathering some of it, he tasted it. Scarce had the juices of the plant reached his palate⑨ when he found himself agitated with a longing desire for the water. He could no longer restrain himself, but bidding farewell to earth, he plunged into the stream. The gods of the water received him graciously, and admitted him to the honor of their society. They obtained the consent of Oceanus and Tethys, the sovereigns of the sea, that all that was mortal in him should be washed away. A hundred rivers poured their waters over him. Then he lost all sense of his former nature and all consciousness. When he recovered, he found himself changed in form and mind. His hair was sea-green, and trailed behind him on the water; his shoulders grew broad, and what had been thighs and legs assumed the form of a fish's tail. The sea-gods complimented him on the change of his appearance, and he fancied himself rather a good-looking personage.

One day Glaucus saw the beautiful maiden Scylla⑩, the favorite of the water-nymphs, rambling on the shore, and when she had found a sheltered nook, laving⑪ her limbs in the clear water. He fell in love with her, and showing himself on the surface, spoke to her, saying such

---

① Eleusinian /ˌɛljuːˈsɪnɪən/: of Eleusis; Eleusis /ɪˈljuːsɪs/是古希腊城镇,即今希腊阿提卡州的埃莱夫西纳(Elefsina),在雅典西北方向不远处。
② mysteries: 秘密仪式
③ allegory /ˈælɪgəri/: 寓言
④ seed-corn: 谷种,粮种
⑤ Glaucus: /ˈglɔːkəs/
⑥ sort: 把……分类
⑦ pasturage /ˈpɑːstʃərɪdʒ/: 放牧
⑧ fin: 鱼鳍
⑨ palate /ˈpælɪt/: 腭,即口腔上壁。
⑩ Scylla: /ˈsɪlə/
⑪ lave: 洗

things as he thought most likely to win her to stay; for she turned to run immediately on the sight of him, and ran till she had gained a cliff① overlooking the sea. Here she stopped and turned round to see whether it was a god or a sea animal, and observed with wonder his shape and color. Glaucus partly emerging from the water, and supporting himself against a rock, said, "Maiden, I am no monster, nor a sea animal, but a god; and neither Proteus nor Triton② ranks higher than I. Once I was a mortal, and followed the sea for a living; but now I belong wholly to it." Then he told the story of his metamorphosis③, and how he had been promoted to his present dignity, and added, "But what avails all this if it fails to move your heart?" He was going on in this strain④, but Scylla turned and hastened away.

Glaucus was in despair, but it occurred to him to consult the enchantress Circe⑤. Accordingly he repaired to her island—the same where afterwards Ulysses⑥ landed, as we shall see in one of our later stories. After mutual salutations, he said, "Goddess, I entreat your pity; you alone can relieve the pain I suffer. The power of herbs I know as well as any one, for it is to them I owe my change of form. I love Scylla. I am ashamed to tell you how I have sued and promised to her, and how scornfully she has treated me. I beseech you to use your incantations⑦, or potent herbs, if they are more prevailing⑧, not to cure me of my love,—for that I do not wish,—but to make her share it and yield me a like⑨ return." To which Circe replied, for she was not insensible to the attractions of the sea-green deity, "You had better pursue a willing object; you are worthy to be sought, instead of having to seek in vain. Be not diffident⑩, know your own worth. I protest to you that even I, goddess though I be, and learned in the virtues of plants and spells⑪, should not know how to refuse you. If she scorns you scorn her; meet one who is ready to meet you half way, and thus make a due return to both at once." To these words Glaucus replied, "Sooner shall trees grow at the bottom of the ocean, and sea-weed on the top of the mountains, than I will cease to love Scylla, and her alone."

The goddess was indignant, but she could not punish him, neither did she wish to do so, for she liked him too well; so she turned all her wrath against her rival, poor Scylla. She took plants of poisonous powers and mixed them together, with incantations and charms. Then she passed through the crowd of gambolling⑫ beasts, the victims of her art, and proceeded to the coast of

---

① gain a cliff：爬上悬崖
② Proteus /ˈprəʊtɪəs/ and Triton：/ˈtraɪtn/：sons of Neptune, minor sea gods. 参见 *The Age of Fable* 第 22 章中的 "The Water Deities" 小节。
③ metamorphosis /ˌmetəˈmɔːfəsɪs/：变形
④ strain：语气，口气
⑤ Circe：/ˈsɜːsi/
⑥ Ulysses /juːˈlɪsiːz/：关于 Ulysses 的故事，参见 *The Age of Fable* 第 29 章和第 30 章。
⑦ incantation /ˌɪnkænˈteɪʃn/：魔法，咒语
⑧ prevailing：占优势的，有力的
⑨ like：相同的，相似的
⑩ diffident /ˈdɪfɪdənt/：缺乏自信的
⑪ learned in the virtues of plants and spells：熟知植物和咒语的功效
⑫ gambol /ˈgæmbl/：跳跃，嬉戏

Sicily, where Scylla lived. There was a little bay on the shore to which Scylla used to resort, in the heat of the day, to breathe the air of the sea, and to bathe in its waters. Here the goddess poured her poisonous mixture, and muttered over it incantations of mighty power. Scylla came as usual and plunged into the water up to her waist. What was her horror to perceive a brood of serpents and barking monsters surrounding her! At first she could not imagine they were a part of herself, and tried to run from them, and to drive them away; but as she ran she carried them with her, and when she tried to touch her limbs, she found her hands touch only the yawning jaws of monsters. Scylla remained rooted to the spot. Her temper grew as ugly as her form, and she took pleasure in devouring hapless mariners① who came within her grasp. Thus she destroyed six of the companions of Ulysses, and tried to wreck the ships of Æneas②, till at last she was turned into a rock, and as such still continues to be a terror to mariners.

Chapter Ⅷ
Pygmalion—Dryope—Venus and Adonis—Apollo and Hyacinthus

Pygmalion

Pygmalion③ saw so much to blame in women that he came at last to abhor the sex④, and resolved to live unmarried. He was a sculptor, and had made with wonderful skill a statue of ivory, so beautiful that no living woman came anywhere near it. It was indeed the perfect semblance of a maiden that seemed to be alive, and only prevented from moving by modesty⑤. His art was so perfect that it concealed itself and its product looked like the workmanship of nature. Pygmalion admired his own work, and at last fell in love with the counterfeit⑥ creation. Oftentimes⑦ he laid his hand upon it as if to assure himself whether it were living or not, and could not even then believe that it was only ivory. He caressed⑧ it, and gave it presents such as young girls love⑨,— bright shells and polished stones, little birds and flowers of various hues, beads and amber. He put raiment⑩ on its limbs, and jewels on its fingers, and a necklace about its neck. To the ears he hung earrings, and strings of pearls upon the breast. Her dress became⑪ her, and she looked not

---

① mariner /ˈmærɪnə/：水手
② Æneas /ɪˈniːæs/：关于 Æneas 的故事，参见 *The Age of Fable* 第 31、第 32、第 33 章。
③ Pygmalion：/pɪɡˈmeɪlɪən/
④ the sex：（此处指）女性
⑤ modesty /ˈmɒdɪsti/：害羞
⑥ counterfeit /ˈkaʊntəfɪt/：假的
⑦ oftentimes /ˈɒfəntaɪmz/：often
⑧ caress /kəˈres/：抚摸
⑨ presents such as young girls love：年轻女孩喜欢的那些礼物
⑩ raiment /ˈreɪmənt/：衣服
⑪ become：适合

less charming than when unattired①. He laid her on a couch spread with cloths of Tyrian dye②, and called her his wife, and put her head upon a pillow of the softest feathers, as if she could enjoy their softness.

The festival of Venus was at hand—a festival celebrated with great pomp③ at Cyprus④. Victims⑤ were offered, the altars smoked, and odor of incense⑥ filled the air. When Pygmalion had performed his part in the solemnities⑦, he stood before the altar and timidly said, "Ye gods, who can do all things, give me, I pray you, for my wife"—he dared not say "my ivory virgin," but said instead—"one like my ivory virgin." Venus, who was present at the festival, heard him and knew the thought he would have uttered; and as an omen⑧ of her favor, caused the flame on the altar to shoot up thrice in a fiery point into the air. When he returned home, he went to see his statue, and leaning over the couch, gave a kiss to the mouth. It seemed to be warm. He pressed its lips again, he laid his hand upon the limbs; the ivory felt soft to his touch and yielded to his fingers⑨ like the wax of Hymettus⑩. While he stands astonished and glad, though doubting, and fears he may be mistaken, again and again with a lover's ardor he touches the object of his hopes. It was indeed alive! The veins when pressed yielded to the finger and again resumed their roundness. Then at last the votary of Venus⑪ found words to thank the goddess, and pressed his lips upon lips as real as his own. The virgin felt the kisses and blushed, and opening her timid eyes to the light, fixed them at the same moment on her lover. Venus blessed the nuptials⑫ she had formed, and from this union Paphos⑬ was born, from whom the city, sacred to Venus, received its name⑭.

Dryope

Dryope and Iole⑮ were sisters. The former was the wife of Andræmon⑯, beloved by her husband, and happy in the birth of her first child. One day the sisters strolled to the bank of a stream that sloped gradually down to the water's edge, while the upland was overgrown with myrtles. They were intending to gather flowers for forming garlands for the altars of the nymphs,

---

① unattired /ˌʌnəˈtaɪəd/: 没有穿衣服的
② Tyrian dye: 紫色或深红色染料;Tyre 是腓尼基 (Phoenicia) 城市,以深红色的染料而闻名。
③ pomp: 节日的盛况
④ Cyprus /ˈsaɪprəs/: 塞浦路斯岛,位于地中海东部。
⑤ victim: 杀死来供奉给神的动物,牺牲
⑥ incense /ˈɪnsens/: 香
⑦ solemnity /səˈlemnɪti/: 仪式
⑧ omen /ˈəʊmən/: 预兆
⑨ yielded to his fingers: 手指按着有弹性
⑩ Hymettus /haɪˈmetəs/: 山名,位于希腊雅典的东南方向,蜜蜂养殖是此地的重要产业。
⑪ the votary of Venus: Pygmalion
⑫ nuptial /ˈnʌpʃl/: 婚姻
⑬ Paphos: /ˈpeɪfɒs/
⑭ Paphos 城位于塞浦路斯西部海岸,传说是 Aphrodite (Venus) 从海水泡沫中诞生的地方,城内有著名的 Aphrodite (Venus) 神庙。
⑮ Dryope: /ˈdraɪəpi/; Iole: /ˈaɪəli/
⑯ Andræmon: /ænˈdriːmən/

and Dryope carried her child at her bosom, precious burden, and nursed[①] him as she walked. Near the water grew a lotus plant, full of purple flowers. Dryope gathered some and offered them to the baby, and Iole was about to do the same, when she perceived blood dropping from the places where her sister had broken them off the stem. The plant was no other than the nymph Lotis[②], who, running from a base pursuer, had been changed into this form. This they learned from the country people when it was too late.

Dryope, horror-struck when she perceived what she had done, would gladly have hastened from the spot, but found her feet rooted to the ground. She tried to pull them away, but moved nothing but her upper limbs. The woodiness[③] crept upward, and by degrees invested[④] her body. In anguish she attempted to tear her hair, but found her hands filled with leaves. The infant felt his mother's bosom begin to harden, and the milk cease to flow. Iole looked on at the sad fate of her sister, and could render no assistance. She embraced the growing trunk, as if she would hold back the advancing wood, and would gladly have been enveloped[⑤] in the same bark. At this moment Andræmon, the husband of Dryope, with her father, approached; and when they asked for Dryope, Iole pointed them to the new-formed lotus. They embraced the trunk of the yet warm tree, and showered their kisses on its leaves.

Now there was nothing left of Dryope but her face. Her tears still flowed and fell on her leaves, and while she could she spoke. "I am not guilty. I deserve not this fate. I have injured no one. If I speak falsely, may my foliage perish with drought and my trunk be cut down and burned. Take this infant and give it to a nurse. Let it often be brought and nursed under my branches, and play in my shade; and when he is old enough to talk, let him be taught to call me mother, and to say with sadness, 'My mother lies hid under this bark.' But bid him be careful of river banks, and beware how he plucks flowers, remembering that every bush he sees may be a goddess in disguise. Farewell, dear husband, and sister, and father. If you retain any love for me, let not the axe wound me, nor the flocks bite and tear my branches. Since I cannot stoop to you, climb up hither and kiss me; and while my lips continue to feel, lift up my child that I may kiss him. I can speak no more, for already the bark advances up my neck, and will soon shoot[⑥] over me. You need not close my eyes, the bark will close them without your aid." Then the lips ceased to move, and life was extinct; but the branches retained for some time longer the vital heat.

Venus and Adonis

Venus, playing one day with her boy Cupid, wounded her bosom with one of his arrows. She pushed him away, but the wound was deeper than she thought. Before it healed she beheld

---

① nurse：喂奶，哺乳

② Lotis：/ˈləʊtɪs/

③ woodiness：木质感

④ invest：包裹住

⑤ envelop /ɪnˈveləp/：包，裹

⑥ shoot：迅速生长

Adonis①, and was captivated with him. She no longer took any interest in her favorite resorts—Paphos, and Cnidos②, and Amathos③, rich in metals. She absented herself even from heaven, for Adonis was dearer to her than heaven. Him she followed and bore him company. She who used to love to recline④ in the shade, with no care but to cultivate her charms⑤, now rambles through the woods and over the hills, dressed like the huntress Diana; and calls her dogs, and chases hares and stags, or other game that it is safe to hunt, but keeps clear of⑥ the wolves and bears, reeking with the slaughter of the herd. She charged⑦ Adonis, too, to beware of such dangerous animals. "Be brave towards the timid," said she; "courage against the courageous is not safe. Beware how you expose yourself to danger and put my happiness to risk. Attack not the beasts that Nature has armed with weapons. I do not value your glory so high as to consent to purchase it by such exposure. Your youth, and the beauty that charms Venus, will not touch the hearts of lions and bristly boars⑧. Think of their terrible claws and prodigious⑨ strength! I hate the whole race of them. Do you ask me why?" Then she told him the story of Atalanta and Hippomenes⑩, who were changed into lions for their ingratitude⑪ to her.⑫

Having given him this warning, she mounted her chariot drawn by swans, and drove away through the air. But Adonis was too noble to heed such counsels. The dogs had roused a wild boar from his lair⑬, and the youth threw his spear and wounded the animal with a sidelong stroke. The beast drew out the weapon with his jaws, and rushed after Adonis, who turned and ran; but the boar overtook him, and buried his tusks⑭ in his side, and stretched him dying upon the plain.

Venus, in her swan-drawn chariot, had not yet reached Cyprus, when she heard coming up through midair the groans of her beloved, and turned her white-winged coursers⑮ back to earth. As she drew near and saw from on high his lifeless body bathed in blood, she alighted and, bending over it, beat her breast and tore her hair. Reproaching the Fates, she said, "Yet theirs shall be but a partial triumph; memorials of my grief shall endure, and the spectacle of your death, my Adonis, and of my lamentations shall be annually renewed. Your blood shall be changed into a flower; that consolation none can envy me." Thus speaking, she sprinkled nectar on the blood; and as they mingled, bubbles rose as in a pool on which raindrops fall, and in an hour's time

---

① Adonis：/ə'dəʊnɪs/

② Cnidos /'naɪdəs/：城市名,位于小亚细亚西南部。

③ Amathos /ə'mæθəs/：塞浦路斯古城

④ recline /rɪ'klaɪn/：躺

⑤ cultivate her charms：梳妆打扮

⑥ keep clear of：远离

⑦ charge：命令,告诫

⑧ boar：野猪

⑨ prodigious /prə'dɪdʒəs/：惊人的,巨大的

⑩ Atalanta：/ˌætə'læntə /；Hippomenes：/hɪ'pɒməniːz/

⑪ ingratitude /ɪn'grætɪtjuːd/：忘恩负义

⑫ Atalanta 和 Hippomenes 被变为狮子的故事在 *The Age of Fable* 第 18 章。

⑬ lair /leə/：动物的窝或躲藏处

⑭ tusk /tʌsk/：（大象、野猪等动物的）长牙,獠牙

⑮ courser /'kɔːsə/：骏马；her white-winged coursers（白翅膀的骏马）指的是给 Venus 拉车的白天鹅。

there sprang up a flower of bloody hue like that of the pomegranate. But it is short-lived. It is said the wind blows the blossoms open, and afterwards blows the petals away; so it is called Anemone①, or Wind Flower, from the cause which assists equally in its production and its decay.

Apollo and Hyacinthus

Apollo was passionately fond of a youth named Hyacinthus②. He accompanied him in his sports, carried the nets when he went fishing, led the dogs when he went to hunt, followed him in his excursions in the mountains, and neglected for him his lyre and his arrows. One day they played a game of quoits③ together, and Apollo, heaving aloft the discus, with strength mingled with skill, sent it high and far. Hyacinthus watched it as it flew, and excited with the sport ran forward to seize it, eager to make his throw, when the quoit bounded from the earth and struck him in the forehead. He fainted and fell. The god, as pale as himself, raised him and tried all his art to stanch the wound and retain the flitting life, but all in vain; the hurt was past the power of medicine. As when one has broken the stem of a lily in the garden it hangs its head and turns its flowers to the earth, so the head of the dying boy, as if too heavy for his neck, fell over on his shoulder. "Thou diest④, Hyacinth," so spoke Phœbus, "robbed of thy youth by me. Thine is the suffering, mine the crime. Would that I could die for thee! But since that may not be, thou shalt⑤ live with me in memory and in song. My lyre shall celebrate thee, my song shall tell thy fate, and thou shalt become a flower inscribed with my regrets." While Apollo spoke, behold the blood which had flowed on the ground and stained the herbage ceased to be blood; but a flower of hue⑥ more beautiful than the Tyrian⑦ sprang up, resembling the lily, if it were not that this is purple and that silvery white.⑧ And this was not enough for Phœbus; but to confer still greater honor, he marked the petals with his sorrow, and inscribed "Ah! ah!" upon them as we see to this day. The flower bears the name of Hyacinthus, and with every returning spring revives the memory of his fate.

It was said that Zephyrus⑨(the West wind), who was also fond of Hyacinthus and jealous of his preference⑩ of Apollo, blew the quoit out of its course⑪ to make it strike Hyacinthus.

---

① anemone /əˈneməni/：植物名，通常在早春开白花。
② Hyacinthus：/ˌhaɪəˈsɪnθəs/
③ quoit：(古希腊、罗马的)铁饼
④ diest：主语是 thou 时 die 的屈折变化形式。
⑤ shalt：主语是 thou 时 shall 的屈折变化形式。
⑥ hue：色彩
⑦ the Tyrian：指古代 Tyre 生产的紫色或深红色染料。
⑧ (原作者注) It is evidently not our modern hyacinth that is here described. It is perhaps some species of iris, or perhaps of larkspur or of pansy. (hyacinth：植物名，大约有 30 个品种，花香，花呈蓝色、紫色或白色。)
⑨ Zephyrus：/ˈzefərəs/
⑩ preference：偏爱
⑪ out of its course：偏离其飞行轨迹

Chapter IX
Ceyx and Halcyone

Ceyx① was king of Thessaly, where he reigned in peace, without violence or wrong. He was son of Hesperus②, the Day-star, and the glow of his beauty reminded one of his father. Halcyone③, the daughter of Æolus④, was his wife, and devotedly attached to him. Now Ceyx was in deep affliction⑤ for the loss of his brother, and direful prodigies⑥ following his brother's death made him feel as if the gods were hostile to him. He thought best, therefore, to make a voyage to Carlos in Ionia⑦, to consult the oracle of Apollo. But as soon as he disclosed his intention to his wife Halcyone, a shudder ran through her frame⑧, and her face grew deadly pale. "What fault of mine, dearest husband, has turned your affection from me? Where is that love of me that used to be uppermost⑨ in your thoughts? Have you learned to feel easy⑩ in the absence of Halcyone? Would you rather have me away?" She also endeavored to discourage him, by describing the violence of the winds, which she had known familiarly when she lived at home in her father's house,—Æolus being the god of the winds, and having as much as he could do to restrain them. "They rush together," said she, "with such fury that fire flashes from the conflict. But if you must go," she added, "dear husband, let me go with you, otherwise I shall suffer not only the real evils which you must encounter, but those also which my fears suggest."

These words weighed heavily on the mind of King Ceyx, and it was no less his own wish than hers to take her with him, but he could not bear to expose her to the dangers of the sea. He answered, therefore, consoling her as well as he could, and finished with these words: "I promise, by the rays of my father the Day-star, that if fate permits I will return before the moon shall have twice rounded her orb." When he had thus spoken, he ordered the vessel to be drawn out of the shiphouse, and the oars and sails to be put aboard. When Halcyone saw these

---

① Ceyx：/'siːɪks/

② Hesperus：Hesperus 本来是昏星（the evening star），但希腊化时期的作家们将其与晨星（Phosphoros /'fɒsfərəs /）等同，所以在这里后面的插入语用 the Day-star。希腊化时期指的是公元前 323 年马其顿国王亚历山大大帝（Alexander the Great）去世至公元前 31 年罗马的安东尼（Anthony）和埃及的克里奥佩特拉（Cleopatra）被打败这段时期。

③ Halcyone：/hæl'saɪəni/

④ Æolus /'iːəʊləs/：风神

⑤ affliction /ə'flɪkʃn/：痛苦

⑥ prodigy /'prɒdɪdʒi/：预兆

⑦ Ionia /aɪ'əʊnɪə/：古代地区名，位于小亚细亚西海岸的中部。

⑧ frame：身躯

⑨ uppermost /'ʌpəməʊst/：占据最高位置的

⑩ easy：舒服的,舒适的

preparations she shuddered, as if with a presentiment① of evil②. With tears and sobs she said farewell, and then fell senseless to the ground.

Ceyx would still have lingered, but now the young men grasped their oars and pulled vigorously through the waves, with long and measured strokes. Halcyone raised her streaming eyes, and saw her husband standing on the deck, waving his hand to her. She answered his signal till the vessel had receded so far that she could no longer distinguish his form from the rest. When the vessel itself could no more be seen, she strained her eyes to catch the last glimmer of the sail, till that too disappeared. Then, retiring to her chamber, she threw herself on her solitary couch.

Meanwhile they glide out of the harbor, and the breeze plays among the ropes. The seamen draw in their oars, and hoist③ their sails. When half or less of their course was passed, as night drew on, the sea began to whiten with swelling waves, and the east wind to blow a gale④. The master⑤ gave the word to take in sail, but the storm forbade obedience, for such is the roar of the winds and waves his orders are unheard. The men, of their own accord, busy themselves to secure the oars, to strengthen the ship, to reef⑥ the sail. While they thus do what to each one seems best, the storm increases. The shouting of the men, the rattling of the shrouds⑦, and the dashing of the waves, mingle with the roar of the thunder. The swelling sea seems lifted up to the heavens, to scatter its foam among the clouds; then sinking away to the bottom assumes the color of the shoal⑧—a Stygian⑨ blackness.

The vessel shares all these changes. It seems like a wild beast that rushes on the spears of the hunters. Rain falls in torrents, as if the skies were coming down to unite with the sea. When the lightning ceases for a moment, the night seems to add its own darkness to that of the storm; then comes the flash, rending the darkness asunder, and lighting up all with a glare. Skill fails, courage sinks, and death seems to come on every wave. The men are stupefied with terror. The thought of parents, and kindred⑩, and pledges left at home, comes over their minds. Ceyx thinks of Halcyone. No name but hers is on his lips, and while he yearns for her, he yet rejoices in her absence⑪. Presently the mast is shattered by a stroke of lightning, the rudder broken, and the triumphant surge curling over looks down upon the wreck, then falls, and crushes it to fragments. Some of the seamen, stunned by the stroke, sink, and rise no more; others cling to fragments of

---

① presentiment /prɪˈzentɪmənt/: 不祥的预感
② evil: 灾难,不幸
③ hoist: 升起
④ gale: 大风
⑤ master: 船长
⑥ reef: 缩 (帆)
⑦ shrouds: (桅的) 左右支索
⑧ shoal: 浅滩
⑨ Stygian /ˈstɪdʒɪən/: 地狱般的
⑩ kindred /ˈkɪndrɪd/: 家人或亲戚
⑪ he yet rejoices in her absence: 他庆幸她没有在场。

the wreck. Ceyx, with the hand that used to grasp the sceptre, holds fast① to a plank, calling for help,—alas, in vain,—upon his father and his father-in-law. But oftenest on his lips was the name of Halcyone. To her his thoughts cling. He prays that the waves may bear his body to her sight, and that it may receive burial at her hands. At length the waters overwhelm him, and he sinks. The Day-star looked dim that night. Since it could not leave the heavens, it shrouded its face with clouds.

In the meanwhile Halcyone, ignorant② of all these horrors, counted the days till her husband's promised return. Now she gets ready the garments which he shall put on, and now what she shall wear when he arrives. To all the gods she offers frequent incense, but more than all to Juno. For her husband, who was no more, she prayed incessantly: that he might be safe; that he might come home; that he might not, in his absence, see any one that he would love better than her. But of all these prayers, the last was the only one destined to be granted. The goddess, at length, could not bear any longer to be pleaded with for one already dead, and to have hands raised to her altars that ought rather to be offering funeral rites. So, calling Iris③, she said, "Iris, my faithful messenger, go to the drowsy dwelling of Somnus④, and tell him to send a vision⑤ to Halcyone in the form of Ceyx, to make known to her the event."

Iris puts on her robe of many colors, and tingeing the sky with her bow⑥, seeks the palace of the King of Sleep⑦. Near the Cimmerian⑧ country, a mountain cave is the abode of the dull god Somnus. Here Phœbus dares not come, either rising, at midday, or setting. Clouds and shadows are exhaled from the ground, and the light glimmers faintly. The bird of dawning⑨, with crested head, never there calls aloud to Aurora, nor watchful dog, nor more sagacious⑩ goose disturbs the silence. No wild beast, nor cattle, nor branch moved with the wind, nor sound of human conversation, breaks the stillness. Silence reigns there; but from the bottom of the rock the River Lethe⑪ flows, and by its murmur invites to sleep. Poppies grow abundantly before the door of the cave, and other herbs, from whose juices Night collects slumbers, which she scatters over the darkened earth. There is no gate to the mansion, to creak⑫ on its hinges, nor any watchman; but in the midst a couch of black ebony, adorned with black plumes and black curtains. There the god reclines, his limbs relaxed with sleep. Around him lie dreams, resembling all various forms, as

---

① fast：紧紧地
② ignorant：不知道的
③ Iris /ˈaɪərɪs/：彩虹女神，诸神的使者。
④ Somnus：/ˈsɒmnəs/
⑤ vision：梦中看到的人或物
⑥ her bow：彩虹
⑦ the King of Sleep：Somnus
⑧ Cimmerian /sɪˈmɪərɪən/：of the Cimmerii（古代的游牧民族、克里米亚最早的居民）
⑨ the bird of dawning：公鸡
⑩ sagacious /səˈɡeɪʃəs/：明智的，聪明的
⑪ Lethe /ˈliːθi/：阴间的河流，人喝其水会忘记过去。
⑫ creak：发出嘎吱声

many as the harvest bears stalks, or the forest leaves, or the seashore sand grains.

As soon as the goddess entered and brushed away the dreams that hovered around her, her brightness lit up all the cave. The god, scarce opening his eyes, and ever and anon dropping his beard upon his breast, at last shook himself free from himself, and leaning on his arm, inquired her errand①,—for he knew who she was. She answered, "Somnus, gentlest of the gods, tranquillizer② of minds and soother③ of care-worn④ hearts, Juno sends you her commands that you despatch a dream to Halcyone, in the city of Trachin⑤, representing her lost husband and all the events of the wreck."

Having delivered her message, Iris hasted away, for she could not longer endure the stagnant air, and as she felt drowsiness creeping over her, she made her escape, and returned by her bow the way she came. Then Somnus called one of his numerous sons,—Morpheus⑥,—the most expert⑦ in counterfeiting⑧ forms, and in imitating the walk, the countenance, and mode of speaking, even the clothes and attitudes⑨ most characteristic of each. But he only imitates men, leaving it to another to personate⑩ birds, beasts, and serpents. Him they call Icelos; and Phantasos is a third, who turns himself into rocks, waters, woods, and other things without life. These wait upon kings and great personages in their sleeping hours, while others move among the common people. Somnus chose, from all the brothers, Morpheus, to perform the command of Iris; then laid his head on his pillow and yielded himself to grateful repose.

Morpheus flew, making no noise with his wings, and soon came to the Hæmonian city⑪, where, laying aside his wings, he assumed the form of Ceyx. Under that form, but pale like a dead man, naked, he stood before the couch of the wretched wife. His beard seemed soaked with water, and water trickled from his drowned locks⑫. Leaning over the bed, tears streaming from his eyes, he said, "Do you recognize your Ceyx, unhappy wife, or has death too much changed my visage⑬? Behold me, know me, your husband's shade⑭, instead of himself. Your prayers, Halcyone, availed me nothing. I am dead. No more deceive yourself with vain hopes of my return. The stormy winds sunk my ship in the Ægean Sea⑮, waves filled my mouth while it called aloud

---

① inquired her errand：询问她的来意

② tranquillizer /ˈtræŋkwɪlaɪzə/：让人平静的人或物

③ soother /ˈsuːðə/：安慰者

④ care-worn：忧心忡忡的

⑤ Trachin /ˈtrætʃɪn/：Thessaly 古城名,位于 Œta 山山脚。

⑥ Morpheus：/ˈmɔːfjuːs/

⑦ expert：有经验的,熟练的

⑧ counterfeit /ˈkauntəfɪt/：模仿

⑨ attitude：姿态

⑩ personate：（为了欺诈的目的）假装是……

⑪ the Hæmonian /hiːˈməʊnɪən/ city：Trachin；Hæmonia /hiːˈməʊnɪə/ is an old name of Thessaly.

⑫ lock：头发

⑬ visage /ˈvɪzɪdʒ/：脸,面部

⑭ shade：鬼魂

⑮ Ægean /iːˈdʒiːən/ Sea：爱琴海,地中海的一部分,位于土耳其和希腊之间。

on you. No uncertain messenger tells you this, no vague rumor brings it to your ears. I come in person, a shipwrecked man, to tell you my fate. Arise! give me tears, give me lamentations, let me not go down to Tartarus unwept." To these words Morpheus added the voice, which seemed to be that of her husband; he seemed to pour forth genuine tears; his hands had the gestures of Ceyx.

Halcyone, weeping, groaned, and stretched out her arms in her sleep, striving to embrace his body, but grasping only the air. "Stay!" she cried; "whither① do you fly? let us go together." Her own voice awakened her. Starting up, she gazed eagerly around, to see if he was still present, for the servants, alarmed by her cries, had brought a light. When she found him not, she smote her breast and rent her garments. She cares not to unbind her hair, but tears it wildly. Her nurse asks what is the cause of her grief. "Halcyone is no more," she answers, "she perished with her Ceyx. Utter not words of comfort, he is shipwrecked and dead. I have seen him, I have recognized him. I stretched out my hands to seize him and detain him. His shade vanished, but it was the true shade of my husband. Not with the accustomed features, not with the beauty that was his, but pale, naked, and with his hair wet with sea-water, he appeared to wretched② me. Here, in this very spot, the sad vision stood,"—and she looked to find the mark of his footsteps. "This it was, this that my presaging mind foreboded, when I implored him not to leave me, to trust himself to the waves. Oh, how I wish, since thou wouldst③ go, thou hadst④ taken me with thee! It would have been far better. Then I should have had no remnant of life to spend without thee, nor a separate death to die. If I could bear to live and struggle to endure, I should be more cruel to myself than the sea has been to me. But I will not struggle, I will not be separated from thee, unhappy husband. This time, at least, I will keep thee company. In death, if one tomb may not include us, one epitaph⑤ shall; if I may not lay my ashes with thine, my name, at least, shall not be separated." Her grief forbade more words, and these were broken with tears and sobs.

It was now morning. She went to the seashore, and sought the spot where she last saw him, on his departure. "While he lingered here, and cast off his tacklings⑥, he gave me his last kiss." While she reviews every object, and strives to recall every incident, looking out over the sea, she descries an indistinct⑦ object floating in the water. At first she was in doubt what it was, but by degrees the waves bore it nearer, and it was plainly the body of a man. Though unknowing of whom, yet, as it was of some shipwrecked one, she was deeply moved, and gave it her tears, saying, "Alas! unhappy one, and unhappy, if such there be, thy wife!" Borne by the waves, it came nearer. As she more and more nearly views it, she trembles more and more. Now, now it approaches the shore. Now marks that she recognizes appear. It is her husband! Stretching out her

---

① whither: to which place
② wretched /'retʃɪd/: 可怜的,不幸的
③ wouldst: 主语是 thou 时 would 的屈折变化形式。
④ hadst: 主语是 thou 时 had 的屈折变化形式。
⑤ epitaph /'epɪtɑːf/: 墓志铭
⑥ tackling /'tæklɪŋ/: 船的索具
⑦ indistinct /ˌɪndɪ'stɪŋkt/: 模糊不清的

trembling hands towards it, she exclaims, "O dearest husband, is it thus you return to me?"

There was built out from the shore a mole①, constructed to break② the assaults of the sea, and stem③ its violent ingress④. She leaped upon this barrier and (it was wonderful she could do so) she flew, and striking the air with wings produced on the instant, skimmed along the surface of the water, an unhappy bird. As she flew, her throat poured forth sounds full of grief, and like the voice of one lamenting. When she touched the mute and bloodless body, she enfolded its beloved limbs with her new-formed wings, and tried to give kisses with her horny beak. Whether Ceyx felt it, or whether it was only the action of the waves, those who looked on doubted, but the body seemed to raise its head. But indeed he did feel it, and by the pitying gods both of them were changed into birds⑤. They mate⑥ and have their young ones. For seven placid⑦ days, in winter time, Halcyone broods over her nest, which floats upon the sea. Then the way is safe to seamen. Æolus guards the winds and keeps them from disturbing the deep⑧. The sea is given up, for the time, to his grandchildren.

Chapter X
Vertumnus and Pomona

The Hamadryads⑨ were Wood-nymphs. Pomona⑩ was of this class, and no one excelled her in love of the garden and the culture⑪ of fruit. She cared not for forests and rivers, but loved the cultivated country, and trees that bear delicious apples. Her right hand bore for its weapon not a javelin, but a pruning-knife⑫. Armed with this, she busied herself at one time to repress the too luxuriant growths⑬, and curtail the branches that straggled out of place⑭; at another, to split the twig and insert therein a graft⑮, making the branch adopt a nursling not its own. She took care, too, that her favorites should not suffer from drought, and led streams of water by them, that the

---

① mole：防波堤
② break：减轻……的力度
③ stem：阻止
④ ingress /ˈɪngres/：进入
⑤ 他俩变成了一种英语叫 halcyon（/ˈhælsɪən/）的鸟。古希腊人认为这种鸟在冬至前后把巢筑在海面上繁殖后代,其间大海风平浪静。
⑥ mate：交配
⑦ placid /ˈplæsɪd/：平静的
⑧ deep：(诗歌用词)大海
⑨ Hamadryad：/ˌhæməˈdraɪəd/
⑩ Pomona：/pəˈməʊnə/
⑪ culture，种植,栽培
⑫ pruning-knife：修剪果树的刀
⑬ repress the too luxuriant growths：抑制住长得太茂盛的桠枝；luxuriant /lʌgˈʒʊəriənt/：(植物、头发)茂盛的
⑭ curtail the branches that straggled out of place：剪短那些长得长长的树枝；curtail /kɜːˈteɪl/：剪短；straggle /ˈstægl/：(植物、树枝等)长得长而不整齐；out of place：在错误的地方
⑮ graft：用于嫁接的嫩枝

thirsty roots might drink. This occupation was her pursuit, her passion; and she was free from that which Venus inspires①. She was not without fear of the country people, and kept her orchard locked, and allowed not men to enter. The Fauns② and Satyrs③ would have given all they possessed to win her, and so would old Sylvanus④, who looks young for his years, and Pan, who wears a garland of pine leaves around his head. But Vertumnus⑤ loved her best of all; yet he sped⑥ no better than the rest. O how often, in the disguise of a reaper, did he bring her corn in a basket, and looked the very image of a reaper! With a hay band tied round him, one would think he had just come from turning over the grass. Sometimes he would have an ox-goad⑦ in his hand, and you would have said he had just unyoked his weary oxen. Now he bore a pruning-hook⑧, and personated a vine-dresser⑨; and again, with a ladder on his shoulder, he seemed as if he was going to gather apples. Sometimes he trudged⑩ along as a discharged⑪ soldier, and again he bore a fishing-rod, as if going to fish. In this way he gained admission to her again and again, and fed his passion with the sight of her.

One day he came in the guise of an old woman, her gray hair surmounted with a cap, and a staff in her hand. She entered the garden and admired the fruit. "It does you credit⑫, my dear," she said, and kissed her, not exactly with an old woman's kiss. She sat down on a bank, and looked up at the branches laden with fruit which hung over her. Opposite was an elm entwined with a vine loaded with swelling grapes. She praised the tree and its associated vine, equally. "But," said she, "if the tree stood alone, and had no vine clinging to it, it would have nothing to attract or offer us but its useless leaves. And equally the vine, if it were not twined round the elm, would lie prostrate on the ground. Why will you not take a lesson from the tree and the vine, and consent to unite yourself with some one? I wish you would. Helen⑬ herself had not more numerous suitors, nor Penelope⑭, the wife of shrewd Ulysses. Even while you spurn them, they court you,—rural deities and others of every kind that frequent⑮ these mountains. But if you are prudent and want to make a

---

① that which Venus inspires：爱情
② Faun /fɔːn/：古代意大利的农村神，外貌像人，但长着山羊的耳朵和尾巴。
③ Satyr /'sætə/：林地之神；在早期的希腊艺术中表现为长着马耳朵和马尾巴的人，在后来的罗马艺术中表现为长着山羊耳朵、尾巴、腿和角的人。
④ Sylvanus /sɪl'vænəs/：古罗马的森林守护神。拉丁语单词 sylvanus 意为"森林的"。
⑤ Vertumnus：/vɜː'tʌmnəs/
⑥ speed：成功
⑦ ox-goad：顶端尖的赶牛棍
⑧ pruning-hook：整枝钩刀
⑨ vine-dresser：葡萄整枝人
⑩ trudge /trʌdʒ/：步履艰难地走
⑪ discharged：（士兵）复原回家的
⑫ It does you credit：它为你增光；credit：荣誉，赞扬
⑬ Helen：西方文学中最著名的美女，其夫是斯巴达（Sparta）的 Menelaus，Helen 被特洛伊（Troy）王子 Paris 勾引到特洛伊后，希腊人与特洛伊人之间爆发了特洛伊战争（the Trojan War）。参见 The Age of Fable 第 27 章。
⑭ Penelope /pə'neləpi/：特洛伊战争中希腊智多星 Ulysses 的妻子，西方文学中最著名的贞妇。参见 The Age of Fable 第 23 章和第 30 章。
⑮ frequent /'friːkwənt/：（及物动词）经常到某地

good alliance①, and will let an old woman advise you,—who loves you better than you have any idea of,—dismiss all the rest and accept Vertumnus, on my recommendation②. I know him as well as he knows himself. He is not a wandering deity, but belongs to these mountains. Nor is he like too many of the lovers nowadays, who love any one they happen to see; he loves you, and you only. Add to this③, he is young and handsome, and has the art of assuming any shape he pleases, and can make himself just what you command him. Moreover, he loves the same things that you do, delights in gardening, and handles your apples with admiration. But now he cares nothing for fruits nor flowers, nor anything else, but only yourself. Take pity on him, and fancy him speaking now with my mouth. Remember that the gods punish cruelty, and that Venus hates a hard heart, and will visit④ such offences sooner or later. To prove this, let me tell you a story, which is well known in Cyprus to be a fact; and I hope it will have the effect to make you more merciful.

"Iphis⑤ was a young man of humble parentage, who saw and loved Anaxarete⑥, a noble lady of the ancient family of Teucer⑦. He struggled long with his passion, but when he found he could not subdue it, he came a suppliant to her mansion. First he told his passion to her nurse, and begged her as she loved her foster-child to favor his suit. And then he tried to win her domestics⑧ to his side. Sometimes he committed his vows to written tablets⑨, and often hung at her door garlands which he had moistened with his tears. He stretched himself on her threshold, and uttered his complaints to the cruel bolts and bars. She was deafer than the surges which rise in the November gale; harder than steel from the German forges⑩, or a rock that still clings to its native cliff. She mocked and laughed at him, adding cruel words to her ungentle treatment, and gave not the slightest gleam of hope.

"Iphis could not any longer endure the torments of hopeless love, and, standing before her doors, he spake⑪ these last words: 'Anaxarete, you have conquered, and shall no longer have to bear my importunities⑫. Enjoy your triumph! Sing songs of joy, and bind your forehead with laurel,—you have conquered! I die; stony heart, rejoice! This at least I can do to gratify you, and force you to praise me; and thus shall I prove that the love of you left me but with life. Nor will I leave it to rumor to tell you of my death. I will come myself, and you shall see me die, and feast your eyes on the spectacle. Yet, O ye gods, who look down on mortal woes, observe my fate! I ask but this: let me be remembered in coming ages, and add those years to my fame which you have reft from my life.' Thus he said, and, turning his pale face and weeping eyes towards her mansion, he fastened a rope to the gatepost, on which he had often hung garlands, and putting his head into the noose, he murmured, 'This garland at least will please you, cruel girl!' and falling hung suspended with his neck broken. As he fell he struck against the gate, and the sound was as the sound of a groan. The servants opened the door and found him dead, and with exclamations of pity raised him and carried him home to his mother, for his father was not living. She received the dead body of her son, and folded the cold form to her bosom, while she poured forth the sad words which bereaved mothers utter. The mournful funeral passed through the town, and the pale corpse was borne on a bier① to the place of the funeral pile. By chance the home of Anaxarete was on the street where the procession② passed, and the lamentations of the mourners met the ears of her whom the avenging deity had already marked for punishment.

"'Let us see this sad procession,' said she, and mounted to a turret, whence through an open window she looked upon the funeral. Scarce had her eyes rested upon the form of Iphis stretched on the bier, when they began to stiffen, and the warm blood in her body to become cold. Endeavoring to step back, she found she could not move her feet; trying to turn away her face, she tried in vain; and by degrees all her limbs became stony like her heart. That you may not doubt the fact, the statue still remains, and stands in the temple of Venus at Salamis③, in the exact form of the lady. Now think of these things, my dear, and lay aside your scorn and your delays, and accept a lover. So may neither the vernal④ frosts blight⑤ your young fruits, nor furious winds scatter your blossoms!"

When Vertumnus had spoken thus, he dropped the disguise of an old woman, and stood before her in his proper⑥ person, as a comely⑦ youth. It appeared to her like the sun bursting through a cloud. He would have renewed his entreaties, but there was no need; his arguments and the sight of his true form prevailed, and the Nymph no longer resisted, but owned a mutual flame.

Chapter XI
Cupid and Psyche

A certain king and queen had three daughters. The charms of the two elder were more than common, but the beauty of the youngest was so wonderful that the poverty of language is unable to

---

① bier /bɪə/：抬尸架

② procession /prə'seʃn/：送葬队伍

③ Salamis /'sæləmɪs/：城市名，位于塞浦路斯岛东海岸。另外，希腊有个岛屿也叫 Salamis，位于雅典以西的海湾中；公元前 480 年，在 Salamis 岛与希腊大陆之间的海峡中，希腊人大败强大的波斯舰队。

④ vernal /'vɜːnl/：春天的

⑤ blight：使枯萎

⑥ proper：自己的，本身的

⑦ comely：漂亮的

express its due praise. The fame of her beauty was so great that strangers from neighboring countries came in crowds to enjoy the sight, and looked on her with amazement, paying her that homage which is due only to Venus herself. In fact Venus found her altars deserted①, while men turned their devotion to this young virgin. As she passed along, the people sang her praises, and strewed her way with chaplets② and flowers.

This perversion of homage due only to the immortal powers to the exaltation of a mortal gave great offence to the real Venus.③ Shaking her ambrosial locks with indignation④, she exclaimed, "Am I then to be eclipsed⑤ in my honors by a mortal girl? In vain then did that royal shepherd, whose judgment was approved by Jove himself, give me the palm of beauty over my illustrious rivals, Pallas and Juno.⑥ But she shall not so quietly usurp⑦ my honors. I will give her cause to repent of so unlawful a beauty."

Thereupon she calls her winged son Cupid, mischievous enough in his own nature, and rouses and provokes him yet more by her complaints. She points out Psyche⑧ to him and says, "My dear son, punish that contumacious⑨ beauty; give thy mother a revenge as sweet as her injuries are great; infuse⑩ into the bosom of that haughty girl a passion for some low, mean, unworthy being, so that she may reap a mortification⑪ as great as her present exultation⑫ and triumph."

Cupid prepared to obey the commands of his mother. There are two fountains in Venus's garden, one of sweet waters, the other of bitter. Cupid filled two amber vases, one from each fountain, and suspending them from the top of his quiver, hastened to the chamber of Psyche, whom he found asleep. He shed a few drops from the bitter fountain over her lips, though the sight of her almost moved him to pity; then touched her side with the point of his arrow. At the touch she awoke, and opened eyes upon Cupid (himself invisible), which so startled him that in his confusion he wounded himself with his own arrow. Heedless of his wound, his whole thought now was to repair the mischief he had done, and he poured the balmy drops of joy over all her silken ringlets.

Psyche, henceforth frowned upon by Venus, derived no benefit from all her charms. True, all eyes were cast eagerly upon her, and every mouth spoke her praises; but neither king, royal youth, nor plebeian⑬ presented himself to demand her in marriage. Her two elder sisters of

① deserted /dɪˈsɜːtɪd/: 被抛弃的,被遗弃的,荒废的
② chaplet /ˈtʃæplɪt/: 花环
③ 这种只有神才配得到的崇敬被错误地用来抬高一个凡人,这让真正的 Venus 深受伤害。perversion /pəˈvɜːʃn/: 错误使用;the immortal powers: 神;exaltation /ˌegzɔːlˈteɪʃn/: 抬高,赞扬;offence: 伤害
④ indignation /ˌɪndɪɡˈneɪʃn/: 愤怒
⑤ eclipse /iˈklɪps/: (通过对比)使……显得暗淡,超越
⑥ 参见 *The Age of Fable* 第 27 章。that royal shepherd: Paris; the palm of beauty: the golden apple "for the fairest"; Pallas /ˈpæləs/: 即 Athena /əˈθiːnə/, Athena 常被叫作 Pallas Athena。
⑦ usurp /juˈzɜːp/: 篡夺
⑧ Psyche: /ˈsaɪki/
⑨ contumacious /ˌkɒntjuˈmeɪʃəs/: 胆大妄为的,抗拒权威的
⑩ infuse /ɪnˈfjuːz/: 注入
⑪ mortification /ˌmɔːtɪfɪˈkeɪʃn/: 极大的苦恼,极大的失望
⑫ exultation /ˌegzʌlˈteɪʃn/: 欢喜
⑬ plebeian /plɪˈbiːən/: 普通人,平民

moderate charms had now long been married to two royal princes; but Psyche, in her lonely apartment, deplored① her solitude, sick of that beauty which, while it procured abundance of flattery, had failed to awaken love.

Her parents, afraid that they had unwittingly② incurred③ the anger of the gods, consulted the oracle of Apollo, and received this answer: "The virgin is destined for the bride of no mortal lover. Her future husband awaits her on the top of the mountain. He is a monster whom neither gods nor men can resist."

This dreadful decree of the oracle filled all the people with dismay, and her parents abandoned themselves to grief. But Psyche said, "Why, my dear parents, do you now lament me? You should rather have grieved when the people showered upon me undeserved honors, and with one voice called me a Venus. I now perceive that I am a victim to that name. I submit. Lead me to that rock to which my unhappy fate has destined me." Accordingly, all things being prepared, the royal maid took her place in the procession, which more resembled a funeral than a nuptial pomp, and with her parents, amid the lamentations of the people, ascended the mountain, on the summit of which they left her alone, and with sorrowful hearts returned home.

While Psyche stood on the ridge of the mountain, panting with fear and with eyes full of tears, the gentle Zephyr④ raised her from the earth and bore her with an easy motion into a flowery dale. By degrees her mind became composed⑤, and she laid herself down on the grassy bank to sleep. When she awoke refreshed with sleep, she looked round and beheld near by a pleasant grove of tall and stately trees. She entered it, and in the midst⑥ discovered a fountain, sending forth clear and crystal waters, and fast by⑦, a magnificent palace whose august⑧ front impressed the spectator that it was not the work of mortal hands, but the happy retreat⑨ of some god. Drawn by admiration and wonder, she approached the building and ventured to enter. Every object she met filled her with pleasure and amazement. Golden pillars supported the vaulted roof, and the walls were enriched with carvings and paintings representing beasts of the chase and rural scenes, adapted to delight the eye of the beholder. Proceeding onward, she perceived that besides the apartments of state⑩ there were others filled with all manner of treasures, and beautiful and precious productions of nature and art.

While her eyes were thus occupied, a voice addressed her, though she saw no one, uttering these words: "Sovereign lady, all that you see is yours. We whose voices you hear are your

---

① deplore /dɪ'plɔː/: 为……而哭泣

② unwittingly /ʌn'wɪtɪŋli/: 不知不觉地

③ incur /ɪn'kəː/ 招致

④ Zephyr /'zefə/: 西风

⑤ composed /kəm'pəʊzd/: 平静的

⑥ midst: middle

⑦ fast by: 就在旁边

⑧ august /ɔː'gʌst/: 庄严的,雄伟的

⑨ retreat /rɪ'triːt/: 隐居场所

⑩ state: 辉煌,豪华,威严

servants and shall obey all your commands with our utmost care and diligence. Retire, therefore, to your chamber and repose on your bed of down①, and when you see fit repair to the bath. Supper awaits you in the adjoining alcove when it pleases you to take your seat there."

Psyche gave ear to the admonitions② of her vocal attendants, and after repose and the refreshment of the bath, seated herself in the alcove, where a table immediately presented itself, without any visible aid from waiters or servants, and covered with the greatest delicacies of food and the most nectareous③ wines. Her ears too were feasted with music from invisible performers; of whom one sang, another played on the lute, and all closed in the wonderful harmony of a full chorus.

She had not yet seen her destined husband. He came only in the hours of darkness and fled before the dawn of morning, but his accents were full of love, and inspired a like passion in her. She often begged him to stay and let her behold him, but he would not consent. On the contrary he charged④ her to make no attempt to see him, for it was his pleasure, for the best of reasons, to keep concealed. "Why should you wish to behold me?" he said; "have you any doubt of my love? have you any wish ungratified? If you saw me, perhaps you would fear me, perhaps adore me, but all I ask of you⑤ is to love me. I would rather you would love me as an equal than adore me as a god."

This reasoning somewhat quieted Psyche for a time, and while the novelty⑥ lasted she felt quite happy. But at length the thought of her parents, left in ignorance of her fate, and of her sisters, precluded⑦ from sharing with her the delights of her situation, preyed on her mind and made her begin to feel her palace as but a splendid prison. When her husband came one night, she told him her distress, and at last drew from him an unwilling consent that her sisters should be brought to see her.

So, calling Zephyr, she acquainted him with her husband's commands, and he, promptly obedient, soon brought them across the mountain down to their sister's valley. They embraced her and she returned their caresses. "Come," said Psyche, "enter with me my house and refresh yourselves with whatever your sister has to offer." Then taking their hands she led them into her golden palace, and committed them to the care of her numerous train of attendant voices, to refresh them in her baths and at her table, and to show them all her treasures. The view of these celestial delights caused envy to enter their bosoms, at seeing their young sister possessed of⑧ such state⑨ and splendor, so much exceeding their own.

They asked her numberless questions, among others what sort of a person her husband was. Psyche replied that he was a beautiful youth, who generally spent the daytime in hunting upon the

---

① down：羽绒，鸭绒

② admonition /ˌædməˈnɪʃn/：告诫，警告

③ nectareous /nekˈteərɪəs/：甘美的

④ charge：告诫，命令

⑤ of you：from you

⑥ novelty /ˈnʌvəlti/：新奇感

⑦ preclude /prɪˈkluːd/：阻止

⑧ possessed of：拥有

⑨ state：堂皇，豪华

mountains. The sisters, not satisfied with this reply, soon made her confess that she had never seen him. Then they proceeded to fill her bosom with dark suspicions. "Call to mind," they said, "the Pythian oracle① that declared you destined to marry a direful and tremendous monster. The inhabitants of this valley say that your husband is a terrible and monstrous serpent, who nourishes you for a while with dainties② that he may by and by devour you. Take our advice. Provide yourself with a lamp and a sharp knife; put them in concealment that your husband may not discover them, and when he is sound asleep, slip out of bed, bring forth your lamp, and see for yourself whether what they say is true or not. If it is, hesitate not to cut off the monster's head, and thereby recover your liberty."

Psyche resisted these persuasions as well as she could, but they did not fail to have their effect on her mind, and when her sisters were gone, their words and her own curiosity were too strong for her to resist. So she prepared her lamp and a sharp knife, and hid them out of sight of her husband. When he had fallen into his first sleep, she silently rose and uncovering her lamp beheld not a hideous monster, but the most beautiful and charming of the gods, with his golden ringlets wandering over his snowy neck and crimson cheek, with two dewy wings on his shoulders, whiter than snow, and with shining feathers like the tender blossoms of spring. As she leaned the lamp over to have a nearer view of his face a drop of burning oil fell on the shoulder of the god, startled with which he opened his eyes and fixed them full upon her; then, without saying one word, he spread his white wings and flew out of the window. Psyche, in vain endeavoring to follow him, fell from the window to the ground. Cupid, beholding her as she lay in the dust, stopped his flight for an instant and said, "O foolish Psyche, is it thus you repay my love? After having disobeyed my mother's commands and made you my wife, will you think me a monster and cut off my head? But go; return to your sisters, whose advice you seem to think preferable to mine. I inflict no other punishment on you than to leave you forever. Love cannot dwell with suspicion." So saying, he fled away, leaving poor Psyche prostrate on the ground, filling the place with mournful lamentations.

When she had recovered some degree of composure③ she looked around her, but the palace and gardens had vanished, and she found herself in the open field not far from the city where her sisters dwelt. She repaired thither and told them the whole story of her misfortunes, at which, pretending to grieve, those spiteful creatures inwardly④ rejoiced. "For now," said they, "he will perhaps choose one of us." With this idea, without saying a word of her intentions, each of them rose early the next morning and ascended the mountains, and having reached the top, called upon Zephyr to receive her and bear her to his lord; then leaping up, and not being sustained by Zephyr, fell down the precipice⑤ and was dashed to pieces.

Psyche meanwhile wandered day and night, without food or repose, in search of her husband. Casting her eyes on a lofty mountain having on its brow a magnificent temple, she sighed and said

---

① the Pythian oracle: oracle of Apollo; Pythian /ˈpɪθɪən/: of Delphi, of the oracle of Apollo

② dainty /ˈdeɪnti/: 美味佳肴

③ composure /kəmˈpəʊʒə/: 平静

④ inwardly /ˈɪnwədli/: 在心里

⑤ precipice /ˈpresɪpɪs/: 悬崖

to herself, "Perhaps my love, my lord, inhabits there," and directed her steps thither.

She had no sooner entered than she saw heaps of corn, some in loose ears and some in sheaves, with mingled ears of barley. Scattered about, lay sickles and rakes, and all the instruments of harvest, without order, as if thrown carelessly out of the weary reapers' hands in the sultry① hours of the day.

This unseemly② confusion the pious Psyche put an end to, by separating and sorting everything to its proper place and kind, believing that she ought to neglect none of the gods, but endeavor by her piety to engage③ them all in her behalf. The holy Ceres, whose temple it was, finding her so religiously employed, thus spoke to her: "O Psyche, truly worthy of our pity, though I cannot shield you from the frowns of Venus, yet I can teach you how best to allay her displeasure. Go, then, and voluntarily surrender yourself to your lady and sovereign, and try by modesty and submission to win her forgiveness, and perhaps her favor will restore you the husband you have lost."

Psyche obeyed the commands of Ceres and took her way to the temple of Venus, endeavoring to fortify her mind and ruminating④ on what she should say and how best propitiate⑤ the angry goddess, feeling that the issue was doubtful and perhaps fatal.

Venus received her with angry countenance⑥. "Most undutiful and faithless of servants," said she, "do you at last remember that you really have a mistress? Or have you rather come to see your sick husband, yet laid up⑦ of the wound given him by his loving wife? You are so ill-favored⑧ and disagreeable that the only way you can merit your lover must be by dint of⑨ industry⑩ and diligence⑪. I will make trial of your housewifery." Then she ordered Psyche to be led to the storehouse of her temple, where was laid up a great quantity of wheat, barley, millet⑫, vetches⑬, beans, and lentils⑭ prepared for food for her pigeons, and said, "Take and separate all these grains, putting all of the same kind in a parcel by themselves, and see that you get it done before evening." Then Venus departed and left her to her task.

But Psyche, in a perfect consternation⑮ at the enormous work, sat stupid and silent, without

---

① sultry /ˈsʌltri/: 酷热的
② unseemly: 不合适的,不得体的
③ engage: 争取过来
④ ruminate /ˈruːmɪneɪt/: 深思
⑤ propitiate /prəˈpɪʃieɪt/: 安抚,抚慰
⑥ countenance /ˈkaʊntənəns/: 表情
⑦ laid up: 生病的
⑧ ill-favored: 让人不快的,令人讨厌的
⑨ by dint of: 凭借,通过
⑩ industry: 勤奋
⑪ diligence /ˈdɪlɪdʒəns/: 勤奋,努力
⑫ millet /ˈmɪlɪt/: 小米
⑬ vetch: 野豌豆
⑭ lentil: 小扁豆
⑮ consternation /ˌkɒnstəˈneɪʃn/: 惊讶,因为惊讶而不知所措

moving a finger to the inextricable① heap.

While she sat despairing, Cupid stirred up the little ant, a native of the fields, to take compassion② on her. The leader of the ant hill③, followed by whole hosts of his six-legged subjects④, approached the heap, and with the utmost diligence, taking grain by grain, they separated the pile, sorting each kind to its parcel; and when it was all done, they vanished out of sight in a moment.

Venus at the approach of twilight returned from the banquet of the gods, breathing odors and crowned with roses. Seeing the task done, she exclaimed, "This is no work of yours, wicked one, but his, whom to your own and his misfortune you have enticed." So saying, she threw her a piece of black bread for her supper and went away.

Next morning Venus ordered Psyche to be called and said to her, "Behold yonder grove which stretches along the margin of the water. There you will find sheep feeding without a shepherd, with golden-shining fleeces on their backs. Go, fetch me a sample of that precious wool gathered from every one of their fleeces."

Psyche obediently went to the riverside, prepared to do her best to execute the command. But the river god inspired the reeds with harmonious murmurs, which seemed to say, "O maiden, severely tried, tempt not the dangerous flood, nor venture among the formidable rams on the other side, for as long as they are under the influence of the rising sun, they burn with a cruel rage to destroy mortals with their sharp horns or rude teeth. But when the noontide sun has driven the cattle to the shade, and the serene spirit of the flood has lulled them to rest, you may then cross in safety, and you will find the woolly gold sticking to the bushes and the trunks of the trees."

Thus the compassionate⑤ river god gave Psyche instructions how to accomplish her task, and by observing his directions she soon returned to Venus with her arms full of the golden fleece; but she received not the approbation⑥ of her implacable⑦ mistress, who said, "I know very well it is by none of your own doings that you have succeeded in this task, and I am not satisfied yet that you have any capacity to make yourself useful. But I have another task for you. Here, take this box and go your way to the infernal shades⑧, and give this box to Proserpine⑨ and say, 'My mistress Venus desires you to send her a little of your beauty, for in tending her sick son she has lost some of her own.' Be not too long on your errand, for I must paint myself with it to appear at the circle of the gods and goddesses this evening."

---

① inextricable /ɪnˈekstrɪkəbl/：解决不了的，混乱之极的
② compassion /kəmˈpæʃn/：同情，怜悯
③ ant hill：蚁垤（dié）
④ 蚂蚁有 6 条腿。
⑤ compassionate /kəmˈpæʃənət/：有同情心的
⑥ approbation /ˌæprəˈbeɪʃn/：认可
⑦ implacable /ɪmˈplækəbl/：安抚不了的
⑧ infernal shades：阴间
⑨ Proserpine：参见 *The Age of Fable* 第 7 章。

Psyche was now satisfied that her destruction was at hand, being obliged to go with her own feet directly down to Erebus. Wherefore, to make no delay of what was not to be avoided, she goes to the top of a high tower to precipitate herself headlong, thus to descend the shortest way to the shades below. But a voice from the tower said to her, "Why, poor unlucky girl, dost① thou design to put an end to thy days in so dreadful a manner? And what cowardice makes thee sink under this last danger who hast been so miraculously supported in all thy former②?" Then the voice told her how by a certain cave she might reach the realms of Pluto, and how to avoid all the dangers of the road, to pass by Cerberus③, the three-headed dog, and prevail on Charon④, the ferryman, to take her across the black river⑤ and bring her back again. But the voice added, "When Proserpine has given you the box filled with her beauty, of all things this is chiefly to be observed by you, that you never once open or look into the box nor allow your curiosity to pry into the treasure of the beauty of the goddesses."

Psyche, encouraged by this advice, obeyed it in all things, and taking heed to her ways travelled safely to the kingdom of Pluto. She was admitted to the palace of Proserpine, and without accepting the delicate seat or delicious banquet that was offered her, but contented with coarse bread for her food, she delivered her message from Venus. Presently the box was returned to her, shut and filled with the precious commodity⑥. Then she returned the way she came, and glad was she to come out once more into the light of day.

But having got so far successfully through her dangerous task, a longing desire seized her to examine the contents of the box. "What," said she, "shall I, the carrier of this divine beauty, not take the least bit to put on my cheeks to appear to more advantage in the eyes of my beloved husband!" So she carefully opened the box, but found nothing there of any beauty at all, but an infernal and truly Stygian⑦ sleep, which being thus set free from its prison, took possession of her, and she fell down in the midst of the road, a sleepy corpse without sense or motion.

But Cupid, being now recovered from his wound, and not able longer to bear the absence of his beloved Psyche, slipping through the smallest crack of the window of his chamber which happened to be left open, flew to the spot where Psyche lay, and gathering up the sleep from her body closed it again in the box, and waked Psyche with a light touch of one of his arrows. "Again," said he, "hast thou almost perished by the same curiosity. But now perform exactly the task imposed on you by my mother, and I will take care of the rest."

Then Cupid, as swift as lightning penetrating the heights of heaven, presented himself before

① dost：主语是 thou 时 do 的屈折变化形式。
② who hast been so miraculously supported in all thy former：定语从句，修饰前面的 thee. hast：主语是 thou 时 have 的屈折变化形式。
③ Cerberus /ˈsɜːbərəs/：参见 *The Age of Fable* 第 32 章。
④ Charon /ˈkeərən/：参见 *The Age of Fable* 第 32 章。
⑤ the black river：即阴间的河流 the Cocytus，参见 *The Age of Fable* 第 32 章。
⑥ commodity /kəˈmɒdɪti/：有用或有价值的物品
⑦ Stygian /ˈstɪdʒɪən/：死亡的，死一般的

Jupiter with his supplication①. Jupiter lent a favoring ear, and pleaded the cause of the lovers so earnestly with Venus that he won her consent. On this he sent Mercury to bring Psyche up to the heavenly assembly, and when she arrived, handing her a cup of ambrosia, he said, "Drink this, Psyche, and be immortal; nor shall Cupid ever break away from the knot in which he is tied, but these nuptials shall be perpetual."

Thus Psyche became at last united to Cupid, and in due time they had a daughter born to them whose name was Pleasure.

Chapter XII
Cadmus—The Myrmidons

Cadmus

Jupiter, under the disguise of a bull, had carried away Europa②, the daughter of Agenor③, king of Phœnicia④. Agenor commanded his son Cadmus⑤ to go in search of his sister, and not to return without her. Cadmus went and sought long and far for his sister, but could not find her, and not daring to return unsuccessful, consulted the oracle of Apollo to know what country he should settle in. The oracle informed him that he should find a cow in the field, and should follow her wherever she might wander, and where she stopped, should build a city and call it Thebes⑥. Cadmus had hardly left the Castalian⑦ cave, from which the oracle was delivered, when he saw a young cow slowly walking before him. He followed her close, offering at the same time his prayers to Phœbus. The cow went on till she passed the shallow channel of Cephisus⑧ and came out into the plain of Panope. There she stood still, and raising her broad forehead to the sky, filled the air with her lowings. Cadmus gave thanks, and stooping down kissed the foreign soil, then lifting his eyes, greeted the surrounding mountains. Wishing to offer a sacrifice to Jupiter, he sent his

---

① supplication /ˌsʌplɪˈkeɪʃn/：恳求，哀求
② Europa /juəˈrəʊpə/：Europa 是 Phœnicia 国王 Agenor 的女儿，有一天她在 Tyre 的海滩上玩耍时被 Jupiter 看到了。Jupiter 爱上了她。为了得到她，Jupiter 把自己变成一头雪白的公牛，来到她的身边。Europa 非常喜欢这头雪白的公牛，于是坐到公牛的背上。Jupiter 马上跳入大海，游到克里特岛。Europa 为 Jupiter 生了 3 个儿子。参见 *The Age of Fable* 第 14 章 Minerva 和 Arachne 比赛的故事。
③ Agenor：/əˈdʒiːnɔː/
④ Phœnicia /fəˈnɪʃə/：地中海东海岸古国名，汉语翻译为"腓尼基"，大致相当于今天的黎巴嫩及叙利亚和以色列靠近黎巴嫩的部分地区。
⑤ Cadmus：/ˈkædməs/
⑥ Thebes /θiːbz/：希腊城市名，位于今中希腊大区维奥蒂亚州（Boeotia 或 Voiotia），雅典西北方向。古埃及也有座城市叫 Thebes，位于开罗以南将近 700 公里的尼罗河两岸，曾是古埃及第十八朝代的都城。
⑦ Castalia /kæˈsteɪlɪə/：溪流名，位于 Delphi 东北方向不远处。
⑧ Cephisus /sɪˈfɪsəs/：也可拼写为 Kifisos，希腊河流名，流经中希腊大区维奥蒂亚州北部。

servants to seek pure water for a libation①. Near by there stood an ancient grove which had never been profaned by the axe, in the midst of which was a cave, thick covered with the growth of bushes, its roof forming a low arch, from beneath which burst forth a fountain of purest water. In the cave lurked a horrid serpent with a crested② head and scales glittering like gold. His eyes shone like fire, his body was swollen with venom, he vibrated a triple tongue, and showed a triple row of teeth. No sooner had the Tyrians③ dipped their pitchers in the fountain, and the in-gushing waters made a sound, than the glittering serpent raised his head out of the cave and uttered a fearful hiss. The vessels fell from their hands, the blood left their cheeks, they trembled in every limb. The serpent, twisting his scaly body in a huge coil, raised his head so as to overtop the tallest trees, and while the Tyrians from terror could neither fight nor fly, slew some with his fangs, others in his folds, and others with his poisonous breath.

Cadmus, having waited for the return of his men till midday, went in search of them. His covering was a lion's hide④, and besides his javelin he carried in his hand a lance, and in his breast a bold heart, a surer reliance than either. When he entered the wood, and saw the lifeless bodies of his men, and the monster with his bloody jaws, he exclaimed, "O faithful friends, I will avenge you, or share your death." So saying he lifted a huge stone and threw it with all his force at the serpent. Such a block⑤ would have shaken the wall of a fortress, but it made no impression on the monster. Cadmus next threw his javelin, which met with better success, for it penetrated the serpent's scales, and pierced through to his entrails⑥. Fierce with pain, the monster turned back his head to view the wound, and attempted to draw out the weapon with his mouth, but broke it off, leaving the iron point rankling⑦ in his flesh. His neck swelled with rage, bloody foam covered his jaws, and the breath of his nostrils poisoned the air around. Now he twisted himself into a circle, then stretched himself out on the ground like the trunk of a fallen tree. As he moved onward, Cadmus retreated before him, holding his spear opposite to the monster's opened jaws. The serpent snapped at the weapon and attempted to bite its iron point. At last Cadmus, watching his chance, thrust the spear at a moment when the animal's head thrown back came against the trunk of a tree, and so succeeded in pinning him to its side. His weight bent the tree as he struggled in the agonies of death.

While Cadmus stood over his conquered foe, contemplating its vast size, a voice was heard (from whence he knew not, but he heard it distinctly⑧) commanding him to take the dragon's teeth and sow them in the earth. He obeyed. He made a furrow in the ground, and planted the teeth, destined to

---

① libation /laɪ'beɪʃn/：奠酒
② crested /'krestɪd/：长着羽冠的
③ the Tyrians /'tɪrɪən/：Cadmus 和他的同伴们来自 Phœnicia 的城市 Tyre，故称 the Tyrians。
④ hide：兽皮
⑤ block：一块石头
⑥ entrail /'entreɪl/：内脏
⑦ rankle /'ræŋkl/：引起疼痛
⑧ distinctly /dɪ'stɪŋktli/：清楚地

produce a crop of men. Scarce had he done so when the clods① began to move, and the points of spears to appear above the surface. Next helmets with their nodding plumes came up, and next the shoulders and breasts and limbs of men with weapons, and in time a harvest of armed warriors. Cadmus, alarmed, prepared to encounter a new enemy, but one of them said to him, "Meddle not with our civil war." With that he who had spoken smote one of his earth-born brothers with a sword, and he himself fell pierced with an arrow from another. The latter fell victim to a fourth, and in like manner the whole crowd dealt with each other till all fell, slain with mutual wounds, except five survivors. One of these cast away his weapons and said, "Brothers, let us live in peace!" These five joined with Cadmus in building his city, to which they gave the name of Thebes.

Cadmus obtained in marriage Harmonia②, the daughter of Venus. The gods left Olympus to honor the occasion with their presence, and Vulcan presented the bride with a necklace of surpassing brilliancy, his own workmanship. But a fatality③ hung over the family of Cadmus in consequence of his killing the serpent sacred to Mars. Semele and Ino④, his daughters, and Actæon⑤ and Pentheus⑥, his grandchildren, all perished unhappily, and Cadmus and Harmonia quitted Thebes, now grown odious to them, and emigrated to the country of the Enchelians, who received them with honor and made Cadmus their king. But the misfortunes of their children still weighed upon their minds; and one day Cadmus exclaimed, "If a serpent's life is so dear to the gods, I would I were myself a serpent." No sooner had he uttered the words than he began to change his form. Harmonia beheld it and prayed to the gods to let her share his fate. Both became serpents. They live in the woods, but mindful of their origin, they neither avoid the presence of man nor do they ever injure any one.

There is a tradition that Cadmus introduced into Greece the letters of the alphabet which were invented by the Phœnicians⑦.

The Myrmidons

The Myrmidons⑧ were the soldiers of Achilles⑨, in the Trojan War⑩. From them all zealous and unscrupulous⑪ followers of a political chief are called by that name, down to this day. But the origin of the Myrmidons would not give one the idea of a fierce and bloody race, but rather of a laborious⑫ and peaceful one.

---

① clod: 土块
② Harmonia: /hɑːˈməʊnɪə/
③ fatality /fəˈtælɪti/: 灾难，厄运
④ Semele: /ˈsemɪli/; Ino: /ˈaɪnəʊ/
⑤ Actæon: 参见 *The Age of Fable* 第 4 章。
⑥ Pentheus: 参见 *The Age of Fable* 第 21 章。
⑦ Phœnician /fəˈnɪʃn/: 腓尼基人；希腊语字母表是在腓尼基字母表的基础上创造出来的。
⑧ Myrmidon: /ˈməːmɪdən/
⑨ Achilles /əˈkɪliːz/: 参见 *The Age of Fable* 第 27 章。
⑩ the Trojan War: 参见 *The Age of Fable* 第 27、第 28 章。
⑪ unscrupulous /ʌnˈskruːpjuləs/: 不讲原则的
⑫ laborious /ləˈbɔːrɪəs/: 勤劳的，勤奋的

Cephalus, king of Athens①, arrived in the island of Ægina② to seek assistance of his old friend and ally Æacus③, the king, in his war with Minos④, king of Crete⑤. Cephalus was most kindly received, and the desired assistance readily promised. "I have people enough," said Æacus, "to protect myself and spare you such a force as you need." "I rejoice to see it," replied Cephalus, "and my wonder has been raised, I confess, to find such a host of youths as I see around me, all apparently of about the same age. Yet there are many individuals whom I previously knew, that I look for now in vain. What has become of them?" Æacus groaned, and replied with a voice of sadness, "I have been intending to tell you, and will now do so, without more delay, that you may see how from the saddest beginning a happy result sometimes flows. Those whom you formerly knew are now dust and ashes! A plague sent by angry Juno devastated⑥ the land. She hated it because it bore the name of one of her husband's female favorites.⑦ While the disease appeared to spring from natural causes we resisted it, as we best might, by natural remedies; but it soon appeared that the pestilence was too powerful for our efforts, and we yielded. At the beginning the sky seemed to settle down upon the earth, and thick clouds shut in the heated air. For four months together a deadly south wind prevailed. The disorder affected the wells and springs; thousands of snakes crept over the land and shed their poison in the fountains. The force of the disease was first spent on the lower animals—dogs, cattle, sheep, and birds. The luckless ploughman wondered to see his oxen fall in the midst of their work, and lie helpless in the unfinished furrow. The wool fell from the bleating⑧ sheep, and their bodies pined away. The horse, once foremost⑨ in the race, contested the palm⑩ no more, but groaned at his stall and died an inglorious death. The wild boar forgot his rage, the stag his swiftness, the bears no longer attacked the herds. Everything languished; dead bodies lay in the roads, the fields, and the woods; the air was poisoned by them. I tell you what is hardly credible, but neither dogs nor birds would touch them, nor starving wolves. Their decay spread the infection. Next the disease attacked the country⑪ people, and then the dwellers in the city. At first the cheek was flushed, and the breath drawn with difficulty. The tongue grew rough and swelled, and the dry mouth stood open with its veins enlarged and gasped for the air. Men could not bear the heat of their clothes or their beds, but preferred to lie on the bare ground; and the

---

① Athens /ˈæθɪnz/：雅典，位于希腊阿提卡大区阿提卡州（Attica 或 Attiki）。

② Ægina /ɪˈdʒaɪnə/：希腊岛屿名，属于阿提卡大区阿提卡州，位于萨罗尼科斯弯（the Saronic Gulf），在雅典西南方向约 27 公里处。

③ Æacus：/ˈiːəkəs/

④ Minos：/ˈmaɪnɒs/

⑤ Crete /kriːt/：克里特岛，位于希腊大陆以南的地中海东部，是希腊最大的岛屿，今希腊的克里特大区包含该岛及其周围的一些小岛。

⑥ devastate /ˈdevəsteɪt/：破坏，蹂躏

⑦ Ægina /ɪˈdʒaɪnə/ 是 Jupiter 所爱的一个仙女，Jupiter 将她虏到一个岛，于是这个岛便以她的名字命名为 Ægina。

⑧ bleat：（羊）咩（miē）咩地叫

⑨ foremost /ˈfɔːməʊst/：第一的，最杰出的，最好的

⑩ palm：（象征胜利的）棕榈枝

⑪ country：乡下

ground did not cool them, but, on the contrary, they heated the spot where they lay. Nor could the physicians① help, for the disease attacked them also, and the contact of the sick gave them infection, so that the most faithful were the first victims. At last all hope of relief vanished, and men learned to look upon death as the only deliverer from disease. Then they gave way to every inclination②, and cared not to ask what was expedient③, for nothing was expedient. All restraint laid aside, they crowded around the wells and fountains and drank till they died, without quenching thirst. Many had not strength to get away from the water, but died in the midst of the stream, and others would drink of it notwithstanding. Such was their weariness of their sick beds that some would creep forth, and if not strong enough to stand, would die on the ground. They seemed to hate their friends, and got away from their homes, as if, not knowing the cause of their sickness, they charged it on the place of their abode. Some were seen tottering along the road, as long as they could stand, while others sank on the earth, and turned their dying eyes around to take a last look, then closed them in death.

"What heart had I left me, during all this, or what ought I to have had, except to hate life and wish to be with my dead subjects? On all sides lay my people strewn like over-ripened apples beneath the tree, or acorns under the storm-shaken oak. You see yonder a temple on the height. It is sacred to Jupiter. O how many offered prayers there, husbands for wives, fathers for sons, and died in the very act of supplication! How often, while the priest made ready for sacrifice, the victim fell, struck down by disease without waiting for the blow! At length all reverence for sacred things was lost. Bodies were thrown out unburied, wood was wanting for funeral piles, men fought with one another for the possession of them. Finally there were none left to mourn; sons and husbands, old men and youths, perished alike unlamented.

"Standing before the altar I raised my eyes to heaven. 'O Jupiter,' I said, 'if thou art④ indeed my father, and art not ashamed of thy offspring, give me back my people, or take me also away!' At these words a clap of thunder was heard. 'I accept the omen,' I cried; 'O may it be a sign of a favorable disposition⑤ towards me!' By chance there grew by the place where I stood an oak with wide-spreading branches, sacred to Jupiter. I observed a troop of ants busy with their labor, carrying minute⑥ grains in their mouths and following one another in a line up the trunk of the tree. Observing their numbers with admiration, I said, 'Give me, O father, citizens as numerous as these, and replenish⑦ my empty city.' The tree shook and gave a rustling sound with its branches, though no wind agitated them. I trembled in every limb, yet I kissed the earth and the tree. I would not confess to myself that I hoped, yet I did hope. Night came on and sleep took possession of my frame oppressed with cares. The tree stood before me in

① physician /fɪˈzɪʃn/：医生
② 于是他们便随心所欲。
③ expedient /ɪkˈspiːdɪənt/：有利的，适合的
④ art：主语是 thou 时动词 be 的屈折变化形式。
⑤ disposition /ˌdɪspəˈzɪʃn/：性质，本质
⑥ minute /maɪˈnjuːt/：非常小的
⑦ replenish /rɪˈplenɪʃ/：使住满人

my dreams, with its numerous branches all covered with living, moving creatures. It seemed to shake its limbs and throw down over the ground a multitude of those industrious[①] grain-gathering animals, which appeared to gain in size, and grow larger and larger, and by and by to stand erect, lay aside their superfluous[②] legs and their black color, and finally to assume the human form. Then I awoke, and my first impulse was to chide the gods who had robbed me of a sweet vision and given me no reality in its place. Being still in the temple, my attention was caught by the sound of many voices without[③]; a sound of late[④] unusual to my ears. While I began to think I was yet dreaming, Telamon, my son, throwing open the temple gates, exclaimed: 'Father, approach, and behold things surpassing even your hopes!' I went forth; I saw a multitude of men, such as I had seen in my dream, and they were passing in procession in the same manner. While I gazed with wonder and delight they approached and kneeling hailed me as their king. I paid my vows to Jove, and proceeded to allot[⑤] the vacant city to the new-born race, and to parcel out[⑥] the fields among them. I called them Myrmidons, from the ant (myrmex[⑦]) from which they sprang. You have seen these persons; their dispositions resemble those which they had in their former shape. They are a diligent and industrious race, eager to gain, and tenacious[⑧] of their gains. Among them you may recruit[⑨] your forces. They will follow you to the war, young in years and bold in heart."

Chapter XIII
Nisus and Scylla—Echo and Narcissus—Clytie—Hero and Leander

Nisus and Scylla

Minos, king of Crete, made war upon Megara[⑩]. Nisus[⑪] was king of Megara, and Scylla[⑫] was his daughter. The siege[⑬] had now lasted six months and the city still held out, for it was decreed

---

① industrious /ɪnˈdʌstrɪəs/: 勤劳的

② superfluous /suːˈpɜːfluəs/: 多余的,不需要的

③ without: 在外面

④ of late: 最近

⑤ allot /əˈlɒt/: 分配

⑥ parcel out: 分配

⑦ myrmex (μύρμηξ): (希腊语)蚂蚁

⑧ tenacious /tɪˈneɪʃəs / of: 紧紧抓住……不放的

⑨ recruit /rɪˈkruːt/: 招募

⑩ Megara /ˈmegərə/: 希腊古代地区名,位于科林斯地峡(the Isthmus of Corinth /ˈkɒrɪnθ/)东端,今属于阿提卡大区阿提卡州;因其第一任国王名叫 Nisus,所以它最初叫 Nisa。

⑪ Nisus: /ˈnaɪsəs/

⑫ Scylla: /ˈsɪlə/

⑬ siege /siːdʒ/: 包围

by fate that it should not be taken so long as a certain purple lock①, which glittered among the hair of King Nisus, remained on his head. There was a tower on the city walls, which overlooked the plain where Minos and his army were encamped. To this tower Scylla used to repair, and look abroad over the tents of the hostile army②. The siege had lasted so long that she had learned to distinguish the persons③ of the leaders. Minos, in particular, excited her admiration. Arrayed in his helmet, and bearing his shield, she admired his graceful deportment④; if he threw his javelin skill seemed combined with force in the discharge⑤; if he drew his bow Apollo himself could not have done it more gracefully. But when he laid aside his helmet, and in his purple robes bestrode his white horse with its gay caparisons⑥, and reined in its foaming mouth, the daughter of Nisus was hardly mistress of herself⑦; she was almost frantic⑧ with admiration. She envied the weapon that he grasped, the reins that he held. She felt as if she could, if it were possible, go to him through the hostile ranks; she felt an impulse to cast herself down from the tower into the midst of his camp, or to open the gates to him, or to do anything else, so only it might gratify Minos. As she sat in the tower, she talked thus with herself: "I know not whether to rejoice or grieve at this sad war. I grieve that Minos is our enemy; but I rejoice at any cause that brings him to my sight. Perhaps he would be willing to grant us peace, and receive me as a hostage⑨. I would fly down, if I could, and alight in his camp, and tell him that we yield ourselves to his mercy. But then, to betray my father! No! rather would I never see Minos again. And yet no doubt it is sometimes the best thing for a city to be conquered, when the conqueror is clement⑩ and generous. Minos certainly has right on his side. I think we shall be conquered; and if that must be the end of it, why should not love unbar the gates to him, instead of leaving it to be done by war? Better spare delay and slaughter if we can. And O if any one should wound or kill Minos! No one surely would have the heart to do it; yet ignorantly, not knowing him, one might. I will, I will surrender myself to him, with my country as a dowry, and so put an end to the war. But how? The gates are guarded, and my father keeps the keys; he only stands in my way⑪. O that it might please the gods to take him away! But why ask the gods to do it? Another woman, loving as I do, would remove with her own hands whatever stood in the way of her love. And can any other woman dare more than I? I would encounter fire and sword to gain my object; but here there is no need of fire and sword. I only need my father's purple lock. More precious than gold to me, that will give me all I wish."

---

① lock：头发
② the hostile army：敌军
③ person：容貌，外貌
④ deportment /dɪˈpɔːtmənt/：风度，举止
⑤ discharge /ˈdɪstʃɑːdʒ/：投掷
⑥ caparison /kəˈpærɪsən/：（铺在马鞍上做装饰的）马衣
⑦ the daughter of Nisus was hardly mistress of herself：Nisus 的女儿几乎无法控制住自己。
⑧ frantic /ˈfræntɪk/：疯狂的
⑨ hostage /ˈhɒstɪdʒ/：人质
⑩ clement /ˈklemənt/：仁慈的
⑪ he only stands in my way：他是我唯一的障碍。

While she thus reasoned night came on, and soon the whole palace was buried in sleep. She entered her father's bedchamber① and cut off the fatal lock; then passed out of the city and entered the enemy's camp. She demanded to be led to the king, and thus addressed him: "I am Scylla, the daughter of Nisus. I surrender to you my country and my father's house. I ask no reward but yourself; for love of you I have done it. See here the purple lock! With this I give you my father and his kingdom." She held out her hand with the fatal spoil. Minos shrunk back and refused to touch it. "The gods destroy thee, infamous② woman," he exclaimed; "disgrace of our time! May neither earth nor sea yield thee a resting-place! Surely, my Crete, where Jove himself was cradled, shall not be polluted with such a monster!" Thus he said, and gave orders that equitable terms③ should be allowed to the conquered city, and that the fleet should immediately sail from the island.

Scylla was frantic. "Ungrateful man," she exclaimed, "is it thus you leave me? —me who have given you victory,—who have sacrificed for you parent and country! I am guilty, I confess, and deserve to die, but not by your hand." As the ships left the shore, she leaped into the water, and seizing the rudder④ of the one which carried Minos, she was borne along an unwelcome companion of their course. A sea-eagle soaring aloft,—it was her father who had been changed into that form,—seeing her, pounced down upon her, and struck her with his beak and claws. In terror she let go the ship and would have fallen into the water, but some pitying deity changed her into a bird⑤. The sea-eagle still cherishes the old animosity⑥; and whenever he espies her in his lofty flight you may see him dart down upon her, with beak and claws, to take vengeance for the ancient crime.

Echo and Narcissus

Echo⑦ was a beautiful nymph, fond of the woods and hills, where she devoted herself to woodland sports. She was a favorite of Diana, and attended her in the chase. But Echo had one failing⑧; she was fond of talking, and whether in chat or argument, would have the last word. One day Juno was seeking her husband, who, she had reason to fear, was amusing himself among the nymphs. Echo by her talk contrived to detain the goddess till the nymphs made their escape. When Juno discovered it, she passed sentence upon Echo in these words: "You shall forfeit⑨ the use of that tongue with which you have cheated me, except for that one purpose you are so fond of—reply. You shall still have the last word, but no power to speak first."

---

① bedchamber: 卧室
② infamous /ˈɪnfəməs/: 臭名昭著的,邪恶的
③ equitable terms: 公正的条款,平等的条款; equitable /ˈekwɪtəbl/: 公平的,公正的
④ rudder /ˈrʌdə/: 船舵
⑤ an egret
⑥ cherish the old animosity: 心怀旧时的仇恨;animosity /ˌænɪˈmɒsɪti/: 敌意,仇恨
⑦ Echo: /ˈekəʊ/
⑧ failing: 弱点,性格缺陷
⑨ forfeit /ˈfɔːfɪt/: 失去,被剥夺

This nymph saw Narcissus[1], a beautiful youth, as he pursued the chase upon the mountains. She loved him and followed his footsteps. O how she longed to address him in the softest accents, and win him to converse! but it was not in her power. She waited with impatience for him to speak first, and had her answer ready. One day the youth, being separated from his companions, shouted aloud, "Who's here?" Echo replied, "Here." Narcissus looked around, but seeing no one called out, "Come." Echo answered, "Come." As no one came, Narcissus called again, "Why do you shun me?" Echo asked the same question. "Let us join one another," said the youth. The maid answered with all her heart in the same words, and hastened to the spot, ready to throw her arms about his neck. He started back, exclaiming, "Hands off! I would rather die than you should have me!" "Have me," said she; but it was all in vain. He left her, and she went to hide her blushes in the recesses of the woods[2]. From that time forth she lived in caves and among mountain cliffs. Her form faded with grief, till at last all her flesh shrank away. Her bones were changed into rocks and there was nothing left of her but her voice. With that she is still ready to reply to any one who calls her, and keeps up her old habit of having the last word.

Narcissus's cruelty in this case was not the only instance. He shunned all the rest of the nymphs, as he had done poor Echo. One day a maiden who had in vain endeavored to attract him uttered a prayer that he might some time or other feel what it was to love and meet no return of affection. The avenging goddess heard and granted the prayer.

There was a clear fountain, with water like silver, to which the shepherds never drove their flocks, nor the mountain goats resorted, nor any of the beasts of the forest; neither was it defaced[3] with fallen leaves or branches; but the grass grew fresh around it, and the rocks sheltered it from the sun. Hither came one day the youth, fatigued with hunting, heated and thirsty. He stooped down to drink, and saw his own image in the water; he thought it was some beautiful water-spirit[4] living in the fountain. He stood gazing with admiration at those bright eyes, those locks curled like the locks of Bacchus or Apollo, the rounded cheeks, the ivory neck, the parted lips, and the glow of health and exercise over all. He fell in love with himself. He brought his lips near to take a kiss; he plunged his arms in to embrace the beloved object. It fled at the touch, but returned again after a moment and renewed the fascination. He could not tear himself away; he lost all thought of food or rest, while he hovered over the brink of the fountain gazing upon his own image. He talked with the supposed spirit: "Why, beautiful being, do you shun me? Surely my face is not one to repel you. The nymphs love me, and you yourself look not indifferent upon me. When I stretch forth my arms you do the same; and you smile upon me and answer my beckonings with the like." His tears fell into the water and disturbed the image. As he saw it depart, he exclaimed, "Stay, I entreat you! Let me at least

---

① Narcissus /nɑːˈsɪsəs/

② the recesses of the woods：森林的深处

③ deface /dɪˈfeɪs/：弄脏……的表面

④ water-spirit：水中精灵

gaze upon you, if I may not touch you." With this, and much more of the same kind, he cherished the flame that consumed him, so that by degrees he lost his color, his vigor, and the beauty which formerly had so charmed the nymph Echo. She kept near him, however, and when he exclaimed, "Alas! alas!" she answered him with the same words. He pined away and died; and when his shade passed the Stygian river①, it leaned over the boat to catch a look of itself in the waters. The nymphs mourned for him, especially the water-nymphs; and when they smote their breasts Echo smote hers also. They prepared a funeral pile and would have burned the body, but it was nowhere to be found; but in its place a flower, purple within, and surrounded with white leaves, which bears the name and preserves the memory of Narcissus.

Clytie

Clytie② was a water-nymph and in love with Apollo, who made her no return. So she pined away, sitting all day long upon the cold ground, with her unbound tresses③ streaming over her shoulders. Nine days she sat and tasted neither food nor drink, her own tears and the chilly dew her only food. She gazed on the sun when he rose, and as he passed through his daily course to his setting; she saw no other object, her face turned constantly on him. At last, they say, her limbs rooted in the ground, her face became a flower④ which turns on its stem so as always to face the sun throughout its daily course; for it retains to that extent the feeling of the nymph from whom it sprang.

Hero and Leander

Leander⑤ was a youth of Abydos⑥, a town of the Asian side of the strait⑦ which separates Asia and Europe. On the opposite shore, in the town of Sestos⑧, lived the maiden Hero⑨, a priestess⑩ of Venus. Leander loved her, and used to swim the strait nightly⑪ to enjoy the company of his mistress, guided by a torch which she reared upon the tower for the purpose. But one night a tempest arose and the sea was rough; his strength failed, and he was drowned. The waves bore his body to the European shore, where Hero became aware of his death, and in her despair cast herself down from the tower into the sea and perished.

---

① the Stygian river: 阴间的河流 the Cocytus; 参见 *The Age of Fable* 第 32 章。
② Clytie: /ˈklɪtɪiː/
③ tress /tres/: 女性的长头发
④ a flower: 向日葵
⑤ Leander: /lɪˈændə/
⑥ Abydos: /əˈbaɪdɒs/
⑦ the strait: 即 the Hellespont /ˈhelɪspɒnt /; the Hellespont 现在叫达达尼尔海峡（the Dardanelles /ˌdɑːdəˈnelz /），连接爱琴海（the Aegean Sea）和马尔马拉海（the Sea of Marmara）; 该海峡最窄处仅 1.2 千米, 最宽处 6 千米。参见 *The Age of Fable* 第 17 章。
⑧ Sestos: /ˈsestɒs/
⑨ Hero: /ˈhɪərəʊ/
⑩ priestess /ˈpriːstɪs/: 女祭司
⑪ nightly: 每天晚上, 在夜间

Chapter XIV
Minerva—Niobe

Minerva

　　Minerva[1], the goddess of wisdom, was the daughter of Jupiter. She was said to have leaped forth from his brain, mature, and in complete armor. She presided over the useful and ornamental arts, both those of men—such as agriculture and navigation—and those of women,—spinning, weaving, and needlework. She was also a warlike divinity; but it was defensive war only that she patronized[2], and she had no sympathy with Mars's savage love of violence and bloodshed. Athens was her chosen seat, her own city, awarded to her as the prize of a contest with Neptune, who also aspired to[3] it. The tale ran that in the reign of Cecrops[4], the first king of Athens, the two deities contended for the possession of the city. The gods decreed that it should be awarded to that one who produced the gift most useful to mortals. Neptune gave the horse; Minerva produced the olive. The gods gave judgment that the olive was the more useful of the two, and awarded the city to the goddess; and it was named after her, Athens, her name in Greek being Athene.

　　There was another contest, in which a mortal dared to come in competition with Minerva. That mortal was Arachne[5], a maiden who had attained such skill in the arts of weaving and embroidery that the nymphs themselves would leave their groves and fountains to come and gaze upon her work. It was not only beautiful when it was done, but beautiful also in the doing. To watch her, as she took the wool in its rude state and formed it into rolls, or separated it with her fingers and carded[6] it till it looked as light and soft as a cloud, or twirled the spindle with skilful touch, or wove the web, or, after it was woven, adorned it with her needle, one would have said that Minerva herself had taught her. But this she denied, and could not bear to be thought a pupil even of a goddess. "Let Minerva try her skill with mine," said she; "if beaten I will pay the penalty[7]." Minerva heard this and was displeased. She assumed the form of an old woman and went and gave Arachne some friendly advice. "I have had much experience," said she, "and I hope you will not despise my counsel. Challenge your fellow-mortals as you will, but do not compete with a goddess. On the contrary, I advise you to ask her forgiveness for what you have said, and as she is merciful perhaps she will pardon you." Arachne stopped her spinning and

---

① Minerva /mɪˈnɜːvə/

② patronize /ˈpeɪtrənaɪz/：支持，鼓励

③ aspire to：非常渴望拥有

④ Cecrops：/ˈsiːkrɒps/

⑤ Arachne /əˈrækni/：该词在古希腊语中的意思是"蜘蛛"。

⑥ card：梳理（毛、棉等）

⑦ pay the penalty：受惩罚；penalty /ˈpenəlti/：惩罚，处罚

looked at the old dame with anger in her countenance. "Keep your counsel," said she, "for your daughters or handmaids; for my part I know what I say, and I stand to it. I am not afraid of the goddess; let her try her skill, if she dare venture." "She comes," said Minerva; and dropping her disguise stood confessed①. The nymphs bent low in homage, and all the bystanders paid reverence. Arachne alone was unterrified. She blushed, indeed; a sudden color dyed her cheek, and then she grew pale. But she stood to her resolve, and with a foolish conceit of her own skill rushed on her fate. Minerva forbore no longer nor interposed any further advice. They proceed to the contest. Each takes her station and attaches the web to the beam. Then the slender shuttle is passed in and out among the threads. The reed② with its fine teeth strikes up the woof③ into its place and compacts④ the web. Both work with speed; their skilful hands move rapidly, and the excitement of the contest makes the labor light. Wool of Tyrian dye is contrasted with that of other colors, shaded off into one another so adroitly⑤ that the joining deceives the eye. Like the bow⑥, whose long arch tinges the heavens, formed by sunbeams reflected from the shower, in which, where the colors meet they seem as one, but at a little distance from the point of contact are wholly different.

Minerva wrought on her web the scene of her contest with Neptune⑦. Twelve of the heavenly powers⑧ are represented, Jupiter, with august gravity⑨, sitting in the midst. Neptune, the ruler of the sea, holds his trident, and appears to have just smitten the earth, from which a horse has leaped forth. Minerva depicted herself with helmed head, her Ægis covering her breast. Such was the central circle; and in the four corners were represented incidents illustrating the displeasure of the gods at such presumptuous⑩ mortals as had dared to contend with them. These were meant as warnings to her rival to give up the contest before it was too late.

Arachne filled her web with subjects designedly⑪ chosen to exhibit the failings⑫ and errors of the gods. One scene represented Leda⑬ caressing the swan, under which form Jupiter had

---

① confess：暴露身份
② reed：筘（kòu）；筘是"织布机上的主要机件之一，由薄长的钢片（筘齿）按一定的密度排列后予以固定,形状像梳子。经线从筘缝中依次穿过。纬线通过经线后,筘即将纬线并紧（也称"打纬"）而成织品。筘的长度即是织品横幅的宽度。"（《汉语大词典》）
③ woof /wuːf/：（纺织术语）纬线
④ compact /kəmˈpækt/：使紧密结合
⑤ adroitly /əˈdrɔɪtli/：熟练地
⑥ bow：rainbow
⑦ 参见故事第 1 段。
⑧ Twelve of the heavenly powers：The twelve most important gods and goddesses in Greece（Rome）are Zeus（Jupiter）, Hera（Juno）, Poseidon（Neptune）, Athena /Athene（Minerva）, Apollo, Artemis（Diana）, Aphrodite（Venus）, Hermes（Mercury）, Demeter（Ceres）, Dionysus（Bacchus）, Hephaestus（Vulcan）, and Ares（Mars）.
⑨ gravity /ˈɡrævəti/：严肃
⑩ presumptuous /prɪˈzʌmptʃuəs/：胆大妄为的,胆大包天的,放肆的
⑪ designedly /dɪˈzaɪnɪdli/：有意地,故意地
⑫ failing：弱点,短处
⑬ Leda /ˈliːdə/：Leda 是 Jupiter 之所爱,为了勾引她,Jupiter 将自己变为一只天鹅。

disguised himself; and another, Danaë① in the brazen tower in which her father had imprisoned her, but where the god② effected③ his entrance in the form of a golden shower. Still another depicted Europa④ deceived by Jupiter under the disguise of a bull. Encouraged by the tameness of the animal Europa ventured to mount his back, whereupon Jupiter advanced into the sea and swam with her to Crete. You would have thought it was a real bull, so naturally was it wrought, and so natural the water in which it swam. She seemed to look with longing eyes back upon the shore she was leaving, and to call to her companions for help. She appeared to shudder with terror at the sight of the heaving waves, and to draw back her feet from the water.

Arachne filled her canvas⑤ with similar subjects, wonderfully well done, but strongly marking her presumption and impiety⑥. Minerva could not forbear to admire, yet felt indignant at the insult. She struck the web with her shuttle and rent it in pieces; she then touched the forehead of Arachne and made her feel her guilt and shame. She could not endure it and went and hanged herself. Minerva pitied her as she saw her suspended by a rope. "Live," she said, "guilty woman! and that⑦ you may preserve the memory of this lesson, continue to hang, both you and your descendants, to all future times." She sprinkled her with the juices of aconite⑧, and immediately her hair came off, and her nose and ears likewise. Her form shrank up, and her head grew smaller yet; her fingers cleaved to her side and served for legs. All the rest of her is body, out of which she spins her thread, often hanging suspended by it, in the same attitude⑨ as when Minerva touched her and transformed her into a spider.

Niobe

The fate of Arachne was noised abroad through all the country, and served as a warning to all presumptuous mortals not to compare themselves with the divinities. But one, and she a matron⑩ too, failed to learn the lesson of humility⑪. It was Niobe⑫, the queen of Thebes. She had indeed

---

① Danaë /ˈdæneɪiː/：Danaë 是国王 Acrisius 的女儿，神谕预言说 Danaë 的儿子会杀死 Acrisius，于是 Acrisius 把 Danaë 关进一座铜塔，以便没有男人可以接近她。Jupiter 化作一阵金雨，飞入铜塔与 Danaë 相会。他们的儿子 Perseus 是希腊的大英雄。参见 *The Age of Fable* 第 15 章。

② the god：Jupiter

③ effect：完成，实施

④ Europa /juəˈrəupə/：Jupiter 之所爱，为了勾引她，Jupiter 将自己变为一头漂亮而温顺的公牛。参见 *The Age of Fable* 第 12 章 Cadmus 的故事。

⑤ canvas /ˈkænvəs/：刺绣用的底布

⑥ impiety /ɪmˈpaɪəti/：对神的不敬

⑦ that：so that

⑧ aconite /ˈækənaɪt/：植物名，有毒

⑨ attitude：姿态

⑩ matron /ˈmeɪtrən/：在怀孕、生产等方面经验丰富的已婚妇女

⑪ humility /hjuˈmɪlɪti/：谦卑，谦逊

⑫ Niobe：/ˈnaɪəubi/

much to be proud of; but it was not her husband's fame[1], nor her own beauty, nor their great descent[2], nor the power of their kingdom that elated[3] her. It was her children; and truly the happiest of mothers would Niobe have been if only she had not claimed to be so. It was on occasion of the annual celebration in honor of Latona and her offspring, Apollo and Diana,—when the people of Thebes were assembled, their brows crowned with laurel, bearing frankincense[4] to the altars and paying their vows,—that Niobe appeared among the crowd. Her attire[5] was splendid with gold and gems, and her aspect[6] beautiful as the face of an angry woman can be. She stood and surveyed the people with haughty looks. "What folly," said she, "is this! —to prefer beings whom you never saw to those who stand before your eyes! Why should Latona be honored with worship, and none be paid to me? My father was Tantalus[7], who was received as a guest at the table of the gods; my mother was a goddess. My husband built and rules this city, Thebes, and Phrygia is my paternal inheritance. Wherever I turn my eyes I survey the elements of my power; nor is my form[8] and presence[9] unworthy of a goddess. To all this let me add I have seven sons and seven daughters, and look for sons-in-law and daughters-in-law of pretensions worthy of my alliance[10]. Have I not cause for pride? Will you prefer to me this Latona, the Titan's daughter, with her two children? I have seven times as many. Fortunate indeed am I, and fortunate I shall remain! Will any one deny this? My abundance[11] is my security. I feel myself too strong for Fortune to subdue. She may take from me much; I shall still have much left. Were I to lose some of my children, I should hardly be left as poor as Latona with her two only. Away with you from these solemnities,—put off the laurel from your brows,—have done with this worship!" The people obeyed, and left the sacred services uncompleted.

The goddess was indignant. On the Cynthian mountain[12] top where she dwelt she thus addressed her son and daughter: "My children, I who have been so proud of you both, and have been used to hold myself second to none of the goddesses except Juno alone, begin now to doubt whether I am indeed a goddess. I shall be deprived of my worship altogether unless you protect me." She was proceeding in this strain[13], but Apollo interrupted her. "Say no more," said he;

---

① Niobe 的丈夫是 Amphion /æmˈphaɪən/, Thebes 的国王, 著名的音乐家。参见 *The Age of Fable* 第 24 章 Amphion 的故事。

② descent /dɪˈsent/: 血统

③ elate /ɪˈleɪt/: 使骄傲, 使得意

④ frankincense /ˈfræŋkɪnsens/: 乳香

⑤ attire /əˈtaɪə/: 服装, 衣着

⑥ aspect /ˈæspekt/: 外表

⑦ Tantalus /ˈtæntələs/: 参见 *The Age of Fable* 第 24 章关于 Tantalus 的注释。

⑧ form: 美丽, 美貌

⑨ presence /ˈprezəns/: 高贵的气质

⑩ sons-in-law and daughters-in-law of pretensions worthy of my alliance: 有资格跟我家联姻的女婿和儿媳; pretension /prɪˈtenʃn/: 资格

⑪ abundance /əˈbʌndəns/: 富足

⑫ the Cynthian mountain: 即 Mount Cynthus /ˈsɪnθəs/, 位于希腊爱琴海中的 Delos 岛, 是 Apollo 和 Diana 的出生地, 所以 Apollo 又叫 Cynthius /ˈsɪnθɪəs/, Diana 又叫 Cynthia /ˈsɪnθɪə/。

⑬ strain: 语气

"speech only delays punishment." So said Diana also. Darting through the air, veiled in clouds, they alighted on the towers of the city. Spread out before the gates was a broad plain, where the youth of the city pursued their warlike sports. The sons of Niobe were there with the rest,—some mounted on spirited horses richly caparisoned, some driving gay chariots. Ismenos, the first-born, as he guided his foaming steeds, struck with an arrow from above, cried out, "Ah me!" dropped the reins, and fell lifeless. Another, hearing the sound of the bow,—like a boatman who sees the storm gathering and makes all sail for the port,—gave the reins to his horses and attempted to escape. The inevitable arrow overtook him as he fled. Two others, younger boys, just from their tasks had gone to the playground to have a game of wrestling. As they stood breast to breast, one arrow pierced them both. They uttered a cry together, together cast a parting look around them, and together breathed their last. Alphenor, an elder brother, seeing them fall, hastened to the spot to render assistance, and fell stricken in the act of brotherly duty. One only was left, Ilioneus. He raised his arms to heaven to try whether prayer might not avail. "Spare me, ye gods!" he cried, addressing all, in his ignorance that all needed not his intercessions①; and Apollo would have spared him, but the arrow had already left the string, and it was too late.

The terror of the people and grief of the attendants soon made Niobe acquainted with what had taken place. She could hardly think it possible; she was indignant that the gods had dared, and amazed that they had been able to do it. Her husband, Amphion, overwhelmed with the blow, destroyed② himself. Alas! how different was this Niobe from her who had so lately driven away the people from the sacred rites, and held her stately course through the city, the envy of her friends, now the pity even of her foes! She knelt over the lifeless bodies, and kissed now one, now another of her dead sons. Raising her pallid arms to heaven, "Cruel Latona," said she, "feed full your rage with my anguish! Satiate③ your hard heart, while I follow to the grave my seven sons. Yet where is your triumph? Bereaved as I am, I am still richer than you, my conqueror." Scarce had she spoken, when the bow sounded and struck terror into all hearts except Niobe's alone. She was brave from excess of grief. The sisters stood in garments of mourning over the biers of their dead brothers. One fell, struck by an arrow, and died on the corpse she was bewailing. Another, attempting to console her mother, suddenly ceased to speak, and sank lifeless to the earth. A third tried to escape by flight, a fourth by concealment, another stood trembling, uncertain what course to take. Six were now dead, and only one remained, whom the mother held clasped in her arms, and covered as it were with her whole body. "Spare me one, and that the youngest! O spare me one of so many!" she cried; and while she spoke, that one fell dead. Desolate she sat, among sons, daughters, husband, all dead, and seemed torpid④ with grief. The breeze moved not her hair, no color was on her cheek, her eyes glared fixed and immovable, there was no sign of life about her. Her very tongue cleaved to

---

① intercession /ˌɪntəˈseʃn/：求情，说情
② destroy：杀死
③ satiate /ˈseɪʃieɪt/：使满足
④ torpid /ˈtɔːpɪd/：麻木的

the roof of her mouth, and her veins ceased to convey the tide of life①. Her neck bent not, her arms made no gesture, her foot no step. She was changed to stone, within and without②. Yet tears continued to flow; and borne on a whirlwind to her native mountain, she still remains, a mass of rock, from which a trickling stream flows, the tribute of her never-ending grief.

Chapter XV
The Grææ and the Gorgons—Perseus—Medusa—Atlas—Andromeda

The Grææ and the Gorgons

The Græ③ were three sisters who were gray-haired from their birth, whence their name④. The Gorgons⑤ were monstrous females with huge teeth like those of swine, brazen claws, and snaky hair. None of these beings make much figure⑥ in mythology except Medusa⑦, the Gorgon, whose story we shall next advert⑧ to. We mention them chiefly to introduce an ingenious⑨ theory of some modern writers, namely, that the Gorgons and Græ were only personifications⑩ of the terrors of the sea, the former denoting the strong billows⑪ of the wide open main⑫, and the latter the white-crested waves that dash against the rocks of the coast. Their names in Greek signify the above epithets⑬.

Perseus and Medusa

Perseus⑭ was the son of Jupiter and Danaë⑮. His grandfather Acrisius⑯, alarmed⑰ by an oracle which had told him that his daughter's child would be the instrument of his death, caused

---

① the tide of life：血液
② within and without：里面和外面
③ Græ：/ˈgriːiː/
④ 古希腊语单词 γραῖα 的意思是"老妇人"，变为复数形式是 γραῖαι，转写为拉丁语就是 græ。
⑤ Gorgon /ˈgɔːgən/：古希腊语形容词 γοργός 的意思是"可怕的，残忍的，猛烈的"，其中性形式是 γοργόν，转写为拉丁语就是 gorgon。
⑥ make much figure：给人留下深刻印象
⑦ Medusa：/mɪˈdjuːzə/
⑧ advert /ədˈvəːt / to：提到
⑨ ingenious /ɪnˈdʒiːnɪəs/：巧妙的
⑩ personification /pəˌsɒnɪfɪˈkeɪʃn/：化身，拟人
⑪ billow：巨浪
⑫ main：(诗)大海
⑬ epithet /ˈepɪθet/：描述某人或某物特点的单词或短语；在这里，Gorgon 指的是 the strong billows of the wide open main 中的 strong 一词，意思是"猛烈的"；Græ 指的是 the white-crested waves 中的 white-crested 一词，意思是"白色顶端的，白色羽冠的"。
⑭ Perseus：/ˈpɜːsjuːs/
⑮ 参见 The Age of Fable 第 14 章关于 Danaë 注释。
⑯ Acrisius：/əˈkrɪsɪəs/
⑰ alarm /əˈlɑːm/：使警觉，使惊恐

the mother and child to be shut up in a chest① and set adrift on the sea. The chest floated towards Seriphus②, where it was found by a fisherman who conveyed the mother and infant to Polydectes③, the king of the country, by whom they were treated with kindness. When Perseus was grown up Polydectes sent him to attempt the conquest of Medusa, a terrible monster who had laid waste④ the country. She was once a beautiful maiden whose hair was her chief glory, but as she dared to vie in beauty with Minerva, the goddess deprived her of her charms and changed her beautiful ringlets into hissing serpents. She became a cruel monster of so frightful an aspect that no living thing could behold her without being turned into stone. All around the cavern where she dwelt might be seen the stony figures of men and animals which had chanced to catch a glimpse of her and had been petrified⑤ with the sight. Perseus, favored by Minerva and Mercury, the former of whom lent him her shield and the latter his winged shoes, approached Medusa while she slept, and taking care not to look directly at her, but guided by her image reflected in the bright shield which he bore, he cut off her head and gave it to Minerva, who fixed it in the middle of her Ægis.

Perseus and Atlas

After the slaughter of Medusa, Perseus, bearing with him the head of the Gorgon, flew far and wide, over land and sea. As night came on, he reached the western limit of the earth, where the sun goes down. Here he would gladly have rested till morning. It was the realm of King Atlas⑥, whose bulk⑦ surpassed that of all other men. He was rich in flocks and herds and had no neighbor or rival to dispute his state. But his chief pride was in his gardens, whose fruit was of gold, hanging from golden branches, half hid with golden leaves. Perseus said to him, "I come as a guest. If you honor illustrious descent, I claim Jupiter for my father; if mighty deeds, I plead the conquest of the Gorgon. I seek rest and food." But Atlas remembered that an ancient prophecy had warned him that a son of Jove should one day rob him of his golden apples. So he answered, "Begone! or neither your false claims of glory nor parentage shall protect you;" and he attempted to thrust him out. Perseus, finding the giant too strong for him, said, "Since you value my friendship so little, deign to accept a present;" and turning his face away, he held up the Gorgon's head. Atlas, with all his bulk, was changed into stone. His beard and hair became forests, his arms and shoulders cliffs, his head a summit, and his bones rocks. Each part

---

① chest：箱子，盒子
② Seriphus /ˈserɪfəs/：希腊岛屿名，是基克拉泽斯群岛（the Cyclades）中的一个岛，属于今希腊南爱琴大区基克拉泽斯州。
③ Polydectes：/ˌpɒlɪˈdektiːs/
④ lay waste：破坏，蹂躏
⑤ petrify /ˈpetrɪfaɪ/：把……变为石头
⑥ Atlas：/ˈætləs/
⑦ bulk：身躯

increased in bulk till he became a mountain, ① and (such was the pleasure of the gods) heaven with all its stars rests upon his shoulders.

The Sea-Monster

Perseus, continuing his flight, arrived at the country of the Æthiopians, of which Cepheus② was king. Cassiopeia③ his queen, proud of her beauty, had dared to compare herself to the Sea-Nymphs, which roused their indignation to such a degree that they sent a prodigious④ sea-monster to ravage⑤ the coast. To appease the deities, Cepheus was directed by the oracle to expose his daughter Andromeda⑥ to be devoured by the monster. As Perseus looked down from his aerial⑦ height he beheld the virgin chained to a rock, and waiting the approach of the serpent. She was so pale and motionless that if it had not been for her flowing tears and her hair that moved in the breeze, he would have taken her for a marble statue. He was so startled at the sight that he almost forgot to wave his wings. As he hovered over her he said, "O virgin, undeserving of those chains, but rather of such as bind fond lovers together, tell me, I beseech you, your name, and the name of your country, and why you are thus bound." At first she was silent from modesty, and, if she could, would have hid her face with her hands; but when he repeated his questions, for fear she might be thought guilty of some fault which she dared not tell, she disclosed her name and that of her country, and her mother's pride of beauty. Before she had done speaking, a sound was heard off upon the water, and the sea-monster appeared, with his head raised above the surface, cleaving the waves with his broad breast. The virgin shrieked, the father and mother who had now arrived at the scene, wretched both, but the mother more justly so, stood by, not able to afford protection, but only to pour forth lamentations and to embrace the victim. Then spoke Perseus: "There will be time enough for tears; this hour is all we have for rescue. My rank as the son of Jove and my renown as the slayer of the Gorgon might make me acceptable as a suitor; but I will try to win her by services rendered, if the gods will only be propitious⑧. If she be rescued by my valor, I demand that she be my reward." The parents consent (how could they hesitate?) and promise a royal dowry with her.

And now the monster was within the range of a stone thrown by a skilful slinger⑨, when with a sudden bound the youth soared into the air. As an eagle, when from his lofty flight he sees a serpent basking in the sun, pounces upon him and seizes him by the neck to prevent him from

---

① 阿特拉斯山脉 (the Atlas Mountains) 位于非洲西北部,穿过摩洛哥 (Morocco)、阿尔及利亚 (Algeria) 北部、突尼斯 (Tunisia)。

② Cepheus：/ˈsiːfjuːs/

③ Cassiopeia：/ˌkæsɪəʊˈpiːə/

④ prodigious /prəˈdɪdʒɪəs/：可怕的,巨大的

⑤ ravage /ˈrævɪdʒ/：破坏,蹂躏

⑥ Andromeda：/ænˈdrɒmɪdə/

⑦ aerial /ˈeərɪəl/：空中的

⑧ propitious /prəʊˈpɪʃəs/：心怀好意的,仁慈的

⑨ slinger /ˈslɪŋə/：投石器使用者

turning his head round and using his fangs, so the youth darted down upon the back of the monster and plunged his sword into its shoulder. Irritated by the wound, the monster raised himself in the air, then plunged into the depth; then, like a wild boar surrounded by a pack of barking dogs, turned swiftly from side to side, while the youth eluded its attacks by means of his wings. Wherever he can find a passage for his sword between the scales he makes a wound, piercing now the side, now the flank, as it slopes towards the tail. The brute spouts① from his nostrils water mixed with blood. The wings of the hero are wet with it, and he dares no longer trust to them. Alighting on a rock which rose above the waves, and holding on by a projecting fragment, as the monster floated near he gave him a death stroke. The people who had gathered on the shore shouted so that the hills reëchoed the sound. The parents, transported② with joy, embraced their future son-in-law, calling him their deliverer③ and the savior④ of their house, and the virgin, both cause and reward of the contest, descended from the rock.

The Wedding Feast

The joyful parents, with Perseus and Andromeda, repaired to the palace, where a banquet was spread for them, and all was joy and festivity⑤. But suddenly a noise was heard of warlike clamor, and Phineus⑥, the betrothed⑦ of the virgin, with a party of his adherents⑧, burst in, demanding the maiden as his own. It was in vain that Cepheus remonstrated⑨—"You should have claimed her when she lay bound to the rock, the monster's victim. The sentence of the gods dooming her to such a fate dissolved all engagements, as death itself would have done." Phineus made no reply, but hurled his javelin at Perseus, but it missed its mark and fell harmless. Perseus would have thrown his in turn, but the cowardly assailant⑩ ran and took shelter behind the altar. But his act was a signal for an onset by his band upon the guests of Cepheus. They defended themselves and a general conflict ensued, the old king retreating from the scene after fruitless expostulations⑪, calling the gods to witness that he was guiltless of this outrage⑫ on the rights of hospitality.

Perseus and his friends maintained for some time the unequal contest; but the numbers of the assailants were too great for them, and destruction seemed inevitable, when a sudden thought struck Perseus⑬,—"I will make my enemy defend me." Then with a loud voice he exclaimed, "If

---

① spout /spaʊt/：喷出
② transport /træn'spɔːt/：使欣喜若狂
③ deliverer /dɪ'lɪvərə/：救命恩人
④ savior /'seɪvɪə/：救星
⑤ festivity /fe'stɪvɪti/：欢乐，喜悦
⑥ Phineus：/'fɪnjuːs/
⑦ betrothed /bɪ'trəʊðd/：未婚夫
⑧ adherent /əd'hɪərənt/：支持者，追随者
⑨ remonstrate /'remənstreɪt/：抗议
⑩ assailant /ə'seɪlənt/：进攻者，攻击者
⑪ expostulation /ɪkˌspɒstju'leɪʃn/：抗议
⑫ outrage /'aʊtreɪdʒ/：伤害
⑬ a sudden thought struck Perseus：Perseus 突然想到一个主意。

I have any friend here let him turn away his eyes!" and held aloft the Gorgon's head. "Seek not to frighten us with your jugglery①," said Thescelus, and raised his javelin in act to throw, and became stone in the very attitude. Ampyx was about to plunge his sword into the body of a prostrate foe, but his arm stiffened and he could neither thrust forward nor withdraw it. Another, in the midst of a vociferous② challenge, stopped, his mouth open, but no sound issuing. One of Perseus's friends, Aconteus, caught sight of the Gorgon and stiffened like the rest. Astyages struck him with his sword, but instead of wounding, it recoiled③ with a ringing noise.

Phineus beheld this dreadful result of his unjust aggression, and felt confounded. He called aloud to his friends, but got no answer; he touched them and found them stone. Falling on his knees and stretching out his hands to Perseus, but turning his head away he begged for mercy. "Take all," said he, "give me but my life." "Base coward," said Perseus, "thus much I will grant you; no weapon shall touch you; moreover, you shall be preserved in my house as a memorial of these events." So saying, he held the Gorgon's head to the side where Phineus was looking, and in the very form in which he knelt, with his hands outstretched and face averted, he became fixed immovably, a mass of stone!

Chapter XVI
Monsters: Giants, Sphinx, Pegasus and Chimæra, Centaurs, Pygmies and Griffin or Gryphon

The Giants

Monsters, in the language of mythology, were beings of unnatural proportions④ or parts, usually regarded with terror, as possessing immense strength and ferocity⑤, which they employed for the injury and annoyance⑥ of men. Some of them were supposed to combine the members⑦ of different animals; such were the Sphinx⑧ and Chimæra⑨; and to these all the terrible qualities of wild beasts were attributed, together with human sagacity and faculties⑩. Others, as the giants, differed from men chiefly in their size; and in this particular we must recognize a wide distinction

---

① jugglery /'dʒʌɡləri/：假装的魔法，花招
② vociferous /vəʊ'sɪfərəs/：大声的
③ recoil /rɪ'kɔɪl/：弹回
④ proportion /prə'pɔːʃn/：比例
⑤ ferocity /fɪ'rɒsəti/：凶猛，残忍
⑥ annoyance /ə'nɔɪəns/：骚扰，打扰
⑦ member：（身体的）部分，器官
⑧ Sphinx：/sfɪŋks/
⑨ Chimæra：/kaɪ'mɪərə/
⑩ sagacity /sə'ɡæsɪti/：智慧；faculty /'fækəlti/：能力

among them. The human giants, if so they may be called, such as the Cyclopes①, Antæus②, Orion③, and others, must be supposed not to be altogether④ disproportioned⑤ to human beings, for they mingled in love and strife with them. But the superhuman giants, who warred with the gods, were of vastly larger dimensions⑥. Tityus⑦, we are told, when stretched on the plain, covered nine acres, and Enceladus⑧ required the whole of Mount Ætna to be laid upon him to keep him down.

We have already spoken of the war which the giants waged against the gods, and of its result. While this war lasted the giants proved a formidable enemy. Some of them, like Briareus⑨, had a hundred arms; others, like Typhon⑩, breathed out fire. At one time they put the gods to such fear that they fled into Egypt and hid themselves under various forms. Jupiter took the form of a ram, whence he was afterwards worshipped in Egypt as the god Ammon⑪, with curved horns. Apollo became a crow, Bacchus a goat, Diana a cat, Juno a cow, Venus a fish, Mercury a bird. At another time the giants attempted to climb up into heaven, and for that purpose took up the mountain Ossa and piled it on Pelion⑫. They were at last subdued by thunderbolts, which Minerva invented, and taught Vulcan and his Cyclopes to make for Jupiter.

The Sphinx

Laius⑬, king of Thebes, was warned by an oracle that there was danger to his throne and life if his new-born son should be suffered⑭ to grow up. He therefore committed the child to the care of a herdsman with orders to destroy⑮ him; but the herdsman, moved with pity, yet not daring entirely to disobey, tied up the child by the feet and left him hanging to the branch of a tree. In this condition the infant was found by a peasant, who carried him to his master and mistress, by whom he was adopted and called Œdipus⑯, or Swollen-foot.

Many years afterwards Laius being on his way to Delphi, accompanied only by one attendant, met in a narrow road a young man also driving in a chariot. On his refusal to leave the way at their

---

① Cyclopes /saɪˈkləʊpiːz/：巨人，只有一只眼睛，位于额头中间。参见 *The Age of Fable* 第 29 章。

② Antæus /ænˈtiːəs/：巨人。参见 *The Age of Fable* 第 19 章。

③ Orion /əˈraɪən/：巨人，英俊的猎人。参见 *The Age of Fable* 第 26 章。

④ altogether：完全地

⑤ disproportioned /ˌdɪsprəˈpɔːʃənd/：不相称的

⑥ dimension /dɪˈmenʃn/：尺寸

⑦ Tityus：/ˈtaɪtɪəs/

⑧ Enceladus：/enˈselədəs/

⑨ Briareus：/braɪˈeərɪəs/

⑩ Typhon：/ˈtaɪfɒn/

⑪ Ammon：/ˈæmən/

⑫ Pelion /ˈpiːlɪən/：希腊山名，位于今色萨利大区马格尼西亚州（Magnesia 或 Magnisia），该山在帕加西迪科斯湾（the Pagasetic Gulf）与爱琴海之间形成一个钩状半岛。

⑬ Laius：/ˈlaɪəs/

⑭ suffer：允许

⑮ destroy：杀死

⑯ Œdipus：/ˈiːdɪpəs/

command the attendant killed one of his horses, and the stranger, filled with rage, slew both Laius and his attendant. The young man was Œdipus, who thus unknowingly became the slayer of his own father.

Shortly after this event the city of Thebes was afflicted with a monster which infested the highroad. It was called the Sphinx. It had the body of a lion and the upper part of a woman. It lay crouched on the top of a rock, and arrested① all travellers who came that way, proposing to them a riddle, with the condition that those who could solve it should pass safe, but those who failed should be killed. Not one had yet succeeded in solving it, and all had been slain. Œdipus was not daunted by these alarming accounts, but boldly advanced to the trial. The Sphinx asked him, "What animal is that which in the morning goes on four feet, at noon on two, and in the evening upon three?" Œdipus replied, "Man, who in childhood creeps on hands and knees, in manhood walks erect, and in old age with the aid of a staff②." The Sphinx was so mortified③ at the solving of her riddle that she cast herself down from the rock and perished.

The gratitude of the people for their deliverance was so great that they made Œdipus their king, giving him in marriage their queen Jocasta④. Œdipus, ignorant of his parentage, had already become the slayer of his father; in marrying the queen he became the husband of his mother. These horrors remained undiscovered, till at length Thebes was afflicted with famine and pestilence, and the oracle being consulted, the double crime of Œdipus came to light. Jocasta put an end to her own life, and Œdipus, seized with madness, tore out his eyes and wandered away from Thebes, dreaded and abandoned by all except his daughters, who faithfully adhered to him, till after a tedious⑤ period of miserable wandering he found the termination of his wretched life.

Pegasus and Chimæra

When Perseus cut off Medusa's head, the blood sinking into the earth produced the winged horse Pegasus⑥. Minerva caught him and tamed him and presented him to the Muses. The fountain Hippocrene⑦, on the Muses' mountain Helicon, was opened by a kick from his hoof.

The Chimæra was a fearful monster, breathing fire. The fore⑧ part of its body was a compound of the lion and the goat, and the hind⑨ part a dragon's. It made great havoc⑩ in Lycia, so that the king, Iobates⑪, sought for some hero to destroy it. At that time there arrived at his

---

① arrest：拦下
② staff：拐杖
③ mortify /ˈmɔːtɪfaɪ/：使感到受辱
④ Jocasta：/dʒəʊˈkæstə/
⑤ tedious /ˈtiːdɪəs/：漫长而疲劳的
⑥ Pegasus：/ˈpeɡəsəs/
⑦ Hippocrene：/ˌhɪpəʊˈkriːni/
⑧ fore：前面的
⑨ hind /haɪnd/：后面的
⑩ havoc /ˈhævək/：破坏
⑪ Iobates：/ˌaɪəˈbætiːz/

court a gallant young warrior, whose name was Bellerophon①. He brought letters from Prœtus②, the son-in-law of Iobates, recommending Bellerophon in the warmest terms as an unconquerable hero, but added at the close a request to his father-in-law to put him to death. The reason was that Prœtus was jealous of him, suspecting that his wife Antea③ looked with too much admiration on the young warrior. From this instance of Bellerophon being unconsciously the bearer of his own death warrant, the expression "Bellerophontic letters" arose, to describe any species of communication which a person is made the bearer of, containing matter prejudicial④ to himself.

Iobates, on perusing the letters, was puzzled what to do, not willing to violate the claims of hospitality, yet wishing to oblige⑤ his son-in-law. A lucky thought occurred to him, to send Bellerophon to combat with the Chimæra. Bellerophon accepted the proposal, but before proceeding to the combat consulted the soothsayer⑥ Polyidus, who advised him to procure if possible the horse Pegasus for the conflict. For this purpose he directed him to pass the night in the temple of Minerva. He did so, and as he slept Minerva came to him and gave him a golden bridle. When he awoke the bridle remained in his hand. Minerva also showed him Pegasus drinking at the well of Pirene⑦, and at sight of the bridle the winged steed came willingly and suffered himself to be taken. Bellerophon mounted him, rose with him into the air, soon found the Chimæra, and gained an easy victory over the monster.

After the conquest of the Chimæra Bellerophon was exposed to further trials and labors by his unfriendly host, but by the aid of Pegasus he triumphed in them all, till at length Iobates, seeing that the hero was a special favorite of the gods, gave him his daughter in marriage and made him his successor on the throne. At last Bellerophon by his pride and presumption drew upon himself the anger of the gods; it is said he even attempted to fly up into heaven on his winged steed, but Jupiter sent a gadfly which stung Pegasus and made him throw his rider, who became lame and blind in consequence. After this Bellerophon wandered lonely through the Aleian field⑧, avoiding the paths of men, and died miserably.

The Centaurs

These monsters were represented as men from the head to the loins⑨, while the remainder⑩ of the body was that of a horse. The ancients were too fond of a horse to consider the union of his nature with man's as forming a very degraded compound, and accordingly the Centaur⑪ is the

---

① Bellerophon：/bəˈlerəfən/
② Prœtus：/ˈpriːtəs/
③ Antea：/ænˈtiːə/
④ prejudicial /ˌpredʒuˈdɪʃl / to：对……不利的
⑤ oblige：帮……的忙
⑥ soothsayer /ˈsuːθˌseɪə/：预言者
⑦ Pirene /pɪˈriːnə/：希腊泉水名,位于科林斯（Corinth）。
⑧ the Aleian field：位于今天土耳其南部地中海以北。
⑨ loin：（常用复数）腰
⑩ remainder /rɪˈmeɪndə/：剩余部分,其余部分
⑪ Centaur：/ˈsentɔː/

only one of the fancied① monsters of antiquity to which any good traits are assigned. The Centaurs were admitted to the companionship of man, and at the marriage of Pirithous② with Hippodamia③ they were among the guests. At the feast Eurytion, one of the Centaurs, becoming intoxicated④ with the wine, attempted to offer violence to the bride; the other Centaurs followed his example, and a dreadful conflict arose in which several of them were slain. This is the celebrated battle of the Lapithæ⑤ and Centaurs, a favorite subject with the sculptors and poets of antiquity.

But not all the Centaurs were like the rude guests of Pirithous. Chiron⑥ was instructed by Apollo and Diana, and was renowned for his skill in hunting, medicine, music, and the art of prophecy. The most distinguished heroes of Grecian story were his pupils. Among the rest the infant Æsculapius⑦ was intrusted to his charge⑧ by Apollo, his father. When the sage returned to his home bearing the infant, his daughter Ocyroe came forth to meet him, and at sight of the child burst forth into a prophetic strain⑨ (for she was a prophetess), foretelling the glory that he was to achieve. Æsculapius when grown up became a renowned physician, and even in one instance succeeded in restoring the dead to life. Pluto resented this, and Jupiter, at his request, struck the bold physician with lightning, and killed him, but after his death received him into the number of the gods.

Chiron was the wisest and justest of all the Centaurs, and at his death Jupiter placed him among the stars as the constellation Sagittarius⑩.

The Pygmies

The Pygmies⑪ were a nation of dwarfs, so called from a Greek word which means the cubit⑫ or measure of about thirteen inches⑬, which was said to be the height of these people. They lived near the sources of the Nile, or according to others, in India. Homer⑭ tells us that the cranes⑮ used to migrate every winter to the Pygmies' country, and their appearance was the signal of bloody warfare to the puny⑯ inhabitants, who had to take up arms to defend their cornfields against the rapacious⑰ strangers. The Pygmies and their enemies the Cranes form the subject of several

---

① fancied /ˈfænsɪd/：想象的，存在于想象中的

② Pirithous：/paɪˈrɪθəʊəs/

③ Hippodamia：/ˌhɪpəʊdəˈmaɪə/

④ intoxicate /ɪnˈtɒksɪkeɪt/：使喝醉

⑤ Lapithæ /ˈlæpɪθiː/：居住在希腊 Thessaly 北部的部落，Pirithous 是该部落的国王。

⑥ Chiron：/ˈkaɪərən/

⑦ Æsculapius：/ˌiːskjuːˈleɪpɪəs/

⑧ charge：照顾，监护

⑨ strain：滔滔不绝的一通话

⑩ Sagittarius：参见 The Age of Fable 第 5 章关于 the twelve signs of the zodiac 的注释。

⑪ Pygmy：/ˈpɪgmi/

⑫ cubit /ˈkjuːbɪt/：古代的长度单位

⑬ 1 英寸（inch）等于 2.54 厘米，13 英寸约等于 33 厘米。

⑭ Homer /ˈhəʊmə/：古希腊史诗诗人，著有《伊利亚特》（The Iliad）和《奥德赛》（The Odyssey）两部英雄史诗。

⑮ crane：鹤

⑯ puny /ˈpjuːni/：矮小的

⑰ rapacious /rəˈpeɪʃəs/：贪婪的，强取的

works of art.

Later writers tell of an army of Pygmies which finding Hercules[①] asleep made preparations to attack him, as if they were about to attack a city. But the hero, awaking, laughed at the little warriors, wrapped some of them up in his lion's skin, and carried them to Eurystheus[②].

The Griffin or Gryphon

The Griffin[③] is a monster with the body of a lion, the head and wings of an eagle, and back covered with feathers. Like birds it builds its nest, and instead of an egg lays an agate[④] therein. It has long claws and talons of such a size that the people of that country make them into drinking-cups. India was assigned as the native country of the Griffins. They found gold in the mountains and built their nests of it, for which reason their nests were very tempting[⑤] to the hunters, and they were forced to keep vigilant guard over them. Their instinct led them to know where buried treasures lay, and they did their best to keep plunderers[⑥] at a distance. The Arimaspians[⑦], among whom the Griffins flourished, were a one-eyed people of Scythia.

Chapter XVII
The Golden Fleece—Medea

The Golden Fleece

In very ancient times there lived in Thessaly a king and queen named Athamas[⑧] and Nephele[⑨]. They had two children, a boy and a girl. After a time Athamas grew indifferent[⑩] to his wife, put her away, and took another. Nephele suspected danger to her children from the influence of the step-mother, and took measures to send them out of her reach. Mercury assisted her, and gave her a ram[⑪] with a golden fleece, on which she set the two children, trusting that the ram would convey them to a place of safety. The ram vaulted into the air with the children on his back, taking his

---

① Hercules /ˈhɜːkjuliːz/：参见 *The Age of Fable* 第 19 章。
② Eurystheus /juəˈrɪsθɪəs/：Argos 国王，参见 *The Age of Fable* 第 19 章。
③ Griffin：/ˈɡrɪfɪn/
④ agate /ˈæɡət/：玛瑙
⑤ tempting：有吸引力的
⑥ plunderer /ˈplʌndərə/：掠夺者，抢劫者
⑦ the Arimaspians /ˌærɪˈmæspɪənz/：传说中居住在 Scythia 北部的部落。关于 Scythia，参见 *The Age of Fable* 第 4 章的相关注释。
⑧ Athamas：/ˈæθəməs/
⑨ Nephele：/ˈnefɪli/
⑩ indifferent /ɪnˈdɪfərənt/：不感兴趣的，冷淡的
⑪ ram：公羊

course to the East, till when crossing the strait that divides Europe and Asia①, the girl, whose name was Helle②, fell from his back into the sea, which from her was called the Hellespont,—now the Dardanelles. The ram continued his career till he reached the kingdom of Colchis③, on the eastern shore of the Black Sea, where he safely landed the boy Phryxus④, who was hospitably received by Æetes⑤, king of the country. Phryxus sacrificed the ram to Jupiter, and gave the Golden Fleece to Æetes, who placed it in a consecrated⑥ grove, under the care of a sleepless dragon.

There was another kingdom in Thessaly near to that of Athamas, and ruled over by a relative of his. The king Æson⑦, being tired of the cares of government, surrendered his crown to his brother Pelias⑧ on condition that he should hold it only during the minority⑨ of Jason⑩, the son of Æson. When Jason was grown up and came to demand the crown from his uncle, Pelias pretended to be willing to yield it, but at the same time suggested to the young man the glorious adventure of going in quest of the Golden Fleece, which it was well known was in the kingdom of Colchis, and was, as Pelias pretended⑪, the rightful property of their family. Jason was pleased with the thought, and forthwith made preparations for the expedition. At that time the only species of navigation known to the Greeks consisted of small boats or canoes hollowed out from trunks of trees, so that when Jason employed Argus⑫ to build him a vessel capable of containing fifty men, it was considered a gigantic undertaking. It was accomplished, however, and the vessel named "Argo⑬," from the name of the builder. Jason sent his invitation to all the adventurous young men of Greece, and soon found himself at the head of a band of bold youths, many of whom afterwards were renowned among the heroes and demigods of Greece. Hercules, Theseus⑭, Orpheus⑮, and Nestor⑯ were among them. They are called the Argonauts⑰, from the name of their vessel.

The "Argo" with her crew of heroes left the shores of Thessaly and having touched at the

---

① the strait that divides Europe and Asia：参见 *The Age of Fable* 第 13 章关于 the strait 的注释。

② Helle：/ˈheli/

③ Colchis /ˈkɒlkɪs/：古代地区名, 位于黑海东端, 高加索山（the Caucasus）以南, 即今天格鲁吉亚（Georgia）西部。

④ Phryxus：/ˈfrɪksəs/

⑤ Æetes：/iːˈiːtiːz/

⑥ consecrated /ˈkɒnsɪkreɪtɪd/：神圣的

⑦ Æson：/ˈiːsɒn/

⑧ Pelias：/ˈpiːlɪæs/

⑨ minority /maɪˈnɒrɪti/：未成年阶段

⑩ Jason：/ˈdʒeɪsn/

⑪ pretend /prɪˈtend/：宣称

⑫ Argus：/ˈɑːgəs/：此处的 Agrus 不是 *The Age of Fable* 第 4 章 Io 的故事中的那个长了一百只眼睛的 Argus。

⑬ Argo：/ˈɑːgəʊ/

⑭ Theseus /ˈθiːsjuːs/：参见 *The Age of Fable* 第 20 章。

⑮ Orpheus /ˈɔːfjuːs/：参见 *The Age of Fable* 第 24 章。

⑯ Nestor /ˈnestɔː/：参见 *The Age of Fable* 第 27 章。

⑰ Argonaut：/ˈɑːgənɔːt/

Island of Lemnos①, thence crossed to Mysia② and thence to Thrace③. Here they found the sage Phineus④, and from him received instruction as to their future course. It seems the entrance of the Euxine Sea was impeded⑤ by two small rocky islands, which floated on the surface, and in their tossings and heavings occasionally came together, crushing and grinding to atoms any object that might be caught between them. They were called the Symplegades⑥, or Clashing Islands. Phineus instructed the Argonauts how to pass this dangerous strait. When they reached the islands they let go a dove, which took her way between the rocks, and passed in safety, only losing some feathers of her tail. Jason and his men seized the favorable moment of the rebound⑦, plied their oars with vigor, and passed safe through, though the islands closed behind them, and actually grazed⑧ their stern⑨. They now rowed along the shore till they arrived at the eastern end of the sea, and landed at the kingdom of Colchis.

Jason made known his message to the Colchian king, Æetes, who consented to give up the golden fleece if Jason would yoke to the plough two fire-breathing bulls with brazen feet, and sow the teeth of the dragon which Cadmus had slain, and from which it was well known that a crop of armed men would spring up, who would turn their weapons against their producer⑩. Jason accepted the conditions, and a time was set for making the experiment. Previously, however, he found means to plead his cause to Medea⑪, daughter of the king. He promised her marriage, and as they stood before the altar of Hecate⑫, called the goddess to witness his oath. Medea yielded, and by her aid, for she was a potent sorceress, he was furnished with a charm⑬, by which he could encounter safely the breath of the fire-breathing bulls and the weapons of the armed men.

At the time appointed, the people assembled at the grove of Mars, and the king assumed his royal seat, while the multitude covered the hill-sides. The brazen-footed bulls rushed in, breathing fire from their nostrils that burned up the herbage as they passed. The sound was like the roar of a furnace, and the smoke like that of water upon quick-lime⑭. Jason advanced boldly to meet them. His friends, the chosen heroes of Greece, trembled to behold him. Regardless of the burning breath, he soothed their rage with his voice, patted their necks with fearless hand,

---

① Lemnos /ˈlemnɒs/：希腊岛屿名,位于爱琴海北部,属于今希腊北爱琴大区莱斯沃斯州（Lesvos）。

② Mysia /ˈmɪsɪə/：古代地区名,在今天的土耳其,北临马尔马拉海,西临爱琴海。

③ Thrace /θreɪs/：古代地区名,位于巴尔干半岛东南部。在古希腊,Thrace 指位于多瑙河（the Danube River)以南、爱琴海以北、黑海和马尔马拉海以西、瓦达尔河(Vadar River) 东边山脉以东的巴尔干地区。

④ Phineus /ˈfɪnjuːs/：参见 Argonautica 中的相关选段。

⑤ impede /ɪmˈpiːd/：挡住,阻挡

⑥ Symplegades /sɪmˈpleɡədiːz/：参见 Argonautica 中的选段。

⑦ rebound：反弹

⑧ graze：轻轻地碰撞

⑨ stern：船尾

⑩ 参见 The Age of Fable 第 12 章。

⑪ Medea /mɪˈdɪə/：参见 Argonautica 中的相关选段。

⑫ Hecate /ˈhekəti/：主管巫术和魔法的女神。

⑬ charm：随身护符

⑭ quick-lime：生石灰

and adroitly① slipped over them the yoke, and compelled them to drag the plough. The Colchians were amazed; the Greeks shouted for joy. Jason next proceeded to sow the dragon's teeth and plough them in. And soon the crop of armed men sprang up, and, wonderful to relate! no sooner had they reached the surface than they began to brandish their weapons and rush upon Jason. The Greeks trembled for their hero, and even she who had provided him a way of safety and taught him how to use it, Medea herself, grew pale with fear. Jason for a time kept his assailants at bay with his sword and shield, till, finding their numbers overwhelming, he resorted to the charm which Medea had taught him, seized a stone and threw it in the midst of his foes. They immediately turned their arms against one another, and soon there was not one of the dragon's brood left alive. The Greeks embraced their hero, and Medea, if she dared, would have embraced him too.

It remained to lull to sleep the dragon that guarded the fleece, and this was done by scattering over him a few drops of a preparation which Medea had supplied. At the smell he relaxed his rage, stood for a moment motionless, then shut those great round eyes, that had never been known to shut before, and turned over on his side, fast asleep. Jason seized the fleece and with his friends and Medea accompanying, hastened to their vessel before Æetes the king could arrest their departure, and made the best of their way back to Thessaly, where they arrived safe, and Jason delivered the fleece to Pelias, and dedicated the "Argo" to Neptune. What became of the fleece afterwards we do not know, but perhaps it was found after all, like many other golden prizes, not worth the trouble it had cost to procure it.

Medea and Æson

Amid the rejoicings for the recovery of the Golden Fleece, Jason felt that one thing was wanting, the presence of Æson, his father, who was prevented by his age and infirmities② from taking part in them. Jason said to Medea, "My spouse, would that your arts, whose power I have seen so mighty for my aid, could do me one further service, take some years from my life and add them to my father's." Medea replied, "Not at such a cost shall it be done, but if my art avails me, his life shall be lengthened without abridging③ yours." The next full moon she issued forth④ alone, while all creatures slept; not a breath stirred the foliage⑤, and all was still. To the stars she addressed her incantations⑥, and to the moon; to Hecate, the goddess of the underworld, and to Tellus⑦ the goddess of the earth, by whose power plants potent for enchantment are produced. She invoked the gods of the woods and caverns, of mountains and valleys, of lakes and rivers, of winds and vapors. While she spoke the stars shone brighter, and presently a chariot descended

---

① adroitly /əˈdrɔɪtli/：机敏地
② infirmity /ɪnˈfɜːmɪti/：虚弱
③ abridge /əˈbrɪdʒ/：缩短
④ issue forth：出去
⑤ foliage /ˈfəʊlɪɪdʒ/：树叶
⑥ incantation /ˌɪnkænˈteɪʃn/：咒语
⑦ Tellus：/ˈteləs/

through the air, drawn by flying serpents. She ascended it, and borne aloft made her way to distant regions, where potent plants grew which she knew how to select for her purpose. Nine nights she employed in her search, and during that time came not within the doors of her palace nor under any roof, and shunned all intercourse① with mortals.

She next erected two altars, the one to Hecate, the other to Hebe②, the goddess of youth, and sacrificed a black sheep, pouring libations of milk and wine. She implored Pluto and his stolen bride③ that they would not hasten to take the old man's life. Then she directed that Æson should be led forth, and having thrown him into a deep sleep by a charm, had him laid on a bed of herbs, like one dead. Jason and all others were kept away from the place, that no profane eyes might look upon her mysteries. Then, with streaming hair, she thrice moved round the altars, dipped flaming twigs in the blood, and laid them thereon to burn. Meanwhile the cauldron④ with its contents was got ready. In it she put magic herbs, with seeds and flowers of acrid⑤ juice, stones from the distant east, and sand from the shore of all-surrounding ocean; hoar⑥ frost, gathered by moonlight, a screech owl's⑦ head and wings, and the entrails⑧ of a wolf. She added fragments of the shells of tortoises, and the liver of stags,—animals tenacious of life⑨,—and the head and beak of a crow, that outlives nine generations of men. These with many other things "without a name" she boiled together for her purposed work, stirring them up with a dry olive branch; and behold! the branch when taken out instantly became green, and before long was covered with leaves and a plentiful growth of young olives; and as the liquor boiled and bubbled, and sometimes ran over, the grass wherever the sprinklings fell shot forth with a verdure like that of spring.

Seeing that all was ready, Medea cut the throat of the old man and let out all his blood, and poured into his mouth and into his wound the juices of her cauldron. As soon as he had completely imbibed⑩ them, his hair and beard laid by their whiteness and assumed the blackness of youth; his paleness and emaciation⑪ were gone; his veins were full of blood, his limbs of vigor and robustness. Æson is amazed at himself, and remembers that such as he now is, he was in his youthful days, forty years before.

Medea used her arts here for a good purpose, but not so in another instance, where she made them the instruments of revenge. Pelias, our readers will recollect, was the usurping⑫ uncle of Jason, and had kept him out of his kingdom. Yet he must have had some good qualities,

---

① intercourse /ˈɪntəkɔːs/：交流
② Hebe：参见 *The Age of Fable* 第 19 章。
③ his stolen bride：即 Proserpine，参见 *The Age of Fable* 第 7 章。
④ cauldron /ˈkɔːldrən/：大锅
⑤ acrid /ˈækrɪd/：辛辣的
⑥ hoar /hɔː/：灰白的
⑦ screech owl：长耳鸮，鸮（xiāo）即猫头鹰。
⑧ entrails /ˈentreɪlz/：(动物或人的)内脏
⑨ tenacious of life：生命力强的;tenacious /tɪˈneɪʃəs/：抓得紧的,顽强的
⑩ imbibe /ɪmˈbaɪb/：喝,吸入
⑪ emaciation /ɪˌmeɪsɪˈeɪʃn/：消瘦,衰弱
⑫ usurp /juˈzɜːp/：篡位

for his daughters loved him, and when they saw what Medea had done for Æson, they wished her to do the same for their father. Medea pretended to consent, and prepared her cauldron as before. At her request an old sheep was brought and plunged into the cauldron. Very soon a bleating was heard in the kettle, and when the cover was removed, a lamb jumped forth and ran frisking away into the meadow. The daughters of Pelias saw the experiment with delight, and appointed a time for their father to undergo the same operation. But Medea prepared her cauldron for him in a very different way. She put in only water and a few simple herbs. In the night she with the sisters entered the bed chamber of the old king, while he and his guards slept soundly under the influence of a spell cast upon them by Medea. The daughters stood by the bedside with their weapons drawn, but hesitated to strike, till Medea chid their irresolution①. Then turning away their faces, and giving random blows, they smote him with their weapons. He, starting from his sleep, cried out, "My daughters, what are you doing? Will you kill your father?" Their hearts failed them and their weapons fell from their hands, but Medea struck him a fatal blow, and prevented his saying more.

Then they placed him in the cauldron, and Medea hastened to depart in her serpent-drawn chariot before they discovered her treachery, or their vengeance would have been terrible. She escaped, however, but had little enjoyment of the fruits of her crime. Jason, for whom she had done so much, wishing to marry Creusa②, princess of Corinth③, put away Medea. She, enraged at his ingratitude, called on the gods for vengeance, sent a poisoned robe as a gift to the bride, and then killing her own children, and setting fire to the palace, mounted her serpent-drawn chariot and fled to Athens, where she married King Ægeus④, the father of Theseus, and we shall meet her again when we come to the adventures of that hero.

There is another story of Medea almost too revolting⑤ for record even of a sorceress, a class of persons to whom both ancient and modern poets have been accustomed to attribute every degree of atrocity. In her flight from Colchis she had taken her young brother Absyrtus⑥ with her. Finding the pursuing vessels of Æetes gaining upon the Argonauts, she caused the lad to be killed and his limbs to be strewn over the sea. Æetes on reaching the place found these sorrowful traces of his murdered son; but while he tarried⑦ to collect the scattered fragments and bestow upon them an honorable interment⑧, the Argonauts escaped.

---

① irresolution /ˌɪrezəˈluːʃn/：犹豫不决

② Creusa：/krɪˈuːzə/

③ Corinth /ˈkɒrɪnθ/：希腊古城名，位于今希腊伯罗奔尼撒大区科林西亚州（Corinthia 或 Korinthia），在现代 Corinth 城西南方向不远处。

④ Ægeus：/ˈiːdʒuːs/

⑤ revolting /rɪˈvəʊltɪŋ/：恐怖的，令人作呕的

⑥ Absyrtus：/əbˈsɜːtəs/

⑦ tarry /ˈtæri/：停留

⑧ interment /ɪnˈtɜːmənt/：葬礼，埋葬

Chapter XVIII
Meleager and Atalanta

Meleager

One of the heroes of the Argonautic expedition was Meleager①, son of Œneus② and Althea③, king and queen of Calydon④. Althea, when her son was born, beheld the three destinies⑤, who, as they spun their fatal thread, foretold that the life of the child should last no longer than a brand⑥ then burning upon the hearth. Althea seized and quenched the brand, and carefully preserved it for years, while Meleager grew to boyhood, youth, and manhood. It chanced, then, that Œneus, as he offered sacrifices to the gods, omitted to pay due honors to Diana; and she, indignant at the neglect, sent a wild boar of enormous size to lay waste the fields of Calydon. Its eyes shone with blood and fire, its bristles stood like threatening spears, its tusks were like those of Indian elephants. The growing corn was trampled⑦, the vines and olive trees laid waste, the flocks and herds were driven in wild confusion by the slaughtering foe. All common aid seemed vain; but Meleager called on the heroes of Greece to join in a bold hunt for the ravenous monster. Theseus and his friend Pirithous⑧, Jason, Peleus⑨, afterwards the father of Achilles, Telamon⑩ the father of Ajax⑪, Nestor, then a youth, but who in his age⑫ bore arms with Achilles and Ajax in the Trojan war,—these and many more joined in the enterprise. With them came Atalanta⑬, the daughter of Iasius⑭, king of Arcadia. A buckle⑮ of polished gold confined⑯ her vest, an ivory quiver hung on her left shoulder, and her left hand bore the bow. Her face blent feminine beauty with the best graces of martial⑰ youth. Meleager saw and loved.

But now already they were near the monster's lair. They stretched strong nets from tree; they

---

① Meleager: /ˌmelɪˈeɪgə/

② Œneus: /ˈiːnjuːs/

③ Althea: /əlˈθiːə/

④ Calydon /ˈkælɪdən/: 希腊古城名,位于今希腊西希腊大区埃托利亚-阿卡纳尼亚州（Aetolia and Akarnania）迈索隆吉市（Mesolongi）附近。

⑤ the three destinies: 三位命运女神（the Three Fates）。参见 *The Age of Fable* 第 1 章。

⑥ brand: 燃烧的木头

⑦ trample /ˈtræmpl/: 踩倒,践踏

⑧ Theseus and his friend Pirithous: 参见 *The Age of Fable* 第 20 章。

⑨ Peleus: /ˈpiːljuːs/

⑩ Telamon: /ˈteləmən/

⑪ Ajax: /ˈeɪdʒæks/

⑫ age: 年老,高龄,耄耋之年

⑬ Atalanta: /ˌætəˈlæntə/

⑭ Iasius: /ˈaɪəsɪəs/

⑮ buckle /ˈbʌkl/: （像小轿车上的安全带一样的）带子

⑯ confine /kənˈfaɪn/: 固定住

⑰ martial /ˈmɑːʃl/: 尚武的,勇敢的

uncoupled① their dogs, they tried to find the footprints of their quarry② in the grass. From the wood was a descent③ to marshy ground. Here the boar, as he lay among the reeds, heard the shouts of his pursuers, and rushed forth against them. One and another is thrown down and slain④. Jason throws his spear, with a prayer to Diana for success; and the favoring goddess allows the weapon to touch, but not to wound, removing the steel point of the spear in its flight. Nestor, assailed, seeks and finds safety in the branches of a tree. Telamon rushes on, but stumbling at a projecting root, falls prone. But an arrow from Atalanta at length for the first time tastes the monster's blood. It is a slight wound, but Meleager sees and joyfully proclaims it. Anceus, excited to envy by the praise given to a female, loudly proclaims his own valor, and defies alike the boar and the goddess who had sent it; but as he rushes on, the infuriated beast lays him low⑤ with a mortal wound. Theseus throws his lance, but it is turned aside by a projecting bough. The dart of Jason misses its object, and kills instead one of their own dogs. But Meleager, after one unsuccessful stroke, drives his spear into the monster's side, then rushes on and despatches him with repeated blows.

Then rose a shout from those around; they congratulated the conqueror, crowding to touch his hand. He, placing his foot upon the head of the slain boar, turned to Atalanta and bestowed on her the head and the rough hide which were the trophies⑥ of his success. But at this, envy excited the rest to strife. Plexippus and Toxeus⑦, the brothers of Meleager's mother, beyond the rest opposed the gift, and snatched from the maiden the trophy she had received. Meleager, kindling with rage at the wrong done to himself, and still more at the insult offered to her whom he loved, forgot the claims of kindred, and plunged his sword into the offenders' hearts.

As Althea bore gifts of thankfulness to the temples for the victory of her son, the bodies of her murdered brothers met her sight. She shrieks, and beats her breast, and hastens to change the garments of rejoicing for those of mourning. But when the author of the deed is known, grief gives way to the stern desire of vengeance on her son. The fatal brand, which once she rescued from the flames, the brand which the destinies had linked with Meleager's life, she brings forth, and commands a fire to be prepared. Then four times she essays to place the brand upon the pile; four times draws back, shuddering at the thought of bringing destruction on her son. The feelings of the mother and the sister contend within her. Now she is pale at the thought of the proposed deed, now flushed again with anger at the act of her son. As a vessel, driven in one direction by the wind, and in the opposite by the tide, the mind of Althea hangs suspended in uncertainty. But now the sister prevails above the mother, and she begins as she holds the fatal wood: "Turn, ye Furies, goddesses of punishment! turn to behold the sacrifice I bring! Crime must atone for crime. Shall

---

① uncouple /ʌnˈkʌpl/：解开（栓狗的绳索）
② quarry /ˈkwɒri/：（被猎人、猎狗、猎食动物等追逐的）猎物
③ descent /dɪˈsent/：下坡路
④ 一只接一只的猎狗被野猪扑倒，然后被它杀死。
⑤ lay... low：把……扑倒在地
⑥ trophy /ˈtrəʊfi/：战利品，纪念品
⑦ Plexippus：/ˈpleksɪpəs/；Toxeus：/ˈtɒksəs/

Œneus rejoice in his victor son, while the house of Thestius① is desolate②? But, alas! to what deed am I borne along? Brothers forgive a mother's weakness! my hand fails me. He deserves death, but not that I should destroy him. But shall he then live, and triumph, and reign over Calydon, while you, my brothers, wander unavenged among the shades③? No! thou hast lived by my gift; die, now, for thine own crime. Return the life which twice I gave thee, first at thy birth, again when I snatched this brand from the flames. O that thou hadst then died! Alas! evil is the conquest; but, brothers, ye have conquered." And, turning away her face, she threw the fatal wood upon the burning pile.

It gave, or seemed to give, a deadly groan. Meleager, absent and unknowing of the cause, felt a sudden pang. He burns, and only by courageous pride conquers the pain which destroys him. He mourns only that he perishes by a bloodless and unhonored death. With his last breath he calls upon his aged father, his brother, and his fond sisters, upon his beloved Atalanta, and upon his mother, the unknown cause of his fate. The flames increase, and with them the pain of the hero. Now both subside; now both are quenched. The brand is ashes, and the life of Meleager is breathed forth to the wandering winds.

Althea, when the deed was done, laid violent hands upon herself. The sisters of Meleager mourned their brother with uncontrollable grief; till Diana, pitying the sorrows of the house that once had aroused her anger, turned them into birds④.

Atalanta

The innocent cause of so much sorrow was a maiden whose face you might truly say was boyish for a girl, yet too girlish for a boy. Her fortune had been told, and it was to this effect⑤: "Atalanta, do not marry; marriage will be your ruin." Terrified by this oracle, she fled the society of men, and devoted herself to the sports of the chase. To all suitors (for she had many) she imposed a condition which was generally effectual⑥ in relieving her of their persecutions, —"I will be the prize of him who shall conquer me in the race⑦; but death must be the penalty of all who try and fail." In spite of this hard condition some would try. Hippomenes⑧ was to be judge of the race. "Can it be possible that any will be so rash⑨ as to risk so much for a wife?" said he. But when he saw her lay aside her robe for the race, he changed his mind, and said, "Pardon me, youths, I knew not the prize you were competing for." As he surveyed them he wished them all to be beaten, and swelled with envy of any one that seemed at all likely to win. While such were his

---

① Thestius /'θiːstɪəs/: father of Althea, Plexippus, and Toxeus
② desolate /'desələt/: 不幸的,可怜的
③ shade: 鬼魂
④ guinea /'ɡɪni/ hens (珍珠鸡)
⑤ to this effect: 大意是这样的
⑥ effectual /ɪ'fektʃuəl/: 有效的
⑦ race: 跑步比赛
⑧ Hippomenes: /hɪ'pɒməniːz/
⑨ rash: 鲁莽的

thoughts, the virgin darted forward. As she ran she looked more beautiful than ever. The breezes seemed to give wings to her feet; her hair flew over her shoulders, and the gay fringe① of her garment fluttered behind her. A ruddy② hue tinged the whiteness of her skin, such as a crimson curtain casts on a marble wall. All her competitors were distanced③, and were put to death without mercy. Hippomenes, not daunted by this result, fixing his eyes on the virgin, said, "Why boast of beating those laggards④? I offer myself for the contest." Atalanta looked at him with a pitying countenance, and hardly knew whether she would rather conquer him or not. "What god can tempt one so young and handsome to throw himself away? I pity him, not for his beauty (yet he is beautiful), but for his youth. I wish he would give up the race, or if he will be so mad, I hope he may outrun me." While she hesitates, revolving these thoughts, the spectators grow impatient for the race, and her father prompts her to prepare. Then Hippomenes addressed a prayer to Venus: "Help me, Venus, for you have led me on." Venus heard and was propitious⑤.

In the garden of her temple, in her own island of Cyprus, is a tree with yellow leaves and yellow branches and golden fruit. Hence she gathered three golden apples, and, unseen by any one else, gave them to Hippomenes, and told him how to use them. The signal is given; each starts from the goal⑥ and skims over the sand. So light their tread, you would almost have thought they might run over the river surface or over the waving grain without sinking. The cries of the spectators cheered Hippomenes,—"Now, now, do your best! haste, haste! you gain on her! relax not! one more effort!" It was doubtful whether the youth or the maiden heard these cries with the greater pleasure. But his breath began to fail him, his throat was dry, the goal yet far off. At that moment he threw down one of the golden apples. The virgin was all amazement. She stopped to pick it up. Hippomenes shot ahead. Shouts burst forth from all sides. She redoubled her efforts, and soon overtook him. Again he threw an apple. She stopped again, but again came up with him. The goal was near; one chance only remained. "Now, goddess," said he, "prosper your gift!" and threw the last apple off at one side. She looked at it, and hesitated; Venus impelled her to turn aside for it. She did so, and was vanquished. The youth carried off his prize.

But the lovers were so full of their own happiness that they forgot to pay due honor to Venus; and the goddess was provoked⑦ at their ingratitude⑧. She caused them to give offence to Cybele⑨. That powerful goddess was not to be insulted with impunity⑩. She took from them their human form and turned them into animals of characters resembling their own: of the huntress-heroine,

---

① fringe /frɪndʒ/：穗状饰物，流苏
② ruddy /ˈrʌdi/：红润的
③ distance：(在跑步比赛中)把……远远地甩在后面
④ laggard /ˈlæɡəd/：跑得慢的人，懒散的人，落后的人
⑤ propitious /prəʊˈpɪʃəs/：打算给予关照的
⑥ goal：(古罗马)跑步比赛的起点
⑦ provoke /prəˈvəʊk/：激怒
⑧ ingratitude /ɪnˈɡrætɪtjuːd/：忘恩负义
⑨ Cybele：/ˈsɪbəliː/
⑩ impunity /ɪmˈpjuːnɪti/：不受惩罚

triumphing in the blood of her lovers, she made a lioness, and of her lord and master a lion, and yoked them to her car, where they are still to be seen in all representations, in statuary① or painting, of the goddess Cybele.

Cybele is the Latin name of the goddess called by the Greeks Rhea and Ops. She was the wife of Cronos and mother of Zeus. In works of art she exhibits the matronly air which distinguishes Juno and Ceres. Sometimes she is veiled, and seated on a throne with lions at her side, at other times riding in a chariot drawn by lions. She wears a mural② crown, that is, a crown whose rim is carved in the form of towers and battlements③. Her priests were called Corybantes④.

Chapter XIX
Hercules—Hebe and Ganymede

Hercules

Hercules⑤ was the son of Jupiter and Alcmena⑥. As Juno was always hostile⑦ to the offspring of her husband by mortal mothers, she declared war against Hercules from his birth. She sent two serpents to destroy him as he lay in his cradle, but the precocious⑧ infant strangled⑨ them with his own hands. He was, however, by the arts⑩ of Juno rendered subject to Eurystheus⑪ and compelled to perform all his commands. Eurystheus enjoined⑫ upon him a succession of desperate adventures, which are called the "Twelve Labors of Hercules." The first was the fight with the Nemean lion. The valley of Nemea⑬ was infested by a terrible lion. Eurystheus ordered Hercules to bring him the skin of this monster. After using in vain his club⑭ and arrows against the lion, Hercules strangled the animal with his hands. He returned carrying the dead lion on his shoulders; but Eurystheus was so frightened at the sight of it and at this proof of the prodigious⑮ strength of the hero, that he ordered him to deliver the account of his exploits in future outside the town.

---

① statuary /ˈstætjuəri/：雕塑

② mural /ˈmjuərəl/：似墙的

③ battlement /ˈbætlmənt/：雉堞，城垛

④ Corybantes：/ˌkɒrɪˈbænti:z/

⑤ Hercules /ˈhɜːkjuli:z/：关于 Hercules 的更详细的故事，参见 *The Library* 中的选段"Hercules"。

⑥ Alcmena：/ælkˈmi:nə/

⑦ hostile /ˈhɒstaɪl/：有敌意的，不友好的

⑧ precocious /prɪˈkəʊʃəs/：早熟的

⑨ strangle /ˈstræŋgl/：扼死

⑩ arts：阴谋诡计，手腕

⑪ Eurystheus：/juəˈrɪsθɪəs/

⑫ enjoin /ɪnˈdʒɔɪn/：强加

⑬ Nemea /nɪˈmi:ə/：古希腊一个树林茂盛的地区，位于今希腊伯罗奔尼撒大区阿尔戈利斯州（Argolis）的 Argos 附近。

⑭ club：（从一端向另一端逐渐变粗的）棍棒

⑮ prodigious /prəˈdɪdʒəs/：惊人的，巨大的

His next labor was the slaughter of the Hydra①. This monster ravaged the country of Argos②, and dwelt in a swamp near the well of Amymone③. This well had been discovered by Amymone when the country was suffering from drought, and the story was that Neptune, who loved her, had permitted her to touch the rock with his trident, and a spring of three outlets④ burst forth. Here the Hydra took up his position, and Hercules was sent to destroy him. The Hydra had nine heads, of which the middle one was immortal. Hercules struck off its heads with his club, but in the place of the head knocked off, two new ones grew forth each time. At length with the assistance of his faithful servant Iolaus, he burned away the heads of the Hydra, and buried the ninth or immortal one under a huge rock.

Another labor was the cleaning of the Augean⑤ stables. Augeas, king of Elis⑥, had a herd of three thousand oxen, whose stalls had not been cleansed for thirty years. Hercules brought the rivers Alpheus⑦ and Peneus⑧ through them, and cleansed them thoroughly in one day.

His next labor was of a more delicate kind. Admeta⑨, the daughter of Eurystheus, longed to obtain the girdle⑩ of the queen of the Amazons⑪, and Eurystheus ordered Hercules to go and get it. The Amazons were a nation of women. They were very warlike and held several flourishing cities. It was their custom to bring up only the female children; the boys were either sent away to the neighboring nations or put to death. Hercules was accompanied by a number of volunteers, and after various adventures at last reached the country of the Amazons. Hippolyta⑫, the queen, received him kindly, and consented to yield him her girdle, but Juno, taking the form of an Amazon, went and persuaded the rest that the strangers were carrying off their queen. They instantly armed and came in great numbers down to the ship. Hercules, thinking that Hippolyta had acted treacherously, slew her, and taking her girdle made sail⑬ homewards.

Another task enjoined him was to bring to Eurystheus the oxen of Geryon⑭, a monster with three bodies, who dwelt in the island Erytheia⑮ (the red), so called because it lay at the west,

---

① Hydra：/ˈhaɪdrə/

② Argos /ˈɑːɡɒs/：希腊城市名,位于今希腊伯罗奔尼撒大区阿尔戈利斯州（Argolis）。

③ Amymone：/ˌæmɪˈməʊni/

④ outlet：出口

⑤ Augean /ɔːˈdʒiːən/：of Augeas /ɔːˈdʒiːæs/

⑥ Elis /ˈiːlɪs/：古希腊地区名,位于伯罗奔尼撒半岛西北角,相当于今天西希腊大区的伊利亚州（Ilia）,因举办古希腊的奥林匹克运动会而著名。参见 The Age of Fable 第 20 章。

⑦ Alpheus：希腊伯罗奔尼撒半岛的主要河流之一,流经 Arcadia 和 Elis,一部分流经地下。

⑧ Peneus /ˈpiːnjuːs/：希腊 Thessaly 地区的河流,以河神 Peneus 的名字命名,Peneus 就是 The Age of Fable 第 3 章中 Daphne 的父亲。该河发源于 Pindus 山,注入爱琴海。

⑨ Admeta：/ədˈmiːtə/

⑩ girdle：/ˈɡɜːdl/：腰带

⑪ Amazon /ˈæməzən/：该词在希腊语中的意思是"没有乳房的","a-"是表示否定的前缀,"mazon"的意思是"乳房"。据说为了拉弓射箭,她们割掉她们的右乳房。

⑫ Hippolyta：/hɪˈpɒlɪtə/

⑬ make sail：扬帆起航

⑭ Geryon：/ˈɡerɪən/

⑮ Erytheia /erɪˈθiːɪə/：传说中的一个岛屿,位于遥远的西方。也有人认为该岛在西班牙加的斯（Cadiz）附近。

under the rays of the setting sun. This description is thought to apply to Spain, of which Geryon was king. After traversing various countries, Hercules reached at length the frontiers of Libya① and Europe, where he raised the two mountains of Calpe and Abyla, as monuments of his progress, or, according to another account, rent one mountain into two and left half on each side, forming the straits of Gibraltar②, the two mountains being called the Pillars of Hercules③. The oxen were guarded by the giant Eurytion and his two-headed dog, but Hercules killed the giant and his dog and brought away the oxen in safety to Eurystheus.

The most difficult labor of all was getting the golden apples of the Hesperides④, for Hercules did not know where to find them. These were the apples which Juno had received at her wedding from the goddess of the Earth, and which she had intrusted to the keeping of the daughters of Hesperus⑤, assisted by a watchful dragon. After various adventures Hercules arrived at Mount Atlas⑥ in Africa. Atlas was one of the Titans who had warred against the gods, and after they were subdued, Atlas was condemned to bear on his shoulders the weight of the heavens. He was the father of the Hesperides, and Hercules thought might, if any one could, find the apples and bring them to him. But how to send Atlas away from his post, or bear up the heavens while he was gone? Hercules took the burden on his own shoulders, and sent Atlas to seek the apples. He returned with them, and though somewhat reluctantly, took his burden upon his shoulders again, and let Hercules return with the apples to Eurystheus.

A celebrated exploit⑦ of Hercules was his victory over Antæus. Antæus, the son of Terra⑧, the Earth, was a mighty giant and wrestler⑨, whose strength was invincible so long as he remained in contact with his mother Earth. He compelled all strangers who came to his country to wrestle with him, on condition that if conquered (as they all were) they should be put to death. Hercules encountered him, and finding that it was of no avail to throw him, for he always rose with renewed strength from every fall, he lifted him up from the earth and strangled him in the air.

Cacus⑩ was a huge giant, who inhabited a cave on Mount Aventine⑪, and plundered the surrounding country. When Hercules was driving home the oxen of Geryon, Cacus stole part of the cattle, while the hero slept. That their footprints might not serve to show where they had been driven, he dragged them backward by their tails to his cave; so their tracks all seemed to show

---

① Libya /ˈlɪbɪə/：在希腊神话中该词通常指整个北非地区，而非今天的北非国家利比亚。

② Gibraltar /dʒɪˈbrɔːltə/：直布罗陀海峡，连接大西洋和地中海的狭窄海峡。

③ the Pillars of Hercules：指直布罗陀海峡（the Strait of Gibralter）最东端的两个海角。在古代，北边的海角叫 Calpe /ˈkælpi/，南边的海角叫 Abyla /əˈbɪlə/。

④ Hesperides /heˈsperɪdiːz/：Hesperides 总共有 3 个，住在西边的 Atlas 山脚下。她们的职责是看守一个长金苹果的园子。这些金苹果是 Juno 嫁给 Jupiter 时得到的礼物。

⑤ the daughters of Hesperus /ˈhespərəs/：the Hesperides

⑥ Mount Atlas：参见第 *The Age of Fable* 15 章关于"阿特拉斯山脉（the Atlas Mountains）"的注释。

⑦ exploit / /ˈeksplɔɪt/：业绩

⑧ Terra /ˈterə/：The meaning of the Latin word "terra" is "earth."

⑨ wrestler /ˈreslə/：摔跤手

⑩ Cacus：/ˈkækəs/

⑪ Mount Aventine：参见 *The Age of Fable* 第 33 章关于 Capitolinus 的注释。

that they had gone in the opposite direction. Hercules was deceived by this stratagem①, and would have failed to find his oxen, if it had not happened that in driving the remainder of the herd past the cave where the stolen ones were concealed, those within began to low, and were thus discovered. Cacus was slain by Hercules.

The last exploit we shall record was bringing Cerberus② from the lower world③. Hercules descended into Hades④, accompanied by Mercury and Minerva. He obtained permission from Pluto to carry Cerberus to the upper air⑤, provided he could do it without the use of weapons; and in spite of the monster's struggling, he seized him, held him fast⑥, and carried him to Eurystheus, and afterwards brought him back again. When he was in Hades he obtained the liberty of Theseus⑦, his admirer and imitator, who had been detained a prisoner there for an unsuccessful attempt to carry off Proserpine.

Hercules in a fit of madness killed his friend Iphitus, and was condemned for this offence to become the slave of Queen Omphale⑧ for three years. While in this service the hero's nature seemed changed. He lived effeminately⑨, wearing at times the dress of a woman, and spinning wool with the hand-maidens of Omphale, while the queen wore his lion's skin. When this service was ended he married Dejanira⑩ and lived in peace with her three years. On one occasion as he was travelling with his wife, they came to a river, across which the Centaur Nessus⑪ carried travellers for a stated⑫ fee. Hercules himself forded⑬ the river, but gave Dejanira to Nessus to be carried across. Nessus attempted to run away with her, but Hercules heard her cries and shot an arrow into the heart of Nessus. The dying Centaur told Dejanira to take a portion of his blood and keep it, as it might be used as a charm to preserve the love of her husband.

Dejanira did so and before long fancied she had occasion to use it. Hercules in one of his conquests had taken prisoner a fair maiden, named Iole, of whom he seemed more fond than Dejanira approved. When Hercules was about to offer sacrifices to the gods in honor of his victory, he sent to his wife for a white robe to use on the occasion. Dejanira, thinking it a good opportunity to try her love-spell, steeped the garment in the blood of Nessus. We are to suppose she took care to wash out all traces of it, but the magic power remained, and as soon as the garment became warm on the body of Hercules the poison penetrated into all his limbs and caused him the most

---

① stratagem /ˈstrætədʒəm/：计谋，计策

② Cerberus /ˈsɜːbərəs/：参见 *The Age of Fable* 第 32 章。

③ the lower world：阴间

④ Hades /ˈheɪdiːz/：阴间

⑤ the upper air：阳间

⑥ fast：紧紧地

⑦ 关于 Theseus 的故事，参见 *The Age of Fable* 第 20 章。

⑧ Omphale /ˈɒmfəli/：小亚细亚古国 Lydia 的女王。

⑨ effeminately /ɪˈfemɪnətli/：像女人一样地

⑩ Dejanira /ˌdedʒəˈnaɪərə/：也可拼写为 Deianira /ˌdiːəˈnaɪərə/。

⑪ Nessus：/ˈnesəs/

⑫ stated /ˈsteɪtɪd/：固定的，规定的

⑬ ford：涉水而过

intense agony. In his frenzy he seized Lichas, who had brought him the fatal robe, and hurled him into the sea. He wrenched off the garment, but it stuck to his flesh, and with it he tore away whole pieces of his body. In this state he embarked on board a ship and was conveyed home. Dejanira, on seeing what she had unwittingly done, hung herself. Hercules, prepared to die, ascended Mount Œta①, where he built a funeral pile of trees, gave his bow and arrows to Philoctetes②, and laid himself down on the pile, his head resting on his club, and his lion's skin spread over him. With a countenance as serene③ as if he were taking his place at a festal board④ he commanded Philoctetes to apply the torch. The flames spread apace⑤ and soon invested⑥ the whole mass.

The gods themselves felt troubled at seeing the champion⑦ of the earth so brought to his end. But Jupiter with cheerful countenance thus addressed them: "I am pleased to see your concern, my princes, and am gratified to perceive that I am the ruler of a loyal people, and that my son enjoys your favor. For although your interest in him arises from his noble deeds, yet it is not the less gratifying to me. But now I say to you, Fear not. He who conquered all else is not to be conquered by those flames which you see blazing on Mount Œta. Only his mother's share in him can perish;⑧ what he derived from me is immortal. I shall take him, dead to earth, to the heavenly shores, and I require of you all to receive him kindly. If any of you feel grieved at his attaining this honor, yet no one can deny that he has deserved it." The gods all gave their assent; Juno only heard the closing words with some displeasure that she should be so particularly pointed at, yet not enough to make her regret the determination of her husband. So when the flames had consumed the mother's share of Hercules, the diviner part, instead of being injured thereby, seemed to start forth with new vigor, to assume a more lofty port⑨ and a more awful dignity. Jupiter enveloped⑩ him in a cloud, and took him up in a four-horse chariot to dwell among the stars⑪. As he took his place in heaven, Atlas felt the added weight.

Juno, now reconciled to him, gave him her daughter Hebe in marriage.

Hebe and Ganymede

Hebe, the daughter of Juno, and goddess of youth, was cup-bearer⑫ to the gods. The usual story is that she resigned her office on becoming the wife of Hercules. But there is another

---

① Œta /ˈiːtə/：参见 *The Age of Fable* 第 5 章关于 Œte 的注释。

② Philoctetes：/ˌfɪlək'tiːtiːz/

③ serene /sɪ'riːn/：平静的

④ festal board：宴会桌

⑤ apace：迅速地

⑥ invest：包围

⑦ champion：勇士

⑧ Hercules 的母亲 Alcmena 是个凡人。

⑨ port：举止，风度

⑩ envelop /ɪn'veləp/：包裹

⑪ Hercules 变成了武仙星座（Hercules）。

⑫ cup-bearer：侍酒者

statement which our countryman Crawford①, the sculptor, has adopted in his group② of Hebe and Ganymede③, now in the Athenæum④ gallery. According to this, Hebe was dismissed from her office in consequence of a fall which she met with one day when in attendance on⑤ the gods. Her successor was Ganymede, a Trojan boy, whom Jupiter, in the disguise of an eagle, seized and carried off from the midst of his playfellows on Mount Ida, bore up to heaven, and installed in the vacant place.

Chapter XX
Theseus—Dædalus—Castor and Pollux

Theseus

Theseus⑥ was the son of Ægeus⑦, king of Athens, and of Æthra⑧, daughter of the king of Trœzen⑨. He was brought up at Trœzen, and when arrived at manhood was to proceed to Athens and present himself to his father. Ægeus on parting from Æthra, before the birth of his son, placed his sword and shoes under a large stone and directed her to send his son to him when he became strong enough to roll away the stone and take them from under it. When she thought the time had come, his mother led Theseus to the stone, and he removed it with ease and took the sword and shoes. As the roads were infested with robbers, his grandfather pressed⑩ him earnestly to take the shorter and safer way to his father's country—by sea; but the youth, feeling in himself the spirit and the soul of a hero, and eager to signalize⑪ himself like Hercules, with whose fame all Greece then rang, by destroying the evil-doers and monsters that oppressed the country, determined on the more perilous and adventurous journey by land.⑫

His first day's journey brought him to Epidaurus⑬, where dwelt a man named Periphetes⑭,

---

① Crawford /ˈkrɔːfəd/, Thomas：美国新古典主义雕刻家，1814 年 3 月生于美国纽约，1857 年 10 月卒于英国伦敦。

② group：（雕塑或绘画中的）群像

③ Ganymede /ˈɡænɪmiːd/：参见 *Homeric Hymns* 中的选段"To Aphrodite"。

④ Athenæum /ˌæθɪˈniːəm/：这里指的是 Boston Athenæum，即波士顿图书馆，位于美国马萨诸塞州波士顿市。波士顿图书馆美术馆成立于 1827 年，重点收藏新英格兰地区艺术家的作品。

⑤ in attendance on：侍候

⑥ Theseus：/ˈθiːsjuːs/

⑦ Ægeus：/ˈiːdʒuːs/

⑧ Æthra：/ˈiːθrə/

⑨ Trœzen /ˈtriːzən/：希腊古城名，位于希腊伯罗奔尼撒半岛东北部，属于今天希腊阿提卡大区阿提卡州。

⑩ press：极力劝说，敦促

⑪ signalize /ˈsɪɡnəlaɪz/：使著名

⑫ Athens 在希腊的萨罗尼科斯湾（Saronic Gulf）以北，Trœzen 在该湾以南，所以从 Trœzen 到 Athens 走水路比走陆路近得多。

⑬ Epidaurus /ˌepɪˈdɔːrəs/：希腊古城名，位于伯罗奔尼撒半岛东北部，在今希腊伯罗奔尼撒大区阿尔戈利斯州东北部海岸，曾是重要的商贸中心。Trœzen 在其东南方向，两城之间路程不远。

⑭ Periphetes：/ˌperɪˈfiːtiːz/

a son of Vulcan. This ferocious① savage② always went armed with a club of iron, and all travellers stood in terror of his violence. When he saw Theseus approach he assailed him, but speedily fell beneath the blows of the young hero, who took possession of his club and bore it ever afterwards as a memorial of his first victory.

Several similar contests with the petty tyrants and marauders③ of the country followed, in all of which Theseus was victorious. One of these evil-doers was called Procrustes④, or the Stretcher. He had an iron bedstead⑤, on which he used to tie all travellers who fell into his hands. If they were shorter than the bed, he stretched their limbs to make them fit it; if they were longer than the bed, he lopped off a portion. Theseus served⑥ him as he had served others.

Having overcome all the perils of the road, Theseus at length reached Athens, where new dangers awaited him. Medea⑦, the sorceress, who had fled from Corinth after her separation from Jason, had become the wife of Ægeus, the father of Theseus. Knowing by her arts who he was, and fearing the loss of her influence with her husband if Theseus should be acknowledged as his son, she filled the mind of Ægeus with suspicions of the young stranger, and induced⑧ him to present him a cup of poison; but at the moment when Theseus stepped forward to take it, the sight of the sword which he wore discovered⑨ to his father who he was, and prevented the fatal draught. Medea, detected in her arts, fled once more from deserved punishment, and arrived in Asia, where the country afterwards called Media⑩ received its name from her. Theseus was acknowledged by his father, and declared his successor.

The Athenians were at that time in deep affliction⑪, on account of the tribute⑫ which they were forced to pay to Minos, king of Crete. This tribute consisted of seven youths and seven maidens, who were sent every year to be devoured by the Minotaur⑬, a monster with a bull's body and a human head. It was exceedingly strong and fierce, and was kept in a labyrinth⑭ constructed by Dædalus⑮, so artfully contrived⑯ that whoever was enclosed in it could by no means find his way out unassisted. Here the Minotaur roamed, and was fed with human victims.

---

① ferocious /fəˈrəʊʃəs/：野蛮的，凶残的

② savage：野蛮、凶残之人

③ marauder /məˈrɔːdə/：打劫者

④ Procrustes：/prəʊˈkrʌstiːz/

⑤ bedstead /ˈbedsted/：床架

⑥ serve：对待

⑦ 参见 The Age of Fable 第 17 章。

⑧ induce /ɪnˈdjuːs/：劝说

⑨ discover：泄露，透露

⑩ Media /ˈmiːdɪə/：古国名，位于今伊朗的西北部。

⑪ affliction /əˈflɪkʃn/：苦难，灾难

⑫ tribute /ˈtrɪbjuːt/：贡品

⑬ Minotaur /ˈmɪnətɔː/：Minotaur 的真实名字是 Asterius /əˈstɪrɪəs/，是 Minos 的妻子 Pasiphae 与她所迷恋的一头公牛交配后生下的怪物。Minotaur 在拉丁语中拼写为 Minotaurus，意思是"Minos 的公牛（taurus）"。

⑭ labyrinth /ˈlæbərɪnθ/：迷宫

⑮ Dædalus：/ˈdiːdələs/

⑯ contrive /kənˈtraɪv/：设计

Theseus resolved to deliver his countrymen from this calamity, or to die in the attempt. Accordingly, when the time of sending off the tribute came, and the youths and maidens were, according to custom, drawn by lot to be sent, he offered himself as one of the victims, in spite of the entreaties of his father. The ship departed under black sails, as usual, which Theseus promised his father to change for white, in case of his returning victorious. When they arrived in Crete, the youths and maidens were exhibited before Minos; and Ariadne①, the daughter of the king, being present, became deeply enamored of Theseus, by whom her love was readily returned. She furnished him with a sword, with which to encounter the Minotaur, and with a clew② of thread by which he might find his way out of the labyrinth. He was successful, slew the Minotaur, escaped from the labyrinth, and taking Ariadne as the companion of his way, with his rescued companions sailed for Athens. On their way they stopped at the island of Naxos③, where Theseus abandoned Ariadne, leaving her asleep. His excuse for this ungrateful treatment of his benefactress④ was that Minerva appeared to him in a dream and commanded him to do so.

On approaching the coast of Attica⑤, Theseus forgot the signal⑥ appointed by his father, and neglected to raise the white sails, and the old king, thinking his son had perished, put an end to his own life. Theseus thus became king of Athens.

One of the most celebrated of the adventures of Theseus is his expedition against the Amazons. He assailed them before they had recovered from the attack of Hercules, and carried off their queen Antiope⑦. The Amazons in their turn invaded the country of Athens and penetrated into the city itself; and the final battle in which Theseus overcame them was fought in the very midst of the city. This battle was one of the favorite subjects of the ancient sculptors, and is commemorated in several works of art that are still extant.

The friendship between Theseus and Pirithous was of a most intimate nature, yet it originated in the midst of arms⑧. Pirithous had made an irruption⑨ into the plain of Marathon⑩, and carried off the herds of the king of Athens. Theseus went to repel the plunderers⑪. The moment Pirithous beheld him, he was seized with admiration; he stretched out his hand as a token of peace, and cried, "Be judge thyself—what satisfaction⑫ dost thou require?" "Thy friendship," replied the

---

① Ariadne /ˌærɪˈædni/：参见 *The Age of Fable* 第 21 章。

② clew /kluː/：线团

③ Naxos /ˈnæksɒs/：希腊岛屿名，位于爱琴海南部，属于今希腊南爱琴大区基克拉泽斯州。

④ benefactress /ˈbenɪfæktrɪs/：女恩人

⑤ Attica /ˈætɪkə/：希腊古地区名，东部和南部临海，雅典（Athens）是其主要城市。古代的 Attica 比今希腊的阿提卡大区小一些。

⑥ signal /ˈsɪɡnl/：信号，暗号

⑦ Antiope：/ænˈtaɪəpiː/

⑧ arms：战争

⑨ irruption /ɪˈrʌpʃn/：入侵

⑩ Marathon /ˈmærəθən/：希腊平原名，位于今希腊的阿提卡大区阿提卡州，公元前 490 年希腊人在此地打败波斯人。

⑪ plunderer /ˈplʌndərə/：掠夺者，抢劫者

⑫ satisfaction：补偿

Athenian①, and they swore inviolable② fidelity. Their deeds corresponded to their professions③, and they ever continued true brothers in arms. Each of them aspired to espouse a daughter of Jupiter. Theseus fixed his choice on Helen, then but a child, afterwards so celebrated as the cause of the Trojan war, and with the aid of his friend he carried her off. Pirithous aspired to the wife of the monarch of Erebus④; and Theseus, though aware of the danger, accompanied the ambitious lover in his descent to the underworld. But Pluto seized and set them on an enchanted rock at his palace gate, where they remained till Hercules arrived and liberated Theseus, leaving Pirithous to his fate.

After the death of Antiope, Theseus married Phædra⑤, daughter of Minos, king of Crete. Phædra saw in Hippolytus⑥, the son of Theseus, a youth endowed with all the graces and virtues of his father, and of an age corresponding to her own. She loved him, but he repulsed her advances⑦, and her love was changed to hate. She used her influence over her infatuated husband to cause him to be jealous of his son, and he imprecated⑧ the vengeance of Neptune upon him. As Hippolytus was one day driving his chariot along the shore, a sea-monster raised himself above the waters, and frightened the horses so that they ran away and dashed the chariot to pieces. Hippolytus was killed, but by Diana's assistance Æsculapius restored him to life. Diana removed Hippolytus from the power of his deluded⑨ father and false stepmother, and placed him in Italy under the protection of the nymph Egeria⑩.

Theseus at length lost the favor of his people, and retired to the court of Lycomedes⑪, king of Scyros⑫, who at first received him kindly, but afterwards treacherously slew him. In a later age the Athenian general Cimon⑬ discovered the place where his remains⑭ were laid, and caused them to be removed to Athens, where they were deposited⑮ in a temple called the Theseum⑯, erected in honor of the hero.

Olympic and Other Games

It seems not inappropriate to mention here the other celebrated national games of the Greeks. The first and most distinguished were the Olympic, founded, it was said, by Jupiter himself. They

---

① the Athenian：Theseus

② inviolable /ɪnˈvaɪələbl/：不可违背的

③ 他们说到做到。profession：承诺,誓言

④ the wife of the monarch of Erebus：Proserpine, 参见 *The Age of Fable* 第7章。

⑤ Phædra：/ˈfiːdrə/

⑥ Hippolytus：/hɪˈpɒlɪtəs/

⑦ advance：（对异性的）追求,挑逗

⑧ imprecate /ˈɪmprɪkeɪt/：祈求

⑨ deluded /dɪˈluːdɪd/：受蒙蔽的,被欺骗的

⑩ Egeria：/ɪˈdʒɪərɪə/

⑪ Lycomedes：/ˌlaɪkəˈmiːdiːz/

⑫ Scyros /ˈskɪrɒs/：希腊岛屿名,位于埃维亚岛（Euboea 或 Evvoia）以东的爱琴海,属于今希腊中希腊大区埃维亚州。

⑬ Cimon /ˈsaɪmən/：公元前5世纪雅典著名的将军、政治家。

⑭ remains：遗骨

⑮ deposit /dɪˈpɒzɪt/：安放

⑯ Theseum：/θɪˈsiːəm/

were celebrated at Olympia① in Elis. Vast numbers of spectators flocked to them from every part of Greece, and from Asia, Africa, and Sicily. They were repeated every fifth year in midsummer, and continued five days. They gave rise to the custom of reckoning time and dating events by Olympiads②. The first Olympiad is generally considered as corresponding with the year 776 B.C. The Pythian③ games were celebrated in the vicinity④ of Delphi, the Isthmian⑤ on the Corinthian isthmus⑥, the Nemean at Nemea, a city of Argolis⑦.

The exercises in these games were of five sorts: running, leaping, wrestling, throwing the quoit, and hurling the javelin, or boxing. Besides these exercises of bodily strength and agility⑧, there were contests in music, poetry, and eloquence. Thus these games furnished poets, musicians, and authors the best opportunities to present their productions to the public, and the fame of the victors was diffused⑨ far and wide.

Dædalus

The labyrinth from which Theseus escaped by means of the clew of Ariadne was built by Dædalus, a most skilful artificer⑩. It was an edifice⑪ with numberless winding⑫ passages and turnings opening into one another, and seeming to have neither beginning nor end, like the river Mæander⑬, which returns on itself, and flows now onward, now backward, in its course to the sea. Dædalus built the labyrinth for King Minos, but afterwards lost the favor of the king, and was shut up in a tower. He contrived to make his escape from his prison, but could not leave the island by sea, as the king kept strict watch on all the vessels, and permitted none to sail without being carefully searched. "Minos may control the land and sea," said Dædalus, "but not the regions of the air. I will try that way." So he set to work to fabricate⑭ wings for himself and his young son Icarus⑮. He wrought⑯ feathers together, beginning with the smallest and adding larger, so as to

---

① Olympia /ə'lɪmpɪə/: 希腊城市名,位于伯罗奔尼撒半岛西部,属于今希腊西希腊大区伊利亚州。

② Olympiad /ə'lɪmpɪæd/: 两届奥林匹克运动会之间的四年,古希腊人用以计算时间。

③ Pythian /'pɪθɪən/: of Delphi

④ vicinity /vɪ'sɪnɪti/ 附近地区

⑤ Isthmian /'ɪsθmɪən/: 科林斯地峡的

⑥ the Corinthian isthmus: 科林斯地峡,连接希腊大陆和伯罗奔尼撒半岛; isthmus /'ɪsθməs/: 地峡,海洋中连接两块陆地的狭窄陆地。

⑦ Argolis /'ɑːgəlɪs/: 古希腊地区名,位于伯罗奔尼撒半岛东北部,是向东伸入爱琴海的一个狭窄、多山的半岛,大致相当于今天希腊伯罗奔尼撒大区的阿尔戈利斯州 (Argolis)。

⑧ agility /ə'dʒɪləti/: 灵活性

⑨ diffuse /dɪ'fjuːz/: 传播

⑩ artificer /ɑː'tɪfɪsə/: 工匠

⑪ edifice /'edɪfɪs/: 庞大而复杂的建筑

⑫ winding /'waɪndɪŋ/: 弯弯曲曲的

⑬ Mæander /mɪ'ændə/: 古代河流名,即今土耳其西南部的 Menderes 河。该河多弯,由此而产生的英语单词 meander 当动词时意思是"(河流)蜿蜒",当名词时意思是"(河流的)拐弯处"。

⑭ fabricate /'fæbrɪkeɪt/: 制作

⑮ Icarus: /'aɪkərəs/

⑯ wrought: work 的过去式

form an increasing surface. The larger ones he secured with thread and the smaller with wax, and gave the whole a gentle curvature① like the wings of a bird. Icarus, the boy, stood and looked on, sometimes running to gather up the feathers which the wind had blown away, and then handling the wax and working it over with his fingers, by his play impeding② his father in his labors. When at last the work was done, the artist③, waving his wings, found himself buoyed upward, and hung suspended, poising himself on the beaten air. He next equipped his son in the same manner, and taught him how to fly, as a bird tempts her young ones from the lofty nest into the air. When all was prepared for flight he said, "Icarus, my son, I charge you to keep at a moderate④ height, for if you fly too low the damp⑤ will clog⑥ your wings, and if too high the heat will melt them. Keep near me and you will be safe." While he gave him these instructions and fitted the wings to his shoulders, the face of the father was wet with tears, and his hands trembled. He kissed the boy, not knowing that it was for the last time. Then rising on his wings, he flew off, encouraging him to follow, and looked back from his own flight to see how his son managed his wings. As they flew the ploughman stopped his work to gaze, and the shepherd leaned on his staff and watched them, astonished at the sight, and thinking they were gods who could thus cleave the air.

They passed Samos⑦ and Delos⑧ on the left and Lebynthos⑨ on the right, when the boy, exulting in his career, began to leave the guidance of his companion and soar upward as if to reach heaven. The nearness of the blazing sun softened the wax which held the feathers together, and they came off. He fluttered⑩ with his arms, but no feathers remained to hold the air. While his mouth uttered cries to his father it was submerged⑪ in the blue waters of the sea, which thenceforth was called by his name.⑫ His father cried, "Icarus, Icarus, where are you?" At last he saw the feathers floating on the water, and bitterly lamenting his own arts, he buried the body and called the land Icaria⑬ in memory of his child. Dædalus arrived safe in Sicily, where he built a temple to Apollo, and hung up his wings, an offering to the god.

Dædalus was so proud of his achievements that he could not bear the idea of a rival. His sister

---

① curvature /ˈkɜːvətʃə/：曲线

② impede /ɪmˈpiːd/：妨碍

③ artist：工匠

④ moderate /ˈmɒdərət/：中等的，适度的

⑤ damp /dæmp/：湿气，雾气

⑥ clog /klɒg/：妨碍

⑦ Samos /ˈseɪmɒs/：希腊岛屿名，位于爱琴海，靠近土耳其西海岸，属于今希腊北爱琴大区萨摩斯州（Samos）。

⑧ Delos /ˈdiːlɒs/：希腊岛屿名，属于今希腊南爱琴大区基克拉泽斯州，位于 Samos 以西，北纬 37 度 30 分附近，与 Samos 几乎在同一纬度上。

⑨ Lebynthos /ˈlebɪnθəs/：希腊古代岛屿名，现在叫 Levitha /ləˈvɪθə/，是位于爱琴海东部、Samos 岛以南北纬 37 度的一个小岛。

⑩ flutter /ˈflʌtə/：扇动（翅膀等）

⑪ submerge /səbˈmɜːdʒ/：淹没在水里

⑫ 这片海域被称作 the Icarian /ɪˈkeərɪən/ Sea。The Icarian Sea 是爱琴海的一部分，指的是希俄斯岛（Chios 或 Khios）以南、基克拉泽斯群岛（the Cyclades）以东、土耳其以西的海域。

⑬ Icaria /aɪˈkeərɪə/：希腊岛屿名，位于 Samos 西南方向不远处，属于今天希腊北爱琴大区萨摩斯州（Samos）。

had placed her son Perdix① under his charge to be taught the mechanical arts. He was an apt scholar② and gave striking evidences of ingenuity③. Walking on the seashore he picked up the spine of a fish. Imitating it, he took a piece of iron and notched④ it on the edge, and thus invented the saw. He put two pieces of iron together, connecting them at one end with a rivet⑤, and sharpening the other ends, and made a pair of compasses⑥. Dædalus was so envious of his nephew's performances that he took an opportunity, when they were together one day on the top of a high tower, to push him off. But Minerva, who favors ingenuity, saw him falling, and arrested his fate by changing him into a bird called after his name, the Partridge⑦. This bird does not build his nest in the trees, nor take lofty flights, but nestles⑧ in the hedges⑨, and mindful of his fall, avoids high places.

Castor and Pollux

Castor and Pollux⑩ were the offspring of Leda and the Swan, under which disguise Jupiter had concealed himself⑪. Leda gave birth to an egg from which sprang the twins. Helen, so famous afterwards as the cause of the Trojan war, was their sister.

When Theseus and his friend Pirithous had carried off Helen from Sparta, the youthful heroes Castor and Pollux, with their followers, hastened to her rescue. Theseus was absent from Attica and the brothers were successful in recovering their sister.

Castor was famous for taming and managing horses, and Pollux for skill in boxing. They were united by the warmest affection and inseparable in all their enterprises. They accompanied the Argonautic expedition⑫. During the voyage a storm arose, and Orpheus⑬ prayed to the Samothracian⑭ gods, and played on his harp, whereupon the storm ceased and stars appeared on the heads of the brothers. From this incident, Castor and Pollux came afterwards to be considered the patron deities⑮ of seamen and voyagers, and the lambent⑯ flames, which in certain states of

---

① Perdix：/'pɜːdɪks/

② scholar：学生

③ ingenuity /ˌɪndʒɪ'njuːəti/：发明创造的能力

④ notch：在……上开锯齿状槽口

⑤ rivet /'rɪvɪt/：铆钉

⑥ compasses：圆规

⑦ Partridge：这种鸟在希腊语和拉丁语中叫 πέρδιξ（perdix），在英语中叫 partridge。

⑧ nestle /'nesl/：筑巢

⑨ hedge：（灌木、小树构成的）树篱

⑩ Castor：/'kɑːstə/；Pollux：/'pɒləks/

⑪ 参见 The Age of Fable 第 14 章关于 Leda 的注释。

⑫ the Argonautic expedition：参见 The Age of Fable 第 17 章。

⑬ Orpheus：参见 The Age of Fable 第 24 章。

⑭ Samothracian /ˌsæmə'θreɪʃn/：of Samothrace /ˌsæmə'θreɪs/；Samothrace：希腊岛屿名，位于爱琴海东北角，属于今希腊东马其顿和色雷斯大区埃夫罗斯州（Evros）。

⑮ the patron deities：保护神

⑯ lambent /'læmbənt/：闪烁的，轻轻摇曳的

the atmosphere play round the sails and masts of vessels, were called by their names①.

After the Argonautic expedition, we find Castor and Pollux engaged in a war with Idas and Lynceus②. Castor was slain, and Pollux, inconsolable③ for the loss of his brother, besought Jupiter to be permitted to give his own life as a ransom for him. Jupiter so far consented as to allow the two brothers to enjoy the boon of life alternately④, passing one day under the earth and the next in the heavenly abodes. According to another form of the story, Jupiter rewarded the attachment⑤ of the brothers by placing them among the stars as Gemini the Twins⑥.

They received divine honors under the name of Dioscuri⑦ (sons of Jove). They were believed to have appeared occasionally in later times, taking part with one side or the other, in hard-fought fields, and were said on such occasions to be mounted on magnificent white steeds. Thus in the early history of Rome they are said to have assisted the Romans at the battle of Lake Regillus⑧, and after the victory a temple was erected in their honor on the spot where they appeared.

Chapter XXI
Bacchus—Ariadne

Bacchus

Bacchus⑨ was the son of Jupiter and Semele⑩. Juno, to gratify her resentment⑪ against Semele, contrived a plan for her destruction. Assuming the form of Beroë, her aged nurse, she insinuated⑫ doubts whether it was indeed Jove himself who came as a lover. Heaving a sigh, she said, "I hope it will turn out so, but I can't help being afraid. People are not always what they pretend to be. If he is indeed Jove, make him give some proof of it. Ask him to come arrayed in all his splendors, such as he wears in heaven. That will put the matter beyond a doubt." Semele was persuaded to try the experiment. She asks a favor, without naming what it is. Jove gives his promise, and confirms it with the irrevocable⑬ oath, attesting⑭ the river Styx, terrible to the gods

---

① Castor and Pollux：(暴风雨中出现在桅杆等上方的)电击发光

② Idas /ˈaɪdæs / and Lynceus /ˈlɪŋkɪəs /：two of the Argonauts and sons of Aphareus /ˈæfərɪəs/

③ inconsolable /ˌɪnkənˈsəʊləbl/：不能被安慰的,悲痛欲绝的

④ alternately /ɔːlˈtɜːnətli/：交替地

⑤ attachment /əˈtætʃmənt/：友谊,友爱

⑥ Gemini the Twins：参见 The Age of Fable 第 5 章关于 the twelve signs of the zodiac 的注释。

⑦ Dioscuri /ˌdaɪɒsˈkjuəri/

⑧ Lake Regillus /ˈredʒɪləs/：意大利湖泊名,公元前 496 年,罗马人在此打败拉丁人。

⑨ Bacchus /ˈbækəs/：参见 The Homeric Hymns 中的选段"To Dionysus"。

⑩ Semele：/ˈsemɪli/

⑪ resentment /rɪˈzentmənt/：不满,怨恨

⑫ insinuate /ɪnˈsɪnjuːeɪt/：暗示

⑬ irrevocable /ɪˈrevəkəbl/：不可取消的,不可改变的

⑭ attest /əˈtest/：请……作证

themselves. Then she made known her request. The god would have stopped her as she spake①, but she was too quick for him. The words escaped, and he could neither unsay② his promise nor her request. In deep distress he left her and returned to the upper regions. There he clothed himself in his splendors, not putting on all his terrors, as when he overthrew the giants, but what is known among the gods as his lesser panoply③. Arrayed in this, he entered the chamber of Semele. Her mortal frame could not endure the splendors of the immortal radiance. She was consumed to ashes.

Jove took the infant Bacchus and gave him in charge to the Nysæan④ nymphs, who nourished his infancy and childhood, and for their care were rewarded by Jupiter by being placed, as the Hyades⑤, among the stars. When Bacchus grew up he discovered the culture⑥ of the vine and the mode⑦ of extracting⑧ its precious juice; but Juno struck him with madness, and drove him forth a wanderer through various parts of the earth. In Phrygia the goddess Rhea cured him and taught him her religious rites, and he set out on a progress through Asia, teaching the people the cultivation of the vine. The most famous part of his wanderings is his expedition to India, which is said to have lasted several years. Returning in triumph, he undertook to introduce his worship into Greece, but was opposed by some princes, who dreaded its introduction on account of the disorders and madness it brought with it.

As he approached his native city Thebes⑨, Pentheus⑩ the king, who had no respect for the new worship, forbade its rites to be performed. But when it was known that Bacchus was advancing, men and women, but chiefly the latter, young and old, poured forth to meet him and to join his triumphal march.

It was in vain Pentheus remonstrated⑪, commanded, and threatened. "Go," said he to his attendants, "seize this vagabond leader of the rout⑫ and bring him to me. I will soon make him confess his false claim of heavenly parentage and renounce⑬ his counterfeit⑭ worship." It was in vain his nearest friends and wisest counsellors remonstrated and begged him not to oppose the god. Their remonstrances only made him more violent.

But now the attendants returned whom he had despatched to seize Bacchus. They had been

---

① spake: spoke

② unsay /ˈʌnˈseɪ/: 收回,取消

③ panoply /ˈpænəpli/: 全套盔甲

④ Nysæan /ˈnɪsiːən/: 居住在 Nysa 山上的;Nysa /ˈnɪsə/: 传说中的山,具体位置不详。

⑤ Hyades /ˈhaɪədiːz/: 位于金牛星座中的一个星团,过去人们认为该星团与太阳一起升起预示着要下雨。

⑥ culture: 栽培,培育

⑦ mode: 方法

⑧ extract /ɪkˈstrækt/: 榨取(果汁、油等)

⑨ His mother, Semele, is the daughter of Cadmus, the founder of Thebes, and Harmonia. See Chapter XII in *The Age of Fable*.

⑩ Pentheus: /ˈpenθjuːs/

⑪ remonstrate /ˈremənstreɪt/: 反对

⑫ rout: 嘈杂的人群,乌合之众

⑬ renounce /rɪˈnaʊns/: 放弃

⑭ counterfeit /ˈkaʊntəfɪt/: 假冒的,虚假的

driven away by the Bacchanals①, but had succeeded in taking one of them prisoner, whom, with his hands tied behind him, they brought before the king. Pentheus, beholding him with wrathful② countenance, said, "Fellow! you shall speedily be put to death, that your fate may be a warning to others; but though I grudge the delay of your punishment, speak, tell us who you are, and what are these new rites you presume to celebrate."

The prisoner, unterrified, responded, "My name is Acetes③; my country is Mæonia④; my parents were poor people, who had no fields or flocks to leave me, but they left me their fishing rods and nets and their fisherman's trade. This I followed for some time, till growing weary of remaining in one place, I learned the pilot's art and how to guide my course by the stars. It happened as I was sailing for Delos we touched at the island of Dia⑤ and went ashore. Next morning I sent the men for fresh water, and myself mounted the hill to observe the wind; when my men returned bringing with them a prize, as they thought, a boy of delicate⑥ appearance, whom they had found asleep. They judged he was a noble youth, perhaps a king's son, and they might get a liberal⑦ ransom⑧ for him. I observed his dress, his walk, his face. There was something in them which I felt sure was more than mortal. I said to my men, 'What god there is concealed in that form I know not, but some one there certainly is. Pardon us, gentle deity, for the violence we have done you, and give success to our undertakings.' Dictys, one of my best hands for climbing the mast and coming down by the ropes, and Melanthus, my steersman, and Epopeus, the leader of the sailor's cry, one and all exclaimed, 'Spare your prayers for us.' So blind is the lust of gain! When they proceeded to put him on board I resisted them. 'This ship shall not be profaned by such impiety⑨,' said I. 'I have a greater share in her⑩ than any of you.' But Lycabas, a turbulent⑪ fellow, seized me by the throat and attempted to throw me overboard⑫, and I scarcely saved myself by clinging to the ropes. The rest approved the deed.

"Then Bacchus (for it was indeed he), as if shaking off his drowsiness⑬, exclaimed, 'What are you doing with me? What is this fighting about? Who brought me here? Where are you going to carry me?' One of them replied, 'Fear nothing; tell us where you wish to go and we will take you

①　Bacchanal /ˈbækənl/: Bacchus 的追随者
②　wrathful /ˈrɒθfəl/: 愤怒的
③　Acetes /əˈsiːtiːz/: Acetes 讲述的关于 Bacchus 的故事，参见 *The Homeric Hymns* 中的赞歌"To Dionysus"。
④　Mæonia /miːˈəʊnɪə/: 即 Lydia /ˈlɪdɪə/，Lydia 是位于小亚细亚的一个古国。由于意大利西部古国 Etruria /ɪˈtruərɪə/ 的居民是从 Lydia 迁移过来的，所以 Mæonia 和 Lydia 也可用来指 Etruria。Etruria 位于意大利西部，相当于今意大利的托斯卡纳区（Tuscany 或 Toscana）和翁布里亚区（Umbria）区的部分地区。Etruria 又叫 Tyrrhenia /tɪˈriːnɪə/。Etruria 的形容词是 Etruscan /ɪˈtrʌskən/。
⑤　Dia /ˈdaɪə/: 希腊小岛名，位于克里特岛（Crete）以北不远处，属于今希腊克里特大区伊拉克利翁州（Iraklio）。
⑥　delicate /ˈdelɪkət/: 漂亮的，迷人的
⑦　liberal /ˈlɪbərəl/: 丰厚的
⑧　ransom /ˈrænsəm/: 赎金
⑨　impiety /ɪmˈpaɪəti/: 对神的不敬
⑩　her: the ship
⑪　turbulent /ˈtɜːbjulənt/: 不守规矩的
⑫　throw me overboard /ˈəʊvəbɔːd/: 把我从船上扔到海里
⑬　drowsiness /ˈdraʊsɪnəs/: 瞌睡

there.' 'Naxos is my home,' said Bacchus; 'take me there and you shall be well rewarded.' They promised so to do, and told me to pilot the ship to Naxos. Naxos lay to the right, and I was trimming① the sails to carry us there, when some by signs and others by whispers signified to me their will that I should sail in the opposite direction, and take the boy to Egypt to sell him for a slave. I was confounded and said, 'Let some one else pilot the ship;' withdrawing myself from any further agency② in their wickedness. They cursed me, and one of them, exclaiming, 'Don't flatter yourself that we depend on you for our safety,' took my place as pilot, and bore③ away from Naxos.

"Then the god, pretending that he had just become aware of their treachery, looked out over the sea and said in a voice of weeping, 'Sailors, these are not the shores you promised to take me to; yonder island is not my home. What have I done that you should treat me so? It is small glory you will gain by cheating a poor boy.' I wept to hear him, but the crew laughed at both of us, and sped the vessel fast over the sea. All at once—strange as it may seem, it is true,—the vessel stopped, in the mid sea, as fast as if it was fixed on the ground. The men, astonished, pulled at their oars, and spread more sail, trying to make progress by the aid of both, but all in vain. Ivy twined round the oars and hindered their motion, and clung to the sails, with heavy clusters of berries. A vine, laden with grapes, ran up the mast, and along the sides of the vessel. The sound of flutes was heard and the odor of fragrant wine spread all around. The god himself had a chaplet of vine leaves, and bore in his hand a spear wreathed with ivy. Tigers crouched at his feet, and forms of lynxes and spotted panthers played around him. The men were seized with terror or madness; some leaped overboard; others preparing to do the same beheld their companions in the water undergoing a change, their bodies becoming flattened and ending in a crooked tail. One exclaimed, 'What miracle is this!' and as he spoke his mouth widened, his nostrils expanded, and scales covered all his body. Another, endeavoring to pull the oar felt his hands shrink up and presently to be no longer hands but fins; another, trying to raise his arms to a rope, found he had no arms, and curving his mutilated body, jumped into the sea. What had been his legs became the two ends of a crescent-shaped④ tail. The whole crew became dolphins and swam about the ship, now upon the surface, now under it, scattering the spray, and spouting the water from their broad nostrils. Of twenty men I alone was left. Trembling with fear, the god cheered me. 'Fear not,' said he; 'steer towards Naxos.' I obeyed, and when we arrived there, I kindled the altars and celebrated the sacred rites of Bacchus."

Pentheus here exclaimed, "We have wasted time enough on this silly story. Take him away and have him executed⑤ without delay." Acetes was led away by the attendants and shut up fast⑥ in prison; but while they were getting ready the instruments of execution the prison doors came

---

① trim：调整船帆以适应风向

② agency /'eɪdʒənsi/：行动,操作

③ bear：(船)朝指定方向航行

④ crescent-shaped：月牙状的; crescent /'kresənt/：月牙

⑤ execute /'eksɪkjuːt/：处死,处决

⑥ fast：牢固地

open of their own accord① and the chains fell from his limbs, and when they looked for him he was nowhere to be found.

Pentheus would take no warning, but instead of sending others, determined to go himself to the scene of the solemnities. The mountain Citheron② was all alive with worshippers, and the cries of the Bacchanals resounded on every side. The noise roused the anger of Pentheus as the sound of a trumpet does the fire③ of a war-horse. He penetrated through the wood and reached an open space where the chief scene of the orgies④ met his eyes. At the same moment the women saw him; and first among them his own mother, Agave⑤, blinded by the god, cried out, "See there the wild boar, the hugest monster that prowls⑥ in these woods! Come on, sisters! I will be the first to strike the wild boar." The whole band rushed upon him, and while he now talks less arrogantly, now excuses himself, and now confesses his crime and implores pardon, they press upon him and wound him. In vain he cries to his aunts⑦ to protect him from his mother. Autonoë⑧ seized one arm, Ino the other, and between them he was torn to pieces, while his mother shouted, "Victory! Victory! we have done it; the glory is ours!"

So the worship of Bacchus was established in Greece.

Ariadne

We have seen in the story of Theseus how Ariadne⑨, the daughter of King Minos, after helping Theseus to escape from the labyrinth, was carried by him to the island of Naxos and was left there asleep, while the ungrateful Theseus pursued his way home without her. Ariadne, on waking and finding herself deserted⑩, abandoned herself to grief. But Venus took pity on her, and consoled her with the promise that she should have an immortal lover, instead of the mortal one she had lost.

The island where Ariadne was left was the favorite island of Bacchus, the same that he wished the Tyrrhenian⑪ mariners⑫ to carry him to, when they so treacherously attempted to make prize of⑬ him. As Ariadne sat lamenting her fate, Bacchus found her, consoled her, and made her his wife. As a marriage present he gave her a golden crown, enriched with gems, and when she died, he took her crown and threw it up into the sky. As it mounted the gems grew brighter and were

---

① of their own accord：自动地

② 参见 *The Age of Fable* 第 24 章关于 Cithæron 的注释。

③ fire：热情，激情

④ orgy /ˈɔːdʒɪ/：祭神仪式

⑤ Agave：/əˈɡeɪvi/

⑥ prowl：游荡

⑦ his aunts：Agave, Autonoë, and Ino are all daughters of Cadmus, king of Thebes. See Chapter XII in *The Age of Fable*.

⑧ Autonoë：/ɔːˈtəʊnəʊi/

⑨ Ariadne /ˌærɪˈædni/：参见 *The Age of Fable* 第 20 章。

⑩ deserted /dɪˈzɜːtɪd/：被抛弃的

⑪ Tyrrhenian：Etruscan. 参见本章关于 Mæonia 的注释。

⑫ mariner /ˈmærɪnə/：水手

⑬ make prize of：捕获

turned into stars, and preserving its form Ariadne's crown remains fixed in the heavens as a constellation①, between the kneeling Hercules② and the man who holds the serpent③.

Chapter XXII
The Rural Deities—Erisichthon—Rhœcus— The Water Deities—The Camenæ—The Winds

The Rural Deities

Pan④, the god of woods and fields, of flocks and shepherds, dwelt in grottos⑤, wandered on the mountains and in valleys, and amused himself with the chase or in leading the dances of the nymphs. He was fond of music, and as we have seen, the inventor of the syrinx⑥, or shepherd's pipe, which he himself played in a masterly manner. Pan, like other gods who dwelt in forests, was dreaded by those whose occupations⑦ caused them to pass through the woods by night, for the gloom⑧ and loneliness of such scenes dispose⑨ the mind to superstitious⑩ fears. Hence sudden fright without any visible cause was ascribed to Pan, and called a Panic⑪ terror.

As the name of the god signifies "all," Pan came to be considered a symbol of the universe and personification of Nature; and later still to be regarded as a representative of all the gods and of heathenism⑫ itself.

Sylvanus⑬ and Faunus⑭ were Latin divinities, whose characteristics are so nearly the same as those of Pan that we may safely consider them as the same personage under different names.

The wood-nymphs, Pan's partners in the dance, were but one class of nymphs. There were besides them the Naiads⑮, who presided over brooks and fountains, the Oreads⑯, nymphs of

---

① 即北冕星座（Corona Borealis）。

② Hercules：武仙星座；参见 *The Age of Fable* 第 19 章。

③ the man who holds the serpent：即蛇夫星座（Ophiuchus /ɒˈfjuːkəs /）。

④ Pan：/pæn/

⑤ grotto /ˈɡrɒtəʊ/：洞穴

⑥ 参见 *The Age of Fable* 第 4 章。

⑦ occupation /ˌɒkjuˈpeɪʃn/：职业

⑧ gloom：黑暗

⑨ dispose /dɪˈspəʊz/：使有某种倾向

⑩ superstitious /ˌsuːpəˈstɪʃəs/：非常的,极度的

⑪ panic 的意思是"惶恐,惊恐"。

⑫ heathenism /ˈhiːðənɪzəm/：异教信仰

⑬ Sylvanus：/sɪlˈvænəs/

⑭ Faunus：/ˈfɔːnəs/

⑮ Naiad：/ˈnaɪæd/

⑯ Oread：/ˈɔːrɪæd/

mountains and grottos, and the Nereids①, sea-nymphs. The three last named② were immortal, but the wood-nymphs, called Dryads③ or Hamadryads④, were believed to perish with the trees which had been their abode⑤ and with which they had come into existence. It was therefore an impious act wantonly⑥ to destroy a tree, and in some aggravated cases was severely punished, as in the instance of Erisichthon⑦, which we are about to record⑧.

Erisichthon

Erisichthon was a profane⑨ person and a despiser⑩ of the gods. On one occasion he presumed to violate with the axe a grove sacred to Ceres. There stood in this grove a venerable⑪ oak so large that it seemed a wood in itself, its ancient trunk towering aloft, whereon votive⑫ garlands were often hung and inscriptions carved expressing the gratitude of suppliants to the nymph of the tree. Often had the Dryads danced round it hand in hand. Its trunk measured fifteen cubits round, and it overtopped the other trees as they overtopped the shrubbery. But for all that, Erisichthon saw no reason why he should spare it and he ordered his servants to cut it down. When he saw them hesitate he snatched an axe from one, and thus impiously exclaimed: "I care not whether it be a tree beloved of⑬ the goddess or not; were it the goddess herself it should come down if it stood in my way." So saying, he lifted the axe and the oak seemed to shudder and utter a groan. When the first blow fell upon the trunk blood flowed from the wound. All the bystanders were horror-struck, and one of them ventured to remonstrate and hold back the fatal axe. Erisichthon, with a scornful look, said to him, "Receive the reward of your piety;" and turned against him the weapon which he had held aside from the tree, gashed⑭ his body with many wounds, and cut off his head. Then from the midst of the oak came a voice, "I who dwell in this tree am a nymph beloved of Ceres, and dying by your hands forewarn you that punishment awaits you." He desisted⑮ not from his crime, and at last the tree, sundered by repeated blows and drawn by ropes, fell with a crash and prostrated a great part of the grove in its fall.

The Dryads, in dismay at the loss of their companion and at seeing the pride of the forest⑯

---

① Nereid: /ˈnɪəriːɪd/
② last named: 最后提到的
③ Dryad: /ˈdraɪəd/
④ Hamadryad: /ˌhæməˈdraɪəd/
⑤ abode /əˈbəʊd/: 住所
⑥ wantonly /ˈwɒntənli/: 毫无理由地
⑦ Erisichthon: /ˌerɪˈsɪkθən/
⑧ record: 讲述
⑨ profane /prəˈfeɪn/: 亵渎神灵的
⑩ despiser /dɪˈspaɪzə/: 鄙视者
⑪ venerable /ˈvenərəbl/: 古老的
⑫ votive /ˈvəʊtɪv/: 许愿的
⑬ of: by
⑭ gash /ɡæʃ/: 砍
⑮ desist /dɪˈzɪst/: 停止
⑯ the pride of the forest: the oak

laid low, went in a body① to Ceres, all clad in garments of mourning, and invoked punishment upon Erisichthon. She nodded her assent, and as she bowed her head the grain ripe for harvest in the laden fields bowed also. She planned a punishment so dire that one would pity him, if such a culprit② as he could be pitied,—to deliver him over to Famine. As Ceres herself could not approach Famine, for the Fates have ordained that these two goddesses shall never come together, she called an Oread from her mountain and spoke to her in these words: "There is a place in the farthest part of ice-clad③ Scythia, a sad and sterile④ region without trees and without crops. Cold dwells there, and Fear and Shuddering, and Famine. Go and tell the last⑤ to take possession of the bowels of Erisichthon. Let not abundance subdue her, nor the power of my gifts drive her away.⑥ Be not alarmed at the distance" (for Famine dwells very far from Ceres), "but take my chariot. The dragons are fleet⑦ and obey the rein, and will take you through the air in a short time." So she gave her the reins, and she drove away and soon reached Scythia. On arriving at Mount Caucasus she stopped the dragons and found Famine in a stony field, pulling up with teeth and claws the scanty⑧ herbage. Her hair was rough, her eyes sunk, her face pale, her lips blanched, her jaws covered with dust, and her skin drawn tight, so as to show all her bones. As the Oread saw her afar off (for she did not dare to come near), she delivered the commands of Ceres; and, though she stopped as short a time as possible, and kept her distance as well as she could, yet she began to feel hungry, and turned the dragons' heads and drove back to Thessaly.

Famine obeyed the commands of Ceres and sped through the air to the dwelling of Erisichthon, entered the bedchamber of the guilty man, and found him asleep. She enfolded him with her wings and breathed herself into him, infusing her poison into his veins. Having discharged her task, she hastened to leave the land of plenty and returned to her accustomed haunts. Erisichthon still slept, and in his dreams craved food, and moved his jaws as if eating. When he awoke, his hunger was raging. Without a moment's delay he would have food set before him, of whatever kind earth, sea, or air produces; and complained of hunger even while he ate. What would have sufficed⑨ for a city or a nation, was not enough for him. The more he ate the more he craved. His hunger was like the sea, which receives all the rivers, yet is never filled; or like fire, that burns all the fuel that is heaped upon it, yet is still voracious⑩ for more.

His property rapidly diminished under the unceasing demands of his appetite, but his hunger

---

① in a body：一起
② culprit /ˈkʌlprɪt/：罪犯，犯有重罪之人
③ ice-clad：被冰覆盖的
④ sterile /ˈsteraɪl/：荒芜的
⑤ the last：Famine
⑥ her：Famine
⑦ fleet：速度快的
⑧ scanty /ˈskænti/：稀少的
⑨ suffice /səˈfaɪs/：足够
⑩ voracious /vəˈreɪʃəs/：贪吃的，贪得无厌的

continued unabated①. At length he had spent all and had only his daughter left, a daughter worthy of a better parent. Her too he sold. She scorned to be the slave of a purchaser and as she stood by the seaside raised her hands in prayer to Neptune. He heard her prayer, and though her new master was not far off and had his eye upon her a moment before, Neptune changed her form and made her assume that of a fisherman busy at his occupation. Her master, looking for her and seeing her in her altered form, addressed her and said, "Good fisherman, whither went the maiden whom I saw just now, with hair dishevelled and in humble garb, standing about where you stand? Tell me truly; so may your luck be good and not a fish nibble② at your hook and get away." She perceived that her prayer was answered and rejoiced inwardly at hearing herself inquired of about herself. She replied, "Pardon me, stranger, but I have been so intent upon my line③ that I have seen nothing else; but I wish I may never catch another fish if I believe any woman or other person except myself to have been hereabouts for some time." He was deceived and went his way, thinking his slave had escaped. Then she resumed her own form. Her father was well pleased to find her still with him, and the money too that he got by the sale of her; so he sold her again. But she was changed by the favour of Neptune as often as she was sold, now into a horse, now a bird, now an ox, and now a stag—got away from her purchasers and came home. By this base method the starving father procured food; but not enough for his wants, and at last hunger compelled him to devour his limbs, and he strove to nourish his body by eating his body, till death relieved him from the vengeance of Ceres.

Rhœcus

The Hamadryads could appreciate④ services as well as punish injuries. The story of Rhœcus⑤ proves this. Rhœcus, happening to see an oak just ready to fall, ordered his servants to prop⑥ it up. The nymph, who had been on the point of perishing with the tree, came and expressed her gratitude to him for having saved her life and bade him ask what reward he would. Rhœcus boldly asked her love and the nymph yielded to his desire. She at the same time charged him to be constant⑦ and told him that a bee should be her messenger and let him know when she would admit his society⑧. One time the bee came to Rhœcus when he was playing at draughts⑨ and he carelessly brushed it away. This so incensed⑩ the nymph that she deprived him of sight.

---

① unabated /ˌʌnəˈbeɪtɪd/: 没有减弱的,没有减退的

② nibble /ˈnɪbl/: 一点一点地咬

③ line: 鱼线

④ appreciate /əˈpriːʃieɪt/: 感谢

⑤ Rhœcus: /ˈriːkəs/

⑥ prop: 支撑

⑦ constant /ˈkɒnstənt/: 专一的,坚贞的

⑧ society: 陪伴

⑨ draughts /drɑːfts/: 一种类似于象棋的游戏

⑩ incense /ɪnˈsens/: 激怒

The Water Deities

Oceanus and Tethys① were the Titans who ruled over the watery elements②. When Jove and his brothers overthrew the Titans and assumed their power, Neptune and Amphitrite succeeded to the dominion of the waters in place of Oceanus and Tethys.

Neptune

Neptune was the chief of the water deities. The symbol of his power was the trident, or spear with three points, with which he used to shatter rocks, to call forth or subdue storms, to shake the shores and the like. He created the horse and was the patron of horse races. His own horses had brazen hoofs and golden manes. They drew his chariot over the sea, which became smooth before him, while the monsters of the deep③ gambolled④ about his path.

Amphitrite

Amphitrite⑤ was the wife of Neptune. She was the daughter of Nereus and Doris, and the mother of Triton. Neptune, to pay his court to⑥ Amphitrite, came riding on a dolphin. Having won her he rewarded the dolphin by placing him among the stars⑦.

Nereus and Doris

Nereus and Doris⑧ were the parents of the Nereids, the most celebrated of whom were Amphitrite, Thetis⑨, the mother of Achilles, and Galatea, who was loved by the Cyclops Polyphemus⑩. Nereus was distinguished for his knowledge and his love of truth and justice, whence⑪ he was termed an elder; the gift of prophecy was also assigned to him.

Triton and Proteus

Triton⑫ was the son of Neptune and Amphitrite, and the poets make him his father's trumpeter⑬. Proteus was also a son of Neptune. He, like Nereus, is styled⑭ a sea-elder for his wisdom and knowledge of future events. His peculiar power was that of changing his shape at will.

---

① Oceanus：/əʊˈsɪənəs/；Tethys：/ˈteθɪs/
② elements：在西方，古人认为宇宙是由四种元素（elements）构成的，这四种元素是气（air）、水（water）、火（fire）、土（earth）。这里的 watery elements 指的就是 the waters。
③ the deep：the ocean
④ gambol /ˈgæmbl/：跳跃，嬉戏
⑤ Amphitrite：/ˈæmfɪtraɪti/
⑥ to pay court to：向……求爱
⑦ 即海豚星座（the Dolfin）。
⑧ Nereus：/ˈnɪərjuːs/；Doris：/ˈdɔːrɪs/
⑨ Thetis：/ˈθetɪs/
⑩ Polyphemus：参见 *The Age of Fable* 第 26 章和第 29 章。
⑪ whence：（连词）因此
⑫ Triton：/ˈtraɪtn/
⑬ trumpeter /ˈtrʌmpɪtə/：号手
⑭ style：叫，称呼

Thetis

Thetis, the daughter of Nereus and Doris, was so beautiful that Jupiter himself sought her in marriage; but having learned from Prometheus the Titan that Thetis should bear a son who should grow greater than his father, Jupiter desisted from his suit[①] and decreed that Thetis should be the wife of a mortal. By the aid of Chiron the Centaur, Peleus succeeded in winning the goddess for his bride and their son was the renowned Achilles. In our chapter on the Trojan war it will appear that Thetis was a faithful mother to him, aiding him in all difficulties, and watching over his interests from the first to the last.

Leucothea and Palæmon

Ino, the daughter of Cadmus and wife of Athamas, flying from her frantic husband with her little son Melicertes[②] in her arms, sprang from a cliff into the sea. The gods, out of compassion, made her a goddess of the sea, under the name of Leucothea[③], and him a god, under that of Palæmon[④]. Both were held powerful to save from shipwreck and were invoked by sailors. Palæmon was usually represented riding on a dolphin. The Isthmian games[⑤] were celebrated in his honor. He was called Portunus[⑥] by the Romans, and believed to have jurisdiction[⑦] of the ports and shores.

The Camenæ[⑧]

By this name the Latins designated[⑨] the Muses, but included under it also some other deities, principally nymphs of fountains. Egeria was one of them, whose fountain and grotto are still shown. It was said that Numa[⑩], the second king of Rome, was favored by this nymph with secret interviews, in which she taught him those lessons of wisdom and of law which he embodied in the institutions of his rising nation. After the death of Numa the nymph pined away and was changed into a fountain.

The Winds

When so many less active agencies were personified, it is not to be supposed that the winds failed to be so. They were Boreas[⑪] or Aquilo[⑫], the north wind; Zephyrus[⑬] or Favonius[⑭], the

---

① suit：求爱,对女人的追求
② Melicertes：/ˌmelɪˈsɜːtiːz/
③ Leucothea：/ljuˈkɒθɪə/
④ Palæmon：/pəˈliːmɒn/
⑤ The Isthmian games：科林斯地峡运动会。参见 *The Age of Fable* 第 20 章。
⑥ Portunus：/ˈpɔːtənəs/
⑦ jurisdiction /ˌdʒuərɪsˈdɪkʃn/：管辖权,控制权
⑧ Camenæ：/kəˈmiːniː/
⑨ designate /ˈdezɪgneɪt/：称呼
⑩ Numa：参见 *The Age of Fable* 第 1 章的注释。
⑪ Boreas：/ˈbɔːrɪəs/
⑫ Aquilo：/əˈkwɪləʊ/
⑬ Zephyrus：/ˈzefərəs/
⑭ Favonius：/fəˈvəʊnɪəs/

west; Notus[1] or Auster[2], the south; and Eurus[3], the east. The first two have been chiefly celebrated by the poets, the former as the type of rudeness, the latter of gentleness. Boreas loved the nymph Orithyia[4], and tried to play the lover's part, but met with poor success. It was hard for him to breathe gently, and sighing was out of the question. Weary at last of fruitless endeavors, he acted out his true character, seized the maiden and carried her off. Their children were Zetes and Calais, winged warriors, who accompanied the Argonautic expedition, and did good service in an encounter[5] with those monstrous birds the Harpies[6].

Chapter XXIII
Achelous and Hercules—Admetus and Alcestis—Antigone—Penelope

Achelous and Hercules

The river-god Achelous[7] told the story of Erisichthon to Theseus and his companions, whom he was entertaining at his hospitable board[8], while they were delayed on their journey by the overflow[9] of his waters. Having finished his story, he added, "But why should I tell of other persons' transformations when I myself am an instance of the possession of this power? Sometimes I become a serpent, and sometimes a bull, with horns on my head. Or I should say I once could do so; but now I have but one horn, having lost one." And here he groaned and was silent.

Theseus asked him the cause of his grief, and how he lost his horn. To which question the river-god replied as follows: "Who likes to tell of his defeats? Yet I will not hesitate to relate mine, comforting myself with the thought of the greatness of my conqueror, for it was Hercules. Perhaps you have heard of the fame of Dejanira, the fairest of maidens, whom a host of suitors strove to win. Hercules and myself were of the number[10], and the rest yielded to us two. He urged in his behalf his descent from Jove and his labors by which he had exceeded the exactions[11] of Juno, his step-mother[12]. I, on the other hand, said to the father of the maiden, 'Behold me, the king of the waters that flow through your land. I am no stranger from a foreign shore, but belong to

---

① Notus: /ˈnəʊtəs/

② Auster: /ˈɔːstə/

③ Eurus: /ˈjuərəs/

④ Orithyia: /ˌɒrɪˈθɪɪə/

⑤ encounter /ɪnˈkaʊntə/: 战斗

⑥ Zetes: /ˈziːtiːz/, Calais: /kəˈleɪɪs/, and the Harpies /ˈhɑːpɪz/: 参见 *Argonautica* 中的 "Phineus and the Harpies" 选段。

⑦ Achelous: /ˌækɪˈləʊəs/

⑧ board: 餐桌

⑨ overflow /ˌəʊvəˈfləʊ/: 泛滥, 溢出

⑩ number: 一群人

⑪ exactions /ɪɡˈzækʃnz/: (复数) 苛刻的要求

⑫ 参见 *The Age of Fable* 第 19 章和 *The Library* 中的 "Hercules" 选段。

the country, a part of your realm. Let it not stand in my way that royal Juno owes me no enmity[①] nor punishes me with heavy tasks. As for this man, who boasts himself the son of Jove, it is either a false pretence[②], or disgraceful to him if true, for it cannot be true except by his mother's shame.' As I said this Hercules scowled[③] upon me, and with difficulty restrained his rage. 'My hand will answer better than my tongue,' said he. 'I yield to you the victory in words, but trust my cause to the strife of deeds.' With that he advanced towards me, and I was ashamed, after what I had said, to yield. I threw off my green vesture and presented myself for the struggle. He tried to throw me, now attacking my head, now my body. My bulk was my protection, and he assailed me in vain. For a time we stopped, then returned to the conflict. We each kept our position, determined not to yield, foot to foot, I bending over him, clenching his hand in mine, with my forehead almost touching his. Thrice Hercules tried to throw me off, and the fourth time he succeeded, brought me to the ground, and himself upon my back. I tell you the truth, it was as if a mountain had fallen on me. I struggled to get my arms at liberty, panting and reeking with perspiration[④]. He gave me no chance to recover, but seized my throat. My knees were on the earth and my mouth in the dust.

"Finding that I was no match for him in the warrior's art[⑤], I resorted to others and glided away in the form of a serpent. I curled my body in a coil and hissed at him with my forked tongue. He smiled scornfully at this, and said, 'It was the labor of my infancy to conquer snakes.' So saying he clasped my neck with his hands. I was almost choked, and struggled to get my neck out of his grasp. Vanquished in this form, I tried what alone remained to me and assumed the form of a bull. He grasped my neck with his arm, and dragging my head down to the ground, overthrew me on the sand. Nor was this enough. His ruthless hand rent my horn from my head. The Naiades took it, consecrated it, and filled it with fragrant flowers. Plenty[⑥] adopted my horn and made it her own, and called it 'Cornucopia[⑦].'"

There is another account of the origin of the Cornucopia. Jupiter at his birth was committed by his mother Rhea to the care of the daughters of Melisseus[⑧], a Cretan king. They fed the infant deity with the milk of the goat Amalthea[⑨]. Jupiter broke off one of the horns of the goat and gave it to his nurses, and endowed it with the wonderful power of becoming filled with whatever the possessor might wish.

---

① enmity /ˈenmɪti/：敌意,憎恨

② pretence /prɪˈtens/：声称

③ scowl /skaʊl/：怒目而视

④ perspiration /ˌpɜːspɪˈreɪʃn/：汗水

⑤ the warrior's art：打斗

⑥ Plenty：丰饶女神

⑦ Cornucopia /ˌkɔːnjuˈkəʊpɪə/：丰饶角（装满鲜花、水果和谷物的羊角）；拉丁语单词 Cornucopia 由 cornu 和 copia 两个词构成,cornu 的意思是"角",copia 的意思是"丰饶,富足"。

⑧ Melisseus：/mɪˈlɪsɪəs/

⑨ Amalthea /ˌæməlˈθiːə/：Jupiter 的父亲 Saturn 害怕被自己的孩子推翻,所以他的孩子一出生他就立刻吃掉他们。Jupiter 出生时,他的母亲 Rhea 把一块石头包裹在襁褓里,拿给 Saturn 吞食。Saturn 没有察觉这个骗局,吞食了包在襁褓里的石头。Rhea 把 Jupiter 秘密地送到克里特岛。在那里,Jupiter 靠吃一只叫 Amalthea 的羊的奶长大。

Admetus and Alcestis

Æsculapius①, the son of Apollo, was endowed by his father with such skill in the healing art② that he even restored the dead to life. At this Pluto took alarm, and prevailed on Jupiter to launch a thunderbolt at Æsculapius. Apollo was indignant at the destruction of his son, and wreaked his vengeance on the innocent workmen who had made the thunderbolt. These were the Cyclopes, who have their workshop under Mount Ætna, from which the smoke and flames of their furnaces are constantly issuing. Apollo shot his arrows at the Cyclopes, which so incensed Jupiter that he condemned him as a punishment to become the servant of a mortal for the space of one year. Accordingly Apollo went into the service of Admetus③, king of Thessaly, and pastured his flocks for him on the verdant④ banks of the river Amphrysos⑤.

Admetus was a suitor, with others, for the hand of Alcestis⑥, the daughter of Pelias⑦, who promised her to him who should come for her in a chariot drawn by lions and boars. This task Admetus performed by the assistance of his divine herdsman⑧, and was made happy in the possession of Alcestis. But Admetus fell ill, and being near to death, Apollo prevailed on the Fates to spare him on condition that some one would consent to die in his stead⑨. Admetus, in his joy at this reprieve⑩, thought little of the ransom, and perhaps remembering the declarations of attachment⑪ which he had often heard from his courtiers⑫ and dependents⑬ fancied that it would be easy to find a substitute⑭. But it was not so. Brave warriors, who would willingly have perilled⑮ their lives for their prince⑯, shrunk from the thought of dying for him on the bed of sickness; and old servants who had experienced his bounty⑰ and that of his house⑱ from their childhood up, were not willing to lay down the scanty⑲ remnant of their days to show their gratitude. Men asked, "Why does not one of his parents do it? They cannot in the course of nature live much longer, and

---

① Æsculapius: /ˌiːskjuˈleɪpɪəs/
② the healing art: 医术
③ Admetus: /ædˈmiːtəs/
④ verdant /ˈvɜːdənt/: 长满绿色草木的
⑤ Amphrysos: /æmˈfrɪsəs/
⑥ Alcestis: /ælˈsestɪs/
⑦ Pelias: 参见 *The Age of Fable* 第 17 章。
⑧ his divine herdsman: Apollo
⑨ in his stead: 代替他
⑩ reprieve /rɪˈpriːv/: 暂缓
⑪ attachment /əˈtætʃmənt/: 爱,忠诚
⑫ courtier /ˈkɔːtɪə/: 朝臣,奉承者
⑬ dependent /dɪˈpendənt/: 扈从,随从
⑭ substitute /ˈsʌbstɪtjuːt/: 替身
⑮ peril: 使面临危险
⑯ prince: 君主,国王
⑰ bounty: 慷慨
⑱ house: (皇族、王族或贵族的)家族
⑲ scanty /ˈskænti/: 不多的

who can feel like them the call to rescue the life they gave from an untimely[①] end？" But the parents, distressed though they were at the thought of losing him, shrunk from the call. Then Alcestis, with a generous self-devotion, proffered herself as the substitute. Admetus, fond as he was of life, would not have submitted to receive it at such a cost; but there was no remedy. The condition imposed by the Fates had been met, and the decree was irrevocable. Alcestis sickened as Admetus revived, and she was rapidly sinking to the grave.

Just at this time Hercules arrived at the palace of Admetus, and found all the inmates[②] in great distress for the impending[③] loss of the devoted wife and beloved mistress. Hercules, to whom no labor was too arduous[④], resolved to attempt her rescue. He went and lay in wait at the door of the chamber of the dying queen, and when Death came for his prey, he seized him and forced him to resign[⑤] his victim. Alcestis recovered, and was restored to her husband.

Antigone

A large proportion both of the interesting persons and of the exalted[⑥] acts of legendary Greece belongs to the female sex. Antigone[⑦] was as bright an example of filial[⑧] and sisterly fidelity as was Alcestis of connubial[⑨] devotion. She was the daughter of Œdipus[⑩] and Jocasta, who with all their descendants were the victims of an unrelenting[⑪] fate, dooming them to destruction. Œdipus in his madness had torn out his eyes, and was driven forth from his kingdom Thebes, dreaded and abandoned by all men, as an object of divine vengeance. Antigone, his daughter, alone shared his wanderings and remained with him till he died, and then returned to Thebes.

Her brothers, Eteocles[⑫] and Polynices[⑬], had agreed to share the kingdom between them, and reign alternately[⑭] year by year. The first year fell to the lot of Eteocles, who, when his time expired, refused to surrender the kingdom to his brother. Polynices fled to Adrastus[⑮], king of Argos, who gave him his daughter in marriage, and aided him with an army to enforce his claim to the kingdom. This led to the celebrated expedition of the "Seven against Thebes,"[⑯] which

---

① untimely /ʌn'taɪmli/：过早的
② inmate：共同居住在同一栋房屋里的人
③ impending /ɪm'pendɪŋ/：即将发生的
④ arduous /'ɑːdjuəs/：艰难的
⑤ resign /rɪ'zaɪn/：放弃
⑥ exalted /ɪg'zɔːltɪd/：崇高的
⑦ Antigone：/æn'tɪgəni/
⑧ filial /'fɪlɪəl/：子女的
⑨ connubial /kə'njuːbɪəl/：婚姻的
⑩ 关于 Œdipus，参见 *The Age of Fable* 第 16 章中 Sphinx 的故事。
⑪ unrelenting /ˌʌnrɪ'lentɪŋ/：冷酷无情的,严厉的
⑫ Eteocles：/ɪ'tiːəkliːz/
⑬ Polynices：/ˌpɒlɪ'naɪsiːz/
⑭ alternately /ɔːl'tɜːnɪtli/：交替地,轮流地
⑮ Adrastus：/ə'dræstəs/
⑯ Seven against Thebes：率军攻打 Thebes 的 7 位将领是 Adrastus, Amphiaraus, Capaneus, Hippomedon, Parthenopaeus, Polynices, Tydeus。

furnished ample materials for the epic and tragic poets of Greece.

Amphiaraus[1], the brother-in-law of Adrastus, opposed the enterprise, for he was a soothsayer, and knew by his art that no one of the leaders except Adrastus would live to return. But Amphiaraus, on his marriage to Eriphyle[2], the king's sister, had agreed that whenever he and Adrastus should differ in opinion, the decision should be left to Eriphyle. Polynices, knowing this, gave Eriphyle the collar[3] of Harmonia, and thereby gained her to his interest. This collar or necklace was a present which Vulcan had given to Harmonia on her marriage with Cadmus, and Polynices had taken it with him on his flight from Thebes. Eriphyle could not resist so tempting a bribe, and by her decision the war was resolved on, and Amphiaraus went to his certain fate. He bore his part bravely in the contest, but could not avert his destiny. Pursued by the enemy, he fled along the river, when a thunderbolt launched by Jupiter opened the ground, and he, his chariot, and his charioteer were swallowed up.

It would not be in place[4] here to detail[5] all the acts of heroism or atrocity which marked the contest; but we must not omit to record the fidelity of Evadne[6] as an offset[7] to the weakness of Eriphyle. Capaneus[8], the husband of Evadne, in the ardor of the fight declared that he would force his way into the city in spite of Jove himself. Placing a ladder against the wall he mounted, but Jupiter, offended at his impious language, struck him with a thunderbolt. When his obsequies[9] were celebrated, Evadne cast herself on his funeral pile and perished.

Early in the contest Eteocles consulted the soothsayer Tiresias[10] as to the issue. Tiresias in his youth had by chance seen Minerva bathing. The goddess in her wrath deprived him of his sight, but afterwards relenting gave him in compensation the knowledge of future events. When consulted by Eteocles, he declared that victory should fall to Thebes if Menœceus[11], the son of Creon[12], gave himself a voluntary victim. The heroic youth, learning the response, threw away his life in the first encounter.

The siege continued long, with various success. At length both hosts agreed that the brothers should decide their quarrel by single combat. They fought and fell by each other's hands. The armies then renewed the fight, and at last the invaders were forced to yield, and fled, leaving their dead unburied. Creon, the uncle of the fallen princes, now become king, caused Eteocles to be buried with distinguished honor, but suffered the body of Polynices to lie where it fell, forbidding

---

① Amphiaraus：/ˌæmfɪəˈreɪəs/

② Eriphyle：/ˌerɪˈfɪli/

③ collar：项链；关于 Harmonia 的项链,参见 *The Age of Fable* 第 12 章 Cadmus 的故事。

④ in place：适合的,恰当的

⑤ detail：详细地叙述或描写

⑥ Evadne：/ɪˈvædni/

⑦ offset：衬托

⑧ Capaneus：/kəˈpænjuːs/

⑨ obsequies /ˈɒbsɪkwɪz/：葬礼

⑩ Tiresias：/taɪˈriːsɪæz/；关于 Tiresias 故事的另一种说法,参见 *The Metamorphoses* 中的"Tiresias"选段。

⑪ Menœceus：/mɪˈniːsjuːs/

⑫ Creon：/ˈkriːɒn/

every one on pain of death① to give it burial.

Antigone, the sister of Polynices, heard with indignation the revolting edict② which consigned③ her brother's body to the dogs and vultures, depriving it of those rites which were considered essential to the repose④ of the dead. Unmoved by the dissuading counsel of an affectionate but timid sister⑤, and unable to procure⑥ assistance, she determined to brave⑦ the hazard, and to bury the body with her own hands. She was detected in the act, and Creon gave orders that she should be buried alive, as having deliberately⑧ set at naught⑨ the solemn edict of the city. Her lover, Hæmon⑩, the son of Creon, unable to avert her fate, would not survive her, and fell by his own hand.

Penelope

Penelope⑪ is another of those mythic heroines whose beauties were rather those of character and conduct than of person⑫. She was the daughter of Icarius⑬, a Spartan⑭ prince. Ulysses⑮, king of Ithaca⑯, sought her in marriage, and won her, over all competitors. When the moment came for the bride to leave her father's house, Icarius, unable to bear the thoughts of parting with his daughter, tried to persuade her to remain with him, and not accompany her husband to Ithaca. Ulysses gave Penelope her choice, to stay or go with him. Penelope made no reply, but dropped her veil over her face. Icarius urged her no further, but when she was gone erected a statue to Modesty⑰ on the spot where they parted.

Ulysses and Penelope had not enjoyed their union more than a year when it was interrupted by the events which called Ulysses to the Trojan war. During his long absence⑱, and when it was doubtful whether he still lived, and highly improbable that he would ever return, Penelope was

---

① on pain of death：以处死作为处罚

② edict /ˈiːdɪkt/：法令

③ consign /kənˈsaɪn/：把……交给

④ repose：安息

⑤ an affectionate but timid sister：Ismene /ɪsˈmiːni/, sister of Antigone

⑥ procure /prəˈkjuə/：获取，获得

⑦ brave：勇敢地面对

⑧ deliberately /dɪˈlɪbərətli/：故意地

⑨ set at naught：蔑视

⑩ Hæmon：/ˈhiːmɒn/

⑪ Penelope /pəˈneləpi/：参见 *The Age of Fable* 第 30 章和 Homer 的史诗 *The Odyssey* 中的选段 "The Killing of the Wooers"。

⑫ 她的美是性格和品行之美，而非长相之美。

⑬ Icarius：/aɪˈkeərɪəs/

⑭ Spartan /ˈspɑːtən/：of Sparta；Sparta /ˈspɑːtə/：古希腊城邦名，位于伯罗奔尼撒半岛南部，在今希腊的伯罗奔尼撒大区拉科尼亚州（Laconia）。

⑮ Ulysses /juːˈlɪsiːz/：参见 *The Age of Fable* 第 29 章和第 30 章和 Homer 的史诗 *The Odyssey* 中的选段 "The Killing of the Wooers"。

⑯ Ithaca /ˈɪθəkə/：希腊岛屿名，位于希腊以西的伊奥尼亚海（Ionian Sea），是伊奥尼亚群岛（Ionian Islands）中的一个岛，属于今希腊伊奥尼亚群岛大区凯法利尼亚州（Kefallinia）。

⑰ Modesty：希腊神话中的谦逊、谨慎、朴实女神。

⑱ 20 年

importuned by numerous suitors, from whom there seemed no refuge but in choosing one of them for her husband. Penelope, however, employed every art to gain time, still hoping for Ulysses' return. One of her arts of delay was engaging in the preparation of a robe for the funeral canopy of Laertes①, her husband's father. She pledged herself to make her choice among the suitors when the robe was finished. During the day she worked at the robe, but in the night she undid the work of the day. This is the famous Penelope's web, which is used as a proverbial expression for anything which is perpetually doing but never done. The rest of Penelope's history will be told when we give an account of her husband's adventures.

Chapter XXIV
Orpheus and Eurydice—Aristæus—Amphion—Linus— Thamyris—Marsyas—Melampus—Musæus

Orpheus and Eurydice

Orpheus② was the son of Apollo and the Muse Calliope③. He was presented by his father with a lyre and taught to play upon it, which he did to such perfection that nothing could withstand the charm of his music. Not only his fellow-mortals but wild beasts were softened by his strains④, and gathering round him laid by their fierceness, and stood entranced⑤ with his lay⑥. Nay, the very trees and rocks were sensible to the charm. The former crowded round him and the latter relaxed somewhat of their hardness, softened by his notes⑦.

Hymen had been called to bless with his presence the nuptials of Orpheus with Eurydice⑧; but though he attended, he brought no happy omens with him. His very torch smoked and brought tears into their eyes. In coincidence with such prognostics⑨, Eurydice, shortly after her marriage, while wandering with the nymphs, her companions, was seen by the shepherd Aristæus⑩, who was struck with her beauty and made advances to her. She fled, and in flying⑪ trod upon a snake in the grass, was bitten in the foot, and died. Orpheus sang his grief to all who breathed the upper air, both gods and men, and finding it all unavailing resolved to seek his wife in the regions of the

---

① Laertes：/leɪˈɜːtiːz/
② Orpheus：/ˈɔːfjuːs/
③ Calliope /kəˈlaɪəpi/：the Muse of epic poetry
④ strain：乐曲，旋律
⑤ entrance /ɪnˈtrɑːns/：使出神，使神魂颠倒
⑥ lay：歌曲，曲调
⑦ note：歌曲，旋律，曲调
⑧ Eurydice：/juəˈrɪdɪsi/
⑨ prognostic /prɒɡˈnɒstɪk/：预兆
⑩ Aristæus：/ˌærɪsˈtiːəs/
⑪ fly：逃跑

dead. He descended by a cave situated on the side of the promontory of Tænarus① and arrived at the Stygian realm②. He passed through crowds of ghosts and presented himself before the throne of Pluto and Proserpine. Accompanying the words with the lyre, he sung③, "O deities of the underworld, to whom all we who live must come, hear my words, for they are true. I come not to spy out the secrets of Tartarus④, nor to try my strength against the three-headed dog⑤ with snaky hair who guards the entrance. I come to seek my wife, whose opening years⑥ the poisonous viper's fang has brought to an untimely end. Love has led me here, Love, a god all powerful with us who dwell on the earth, and, if old traditions say true, not less so here. I implore you by these abodes full of terror, these realms of silence and uncreated things, unite again the thread of Eurydice's life⑦. We all are destined to you, and sooner or later must pass to your domain. She too, when she shall have filled her term of life, will rightly be yours. But till then grant her to me, I beseech you. If you deny me I cannot return alone; you shall triumph in the death of us both."

As he sang these tender strains, the very ghosts shed tears. Tantalus⑧, in spite of his thirst, stopped for a moment his efforts for water, Ixion's wheel stood still⑨, the vulture ceased to tear the giant's liver⑩, the daughters of Danaüs rested from their task of drawing water in a sieve⑪, and Sisyphus⑫ sat on his rock to listen. Then for the first time, it is said, the cheeks of the Furies were wet with tears. Proserpine could not resist, and Pluto himself gave way. Eurydice was called. She came from among the new-arrived ghosts, limping⑬ with her wounded foot. Orpheus was permitted to take her away with him on one condition, that he should not turn around to look at her till they should have reached the upper air. Under this condition they proceeded on their way, he leading, she following, through passages dark and steep, in total silence, till they had nearly reached the outlet into the cheerful upper world, when Orpheus, in a moment of forgetfulness, to

---

① Tænarus /tiːˈneərəs/：即今希腊大陆最南端的马塔潘角（Cape Matapan），位于伯罗奔尼撒大区拉科尼亚州；在马塔潘角最末端有一个洞，古希腊人认为该洞是通往阴间的入口。此处建有海神 Neptune（Poseidon）的神庙。

② the Stygian realm：阴间

③ sung 也是 sing 的过去式形式，但不常用。

④ spy out the secrets of Tartarus：刺探阴间的机密

⑤ the three-headed dog：即 Cerberus，参见 *The Age of Fable* 第 32 章。

⑥ opening years：青春年华

⑦ unite again the thread of Eurydice's life：把 Eurydice 的生命之线接上；参见 *The Age of Fable* 第 1 章关于 the Fates 的叙述。

⑧ Tantalus /ˈtæntələs/：Tantalus 是 Phrygia 国王，诸神的朋友；他与诸神关系密切，所以常与他们一起进餐。他向凡人泄露了诸神的秘密，所以他在阴间遭受严厉的惩罚。他站在水里，水就在他的下巴下面，但当他低头喝水时，水立刻流走。水果就挂在他头顶上的树枝上，但当他伸手想摘水果时，树枝立刻就被风吹开。他永远处于口渴的状态。

⑨ Ixion /ɪkˈsaɪən/：Ixion 试图勾引 Jupiter 的老婆 Juno，于是受到 Jupiter 的惩罚。在阴间，他被捆绑在一个燃烧的、不停转动的轮子上。

⑩ the giant：Tityus；参见 *The Age of Fable* 第 32 章关于巨人 Tityus 的叙述。

⑪ Danaüs /ˈdæneɪəs/：Danaüs 有 50 个女儿，他命令他的女儿们新婚之夜杀掉她们的新郎。其中 49 人杀死了她们的新郎，在阴间她们遭受惩罚，用筛子不停地打水。

⑫ Sisyphus /ˈsɪsɪfəs/：Sisyphus 是 Corinth 国王，也在阴间受惩罚。他总是把一块巨石从山脚推往山顶。当他把巨石推到山顶时，巨石立刻从山顶滚回山脚，他不得不下山再次把巨石推往山顶。这一惩罚永不停止，Sisyphus 永远都在往山顶推那块巨石。

⑬ limp：一瘸一拐地走

assure himself that she was still following, cast a glance behind him, when instantly she was borne away. Stretching out their arms to embrace each other, they grasped only the air! Dying now a second time, she yet cannot reproach her husband, for how can she blame his impatience to behold her? "Farewell," she said, "a last farewell,"—and was hurried away, so fast that the sound hardly reached his ears.

Orpheus endeavored to follow her, and besought permission to return and try once more for her release; but the stern ferryman① repulsed him and refused passage. Seven days he lingered about the brink, without food or sleep; then bitterly accusing of cruelty the powers of Erebus, he sang his complaints to the rocks and mountains, melting the hearts of tigers and moving the oaks from their stations. He held himself aloof② from womankind, dwelling constantly on the recollection③ of his sad mischance④. The Thracian maidens tried their best to captivate him, but he repulsed their advances. They bore with⑤ him as long as they could; but finding him insensible one day, excited by the rites of Bacchus, one of them exclaimed, "See yonder our despiser⑥!" and threw at him her javelin. The weapon, as soon as it came within the sound of his lyre, fell harmless at his feet. So did also the stones that they threw at him. But the women raised a scream and drowned the voice of the music, and then the missiles reached him and soon were stained with his blood. The maniacs⑦ tore him limb from limb, and threw his head and his lyre into the river Hebrus⑧, down which they floated, murmuring sad music, to which the shores responded a plaintive⑨ symphony. The Muses gathered up the fragments of his body and buried them at Libethra⑩, where the nightingale⑪ is said to sing over his grave more sweetly than in any other part of Greece. His lyre was placed by Jupiter among the stars⑫. His shade passed a second time to Tartarus, where he sought out his Eurydice and embraced her with eager arms. They roam the happy fields together now, sometimes he leading, sometimes she; and Orpheus gazes as much as he will upon her, no longer incurring⑬ a penalty for a thoughtless glance.

Aristæus, the Bee-Keeper

Man avails himself of the instincts of the inferior animals for his own advantage. Hence sprang

---

① the stern ferryman: 指 Charon; 参见 *The Age of Fable* 第 32 章。
② aloof: 远离
③ recollection /ˌrekəˈlekʃn/: 回忆
④ mischance /mɪsˈtʃɑːns/: 厄运, 灾难
⑤ bear with: 容忍, 对……有耐心
⑥ our despiser: 蔑视我们的人
⑦ maniac /ˈmeɪnɪæk/: 疯狂的人
⑧ Hebrus /ˈhiːbrəs/: 即今希腊最东北端希腊与土耳其之间的界河埃夫罗斯河 (Evros), 该河发源于保加利亚, 在保加利亚境内叫马里查河 (Maritsa), 在土耳其境内叫梅里奇河 (Meriç)。
⑨ plaintive /ˈpleɪntɪv/: 悲伤的, 忧伤的
⑩ Libethra /lɪˈbeθrə/: 希腊古城名, 位于奥林匹斯山山脚下。
⑪ nightingale /ˈnaɪtɪŋgeɪl/: 夜莺; 在筑巢和繁殖季节, 雄性夜莺昼夜鸣叫, 鸣叫声美妙动听。
⑫ 即天琴座 (Lyra /ˈlaɪərə/)。
⑬ incur /ɪnˈkɜː/: 招致

the art of keeping bees. Honey must first have been known as a wild product, the bees building their structures in hollow trees or holes in the rocks, or any similar cavity① that chance offered. Thus occasionally the carcass② of a dead animal would be occupied by the bees for that purpose. It was no doubt from some such incident that the superstition arose that the bees were engendered by the decaying flesh of the animal; and Virgil③, in the following story, shows how this supposed fact may be turned to account for renewing the swarm when it has been lost by disease or accident.

Aristæus, who first taught the management of bees, was the son of the water-nymph Cyrene④. His bees had perished, and he resorted for aid to his mother. He stood at the river side and thus addressed her: "O mother, the pride of my life⑤ is taken from me! I have lost my precious bees. My care and skill have availed me nothing, and you, my mother, have not warded off⑥ from me the blow of misfortune." His mother heard these complaints as she sat in her palace at the bottom of the river, with her attendant nymphs around her. They were engaged in female occupations, spinning and weaving, while one told stories to amuse the rest. The sad voice of Aristæus interrupting their occupation, one of them put her head above the water and seeing him, returned and gave information to his mother, who ordered that he should be brought into her presence. The river at her command opened itself and let him pass in, while it stood curled like a mountain on either side. He descended to the region where the fountains of the great rivers lie; he saw the enormous receptacles⑦ of waters and was almost deafened with the roar, while he surveyed them hurrying off in various directions to water the face of the earth. Arriving at his mother's apartment, he was hospitably received by Cyrene and her nymphs, who spread their table with the richest dainties. They first poured out libations to Neptune, then regaled⑧ themselves with the feast, and after that Cyrene thus addressed him: "There is an old prophet named Proteus⑨, who dwells in the sea and is a favorite of Neptune, whose herd of sea-calves⑩ he pastures. We nymphs hold him in great respect, for he is a learned sage and knows all things, past, present, and to come⑪. He can tell you, my son, the cause of the mortality⑫ among your bees, and how you may remedy it. But he will not do it voluntarily, however you may entreat him. You must compel him by force. If you seize him and chain him, he will answer your questions in order to get released, for he cannot by all his arts get away if you hold fast the chains. I will carry you to his cave, where he comes at noon to take his midday repose. Then you may easily secure him. But when he finds himself

①　cavity /ˈkævɪti/：洞

②　carcass /ˈkɑːkəs/：动物的尸体

③　Virgil /ˈvɜːdʒɪl/：古罗马诗人，代表作是史诗 *The Aeneid*。

④　Cyrene：/saɪˈriːni/

⑤　the pride of my life：my bees

⑥　ward off：挡开，避开

⑦　receptacle /rɪˈseptəkl/：容器，贮藏器，贮藏处

⑧　regale /rɪˈɡeɪl/：（用美味佳肴）款待

⑨　Proteus：参见 *The Age of Fable* 第 22 章。

⑩　sea-calf：斑海豹

⑪　to come：未来的

⑫　mortality /mɔːˈtælɪti/：大规模的死亡

captured, his resort is to a power he possesses of changing himself into various forms. He will become a wild boar or a fierce tiger, a scaly① dragon or lion with yellow mane. Or he will make a noise like the crackling of flames or the rush of water, so as to tempt you to let go the chain, when he will make his escape. But you have only to keep him fast bound, and at last when he finds all his arts unavailing, he will return to his own figure and obey your commands." So saying she sprinkled her son with fragrant nectar, the beverage of the gods, and immediately an unusual vigor filled his frame, and courage his heart, while perfume breathed all around him.

The nymph led her son to the prophet's cave and concealed him among the recesses of the rocks, while she herself took her place behind the clouds. When noon came and the hour when men and herds retreat from the glaring sun to indulge in quiet slumber, Proteus issued② from the water, followed by his herd of sea-calves which spread themselves along the shore. He sat on the rock and counted his herd; then stretched himself on the floor of the cave and went to sleep. Aristæus hardly allowed him to get fairly asleep before he fixed the fetters on him and shouted aloud. Proteus, waking and finding himself captured, immediately resorted to his arts, becoming first a fire, then a flood, then a horrible wild beast, in rapid succession. But finding all would not do, he at last resumed his own form and addressed the youth in angry accents: "Who are you, bold youth, who thus invade my abode, and what do you want of me?" Aristæus replied, "Proteus, you know already, for it is needless for any one to attempt to deceive you. And do you also cease your efforts to elude me. I am led hither by divine assistance, to know from you the cause of my misfortune and how to remedy it." At these words the prophet, fixing on him his gray eyes with a piercing look, thus spoke: "You receive the merited reward of your deeds, by which Eurydice met her death, for in flying from you she trod upon a serpent, of whose bite she died. To avenge her death, the nymphs, her companions, have sent this destruction to your bees. You have to appease their anger, and thus it must be done: Select four bulls, of perfect form and size, and four cows of equal beauty, build four altars to the nymphs, and sacrifice the animals, leaving their carcasses in the leafy grove. To Orpheus and Eurydice you shall pay such funeral honors as may allay their resentment. Returning after nine days, you will examine the bodies of the cattle slain and see what will befall③." Aristæus faithfully obeyed these directions. He sacrificed the cattle, he left their bodies in the grove, he offered funeral honors to the shades of Orpheus and Eurydice; then returning on the ninth day he examined the bodies of the animals, and, wonderful to relate! a swarm of bees had taken possession of one of the carcasses and were pursuing their labors there as in a hive④.

The following are other celebrated mythical poets and musicians, some of whom were hardly inferior to Orpheus himself:

---

① scaly /ˈskeɪli/: 长鳞片的

② issue /ˈɪʃuː/: 出来

③ befall /bɪˈfɔːl/: happen

④ hive: 蜂房

Amphion

Amphion was the son of Jupiter and Antiope①, queen of Thebes. With his twin brother Zethus② he was exposed at birth on Mount Cithæron③, where they grew up among the shepherds, not knowing their parentage. Mercury gave Amphion a lyre and taught him to play upon it, and his brother occupied himself in hunting and tending the flocks. Meanwhile Antiope, their mother, who had been treated with great cruelty by Lycus④, the usurping king of Thebes, and by Dirce⑤, his wife, found means to inform her children of their rights and to summon them to her assistance. With a band of their fellow-herdsmen they attacked and slew Lycus, and tying Dirce by the hair of her head to a bull, let him⑥ drag her till she was dead. Amphion, having become king of Thebes, fortified the city with a wall. It is said that when he played on his lyre the stones moved of their own accord and took their places in the wall.

Linus

Linus⑦ was the instructor of Hercules in music, but having one day reproved⑧ his pupil rather harshly, he roused the anger of Hercules, who struck him with his lyre and killed him.

Thamyris

An ancient Thracian bard, who in his presumption challenged the Muses to a trial of skill, and being overcome⑨ in the contest, was deprived by them of his sight.⑩

Marsyas

Minerva invented the flute, and played upon it to the delight of all the celestial auditors⑪; but the mischievous urchin⑫ Cupid having dared to laugh at the queer face which the goddess made while playing, Minerva threw the instrument indignantly away, and it fell down to earth, and was found by Marsyas⑬. He blew upon it, and drew from it such ravishing sounds that he was

---

① Antiope：/ænˈtaɪəpiː/

② Zethus：/ˈzeθəs/

③ Cithæron /sɪˈθiːrɒn/：也可拼写为 Citheron，希腊山脉名，位于维奥蒂亚（Boeotia 或 Voiotia）和阿提卡（Attica）之间；该山脉在希腊神话中是非常著名的，Actæon 被变为鹿的故事（参见 *The Age of Fable* 第 4 章）以及 Pentheus 被两位小姨撕成碎片的故事（参见 *The Age of Fable* 第 21 章）都发生在这里；Œdipus 出生时也是被抛弃在这里（参见 *The Age of Fable* 第 16 章）。

④ Lycus /ˈlaɪkəs/

⑤ Dirce：/ˈdɜːsi/

⑥ him：the bull

⑦ Linus：/ˈlaɪnəs/

⑧ reprove /rɪˈpruːv/：责备

⑨ overcome /ˌəʊvəˈkʌm/：击败，打败

⑩ Thamyris：/ˈθæmərɪs/

⑪ auditor /ˈɔːdɪtə/：听者

⑫ urchin /ˈɜːtʃɪn/：调皮的孩子，淘气的孩子

⑬ Marsyas：/ˈmɑːsaɪəs/

tempted to challenge Apollo himself to a musical contest. The god of course triumphed, and punished Marsyas by flaying[①] him alive.

Melampus

Melampus[②] was the first mortal endowed with prophetic powers. Before his house there stood an oak tree containing a serpent's nest. The old serpents were killed by the servants, but Melampus took care of the young ones and fed them carefully. One day when he was asleep under the oak the serpents licked his ears with their tongues. On awaking he was astonished to find that he now understood the language of birds and creeping things[③]. This knowledge enabled him to foretell future events, and he became a renowned soothsayer. At one time his enemies took him captive and kept him strictly imprisoned. Melampus in the silence of the night heard the woodworms[④] in the timbers talking together, and found out by what they said that the timbers were nearly eaten through and the roof would soon fall in. He told his captors and demanded to be let out, warning them also. They took his warning, and thus escaped destruction, and rewarded Melampus and held him in high honor.

Musæus

A semi-mythological[⑤] personage who was represented by one tradition to be the son of Orpheus. He is said to have written sacred poems and oracles.[⑥]

Chapter XXV
Arion—Ibycus—Simonides—Sappho

The poets whose adventures compose this chapter were real persons some of whose works yet remain, and their influence on poets who succeeded them is yet more important than their poetical remains.

Arion

Arion[⑦] was a famous musician, and dwelt in the court of Periander[⑧], king of Corinth, with whom he was a great favorite. There was to be a musical contest in Sicily[⑨], and Arion longed to

---

① flay：剥皮
② Melampus：/mɪˈlæmpəs/
③ creeping things：爬行动物
④ woodworm /ˈwudwɜːm/：木蛀虫
⑤ semi-mythological：半神化的
⑥ Musæus：/mjuˈsiːəs/
⑦ Arion：/əˈraɪən/
⑧ Periander：/ˌperɪˈændə/
⑨ 西西里岛位于希腊以西的地中海上,两者之间是伊奥尼亚海（the Ionian Sea）。

compete for the prize. He told his wish to Periander, who besought① him like a brother to give up the thought. "Pray stay with me," he said, "and be contented. He who strives to win may lose." Arion answered, "A wandering life best suits the free heart of a poet. The talent which a god bestowed on me, I would fain② make a source of pleasure to others. And if I win the prize, how will the enjoyment of it be increased by the consciousness of my widespread fame!" He went, won the prize, and embarked with his wealth in a Corinthian ship for home. On the second morning after setting sail, the wind breathed mild and fair. "O Periander," he exclaimed, "dismiss your fears! Soon shall you forget them in my embrace. With what lavish offerings will we display our gratitude to the gods, and how merry will we be at the festal board!" The wind and sea continued propitious. Not a cloud dimmed the firmament③. He had not trusted too much to the ocean—but he had to man. He overheard the seamen exchanging hints with one another, and found they were plotting to possess themselves of his treasure. Presently they surrounded him loud and mutinous④, and said, "Arion, you must die! If you would have a grave on shore, yield yourself to die on this spot; but if otherwise, cast yourself into the sea." "Will nothing satisfy you but my life?" said he. "Take my gold, and welcome, I willingly buy my life at that price." "No, no; we cannot spare you. Your life would be too dangerous to us. Where could we go to escape from Periander, if he should know that you had been robbed by us? Your gold would be of little use to us, if on returning home, we could never more be free from fear." "Grant me, then," said he, "a last request, since nought⑤ will avail to save my life, that I may die, as I have lived, as becomes a bard. When I shall have sung my death song, and my harp-strings shall have ceased to vibrate, then I will bid farewell to life, and yield uncomplaining to my fate." This prayer, like the others, would have been unheeded,—they thought only of their booty,—but to hear so famous a musician, that moved their rude hearts. "Suffer⑥ me," he added, "to arrange my dress. Apollo will not favor me unless I be clad in my minstrel⑦ garb⑧."

He clothed his well-proportioned⑨ limbs in gold and purple fair to see⑩, his tunic fell around him in graceful folds, jewels adorned his arms, his brow was crowned with a golden wreath, and over his neck and shoulders flowed his hair perfumed with odors. His left hand held the lyre, his right the ivory wand with which he struck its chords. Like one inspired, he seemed to drink the morning air and glitter in the morning ray. The seamen gazed with admiration. He strode forward to the vessel's side and looked down into the deep blue sea. Addressing his lyre, he sang, "Companion of my voice, come with me to the realm of shades⑪. Though Cerberus may growl, we

---

① beseech /bɪˈsiːtʃ/：恳求；besought 是 beseech 的过去式和过去分词形式。

② fain：（用在 would 之后）高兴地，乐意地

③ firmament /ˈfɜːməmənt/：天空，苍穹

④ mutinous /ˈmjuːtɪnəs/：图谋不轨的

⑤ nought /nɔːt/：nothing

⑥ suffer：允许

⑦ minstrel /ˈmɪnstrəl/：音乐家，歌手，诗人

⑧ garb：服装

⑨ well-proportioned /prəˈpɔːʃənd/：匀称的

⑩ fair to see：看上去漂亮的，悦目的；fair to see 是定语，修饰前面的 gold and purple。

⑪ the realm of shades：阴间

know the power of song can tame his rage. Ye heroes of Elysium, who have passed the darkling flood①,—ye happy souls, soon shall I join your band. Yet can ye relieve my grief? Alas, I leave my friend behind me. Thou, who didst find thy Eurydice, and lose her again as soon as found②; when she had vanished like a dream, how didst thou hate the cheerful light! I must away, but I will not fear. The gods look down upon us. Ye who slay me unoffending, when I am no more, your time of trembling shall come. Ye Nereids, receive your guest, who throws himself upon your mercy!" So saying, he sprang into the deep sea. The waves covered him, and the seamen held on their way, fancying themselves safe from all danger of detection.

But the strains of his music had drawn round him the inhabitants of the deep③ to listen, and Dolphins followed the ship as if chained by a spell④. While he struggled in the waves, a Dolphin offered him his back⑤, and carried him mounted thereon safe to shore. At the spot where he landed, a monument of brass was afterwards erected upon the rocky shore, to preserve the memory of the event.

When Arion and the dolphin parted, each to his own element⑥, Arion thus poured forth his thanks: "Farewell, thou faithful, friendly fish! Would that I could reward thee; but thou canst not wend⑦ with me, nor I with thee. Companionship we may not have. May Galatea, queen of the deep, accord thee her favor, and thou, proud of the burden, draw her chariot over the smooth mirror of the deep."

Arion hastened from the shore, and soon saw before him the towers of Corinth. He journeyed on, harp in hand, singing as he went, full of love and happiness, forgetting his losses, and mindful only of what remained, his friend and his lyre. He entered the hospitable halls, and was soon clasped in the embrace of Periander. "I come back to thee, my friend," he said. "The talent which a god bestowed has been the delight of thousands, but false knaves have stripped me of my well-earned treasure; yet I retain the consciousness of wide spread fame." Then he told Periander all the wonderful events that had befallen him, who heard him with amazement. "Shall such wickedness triumph?" said he. "Then in vain is power lodged in my hands. That we may discover the criminals, you must remain here in concealment, and so they will approach without suspicion." When the ship arrived in the harbor, he summoned the mariners before him. "Have you heard anything of Arion?" he inquired. "I anxiously look for his return." They replied, "We left him well and prosperous in Tarentum⑧." As they said these words, Arion stepped forth and faced them. His well-proportioned limbs were arrayed in gold and purple fair to see, his tunic fell around him in graceful folds, jewels adorned his arms, his brow was crowned with a golden

---

① the darkling flood: 阴间的河流 the Cocytus; flood: 河流，溪流

② 参见 The Age of Fable 第 24 章。

③ the deep: 大海

④ spell: 咒语

⑤ his back: its back

⑥ each to his own element: Arion 回到陆地，海豚游回大海。参见 The Age of Fable 第 22 章关于 element 的注解。

⑦ wend /wend/: 走

⑧ Tarentum /təˈrentəm/: 即今意大利南部港口城市塔兰托（Taranto），属于普利亚区（Puglia）。公元前 8 世纪到公元前 6 世纪期间，希腊人在意大利南部沿海建立了一些城市（殖民地），这些城市被统称为"大希腊"（Magna Graecia）。公元前 6 世纪后，由于内部不和及本地人的攻打，"大希腊"渐渐衰落。Tarentum 是"大希腊"非常富裕的一座城市，当时以生产紫色染料而著称。

wreath, and over his neck and shoulders flowed his hair perfumed with odors; his left hand held the lyre, his right the ivory wand with which he struck its chords. They fell prostrate at his feet, as if a lightning bolt had struck them. "We meant to murder him, and he has become a god. O Earth, open and receive us!" Then Periander spoke. "He lives, the master of the lay①! Kind Heaven protects the poet's life. As for you, I invoke not the spirit of vengeance; Arion wishes not your blood. Ye slaves of avarice②, begone! Seek some barbarous land, and never may aught③ beautiful delight your souls!"

Ibycus

In order to understand the story of Ibycus④ which follows it is necessary to remember, first, that the theatres of the ancients were immense fabrics⑤ capable of containing from ten to thirty thousand spectators, and as they were used only on festival occasions, and admission was free to all, they were usually filled. They were without roofs and open to the sky, and the performances were in the daytime. Secondly, the appalling⑥ representation of the Furies⑦ is not exaggerated in the story. It is recorded that Æschylus⑧, the tragic poet, having on one occasion represented the Furies in a chorus⑨ of fifty performers, the terror of the spectators was such that many fainted and were thrown into convulsions⑩, and the magistrates⑪ forbade a like⑫ representation for the future.

Ibycus, the pious poet, was on his way to the chariot races and musical competitions held at the Isthmus of Corinth⑬, which attracted all of Grecian lineage⑭. Apollo had bestowed on him the gift of song, the honeyed lips of the poet, and he pursued his way with lightsome⑮ step, full of the god. Already the towers of Corinth crowning the height appeared in view, and he had entered with pious awe the sacred grove of Neptune. No living object was in sight, only a flock of cranes flew overhead taking the same course as himself in their migration⑯ to a southern clime⑰. "Good luck

---

① lay：歌曲,旋律
② avarice /ˈævərɪs/：贪婪
③ aught /ɔːt/：anything
④ Ibycus：/ˈɪbɪkəs/
⑤ fabric /ˈfæbrɪk/：建筑物
⑥ appalling /əˈpɔːlɪŋ/：可怕的,恐怖的
⑦ the Furies：参见 *The Age of Fable* 第 1 章关于 the Furies 的叙述。
⑧ Æschylus /ˈiːskɪləs/：古希腊悲剧诗人,著有 *Prometheus Bound* 等悲剧作品。
⑨ chorus /ˈkɔːrəs/：合唱队是古希腊悲剧的组成部分,最初由 50 位演员组成,后来减到 12 位,后来又增加到 15 位。在古希腊悲剧的表演中,演员戴着面具表演,合唱队的成员戴相同的面具。
⑩ convulsion /kənˈvʌlʃn/：抽风,惊厥
⑪ magistrate /ˈmædʒɪstrət/：行政官
⑫ like：类似的
⑬ Ibycus 前往参加的是科林斯地峡运动会（the Isthmian Games）,在该运动会上,除了有体育竞技外,还有诗歌和音乐比赛。马车比赛（chariot races）也是其中的一个项目。Ibycus 是一位来自"大希腊"Rhegium /ˈriːdʒɪəm/ 的诗人。Rhegium 即今意大利南部城市雷焦卡拉布里亚（Reggio di Calabria）,属于意大利卡拉布里亚区（Calabria）,与西西里（Sicily）城市 Messina 隔狭窄的梅西纳海峡（the Strait of Messina）相望。
⑭ lineage /ˈlɪniɪdʒ/：血统
⑮ lightsome /ˈlaɪtsəm/：轻快的
⑯ migration /maɪˈɡreɪʃn/：（候鸟的）迁徙
⑰ clime：（按气候划分的）地区

to you, ye friendly squadrons," he exclaimed, "my companions from across the sea. I take your company for a good omen. We come from far and fly in search of hospitality. May both of us meet that kind reception which shields the stranger guest from harm!"

He paced briskly on, and soon was in the middle of the wood. There suddenly, at a narrow pass, two robbers stepped forth and barred his way. He must yield or fight. But his hand, accustomed to the lyre, and not to the strife of arms, sank powerless. He called for help on men and gods, but his cry reached no defender's ear. "Then here must I die," said he, "in a strange land, unlamented, cut off by the hand of outlaws, and see none to avenge my cause." Sore wounded, he sank to the earth, when hoarse① screamed the cranes overhead. "Take up my cause, ye cranes," he said, "since no voice but yours answers to my cry." So saying he closed his eyes in death.

The body, despoiled and mangled, was found, and though disfigured② with wounds, was recognized by the friend in Corinth who had expected him as a guest. "Is it thus I find you restored to me?" he exclaimed. "I who hoped to entwine your temples③ with the wreath of triumph in the strife④ of song!"

The guests assembled at the festival heard the tidings⑤ with dismay. All Greece felt the wound, every heart owned its loss. They crowded round the tribunal⑥ of the magistrates, and demanded vengeance on the murderers and expiation⑦ with their blood.

But what trace or mark shall point out the perpetrator⑧ from amidst the vast multitude attracted by the splendor of the feast? Did he fall by the hands of robbers or did some private enemy slay him? The all-discerning⑨ sun alone can tell, for no other eye beheld it. Yet not improbably the murderer even now walks in the midst of the throng, and enjoys the fruits of his crime, while vengeance seeks for him in vain. Perhaps in their own temple's enclosure he defies the gods, mingling freely in this throng of men that now presses into the amphitheatre⑩.

For now crowded together, row on row, the multitude fill the seats till it seems as if the very fabric would give way⑪. The murmur of voices sounds like the roar of the sea, while the circles widening in their ascent rise tier on tier, as if they would reach the sky.

And now the vast assemblage listens to the awful voice of the chorus personating⑫ the Furies, which in solemn guise advances with measured step, and moves around the circuit of the theatre. Can they be mortal women who compose that awful group, and can that vast concourse⑬ of silent

---

① hoarse：hoarsely

② disfigure /dɪsˈfɪɡə/：毁坏……的外形

③ temple：太阳穴

④ strife：比赛

⑤ tidings /ˈtaɪdɪŋz/：news

⑥ tribunal /traɪˈbjuːnl/：行政官的坐席

⑦ expiation /ˌekspɪˈeɪʃn/：赎罪，抵罪

⑧ perpetrator /ˈpɜːpɪtreɪtə/：犯罪的人

⑨ all-discerning /dɪˈsɜːnɪŋ/：洞察一切的

⑩ amphitheatre /ˈæmfɪθɪətə/：古希腊、罗马的椭圆形或圆形露天竞技场

⑪ give way：垮塌

⑫ personate /ˈpɜːsəneɪt/：扮演

⑬ concourse /ˈkɒŋkɔːs/：人群

forms be living beings?

The choristers①, clad in black, bore in their fleshless hands torches blazing with a pitchy flame. Their cheeks were bloodless, and in place of hair writhing and swelling serpents curled around their brows. Forming a circle, these awful beings sang their hymns, rending the hearts of the guilty, and enchaining all their faculties. It rose and swelled, overpowering the sound of the instruments, stealing the judgment, palsying the heart, curdling the blood.

"Happy the man who keeps his heart pure from guilt and crime! Him we avengers touch not; he treads the path of life secure from us. But woe! woe! to him who has done the deed of secret murder. We the fearful family of Night fasten ourselves upon his whole being. Thinks he by flight to escape us? We fly still faster in pursuit, twine our snakes around his feet, and bring him to the ground. Unwearied we pursue; no pity checks our course; still on and on, to the end of life, we give him no peace nor rest." Thus the Eumenides② sang, and moved in solemn cadence③, while stillness like the stillness of death sat over the whole assembly as if in the presence of superhuman beings; and then in solemn march completing the circuit of the theatre, they passed out at the back of the stage.

Every heart fluttered between illusion and reality, and every breast panted with undefined terror, quailing④ before the awful power that watches secret crimes and winds⑤ unseen the skein⑥ of destiny. At that moment a cry burst forth from one of the uppermost benches—"Look! look! comrade, yonder are the cranes of Ibycus!" And suddenly there appeared sailing across the sky a dark object which a moment's inspection showed to be a flock of cranes flying directly over the theatre. "Of Ibycus! did he say?" The beloved name revived the sorrow in every breast. As wave follows wave over the face of the sea, so ran from mouth to mouth the words, "Of Ibycus! him whom we all lament, whom some murderer's hand laid low! What have the cranes to do with him?" And louder grew the swell of voices, while like a lightning's flash the thought sped through every heart, "Observe the power of the Eumenides! The pious poet shall be avenged! the murderer has informed against himself. Seize the man who uttered that cry and the other to whom he spoke!"

The culprit⑦ would gladly have recalled⑧ his words, but it was too late. The faces of the murderers, pale with terror, betrayed their guilt. The people took them before the judge, they confessed their crime, and suffered the punishment they deserved.

---

① chorister /ˈkɒrɪstə/：合唱队成员

② the Eumenides /juːˈmenɪdiːz/：the Furies

③ cadence /ˈkeɪdəns/：节奏；在古希腊的悲剧中，合唱队（the chorus）描述剧中的情节并加以评论，同时伴以歌唱、舞蹈和朗诵。

④ quail /kweɪl/：畏缩

⑤ wind /waɪnd/：绕（线团等）

⑥ skein /skeɪn/：一绞线

⑦ culprit /ˈkʌlprɪt/：罪犯

⑧ recall：收回

Simonides

Simonides① was one of the most prolific② of the early poets of Greece, but only a few fragments of his compositions have descended to us. He wrote hymns③, triumphal odes④, and elegies⑤. In the last species of composition he particularly excelled⑥. His genius was inclined to the pathetic, and none could touch with truer effect the chords of human sympathy. The "Lamentation of Danaë⑦," the most important of the fragments which remain of his poetry, is based upon the tradition that Danaë and her infant son were confined by order of her father, Acrisius, in a chest and set adrift on the sea. The chest floated towards the island of Seriphus, where both were rescued by Dictys, a fisherman, and carried to Polydectes, king of the country, who received and protected them. The child, Perseus, when grown up became a famous hero, whose adventures have been recorded in a previous chapter.

Simonides passed much of his life at the courts of princes, and often employed his talents in panegyric⑧ and festal⑨ odes⑩, receiving his reward from the munificence⑪ of those whose exploits⑫ he celebrated. This employment was not derogatory⑬, but closely resembles that of the earliest bards⑭, such as Demodocus⑮, described by Homer, or of Homer himself, as recorded by tradition.

On one occasion, when residing at the court of Scopas⑯, king of Thessaly, the prince desired him to prepare a poem in celebration of his exploits, to be recited at a banquet. In order to diversify his theme, Simonides, who was celebrated for his piety, introduced into his poem the exploits of Castor and Pollux⑰. Such digressions⑱ were not unusual with the poets on similar occasions, and one might suppose an ordinary mortal might have been content to share the praises of the sons of Leda⑲. But vanity is exacting⑳; and as Scopas sat at his festal board among his

---

① Simonides /saɪˈmɒnɪdiːz/：希腊诗人，出生在凯阿岛（Cea 或 Kea）。凯阿岛是基克拉泽斯群岛中离阿提卡最近的一个大岛，属于今希腊南爱琴大区基克拉泽斯州。

② prolific /prəˈlɪfɪk/：多产的，作品多的

③ hymn：赞美神的歌曲

④ triumphal ode：凯旋颂歌，用来赞颂凯旋的运动会获胜者

⑤ elegy /ˈelədʒi/：哀悼死者的歌曲

⑥ excel /ɪkˈsel/：（在某方面）突出，杰出

⑦ 参见 *The Age of Fable* 第 15 章。

⑧ panegyric /ˌpænɪˈdʒɪrɪk/：颂扬的

⑨ festal /ˈfestl/：节日的

⑩ ode：颂歌

⑪ munificence /mjuːˈnɪfɪsəns/：慷慨，大方

⑫ exploit：丰功伟绩

⑬ 这个职业没有什么不光彩的。derogatory /dɪˈrɒɡətəri/：不光彩的，有辱人格的

⑭ bard：吟游诗人

⑮ Demodocus /dɪˈmɒdəkəs/：Demodocus 出现在 *The Odyssey* 第 8 卷，在 Alcinous 的宫廷宴会上唱歌。参见 *The Age of Fable* 第 30 章及 *The Odyssey* 中的"The Love of Mars and Venus"选段。

⑯ Scopas：/ˈskəʊpəs/

⑰ 参见 *The Age of Fable* 第 20 章。

⑱ digression /daɪˈɡreʃn/：离题

⑲ the sons of Leda：Castor and Pollux

⑳ exacting /ɪɡˈzæktɪŋ/：难满足的

courtiers and sycophants①, he grudged② every verse that did not rehearse his own praises. When Simonides approached to receive the promised reward Scopas bestowed but half the expected sum, saying, "Here is payment for my portion of thy performance; Castor and Pollux will doubtless compensate thee for so much as relates to them." The disconcerted③ poet returned to his seat amidst the laughter which followed the great man's jest. In a little time he received a message that two young men on horseback were waiting without④ and anxious to see him. Simonides hastened to the door, but looked in vain for the visitors. Scarcely, however, had he left the banqueting hall when the roof fell in with a loud crash, burying Scopas and all his guests beneath the ruins. On inquiring as to the appearance of the young men who had sent for him, Simonides was satisfied that they were no other than Castor and Pollux themselves.

Sappho

Sappho⑤ was a poetess who flourished⑥ in a very early age of Greek literature. Of her works few fragments remain, but they are enough to establish her claim to eminent poetical genius. The story of Sappho commonly alluded to⑦ is that she was passionately in love with a beautiful youth named Phaon⑧, and failing to obtain a return of affection she threw herself from the promontory of Leucadia⑨ into the sea, under a superstition that those who should take that "Lover's-leap" would, if not destroyed⑩, be cured of their love.

Chapter ⅩⅩⅥ
Endymion—Orion—Aurora and Tithonus—Acis and Galatea

Endymion

Endymion⑪ was a beautiful youth who fed his flock on Mount Latmos⑫. One calm, clear night Diana, the moon, looked down and saw him sleeping. The cold heart of the virgin goddess was

---

① sycophant /ˈsɪkəfənt/：吹牛拍马之人

② grudge /ɡrʌdʒ/：怨恨

③ disconcerted /ˌdɪskənˈsɜːtɪd/：窘迫的

④ without：在外面

⑤ Sappho /ˈsæfəʊ/：希腊女诗人，出生在莱斯沃斯岛（Lesbos /ˈlezbɒs /或 Lesvos）。莱斯沃斯岛属于今希腊北爱琴大区，离土耳其海岸很近。

⑥ flourish /ˈflʌrɪʃ/：（作家等）处于名声的顶峰

⑦ allude to：提到

⑧ Phaon /ˈfeɪɒn/：Phaon 是传说中的船夫，他让化装成老妇人的 Venus 免费坐船，所以 Venus 赐予他青春和美貌。

⑨ Leucadia /ljuˈkeɪdɪə/：即 Lefkada /lefˈkædə /或 Lefkas /ˈlefkəs/，希腊大陆以西伊奥尼亚海（Ionian Sea）中的一个岛屿，属于今希腊伊奥尼亚群岛大区莱夫卡扎州，与希腊大陆之间只有一条非常狭窄的海峡。

⑩ destroyed：killed

⑪ Endymion：/enˈdɪmɪən/

⑫ Latmos /ˈlætməs/：山名，位于今土耳其西部，在土耳其叫 Beşparmak Mountains。

warmed by his surpassing① beauty, and she came down to him, kissed him, and watched over him while he slept.

Another story was that Jupiter bestowed on him the gift of perpetual youth united with perpetual sleep. Of one so gifted we can have but few adventures to record. Diana, it was said, took care that his fortunes should not suffer by his inactive life, for she made his flock increase, and guarded his sheep and lambs from the wild beasts.

Orion

Orion② was the son of Neptune. He was a handsome giant and a mighty hunter. His father gave him the power of wading through the depths of the sea, or, as others say, of walking on its surface.

Orion loved Merope③, the daughter of Œnopion④, king of Chios⑤, and sought her in marriage. He cleared the island of wild beasts, and brought the spoils of the chase as presents to his beloved; but as Œnopion constantly deferred⑥ his consent, Orion attempted to gain possession of the maiden by violence. Her father, incensed at this conduct, having made Orion drunk, deprived him of his sight and cast him out on the seashore. The blinded hero followed the sound of a Cyclops' hammer till he reached Lemnos, and came to the forge of Vulcan, who, taking pity on him, gave him Kedalion⑦, one of his men, to be his guide to the abode of the sun. Placing Kedalion on his shoulders, Orion proceeded to the east, and there meeting the sun-god, was restored to sight by his beam.

After this he dwelt as a hunter with Diana, with whom he was a favorite, and it is even said she was about to marry him. Her brother⑧ was highly displeased and often chid her, but to no purpose⑨. One day, observing Orion wading through the sea with his head just above the water, Apollo pointed it out to his sister and maintained⑩ that she could not hit that black thing on the sea. The archer-goddess⑪ discharged a shaft with fatal aim. The waves rolled the dead body of Orion to the land, and bewailing her fatal error with many tears, Diana placed him among the stars, where he appears as a giant, with a girdle, sword, lion's skin, and club.⑫ Sirius⑬, his dog, follows him, and the Pleiads⑭ fly before him.

---

① surpassing /sə'pɑːsɪŋ/: 无与伦比的

② Orion: /ə'raɪən/

③ Merope: /'merəpi/

④ Œnopion: /iː'nəʊpɪən/

⑤ Chios /'kaɪɒs/: 希腊岛屿名,位于爱琴海,距离土耳其西海岸非常近,属于今希腊北爱琴大区希俄斯州。

⑥ defer /dɪ'fɜː/: 推迟

⑦ Kedalion: /kə'deɪlɪən/

⑧ Her brother: Apollo

⑨ to no purpose: 没有任何效果

⑩ maintain: 断言

⑪ The archer-goddess: Diana

⑫ 即猎户星座（Orion）。

⑬ Sirius /'sɪrɪəs/: 即天狼星。

⑭ Pleiads /'plaɪədz/: 昴星团

The Pleiads were daughters of Atlas, and nymphs of Diana's train①. One day Orion saw them and became enamoured and pursued them. In their distress they prayed to the gods to change their form, and Jupiter in pity turned them into pigeons, and then made them a constellation in the sky. Though their number was seven, only six stars are visible, for Electra②, one of them, it is said left her place that she might not behold the ruin of Troy, for that city was founded by her son Dardanus③. The sight had such an effect on her sisters that they have looked pale ever since.

Aurora and Tithonus

The goddess of the Dawn④, like her sister the Moon⑤, was at times inspired with the love of mortals. Her greatest favorite was Tithonus⑥, son of Laomedon⑦, king of Troy. She stole him away, and prevailed on Jupiter to grant him immortality; but, forgetting to have youth joined in the gift, after some time she began to discern, to her great mortification⑧, that he was growing old. When his hair was quite white she left his society; but he still had the range⑨ of her palace, lived on ambrosial food, and was clad in celestial raiment. At length he lost the power of using his limbs, and then she shut him up in his chamber, whence his feeble voice might at times be heard. Finally she turned him into a grasshopper⑩.

Memnon⑪ was the son of Aurora and Tithonus. He was king of the Æthiopians, and dwelt in the extreme east, on the shore of Ocean. He came with his warriors to assist the kindred of his father in the war of Troy. King Priam received him with great honors, and listened with admiration to his narrative of the wonders of the ocean shore.

The very day after his arrival, Memnon, impatient of repose, led his troops to the field. Antilochus⑫, the brave son of Nestor, fell by his hand, and the Greeks were put to flight, when Achilles appeared and restored the battle. A long and doubtful contest ensued between him and the son of Aurora; at length victory declared for Achilles, Memnon fell, and the Trojans fled in dismay.

Aurora, who from her station in the sky had viewed with apprehension⑬ the danger of her son, when she saw him fall, directed his brothers, the Winds, to convey his body to the banks of the river Esepus in Paphlagonia⑭. In the evening Aurora came, accompanied by the Hours and the

---

① train：随行人员，随从
② Electra：/ɪˈlektrə/
③ Dardanus /ˈdɑːdənəs/：son of Zeus and Electra and builder of Troy
④ The goddess of the Dawn：Aurora /ɔːˈrɔːrə/
⑤ the Moon：Diana
⑥ Tithonus /tɪˈθəʊnəs/：参见 The Homeric Hymns 中的"To Aphrodite"选段。
⑦ Laomedon：/leɪˈɒmɪdən/
⑧ mortification /ˌmɔːtɪfɪˈkeɪʃn/：极度的失望，极大的烦恼
⑨ range：走动，行走
⑩ grasshopper /ˈɡrɑːshɒpə/：蚱蜢
⑪ Memnon：/ˈmemnɒn/
⑫ Antilochus：/ənˈtɪləkəs/
⑬ apprehension /ˌæprɪˈhenʃn/：不安，焦虑
⑭ Paphlagonia /ˌpæfləˈɡəʊnɪə/：古代地区名，位于小亚细亚，北临黑海。

Pleiads, and wept and lamented over her son. Night, in sympathy with her grief, spread the heaven with clouds; all nature mourned for the offspring of the Dawn. The Æthiopians raised his tomb on the banks of the stream in the grove of the Nymphs, and Jupiter caused the sparks and cinders of his funeral pile to be turned into birds, which, dividing into two flocks, fought over the pile till they fell into the flame. Every year at the anniversary of his death they return and celebrate his obsequies in like manner. Aurora remains inconsolable for the loss of her son. Her tears still flow, and may be seen at early morning in the form of dew-drops on the grass.

Acis and Galatea

Scylla was a fair virgin of Sicily, a favorite of the Sea-Nymphs. She had many suitors, but repelled[①] them all, and would go to the grotto of Galatea[②], and tell her how she was persecuted. One day the goddess, while Scylla dressed her hair, listened to the story, and then replied, "Yet, maiden, your persecutors are of the not ungentle race of men, whom, if you will, you can repel; but I, the daughter of Nereus[③], and protected by such a band of sisters[④], found no escape from the passion of the Cyclops[⑤] but in the depths of the sea;" and tears stopped her utterance, which when the pitying maiden had wiped away with her delicate finger, and soothed the goddess, "Tell me, dearest," said she, "the cause of your grief." Galatea then said, "Acis[⑥] was the son of Faunus and a Naiad. His father and mother loved him dearly, but their love was not equal to mine. For the beautiful youth attached himself to me alone, and he was just sixteen years old, the down[⑦] just beginning to darken his cheeks. As much as I sought his society, so much did the Cyclops seek mine; and if you ask me whether my love for Acis or my hatred of Polyphemus[⑧] was the stronger, I cannot tell you; they were in equal measure. O Venus, how great is thy power! this fierce giant, the terror of the woods, whom no hapless stranger escaped unharmed, who defied even Jove himself, learned to feel what love was, and, touched with a passion for me, forgot his flocks and his well-stored caverns. Then for the first time he began to take some care of his appearance, and to try to make himself agreeable[⑨]; he harrowed those coarse locks[⑩] of his with a comb, and mowed his beard with a sickle, looked at his harsh features in the water, and composed his countenance. His love of slaughter, his fierceness and thirst of blood prevailed no more, and ships that touched at his island went away in safety. He paced up and down the seashore, imprinting huge tracks with his heavy tread, and, when weary, lay tranquilly[⑪] in his cave.

---

① repel /rɪ'pel/：用粗暴的语言或举动来拒绝他人的追求
② Galatea：/ˌgælə'tɪə/
③ Nereus：/'nɪərjuːs/
④ such a band of sisters：the Nereids, sea-nymphs and daughters of Nereus
⑤ the Cyclops：参见 *The Age of Fable* 第 29 章。
⑥ Acis：/'æsɪs/
⑦ down：汗毛
⑧ Polyphemus /ˌpɒlɪ'fiːməs/：参见 *The Age of Fable* 第 29 章。
⑨ agreeable /ə'griːəbl/：令人愉悦的
⑩ lock：头发
⑪ tranquilly /'træŋkwɪli/：安静地

"There is a cliff which projects① into the sea, which washes it on either side. Thither one day the huge Cyclops ascended, and sat down while his flocks spread themselves around. Laying down his staff, which would have served for a mast to hold a vessel's sail, and taking his instrument compacted② of numerous pipes, he made the hills and the waters echo the music of his song. I lay hid under a rock by the side of my beloved Acis, and listened to the distant strain. It was full of extravagant praises of my beauty, mingled with passionate reproaches of my coldness and cruelty.

"When he had finished he rose up, and, like a raging bull that cannot stand still, wandered off into the woods. Acis and I thought no more of him, till on a sudden he came to a spot which gave him a view of us as we sat. 'I see you,' he exclaimed, 'and I will make this the last of your love-meetings.' His voice was a roar such as an angry Cyclops alone could utter. Ætna trembled at the sound. I, overcome with terror, plunged into the water. Acis turned and fled, crying, 'Save me, Galatea, save me, my parents!' The Cyclops pursued him, and tearing a rock from the side of the mountain hurled it at him. Though only a corner of it touched him, it overwhelmed③ him.

"All that fate left in my power I did for Acis. I endowed him with the honors of his grandfather, the river-god. The purple blood flowed out from under the rock, but by degrees grew paler and looked like the stream of a river rendered turbid④ by rains, and in time it became clear. The rock cleaved open, and the water, as it gushed from the chasm⑤, uttered a pleasing murmur."

Thus Acis was changed into a river, and the river retains the name of Acis⑥.

Chapter XXVII
The Trojan War

Minerva was the goddess of wisdom, but on one occasion she did a very foolish thing; she entered into competition with Juno and Venus for the prize of beauty. It happened thus: At the nuptials of Peleus and Thetis⑦ all the gods were invited with the exception of Eris⑧, or Discord.

---

① project /prə'dʒekt/: 突出
② compact /kəm'pækt/: 组成，构成
③ overwhelm /ˌəʊvə'welm/: 掩埋，覆盖
④ turbid /'tɜːbɪd/: 混浊的
⑤ chasm /'kæzəm/: 深的缝隙
⑥ Acis 是意大利西西里岛的一条河，在埃特纳火山（Ætna）附近。
⑦ Peleus /'piːljuːs / and Thetis /'θetɪs/: parents of Achilles
⑧ Eris: /'erɪs/

Enraged at her exclusion①, the goddess threw a golden apple among the guests, with the inscription②, "For the fairest." Thereupon Juno, Venus, and Minerva each claimed the apple. Jupiter, not willing to decide in so delicate③ a matter, sent the goddesses to Mount Ida④, where the beautiful shepherd Paris⑤ was tending his flocks, and to him was committed the decision. The goddesses accordingly appeared before him. Juno promised him power and riches, Minerva glory and renown in war, and Venus the fairest of women for his wife, each attempting to bias⑥ his decision in her own favor. Paris decided in favor of Venus and gave her the golden apple, thus making the two other goddesses his enemies. Under the protection of Venus, Paris sailed to Greece, and was hospitably received by Menelaus⑦, king of Sparta⑧. Now Helen⑨, the wife of Menelaus, was the very woman whom Venus had destined for Paris, the fairest of her sex. She had been sought as a bride by numerous suitors, and before her decision was made known, they all, at the suggestion of Ulysses⑩, one of their number, took an oath that they would defend her from all injury and avenge her cause if necessary. She chose Menelaus, and was living with him happily when Paris became their guest. Paris, aided by Venus, persuaded her to elope with him, and carried her to Troy⑪, whence arose the famous Trojan⑫ war, the theme of the greatest poems of antiquity⑬, those of Homer and Virgil.

Menelaus called upon his brother chieftains of Greece⑭ to fulfil their pledge, and join him in his efforts to recover⑮ his wife. They generally came forward, but Ulysses, who had married Penelope, and was very happy in his wife and child, had no disposition⑯ to embark⑰ in such a troublesome affair. He therefore hung back⑱ and Palamedes⑲ was sent to urge him. When Palamedes arrived at Ithaca⑳ Ulysses pretended to be mad. He yoked an ass and an ox together to

---

① exclusion /ɪksˈkluːʒn/：被排斥，被排除在外
② inscription /ɪnˈskrɪpʃn/：刻在石头、金属等之上的文字
③ delicate /ˈdelɪkət/：需要慎重处理的
④ Mount Ida：参见 *The Age of Fable* 第 5 章关于 Ida 的注释。
⑤ Paris：/ˈpærɪs/
⑥ bias /ˈbaɪəs/：影响
⑦ Menelaus：/ˌmenɪˈleɪəs/
⑧ Sparta /ˈspɑːtə/：Sparta 位于伯罗奔尼撒半岛半岛南部，是古希腊非常强大的城邦，其居民以纪律严明、骁勇善战而闻名。
⑨ Helen：/ˈhelɪn/
⑩ Ulysses：/juːˈlɪsiːz/
⑪ Troy /trɔɪ/：又叫 Ilium /ˈɪlɪəm/，位于小亚细亚西北部，达达尼尔海峡（the Dardanelles）南部入口附近，距离爱琴海海岸不远。
⑫ Trojan /ˈtrəʊdʒən/：of Troy
⑬ antiquity /ænˈtɪkwɪtɪ/：古代
⑭ his brother chieftains of Greece：与他级别相同的希腊首领们
⑮ recover：夺回
⑯ disposition /ˌdɪspəˈzɪʃn/：意向，倾向
⑰ embark（in, on, upon）：从事，参与
⑱ hang back：不愿意行动
⑲ Palamedes：/ˌpæləˈmiːdiːz/
⑳ Ithaca：参见 *The Age of Fable* 第 23 章关于 Ithaca 的注释。

the plough and began to sow salt. Palamedes, to try him, placed the infant Telemachus① before the plough, whereupon the father turned the plough aside, showing plainly that he was no madman, and after that could no longer refuse to fulfil his promise. Being now himself gained for the undertaking, he lent his aid to bring in other reluctant② chiefs, especially Achilles③. This hero was the son of that Thetis at whose marriage the apple of Discord had been thrown among the goddesses. Thetis was herself one of the immortals, a sea-nymph, and knowing that her son was fated to perish before Troy if he went on the expedition, she endeavored to prevent his going. She sent him away to the court of King Lycomedes④, and induced⑤ him to conceal himself in the disguise of a maiden among the daughters of the king. Ulysses, hearing he was there, went disguised as a merchant to the palace and offered for sale female ornaments, among which he had placed some arms. While the king's daughters were engrossed⑥ with the other contents of the merchant's pack, Achilles handled the weapons and thereby betrayed himself to the keen eye of Ulysses, who found no great difficulty in persuading him to disregard⑦ his mother's prudent counsels and join his countrymen in the war.

Priam⑧ was king of Troy, and Paris, the shepherd and seducer of Helen, was his son. Paris had been brought up in obscurity⑨, because there were certain ominous forebodings connected with him from his infancy that he would be the ruin of the state. These forebodings seemed at length likely to be realized, for the Grecian armament⑩ now in preparation was the greatest that had ever been fitted out⑪. Agamemnon⑫, king of Mycenæ⑬, and brother of the injured Menelaus, was chosen commander-in-chief. Achilles was their most illustrious warrior. After him ranked Ajax⑭, gigantic in size and of great courage, but dull of intellect; Diomede⑮, second only to Achilles in all the qualities of a hero; Ulysses, famous for his sagacity⑯; and Nestor⑰, the oldest of the Grecian chiefs, and one to whom they all looked up for counsel. But Troy was no feeble

---

① Telemachus：/tɪˈleməkəs/

② reluctant /rɪˈlʌktənt/：不情愿的

③ Achilles：/əˈkɪliːz/

④ Lycomedes /ˌlaɪkəˈmiːdiːz/：Skyros 的国王，Skyros /ˈskaɪrəs/是希腊岛屿，位于埃维亚（Euboea 或 Evvia）岛以东的爱琴海，属于今希腊中希腊大区埃维亚州。

⑤ induce /ɪnˈdjuːs/：教导

⑥ be engrossed /ɪnˈɡrəʊst / with：全神贯注于

⑦ disregard /ˈdɪsrɪˈɡɑːd/：不顾

⑧ Priam：/ˈpraɪəm/

⑨ obscurity /əbˈskjuərɪti/：默默无闻

⑩ armament /ˈɑːməmənt/：军队

⑪ fit out：装备所需的一切

⑫ Agamemnon：/ˌæɡəˈmemnən/

⑬ Mycenæ /maɪˈsiːni/：古希腊城市，位于伯罗奔尼撒半岛东北部伯罗奔尼撒大区阿尔戈利斯州（Argolis），曾有灿烂的文明。

⑭ Ajax：/ˈeɪdʒæks/

⑮ Diomede /ˈdaɪəmiːd/：也可写为 Diomedes /ˌdaɪəˈmiːdiːz/或 Diomed /ˈdaɪəmed /。

⑯ sagacity /səˈɡæsɪti/：睿智

⑰ Nestor：/ˈnestɔː/

enemy. Priam, the king, was now old, but he had been a wise prince and had strengthened his state by good government at home and numerous alliances with his neighbors. But the principal stay① and support of his throne was his son Hector②, one of the noblest characters painted③ by heathen antiquity④. He felt, from the first, a presentiment⑤ of the fall of his country, but still persevered in his heroic resistance, yet by no means justified the wrong which brought this danger upon her. He was united in marriage with Andromache⑥, and as a husband and father his character was not less admirable than as a warrior. The principal leaders on the side of the Trojans, besides Hector, were Æneas and Deiphobus, Glaucus and Sarpedon⑦.

After two years of preparation the Greek fleet and army assembled in the port of Aulis⑧ in Bœotia⑨. Here Agamemnon in hunting killed a stag which was sacred to Diana, and the goddess in return visited the army with pestilence, and produced a calm⑩ which prevented the ships from leaving the port. Calchas⑪, the soothsayer, thereupon announced that the wrath of the virgin goddess could only be appeased by the sacrifice of a virgin on her altar, and that none other but the daughter of the offender would be acceptable. Agamemnon, however reluctant, yielded his consent, and the maiden Iphigenia⑫ was sent for under the pretence that she was to be married to Achilles. When she was about to be sacrificed the goddess relented and snatched her away, leaving a hind⑬ in her place, and Iphigenia, enveloped in a cloud, was carried to Tauris⑭, where Diana made her priestess of her temple.

The wind now proving fair the fleet made sail and brought the forces to the coast of Troy. The Trojans came to oppose their landing, and at the first onset⑮ Protesilaus⑯ fell by the hand of Hector. Protesilaus had left at home his wife, Laodamia⑰, who was most tenderly attached to him. When the news of his death reached her she implored the gods to be allowed to converse with him only three hours. The request was granted. Mercury led Protesilaus back to the upper world, and when he died a second time Laodamia died with him. There was a story that the nymphs planted

---

① stay：支柱

② Hector：/ˈhektə/

③ paint：刻画，描述

④ antiquity：古人，古代作家

⑤ presentiment /prɪˈzentɪmənt/：（对不幸事件的）预感

⑥ Andromache：/ænˈdrɒməki/

⑦ Æneas：/ɪˈniːæs /；Deiphobus：/dɪˈɪfəbəs /；Glaucus：/ˈɡlɔːkəs /；Sarpedon：/sɑːˈpiːdən/

⑧ Aulis /ˈɔːlɪs/：古希腊港口名，即今天的阿夫利佐斯（Avlidos）。按照今希腊的行政区域划分，阿夫利佐斯不属于维奥蒂亚州，而属于中希腊大区埃维亚州。埃维亚州除了埃维亚岛等岛屿外，还有一小部分位于希腊大陆，即维奥蒂亚州以东的沿海地区，阿夫利佐斯位于这个区域的南部。

⑨ Bœotia /biːˈəʊʃɪə/：古希腊地区名，比今希腊的中希腊大区维奥蒂亚州（Bœotia 或 Voiotia）大。

⑩ calm：（海上）无风

⑪ Calchas：/ˈkælkəs/

⑫ Iphigenia /ɪˌfɪdʒɪˈnaɪə/：daughter of Agamemnon and Clytemnestra

⑬ hind /haɪnd/：3 岁或 3 岁以上的红色雌鹿

⑭ Tauris /ˈtɔːrɪs/：即现在黑海正北边的克里米亚（Crimea），又叫 Taurica。

⑮ onset /ˈɒnset/：进攻

⑯ Protesilaus：/prəˌtesɪˈleɪəs/

⑰ Laodamia：/ˌleɪəʊdəˈmaɪə/

elm trees round his grave which grew very well till they were high enough to command a view of Troy, and then withered away, while fresh branches sprang from the roots.

The Iliad

The war continued without decisive results for nine years. Then an event occurred which seemed likely to be fatal to the cause of the Greeks, and that was a quarrel between Achilles and Agamemnon. It is at this point that the great poem of Homer, *The Iliad*①, begins. The Greeks, though unsuccessful against Troy, had taken the neighboring and allied cities, and in the division of the spoil② a female captive, by name Chryseis③, daughter of Chryses④, priest of Apollo, had fallen to the share of Agamemnon. Chryses came bearing the sacred emblems of his office, and begged the release of his daughter. Agamemnon refused. Thereupon Chryses implored Apollo to afflict the Greeks till they should be forced to yield their prey. Apollo granted the prayer of his priest, and sent pestilence into the Grecian camp. Then a council was called to deliberate⑤ how to allay the wrath of the gods and avert the plague. Achilles boldly charged their misfortunes upon Agamemnon as caused by his withholding⑥ Chryseis. Agamemnon, enraged, consented to relinquish⑦ his captive, but demanded that Achilles should yield to him in her stead Briseis⑧, a maiden who had fallen to Achilles' share in the division of the spoil. Achilles submitted, but forthwith declared that he would take no further part in the war. He withdrew his forces from the general camp and openly avowed his intention of returning home to Greece.

The gods and goddesses interested themselves as much in this famous war as the parties themselves. It was well known to them that fate had decreed that Troy should fall, at last, if her enemies should persevere and not voluntarily abandon the enterprise. Yet there was room enough left for chance to excite by turns the hopes and fears of the powers above⑨ who took part with either side. Juno and Minerva, in consequence of the slight⑩ put upon their charms by Paris, were hostile⑪ to the Trojans; Venus for the opposite cause favored them. Venus enlisted⑫ her admirer Mars⑬ on the same side, but Neptune favored the Greeks. Apollo was neutral, sometimes taking one side, sometimes the other, and Jove himself, though he loved the good King Priam, yet

---

① *The Iliad* /ˈɪliæd/：古希腊诗人荷马（Homer）写的史诗，共 24 卷。Iliad 一词源自 Troy 的另一个名字 Ilium。
② spoil：掠夺来的赃物
③ Chryseis：/kraɪˈsiːɪs/
④ Chryses：/ˈkraɪsiːz/
⑤ deliberate /dɪˈlɪbəreɪt/：商议
⑥ withhold：扣留
⑦ relinquish /rɪˈlɪŋkwɪʃ/：放弃，释放
⑧ Briseis：/braɪˈsiːɪs/
⑨ the powers above：天上的诸神
⑩ slight：轻视，冒犯
⑪ hostile /ˈhɒstaɪl/：敌对的，有敌意的
⑫ enlist /ɪnˈlɪst/：谋取……的支持和帮助
⑬ her admirer Mars：参见 *The Odyssey* 中的"The Love of Mars and Venus"选段。

exercised a degree of impartiality①; not, however, without exceptions.

Thetis, the mother of Achilles, warmly resented the injury done to her son. She repaired immediately to Jove's palace and besought him to make the Greeks repent of their injustice to Achilles by granting success to the Trojan arms. Jupiter consented, and in the battle which ensued② the Trojans were completely successful. The Greeks were driven from the field and took refuge in their ships.

Then Agamemnon called a council of his wisest and bravest chiefs. Nestor advised that an embassy③ should be sent to Achilles to persuade him to return to the field; that Agamemnon should yield the maiden, the cause of the dispute, with ample gifts to atone for④ the wrong he had done. Agamemnon consented, and Ulysses, Ajax, and Phœnix⑤ were sent to carry to Achilles the penitent⑥ message. They performed that duty, but Achilles was deaf to their entreaties. He positively refused to return to the field, and persisted in his resolution to embark for Greece without delay.

The Greeks had constructed a rampart⑦ around their ships, and now instead of besieging Troy they were in a manner besieged themselves, within their rampart. The next day after the unsuccessful embassy to Achilles, a battle was fought, and the Trojans, favored by Jove, were successful, and succeeded in forcing a passage through the Grecian rampart, and were about to set fire to the ships. Neptune, seeing the Greeks so pressed, came to their rescue. He appeared in the form of Calchas the prophet, encouraged the warriors with his shouts, and appealed to each individually till he raised their ardor to such a pitch that they forced the Trojans to give way. Ajax performed prodigies⑧ of valor, and at length encountered Hector. Ajax shouted defiance, to which Hector replied, and hurled his lance at the huge warrior. It was well aimed and struck Ajax, where the belts that bore his sword and shield crossed each other on the breast. The double guard prevented its penetrating and it fell harmless. Then Ajax, seizing a huge stone, one of those that served to prop the ships, hurled it at Hector. It struck him in the neck and stretched him on the plain. His followers instantly seized him and bore him off, stunned and wounded.

While Neptune was thus aiding the Greeks and driving back the Trojans, Jupiter saw nothing of what was going on, for his attention had been drawn from the field by the wiles of Juno. That goddess had arrayed herself in all her charms, and to crown all had borrowed of Venus her girdle, called "Cestus⑨," which had the effect to heighten the wearer's charms to such a degree that they were quite irresistible. So prepared, Juno went to join her husband, who sat on Olympus

---

① impartiality /ɪmˌpɑːʃɪˈælɪti/：公正

② ensue /ɪnˈsjuː/：follow

③ embassy /ˈembəsi/：特别使团

④ atone for：补偿

⑤ Phœnix：/ˈfiːnɪks/

⑥ penitent /ˈpenɪtənt/：表示悔恨的

⑦ rampart /ˈræmpɑːt/：用于防御的土堆或墙

⑧ prodigy /ˈprɒdɪdʒi/：令人惊讶的事,非同寻常之事

⑨ Cestus：/ˈsestəs/

watching the battle. When he beheld her she looked so charming that the fondness of his early love revived, and, forgetting the contending armies and all other affairs of state, he thought only of her and let the battle go as it would.①

But this absorption did not continue long, and when, upon turning his eyes downward, he beheld Hector stretched on the plain almost lifeless from pain and bruises②, he dismissed Juno in a rage, commanding her to send Iris③ and Apollo to him. When Iris came he sent her with a stern message to Neptune, ordering him instantly to quit the field. Apollo was despatched to heal Hector's bruises and to inspirit④ his heart. These orders were obeyed with such speed that, while the battle still raged, Hector returned to the field and Neptune betook himself to his own dominions.

An arrow from Paris's bow wounded Machaon⑤, son of Æsculapius⑥, who inherited his father's art of healing, and was therefore of great value to the Greeks as their surgeon, besides being one of their bravest warriors. Nestor took Machaon in his chariot and conveyed him from the field. As they passed the ships of Achilles, that hero, looking out over the field, saw the chariot of Nestor and recognized the old chief, but could not discern who the wounded chief was. So calling Patroclus⑦, his companion and dearest friend, he sent him to Nestor's tent to inquire.

Patroclus, arriving at Nestor's tent, saw Machaon wounded, and having told the cause of his coming would have hastened away, but Nestor detained him, to tell him the extent of the Grecian calamities. He reminded him also how, at the time of departing for Troy, Achilles and himself had been charged by their respective fathers with different advice: Achilles to aspire to the highest pitch of glory, Patroclus, as the elder, to keep watch over his friend, and to guide his inexperience. "Now," said Nestor, "is the time for such influence. If the gods so please, thou mayest win him back to the common cause; but if not let him at least send his soldiers to the field, and come thou, Patroclus, clad in his armor, and perhaps the very sight of it may drive back the Trojans."

Patroclus was strongly moved with this address⑧, and hastened back to Achilles, revolving in his mind all he had seen and heard. He told the prince the sad condition of affairs at the camp of their late associates⑨: Diomede, Ulysses, Agamemnon, Machaon, all wounded, the rampart broken down, the enemy among the ships preparing to burn them, and thus to cut off all means of return to Greece. While they spoke the flames burst forth from one of the ships. Achilles, at the

---

① 参见 *The Iliad* 选段"Deception of Jupiter by Juno"。
② bruise /bruːz/：瘀伤
③ Iris /ˈaɪərɪs/：彩虹女神,诸神的信使。
④ inspirit：鼓舞,使振奋
⑤ Machaon：/məˈkeɪɒn/
⑥ Æsculapius：参见 *The Age of Fable* 第16章。
⑦ Patroclus：/pəˈtrɒkləs/
⑧ address：一番话
⑨ associate /əˈsəʊʃiət/：同伴

sight, relented so far as to grant Patroclus his request to lead the Myrmidons① (for so were Achilles' soldiers called) to the field, and to lend him his armor, that he might thereby strike more terror into the minds of the Trojans. Without delay the soldiers were marshalled, Patroclus put on the radiant armor and mounted the chariot of Achilles, and led forth the men ardent for battle. But before he went, Achilles strictly charged him that he should be content with repelling the foe. "Seek not," said he, "to press the Trojans without me, lest thou add still more to the disgrace already mine." Then exhorting② the troops to do their best he dismissed them full of ardor to the fight. Patroclus and his Myrmidons at once plunged into the contest where it raged hottest; at the sight of which the joyful Grecians shouted and the ships reëchoed the acclaim③. The Trojans, at the sight of the well-known armor, struck with terror, looked everywhere for refuge. First those who had got possession of the ship and set it on fire left and allowed the Grecians to retake it and extinguish the flames. Then the rest of the Trojans fled in dismay. Ajax, Menelaus, and the two sons of Nestor④ performed prodigies of valor. Hector was forced to turn his horses' heads and retire from the enclosure, leaving his men entangled in the fosse⑤ to escape as they could. Patroclus drove them before him, slaying many, none daring to make a stand⑥ against him.

At last Sarpedon, son of Jove, ventured to oppose himself in fight to Patroclus. Jupiter looked down upon him and would have snatched him from the fate which awaited him, but Juno hinted that if he did so it would induce all others of the inhabitants of heaven to interpose in like manner whenever any of their offspring were endangered; to which reason Jove yielded. Sarpedon threw his spear, but missed Patroclus, but Patroclus threw his with better success. It pierced Sarpedon's breast and he fell, and, calling to his friends to save his body from the foe, expired. Then a furious contest arose for the possession of the corpse. The Greeks succeeded and stripped Sarpedon of his armor; but Jove would not allow the remains⑦ of his son to be dishonored, and by his command Apollo snatched from the midst of the combatants the body of Sarpedon and committed it to the care of the twin brothers Death and Sleep, by whom it was transported to Lycia, the native land of Sarpedon, where it received due funeral rites.

Thus far Patroclus had succeeded to his utmost wish in repelling the Trojans and relieving his countrymen, but now came a change of fortune. Hector, borne in his chariot, confronted him. Patroclus threw a vast stone at Hector, which missed its aim, but smote Cebriones⑧, the charioteer, and knocked him from the car⑨. Hector leaped from the chariot to rescue his friend, and Patroclus also descended to complete his victory. Thus the two heroes met face to face. At this

---

① the Myrmidons：参见 *The Age of Fable* 第 12 章。

② exhort /ɪgˈzɔːt/：敦促

③ acclaim /əˈkleɪm/：表示欢迎的吼叫

④ the two sons of Nestor：Antilochus /ənˈtɪləkəs/ and Thrasymedes /ˌθræsɪˈmiːdiːz/

⑤ fosse /ˈfɒs/：战壕

⑥ stand：停下来反击,停下来抵抗

⑦ remains：遗体,遗骨

⑧ Cebriones：/ˌsebrɪˈəʊniːz/

⑨ car：chariot

decisive moment the poet, as if reluctant to give Hector the glory, records that Phœbus took part against Patroclus. He struck the helmet from his head and the lance from his hand. At the same moment an obscure① Trojan wounded him in the back, and Hector, pressing forward, pierced him with his spear. He fell mortally wounded.

Then arose a tremendous conflict for the body of Patroclus, but his armor was at once taken possession of by Hector, who retiring a short distance divested himself of② his own armor and put on that of Achilles, then returned to the fight. Ajax and Menelaus defended the body, and Hector and his bravest warriors struggled to capture it. The battle raged with equal fortunes, when Jove enveloped the whole face of heaven with a dark cloud. The lightning flashed, the thunder roared, and Ajax, looking round for some one whom he might despatch to Achilles to tell him of the death of his friend, and of the imminent danger that his remains would fall into the hands of the enemy, could see no suitable messenger. It was then that he exclaimed in those famous lines so often quoted,③

"Father of heaven and earth④! deliver thou
Achaia's⑤ host from darkness; clear the skies;
Give day; and, since thy sovereign will is such,
Destruction with it; but, O, give us day."
　　　　　　　　　　　—Cowper⑥.

Or, as rendered⑦ by Pope⑧,

"... Lord of earth and air⑨!
O king! O father! hear my humble prayer!
Dispel this cloud, the light of heaven restore;
Give me to see and Ajax asks no more;
If Greece must perish we thy will obey,
But let us perish in the face of day."

Jupiter heard the prayer and dispersed the clouds. Then Ajax sent Antilochus⑩ to Achilles with the intelligence⑪ of Patroclus's death, and of the conflict raging for his remains. The Greeks at last succeeded in bearing off the body to the ships, closely pursued by Hector and Æneas and

① obscure /əbˈskjuə/：没有名气的
② divest /daɪˈvest/ himself of：脱掉
③ 引文引自 The Iliad 第 17 卷。
④ Father of heaven and earth：Jupiter
⑤ Achaia (Achaea) /əˈkiə/：古希腊地区名，位于伯罗奔尼撒半岛北部海岸。该词常用来指希腊。古代的 Achaia 与今希腊西希腊大区的阿哈伊亚州（Achaia 或 Achaea）大致相当。
⑥ William Cowper：荷马史诗的英语译者,他用素体诗（blank verse）翻译的荷马史诗 1791 年出版,以忠实于荷马的古希腊原文而著称。
⑦ render /ˈrendə/：翻译
⑧ Alexander Pope：18 世纪英国诗人,荷马史诗的英语译者,他用英雄双行体（heroic couplet）翻译的荷马史诗 1715 年出版。
⑨ Lord of earth and air：Jupiter
⑩ Antilochus：参见本章关于 the two sons of Nestor 的注释。
⑪ intelligence /ɪnˈtelɪdʒəns/：消息,信息

the rest of the Trojans.

Achilles heard the fate of his friend with such distress that Antilochus feared for a while that he would destroy himself. His groans reached the ears of his mother, Thetis, far down in the deeps of ocean where she abode, and she hastened to him to inquire the cause. She found him overwhelmed with self-reproach that he had indulged his resentment so far, and suffered his friend to fall a victim to it. But his only consolation was the hope of revenge. He would fly instantly in search of Hector. But his mother reminded him that he was now without armor, and promised him, if he would but wait till the morrow①, she would procure for him a suit of armor from Vulcan more than equal to that he had lost. He consented, and Thetis immediately repaired to Vulcan's palace. She found him busy at his forge making tripods for his own use, so artfully constructed that they moved forward of their own accord when wanted, and retired again when dismissed. On hearing the request of Thetis, Vulcan immediately laid aside his work and hastened to comply with her wishes. He fabricated a splendid suit of armor for Achilles, first a shield adorned with elaborate devices②, then a helmet crested with gold, then a corselet③ and greaves④ of impenetrable⑤ temper⑥, all perfectly adapted to his form⑦, and of consummate⑧ workmanship. It was all done in one night, and Thetis, receiving it, descended with it to earth, and laid it down at Achilles' feet at the dawn of day.

The first glow of pleasure that Achilles had felt since the death of Patroclus was at the sight of this splendid armor. And now, arrayed in it, he went forth into the camp, calling all the chiefs to council. When they were all assembled he addressed them. Renouncing⑨ his displeasure against Agamemnon and bitterly lamenting the miseries that had resulted from it, he called on them to proceed at once to the field. Agamemnon made a suitable reply, laying all the blame on Ate⑩, the goddess of discord; and thereupon complete reconcilement⑪ took place between the heroes.

Then Achilles went forth to battle inspired with a rage and thirst for vengeance that made him irresistible. The bravest warriors fled before him or fell by his lance. Hector, cautioned by Apollo, kept aloof; but the god⑫, assuming the form of one of Priam's sons, Lycaon⑬, urged Æneas to

---

① morrow /ˈmɒrəʊ/：morning
② device：图案；参见 The Iliad 选段"The Shield of Achilles"。
③ corselet /ˈkɔːslɪt/：护身盔甲
④ greave：胫甲（用以保护膝盖以下腿部的铠甲）
⑤ impenetrable /ɪmˈpenɪtrəbl/：不能被刺穿的
⑥ temper：（皮革的）质地,坚韧度
⑦ form：体型
⑧ consummate /ˈkɒnsʌmət/：完美的
⑨ renounce /rɪˈnaʊns/：公开宣布放弃
⑩ Ate /ˈɑːti/：daughter of Jupiter and Eris
⑪ reconcilement /ˈrekənsaɪlmənt/：和解
⑫ the god：Apollo
⑬ Lycaon：/laɪˈkeɪɒn/

encounter the terrible warrior. Æneas, though he felt himself unequal, did not decline① the combat. He hurled his spear with all his force against the shield the work of Vulcan. It was formed of five metal plates; two were of brass, two of tin, and one of gold. The spear pierced two thicknesses②, but was stopped in the third. Achilles threw his with better success. It pierced through the shield of Æneas, but glanced③ near his shoulder and made no wound. Then Æneas seized a stone, such as two men of modern times could hardly lift, and was about to throw it, and Achilles, with sword drawn, was about to rush upon him, when Neptune, who looked out upon the contest, moved with pity for Æneas, who he saw would surely fall a victim if not speedily rescued, spread a cloud between the combatants, and lifting Æneas from the ground, bore him over the heads of warriors and steeds to the rear of the battle. Achilles, when the mist cleared away, looked round in vain for his adversary④, and acknowledging the prodigy, turned his arms against other champions⑤. But none dared stand before him, and Priam looking down from the city walls beheld his whole army in full flight towards the city. He gave command to open wide the gates to receive the fugitives, and to shut them as soon as the Trojans should have passed, lest the enemy should enter likewise. But Achilles was so close in pursuit that that would have been impossible if Apollo had not, in the form of Agenor⑥, Priam's son, encountered Achilles for a while, then turned to fly, and taken the way apart from the city. Achilles pursued and had chased his supposed victim far from the walls, when Apollo disclosed himself, and Achilles, perceiving how he had been deluded, gave up the chase.

But when the rest had escaped into the town Hector stood without⑦ determined to await the combat. His old father called to him from the walls and begged him to retire nor tempt the encounter. His mother, Hecuba⑧, also besought him to the same effect, but all in vain. "How can I," said he to himself, "by whose command the people went to this day's contest, where so many have fallen, seek safety for myself against a single foe? But what if I offer him to yield up Helen and all her treasures and ample of our own⑨ beside? Ah, no! It is too late. He would not even hear me through, but slay me while I spoke." While he thus ruminated, Achilles approached, terrible as Mars, his armor flashing lightning as he moved. At that sight Hector's heart failed him and he fled. Achilles swiftly pursued. They ran, still keeping near the walls, till they had thrice encircled the city. As often as Hector approached the walls Achilles intercepted⑩ him and forced him to keep out in a wider circle. But Apollo sustained Hector's strength and would not let him

---

① decline /dɪˈklaɪn/：躲避，回避，婉言拒绝

② thickness：层

③ glance：擦过

④ adversary /ˈædvəsəri/：对手，敌人

⑤ champion /ˈtʃæmpɪən/：参加战斗的人

⑥ Agenor：/əˈdʒiːnɔː/

⑦ without：在外面

⑧ Hecuba：/ˈhekjubə/

⑨ ample of our own：ample treasures of our own；ample /ˈæmpl/：大量的，充足的

⑩ intercept /ˌɪntəˈsept/：拦住

sink in weariness. Then Pallas, assuming the form of Deiphobus, Hector's bravest brother, appeared suddenly at his side. Hector saw him with delight, and thus strengthened stopped his flight and turned to meet Achilles. Hector threw his spear, which struck the shield of Achilles and bounded back. He turned to receive another from the hand of Deiphobus, but Deiphobus was gone. Then Hector understood his doom and said, "Alas! it is plain this is my hour to die! I thought Deiphobus at hand, but Pallas deceived me, and he is still in Troy. But I will not fall inglorious." So saying he drew his falchion① from his side and rushed at once to combat. Achilles, secured behind his shield, waited the approach of Hector. When he came within reach of his spear, Achilles choosing with his eye a vulnerable part where the armor leaves the neck uncovered, aimed his spear at that part and Hector fell, death-wounded, and feebly said, "Spare my body! Let my parents ransom it, and let me receive funeral rites from the sons and daughters of Troy." To which Achilles replied, "Dog, name not ransom nor pity to me, on whom you have brought such dire distress. No! trust me, naught shall save thy carcass② from the dogs. Though twenty ransoms and thy weight in gold③ were offered, I would refuse it all."

So saying he stripped the body of its armor, and fastening cords to the feet tied them behind his chariot, leaving the body to trail along the ground. Then mounting the chariot he lashed the steeds and so dragged the body to and fro before the city. What words can tell the grief of King Priam and Queen Hecuba at this sight! His people could scarce restrain the old king from rushing forth. He threw himself in the dust and besought them each by name to give him way. Hecuba's distress was not less violent. The citizens stood round them weeping. The sound of the mourning reached the ears of Andromache, the wife of Hector, as she sat among her maidens at work, and anticipating evil she went forth to the wall. When she saw the sight there presented, she would have thrown herself headlong from the wall, but fainted and fell into the arms of her maidens. Recovering, she bewailed her fate, picturing to herself her country ruined, herself a captive, and her son dependent for his bread on the charity of strangers.

When Achilles and the Greeks had taken their revenge on the killer of Patroclus they busied themselves in paying due funeral rites to their friend. A pile was erected, and the body burned with due solemnity; and then ensued games of strength and skill, chariot races, wrestling, boxing, and archery. Then the chiefs sat down to the funeral banquet and after that retired to rest. But Achilles neither partook of the feast nor of sleep. The recollection of his lost friend kept him awake, remembering their companionship in toil and dangers, in battle or on the perilous deep④. Before the earliest dawn he left his tent, and joining to his chariot his swift steeds, he fastened Hector's body to be dragged behind. Twice he dragged him around the tomb of Patroclus, leaving him at length stretched in the dust. But Apollo would not permit the body to be torn or disfigured

---

① falchion /ˈfɔːltʃən/：宝剑
② carcass /ˈkɑːkəs/：（贬义）人的尸体,动物的尸体
③ thy weight in gold：和你的体重一样重的黄金
④ deep：（诗歌用词）大海

with all this abuse①, but preserved it free from all taint or defilement②.

While Achilles indulged his wrath in thus disgracing③ brave Hector, Jupiter in pity summoned Thetis to his presence. He told her to go to her son and prevail on him to restore the body of Hector to his friends. Then Jupiter sent Iris to King Priam to encourage him to go to Achilles and beg the body of his son. Iris delivered her message, and Priam immediately prepared to obey. He opened his treasuries④ and took out rich garments and cloths, with ten talents⑤ in gold and two splendid tripods and a golden cup of matchless workmanship. Then he called to his sons and bade them draw forth his litter⑥ and place in it the various articles designed for a ransom to Achilles. When all was ready, the old king with a single companion as aged as himself, the herald⑦ Idæus⑧, drove forth from the gates, parting there with Hecuba, his queen, and all his friends, who lamented him as going to certain death.

But Jupiter, beholding with compassion the venerable king, sent Mercury to be his guide and protector. Mercury, assuming the form of a young warrior, presented himself to the aged couple⑨, and while at the sight of him they hesitated whether to fly or yield, the god approached, and grasping Priam's hand offered to be their guide to Achilles' tent. Priam gladly accepted his offered service, and he, mounting the carriage, assumed the reins and soon conveyed them to the tent of Achilles. Mercury's wand put to sleep all the guards, and without hinderance he introduced⑩ Priam into the tent where Achilles sat, attended by two of his warriors. The old king threw himself at the feet of Achilles, and kissed those terrible hands which had destroyed so many of his sons. "Think, O Achilles," he said, "of thy own father, full of days⑪ like me, and trembling on the gloomy verge of life. Perhaps even now some neighbor chief oppresses him and there is none at hand to succor⑫ him in his distress. Yet doubtless knowing that Achilles lives he still rejoices, hoping that one day he shall see thy face again. But no comfort cheers me, whose bravest sons, so late the flower of Ilium, all have fallen. Yet one I had, one more than all the rest the strength of my age, whom, fighting for his country, thou hast slain. I come to redeem⑬ his body, bringing inestimable⑭ ransom with me. Achilles! reverence⑮ the gods! recollect thy father! for his sake show compassion to me!" These words moved

---

① abuse /əˈbjuːz/：凌辱
② defilement /dɪˈfaɪlmənt/：污损，玷污
③ disgrace：侮辱
④ treasury /ˈtreʒəri/：存放财宝的库房
⑤ talent：雅典人和罗马人使用的重量单位，大约相当于 26 千克。
⑥ litter：马拉的轿子
⑦ herald /ˈherəld/：传令官
⑧ Idæus：/ɪˈdiːəs/
⑨ the aged couple：Priam and Idæus
⑩ introduce：引领
⑪ full of days：年老的
⑫ succor /ˈsʌkə/：帮助
⑬ redeem /rɪˈdiːm/：赎回
⑭ inestimable /ɪnˈestɪməbl/：无价的
⑮ reverence /ˈrevərəns/：尊重

Achilles, and he wept; remembering by turns his absent father and his lost friend. Moved with pity of Priam's silver locks and beard, he raised him from the earth, and thus spake: "Priam, I know that thou hast reached this place conducted by some god, for without aid divine no mortal even in his prime of youth had dared the attempt. I grant thy request, moved thereto by the evident will of Jove." So saying he arose, and went forth with his two friends, and unloaded of its charge the litter, leaving two mantles and a robe for the covering of the body, which they placed on the litter, and spread the garments over it, that not unveiled it should be borne back to Troy. Then Achilles dismissed the old king with his attendants, having first pledged himself to allow a truce① of twelve days for the funeral solemnities.

As the litter approached the city and was descried② from the walls, the people poured forth to gaze once more on the face of their hero. Foremost of all, the mother and the wife of Hector came, and at the sight of the lifeless body renewed their lamentations. The people all wept with them, and to the going down of the sun there was no pause or abatement③ of their grief.

The next day preparations were made for the funeral solemnities. For nine days the people brought wood and built the pile, and on the tenth they placed the body on the summit and applied the torch; while all Troy thronging forth encompassed④ the pile. When it had completely burned, they quenched the cinders⑤ with wine, collected the bones and placed them in a golden urn⑥, which they buried in the earth, and reared a pile of stones over the spot.

Chapter XXVIII
The Fall of Troy—Return of the Greeks—Agamemnon, Orestes, and Electra

The Fall of Troy

The story of the *Iliad* ends with the death of Hector, and it is from the *Odyssey*⑦ and later poems that we learn the fate of the other heroes. After the death of Hector, Troy did not immediately fall, but receiving aid from new allies still continued its resistance. One of these allies was Memnon,

---

① truce /truːs/: 停战

② descry /dɪˈskraɪ/: 看见

③ abatement /əˈbeɪtmənt/: 减轻, 减退

④ encompass /ɪnˈkʌmpəs/: 包围, 围住

⑤ cinder /ˈsɪndə/: 没有燃烧完的木材、木炭或煤炭

⑥ urn /ɜːn/: 骨灰瓮

⑦ *Odyssey*: /ˈɒdɪsi/

the Æthiopian prince, whose story we have already told①. Another was Penthesilea②, queen of the Amazons③, who came with a band of female warriors. All the authorities attest④ their valor and the fearful effect of their war cry. Penthesilea slew many of the bravest warriors, but was at last slain by Achilles. But when the hero bent over his fallen foe, and contemplated her beauty, youth, and valor, he bitterly regretted his victory. Thersites⑤, an insolent⑥ brawler⑦ and demagogue⑧, ridiculed his grief, and was in consequence⑨ slain by the hero.

Achilles by chance had seen Polyxena⑩, daughter of King Priam, perhaps on the occasion of the truce which was allowed the Trojans for the burial of Hector. He was captivated with her charms, and to win her in marriage agreed to use his influence with the Greeks to grant peace to Troy. While in the temple of Apollo, negotiating the marriage, Paris discharged at him a poisoned arrow, which, guided by Apollo, wounded Achilles in the heel, the only vulnerable⑪ part about him. For Thetis his mother had dipped him when an infant in the river Styx, which made every part of him invulnerable except the heel by which she held him.

The body of Achilles so treacherously slain was rescued by Ajax and Ulysses. Thetis directed the Greeks to bestow her son's armor on the hero who of all the survivors should be judged most deserving of it. Ajax and Ulysses were the only claimants⑫; a select number of the other chiefs were appointed to award the prize. It was awarded to Ulysses, thus placing wisdom before valor; whereupon Ajax slew himself. On the spot where his blood sank into the earth a flower sprang up, called the hyacinth, bearing on its leaves the first two letters of the name of Ajax, Ai, the Greek for "woe."⑬ Thus Ajax is a claimant with the boy Hyacinthus⑭ for the honor of giving birth to this flower. There is a species of Larkspur⑮ which represents the hyacinth of the poets in preserving the memory of this event, the Delphinium⑯ Ajacis⑰—Ajax's Larkspur.

It was now discovered that Troy could not be taken but by the aid of the arrows of Hercules. They were in possession of Philoctetes⑱, the friend who had been with Hercules at the last and

---

① 参见 *The Age of Fable* 第 26 章。
② Penthesilea：/ˌpenθesɪˈliːə/
③ the Amazons：参见 *The Age of Fable* 第 19 章。
④ attest：证明，证实
⑤ Thersites：/θɜːˈsaɪtiːz/
⑥ insolent /ˈɪnsələnt/：傲慢的
⑦ brawler /ˈbrɔːlə/：爱吵闹的人，高声喧哗的人
⑧ demagogue /ˈdeməɡɒɡ/：（古希腊）支持普通民众事业的领袖或演说家
⑨ in consequence /ˈkɒnsɪkwəns/：因此
⑩ Polyxena：/pɒˈlɪksɪnə/
⑪ vulnerable /ˈvʌlnərəbl/：易受伤的，脆弱的
⑫ claimant /ˈkleɪmənt/：提出要求的人
⑬ Ajax 在古希腊语中拼写为 Αἴας(Aias)，αἴ(ai)是感叹词，表示叹息或悲痛。
⑭ 参见 *The Age of Fable* 第 8 章。
⑮ Larkspur /ˈlɑːkspə/：翠雀属植物
⑯ delphinium /delˈfɪnɪəm/：（植物）翠雀
⑰ 古希腊语人名 Αἴας 转写为拉丁语是 Ajax，其属格是 Ajacis。
⑱ Philoctetes /ˌfɪlɒkˈtiːtiːz/：参见 *The Age of Fable* 第 19 章。

lighted his funeral pyre. Philoctetes had joined the Grecian expedition against Troy, but had accidentally wounded his foot with one of the poisoned arrows, and the smell from his wound proved so offensive that his companions carried him to the isle of Lemnos and left him there. Diomed was now sent to induce① him to rejoin the army. He succeeded. Philoctetes was cured of his wound by Machaon, and Paris was the first victim of the fatal arrows. In his distress Paris bethought him of one whom in his prosperity he had forgotten. This was the nymph Œnone②, whom he had married when a youth, and had abandoned for the fatal beauty Helen. Œnone, remembering the wrongs she had suffered, refused to heal the wound, and Paris went back to Troy and died. Œnone quickly repented, and hastened after him with remedies, but came too late, and in her grief hung herself.

There was in Troy a celebrated statue of Minerva called the Palladium③. It was said to have fallen from heaven, and the belief was that the city could not be taken so long as this statue remained within it. Ulysses and Diomed entered the city in disguise and succeeded in obtaining the Palladium, which they carried off to the Grecian camp.

But Troy still held out, and the Greeks began to despair of ever subduing it by force, and by advice of Ulysses resolved to resort to stratagem. They pretended to be making preparations to abandon the siege, and a portion of the ships were withdrawn and lay hid behind a neighboring island④. The Greeks then constructed an immense wooden horse, which they gave out⑤ was intended as a propitiatory⑥ offering to Minerva, but in fact was filled with armed men. The remaining Greeks then betook themselves to their ships and sailed away, as if for a final departure. The Trojans, seeing the encampment⑦ broken up and the fleet gone, concluded the enemy to have abandoned the siege. The gates were thrown open, and the whole population issued forth rejoicing at the long-prohibited liberty of passing freely over the scene of the late encampment. The great horse was the chief object of curiosity. All wondered what it could be for. Some recommended to take it into the city as a trophy⑧; others felt afraid of it.

While they hesitate, Laocoön⑨, the priest of Neptune, exclaims, "What madness, citizens, is this? Have you not learned enough of Grecian fraud to be on your guard against it? For my part, I fear the Greeks even when they offer gifts." So saying he threw his lance at the horse's side. It struck, and a hollow sound reverberated⑩ like a groan. Then perhaps the people might have taken his advice and destroyed the fatal horse and all its contents; but just at that moment a group of

---

① induce /ɪnˈdjuːs/: 劝说

② Œnone: /iːˈnəʊni/

③ Palladium: /pəˈleɪdɪəm/

④ This island is called Tenedos, which is not far from Troy.

⑤ give out: 宣称,声明

⑥ propitiatory /prəʊˈpɪʃɪətəri/: 用于谋取好感的,用于安抚被冒犯者的

⑦ encampment /ɪnˈkæmpmənt/: (军队驻扎的)营地

⑧ trophy /ˈtrəʊfi/: 战利品

⑨ Laocoön: /leɪˈɒkəʊɒn/

⑩ reverberate /rɪˈvɜːbəreɪt/: 回响

people appeared, dragging forward one who seemed a prisoner and a Greek. Stupefied with terror, he was brought before the chiefs, who reassured him, promising that his life should be spared on condition of his returning true answers to the questions asked him. He informed them that he was a Greek, Sinon[1] by name, and that in consequence of the malice of Ulysses he had been left behind by his countrymen at their departure. With regard to the wooden horse, he told them that it was a propitiatory offering to Minerva, and made so huge for the express[2] purpose of preventing its being carried within the city; for Calchas the prophet had told them that if the Trojans took possession of it they would assuredly triumph over the Greeks. This language turned the tide of the people's feelings and they began to think how they might best secure the monstrous[3] horse and the favorable auguries[4] connected with it, when suddenly a prodigy occurred which left no room to doubt. There appeared, advancing over the sea, two immense serpents. They came upon the land, and the crowd fled in all directions. The serpents advanced directly to the spot where Laocoön stood with his two sons. They first attacked the children, winding round their bodies and breathing their pestilential breath in their faces. The father, attempting to rescue them, is next seized and involved in the serpents' coils. He struggles to tear them away, but they overpower all his efforts and strangle him and the children in their poisonous folds. This event was regarded as a clear indication of the displeasure of the gods at Laocoön's irreverent[5] treatment of the wooden horse, which they no longer hesitated to regard as a sacred object, and prepared to introduce with due solemnity into the city. This was done with songs and triumphal acclamations[6], and the day closed with festivity. In the night the armed men who were enclosed in the body of the horse, being let out by the traitor Sinon, opened the gates of the city to their friends, who had returned under cover of the night. The city was set on fire; the people, overcome with feasting and sleep, put to the sword, and Troy completely subdued.

King Priam lived to see the downfall of his kingdom and was slain at last on the fatal night when the Greeks took the city. He had armed himself and was about to mingle with the combatants, but was prevailed on by Hecuba, his aged queen, to take refuge with herself and his daughters as a suppliant at the altar of Jupiter. While there, his youngest son Polites[7], pursued by Pyrrhus[8], the son of Achilles, rushed in wounded, and expired at the feet of his father; whereupon Priam, overcome with indignation, hurled his spear with feeble hand against Pyrrhus, and was forthwith slain by him.

Queen Hecuba and her daughter Cassandra[9] were carried captives to Greece. Cassandra had

---

① Sinon: /ˈsaɪnən/
② express /ɪksˈpres/: 明确的
③ monstrous /ˈmɒnstrəs/: 巨大的
④ augury /ˈɔːgjuri/: 预兆
⑤ irreverent /ɪˈrevərənt/: 不尊敬的,不敬神的
⑥ acclamation /ˌækləˈmeɪʃn/: 称赞,欢呼
⑦ Polites: /pəˈlɪtiːz/
⑧ Pyrrhus /ˈpɪrəs/: 又叫 Neoptolemus。
⑨ Cassandra: /kəˈsændrə/

been loved by Apollo, and he gave her the gift of prophecy; but afterwards offended with her, he rendered the gift unavailing by ordaining that her predictions should never be believed. Polyxena, another daughter, who had been loved by Achilles, was demanded by the ghost of that warrior, and was sacrificed by the Greeks upon his tomb.

Menelaus and Helen

Our readers will be anxious to know the fate of Helen, the fair but guilty occasion[1] of so much slaughter. On the fall of Troy Menelaus recovered possession of his wife, who had not ceased to love him, though she had yielded to the might of Venus[2] and deserted[3] him for another. After the death of Paris she aided the Greeks secretly on several occasions, and in particular when Ulysses and Diomed entered the city in disguise to carry off the Palladium. She saw and recognized Ulysses, but kept the secret and even assisted them in obtaining the image[4]. Thus she became reconciled to her husband, and they were among the first to leave the shores of Troy for their native land. But having incurred the displeasure of the gods they were driven by storms from shore to shore of the Mediterranean, visiting Cyprus, Phœnicia, and Egypt. In Egypt they were kindly treated and presented with rich gifts, of which Helen's share was a golden spindle[5] and a basket on wheels. The basket was to hold the wool and spools[6] for the queen's work.

Menelaus and Helen at length arrived in safety at Sparta, resumed their royal dignity, and lived and reigned in splendor; and when Telemachus, the son of Ulysses, in search of his father, arrived at Sparta, he found Menelaus and Helen celebrating the marriage of their daughter Hermione[7] to Neoptolemus[8], son of Achilles.

Agamemnon, Orestes, and Electra

Agamemnon, the general-in-chief of the Greeks, the brother of Menelaus, and who had been drawn into the quarrel to avenge his brother's wrongs, not his own, was not so fortunate in the issue. During his absence his wife Clytemnestra[9] had been false[10] to him, and when his return was expected, she with her paramour[11], Ægisthus[12], laid a plan for his destruction[13], and at the banquet given to celebrate his return, murdered him.

---

① occasion /əˈkeɪʒn/：起因

② the might of Venus：love

③ desert /dɪˈzɜːt/：抛弃

④ image：雕像，塑像

⑤ spindle /ˈspɪndl/：纺锤

⑥ spool：线轴

⑦ Hermione：/hɜːˈmaɪəni/

⑧ Neoptolemus /ˌniːɒpˈtɒləməs/：又叫 Pyrrhus。

⑨ Clytemnestra：/ˌklaɪtɪmˈnestrə/

⑩ false：(夫或妻对对方)不忠实的

⑪ paramour /ˈpærəmʊə/：(已婚者的)非法性伴侣或秘密情人

⑫ Ægisthus：/iːˈdʒɪsθəs/

⑬ destruction：杀害

It was intended by the conspirators to slay his son Orestes① also, a lad not yet old enough to be an object of apprehension②, but from whom, if he should be suffered to grow up, there might be danger. Electra③, the sister of Orestes, saved her brother's life by sending him secretly away to his uncle Strophius④, King of Phocis⑤. In the palace of Strophius Orestes grew up with the king's son Pylades⑥, and formed with him that ardent friendship which has become proverbial. Electra frequently reminded her brother by messengers of the duty of avenging his father's death, and when grown up he consulted the oracle of Delphi, which confirmed him in his design. He therefore repaired in disguise to Argos⑦, pretending to be a messenger from Strophius, who had come to announce the death of Orestes, and brought the ashes of the deceased⑧ in a funeral urn. After visiting his father's tomb and sacrificing upon it, according to the rites of the ancients, he made himself known to his sister Electra, and soon after slew both Ægisthus and Clytemnestra.

This revolting⑨ act, the slaughter of a mother by her son, though alleviated⑩ by the guilt of the victim and the express command of the gods, did not fail to awaken in the breasts of the ancients the same abhorrence⑪ that it does in ours. The Eumenides, avenging deities, seized upon Orestes, and drove him frantic from land to land. Pylades accompanied him in his wanderings and watched over him. At length, in answer to a second appeal to the oracle, he was directed to go to Tauris in Scythia, and to bring thence a statue of Diana which was believed to have fallen from heaven. Accordingly Orestes and Pylades went to Tauris, where the barbarous people were accustomed to sacrifice to the goddess all strangers who fell into their hands. The two friends were seized and carried bound to the temple to be made victims⑫. But the priestess of Diana was no other than Iphigenia, the sister of Orestes, who, our readers will remember, was snatched away by Diana at the moment when she was about to be sacrificed. Ascertaining from the prisoners who they were, Iphigenia disclosed herself to them, and the three made their escape with the statue of the goddess, and returned to Mycenæ.

But Orestes was not yet relieved from the vengeance of the Erinyes. At length he took refuge with Minerva at Athens. The goddess afforded him protection, and appointed the court of Areopagus⑬ to decide his fate. The Erinyes brought forward their accusation, and Orestes made the

---

① Orestes：/ɒˈrestiːz/

② apprehension /ˌæprɪˈhenʃn/：恐惧,不安,忧虑

③ Electra：/ɪˈlektrə/

④ Strophius：/ˈstrəʊfɪəs/

⑤ Phocis /ˈfəʊsɪs/：古希腊地区名,位于希腊中部,大致相当于今希腊中希腊大区弗西奥蒂斯州（Fthiotis）西南部和福基斯州（Phocis 或 Fokis）。Delphi 在其境内。

⑥ Pylades：/ˈpɪlədiːz/

⑦ Agamemnon is the king of Mycenæ, or Argos.

⑧ the deceased /dɪˈsiːst/：死者

⑨ revolting /rɪˈvəʊltɪŋ/：叛逆的,令人作呕的,可怕的

⑩ alleviate /əˈliːvieɪt/：减轻

⑪ abhorrence /əbˈhɒrəns/：憎恨,憎恶

⑫ victim：杀死来献给神当祭品的人或动物

⑬ the court of Areopagus：（古雅典城邦的）最高法院；Areopagus /ˌærɪˈɒpəɡəs/：雅典山名,古雅典城邦最高法院的所在地。

command of the Delphic oracle his excuse. When the court voted and the voices were equally divided, Orestes was acquitted[①] by the command of Minerva.

Chapter XXIX
Adventures of Ulysses

Return of Ulysses

The romantic poem of the *Odyssey* is now to engage[②] our attention. It narrates the wanderings of Ulysses[③](Odysseus[④] in the Greek language) in his return from Troy to his own kingdom Ithaca[⑤].

From Troy the vessels first made[⑥] land at Ismarus[⑦], city of the Ciconians[⑧], where, in a skirmish[⑨] with the inhabitants, Ulysses lost six men from each ship. Sailing thence, they were overtaken by a storm which drove them for nine days along the sea till they reached the country of the Lotus-eaters. Here, after watering[⑩], Ulysses sent three of his men to discover who the inhabitants were. These men on coming among the Lotus-eaters were kindly entertained[⑪] by them, and were given some of their own food, the lotus-plant, to eat. The effect of this food was such that those who partook of it lost all thoughts of home and wished to remain in that country. It was by main force that Ulysses dragged these men away, and he was even obliged to tie them under the benches of the ships.

They next arrived at the country of the Cyclopes[⑫]. The Cyclopes were giants, who inhabited an island of which they were the only possessors. The name means "round eye," and these giants were so called because they had but one eye, and that placed in the middle of the forehead. They dwelt in caves and fed on the wild productions of the island and on what their flocks yielded, for they were shepherds. Ulysses left the main body of his ships at anchor, and with one vessel went to the Cyclopes' island to explore for supplies[⑬]. He landed with his companions, carrying with them a jar of wine for a present, and coming to a large cave they entered it, and finding no one within

---

① acquit /əˈkwɪt/：宣布无罪

② engage：吸引

③ Ulysses：/juːˈlɪsiːz/

④ Odysseus /əˈdɪsjuːs/：史诗标题 *Odyssey* 一词来自于该希腊语名字。

⑤ Ithaca /ˈɪθəkə/：参见 *The Age of Fable* 第 23 章关于 Ithaca 的注释。

⑥ make：抵达，到达

⑦ Ismarus /ɪsˈmærəs/：古代城市名，位于色雷斯（Thrace）爱琴海海岸。

⑧ the Ciconians /sɪˈkəʊnɪənz/：色雷斯部落，居住在色雷斯南部的爱琴海海岸。

⑨ skirmish /ˈskɜːmɪʃ/：小规模战斗

⑩ water：给船补充淡水

⑪ entertain /ˌentəˈteɪn/：款待，招待

⑫ Cyclopes /saɪˈkləʊpiːz/：该词的单数是 Cyclops /ˈsaɪklɒps/，复数形式是 Cyclopes，Cyclops 或 Cyclopses。

⑬ supplies：补给

examined its contents. They found it stored with the richest of the flock, quantities of cheese, pails and bowls of milk, lambs and kids[①] in their pens[②], all in nice order. Presently[③] arrived the master of the cave, Polyphemus[④], bearing an immense bundle of firewood, which he threw down before the cavern's mouth. He then drove into the cave the sheep and goats to be milked, and, entering, rolled to the cave's mouth an enormous rock, that twenty oxen could not draw. Next he sat down and milked his ewes[⑤], preparing a part for cheese, and setting the rest aside for his customary[⑥] drink. Then, turning round his great eye, he discerned the strangers, and growled out to them, demanding who they were, and where from. Ulysses replied most humbly, stating that they were Greeks, from the great expedition that had lately won so much glory in the conquest of Troy; that they were now on their way home, and finished by imploring his hospitality in the name of the gods. Polyphemus deigned no answer[⑦], but reaching out his hand seized two of the Greeks, whom he hurled against the side of the cave, and dashed out their brains. He proceeded to devour them with great relish[⑧], and having made a hearty meal, stretched himself out on the floor to sleep. Ulysses was tempted to seize the opportunity and plunge his sword into him as he slept, but recollected that it would only expose them all to certain destruction, as the rock with which the giant had closed up the door was far beyond their power to remove, and they would therefore be in hopeless imprisonment. Next morning the giant seized two more of the Greeks, and despatched[⑨] them in the same manner as their companions, feasting on their flesh till no fragment was left. He then moved away the rock from the door, drove out his flocks, and went out, carefully replacing the barrier after him. When he was gone Ulysses planned how he might take vengeance for his murdered friends, and effect[⑩] his escape with his surviving companions. He made his men prepare a massive bar of wood cut by the Cyclops for a staff, which they found in the cave. They sharpened the end of it, and seasoned[⑪] it in the fire, and hid it under the straw on the cavern floor. Then four of the boldest were selected, with whom Ulysses joined himself as a fifth. The Cyclops came home at evening, rolled away the stone and drove in his flock as usual. After milking them and making his arrangements as before, he seized two more of Ulysses' companions and dashed their brains out, and made his evening meal upon them as he had on the others. After he had supped[⑫], Ulysses approaching him handed him a bowl of wine, saying, "Cyclops, this is wine; taste and drink after thy meal of men's flesh." He took and drank it, and was hugely delighted with it, and

---

① kid：小山羊

② pen：（牛、羊、鸡等的）圈

③ presently：soon

④ Polyphemus /ˌpɒlɪˈfiːməs/：参见 *The Age of Fable* 第 26 章 "Acis and Galatea" 的故事。

⑤ ewe /juː/：母羊

⑥ customary /ˈkʌstəməri/：平常的，通常的

⑦ deign /deɪn/ no answer：不屑回答

⑧ with great relish：津津有味地；relish /ˈrelɪʃ/：对某种食物的味道特别喜欢

⑨ despatch（dispatch）/dɪˈspætʃ/：杀死

⑩ effect：完成，实现

⑪ season：使（木材）变干、变硬

⑫ sup /sʌp/：吃晚餐

called for more. Ulysses supplied him once again, which pleased the giant so much that he promised him as a favor that he should be the last of the party devoured. He asked his name, to which Ulysses replied, "My name is Noman."

After his supper the giant lay down to repose, and was soon found asleep. Then Ulysses with his four select friends thrust the end of the stake into the fire till it was all one burning coal, then poising it exactly above the giant's only eye, they buried it deeply into the socket①, twirling it round as a carpenter does his auger②. The howling monster with his outcry filled the cavern, and Ulysses with his aids③ nimbly got out of his way and concealed themselves in the cave. He, bellowing, called aloud on all the Cyclopes dwelling in the caves around him, far and near. They on his cry flocked round the den, and inquired what grievous hurt had caused him to sound such an alarm and break their slumbers. He replied, "O friends, I die, and Noman gives the blow." They answered, "If no man hurts thee it is the stroke of Jove, and thou must bear it." So saying, they left him groaning.

Next morning the Cyclops rolled away the stone to let his flock out to pasture, but planted himself in the door of the cave to feel of all as they went out, that Ulysses and his men should not escape with them. But Ulysses had made his men harness the rams of the flock three abreast, with osiers④ which they found on the floor of the cave. To the middle ram of the three one of the Greeks suspended himself, so protected by the exterior⑤ rams on either side. As they passed, the giant felt of the animals' backs and sides, but never thought of their bellies; so the men all passed safe, Ulysses himself being on the last one that passed. When they had got a few paces from the cavern, Ulysses and his friends released themselves from their rams, and drove a good part of the flock down to the shore to their boat. They put them aboard with all haste, then pushed off from the shore, and when at a safe distance Ulysses shouted out, "Cyclops, the gods have well requited⑥ thee for thy atrocious⑦ deeds. Know it is Ulysses to whom thou owest thy shameful loss of sight." The Cyclops, hearing this, seized a rock that projected from the side of the mountain, and rending it from its bed, he lifted it high in the air, then exerting all his force, hurled it in the direction of the voice. Down came the mass, just clearing⑧ the vessel's stern. The ocean, at the plunge of the huge rock, heaved the ship towards the land, so that it barely escaped being swamped⑨ by the waves. When they had with the utmost difficulty pulled off shore, Ulysses was about to hail the giant again, but his friends besought him not to do so. He could not forbear,

---

① socket /ˈsɒkɪt/：眼窝
② auger /ˈɔːɡə/：（木匠使用的）螺旋钻
③ aid：助手
④ osier /ˈəʊzɪə/：柳条
⑤ exterior /ɪkˈstɪərɪə/：外侧的
⑥ requite /rɪˈkwaɪt/：报复，报答
⑦ atrocious /əˈtrəʊʃəs/：野蛮的，残酷的
⑧ clear：越过
⑨ swamp /swɒmp/：淹没

however, letting the giant know that they had escaped his missile①, but waited till they had reached a safer distance than before. The giant answered them with curses, but Ulysses and his friends plied their oars vigorously, and soon regained② their companions.

Ulysses next arrived at the island of Æolus③. To this monarch Jupiter had intrusted the government④ of the winds, to send them forth or retain them at his will. He treated Ulysses hospitably, and at his departure gave him, tied up in a leathern bag, with a silver string, such winds as might be hurtful and dangerous, commanding fair winds to blow the barks⑤ towards their country. Nine days they sped before the wind, and all that time Ulysses had stood at the helm⑥, without sleep. At last quite exhausted he lay down to sleep. While he slept, the crew conferred together about the mysterious bag, and concluded it must contain treasures given by the hospitable king Æolus to their commander. Tempted to secure some portion for themselves, they loosed the string, when immediately the winds rushed forth. The ships were driven far from their course, and back again to the island they had just left. Æolus was so indignant at their folly that he refused to assist them further, and they were obliged to labor over their course once more by means of their oars.

The Læstrygonians

Their next adventure was with the barbarous tribe of Læstrygonians⑦. The vessels all pushed into the harbor, tempted by the secure appearance of the cove⑧, completely land-locked⑨; only Ulysses moored his vessel without⑩. As soon as the Læstrygonians found the ships completely in their power they attacked them, heaving huge stones which broke and overturned them, and with their spears despatched the seamen as they struggled in the water. All the vessels with their crews were destroyed, except Ulysses' own ship, which had remained outside, and finding no safety but in flight, he exhorted his men to ply their oars vigorously, and they escaped.

With grief for their slain companions mixed with joy at their own escape, they pursued their way till they arrived at the Ææan isle⑪, where Circe⑫ dwelt, the daughter of the sun. Landing here, Ulysses climbed a hill, and gazing round saw no signs of habitation except in one spot at the centre of the island, where he perceived a palace embowered with trees. He sent forward one-half of his crew, under the command of Eurylochus⑬, to see what prospect of hospitality they might

---

① his missile /ˈmɪsaɪl/: 他投掷的石头
② regain: 与……会合,与……团聚
③ Æolus: /ˈiːəʊləs/
④ government: 管理,控制
⑤ bark: 船
⑥ helm /helm/: 舵
⑦ Læstrygonians /ˌliːstrɪˈɡəʊnɪənz/: 传说中同类相食的巨人部落
⑧ cove: 小海湾
⑨ land-locked /ˈlændlɒkt/: 被陆地包围的
⑩ without: 在外面
⑪ the Ææan /iːˈiːən/ isle: Ææa /iːˈiːə/, 其地理位置不详。
⑫ Circe: /ˈsɜːsi/
⑬ Eurylochus: /juːˈrɪləkəs/

find. As they approached the palace, they found themselves surrounded by lions, tigers, and wolves, not fierce, but tamed by Circe's art, for she was a powerful magician. All these animals had once been men, but had been changed by Circe's enchantments① into the forms of beasts. The sounds of soft music were heard from within, and a sweet female voice singing. Eurylochus called aloud and the goddess came forth and invited them in; they all gladly entered except Eurylochus, who suspected danger. The goddess conducted her guests to a seat, and had them served with wine and other delicacies. When they had feasted heartily, she touched them one by one with her wand, and they became immediately changed into swine, in "head, body, voice, and bristles②," yet with their intellects③ as before. She shut them in her sties and supplied them with acorns and such other things as swine love.

Eurylochus hurried back to the ship and told the tale. Ulysses thereupon determined to go himself, and try if by any means he might deliver his companions. As he strode onward alone, he met a youth who addressed him familiarly, appearing to be acquainted with his adventures. He announced himself as Mercury, and informed Ulysses of the arts of Circe, and of the danger of approaching her. As Ulysses was not to be dissuaded from his attempt, Mercury provided him with a sprig of the plant Moly④, of wonderful power to resist sorceries, and instructed him how to act. Ulysses proceeded, and reaching the palace was courteously received by Circe, who entertained him as she had done his companions, and after he had eaten and drank, touched him with her wand, saying, "Hence, seek the sty and wallow⑤ with thy friends." But he, instead of obeying, drew his sword and rushed upon her with fury in his countenance. She fell on her knees and begged for mercy. He dictated a solemn oath that she would release his companions and practise no further harm against him or them; and she repeated it, at the same time promising to dismiss them all in safety after hospitably entertaining them. She was as good as her word.⑥ The men were restored to their shapes, the rest of the crew summoned from the shore, and the whole magnificently entertained day after day, till Ulysses seemed to have forgotten his native land, and to have reconciled⑦ himself to an inglorious⑧ life of ease and pleasure.

At length his companions recalled him to nobler sentiments, and he received their admonition gratefully. Circe aided their departure, and instructed them how to pass safely by the coast of the Sirens⑨. The Sirens were sea-nymphs who had the power of charming⑩ by their song all who heard them, so that the unhappy mariners were irresistibly impelled to cast themselves into the sea to

---

① enchantment /ɪnˈtʃɑːntmənt/：魔力，妖术
② bristle /ˈbrɪsl/：猪鬃
③ intellect /ˈɪntəlekt/：智力
④ Moly /ˈməʊli/：白花黑根魔草
⑤ wallow /ˈwɒləʊ/：打滚
⑥ 她说到做到。
⑦ reconcile /ˈrekənsaɪl/：使甘心于
⑧ inglorious /ɪnˈglɔːrɪəs/：可耻的，不光彩的
⑨ Siren：/ˈsaɪərən/
⑩ charm：迷住，（实施魔法以）控制

their destruction. Circe directed Ulysses to fill the ears of his seamen with wax, so that they should not hear the strain; and to cause himself to be bound to the mast, and his people① to be strictly enjoined②, whatever he might say or do, by no means to release him till they should have passed the Sirens' island. Ulysses obeyed these directions. He filled the ears of his people with wax, and suffered them to bind him with cords firmly to the mast. As they approached the Sirens' island, the sea was calm, and over the waters came the notes of music so ravishing③ and attractive that Ulysses struggled to get loose, and by cries and signs to his people begged to be released; but they, obedient to his previous orders, sprang forward and bound him still faster. They held on their course, and the music grew fainter till it ceased to be heard, when with joy Ulysses gave his companions the signal to unseal④ their ears, and they relieved him from his bonds.

Scylla and Charybdis

Ulysses had been warned by Circe of the two monsters Scylla and Charybdis⑤. We have already met with Scylla in the story of Glaucus⑥, and remember that she was once a beautiful maiden and was changed into a snaky monster by Circe. She dwelt in a cave high up on the cliff, from whence she was accustomed to thrust forth her long necks (for she had six heads), and in each of her mouths to seize one of the crew of every vessel passing within reach. The other terror, Charybdis, was a gulf⑦, nearly on a level with the water. Thrice each day the water rushed into a frightful chasm, and thrice was disgorged⑧. Any vessel coming near the whirlpool when the tide was rushing in must inevitably be ingulfed⑨; not Neptune himself could save it.

On approaching the haunt⑩ of the dread⑪ monsters, Ulysses kept strict watch to discover them. The roar of the waters as Charybdis ingulfed them, gave warning at a distance, but Scylla could nowhere be discerned. While Ulysses and his men watched with anxious eyes the dreadful whirlpool, they were not equally on their guard from the attack of Scylla, and the monster, darting forth her snaky heads, caught six of his men, and bore them away, shrieking, to her den. It was the saddest sight Ulysses had yet seen; to behold his friends thus sacrificed and hear their cries, unable to afford them any assistance.

Circe had warned him of another danger. After passing Scylla and Charybdis the next land he

---

① his people: his seamen
② enjoin /ɪnˈdʒɔɪn/：禁止
③ ravishing /ˈrævɪʃɪŋ/：令人销魂的
④ unseal /ˈʌnˈsiːl/：给……拆封
⑤ Scylla：/ˈsɪlə /; Charybdis：/kəˈrɪbdɪs/
⑥ 参见 The Age of Fable 第 7 章。
⑦ gulf：漩涡
⑧ disgorge /dɪsˈɡɔːdʒ/：吐出
⑨ ingulf (engulf) /ɪnˈɡʌlf/：吞没
⑩ haunt /hɔːnt/：(动物的) 出没地
⑪ dread /dred/：可怕的

would make was Thrinakia①, an island whereon were pastured the cattle of Hyperion②, the Sun, tended by his daughters Lampetia and Phaëthusa③. These flocks must not be violated④, whatever the wants of the voyagers might be. If this injunction⑤ were transgressed⑥ destruction was sure to fall on the offenders.

Ulysses would willingly have passed the island of the Sun without stopping, but his companions so urgently pleaded for the rest and refreshment that would be derived from anchoring and passing the night on shore, that Ulysses yielded. He bound them, however, with an oath that they would not touch one of the animals of the sacred flocks and herds, but content themselves with what provision they yet had left of the supply which Circe had put on board. So long as this supply lasted the people kept their oath, but contrary winds⑦ detained them at the island for a month, and after consuming all their stock of provisions, they were forced to rely upon the birds and fishes they could catch. Famine pressed them, and at length one day, in the absence of Ulysses, they slew some of the cattle, vainly attempting to make amends for the deed by offering from them a portion to the offended powers. Ulysses, on his return to the shore, was horror-struck⑧ at perceiving what they had done, and the more so on account of the portentous signs which followed. The skins crept on the ground, and the joints of meat lowed⑨ on the spits⑩ while roasting.

The wind becoming fair they sailed from the island. They had not gone far when the weather changed, and a storm of thunder and lightning ensued. A stroke of lightning shattered their mast, which in its fall killed the pilot. At last the vessel itself came to pieces. The keel and mast floating side by side, Ulysses formed of them a raft, to which he clung, and, the wind changing, the waves bore him to Calypso's island. All the rest of the crew perished.

Calypso

Calypso⑪ was a sea-nymph, which name denotes a numerous class of female divinities of lower rank, yet sharing many of the attributes⑫ of the gods. Calypso received Ulysses hospitably, entertained him magnificently, became enamoured of him, and wished to retain him forever,

---

① Thrinakia /θrɪ'neɪkɪə/：其地理位置不详。

② Hyperion /haɪ'pɪərɪən/：提坦神（the Titans）之一，太阳神（Helios）、月亮女神（Selene）和黎明女神（Eos）的父亲。荷马和其他诗人偶尔会用 Hyperion 这个名字来指太阳神 Helios。Helios, Selene, Eos 是奥林匹斯诸神之前的一代神。

③ Lampetia：/ləm'piːtɪə /；Phaëthusa：/ˌfeɪɪ'θjuːzə/

④ violate /'vaɪəleɪt/：侵犯，亵渎

⑤ injunction /ɪn'dʒʌŋkʃn/：警告

⑥ transgress /trænz'gres/：违背

⑦ contrary winds：逆风

⑧ horror-struck /'hɒrəstrʌk/：惊恐的

⑨ low：（牛）哞哞地叫

⑩ spit：烤肉叉

⑪ Calypso：/kə'lɪpsəʊ/

⑫ attribute /'ætrɪbjuːt/：特点

conferring on him immortality. But he persisted in his resolution① to return to his country and his wife and son. Calypso at last received the command of Jove to dismiss him. Mercury brought the message to her, and found her in her grotto.

Calypso with much reluctance② proceeded to obey the commands of Jupiter. She supplied Ulysses with the means of constructing a raft, provisioned it well for him, and gave him a favoring gale. He sped on his course prosperously for many days, till at length, when in sight of land, a storm arose that broke his mast, and threatened to rend the raft asunder. In this crisis he was seen by a compassionate sea-nymph, who in the form of a cormorant③ alighted on the raft, and presented him a girdle, directing him to bind it beneath his breast, and if he should be compelled to trust himself to the waves, it would buoy him up and enable him by swimming to reach the land.

Chapter XXX
The Phæacians—Fate of the Suitors

The Phæacians

Ulysses clung to the raft while any of its timbers kept together, and when it no longer yielded him support, binding the girdle around him, he swam. Minerva smoothed the billows before him and sent him a wind that rolled the waves towards the shore. The surf beat high on the rocks and seemed to forbid approach; but at length finding calm water at the mouth of a gentle stream, he landed, spent④ with toil, breathless and speechless and almost dead. After some time, reviving, he kissed the soil, rejoicing, yet at a loss what course to take. At a short distance he perceived a wood, to which he turned his steps. There, finding a covert sheltered by intermingling⑤ branches alike from the sun and the rain, he collected a pile of leaves and formed a bed, on which he stretched himself, and heaping the leaves over him, fell asleep.

The land where he was thrown was Scheria⑥, the country of the Phæacians⑦. These people dwelt originally near the Cyclopes; but being oppressed by that savage race, they migrated to the isle of Scheria, under the conduct⑧ of Nausithoüs⑨, their king. They were, the poet tells us, a

---

① resolution /ˌrezəˈluːʃn/：决心
② reluctance /rɪˈlʌktəns/：不情愿
③ cormorant /ˈkɔːmərənt/：鸬鹚，水老鸦
④ spend：使耗尽体力
⑤ intermingle /ˌɪntəˈmɪŋgl/：交织在一起
⑥ Scheria /ˈskiːrɪə/：即今天的科孚岛（Corfu）。科孚岛又叫克基拉岛（Kerkira），是希腊伊奥尼亚群岛中的一个岛，位于希腊和阿尔巴尼亚交界处以西的大海上。该岛离 Ulysses 的家乡 Ithaca 不远。
⑦ Phæacian：/fɪˈeɪʃn/
⑧ conduct /ˈkɒndʌkt/：指导，引导
⑨ Nausithoüs：/ˌnɔːsɪˈθəʊəs/

people akin① to the gods, who appeared manifestly② and feasted among them when they offered sacrifices, and did not conceal themselves from solitary wayfarers③ when they met them. They had abundance of wealth and lived in the enjoyment of it undisturbed by the alarms④ of war, for as they dwelt remote from gain-seeking man, no enemy ever approached their shores, and they did not even require to make use of bows and quivers. Their chief employment was navigation. Their ships, which went with the velocity⑤ of birds, were endued with intelligence; they knew every port and needed no pilot. Alcinoüs⑥, the son of Nausithoüs, was now their king, a wise and just sovereign, beloved by his people.

Now it happened that the very night on which Ulysses was cast ashore on the Phæacian island, and while he lay sleeping on his bed of leaves, Nausicaa⑦, the daughter of the king, had a dream sent by Minerva, reminding her that her wedding-day was not far distant, and that it would be but a prudent preparation for that event to have a general washing of the clothes of the family. This was no slight affair, for the fountains were at some distance, and the garments must be carried thither. On awaking, the princess hastened to her parents to tell them what was on her mind; not alluding to her wedding-day, but finding other reasons equally good. Her father readily assented and ordered the grooms⑧ to furnish forth a wagon for the purpose. The clothes were put therein, and the queen mother placed in the wagon, likewise, an abundant supply of food and wine. The princess took her seat and plied the lash⑨, her attendant virgins following her on foot. Arrived at the river side, they turned out the mules to graze, and unlading⑩ the carriage, bore the garments down to the water, and working with cheerfulness and alacrity⑪ soon despatched⑫ their labor. Then having spread the garments on the shore to dry, and having themselves bathed, they sat down to enjoy their meal; after which they rose and amused themselves with a game of ball, the princess singing to them while they played. But when they had refolded the apparel⑬ and were about to resume their way to the town, Minerva caused the ball thrown by the princess to fall into the water, whereat they all screamed and Ulysses awaked at the sound.

Now we must picture to ourselves Ulysses, a shipwrecked mariner, but a few hours escaped from the waves, and utterly destitute of clothing⑭, awaking and discovering that only a few bushes

① akin：有血缘关系的
② manifestly /ˈmænɪfestli/：明显地（指不隐藏其神的身份）
③ wayfarer /ˈweɪfeərə/：行路人
④ alarm：忧虑，担心
⑤ velocity /vəˈlɒsəti/：快速
⑥ Alcinoüs：/ˌælsɪˈnəʊəs/
⑦ Nausicaa：/nɔːˈsɪkɪə/
⑧ groom：男仆，马夫
⑨ lash：鞭子
⑩ unlade /ʌnˈleɪd/：从……卸下货物
⑪ alacrity /əˈlækrəti/：轻快
⑫ despatch（dispatch）：完成
⑬ apparel /əˈpærəl/：衣服
⑭ destitute of clothing：没有穿衣服的；destitute /ˈdestɪtjuːt/：没有的；缺乏的

were interposed① between him and a group of young maidens whom, by their deportment② and attire③, he discovered to be not mere peasant girls, but of a higher class. Sadly needing help, how could he yet venture, naked as he was, to discover④ himself and make his wants known? It certainly was a case worthy of the interposition⑤ of his patron goddess Minerva, who never failed him at a crisis. Breaking off a leafy branch from a tree, he held it before him and stepped out from the thicket. The virgins at sight of him fled in all directions, Nausicaa alone excepted, for her Minerva aided and endowed⑥ with courage and discernment⑦. Ulysses, standing respectfully aloof, told his sad case, and besought the fair object⑧(whether queen or goddess he professed he knew not) for food and clothing. The princess replied courteously, promising present relief and her father's hospitality when he should become acquainted with the facts. She called back her scattered maidens, chiding their alarm, and reminding them that the Phæacians had no enemies to fear. This man, she told them, was an unhappy wanderer, whom it was a duty to cherish, for the poor and stranger are from Jove. She bade them bring food and clothing, for some of her brother's garments were among the contents of the wagon. When this was done, and Ulysses, retiring to a sheltered place, had washed his body free from the sea-foam, clothed and refreshed himself with food, Pallas dilated⑨ his form⑩ and diffused grace over his ample chest and manly brows.

The princess, seeing him, was filled with admiration, and scrupled⑪ not to say to her damsels⑫ that she wished the gods would send her such a husband. To Ulysses she recommended that he should repair to the city, following herself and train⑬ so far as the way lay through the fields; but when they should approach the city she desired that he would no longer be seen in her company, for she feared the remarks which rude and vulgar people might make on seeing her return accompanied by such a gallant⑭ stranger. To avoid which she directed him to stop at a grove adjoining⑮ the city, in which were a farm and garden belonging to the king. After allowing time for the princess and her companions to reach the city, he was then to pursue his way thither, and would be easily guided by any he might meet to the royal abode.

Ulysses obeyed the directions and in due time proceeded to the city, on approaching which he

---

① interpose /ˌɪntəˈpəʊz/：放置在……之间

② deportment /dɪˈpɔːtmənt/：风度，举止

③ attire /əˈtaɪə/：衣服，衣着

④ discover：暴露，使被看到

⑤ interposition /ˌɪntəpəˈzɪʃn/：介入

⑥ endow /ɪnˈdaʊ/：赋予

⑦ discernment /dɪˈsɜːnmənt/：洞察力

⑧ the fair object：Nausicaa, who is beautiful

⑨ dilate /daɪˈleɪt/：扩大

⑩ form：美

⑪ scruple /ˈskruːpl/：有顾虑

⑫ damsel /ˈdæmzl/：侍女

⑬ train：一群随从

⑭ gallant /ˈɡælənt/：有吸引力的，帅气的

⑮ adjoin /əˈdʒɔɪn/：临近，靠近

met a young woman bearing a pitcher① forth for water. It was Minerva, who had assumed that form. Ulysses accosted her and desired to be directed to the palace of Alcinoüs the king. The maiden replied respectfully, offering to be his guide; for the palace, she informed him, stood near her father's dwelling. Under the guidance of the goddess, and by her power enveloped in a cloud which shielded him from observation, Ulysses passed among the busy crowd, and with wonder observed their harbor, their ships, their forum②(the resort of heroes), and their battlements, till they came to the palace, where the goddess, having first given him some information of the country, king, and people he was about to meet, left him. Ulysses, before entering the courtyard of the palace, stood and surveyed the scene. Its splendor astonished him. Brazen walls stretched from the entrance to the interior house, of which the doors were gold, the doorposts silver, the lintels③ silver ornamented with gold. On either side were figures④ of mastiffs⑤ wrought in gold and silver, standing in rows as if to guard the approach. Along the walls were seats spread through all their length with mantles of finest texture, the work of Phæacian maidens. On these seats the princes sat and feasted, while golden statues of graceful youths held in their hands lighted torches which shed radiance over the scene. Full fifty female menials⑥ served in household offices, some employed to grind the corn, others to wind off the purple wool or ply the loom⑦. For the Phæacian women as far exceeded all other women in household arts as the mariners of that country did the rest of mankind in the management of ships. Without⑧ the court a spacious garden lay, four acres in extent. In it grew many a lofty tree, pomegranate, pear, apple, fig, and olive. Neither winter's cold nor summer's drought arrested their growth, but they flourished in constant succession, some budding while others were maturing. The vineyard was equally prolific. In one quarter you might see the vines, some in blossom, some loaded with ripe grapes, and in another observe the vintagers⑨ treading the wine press⑩. On the garden's borders flowers of all hues bloomed all the year round, arranged with neatest art. In the midst two fountains poured forth their waters, one flowing by artificial channels over all the garden, the other conducted through the courtyard of the palace, whence every citizen might draw his supplies.

Ulysses stood gazing in admiration, unobserved himself, for the cloud which Minerva spread around him still shielded him. At length, having sufficiently observed the scene, he advanced with rapid step into the hall where the chiefs and senators were assembled, pouring libation to Mercury, whose worship followed the evening meal. Just then Minerva dissolved the cloud and disclosed him

---

① pitcher /ˈpɪtʃə/：有手柄和嘴的陶制大罐
② forum /ˈfɔːrəm/：城市的广场或市场
③ lintel /ˈlɪntl/：门楣
④ figure：雕像
⑤ mastiff /ˈmæstɪf/：一种大头、垂耳、高大、强壮的看家狗
⑥ menial /ˈmiːnɪəl/：家仆
⑦ loom：织布机
⑧ without：outside
⑨ vintager /ˈvɪntɪdʒə/：酿酒师
⑩ wine press：榨汁机（用来榨取酿葡萄酒的葡萄汁）

to the assembled chiefs. Advancing to the place where the queen sat, he knelt at her feet and implored her favor and assistance to enable him to return to his native country. Then withdrawing, he seated himself in the manner of suppliants, at the hearth side.

For a time none spoke. At last an aged statesman, addressing the king, said, "It is not fit that a stranger who asks our hospitality① should be kept waiting in suppliant guise, none welcoming him. Let him therefore be led to a seat among us and supplied with food and wine." At these words the king rising gave his hand to Ulysses and led him to a seat, displacing thence his own son to make room for the stranger. Food and wine were set before him and he ate and refreshed himself.

The king then dismissed his guests, notifying them that the next day he would call them to council to consider what had best be done for the stranger.

When the guests had departed and Ulysses was left alone with the king and queen, the queen asked him who he was and whence he came, and (recognizing the clothes which he wore as those which her maidens and herself had made) from whom he received those garments. He told them of his residence in Calypso's isle and his departure thence; of the wreck of his raft, his escape by swimming, and of the relief afforded by the princess. The parents heard approvingly, and the king promised to furnish a ship in which his guest might return to his own land.

The next day the assembled chiefs confirmed the promise of the king. A bark② was prepared and a crew of stout rowers③ selected, and all betook themselves to the palace, where a bounteous④ repast⑤ was provided. After the feast the king proposed that the young men should show their guest their proficiency⑥ in manly sports, and all went forth to the arena⑦ for games of running, wrestling, and other exercises. After all had done their best, Ulysses being challenged to show what he could do, at first declined, but being taunted⑧ by one of the youths, seized a quoit of weight far heavier than any of the Phæacinas had thrown, and sent it farther than the utmost⑨ throw of theirs. All were astonished, and viewed their guest with greatly increased respect.

After the games they returned to the hall, and the herald led in Demodocus⑩, the blind bard. He took for his theme the "Wooden Horse," by means of which the Greeks found entrance into Troy. Apollo inspired him, and he sang so feelingly⑪ the terrors and the exploits of that eventful time that all were delighted, but Ulysses was moved to tears. Observing which, Alcinoüs, when the song was done, demanded of him why at the mention of Troy his sorrows awaked. Had he lost

---

① hospitality /ˌhɒspɪˈtæləti/：对陌生人、客人或来访者的款待
② bark：用人划的大船
③ rower /ˈrəʊə/：桨手，划船的人
④ bounteous /ˈbaʊntɪəs/：丰盛的
⑤ repast /rɪˈpɑːst/：食物
⑥ proficiency /prəˈfɪʃnsi/：熟练，精通，技能
⑦ arena /əˈriːnə/：竞技场
⑧ taunt /tɔːnt/：嘲笑，奚落
⑨ utmost /ˈʌtməʊst/：最远的
⑩ Demodocus：/dɪˈmɒdəkəs/
⑪ feelingly /ˈfiːlɪŋli/：动情地，充满感情地

there a father, or brother, or any dear friend? Ulysses replied by announcing himself by his true name, and at their request, recounted the adventures which had befallen him since his departure from Troy. This narrative raised the sympathy and admiration of the Phæacians for their guest to the highest pitch. The king proposed that all the chiefs should present him with a gift, himself setting the example. They obeyed, and vied① with one another in loading the illustrious stranger with costly gifts.

The next day Ulysses set sail in the Phæacian vessel, and in a short time arrived safe at Ithaca, his own island. When the vessel touched the strand he was asleep. The mariners, without waking him, carried him on shore, and landed with him the chest containing his presents, and then sailed away.

Neptune was so displeased at the conduct of the Phæacians in thus rescuing Ulysses from his hands that on the return of the vessel to port he transformed it into a rock, right opposite the mouth of the harbor.

Fate of the Suitors

Ulysses had now been away from Ithaca for twenty years, and when he awoke he did not recognize his native land. Minerva appeared to him in the form of a young shepherd, informed him where he was, and told him the state of things at his palace. More than a hundred nobles of Ithaca and of the neighboring islands had been for years suing for the hand of Penelope②, his wife, imagining him dead, and lording it③ over his palace and people, as if they were owners of both. That he might be able to take vengeance upon them, it was important that he should not be recognized. Minerva accordingly metamorphosed④ him into an unsightly⑤ beggar, and as such he was kindly received by Eumæus⑥, the swine-herd⑦, a faithful servant of his house.

Telemachus⑧, his son, was absent in quest of his father. He had gone to the courts of the other kings, who had returned from the Trojan expedition. While on the search, he received counsel from Minerva to return home. He arrived and sought Eumæus to learn something of the state of affairs at the palace before presenting himself among the suitors. Finding a stranger with Eumæus, he treated him courteously, though in the garb of a beggar, and promised him assistance. Eumæus was sent to the palace to inform Penelope privately of her son's arrival, for caution was necessary with regard to the suitors, who, as Telemachus had learned, were plotting to intercept⑨ and kill him. When Eumæus was gone, Minerva presented herself to Ulysses, and directed him to make himself known to his son. At the same time she touched him, removed at

---

① vie /vaɪ/：竞争
② Penelope /pəˈneləpi/：参见 *The Age of Fable* 第 23 章。
③ lord it：逞威风
④ metamorphose /ˌmetəˈmɔːfəʊz/：改变……的外形
⑤ unsightly /ʌnˈsaɪtli/：丑陋的，难看的
⑥ Eumæus：/juəˈmiːəs/
⑦ swine-herd /ˈswaɪnhɜːd/：猪倌
⑧ Telemachus：/tɪˈleməkəs/
⑨ intercept /ˌɪntəˈsept/：拦截

once from him the appearance of age and penury, and gave him the aspect of vigorous manhood that belonged to him. Telemachus viewed him with astonishment, and at first thought he must be more than mortal. But Ulysses announced himself as his father, and accounted for the change of appearance by explaining that it was Minerva's doing.

The father and son took counsel together how they should get the better of① the suitors and punish them for their outrages②. It was arranged that Telemachus should proceed to the palace and mingle with the suitors as formerly; that Ulysses should also go as a beggar, a character which in the rude old times had different privileges from what we concede③ to it now. As traveller and storyteller, the beggar was admitted in the halls of chieftains, and often treated like a guest; though sometimes, also, no doubt, with contumely④. Ulysses charged his son not to betray, by any display of unusual interest in him, that he knew him to be other than he seemed, and even if he saw him insulted, or beaten, not to interpose otherwise than he might do for any stranger. At the palace they found the usual scene of feasting and riot⑤ going on. The suitors pretended to receive Telemachus with joy at his return, though secretly mortified at the failure of their plots to take his life. The old beggar was permitted to enter, and provided with a portion from the table. A touching incident occurred as Ulysses entered the courtyard of the palace. An old dog lay in the yard almost dead with age, and seeing a stranger enter, raised his head, with ears erect. It was Argus⑥, Ulysses' own dog, that he had in other days often led to the chase.

As Ulysses sat eating his portion in the hall, the suitors began to exhibit their insolence⑦ to him. When he mildly remonstrated, one of them raised a stool and with it gave him a blow. Telemachus had hard work to restrain his indignation at seeing his father so treated in his own hall, but remembering his father's injunctions, said no more than what became⑧ him as master of the house, though young, and protector of his guests.

Penelope had protracted⑨ her decision in favor of either of her suitors so long that there seemed to be no further pretence⑩ for delay. The continued absence of her husband seemed to prove that his return was no longer to be expected. Meanwhile her son had grown up, and was able to manage his own affairs. She therefore consented to submit the question of her choice to a trial of skill among the suitors. The test selected was shooting with the bow. Twelve rings were arranged in a line, and he whose arrow was sent through the whole twelve was to have the queen for his prize. A bow that one of his brother heroes had given to Ulysses in former times was brought from the armory⑪, and with its quiver full of arrows was laid in the hall. Telemachus had taken care that all

---

① get the better of：战胜
② outrage /ˈaʊtreɪdʒ/：恶行
③ concede /kənˈsiːd/：给予
④ contumely /ˈkɒntjuːmɪli/：侮辱的语言或对待
⑤ riot：浪费的生活
⑥ Argus：/ˈɑːgəs/
⑦ insolence /ˈɪnsələns/：侮辱的行为或举动
⑧ become：适合
⑨ protract /prəˈtrækt/：拖延
⑩ pretence /prɪˈtens/：借口
⑪ armory /ˈɑːməri/：武器库

other weapons should be removed, under pretence that in the heat of competition there was danger, in some rash moment, of putting them to an improper use.

All things being prepared for the trial, the first thing to be done was to bend the bow in order to attach the string. Telemachus endeavored to do it, but found all his efforts fruitless; and modestly confessing that he had attempted a task beyond his strength, he yielded the bow to another. He tried it with no better success, and, amidst the laughter and jeers of his companions, gave it up. Another tried it and another; they rubbed the bow with tallow①, but all to no purpose; it would not bend. Then spoke Ulysses, humbly suggesting that he should be permitted to try; for, said he, "beggar as I am, I was once a soldier, and there is still some strength in these old limbs of mine." The suitors hooted② with derision③, and commanded to turn him out of the hall for his insolence④. But Telemachus spoke up for him, and, merely to gratify the old man, bade him try. Ulysses took the bow, and handled it with the hand of a master. With ease he adjusted the cord to its notch⑤, then fitting an arrow to the bow he drew the string and sped the arrow unerring through the rings.

Without allowing them time to express their astonishment, he said, "Now for another mark!" and aimed direct at the most insolent one of the suitors. The arrow pierced through his throat and he fell dead. Telemachus, Eumæus, and another faithful follower, well armed, now sprang to the side of Ulysses. The suitors, in amazement, looked round for arms, but found none, neither was there any way of escape, for Eumæus had secured the door. Ulysses left them not long in uncertainty; he announced himself as the long-lost chief, whose house they had invaded, whose substance they had squandered⑥, whose wife and son they had persecuted for ten long years; and told them he meant to have ample vengeance. All were slain, and Ulysses was left master of his palace and possessor of his kingdom and his wife.

Chapter XXXI
Adventures of Æneas

The Harpies

We have followed one of the Grecian heroes, Ulysses, in his wanderings on his return home from Troy, and now we propose to share the fortunes of the remnant of the conquered people⑦,

---

① tallow /ˈtæləʊ/：（动物的）脂
② hoot /huːt/：发出蔑视的喊叫，大笑
③ derision /dɪˈrɪʒən/：嘲笑
④ insolence /ˈɪnsələns/：傲慢无礼的行为
⑤ notch /nɒtʃ/：槽口
⑥ squander /ˈskwɒndə/：浪费
⑦ the conquered people：the Trojans

under their chief Æneas①, in their search for a new home, after the ruin of their native city②. On that fatal night when the wooden horse③ disgorged④ its contents of armed men, and the capture⑤ and conflagration⑥ of the city were the result, Æneas made his escape from the scene of destruction, with his father, and his wife, and young son. The father, Anchises⑦, was too old to walk with the speed required, and Æneas took him upon his shoulders. Thus burdened, leading his son and followed by his wife, he made the best of his way out of the burning city; but, in the confusion, his wife was swept away and lost.

On arriving at the place of rendezvous⑧, numerous fugitives⑨, of both sexes, were found, who put themselves under the guidance of Æneas. Some months were spent in preparation, and at length they embarked. They first landed on the neighboring shores of Thrace⑩, and were preparing to build a city, but Æneas was deterred⑪ by a prodigy. Preparing to offer sacrifice, he tore some twigs from one of the bushes. To his dismay the wounded part dropped blood. When he repeated the act a voice from the ground cried out to him, "Spare me, Æneas; I am your kinsman, Polydore⑫, here murdered with many arrows, from which a bush has grown, nourished with my blood." These words recalled to the recollection⑬ of Æneas that Polydore was a young prince of Troy, whom his father had sent with ample treasures to the neighboring land of Thrace, to be there brought up, at a distance from the horrors of war. The king to whom he was sent had murdered him and seized his treasures. Æneas and his companions, considering the land accursed by the stain of such a crime, hastened away.

They next landed on the island of Delos⑭, which was once a floating island, till Jupiter fastened it by adamantine⑮ chains to the bottom of the sea. Apollo and Diana were born there, and the island was sacred to Apollo. Here Æneas consulted the oracle of Apollo, and received an answer, ambiguous as usual, —"Seek your ancient mother; there the race of Æneas shall dwell, and reduce all other nations to their sway⑯." The Trojans heard with joy and immediately began to ask one another, "Where is the spot intended by the oracle?" Anchises remembered that there was a tradition that their forefathers came from Crete and thither they resolved to steer. They arrived at

---

① Æneas: /ɪˈniːæs/

② their native city: Troy

③ the wooden horse: 参见 *The Age of Fable* 第 28 章和 Virgil 的史诗 *The Aeneid* 中的选段"The Trojan Horse"。

④ disgorge /dɪsˈɡɔːdʒ/: 吐出

⑤ capture /ˈkæptʃə/: 夺取,占领

⑥ conflagration /ˌkɒnfləˈɡreɪʃn/: 被火烧,大火

⑦ Anchises /ænˈkaɪsiːz/: 参见 *The Homeric Hymns* 中的"To Aphrodite"选段。

⑧ rendezvous /ˈrɒndɪvuː/: 集合地

⑨ fugitive /ˈfjuːdʒɪtɪv/: 逃离危险、敌人、主人等的人

⑩ Thrace: 参见 *The Age of Fable* 第 17 章关于 Thrace 的注释。

⑪ deter /dɪˈtɜː/: 阻止

⑫ Polydore: /ˌpɒlɪˈdɔːri/

⑬ recollection: 记忆,回忆

⑭ Delos /ˈdiːlɒs/: 参见 *The Age of Fable* 第 20 章关于 Delos 的注释。

⑮ adamantine /ˌædəˈmæntaɪn/: 坚硬的

⑯ sway: 统治

Crete and began to build their city, but sickness broke out among them, and the fields that they had planted failed to yield a crop. In this gloomy aspect of affairs Æneas was warned in a dream to leave the country and seek a western land, called Hesperia①, whence Dardanus②, the true founder of the Trojan race, had originally migrated. To Hesperia, now called Italy, therefore, they directed their future course, and not till after many adventures and the lapse of time sufficient to carry a modern navigator several times round the world, did they arrive there.

Their first landing was at the island of the Harpies③. These were disgusting birds with the heads of maidens, with long claws and faces pale with hunger. They were sent by the gods to torment a certain Phineus, whom Jupiter had deprived of his sight, in punishment of his cruelty; and whenever a meal was placed before him the Harpies darted down from the air and carried it off. They were driven away from Phineus by the heroes of the Argonautic expedition, and took refuge in the island where Æneas now found them.

When they entered the port the Trojans saw herds of cattle roaming over the plain. They slew as many as they wished and prepared for a feast. But no sooner had they seated themselves at the table than a horrible clamor was heard in the air, and a flock of these odious harpies came rushing down upon them, seizing in their talons the meat from the dishes and flying away with it. Æneas and his companions drew their swords and dealt vigorous blows among the monsters, but to no purpose, for they were so nimble it was almost impossible to hit them, and their feathers were like armor impenetrable④ to steel⑤. One of them, perched on a neighboring cliff, screamed out, "Is it thus, Trojans, you treat us innocent birds, first slaughter our cattle and then make war on ourselves?" She then predicted dire sufferings to them in their future course, and having vented her wrath flew away. The Trojans made haste to leave the country, and next found themselves coasting⑥ along the shore of Epirus⑦. Here they landed, and to their astonishment learned that certain Trojan exiles, who had been carried there as prisoners, had become rulers of the country. Andromache, the widow of Hector, became the wife of one of the victorious Grecian chiefs, to whom she bore a son. Her husband dying, she was left regent⑧ of the country, as guardian of her son, and had married a fellow-captive, Helenus⑨, of the royal race of Troy. Helenus and Andromache treated the exiles with the utmost hospitality, and dismissed them loaded with gifts.

---

① Hesperia /heˈspɪərɪə/：Hesperia 意思是"西边的土地"。在希腊人眼里，Hesperia 指意大利；在罗马人眼里，Hesperia 指西班牙。此处指意大利。

② Dardanus：/ˈdɑːdənəs/

③ the Harpies /ˈhɑːpɪz/：参见 *Argonautica* 中的"Phineus and the Harpies"选段。

④ impenetrable /ɪnˈpenɪtrəbl/：刺不穿的

⑤ steel：钢制刀剑

⑥ coast：沿海岸航行

⑦ Epirus /ɪˈpaɪrəs/：地区名，位于阿尔巴尼亚（Albania）南部和希腊西北部，西临伊奥尼亚海（the Ionian Sea）。希腊境内的伊庇鲁斯（Epirus）现在是希腊的一个大区。

⑧ regent /ˈriːdʒənt/：统治者

⑨ Helenus：/ˈhelənəs/

From hence Æneas coasted along the shore of Sicily[①] and passed the country of the Cyclopes. Here they were hailed from the shore by a miserable object, whom by his garments, tattered[②] as they were, they perceived to be a Greek. He told them he was one of Ulysses's companions, left behind by that chief in his hurried departure. He related the story of Ulysses's adventure with Polyphemus, and besought them to take him off with them as he had no means of sustaining his existence where he was but wild berries and roots, and lived in constant fear of the Cyclopes. While he spoke Polyphemus made his appearance; "a terrible monster, shapeless, vast, whose only eye had been put out." He walked with cautious steps, feeling his way with a staff, down to the seaside, to wash his eye-socket in the waves. When he reached the water, he waded out towards them, and his immense height enabled him to advance far into the sea, so that the Trojans, in terror, took to their oars to get out of his way. Hearing the oars, Polyphemus shouted after them, so that the shores resounded, and at the noise the other Cyclopes came forth from their caves and woods and lined the shore, like a row of lofty pine trees. The Trojans plied their oars and soon left them out of sight.

Æneas had been cautioned[③] by Helenus to avoid the strait guarded by the monsters Scylla and Charybdis. There Ulysses, the reader will remember, had lost six of his men, seized by Scylla while the navigators[④] were wholly intent upon avoiding Charybdis. Æneas, following the advice of Helenus, shunned the dangerous pass and coasted along the island of Sicily.

Juno, seeing the Trojans speeding their way prosperously towards their destined shore, felt her old grudge[⑤] against them revive, for she could not forget the slight[⑥] that Paris had put upon her, in awarding the prize of beauty to another. In heavenly minds can such resentments dwell! Accordingly she hastened to Æolus, the ruler of the winds,—the same who supplied Ulysses with favoring gales, giving him the contrary ones tied up in a bag. Æolus obeyed the goddess and sent forth his sons, Boreas, Typhon, and the other winds, to toss[⑦] the ocean. A terrible storm ensued and the Trojan ships were driven out of their course towards the coast of Africa. They were in imminent danger of being wrecked, and were separated, so that Æneas thought that all were lost except his own.

At this crisis[⑧], Neptune, hearing the storm raging, and knowing that he had given no orders for one, raised his head above the waves, and saw the fleet of Æneas driving before the gale[⑨]. Knowing the hostility of Juno, he was at no loss to account for it, but his anger was not the less at

---

① Sicily /ˈsɪsɪli/：地中海面积最大、人口最稠密的岛屿，现在属于意大利。狭窄的墨西拿海峡（the Strait of Messina）把西西里岛（Sicily）与意大利大陆隔开。西西里岛距离北非大陆（突尼斯东北部）大约 160 公里。

② tattered /ˈtætəd/：（衣服）破烂的

③ caution /ˈkɔːʃn/：警告，建议

④ navigator /ˈnævɪɡeɪtə/：（经验丰富的）水手

⑤ grudge /ɡrʌdʒ/：不满，憎恨，恶意

⑥ slight /slaɪt/：不敬，蔑视

⑦ toss：使摇摆，使颠簸

⑧ crisis：麻烦和危险的时刻

⑨ gale：（八、九级的）大风

this interference in his province①. He called the winds and dismissed them with a severe reprimand. He then soothed the waves, and brushed away the clouds from before the face of the sun. Some of the ships which had got on the rocks he pried② off with his own trident, while Triton and a sea-nymph, putting their shoulders under others, set them afloat again. The Trojans, when the sea became calm, sought the nearest shore, which was the coast of Carthage③, where Æneas was so happy as to find that one by one the ships all arrived safe, though badly shaken.

Dido

Carthage, where the exiles④ had now arrived, was a spot on the coast of Africa opposite Sicily, where at that time a Tyrian⑤ colony under Dido⑥, their queen, were laying the foundations of a state destined in later ages to be the rival of Rome itself. Dido was the daughter of Belus⑦, king of Tyre⑧, and sister of Pygmalion⑨, who succeeded his father on the throne. Her husband was Sichæus⑩, a man of immense wealth, but Pygmalion, who coveted⑪ his treasures, caused him to be put to death. Dido, with a numerous body of friends and followers, both men and women, succeeded in effecting⑫ their escape from Tyre, in several vessels, carrying with them the treasures of Sichæus. On arriving at the spot which they selected as the seat of their future home, they asked of⑬ the natives only so much land as they could enclose with a bull's hide. When this was readily granted, she caused the hide to be cut into strips, and with them enclosed a spot on which she built a citadel⑭, and called it Byrsa⑮(a hide). Around this fort the city of Carthage rose, and soon became a powerful and flourishing place.

Such was the state of affairs when Æneas with his Trojans arrived there. Dido received the illustrious exiles with friendliness and hospitality. "Not unacquainted with distress," she said, "I have learned to succor the unfortunate." The queen's hospitality displayed itself in festivities at which games of strength and skill were exhibited. The strangers contended for the palm⑯ with her own subjects, on equal terms, the queen declaring that whether the victor were "Trojan or Tyrian

---

① province：管辖范围

② pry：撬

③ Carthage /ˈkɑːθɪdʒ/：古代的著名城市，位于今北非国家突尼斯（Tunisia）首都突尼斯城（Tunis）市郊。公元前 3 世纪中叶至公元前 2 世纪中叶，Carthage 曾与罗马多次交战，公元前 147 年被罗马击败。

④ exile /ˈeksaɪl/：离乡背井的人，被流放的人

⑤ 参见 The Age of Fable 第 6 章 Tyrian 一词的注解。

⑥ Dido：/ˈdaɪdəʊ/

⑦ Belus：/ˈbeləs/

⑧ Tyre：参见 The Age of Fable 第 6 章 Tyrian 一词的注解。

⑨ 这个 Pygmalion 不是第 8 章中的那个 Pygmalion。

⑩ Sichæus：/ˈsɪkiːəs/

⑪ covet /ˈkʌvɪt/：觊（jì）觎（yú），非常渴望得到

⑫ effect /ɪˈfekt/：完成

⑬ of：from

⑭ citadel /ˈsɪtədl/：城堡，堡垒

⑮ Byrsa /ˈbɜːsə/：古希腊语单词 byrsa（βύρσα）的意思是"牛皮（hide）"。

⑯ palm：（颁发给优胜者的）奖励

should make no difference to her." At the feast which followed the games, Æneas gave at her request a recital① of the closing events of the Trojan history and his own adventures after the fall of the city. Dido was charmed with his discourse and filled with admiration of his exploits. She conceived an ardent passion for him, and he for his part seemed well content to accept the fortunate chance which appeared to offer him at once a happy termination② of his wanderings, a home, a kingdom, and a bride. Months rolled away in the enjoyment of pleasant intercourse, and it seemed as if Italy and the empire destined to be founded on its shores were alike forgotten. Seeing which, Jupiter despatched Mercury with a message to Æneas recalling him to a sense of his high destiny, and commanding him to resume his voyage.

Æneas parted from Dido, though she tried every allurement and persuasion to detain him. The blow to her affection and her pride was too much for her to endure, and when she found that he was gone, she mounted a funeral pile which she had caused to be erected, and having stabbed herself was consumed with the pile. The flames rising over the city were seen by the departing Trojans, and, though the cause was unknown, gave to Æneas some intimation③ of the fatal event.

Palinurus

After touching at the island of Sicily, where Acestes④, a prince of Trojan lineage⑤, bore sway, who gave them a hospitable reception, the Trojans reëmbarked, and held on their course for Italy. Venus now interceded with Neptune to allow her son at last to attain the wished-for goal and find an end of his perils on the deep⑥. Neptune consented, stipulating⑦ only for one life as a ransom for the rest. The victim was Palinurus⑧, the pilot. As he sat watching the stars, with his hand on the helm, Somnus sent by Neptune approached in the guise of Phorbas⑨ and said: "Palinurus, the breeze is fair, the water smooth, and the ship sails steadily on her course. Lie down awhile and take needful rest. I will stand at the helm in your place." Palinurus replied, "Tell me not of smooth seas or favoring winds, —me who have seen so much of their treachery. Shall I trust Æneas to the chances of the weather and the winds?" And he continued to grasp the helm and to keep his eyes fixed on the stars. But Somnus waved over him a branch moistened with Lethæan⑩ dew, and his eyes closed in spite of all his efforts. Then Somnus pushed him overboard and he fell; but keeping his hold upon the helm, it came away with him. Neptune was mindful of his promise and kept the ship on her track without helm or pilot, till Æneas discovered his loss,

---

① recital /rɪˈsaɪtl/：详细的描述
② termination /ˌtɜːmɪˈneɪʃn/：终结，结束
③ intimation /ˌɪntɪˈmeɪʃn/：暗示，提示
④ Acestes：/əˈsestiːz/
⑤ lineage /ˈlɪnɪɪdʒ/：血统
⑥ deep：海
⑦ stipulate /ˈstɪpjuleɪt/：（作为条件）规定，约定
⑧ Palinurus：/ˌpælɪˈnʌrəs/
⑨ Phorbas：/ˈfɔːbəs/
⑩ Lethæan /liːˈθiːən/：Lethe 的形容词，通常拼写为 Lethean。参见 The Age of Fable 第 9 章关于 Lethe 的注释。

and, sorrowing deeply for his faithful steersman, took charge of the ship himself.

The ships at last reached the shores of Italy, and joyfully did the adventurers leap to land. While his people were employed in making their encampment Æneas sought the abode of the Sibyl①. It was a cave connected with a temple and grove, sacred to Apollo and Diana. While Æneas contemplated the scene, the Sibyl accosted him. She seemed to know his errand, and under the influence of the deity of the place, burst forth in a prophetic strain, giving dark intimations of labors and perils through which he was destined to make his way to final success. She closed with the encouraging words which have become proverbial: "Yield not to disasters, but press onward the more bravely." Æneas replied that he had prepared himself for whatever might await him. He had but one request to make. Having been directed in a dream to seek the abode of the dead in order to confer with his father, Anchises, to receive from him a revelation② of his future fortunes and those of his race, he asked her assistance to enable him to accomplish the task. The Sibyl replied, "The descent to Avernus③ is easy: the gate of Pluto stands open night and day; but to retrace one's steps④ and return to the upper air, that is the toil, that the difficulty." She instructed him to seek in the forest a tree on which grew a golden branch. This branch was to be plucked off and borne as a gift to Proserpine, and if fate was propitious it would yield to the hand and quit its parent trunk, but otherwise no force could rend it away. If torn away, another would succeed.

Æneas followed the directions of the Sibyl. His mother, Venus, sent two of her doves to fly before him and show him the way, and by their assistance he found the tree, plucked the branch, and hastened back with it to the Sibyl.

Chapter XXXII
The Infernal Regions—Elysium—The Sibyl

The Infernal Regions

As at the commencement⑤ of our series we have given the pagan account of the creation of the world, so as we approach its conclusion⑥ we present a view of the regions of the dead, depicted by one of their most enlightened poets, who drew his doctrines from their most esteemed philosophers. The region where Virgil⑦ locates the entrance to this abode is perhaps the most strikingly adapted

---

① the Sibyl /ˈsɪbɪl/: Sibyl 本是一个宣布 Apollo 神谕的女祭司的名字,后来这个名字用来表示"女预言家"。

② revelation /ˌrevəˈleɪʃn/: 揭示,展示

③ Avernus /əˈvɜːnəs/: 湖名,位于意大利那不勒斯(Naples)附近,古罗马诗人认为这是阴间的入口。也可用来指阴间。

④ retrace one's steps: 原路返回

⑤ commencement /kəˈmensmənt/: 开始的时候

⑥ conclusion /kənˈkluːʒn/: 结尾

⑦ Virgil: 古罗马诗人,代表作是 Aeneid,这里的第 31、32 和 33 章改写自 Aeneid 这部史诗。Aeneid 一词来自史诗主人公的名字 Æneas。

to excite ideas of the terrific and preternatural① of any on the face of the earth. It is the volcanic region near Vesuvius②, where the whole country③ is cleft with chasms, from which sulphurous④ flames arise, while the ground is shaken with pent-up⑤ vapors, and mysterious sounds issue from the bowels of the earth. The lake Avernus is supposed to fill the crater⑥ of an extinct⑦ volcano. It is circular, half a mile wide, and very deep, surrounded by high banks, which in Virgil's time were covered with a gloomy forest. Mephitic⑧ vapors rise from its waters, so that no life is found on its banks, and no birds fly over it. Here, according to the poet, was the cave which afforded access to the infernal regions, and here Æneas offered sacrifices to the infernal deities, Proserpine, Hecate, and the Furies. Then a roaring was heard in the earth, the woods on the hilltops were shaken, and the howling of dogs announced the approach of the deities. "Now," said the Sibyl, "summon up your courage, for you will need it." She descended into the cave, and Æneas followed. Before the threshold of hell they passed through a group of beings who are enumerated as Griefs and avenging Cares, pale Diseases and melancholy Age, Fear and Hunger that tempt to crime, Toil, Poverty, and Death,—forms horrible to view. The Furies spread their couches there, and Discord, whose hair was of vipers⑨ tied up with a bloody fillet⑩. Here also were the monsters, Briareus, with his hundred arms, Hydras hissing, and Chimæras breathing fire. Æneas shuddered at the sight, drew his sword and would have struck, but the Sibyl restrained him. They then came to the black river Cocytus⑪, where they found the ferryman, Charon⑫, old and squalid⑬, but strong and vigorous, who was receiving passengers of all kinds into his boat, magnanimous⑭ heroes, boys and unmarried girls, as numerous as the leaves that fall at autumn, or the flocks⑮ that fly southward at the approach of winter. They stood pressing for a passage and longing to touch the opposite shore. But the stern ferryman took in only such as he chose, driving the rest back. Æneas, wondering at the sight, asked the Sibyl, "Why this discrimination⑯?" She answered, "Those who are taken on board the bark are the souls of those who have received due⑰

---

① preternatural /ˌpriːtəˈnætʃrəl/：超自然的，不可思议的
② Vesuvius /vɪˈsuːvɪəs/：意大利活火山，位于意大利南部临那不勒斯湾（the Bay of Naples）的平原上。该火山公元79年的大爆发，掩埋了著名的庞贝城（Pompeii）。
③ country：地区
④ sulphurous /ˈsʌlfərəs/：含有硫磺的
⑤ pent-up：被抑制的，被关住的
⑥ crater /ˈkreɪtə/：（碗状的）火山口
⑦ extinct /ɪkˈstɪŋkt/：（火山）死的
⑧ mephitic /mɪˈfɪtɪk/：有毒的
⑨ viper /ˈvaɪpə/：毒蛇
⑩ fillet /ˈfɪlɪt/：束发带
⑪ Cocytus /kəʊˈsaɪtəs/：阴间的河流之一。
⑫ Charon：/ˈkeərən/
⑬ squalid /ˈskwɒlɪd/：肮脏的
⑭ magnanimous /mæɡˈnænɪməs/：有巨大勇气的，勇敢而高尚的
⑮ flock：鸟群
⑯ discrimination /dɪˌskrɪmɪˈneɪʃn/：区别
⑰ due：应有的

burial rites①; the host of others who have remained unburied are not permitted to pass the flood②, but wander a hundred years, and flit to and fro about the shore, till at last they are taken over." Æneas grieved at recollecting some of his own companions who had perished in the storm. At that moment he beheld Palinurus, his pilot, who fell overboard and was drowned. He addressed him and asked him the cause of his misfortune. Palinurus replied that the rudder was carried away, and he, clinging to it, was swept away with it. He besought Æneas most urgently to extend to him his hand and take him in company to the opposite shore. But the Sibyl rebuked him for the wish thus to transgress the laws of Pluto; but consoled him by informing him that the people of the shore where his body had been wafted by the waves should be stirred up by prodigies to give it due burial, and that the promontory should bear the name of Cape Palinurus③, which it does to this day. Leaving Palinurus consoled by these words, they approached the boat. Charon, fixing his eyes sternly upon the advancing warrior, demanded by what right he, living and armed, approached that shore. To which the Sibyl replied that they would commit no violence, that Æneas's only object was to see his father, and finally exhibited the golden branch, at sight of which Charon's wrath relaxed, and he made haste to turn his bark to the shore, and receive them on board. The boat, adapted only to the light freight of bodiless spirits, groaned under the weight of the hero. They were soon conveyed to the opposite shore. There they were encountered by the three-headed dog, Cerberus④, with his necks bristling with snakes. He barked with all his three throats till the Sibyl threw him a medicated⑤ cake which he eagerly devoured, and then stretched himself out in his den and fell asleep. Æneas and the Sibyl sprang to land. The first sound that struck their ears was the wailing of young children, who had died on the threshold of life, and near to these were they who had perished under false charges. Minos⑥ presides over them as judge, and examines the deeds of each. The next class was of those who had died by their own hand, hating life and seeking refuge in death. O how willingly would they now endure poverty, labor, and any other infliction⑦, if they might but return to life! Next were situated the regions of sadness, divided off into retired paths, leading through groves of myrtle. Here roamed those who had fallen victims to unrequited⑧ love, not freed from pain even by death itself. Among these, Æneas thought he descried the form of Dido, with a wound still recent. In the dim light he was for a moment uncertain, but approaching, perceived it was indeed herself. Tears fell from his eyes, and he addressed her in the accents of love. "Unhappy Dido! was then the rumor true that you had perished? and was I, alas! the cause? I call the gods to witness that my departure from you was reluctant, and in obedience to the commands of Jove; nor could I believe that my absence would

---

① burial rite：葬礼

② flood：河流

③ Cape Palinurus：位于意大利城市 Salerno 西南方向,那不勒斯（Naples）南偏东方向。

④ Cerberus：/ˈsɜːbərəs/

⑤ medicated /ˈmedɪkeɪtɪd/：加过药的

⑥ Minos：这里的 Minos 就是 *The Age of Fable* 第 13 章中的 Minos;他是个公正的统治者,所以后来做了阴间的判官。

⑦ infliction /ɪnˈflɪkʃn/：痛苦

⑧ unrequited /ˌʌnrɪˈkwaɪtɪd/：付出爱后没有得到回报的

cost you so dear. Stop, I beseech you, and refuse me not a last farewell." She stood for a moment with averted countenance, and eyes fixed on the ground, and then silently passed on, as insensible to his pleadings as a rock. Æneas followed for some distance; then, with a heavy heart, rejoined his companion and resumed his route.

They next entered the fields where roam the heroes who have fallen in battle. Here they saw many shades of Grecian and Trojan warriors. The Trojans thronged around him, and could not be satisfied with the sight. They asked the cause of his coming, and plied him with innumerable questions. But the Greeks, at the sight of his armor glittering through the murky① atmosphere, recognized the hero, and filled with terror turned their backs and fled, as they used to do on the plains of Troy.

Æneas would have lingered long with his Trojan friends, but the Sibyl hurried him away. They next came to a place where the road divided, the one leading to Elysium②, the other to the regions of the condemned. Æneas beheld on one side the walls of a mighty city, around which Phlegethon③ rolled its fiery waters. Before him was the gate of adamant④ that neither gods nor men can break through. An iron tower stood by the gate, on which Tisiphone⑤, the avenging Fury, kept guard. From the city were heard groans, and the sound of the scourge, the creaking of iron, and the clanking of chains. Æneas, horror-struck, inquired of his guide what crimes were those whose punishments produced the sounds he heard? The Sibyl answered, "Here is the judgment hall of Rhadamanthus⑥, who brings to light crimes done in life, which the perpetrator⑦ vainly thought impenetrably hid. Tisiphone applies her whip of scorpions, and delivers the offender over to her sister Furies." At this moment with horrid clang the brazen gates unfolded, and Æneas saw within a Hydra with fifty heads guarding the entrance. The Sibyl told him that the gulf of Tartarus descended deep, so that its recesses were as far beneath their feet as heaven was high above their heads. In the bottom of this pit, the Titan race, who warred against the gods, lie prostrate⑧; Salmoneus⑨, also, who presumed to vie with Jupiter, and built a bridge of brass over which he drove his chariot that the sound might resemble thunder, launching flaming brands at his people in imitation of lightning, till Jupiter struck him with a real thunderbolt, and taught him the difference between mortal weapons and divine. Here, also, is Tityus⑩, the giant, whose form is so immense that as he lies he stretches over nine acres, while a vulture preys upon his liver, which as fast as it is devoured grows again, so that his punishment will have no end.

---

① murky /ˈmɜːki/：阴暗的，模糊不清的

② Elysium：参见 *The Age of Fable* 第 1 章 the Elysian Plain 的注释。

③ Phlegethon /ˈfledʒɪθən/：阴间的河流之一

④ adamant /ˈædəmənt/：坚硬的物体，金刚石之类的硬石

⑤ Tisiphone /tɪˈsɪfəni/：参见 *The Age of Fable* 第 1 章关于 the Erinyes 的叙述。

⑥ Rhadamanthus /ˌrædəˈmænθəs/：阴间的判官之一。

⑦ perpetrator /ˈpɜːpɪtreɪtə/：犯罪的人

⑧ 参见 *The Age of Fable* 第 1 章。

⑨ Salmoneus：/səlˈməʊnjuːs/

⑩ Tityus：/ˈtaɪtɪəs/

Æneas saw groups seated at tables loaded with dainties, while near by stood a Fury who snatched away the viands① from their lips as fast as they prepared to taste them. Others beheld suspended over their heads huge rocks, threatening to fall, keeping them in a state of constant alarm. These were they who had hated their brothers, or struck their parents, or defrauded② the friends who trusted them, or who, having grown rich, kept their money to themselves, and gave no share to others; the last being the most numerous class. Here also were those who had violated the marriage vow, or fought in a bad cause, or failed in fidelity to their employers. Here was one who had sold his country for gold, another who perverted③ the laws, making them④ say one thing today and another tomorrow.

Ixion was there, fastened to the circumference of a wheel ceaselessly revolving; and Sisyphus, whose task was to roll a huge stone up to a hill-top, but when the steep was well-nigh gained, the rock, repulsed by some sudden force, rushed again headlong down to the plain. Again he toiled at it, while the sweat bathed all his weary limbs, but all to no effect. There was Tantalus, who stood in a pool, his chin level with the water, yet he was parched with thirst, and found nothing to assuage it; for when he bowed his hoary head, eager to quaff, the water fled away, leaving the ground at his feet all dry. Tall trees laden with fruit stooped their heads to him, pears, pomegranates, apples, and luscious⑤ figs; but when with a sudden grasp he tried to seize them winds whirled them high above his reach.⑥

The Sibyl now warned Æneas that it was time to turn from these melancholy regions and seek the city of the blessed. They passed through a middle tract of darkness, and came upon the Elysian fields, the groves where the happy reside. They breathed a freer air, and saw all objects clothed in a purple light. The region has a sun and stars of its own. The inhabitants were enjoying themselves in various ways, some in sports on the grassy turf, in games of strength or skill, others dancing or singing. Orpheus⑦ struck the chords of his lyre, and called forth ravishing sounds. Here Æneas saw the founders of the Trojan state, magnanimous heroes who lived in happier times. He gazed with admiration on the war chariots and glittering arms now reposing in disuse. Spears stood fixed in the ground, and the horses, unharnessed, roamed over the plain. The same pride in splendid armor and generous steeds which the old heroes felt in life, accompanied them here. He saw another group feasting and listening to the strains of music. They were in a laurel grove, whence the great river Po⑧ has its origin, and flows out among men. Here dwelt those who fell by wounds

---

① viand /'vaɪənd/：食物
② defraud /dɪ'frɔːd/：欺骗，诈取
③ pervert /pə'vɜːt/：歪曲
④ them：the laws
⑤ luscious /'lʌʃəs/：甘美的，甜的
⑥ Ixion, Sisyphus, and Tantalus：这几个神话人物的故事参见 *The Age of Fable* 第24章的相关注释。
⑦ 参见 *The Age of Fable* 第24章。
⑧ Po /pəu/：意大利最长的河流，发源于意大利西部边境的阿尔卑斯山（the Alps），流经意大利北部平原，注入亚得里亚海（the Adriatic Sea）。

received in their country's cause, holy priests① also, and poets who have uttered thoughts worthy of Apollo, and others who have contributed to cheer and adorn life by their discoveries in the useful arts, and have made their memory blessed by rendering service to mankind. They wore snow-white fillets about their brows. The Sibyl addressed a group of these, and inquired where Anchises was to be found. They were directed where to seek him, and soon found him in a verdant② valley, where he was contemplating the ranks of his posterity③, their destinies and worthy④ deeds to be achieved in coming times. When he recognized Æneas approaching, he stretched out both hands to him, while tears flowed freely. "Have you come at last," said he, "long expected, and do I behold you after such perils past? O my son, how have I trembled for you as I have watched your career!" To which Æneas replied, "O father! your image was always before me to guide and guard me." Then he endeavored to enfold his father in his embrace, but his arms enclosed only an unsubstantial⑤ image.

Æneas perceived before him a spacious valley, with trees gently waving to the wind, a tranquil landscape, through which the river Lethe flowed. Along the banks of the stream wandered a countless multitude, numerous as insects in the summer air. Æneas, with surprise, inquired who were these. Anchises answered, "They are souls to which bodies are to be given in due time. Meanwhile they dwell on Lethe's bank, and drink oblivion of their former lives." "O father!" said Æneas, "is it possible that any can be so in love with life as to wish to leave these tranquil seats for the upper world⑥?" Anchises replied by explaining the plan of creation. The Creator, he told him, originally made the material of which souls are composed of the four elements, fire, air, earth, and water, all which when united took the form of the most excellent part, fire, and became flame. This material was scattered like seed among the heavenly bodies, the sun, moon, and stars. Of this seed the inferior gods created man and all other animals, mingling it with various proportions of earth, by which its purity was alloyed⑦ and reduced. Thus, the more earth predominates in the composition the less pure is the individual; and we see men and women with their full-grown bodies have not the purity of childhood. So in proportion to the time which the union of body and soul has lasted is the impurity contracted by the spiritual part. This impurity must be purged away after death, which is done by ventilating the souls in the current of winds, or merging them in water, or burning out their impurities by fire. Some few, of whom Anchises intimates⑧ that he is one, are admitted at once to Elysium, there to remain. But the rest, after the impurities of earth are purged away, are sent back to life endowed with new bodies, having had the remembrance of their former lives effectually washed away by the waters of Lethe. Some,

①　priest：祭司

②　verdant /ˈvɜːdənt/：绿色的，草木茂盛的

③　posterity /pɒˈsterɪti/：后代，子孙

④　worthy：有价值的，重要的，值得尊重的

⑤　unsubstantial /ˌʌnsəbˈstænʃl/：无实质的，非物质的

⑥　the upper world：阳间

⑦　alloy /əˈlɔɪ/：（通过添加品质差的物质）使……的质量降低

⑧　intimate /ˈɪntɪmeɪt/：宣布

however, there still are, so thoroughly corrupted, that they are not fit to be intrusted with human bodies, and these are made into brute animals, lions, tigers, cats, dogs, monkeys, etc. This is what the ancients called Metempsychosis①, or the transmigration② of souls; a doctrine which is still held by the natives of India, who scruple③ to destroy the life even of the most insignificant animal, not knowing but it may be one of their relations④ in an altered form.

Anchises, having explained so much, proceeded to point out to Æneas individuals of his race, who were hereafter to be born, and to relate to him the exploits they should perform in the world. After this he reverted to the present, and told his son of the events that remained to him to be accomplished before the complete establishment of himself and his followers in Italy. Wars were to be waged, battles fought, a bride to be won, and in the result a Trojan state founded, from which should rise the Roman power, to be in time the sovereign of the world.

Æneas and the Sibyl then took leave of Anchises, and returned by some short cut⑤, which the poet does not explain, to the upper world.

Elysium

Virgil, we have seen, places his Elysium under the earth, and assigns it for a residence⑥ to the spirits of the blessed. But in Homer Elysium forms no part of the realms of the dead. He places it on the west of the earth, near Ocean⑦, and describes it as a happy land, where there is neither snow, nor cold, nor rain, and always fanned by the delightful breezes of Zephyrus. Hither favored heroes pass without dying and live happy under the rule of Rhadamanthus. The Elysium of Hesiod⑧ and Pindar⑨ is in the Isles of the Blessed, or Fortunate Islands, in the Western Ocean⑩. From these sprang the legend of the happy island Atlantis⑪. This blissful region may have been wholly imaginary, but possibly may have sprung from the reports of some storm-driven mariners who had caught a glimpse of the coast of America.

The Sibyl

As Æneas and the Sibyl pursued their way back to earth, he said to her, "Whether thou be a

---

① Metempsychosis /ˌmetempsaɪˈkəʊsɪs/：投胎转世

② transmigration /ˌtrænzmaɪˈɡreɪʃn/：灵魂转世，人死后灵魂进入另外一个身体

③ scruple /ˈskruːpl/：犹豫，不愿意做

④ relation /rɪˈleɪʃn/：亲戚

⑤ short cut：捷径

⑥ residence /ˈrezɪdəns/：住处，住所

⑦ Ocean：指大西洋

⑧ Hesiod /ˈhesɪəd/：最早的希腊诗人之一，生活在公元前 700 年前后，代表作有《神谱》（*Theogony*）和《工作与日子》（*Works and Days*）。

⑨ Pindar /ˈpɪndə/：古希腊诗人，生于公元前 518 年，卒于公元前 446 年之后，以歌颂古希腊四大运动会的优胜者的颂歌著称于世。关于古希腊四大运动会的相关信息，参见 *The Age of Fable* 第 20 章的"Olympic and Other Games"一节。

⑩ the Western Ocean：指大西洋。

⑪ Atlantis /ətˈlæntɪs/：传说中的岛屿，位于直布罗陀海峡（the Straits of Gibraltar）以西的大西洋海域。据传说，该岛因为地震而被大海吞没。

goddess or a mortal beloved of the gods, by me thou shalt always be held in reverence. When I reach the upper air I will cause a temple to be built to thy honor, and will myself bring offerings." "I am no goddess," said the Sibyl; "I have no claim to sacrifice or offering. I am mortal; yet if I could have accepted the love of Apollo I might have been immortal. He promised me the fulfilment of my wish, if I would consent to be his. I took a handful of sand, and holding it forth, said, 'Grant me to see as many birthdays as there are sand grains in my hand.' Unluckily I forgot to ask for enduring youth. This also he would have granted, could I have accepted his love, but offended at my refusal, he allowed me to grow old. My youth and youthful strength fled long ago. I have lived seven hundred years, and to equal the number of the sand grains I have still to see three hundred springs and three hundred harvests. My body shrinks up as years increase, and in time, I shall be lost to sight, but my voice will remain, and future ages will respect my sayings."

These concluding words of the Sibyl alluded to her prophetic power. In her cave she was accustomed to inscribe on leaves gathered from the trees the names and fates of individuals. The leaves thus inscribed were arranged in order within the cave, and might be consulted by her votaries. But if perchance at the opening of the door the wind rushed in and dispersed the leaves the Sibyl gave no aid to restoring them again, and the oracle was irreparably lost.

The following legend of the Sibyl is fixed at a later date. In the reign of one of the Tarquins[①] there appeared before the king a woman who offered him nine books for sale. The king refused to purchase them, whereupon the woman went away and burned three of the books, and returning offered the remaining books for the same price she had asked for the nine. The king again rejected them; but when the woman, after burning three books more, returned and asked for the three remaining the same price which she had before asked for the nine, his curiosity was excited, and he purchased the books. They were found to contain the destinies of the Roman state. They were kept in the temple of Jupiter Capitolinus[②], preserved in a stone chest, and allowed to be inspected only by especial officers appointed for that duty, who, on great occasions, consulted them and interpreted their oracles to the people.

There were various Sibyls; but the Cumæan[③] Sibyl, of whom Ovid[④] and Virgil write, is the most celebrated of them. Ovid's story of her life protracted[⑤] to one thousand years may be intended to represent the various Sibyls as being only reappearances of one and the same individual.

---

① the Tarquins /ˈtɑːkwɪnz/：古罗马历史上有两个姓 Tarquin 的国王,老 Tarquin 的拉丁语名字是 Tarquinius Priscus,据说公元前 616 年至公元前 579 年在位,小 Tarquin 的拉丁语名字是 Lucius Tarquinius Superbus,公元前 534 年至公元前 510 年在位。

② Capitolinus /ˌkæpɪtəʊˈlɪnəs/：位于台伯河（the Tiber）东岸的古罗马城内有 7 座小山,分别叫 the Palatine Hill, the Capitoline Hill, the Quirinal Hill, the Viminal Hill, the Esquiline Hill, the Caelian Hill, the Aventine Hill。Jupiter 的神庙建在 the Capitoline Hill 上,所以拉丁语形容词 Capitolinus 便成了 Jupiter 的一个代表性修饰词。

③ Cumæan /ˈkjuːmiːən/：Cumæ 的;Cumæ /ˈkjuːmiː/ 是希腊人在意大利建立的最早的定居点,位于今天那不勒斯（Naples）附近。

④ Ovid /ˈɒvɪd/：古罗马诗人,生于公元前 43 年,卒于公元 17 年,代表作是《变形记》（*Metamorphoses*）。

⑤ protract /prəˈtrækt/：延长

Chapter XXXIII
Æneas in Italy

Æneas, having parted from the Sibyl and rejoined his fleet, coasted along the shores of Italy and cast anchor in the mouth of the Tiber①. The poet, having brought his hero to this spot, the destined termination② of his wanderings, invokes his Muse to tell him the situation of things at that eventful moment. Latinus③, third in descent from Saturn④, ruled the country. He was now old and had no male descendant, but had one charming daughter, Lavinia⑤, who was sought in marriage by many neighboring chiefs, one of whom, Turnus⑥, king of the Rutulians⑦, was favored by the wishes of her parents. But Latinus had been warned in a dream by his father Faunus, that the destined husband of Lavinia should come from a foreign land. From that union should spring a race destined to subdue⑧ the world.

Our readers will remember that in the conflict with the Harpies one of those half-human birds had threatened the Trojans with dire sufferings. In particular she predicted that before their wanderings ceased they should be pressed by hunger to devour their tables. This portent now came true; for as they took their scanty meal, seated on the grass, the men placed their hard biscuit on their laps, and put thereon whatever their gleanings⑨ in the woods supplied. Having despatched⑩ the latter they finished by eating the crusts. Seeing which, the boy Iulus⑪ said playfully, "See, we are eating our tables." Æneas caught the words and accepted the omen. "All hail, promised land!" he exclaimed, "this is our home, this our country." He then took measures to find out who were the present inhabitants of the land, and who their rulers. A hundred chosen men were sent to the village of Latinus, bearing presents and a request for friendship and alliance. They went and were favorably received. Latinus immediately concluded that the Trojan hero was no other than the promised son-in-law announced by the oracle. He cheerfully granted his alliance and sent back the messengers mounted on steeds from his stables, and loaded with gifts and friendly messages.

Juno, seeing things go thus prosperously for the Trojans, felt her old animosity⑫ revive, summoned Alecto⑬ from Erebus, and sent her to stir up discord. The Fury first took possession of

---

① the Tiber /ˈtaɪbə/: 台伯河,意大利第二长的河流,发源于亚平宁山,流经罗马,注入第勒尼安海 (the Tyrrhenian Sea)。

② termination /ˌtɜːmɪˈneɪʃn/: 终点

③ Latinus: /ləˈtɪnəs/

④ 参见 The Age of Fable 第 1 章关于 Saturn 的叙述。

⑤ Lavinia: /ləˈvɪnɪə/

⑥ Turnus: /ˈtɜːnəs/

⑦ the Rutulians /ruˈtuːlɪənz/: 意大利中部部落,其都城叫 Ardea,位于罗马东南方向不远处。

⑧ subdue /səbˈdjuː/: 用军事力量征服

⑨ gleanings: 收集物

⑩ dispatch (despatch): 吃完

⑪ Iulus /aɪˈjuːləs/: Aeneas 之子,又叫 Ascanius /æsˈkeɪnɪəs/。

⑫ animosity /ˌænɪˈmɒsɪti/: 敌意,仇恨

⑬ Alecto /əˈlektəʊ/: 参见 The Age of Fable 第 1 章关于 the Erinyes 的叙述。

the queen, Amata①, and roused her to oppose in every way the new alliance. Alecto then speeded to the city of Turnus, and assuming the form of an old priestess, informed him of the arrival of the foreigners and of the attempts of their prince to rob him of his bride. Next she turned her attention to the camp of the Trojans. There she saw the boy Iulus and his companions amusing themselves with hunting. She sharpened the scent② of the dogs, and led them to rouse up from the thicket a tame stag, the favorite of Silvia③, the daughter of Tyrrheus④, the king's herdsman. A javelin from the hand of Iulus wounded the animal, and he had only strength left to run homewards, and died at his mistress's feet. Her cries and tears roused her brothers and the herdsmen, and they, seizing whatever weapons came to hand, furiously assaulted the hunting party. These were protected by their friends, and the herdsmen were finally driven back with the loss of two of their number.

These things were enough to rouse the storm of war, and the queen, Turnus, and the peasants all urged the old king to drive the strangers from the country. He resisted as long as he could, but, finding his opposition unavailing, finally gave way and retreated to his retirement.

Opening the Gates of Janus

It was the custom of the country, when war was to be undertaken, for the chief magistrate, clad in his robes of office, with solemn pomp to open the gates of the temple of Janus⑤, which were kept shut as long as peace endured. His people now urged the old king to perform that solemn office, but he refused to do so. While they contested, Juno herself, descending from the skies, smote the doors with irresistible force, and burst them open. Immediately the whole country was in a flame. The people rushed from every side breathing nothing but war.

Turnus was recognized by all as leader; others joined as allies, chief of whom was Mezentius⑥, a brave and able soldier, but of detestable⑦ cruelty. He had been the chief of one of the neighboring cities, but his people drove him out. With him was joined his son Lausus⑧, a generous youth, worthy of a better sire⑨.

Camilla

Camilla⑩, the favorite of Diana, a huntress and warrior, after the fashion of the Amazons, came with her band of mounted⑪ followers, including a select number of her own sex, and ranged

---

① Amata：/əˈmætə/

② scent：嗅觉

③ Silvia：/ˈsɪlvɪə/

④ Tyrrheus：/ˈtɪrjuːs/

⑤ Janus /ˈdʒeɪnəs/：参见 *The Age of Fable* 第 1 章关于 Janus 的叙述。

⑥ Mezentius：/mɪˈzentɪəs/

⑦ detestable /dɪˈtestəbl/：可憎的

⑧ Lausus：/ˈlɔːsəs/

⑨ sire /ˈsaɪə/：父亲

⑩ Camilla：/kəˈmɪlə/

⑪ mounted /ˈmaʊntɪd/：骑马的

herself on the side of Turnus. This maiden had never accustomed her fingers to the distaff① or the loom, but had learned to endure the toils of war, and in speed to outstrip the wind. It seemed as if she might run over the standing corn without crushing it, or over the surface of the water without dipping her feet. Camilla's history had been singular from the beginning. Her father, Metabus②, driven from his city by civil discord, carried with him in his flight his infant daughter. As he fled through the woods, his enemies in hot pursuit, he reached the bank of the river Amazenus③, which, swelled by rains, seemed to debar④ a passage. He paused for a moment, then decided what to do. He tied the infant to his lance with wrappers of bark, and poising the weapon in his upraised hand thus addressed Diana: "Goddess of the woods! I consecrate this maid to you;" then hurled the weapon with its burden to the opposite bank. The spear flew across the roaring water. His pursuers were already upon him, but he plunged into the river and swam across, and found the spear, with the infant safe on the other side. Thenceforth he lived among the shepherds and brought up his daughter in woodland arts. While a child she was taught to use the bow and throw the javelin. With her sling⑤ she could bring down the crane or the wild swan. Her dress was a tiger's skin. Many mothers sought her for a daughter-in-law, but she continued faithful to Diana and repelled the thought of marriage.

Evander

Such were the formidable⑥ allies that ranged themselves against Æneas. It was night and he lay stretched in sleep on the bank of the river under the open heavens. The god of the stream, Father Tiber, seemed to raise his head above the willows and to say, "O goddess-born⑦, destined possessor of the Latin realms, this is the promised land, here is to be your home, here shall terminate the hostility of the heavenly powers, if only you faithfully persevere. There are friends not far distant. Prepare your boats and row up my stream; I will lead you to Evander⑧, the Arcadian chief, he has long been at strife with Turnus and the Rutulians, and is prepared to become an ally of yours. Rise! offer your vows to Juno, and deprecate her anger⑨. When you have achieved your victory then think of me." Æneas woke and paid immediate obedience to the friendly vision. He sacrificed to Juno, and invoked the god of the river and all his tributary⑩ fountains to lend their aid. Then for the first time a vessel filled with armed warriors floated on the stream of the Tiber. The river smoothed its waves, and bade its current flow gently, while,

---

① distaff /ˈdɪstɑːf/：纺纱杆

② Metabus：/mɪˈtæbəs/

③ Amazenus：/ˌæməˈziːnəs/

④ debar /dɪˈbɑː/：阻止

⑤ sling：投石器

⑥ formidable /ˈfɔːmɪdəbl/：可怕的

⑦ goddess-born：指 Aeneas，他的母亲是 Venus。

⑧ Evander /ɪˈvændə/：按照罗马的传说，Evander 是第一个在未来的罗马建立定居点的人。他来自希腊的 Arcardia，所以被叫作 the Arcadian chief。

⑨ deprecate her anger：请她息怒；deprecate /ˈdeprɪkeɪt/：祈求免予遭受

⑩ tributary /ˈtrɪbjutəri/：支流的

impelled by the vigorous strokes of the rowers, the vessels shot rapidly up the stream.

About the middle of the day they came in sight of the scattered buildings of the infant town, where in after times the proud city of Rome grew, whose glory reached the skies. By chance the old king, Evander, was that day celebrating annual solemnities in honor of Hercules and all the gods. Pallas[1], his son, and all the chiefs of the little commonwealth stood by. When they saw the tall ship gliding onward near the wood, they were alarmed at the sight, and rose from the tables. But Pallas forbade the solemnities to be interrupted, and seizing a weapon, stepped forward to the river's bank. He called aloud, demanding who they were, and what their object[2]. Æneas, holding forth an olive-branch[3], replied, "We are Trojans, friends to you, and enemies to the Rutulians. We seek Evander, and offer to join our arms with yours." Pallas, in amaze at the sound of so great a name, invited them to land, and when Æneas touched the shore he seized his hand, and held it long in friendly grasp. Proceeding through the wood, they joined the king and his party and were most favorably received. Seats were provided for them at the tables, and the repast proceeded.

Infant Rome

When the solemnities were ended all moved towards the city. The king, bending with age, walked between his son and Æneas, taking the arm of one or the other of them, and with much variety of pleasing talk shortening the way. Æneas with delight looked and listened, observing all the beauties of the scene, and learning much of heroes renowned in ancient times. Evander said, "These extensive groves were once inhabited by fauns and nymphs, and a rude race of men who sprang from the trees themselves, and had neither laws nor social culture. They knew not how to yoke the cattle nor raise a harvest, nor provide from present abundance for future want; but browsed like beasts upon the leafy boughs, or fed voraciously on their hunted prey. Such were they when Saturn, expelled from Olympus by his sons, came among them and drew together the fierce savages, formed them into society, and gave them laws. Such peace and plenty ensued that men ever since have called his reign the golden age; but by degrees far other times succeeded, and the thirst of gold and the thirst of blood prevailed. The land was a prey to successive tyrants, till fortune and resistless destiny brought me hither, an exile from my native land, Arcadia[4]."

Having thus said, he showed him the Tarpeian rock[5], and the rude spot then overgrown with bushes where in after times the Capitol rose in all its magnificence. He next pointed to some dismantled walls, and said, "Here stood Janiculum[6], built by Janus, and there Saturnia[7], the town of Saturn." Such discourse brought them to the cottage of poor Evander, whence they saw the

---

① Pallas: /ˈpæləs/

② object: 目的

③ olive-branch: olive-branch 是和平或善意的象征。

④ Arcadia: 参见 *The Age of Fable* 第 1 章关于 Arcadia 的注释。

⑤ the Tarpeian /tɑːˈpɪən/ rock: 古罗马的一处悬崖,位于 the Capitoline Hill 的西南角。

⑥ Janiculum /dʒeɪˈnɪkələm/: 台伯河西岸的小山,正对着东岸的古罗马城,Janus 在此修建城堡,故名 Janiculum。

⑦ Saturnia: /səˈtɜːnɪə/

lowing herds roaming over the plain where now the proud and stately Forum① stands. They entered, and a couch was spread for Æneas, well stuffed with leaves, and covered with the skin of a Libyan bear.

Next morning, awakened by the dawn and the shrill song of birds beneath the eaves of his low mansion, old Evander rose. Clad in a tunic②, and a panther's skin thrown over his shoulders, with sandals on his feet and his good sword girded to his side, he went forth to seek his guest. Two mastiffs followed him, his whole retinue③ and body guard. He found the hero attended by his faithful Achates④, and, Pallas soon joining them, the old king spoke thus:

"Illustrious Trojan, it is but little we can do in so great a cause. Our state is feeble, hemmed in on one side by the river⑤, on the other by the Rutulians. But I propose to ally you with a people numerous and rich, to whom fate has brought you at the propitious moment. The Etruscans⑥ hold the country beyond the river. Mezentius was their king, a monster of cruelty, who invented unheard-of⑦ torments to gratify his vengeance. He would fasten the dead to the living, hand to hand and face to face, and leave the wretched victims to die in that dreadful embrace. At length the people cast him out, him and his house. They burned his palace and slew his friends. He escaped and took refuge with Turnus, who protects him with arms. The Etruscans demand that he shall be given up to deserved punishment, and would ere now have attempted to enforce their demand; but their priests restrain them, telling them that it is the will of heaven that no native of the land shall guide them to victory, and that their destined leader must come from across the sea. They have offered the crown to me, but I am too old to undertake such great affairs, and my son is native-born, which precludes⑧ him from the choice. You, equally by birth and time of life, and fame in arms, pointed out by the gods, have but to appear to be hailed at once as their leader. With you I will join Pallas, my son, my only hope and comfort. Under you he shall learn the art of war, and strive to emulate⑨ your great exploits."

Then the king ordered horses to be furnished for the Trojan chiefs, and Æneas, with a chosen band of followers and Pallas accompanying, mounted and took the way to the Etruscan city, having sent back the rest of his party in the ships. Æneas and his band safely arrived at the Etruscan camp and were received with open arms by Tarchon⑩ and his countrymen.

---

① Forum /ˈfɔːrəm/：古罗马城的著名广场，位于 the Palatine Hill 和 the Captoline Hill 两山的山脚，现尚存遗址。在拉丁语中叫 Forum Romanum（罗马广场）或 Forum Magnum（大广场），也可简称为 Forum。

② tunic /ˈtjuːnɪk/：古希腊人和古罗马人穿的一种短袖束腰外衣，下摆到膝盖，男女通用。

③ retinue /ˈretɪnjuː/：随从，随行人员

④ Achates /əˈkeɪtiːz/：Achates 是 Æneas 的忠实朋友。

⑤ the river：即台伯河。

⑥ Etruscans /ɪˈtrʌskənz/：古罗马建立之前意大利中部最强大的部落。参见 The Age of Fable 第 21 章关于 Mæonia 的注释。

⑦ unheard-of：没有听说过的

⑧ preclude /prɪˈkluːd/：排除

⑨ emulate /ˈemjuleɪt/：尽力模仿

⑩ Tarchon：/ˈtɑːkən/

Nisus and Euryalus

In the meanwhile Turnus had collected his bands and made all necessary preparations for the war. Juno sent Iris to him with a message inciting him to take advantage of the absence of Æneas and surprise① the Trojan camp. Accordingly the attempt was made, but the Trojans were found on their guard, and having received strict orders from Æneas not to fight in his absence, they lay still in their intrenchments②, and resisted all the efforts of the Rutulians to draw them into the field. Night coming on, the army of Turnus, in high spirits at their fancied superiority, feasted and enjoyed themselves, and finally stretched themselves on the field and slept secure.

In the camp of the Trojans things were far otherwise. There all was watchfulness and anxiety and impatience for Æneas's return. Nisus stood guard at the entrance of the camp, and Euryalus③, a youth distinguished above all in the army for graces of person and fine qualities, was with him. These two were friends and brothers in arms. Nisus said to his friend, "Do you perceive what confidence and carelessness the enemy display? Their lights are few and dim, and the men seem all oppressed with wine or sleep. You know how anxiously our chiefs wish to send to Æneas, and to get intelligence from him. Now, I am strongly moved to make my way through the enemy's camp and to go in search of our chief. If I succeed, the glory of the deed will be reward enough for me, and if they judge the service deserves anything more, let them pay it to you."

Euryalus, all on fire with the love of adventure, replied, "Would you, then, Nisus, refuse to share your enterprise with me? And shall I let you go into such danger alone? Not so my brave father brought me up, nor so have I planned for myself when I joined the standard④ of Æneas, and resolved to hold my life cheap in comparison with honor." Nisus replied, "I doubt it not, my friend; but you know the uncertain event of such an undertaking, and whatever may happen to me, I wish you to be safe. You are younger than I and have more of life in prospect. Nor can I be the cause of such grief to your mother, who has chosen to be here in the camp with you rather than stay and live in peace with the other matrons in Acestes' city." Euryalus replied, "Say no more. In vain you seek arguments to dissuade me. I am fixed in the resolution to go with you. Let us lose no time." They called the guard, and committing the watch to them, sought the general's tent. They found the chief officers in consultation, deliberating how they should send notice to Æneas of their situation. The offer of the two friends was gladly accepted, themselves loaded with praises and promised the most liberal rewards in case of success. Iulus especially addressed Euryalus, assuring him of his lasting friendship. Euryalus replied, "I have but one boon to ask. My aged mother is with me in the camp. For me she left the Trojan soil, and would not stay behind with the other matrons at the city of Acestes. I go now without taking leave of her. I could not bear her tears nor set at nought⑤ her

---

① surprise /səˈpraɪz/：突袭

② intrenchment（entrenchment）/ɪnˈtrentʃmənt/：堑壕，用堑壕巩固的防御工事

③ Euryalus：/juəˈraɪələs/

④ standard /ˈstændəd/：部队，军队

⑤ set... at nought：不顾……

entreaties. But do thou, I beseech you, comfort her in her distress. Promise me that and I shall go more boldly into whatever dangers may present themselves." Iulus and the other chiefs were moved to tears, and promised to do all his request. "Your mother shall be mine," said Iulus, "and all that I have promised to you shall be made good to her, if you do not return to receive it."①

The two friends left the camp and plunged at once into the midst of the enemy. They found no watch, no sentinels② posted, but, all about, the sleeping soldiers strewn on the grass and among the wagons. The laws of war at that early day did not forbid a brave man to slay a sleeping foe, and the two Trojans slew, as they passed, such of the enemy as they could without exciting alarm. In one tent Euryalus made prize of a helmet brilliant with gold and plumes. They had passed through the enemy's ranks without being discovered, but now suddenly appeared a troop directly in front of them, which, under Volscens③, their leader, were approaching the camp. The glittering helmet of Euryalus caught their attention, and Volscens hailed the two, and demanded who and whence they were. They made no answer, but plunged into the wood. The horsemen scattered in all directions to intercept their flight. Nisus had eluded pursuit and was out of danger, but Euryalus being missing he turned back to seek him. He again entered the wood and soon came within sound of voices. Looking through the thicket he saw the whole band surrounding Euryalus with noisy questions. What should he do? how extricate④ the youth, or would it be better to die with him.

Raising his eyes to the moon, which now shone clear, he said, "Goddess! favor my effort!" and aiming his javelin at one of the leaders of the troop, struck him in the back and stretched him on the plain with a death-blow. In the midst of their amazement another weapon flew and another of the party fell dead. Volscens, the leader, ignorant whence the darts came, rushed sword in hand upon Euryalus. "You shall pay the penalty of both," he said, and would have plunged the sword into his bosom, when Nisus, who from his concealment saw the peril of his friend, rushed forward exclaiming, "'Twas I⑤, 'twas I; turn your swords against me, Rutulians, I did it; he only followed me as a friend." While he spoke the sword fell, and pierced the comely bosom of Euryalus. His head fell over on his shoulder, like a flower cut down by the plough. Nisus rushed upon Volscens and plunged his sword into his body, and was himself slain on the instant by numberless blows.

Mezentius

Æneas, with his Etrurian⑥ allies, arrived on the scene of action in time to rescue his beleaguered⑦ camp; and now the two armies being nearly equal in strength, the war began in good

---

① Acestes 的母亲是特洛伊人,所以 Aeneas 到达西西里岛 (Sicily) 时受到了他的款待。有些与 Aeneas 随行的特洛伊妇女留在了西西里岛,而 Euryalus 的母亲却与儿子一起来到意大利。

② sentinel /ˈsentɪnl/: 哨兵

③ Volscens: /ˈvɒlsəns/

④ extricate /ˈekstrɪkeɪt/: 使脱离险境

⑤ 'Twas I: It was I

⑥ Etrurian /ɪˈtruərɪən/: Etruscan

⑦ beleaguer /bɪˈliːgə/: 包围

earnest①. We cannot find space for all the details, but must simply record the fate of the principal characters whom we have introduced to our readers. The tyrant Mezentius, finding himself engaged against his revolting subjects, raged like a wild beast. He slew all who dared to withstand him, and put the multitude to flight wherever he appeared. At last he encountered Æneas, and the armies stood still to see the issue. Mezentius threw his spear, which striking Æneas's shield glanced off and hit Anthor②. He was a Grecian by birth, who had left Argos, his native city, and followed Evander into Italy. The poet says of him with simple pathos③ which has made the words proverbial, "He fell, unhappy, by a wound intended for another, looked up at the skies, and dying remembered sweet Argos." Æneas now in turn hurled his lance. It pierced the shield of Mezentius, and wounded him in the thigh. Lausus, his son, could not bear the sight, but rushed forward and interposed himself, while the followers pressed round Mezentius and bore him away. Æneas held his sword suspended over Lausus and delayed to strike, but the furious youth pressed on and he was compelled to deal the fatal blow. Lausus fell, and Æneas bent over him in pity. "Hapless youth," he said, "what can I do for you worthy of your praise? Keep those arms in which you glory, and fear not but that your body shall be restored to your friends, and have due funeral honors." So saying, he called the timid followers and delivered the body into their hands.

Mezentius meanwhile had been borne to the riverside, and washed his wound. Soon the news reached him of Lausus's death, and rage and despair supplied the place of strength. He mounted his horse and dashed into the thickest of the fight, seeking Æneas. Having found him, he rode round him in a circle, throwing one javelin after another, while Æneas stood fenced with his shield, turning every way to meet them. At last, after Mezentius had three times made the circuit, Æneas threw his lance directly at the horse's head. It pierced his temples and he fell, while a shout from both armies rent the skies. Mezentius asked no mercy, but only that his body might be spared the insults of his revolted subjects, and be buried in the same grave with his son. He received the fatal stroke not unprepared, and poured out his life and his blood together.

Pallas, Camilla, Turnus

While these things were doing in one part of the field, in another Turnus encountered the youthful Pallas. The contest between champions④ so unequally matched⑤ could not be doubtful. Pallas bore himself bravely, but fell by the lance of Turnus. The victor almost relented when he saw the brave youth lying dead at his feet, and spared to use the privilege of a conqueror in despoiling⑥ him of his arms. The belt only, adorned with studs⑦ and carvings of gold, he took and

---

① in good earnest：紧张地，认真地
② Anthor：/ˈænθə/
③ pathos /ˈpeɪɒs/：怜悯，同情，悲怆
④ champion /ˈtʃæmpɪən/：战士
⑤ so unequally matched：实力悬殊如此大的
⑥ despoil /dɪˈspɔɪl/：剥夺，抢劫
⑦ stud：腰带上金属或琥珀做的饰钉

clasped round his own body. The rest he remitted① to the friends of the slain.

After the battle there was a cessation of arms② for some days to allow both armies to bury their dead. In this interval Æneas challenged Turnus to decide the contest by single combat, but Turnus evaded the challenge. Another battle ensued, in which Camilla, the virgin warrior, was chiefly conspicuous. Her deeds of valor surpassed those of the bravest warriors, and many Trojans and Etruscans fell pierced with her darts or struck down by her battle-axe. At last an Etruscan named Aruns③, who had watched her long, seeking for some advantage, observed her pursuing a flying enemy whose splendid armor offered a tempting prize. Intent on the chase she observed not her danger, and the javelin of Aruns struck her and inflicted a fatal wound. She fell and breathed her last in the arms of her attendant maidens. But Diana, who beheld her fate, suffered not her slaughter to be unavenged. Aruns, as he stole away, glad, but frightened, was struck by a secret arrow, launched by one of the nymphs of Diana's train, and died ignobly and unknown.

At length the final conflict took place between Æneas and Turnus. Turnus had avoided the contest as long as he could, but at last, impelled by the ill success of his arms and by the murmurs of his followers, he braced himself④ to the conflict. It could not be doubtful. On the side of Æneas were the expressed decree of destiny, the aid of his goddess-mother at every emergency, and impenetrable armor fabricated by Vulcan, at her request, for her son. Turnus, on the other hand, was deserted by his celestial allies, Juno having been expressly⑤ forbidden by Jupiter to assist him any longer. Turnus threw his lance, but it recoiled⑥ harmless from the shield of Æneas. The Trojan hero then threw his, which penetrated the shield of Turnus, and pierced his thigh. Then Turnus's fortitude⑦ forsook him and he begged for mercy; and Æneas would have given him his life, but at the instant his eye fell on the belt of Pallas, which Turnus had taken from the slaughtered youth. Instantly his rage revived, and exclaiming, "Pallas immolates⑧ thee with this blow," he thrust him through with his sword.

Here the poem of the "Æneid" closes, and we are left to infer that Æneas, having triumphed over his foes, obtained Lavinia for his bride. Tradition adds that he founded his city, and called it after her name, Lavinium⑨. His son Iulus founded Alba Longa⑩, which was the birthplace of Romulus and Remus⑪ and the cradle of Rome itself.

---

① remit /rɪˈmɪt/：归还
② a cessation of arms：停战，休战
③ Aruns：/ˈærənz/
④ brace himself：振作起来，打起精神
⑤ expressly /ekˈspresli/：明确地
⑥ recoil：弹回
⑦ fortitude /ˈfɔːtɪtjuːd/：力气，力量
⑧ immolate /ˈɪməleɪt/：杀死
⑨ Lavinium：/ləˈvɪnɪəm/
⑩ Alba Longa /ˈælbə ˈlɒŋɡə/：即 Alba，意大利中部 Latium 地区古城，位于罗马东南方向不远处。
⑪ Romulus /ˈrɒmjuləs/ and Remus /ˈriːməs/：Romulus 和 Remus 是一对双胞胎兄弟，他们是 Alba Longa 国王 Numitor 的孙子。按照传说，Romulus 是罗马城的创建者。

第二部分

希腊罗马神话文学作品选读

Homer

荷马（Homer）是古希腊最伟大的诗人，但关于他的生平和著作尚无定论。学者们根据荷马史诗的语言特点进行猜测，一般认为荷马生活在公元前 9 世纪至公元前 8 世纪之间。西方学者普遍认为荷马是位游吟盲诗人，史诗《伊利亚特》（*The Iliad*）和《奥德赛》（*The Odyssey*）被认为是他的作品。

《伊利亚特》共 24 卷，讲的是十年特洛伊战争最后几十天的故事，以特洛伊主帅赫克托耳（Hector）的阵亡而结束。本读本选取了《伊利亚特》中的 3 个片段：第 1 个选段"Deception of Jupiter by Juno"选自史诗的第 14 卷，第 2 个选段"The Shield of Achilles"选自史诗的第 18 卷，第 3 个选段"The Death of Hector"选自史诗的第 22 卷。

《奥德赛》共 24 卷，讲述参加特洛伊战争的希腊将领奥德修斯（Odysseus）回家的故事。奥德修斯的回家之路充满了各种艰难险阻，但他克服了重重困难，回到了家乡，打败了妻子的众多追求者，终于与家人团聚。本读本选取了《奥德赛》中的两个片段：第 1 个选段"The Love of Mars and Venus"选自史诗的第 8 卷，第 2 个选段"The Killing of the Wooers"选自史诗的第 22 卷。

译者塞缪尔·巴特勒（Samuel Butler）是 19 世纪英国作家，代表作有《埃瑞洪》（*Erewhon*）和《众生之路》（*The Way of All Flesh*）。巴特勒的翻译使用口语化的散文，文体清晰易懂。荷马史诗的英文译本大约有 120 种，其中乔治·查普曼（George Chapman）1616 年的译本受到诗人约翰·济慈（John Keats）的高度赞扬。

The Iliad
Translated into English by Samuel Butler

Deception of Jupiter by Juno

Juno of the golden throne looked down as she stood upon a peak of Olympus and her heart was gladdened at the sight of him who was at once her brother and her brother-in-law①, hurrying hither and thither② amid the fighting. Then she turned her eyes to Jove as he sat on the topmost③ crests④ of many-fountained⑤ Ida⑥, and loathed⑦ him. She set herself to think how she might hoodwink⑧ him, and in the end she deemed that it would be best for her to go to Ida and array⑨ herself in rich attire⑩, in the hope that Jove might become enamoured of her, and wish to embrace⑪ her. While he was thus engaged a sweet and careless sleep might be made to steal over his eyes and senses.

She went, therefore, to the room which her son Vulcan had made her, and the doors of which he had cunningly fastened by means of a secret key so that no other god could open them. Here she entered and closed the doors behind her. She cleansed all the dirt from her fair body with ambrosia, then she anointed⑫ herself with olive oil, ambrosial⑬, very soft, and scented specially for herself—if it were so much as shaken in the bronze-floored house of Jove, the scent⑭ pervaded⑮ the universe of heaven and earth. With this she anointed her delicate skin, and then she plaited the fair ambrosial locks that flowed in a stream of golden tresses from her immortal head. She put on the wondrous robe which Minerva had worked for her with consummate⑯ art, and had embroidered with manifold devices; she fastened it about her bosom with golden clasps, and she girded herself with a girdle that had a hundred tassels⑰; then she fastened her earrings, three brilliant pendants that glistened most beautifully, through the pierced lobes⑱ of her ears, and threw a lovely new veil over her head. She bound her sandals on to her feet, and when she had arrayed herself perfectly to her satisfaction, she left her room and called Venus to come aside and speak to her. "My dear child," said she, "will you do what I am going to ask of you, or will refuse me because you are angry at my being on the Danaan⑲ side, while you are on the Trojan?"

---

① her brother and her brother-in-law：Neptune；Jupiter, Neptune, and Juno are all offspring of Saturn, and Jupiter is the husband of Juno, so Neptune is her brother and her brother-in-law. Both Juno and Neptune support the Greeks.

② hither and thither：here and there

③ topmost /ˈtɒpməʊst/：最高的

④ crest：山顶, 峰顶

⑤ many-fountained：山泉众多的

⑥ 参见 *The Age of Fable* 第 5 章关于 Ida 的注释。

⑦ loathe /ləʊð/：恨, 讨厌, 不喜欢

⑧ hoodwink /ˈhʊdwɪŋk/：欺骗, 蒙蔽

⑨ array /əˈreɪ/：打扮, 装饰

⑩ attire /əˈtaɪə/：服装, 衣着

⑪ embrace：（委婉语）与……发生性关系

⑫ anoint /əˈnɔɪnt/：（用油、软膏、药膏等）涂抹

⑬ ambrosial /æmˈbrəʊzɪəl/：芳香的

⑭ scent：香味

⑮ pervade /pəˈveɪd/：弥漫, 充满, 渗透

⑯ consummate /ˈkɒnsʌmət/：无与伦比的, 完美的

⑰ tassel /ˈtæsəl/：流苏, 穗状坠饰品

⑱ lobe：耳垂

⑲ Danaan /dəˈnæən/：希腊的；the Danaans 本指居住在伯罗奔尼撒半岛 Argos 地区的希腊人, 在荷马的史诗中该词用来指"希腊人"。

Jove's daughter Venus answered, "Juno, august queen of goddesses, daughter of mighty Saturn, say what you want, and I will do it for you at once, if I can, and if it can be done at all."

Then Juno told her a lying[①] tale and said, "I want you to endow me with some of those fascinating charms, the spells of which bring all things mortal and immortal to your feet. I am going to the world's end to visit Oceanus (from whom all we gods proceed) and mother Tethys; they received me in their house, took care of me, and brought me up, having taken me over from Rhaea[②] when Jove imprisoned great Saturn in the depths that are under earth and sea.[③] I must go and see them that I may make peace between them; they have been quarrelling, and are so angry that they have not slept with one another this long while; if I can bring them round and restore them to one another's embraces, they will be grateful to me and love me for ever afterwards."

Thereon laughter-loving Venus said, "I cannot and must not refuse you, for you sleep in the arms of Jove who is our king."

As she spoke she loosed from her bosom the curiously embroidered girdle[④] into which all her charms had been wrought—love, desire, and that sweet flattery which steals the judgement even of the most prudent. She gave the girdle to Juno and said, "Take this girdle wherein all my charms reside and lay it in your bosom. If you will wear it I promise you that your errand, be it what it may, will not be bootless[⑤]."

When she heard this Juno smiled, and still smiling she laid the girdle in her bosom.

Venus now went back into the house of Jove, while Juno darted down from the summits of Olympus. She passed over Pieria[⑥] and fair Emathia[⑦], and went on and on till she came to the snowy ranges of the Thracian horsemen, over whose topmost crests she sped without ever setting foot to ground. When she came to Athos[⑧] she went on over the waves of the sea till she reached Lemnos[⑨], the city of noble Thoas[⑩]. There she met Sleep, own brother[⑪] to Death, and caught him by the hand, saying, "Sleep, you who lord it alike over mortals and immortals, if you ever did me a service in times past, do one for me now, and I shall be grateful to you ever after. Close Jove's keen eyes for me in slumber while I hold him clasped in my embrace, and I will give you a beautiful golden seat, that can never fall to pieces; my clubfooted[⑫] son Vulcan shall make it for you, and he shall give it a footstool for you to rest your fair feet upon when you are at table."

---

① lying /ˈlaɪɪŋ/: 撒谎的,不真实的,欺骗的
② Rhaea: 该名字在 *The Age of Fable* 中拼写为 Rhea。
③ 参见 *The Age of Fable* 第 4 章关于 my foster-parents 的注释。
④ the curiously embroidered girdle: the Cestus; 参见 *The Age of Fable* 第 1 章关于 Venus 的叙述。
⑤ bootless /ˈbuːtlɪs/: 不成功的,无用的
⑥ Pieria /paɪˈɪərɪə/: 希腊地区名,现在是希腊中马其顿大区的一个州。奥林匹斯山位于该地区西部。
⑦ Emathia /ɪˈmæθɪə/: 希腊地区名,现在是希腊中马其顿大区的一个州,位于 Pieria 以北。
⑧ Athos /ˈæθɒs/: 希腊山名,位于半自治的圣山僧侣共和国。
⑨ Lemnos /ˈlemnɒs/: 希腊岛名,位于爱琴海北部,距离土耳其西海岸不远,属于今天希腊北爱琴大区莱斯沃斯州。
⑩ Thoas /ˈθəʊəs/: Bacchus 和 Ariadne 之子,Lemnos 国王。关于 Bacchus 和 Ariadne 的故事,参见 *The Age of Fable* 第 21 章。
⑪ own brother: 亲兄弟;own: 因为血缘而有亲戚关系的
⑫ clubfooted /ˌklʌbˈfutɪd/: 畸形脚的

Then Sleep answered, "Juno, great queen of goddesses, daughter of mighty Saturn, I would lull any other of the gods to sleep without compunction①, not even excepting the waters of Oceanus from whom all of them proceed, but I dare not go near Jove, nor send him to sleep unless he bids me. I have had one lesson already through doing what you asked me, on the day when Jove's mighty son Hercules set sail from Ilius② after having sacked③ the city of the Trojans. At your bidding④ I suffused⑤ my sweet self over the mind of aegis-bearing Jove, and laid him to rest; meanwhile you hatched a plot against Hercules, and set the blasts of the angry winds beating upon the sea, till you took him to the goodly city of Cos⑥ away from all his friends. Jove was furious when he awoke, and began hurling the gods about all over the house; he was looking more particularly for myself, and would have flung me down through space into the sea where I should never have been heard of any more, had not Night who cows⑦ both men and gods protected me. I fled to her and Jove left off⑧ looking for me in spite of his being so angry, for he did not dare do anything to displease Night. And now you are again asking me to do something on which I cannot venture."

And Juno said, "Sleep, why do you take such notions as those into your head? Do you think Jove will be as anxious to help the Trojans, as he was about his own son? Come, I will marry you to one of the youngest of the Graces⑨, and she shall be your own—Pasithea⑩, whom you have always wanted to marry."

Sleep was pleased when he heard this, and answered, "Then swear it to me by the dread⑪ waters of the river Styx; lay one hand on the bounteous earth, and the other on the sheen⑫ of the sea, so that all the gods who dwell down below with Saturn⑬ may be our witnesses, and see that you really do give me one of the youngest of the Graces—Pasithea, whom I have always wanted to marry."

Juno did as he had said. She swore, and invoked all the gods of the nether world⑭, who are called Titans, to witness. When she had completed her oath, the two enshrouded themselves in a thick mist and sped lightly forward, leaving Lemnos and Imbrus⑮ behind them. Presently they

---

① compunction /kəmˈpʌŋkʃn/：内疚，不安，后悔，顾虑
② Ilius /ˈɪlɪəs/：Troy；Troy can also be call Ilion /ˈɪlɪən /，Ilium /ˈɪlɪəm /，Ilios /ˈɪlɪəs /，or Ilius.
③ sack：洗劫，劫掠
④ bidding：命令
⑤ suffuse /səˈfjuːz/：覆盖
⑥ Cos /kɒs/：该城位于今希腊南爱琴大区左泽卡尼索斯州（Dodekanisos）科斯岛（Cos 或 Kos）东部海岸，离土耳其西海岸非常近。
⑦ cow：吓唬，威胁
⑧ leave off：停止
⑨ the Graces：参见 The Age of Fable 第 1 章关于 the Graces 的叙述。
⑩ Pasithea /ˌpæsɪˈθiːə/：Hesiod 认为 the Graces（美惠女神）是三姐妹，即 The Age of Fable 第 1 章中提到的那三位，但在荷马史诗中，the Graces 有数位。
⑪ dread /dred/：可怕的
⑫ sheen：表面的光泽，表面的光辉；the sheen of the sea：熠熠发光的海面
⑬ all the gods who dwell down below with Saturn：参见 The Age of Fable 第 1 章关于 Saturn 被其子 Jupiter 推翻的叙述。
⑭ the nether world：Tartarus，参见 The Age of Fable 第 1 章关于 Tartarus 的注释；nether /ˈneðə/：下面的，地下的
⑮ Imbrus /ˈɪmbrəs/：即今土耳其的格克切岛（Gökçeada）；格克切岛位于希腊的 Lemnos 岛东北方向不远处，是土耳其最大的岛屿，也是土耳其领土的最西端。

reached many-fountained Ida, mother of wild beasts, and Lectum① where they left the sea to go on by land, and the tops of the trees of the forest soughed② under the going of their feet. Here Sleep halted, and ere Jove caught sight of him he climbed a lofty pine-tree—the tallest that reared its head towards heaven on all Ida. He hid himself behind the branches and sat there in the semblance of the sweet-singing bird that haunts the mountains and is called Chalcis③ by the gods, but men call it Cymindis④. Juno then went to Gargarus⑤, the topmost peak of Ida, and Jove, driver of the clouds, set eyes upon her. As soon as he did so he became inflamed with the same passionate desire for her that he had felt when they had first enjoyed each other's embraces, and slept with one another without their dear parents knowing anything about it. He went up to her and said, "What do you want that you have come hither from Olympus—and that too with neither chariot nor horses to convey you?"

Then Juno told him a lying tale and said, "I am going to the world's end, to visit Oceanus, from whom all we gods proceed, and mother Tethys; they received me into their house, took care of me, and brought me up. I must go and see them that I may make peace between them: they have been quarrelling, and are so angry that they have not slept with one another this long time. The horses that will take me over land and sea are stationed on the lowermost⑥ spurs⑦ of many-fountained Ida, and I have come here from Olympus on purpose to consult you. I was afraid you might be angry with me later on, if I went to the house of Oceanus without letting you know."

And Jove said, "Juno, you can choose some other time for paying your visit to Oceanus—for the present let us devote ourselves to love and to the enjoyment of one another. Never yet have I been so overpowered⑧ by passion neither for goddess nor mortal woman as I am at this moment for yourself—not even when I was in love with the wife of Ixion⑨ who bore me Pirithous⑩, peer of gods in counsel, nor yet with Danae the daintily-ancled daughter of Acrisius, who bore me the famed hero Perseus⑪. Then there was the daughter of Phoenix⑫, who bore me Minos and Rhadamanthus: there was Semele⑬, and Alcmena⑭ in Thebes by whom I begot⑮ my lion-hearted

---

① Lectum /ˈlektəm/: 即今土耳其小亚细亚半岛最西端的巴巴角（Cape Baba）。该角是亚洲大陆的最西端。

② sough /saʊ; sʌf/: 发出沙沙声,发出飒飒声

③ Chalcis /ˈkælsɪs /: 欧夜莺

④ Cymindis /sɪˈmɪndɪs/: Chalcis (Χαλκίς)和 Cymindis (κύμινδις) 是同一种鸟的两种名字。

⑤ Gargarus: /ˈgɑːgərəs/

⑥ lowermost /ˈləʊəməʊst/: lowest

⑦ spur: 山坡

⑧ overpower /ˌəʊvəˈpaʊə/: 制伏,压倒

⑨ the wife of Ixion: Dia

⑩ Pirithous: /paɪˈrɪθəʊəs/

⑪ Perseus: 参见 The Age of Fable 第 15 章关于 Persus 的叙述。

⑫ the daughter of Phoenix: Europa;关于 Jupiter 勾引 Europa 的故事,参见 The Age of Fable 第 14 章关于 Europa 的注释;Phoenix/ˈfiːnɪks/是 Agenor 的儿子,所以与 Europa 是兄妹,但有人（如荷马）认为他是 Europa 的父亲。

⑬ 关于 Jupiter 与 Semele 的故事,参见 The Age of Fable 第 21 章。

⑭ 关于 Jupiter 与 Alcmena 的故事,参见 The Age of Fable 第 19 章。

⑮ beget /bɪˈget/: （父亲）生（子女）

son Hercules, while Semele became mother to Bacchus the comforter of mankind. There was queen Ceres① again, and lovely Leto②, and yourself—but with none of these was I ever so much enamoured as I now am with you."

Juno again answered him with a lying tale. "Most dread son of Saturn," she exclaimed, "what are you talking about? Would you have us enjoy one another here on the top of Mount Ida, where everything can be seen? What if one of the ever-living③ gods should see us sleeping together, and tell the others? It would be such a scandal that when I had risen from your embraces I could never show myself inside your house again; but if you are so minded, there is a room which your son Vulcan has made me, and he has given it good strong doors; if you would so have it, let us go thither and lie down."

And Jove answered, "Juno, you need not be afraid that either god or man will see you, for I will enshroud both of us in such a dense golden cloud, that the very sun for all his bright piercing beams shall not see through it."

With this the son of Saturn caught his wife in his embrace; whereon the earth sprouted④ them a cushion⑤ of young grass, with dew-bespangled⑥ lotus, crocus, and hyacinth, so soft and thick that it raised them well above the ground. Here they laid themselves down and overhead they were covered by a fair cloud of gold, from which there fell glittering dew-drops.

Thus, then, did the sire of all things⑦ repose peacefully on the crest of Ida, overcome at once by sleep and love, and he held his spouse in his arms. Meanwhile Sleep made off to the ships of the Achaeans⑧, to tell earth-encircling Neptune, lord of the earthquake. When he had found him he said, "Now, Neptune, you can help the Danaans with a will⑨, and give them victory though it be only for a short time while Jove is still sleeping. I have sent him into a sweet slumber, and Juno has beguiled him into going to bed with her."

The Shield of Achilles

When he⑩ had so said he left her⑪ and went to his bellows⑫, turning them towards the fire and bidding them do their office. Twenty bellows blew upon the melting-pots, and they blew blasts of every kind, some fierce to help him when he had need of them, and others less strong as Vulcan

---

① Ceres 与 Jupiter 生下 Proserpine。
② Leto /ˈliːtəʊ/：即 Latona，与 Jupiter 生下 Apollo 和 Diana。参见 *The Age of Fable* 第 4 章。
③ ever-living：长生不老的
④ sprout：使长出
⑤ cushion /ˈkʊʃn/：垫子
⑥ dew-bespangled /bɪˈspæŋgld/：有闪烁露珠点缀的
⑦ the sire of all things：Jove
⑧ Achaean /əˈkiːən/：来自 Achaia（Achaea）的人,在荷马史诗中,该词通常指"希腊人";关于 Achaia（Achaea）,参见 *The Age of Fable* 第 27 章的注释。
⑨ with a will：热心地,努力地,尽情地
⑩ he：Vulcan
⑪ her：Thetis, mother of Achilles
⑫ bellows /ˈbeləʊz/：（铁匠使用的）风箱

willed it in the course of his work. He threw tough copper into the fire, and tin, with silver and gold; he set his great anvil① on its block, and with one hand grasped his mighty hammer while he took the tongs② in the other.

First he shaped the shield so great and strong, adorning it all over and binding it round with a gleaming circuit in three layers; and the baldric③ was made of silver. He made the shield in five thicknesses④, and with many a wonder did his cunning⑤ hand enrich it.

He wrought the earth, the heavens, and the sea; the moon also at her full and the untiring sun, with all the signs that glorify the face of heaven—the Pleiads⑥, the Hyads⑦, huge Orion⑧, and the Bear⑨, which men also call the Wain and which turns round ever in one place, facing Orion, and alone never dips into the stream of Oceanus.

He wrought also two cities, fair to see and busy with the hum⑩ of men. In the one were weddings and wedding-feasts, and they were going about the city with brides whom they were escorting by torchlight from their chambers. Loud rose the cry of Hymen, and the youths danced to the music of flute and lyre, while the women stood each at her house door to see them.

Meanwhile the people were gathered in assembly, for there was a quarrel, and two men were wrangling⑪ about the blood-money⑫ for a man who had been killed, the one saying before the people that he had paid damages⑬ in full, and the other that he had not been paid. Each was trying to make his own case good, and the people took sides, each man backing the side that he had taken; but the heralds kept them back, and the elders⑭ sate⑮ on their seats of stone in a solemn circle, holding the staves⑯ which the heralds had put into their hands. Then they rose and each in his turn gave judgement, and there were two talents⑰ laid down, to be given to him whose judgement should be deemed the fairest⑱.

About the other city there lay encamped two hosts⑲ in gleaming armour, and they were

① anvil /ˈænvɪl/: (铁匠使用的)砧

② tongs /tɒŋz/: 夹子

③ baldric /ˈbɔːldrɪk/: 用来在身上挂宝剑、盾牌等的装饰精美的带子

④ thickness: 层

⑤ cunning: 巧的, 熟练的

⑥ Pleiads /ˈplaɪədz/: 昴星团

⑦ 参见 *The Age of Fable* 第 21 章关于 Hyades 的注释。

⑧ Orion: 猎户座

⑨ the Bear: 参见 *The Age of Fable* 第 1 章关于 the Bear 的注释和第 4 章关于 the Great and Little Bear 的注释。

⑩ hum: 喧嚣声, 嘈杂声

⑪ wrangle /ˈræŋgl/: (愤怒地或大声地)争吵

⑫ blood-money: 杀人者或其家属支付给被杀者家属的补偿款

⑬ damages: 补偿款

⑭ elder: 经验丰富而有权威的长者

⑮ sate: sat

⑯ stave /steɪv/: 权杖

⑰ talent: (古希腊、罗马等使用的)货币单位

⑱ fair: 公平的

⑲ host: 部队, 军队

divided① whether to sack it, or to spare it and accept the half of what it contained. But the men of the city would not yet consent, and armed themselves for a surprise②; their wives and little children kept guard upon the walls, and with them were the men who were past fighting through age; but the others sallied forth with Mars and Pallas Minerva at their head—both of them wrought in gold and clad in golden raiment, great and fair with their armour as befitting gods, while they that followed were smaller. When they reached the place where they would lay their ambush, it was on a riverbed to which live stock of all kinds would come from far and near to water; here, then, they lay concealed, clad in full armour. Some way off them there were two scouts who were on the look-out for the coming of sheep or cattle, which presently came, followed by two shepherds who were playing on their pipes, and had not so much as a thought of danger. When those who were in ambush saw this, they cut off the flocks and herds and killed the shepherds. Meanwhile the besiegers, when they heard much noise among the cattle as they sat in council, sprang to their horses, and made with all speed towards them; when they reached them they set battle in array by the banks of the river, and the hosts aimed their bronze-shod spears at one another. With them were Strife and Riot, and fell③ Fate who was dragging three men after her, one with a fresh wound, and the other unwounded, while the third was dead, and she was dragging him along by his heel: and her robe was bedrabbled④ in men's blood. They went in and out with one another and fought as though they were living people haling⑤ away one another's dead.

He wrought also a fair fallow⑥ field, large and thrice ploughed already. Many men were working at the plough within it, turning their oxen to and fro, furrow after furrow. Each time that they turned on reaching the headland⑦ a man would come up to them and give them a cup of wine, and they would go back to their furrows looking forward to the time when they should again reach the headland. The part that they had ploughed was dark behind them, so that the field, though it was of gold, still looked as if it were being ploughed—very curious to behold.

He wrought also a field of harvest corn, and the reapers were reaping with sharp sickles in their hands. Swathe⑧ after swathe fell to the ground in a straight line behind them, and the binders bound them in bands of twisted straw. There were three binders, and behind them there were boys who gathered the cut corn in armfuls and kept on bringing them to be bound: among them all the owner of the land stood by in silence and was glad. The servants were getting a meal ready under an oak, for they had sacrificed a great ox, and were busy cutting him⑨ up, while the women were making a porridge of much white barley for the labourers' dinner.

---

① divided：有分歧的,意见不一致的

② surprise：突然袭击

③ fell：凶猛的,残暴的

④ bedrabble /bɪˈdræbl/：(被雨水、稀泥等)弄脏

⑤ hale：拖

⑥ fallow：(土地)犁好等待播种的

⑦ headland：(犁沟尽头或篱笆旁)未犁的土地

⑧ swathe /sweɪð/：一刈幅的作物或牧草

⑨ him：the great ox

He wrought also a vineyard, golden and fair to see, and the vines were loaded with grapes. The bunches overhead were black, but the vines were trained on poles of silver. He ran a ditch of dark metal all round it, and fenced it with a fence of tin; there was only one path to it, and by this the vintagers went when they would gather the vintage. Youths and maidens all blithe① and full of glee②, carried the luscious③ fruit in plaited baskets; and with them there went a boy who made sweet music with his lyre, and sang the Linus-song④ with his clear boyish voice.

He wrought also a herd of horned cattle. He made the cows of gold and tin, and they lowed as they came full speed out of the yards to go and feed among the waving reeds that grow by the banks of the river. Along with the cattle there went four shepherds, all of them in gold, and their nine fleet⑤ dogs went with them. Two terrible lions had fastened on⑥ a bellowing bull that was with the foremost cows, and bellow as he might they haled him, while the dogs and men gave chase⑦: the lions tore through the bull's thick hide⑧ and were gorging on his blood and bowels, but the herdsmen were afraid to do anything, and only hounded⑨ on their dogs; the dogs dared not fasten on the lions but stood by barking and keeping out of harm's way.

The god wrought also a pasture in a fair mountain dell⑩, and large flock of sheep, with a homestead and huts, and sheltered sheepfolds.

Furthermore he wrought a green⑪, like that which Daedalus once made in Cnossus⑫ for lovely Ariadne. Hereon there danced youths and maidens whom all would woo, with their hands on one another's wrists. The maidens wore robes of light linen, and the youths well woven shirts that were slightly oiled. The girls were crowned with garlands, while the young men had daggers of gold that hung by silver baldrics; sometimes they would dance deftly in a ring with merry twinkling feet, as it were a potter sitting at his work and making trial of his wheel to see whether it will run, and sometimes they would go all in line with one another, and much people was gathered joyously about the green. There was a bard also to sing to them and play his lyre, while two tumblers⑬ went about performing in the midst of them when the man struck up with his tune.

All round the outermost rim of the shield he set the mighty stream of the river Oceanus.

Then when he had fashioned the shield so great and strong, he made a breastplate⑭ also that

---

① blithe /blaɪð/：快乐的，欢快的

② glee：快乐，欢快

③ luscious /ˈlʌʃəs/：甜的

④ Linus-song：古希腊的挽歌

⑤ fleet：灵活的，行动敏捷的

⑥ fasten on：死死咬住，紧紧抓住

⑦ give chase：追赶

⑧ hide：牛皮

⑨ hound：唆（sǒu）使，怂勇做坏事

⑩ dell：小峡谷

⑪ green：位于村镇中央的公共草地，用于某种特定目的的草地

⑫ Cnossus /ˈnɒsəs/：古克里特（Crete）城市，国王 Minos 的都城

⑬ tumbler /ˈtʌmblə/：翻跟斗的人

⑭ breastplate /ˈbrestpleɪt/：护胸铠甲

shone brighter than fire. He made helmet, close fitting to the brow, and richly worked, with a golden plume overhanging it; and he made greaves① also of beaten tin.

Lastly, when the famed lame god② had made all the armour, he took it and set it before the mother of Achilles; whereon she darted like a falcon from the snowy summits of Olympus and bore away the gleaming armour from the house of Vulcan.

The Death of Hector

Thus the Trojans in the city,③ scared④ like fawns, wiped the sweat from off them and drank to quench their thirst, leaning against the goodly⑤ battlements⑥, while the Achaeans with their shields laid upon their shoulders drew close up to the walls. But stern fate bade Hector stay where he was before Ilius and the Scaean gates⑦. Then Phoebus Apollo spoke to the son of Peleus⑧ saying, "Why, son of Peleus, do you, who are but man, give chase to me who am immortal? Have you not yet found out that it is a god whom you pursue so furiously? You did not harass⑨ the Trojans whom you had routed⑩, and now they are within their walls, while you have been decoyed⑪ hither away from them. Me you cannot kill, for death can take no hold upon me."

Achilles was greatly angered and said, "You have baulked⑫ me, Far-Darter⑬, most malicious of all gods, and have drawn me away from the wall, where many another man would have bitten the dust ere he got within Ilius; you have robbed me of great glory and have saved the Trojans at no risk to yourself, for you have nothing to fear, but I would indeed have my revenge if it were in my power to do so."

On this, with fell⑭ intent he made towards the city, and as the winning horse in a chariot race strains⑮ every nerve when he⑯ is flying over the plain, even so fast and furiously did the limbs of Achilles bear him onwards. King Priam was first to note him as he scoured⑰ the plain, all radiant as the star which men call Orion's Hound⑱, and whose beams blaze forth in time of

① greave /griːv/：保护小腿的铠甲
② the famed lame god：Vulcan
③ Achilles 重返战场后,特洛伊人（the Trojans）大败,纷纷退回特洛伊城（Troy）。
④ scared /skeəd/：害怕的,胆小的
⑤ goodly /ˈɡʊdli/：相当大的
⑥ battlement /ˈbætlmənt/：城堞,城垛
⑦ the Scaean /ˈskiːən /gates：特洛伊城的西门
⑧ the son of Peleus：Achilles
⑨ harass /ˈhærəs/：蹂躏,连续攻击
⑩ rout /raʊt/：使慌忙撤退,击溃
⑪ decoy /ˈdiːkɔɪ/：引诱
⑫ baulk /bɔːlk/：阻碍,妨碍
⑬ Far-Darter：射箭射得远的人;Far-Darter 是 Apollo 的称号之一。
⑭ fell /fel/：凶恶的,残忍的,可怕的
⑮ strain：拉紧
⑯ he：the winning horse
⑰ scour /ˈskaʊə/：快速穿过（以便搜寻或追逐）
⑱ Orion's Hound：即 Sirius,参见 *The Age of Fable* 第 26 章和 *Argonautica* 选段"Interview of Jason and Medea"关于 Sirius 的注释。

harvest more brilliantly than those of any other that shines by night; brightest of them all though he① be, he yet bodes ill② for mortals, for he brings fire and fever in his train—even so did Achilles' armour gleam on his breast as he sped onwards. Priam raised a cry and beat his head with his hands as he lifted them up and shouted out to his dear son, imploring him to return; but Hector still stayed before the gates, for his heart was set upon doing battle with Achilles. The old man reached out his arms towards him and bade him for pity's sake come within the walls. "Hector," he cried, "my son, stay not to face this man alone and unsupported, or you will meet death at the hands of the son of Peleus, for he is mightier than you. Monster that he is, would indeed that the gods loved him no better than I do, for so, dogs and vultures would soon devour him as he lay stretched on earth, and a load of grief would be lifted from my heart, for many a brave son has he reft③ from me, either by killing them or selling them away in the islands that are beyond the sea: even now I miss two sons from among the Trojans who have thronged within the city, Lycaon and Polydorus④, whom Laothoe⑤ peeress⑥ among women bore me. Should they be still alive and in the hands of the Achaeans, we will ransom them with gold and bronze, of which we have store⑦, for the old man Altes⑧ endowed his daughter richly; but if they are already dead and in the house of Hades, sorrow will it be to us two who were their parents; albeit the grief of others will be more short-lived unless you too perish at the hands of Achilles. Come, then, my son, within the city, to be the guardian of Trojan men and Trojan women, or you will both lose your own life and afford a mighty triumph to the son of Peleus. Have pity also on your unhappy father while life yet remains to him—on me, whom the son of Saturn⑨ will destroy by a terrible doom on the threshold of old age, after I have seen my sons slain and my daughters haled away as captives, my bridal chambers pillaged⑩, little children dashed to earth amid the rage of battle, and my sons' wives dragged away by the cruel hands of the Achaeans; in the end fierce hounds will tear me in pieces at my own gates after some one has beaten the life out of my body with sword or spear—hounds that I myself reared and fed at my own table to guard my gates, but who will yet lap⑪ my blood and then lie all distraught⑫ at my doors. When a young man falls by the sword in battle, he may lie where he is and there is nothing unseemly⑬; let what will be seen, all is honourable in death, but when an old man is slain there is nothing in this world more pitiable than

---

① he: Orion's Hound
② bode ill: (预兆)主凶
③ reft: reave 的过去式和过去分词;reave: 剥夺,抢走
④ Polydorus: /ˌpɒlɪˈdɔːrəs/
⑤ Laothoe /ˌleɪəˈθəʊɪ/: Priam 的配偶之一
⑥ peeress /ˈpɪərɪs/: 有爵位的女子,女贵族
⑦ store: 许多,大量
⑧ Altes /ˈæltiːz/: father of Laothoe and king of the Leleges
⑨ the son of Saturn: Jupiter
⑩ pillage /ˈpɪlɪdʒ/: 洗劫一空
⑪ lap: 舔
⑫ distraught /dɪˈstrɔːt/: 困惑的
⑬ unseemly /ʌnˈsiːmli/: 不体面的,不恰当的

that dogs should defile his grey hair and beard and all that men hide for shame."

The old man tore his grey hair as he spoke, but he moved not the heart of Hector. His mother hard by① wept and moaned aloud as she bared her bosom and pointed to the breast which had suckled him. "Hector," she cried, weeping bitterly the while, "Hector, my son, spurn not this breast, but have pity upon me too; if I have ever given you comfort from my own bosom, think on it now, dear son, and come within the wall to protect us from this man; stand not without② to meet him. Should the wretch kill you, neither I nor your richly dowered③ wife shall ever weep, dear offshoot④ of myself, over the bed on which you lie, for dogs will devour you at the ships of the Achaeans."

Thus did the two with many tears implore their son, but they moved not the heart of Hector, and he stood his ground awaiting huge Achilles as he drew nearer towards him. As serpent in its den upon the mountains, full fed with deadly poisons, waits for the approach of man—he⑤ is filled with fury and his eyes glare terribly as he goes writhing round his den—even so Hector leaned his shield against a tower that jutted out from the wall and stood where he was, undaunted.

"Alas," said he to himself in the heaviness of his heart, "if I go within the gates, Polydamas⑥ will be the first to heap reproach upon me, for it was he that urged me to lead the Trojans back to the city on that awful night when Achilles again came forth against us. I would not listen, but it would have been indeed better if I had done so. Now that my folly has destroyed the host, I dare not look Trojan men and Trojan women in the face, lest a worse man should say, 'Hector has ruined us by his self-confidence.' Surely it would be better for me to return after having fought Achilles and slain him, or to die gloriously here before the city. What, again, if I were to lay down my shield and helmet, lean my spear against the wall and go straight up to noble Achilles? What if I were to promise to give up Helen, who was the fountainhead⑦ of all this war, and all the treasure that Alexandrus⑧ brought with him in his ships to Troy, aye, and to let the Achaeans divide the half of everything that the city contains among themselves? I might make the Trojans, by the mouths of their princes, take a solemn oath that they would hide nothing, but would divide into two shares all that is within the city—but why argue with myself in this way? Were I to go up to him he would show me no kind of mercy; he would kill me then and there as easily as though I were a woman, when I had put off my armour. There is no parleying⑨ with him from some rock or oak tree⑩ as young men and maidens prattle⑪ with one another. Better fight him

---

① hard by：在近旁

② without：在外面

③ richly dowered：嫁妆丰富的

④ offshoot /ˈɒfʃuːt/：后代，子孙

⑤ he：the serpent

⑥ Polydamas /ˌpɒlɪˈdæməs/：足智多谋的特洛伊英雄，和 Hector 诞生于同一个夜晚。当 Achilles 重新披挂上阵后，Polydamas 曾建议 Hector 率领特洛伊人撤回城里暂避。

⑦ fountainhead /ˈfaʊntɪnˈhed/：根源，源泉

⑧ Alexandrus /ˌælɪɡˈzɑːndrəs/：Paris

⑨ parley /ˈpɑːli/：谈判

⑩ him from some rock or oak tree：诞生于岩石或橡树的他，铁石心肠的他；橡树木非常坚硬，常用于建房、造船等。

⑪ prattle /ˈprætl/：闲谈，瞎扯

at once, and learn to which of us Jove will vouchsafe victory."

Thus did he stand and ponder, but Achilles came up to him as it were Mars himself, plumed① lord of battle. From his right shoulder he brandished② his terrible spear of Pelian③ ash④, and the bronze gleamed around him like flashing fire or the rays of the rising sun. Fear fell upon Hector as he beheld him, and he dared not stay longer where he was but fled in dismay from before the gates, while Achilles darted after him at his utmost speed. As a mountain falcon, swiftest of all birds, swoops down upon some cowering dove—the dove flies before him but the falcon with a shrill scream follows close after, resolved to have her—even so did Achilles make straight for Hector with all his might, while Hector fled under the Trojan wall as fast as his limbs could take him.

On they flew along the waggon-road⑤ that ran hard by under the wall, past the look-out station⑥, and past the weather-beaten wild fig-tree, till they came to two fair springs which feed the river Scamander⑦. One of these two springs is warm, and steam rises from it as smoke from a burning fire, but the other even in summer is as cold as hail⑧ or snow, or the ice that forms on water. Here, hard by the springs, are the goodly washing-troughs⑨ of stone, where in the time of peace before the coming of the Achaeans the wives and fair daughters of the Trojans used to wash their clothes. Past these did they fly, the one in front and the other giving chase behind him: good was the man that fled, but better far was he that followed after, and swiftly indeed did they run, for the prize was no mere beast for sacrifice or bullock's hide, as it might be for a common foot-race, but they ran for the life of Hector. As horses in a chariot race speed round the turning-posts when they are running for some great prize—a tripod or woman—at the games in honour of some dead hero, so did these two run full speed three times round the city of Priam. All the gods watched them, and the sire of gods and men⑩ was the first to speak.

"Alas," said he, "my eyes behold a man who is dear to me being pursued round the walls of Troy; my heart is full of pity for Hector, who has burned the thigh-bones of many a heifer in my honour, at one while on the crests of many-valleyed Ida, and again on the citadel of Troy; and now I see noble Achilles in full pursuit of him round the city of Priam. What say you? Consider among yourselves and decide whether we shall now save him or let him fall, valiant though he be, before Achilles, son of Peleus."

Then Minerva said, "Father, wielder⑪ of the lightning, lord of cloud and storm, what mean

① plumed /pluːmd/：头盔用羽毛装饰的
② brandish /ˈbrændɪʃ/：挥舞
③ Pelian /ˈpiːlɪən/：of or from Mount Pelion；关于 Mount Pelion,参见 *The Age of Fable* 第 16 章的注释。
④ ash：梣树;梣树的木质非常坚硬,在古希腊常用于制作兵器、造船等。
⑤ waggon-road：wagon-road
⑥ look-out station：瞭望台
⑦ Scamander /ˈskæməndə/：河流名,发源于 Ida 山,从 Troy 城下流过。
⑧ hail /heɪl/：冰雹
⑨ washing-trough /trɒf/：洗衣槽
⑩ the sire of gods and men：Jupiter
⑪ wielder /ˈwiːldə/：掌管者,使用者,支配者

you? Would you pluck this mortal whose doom has long been decreed out of the jaws of death? Do as you will, but we others shall not be of a mind with you."

And Jove answered, "My child, Trito-born①, take heart. I did not speak in full earnest②, and I will let you have your way. Do without let③ or hindrance as you are minded."

Thus did he urge Minerva who was already eager, and down she darted from the topmost summits of Olympus.

Achilles was still in full pursuit of Hector, as a hound chasing a fawn which he has started④ from its covert⑤ on the mountains, and hunts through glade and thicket; the fawn may try to elude⑥ him by crouching under cover of a bush, but he will scent her out and follow her up until he gets her—even so there was no escape for Hector from the fleet⑦ son of Peleus. Whenever he made a set⑧ to get near the Dardanian⑨ gates and under the walls, that⑩ his people might help him by showering down weapons from above, Achilles would gain on him and head⑪ him back towards the plain, keeping himself always on the city side. As a man in a dream who fails to lay hands upon another whom he is pursuing—the one cannot escape nor the other overtake—even so neither could Achilles come up with Hector, nor Hector break away from Achilles; nevertheless he might even yet have escaped death had not the time come when Apollo, who thus far had sustained his strength and nerved⑫ his running, was now no longer to stay by him. Achilles made signs to the Achaean host, and shook his head to show that no man was to aim a dart at Hector, lest another might win the glory of having hit him and he might himself come in second. Then, at last, as they were nearing the fountains for the fourth time, the father of all⑬ balanced his golden scales⑭ and placed a doom⑮ in each of them, one for Achilles and the other for Hector. As he held the scales by the middle, the doom of Hector fell down deep into the house of Hades⑯—and then Phoebus Apollo left him. Thereon Minerva went close up to the son of Peleus and said, "Noble Achilles, favoured of heaven⑰, we two shall surely take back to the ships a triumph for the Achaeans by

---

① Trito-born /ˈtraɪtəʊˈbɔːn/：第三个出生的；这是 Minerva 的称号之一。

② in full earnest：认真地

③ let：阻碍，妨碍

④ start：惊出

⑤ covert /ˈkʌvət/：动物的隐藏处

⑥ elude /ɪˈluːd/：逃避，逃离

⑦ fleet /fliːt/：快速的，灵活的

⑧ set：倾向，决心

⑨ Dardanian /dɑːˈdeɪnɪən/：Trojan

⑩ that：so that

⑪ head：拦截，阻挡

⑫ nerve /nɜːv/：给……力量，鼓舞

⑬ the father of all：Jupiter

⑭ scale /skeɪl/：天平盘，秤盘

⑮ doom /duːm/：命运

⑯ the house of Hades：阴间

⑰ favoured of heaven：受神宠爱的

slaying Hector, for① all his lust② of battle. Do what Apollo may as he lies grovelling③ before his father, aegis-bearing Jove, Hector cannot escape us longer. Stay here and take breath, while I go up to him and persuade him to make a stand and fight you."

Thus spoke Minerva. Achilles obeyed her gladly, and stood still, leaning on his bronze-pointed ashen④ spear, while Minerva left him and went after Hector in the form and with the voice of Deiphobus⑤. She came close up to him and said, "Dear brother, I see you are hard pressed by Achilles who is chasing you at full speed round the city of Priam, let us await his onset⑥ and stand on our defence."

And Hector answered, "Deiphobus, you have always been dearest to me of all my brothers, children of Hecuba and Priam, but henceforth I shall rate you yet more highly, inasmuch as you have ventured outside the wall for my sake when all the others remain inside."

Then Minerva said, "Dear brother, my father and mother went down on their knees and implored me, as did all my comrades, to remain inside, so great a fear has fallen upon them all; but I was in an agony of grief when I beheld you; now, therefore, let us two make a stand and fight, and let there be no keeping our spears in reserve, that we may learn whether Achilles shall kill us and bear off our spoils to the ships, or whether he shall fall before you."

Thus did Minerva inveigle⑦ him by her cunning, and when the two were now close to one another great Hector was first to speak. "I will no longer fly you, son of Peleus," said he, "as I have been doing hitherto. Three times have I fled round the mighty city of Priam, without daring to withstand you, but now, let me either slay or be slain, for I am in the mind to face you. Let us, then, give pledges to one another by our gods, who are the fittest witnesses and guardians of all covenants⑧; let it be agreed between us that if Jove vouchsafes me the longer stay and I take your life, I am not to treat your dead body in any unseemly fashion, but when I have stripped you of your armour, I am to give up your body to the Achaeans. And do you likewise."

Achilles glared at him and answered, "Fool, prate⑨ not to me about covenants. There can be no covenants between men and lions; wolves and lambs can never be of one mind, but hate each other out and out all through. Therefore there can be no understanding between you and me, nor may there be any covenants between us, till one or other shall fall and glut⑩ grim Mars with his life's blood. Put forth all your strength; you have need now to prove yourself indeed a bold soldier and man of war. You have no more chance, and Pallas Minerva will forthwith vanquish you by my

---

① for：尽管
② lust /lʌst/：渴望
③ grovel /ˈɡrɒvl/：匍匐
④ ashen /ˈæʃən/：用梣树木制作的
⑤ Deiphobus is a brother of Hector.
⑥ onset /ˈɒnset/：进攻
⑦ inveigle /ɪnˈviːɡl/：欺骗，诱惑
⑧ covenant /ˈkʌvənənt/：契约
⑨ prate：长时间瞎谈
⑩ glut /ɡlʌt/：使完全满足

spear: you shall now pay me in full for the grief you have caused me on account of my comrades whom you have killed in battle."

He poised his spear as he spoke and hurled it. Hector saw it coming and avoided it; he watched it and crouched down so that it flew over his head and stuck in the ground beyond; Minerva then snatched it up and gave it back to Achilles without Hector's seeing her; Hector thereon said to the son of Peleus, "You have missed your aim, Achilles, peer of the gods, and Jove has not yet revealed to you the hour of my doom, though you made sure that he had done so. You were a false-tongued① liar when you deemed that I should forget my valour and quail② before you. You shall not drive spear into the back of a runaway—drive it, should heaven so grant you power, drive it into me as I make straight towards you; and now for your own part avoid my spear if you can—would that you might receive the whole of it into your body; if you were once dead the Trojans would find the war an easier matter, for it is you who have harmed them most."

He poised his spear as he spoke and hurled it. His aim was true for he hit the middle of Achilles' shield, but the spear rebounded from it, and did not pierce it. Hector was angry when he saw that the weapon had sped from his hand in vain, and stood there in dismay for he had no second spear. With a loud cry he called Deiphobus and asked him for one, but there was no man; then he saw the truth and said to himself, "Alas! the gods have lured me on to my destruction. I deemed that the hero Deiphobus was by my side, but he is within the wall, and Minerva has inveigled me; death is now indeed exceedingly near at hand and there is no way out of it—for so Jove and his son Apollo the far-darter have willed it, though heretofore they have been ever ready to protect me. My doom has come upon me; let me not then die ingloriously and without a struggle, but let me first do some great thing that shall be told among men hereafter."

As he spoke he drew the keen blade③ that hung so great and strong by his side, and gathering himself together he sprang on Achilles like a soaring eagle which swoops down from the clouds on to some lamb or timid hare—even so did Hector brandish his sword and spring upon Achilles. Achilles mad with rage darted towards him, with his wondrous shield before his breast, and his gleaming helmet, made with four layers of metal, nodding fiercely forward. The thick tresses of gold with which Vulcan had crested the helmet floated round it, and as the evening star that shines brighter than all others through the stillness of night, even such was the gleam of the spear which Achilles poised in his right hand, fraught with the death of noble Hector. He eyed his fair flesh over and over to see where he could best wound it, but all was protected by the goodly armour of which Hector had spoiled④ Patroclus after he had slain him,⑤ save only the throat where the collar-bones divide the neck from the shoulders, and this is a most deadly place: here then did Achilles strike him as he was coming on towards him, and the point of his spear went right through

---

① false-tongued：说假话的
② quail /kweɪl/：退缩
③ blade：宝剑
④ spoil：夺取战死者的武器和盔甲
⑤ 参见 The Age of Fable 第27章。

the fleshy part of the neck, but it did not sever① his windpipe② so that he could still speak. Hector fell headlong, and Achilles vaunted over him saying, "Hector, you deemed that you should come off scatheless③ when you were spoiling Patroclus, and recked④ not of myself who was not with him. Fool that you were: for I, his comrade, mightier far than he, was still left behind him at the ships, and now I have laid you low. The Achaeans shall give him all due funeral rites, while dogs and vultures shall work their will upon yourself."

Then Hector said, as the life ebbed⑤ out of him, "I pray you by your life and knees, and by your parents, let not dogs devour me at the ships of the Achaeans, but accept the rich treasure of gold and bronze which my father and mother will offer you, and send my body home, that the Trojans and their wives may give me my dues of fire when I am dead."

Achilles glared at him and answered, "Dog, talk not to me neither of knees nor parents; would that I could be as sure of being able to cut your flesh into pieces and eat it raw, for the ill you have done me, as I am that nothing shall save you from the dogs—it shall not be, though they bring ten or twenty-fold ransom and weigh it out for me on the spot, with promise of yet more hereafter. Though Priam son of Dardanus⑥ should bid them offer me your weight in gold, even so your mother shall never lay you out⑦ and make lament over the son she bore, but dogs and vultures shall eat you utterly up."

Hector with his dying breath then said, "I know you what you are, and was sure that I should not move you, for your heart is hard as iron; look to it that I bring not heaven's anger upon you on the day when Paris and Phoebus Apollo, valiant though you be, shall slay you at the Scaean gates."

When he had thus said the shrouds of death enfolded him, whereon his soul went out of him and flew down to the house of Hades, lamenting its sad fate that it should enjoy youth and strength no longer. But Achilles said, speaking to the dead body, "Die; for my part I will accept my fate whensoever Jove and the other gods see fit to send it."

As he spoke he drew his spear from the body and set it on one side; then he stripped the blood-stained armour from Hector's shoulders while the other Achaeans came running up to view his wondrous strength and beauty; and no one came near him without giving him a fresh wound. Then would one turn to his neighbour and say, "It is easier to handle Hector now than when he was flinging⑧ fire on to our ships"—and as he spoke he would thrust his spear into him anew⑨.

---

① sever /'sevə/：切断，割断

② windpipe /'wɪndpaɪp/：气管

③ scatheless /'skeɪðləs/：不受伤害的

④ reck：注意到

⑤ ebb：流走

⑥ 关于 Dardanus，参见 *The Age of Fable* 第 26 章的注释。

⑦ lay you out：为你的尸体做火化前的准备

⑧ fling：用力扔

⑨ anew /ə'njuː/：再一次，又一次

The Odyssey

The Love of Mars and Venus

Translated into English by Samuel Butler

Meanwhile the bard① began to sing the loves of Mars and Venus, and how they first began their intrigue② in the house of Vulcan. Mars made Venus many presents, and defiled③ King Vulcan's marriage bed, so the sun, who saw what they were about, told Vulcan. Vulcan was very angry when he heard such dreadful news, so he went to his smithy④ brooding⑤ mischief, got his great anvil into its place, and began to forge some chains which none could either unloose or break, so that they might stay there in that place. When he had finished his snare he went into his bedroom and festooned the bed-posts all over with chains like cobwebs; he also let many hang down from the great beam of the ceiling. Not even a god could see them, so fine⑥ and subtle⑦ were they. As soon as he had spread the chains all over the bed, he made as though he were setting out for the fair state of Lemnos, which of all places in the world was the one he was most fond of. But Mars kept no blind look out, and as soon as he saw him start, hurried off to his house, burning with love for Venus.

Now Venus was just come in from a visit to her father Jove, and was about sitting down when Mars came inside the house, and said as he took her hand in his own, "Let us go to the couch⑧ of Vulcan: he is not at home, but is gone off to Lemnos among the Sintians⑨, whose speech is barbarous."

She was nothing⑩ loth⑪, so they went to the couch to take their rest, whereon they were caught in the toils⑫ which cunning Vulcan had spread for them, and could neither get up nor stir hand or foot, but found too late that they were in a trap. Then Vulcan came up to them, for he had turned

---

① the bard：Demodocus
② intrigue /ɪnˈtriːg/：私通，秘密恋情
③ defile /dɪˈfaɪl/：弄脏，玷污
④ smithy /ˈsmɪði/：铁匠铺
⑤ brood：筹划，思考
⑥ fine：细的
⑦ subtle /ˈsʌtl/：不易被察觉的
⑧ couch：床
⑨ the Sintians /ˈsɪnʃənz/：部落名，居住在 Lemnos 岛等地，他们是爱琴海的非希腊语民族，作为希腊人的荷马（Homer）把他们描述为"whose speech is barbarous"。
⑩ nothing：根本不，一点也不
⑪ loth：不情愿的
⑫ toils：网，陷阱

back before reaching Lemnos, when his scout① the sun told him what was going on. He was in a furious passion, and stood in the vestibule② making a dreadful noise as he shouted to all the gods.

"Father Jove," he cried, "and all you other blessed gods who live for ever, come here and see the ridiculous and disgraceful sight that I will show you. Jove's daughter Venus is always dishonouring me because I am lame. She is in love with Mars, who is handsome and clean built③, whereas I am a cripple—but my parents are to blame for that, not I; they ought never to have begotten me. Come and see the pair together asleep on my bed. It makes me furious to look at them. They are very fond of one another, but I do not think they will lie there longer than they can help, nor do I think that they will sleep much; there, however, they shall stay till her father has repaid me the sum I gave him for his baggage④ of a daughter, who is fair but not honest⑤."

On this the gods gathered to the house of Vulcan. Earth-encircling Neptune came, and Mercury the bringer of luck, and King Apollo, but the goddesses stayed at home all of them for shame. Then the givers of all good things⑥ stood in the doorway, and the blessed gods roared with inextinguishable⑦ laughter, as they saw how cunning Vulcan had been, whereon one would turn towards his neighbour saying:

"Ill deeds do not prosper⑧, and the weak confound⑨ the strong. See how limping⑩ Vulcan, lame as he is, has caught Mars who is the fleetest⑪ god in heaven; and now Mars will be cast in heavy damages⑫."

Thus did they converse, but King Apollo said to Mercury, "Messenger Mercury, giver of good things, you would not care how strong the chains were, would you, if you could sleep with Venus?"

"King Apollo," answered Mercury, "I only wish I might get the chance, though there were three times as many chains—and you might look on, all of you, gods and goddesses, but would sleep with her if I could."

The immortal gods burst out laughing as they heard him, but Neptune took it all seriously, and kept on imploring Vulcan to set Mars free again. "Let him go," he cried, "and I will undertake⑬, as you require, that he shall pay you all the damages that are held reasonable among the immortal gods."

"Do not," replied Vulcan, "ask me to do this; a bad man's bond is bad security; what

---

① scout：侦查员,监视者

② vestibule /ˈvestɪbjuːl/：门厅

③ clean built：体态优美的,身材好的

④ baggage：荡妇

⑤ honest：(女人)贞节的

⑥ the givers of all good things：the gods

⑦ inextinguishable /ˌɪnɪksˈtɪŋgwɪʃəbl/：抑制不住的

⑧ prosper /ˈprɒspə/：成功

⑨ confound /kənˈfaʊnd/：击败,打败

⑩ limping：走路一瘸一拐的

⑪ fleet：灵活的,行动敏捷的

⑫ damages：补偿款

⑬ undertake：保证

remedy could I enforce against you if Mars should go away and leave his debts behind him along with his chains?"

"Vulcan," said Neptune, "if Mars goes away without paying his damages, I will pay you myself." So Vulcan answered, "In this case I cannot and must not refuse you."

Thereon he loosed the bonds that bound them, and as soon as they were free they scampered① off, Mars to Thrace and laughter-loving Venus to Cyprus and to Paphos②, where is her grove and her altar fragrant with burnt offerings. Here the Graces bathed her, and anointed her with oil of ambrosia such as the immortal gods make use of, and they clothed her in raiment③ of the most enchanting beauty.

The Killing of the Wooers
Translated into English by S. H. Butcher and A. Lang

Then Odysseus④ of many counsels⑤ stripped⑥ him of his rags and leaped on to the great threshold with his bow and quiver full of arrows, and poured forth all the swift shafts⑦ there before his feet, and spake⑧ among the wooers⑨:

'Lo⑩, now is this terrible trial⑪ ended at last; and now will I know of another mark, which never yet man has smitten, if perchance I may hit it and Apollo grant me renown.'

With that he pointed the bitter arrow at Antinous⑫. Now he⑬ was about raising to his lips a fair twy-eared⑭ chalice⑮ of gold, and behold, he was handling it to drink of the wine, and death was far from his thoughts. For who among men at feast would deem that one man amongst so many,

---

① scamper /ˈskæmpə/：逃离，跑掉
② Paphos：参见 *The Age of Fable* 第 8 章关于 Paphos 的注释。
③ raiment /ˈreɪmənt/：衣服
④ Odysseus：Greek name of Ulysses
⑤ counsel /ˈkaʊnsl/：建议，指导，观点，计划；Odysseus of many counsels：点子多的 Odysseus（Odysseus is famous for his wisdom.）
⑥ strip：脱去（衣服等）
⑦ shaft /ʃɑːft/：箭
⑧ spake：spoke
⑨ wooer /ˈwuːə/：求婚者，追求者
⑩ lo：(感叹词)看
⑪ this terrible trial：即发生在 *The Odyssey* 第 21 卷中的拉弓、射箭比赛。在 *The Odyssey* 第 21 卷中，Odysseus 的妻子拿出 Odysseus 的弓，向她的求婚者们宣布，她将嫁给能拉开弓、能把箭从 12 个环中射过去的人。求婚者们纷纷尝试，但无人能拉开弓。假装为乞丐、身穿破衣烂衫的 Odysseus 提出想要尝试，遭到求婚者们的漫骂和羞辱，但 Odysseu 之子 Telemachus 坚持给予 Odysseus 尝试的机会。
⑫ Antinous /ænˈtɪnəʊəs/：the most arrogant of the wooers or suitors of Penelope, Odysseus's wife.
⑬ he：Antinous
⑭ twy-eared：(杯子)有两个捏把的；twy-(twi-) /twaɪ/：有两个……的；ear：(杯子上的)耳朵状的捏把
⑮ chalice /ˈtʃælɪs/：酒杯

how hardy① soever he were, would bring on him foul death and black fate? But Odysseus aimed and smote him with the arrow in the throat, and the point passed clean out through his delicate neck, and he fell sidelong and the cup dropped from his hand as he was smitten, and at once through his nostrils there came up a thick jet of slain man's blood, and quickly he spurned② the table from him with his foot, and spilt the food on the ground, and the bread and the roast flesh were defiled③. Then the wooers raised a clamour through the halls when they saw the man fallen, and they leaped from their high seats, as men stirred by fear, all through the hall, peering④ everywhere along the well-builded⑤ walls, and nowhere was there a shield or a mighty spear to lay hold on. Then they reviled⑥ Odysseus with angry words:

'Stranger, thou shootest at men to thy hurt. Never again shalt thou enter other lists⑦, now is utter doom assured thee. Yea, for now hast thou slain the man that was far the best of all the noble youths in Ithaca; wherefore vultures shall devour thee here.'

So each one spake, for indeed they thought that Odysseus had not slain him wilfully⑧; but they knew not in their folly that on their own heads, each and all of them, the bands⑨ of death had been made fast. Then Odysseus of many counsels looked fiercely on them, and spake:

'Ye⑩ dogs, ye said in your hearts that I should never more come home from the land of the Trojans⑪, in that ye wasted my house and lay with the maidservants by force, and traitorously wooed my wife while I was yet alive, and ye had no fear of the gods, that hold the wide heaven, nor of the indignation of men hereafter. But now the bands of death have been made fast upon you one and all.'

Even so he spake, and pale fear gat⑫ hold on the limbs of all, and each man looked about, where he might shun utter doom.

And Eurymachus⑬ alone answered him, and spake: 'If thou art indeed Odysseus of Ithaca, come home again, with right thou speakest thus, of all that the Achaeans have wrought, many infatuate⑭ deeds in thy halls and many in the field. Howbeit, he now lies dead that is to blame for all, Antinous; for he brought all these things upon us, not as longing very greatly for the marriage

---

① hardy /ˈhɑːdi/: 胆子大的

② spurn /spɜːn/: 踢开

③ defile /dɪˈfaɪl/: 弄脏, 污染

④ peer /pɪə/: 盯着看

⑤ well-builded: well-built

⑥ revile /rɪˈvaɪl/: 责骂

⑦ lists: 比武场, 竞技场, 竞赛场

⑧ wilfully /ˈwɪlfuli/: 故意地

⑨ bands: 锁链

⑩ ye /jiː/: 你, 你们

⑪ the land of the Trojans: Troy

⑫ gat: got

⑬ Eurymachus: /juəˈrɪməkəs/

⑭ infatuate /ɪnˈfætjuət/: 非常愚蠢的

nor needing it sore①, but with another purpose, that Cronion② has not fulfilled for him, namely, that he might himself be king over all the land of stablished③ Ithaca, and he was to have lain in wait for thy son and killed him. But now he is slain after his deserving, and do thou spare thy people, even thine own; and we will hereafter go about the township and yield thee amends④ for all that has been eaten and drunken in thy halls, each for himself bringing atonement⑤ of twenty oxen worth, and requiting⑥ thee in gold and bronze till thy heart is softened, but till then none may blame thee that thou art angry.'

Then Odysseus of many counsels looked fiercely on him, and said: 'Eurymachus, not even if ye gave me all your heritage, all that ye now have, and whatsoever else ye might in any wise⑦ add thereto, not even so would I henceforth hold my hands from slaying, ere the wooers had paid for all their transgressions⑧. And now the choice lies before you, whether to fight in fair battle or to fly, if any may avoid death and the fates. But there be some, methinks⑨, that shall not escape from utter doom.'

He spake, and their knees were straightway⑩ loosened and their hearts melted within them. And Eurymachus spake among them yet again:

'Friends, it is plain that this man will not hold his unconquerable hands, but now that he has caught up the polished bow and quiver, he will shoot from the smooth threshold till he has slain us all; wherefore let us take thought for the delight of battle. Draw your blades⑪, and hold up the tables to ward off⑫ the arrows of swift death, and let us all have at him with one accord, and drive him, if it may be, from the threshold and the doorway and then go through the city, and quickly would the cry be raised. Thereby should this man soon have shot his latest⑬ bolt⑭.'

Therewith he drew his sharp two-edged sword of bronze, and leapt on Odysseus with a terrible cry, but in the same moment goodly Odysseus shot the arrow forth and struck him on the breast by the pap⑮, and drave⑯ the swift shaft into his liver. So he let the sword fall from his hand, and

---

① sore /sɔː/: 极端地,非常地
② Cronion /ˈkrəʊnɪən/: Zeus, son of Cronos
③ stablish: establish
④ amends /əˈmendz/: 赔偿
⑤ atonement /əˈtəʊnmənt/: 赔偿
⑥ requite /rɪˈkwaɪt/: 回报
⑦ wise: 方式,方法
⑧ transgression /trænzˈɡreʃn/: 过失,错误
⑨ methinks /mɪˈθɪŋks/: it seems to me
⑩ straightway /ˈstreɪtweɪ/: 立刻,马上
⑪ blade: 剑
⑫ ward off: 挡开
⑬ latest: 最后的
⑭ bolt: 箭
⑮ pap: 奶头
⑯ drave: drove

grovelling① over the table he bowed and fell, and spilt the food and the two-handled② cup on the floor. And in his agony he smote the ground with his brow, and spurning with both his feet he overthrew the high seat, and the mist of death was shed upon his eyes.

Then Amphinomus③ made at renowned Odysseus, setting straight at him, and drew his sharp sword, if perchance he might make him give ground from the door. But Telemachus was beforehand with him, and cast and smote him from behind with a bronze-shod④ spear between the shoulders, and drave it out through the breast, and he fell with a crash and struck the ground full with his forehead. Then Telemachus sprang away, leaving the long spear fixed in Amphinomus, for he greatly dreaded lest one of the Achaeans might run upon him with his blade, and stab him as he drew forth the spear, or smite him with a down⑤ stroke of the sword. So he started and ran and came quickly to his father, and stood by him, and spake winged words⑥:

'Father, lo, now I will bring thee a shield and two spears and a helmet all of bronze, close fitting on the temples⑦, and when I return I will arm myself, and likewise give arms to the swineherd⑧ and the neatherd⑨ yonder: for it is better to be clad in full armour.'

And Odysseus of many counsels answered him saying: 'Run and bring them while I have arrows to defend me, lest they thrust⑩ me from the doorway, one man against them all.'

So he spake, and Telemachus obeyed his dear father, and went forth to the chamber, where his famous weapons were lying. Thence he took out four shields and eight spears, and four helmets of bronze, with thick plumes of horse hair, and he started to bring them and came quickly to his father. Now he girded the gear of bronze about his own body first, and in like manner the two thralls⑪ did on the goodly armour, and stood beside the wise and crafty⑫ Odysseus. Now he, so long as he had arrows to defend him, kept aiming and smote the wooers one by one in his house, and they fell thick one upon another⑬. But when the arrows failed the prince in his archery, he leaned his bow against the doorpost⑭ of the stablished hall, against the shining faces of the entrance. As for him he girt his fourfold shield about his shoulders and bound on his mighty head a well wrought helmet, with horse hair crest⑮, and terribly the plume waved aloft. And he grasped

---

① grovel /ˈɡrɒvl/: 趴
② two-handled: two-eared
③ Amphinomus: /ˌæmfɪˈnəʊməs/
④ bronze-shod: (矛)尖端用铜包裹的
⑤ down: 朝下的
⑥ winged words: 说中要害的话;这个短语从荷马史诗中的短语ἔπεα(words)πτερόεντα(winged)而来。
⑦ temple /ˈtempl/: 太阳穴
⑧ swineherd: Eumaeus
⑨ neatherd /ˈniːthɜːd/: 牧牛人 Philoetius /ˌfɪləˈiːtɪəs/
⑩ thrust: 推
⑪ the two thralls: Eumaeus and Philoetius; thrall /θrɔːl/: 奴仆
⑫ crafty /ˈkrɑːfti/: 狡猾的
⑬ thick: 接二连三地
⑭ doorpost: 门柱
⑮ crest: (盔的)顶饰

two mighty spears tipped with bronze①.

Now there was in the well-builded hall a certain postern② raised above the floor, and there by the topmost level of the threshold of the stablished hall, was a way into an open passage, closed by well-fitted folding doors. So Odysseus bade the goodly swineherd stand near thereto and watch the way, for thither there was but one approach. Then Agelaus③ spake among them, and declared his word to all:

'Friends, will not some man climb up to the postern, and give word to the people, and a cry would be raised straightway; so should this man soon have shot his latest bolt?'

Then Melanthius④, the goatherd⑤, answered him, saying: 'It may in no wise be, prince Agelaus; for the fair gate of the courtyard is terribly nigh, and perilous is the entrance to the passage, and one man, if he were valiant, might keep back a host. But come, let me bring you armour from the inner chamber, that ye may be clad in hauberks⑥, for, methinks, within that room and not elsewhere did Odysseus and his renowned son lay by⑦ the arms.'

Therewith Melanthius, the goatherd, climbed up by the clerestory⑧ of the hall to the inner chambers of Odysseus, whence he took twelve shields and as many spears, and as many helmets of bronze with thick plumes of horse hair, and he came forth and brought them speedily, and gave them to the wooers. Then the knees of Odysseus were loosened and his heart melted within him, when he saw them girding on the armour and brandishing⑨ the long spears in their hands, and great, he saw, was the adventure. Quickly he spake to Telemachus winged words:

'Telemachus, sure I am that one of the women in the halls is stirring up an evil battle against us, or perchance it is Melanthius.'

Then wise Telemachus answered him: 'My father, it is I that have erred⑩ herein and none other is to blame, for I left the well-fitted door of the chamber open, and there has been one of them but too quick to spy it. Go now, goodly Eumaeus, and close the door of the chamber, and mark if it be indeed one of the women that does this mischief, or Melanthius, son of Dolius⑪, as methinks it is.'

Even so they spake one to the other. And Melanthius, the goatherd, went yet again to the chamber to bring the fair armour. But the goodly swineherd was ware⑫ thereof, and quickly he spake to Odysseus who stood nigh him:

---

① spears tipped with bronze: bronze-shod spears
② postern /'pɒstən/: 后门，边门
③ Agelaus: /ˌædʒɪ'leɪəs/
④ Melanthius: /mɪ'lænθɪəs/
⑤ goatherd /'ɡəʊthɜːd/: 羊倌，牧羊人
⑥ hauberk /'hɔːbɜːk/: 保护脖子和肩部的铠甲
⑦ lay by: 存放
⑧ clerestory /'klɪəstɔːri/: 天窗
⑨ brandish /'brændɪʃ/: 挥舞
⑩ err /ɜː/: 犯错
⑪ Dolius: /'dəʊlɪəs/
⑫ ware: 意识到的，知道的

'Son of Laertes, of the seed of Zeus, Odysseus, of many devices①, lo, there again is that baleful② man, whom we ourselves suspect, going to the chamber; do thou tell me truly, shall I slay him if I prove the better man, or bring him hither to thee, that he may pay for the many transgressions that he has devised in thy house?'

Then Odysseus of many counsels answered saying: 'Verily, I and Telemachus will keep the proud wooers within the halls, for all their fury, but do ye twain③ tie his feet and arms behind his back and cast him into the chamber, and close the doors after you, and make fast to his body a twisted rope, and drag him up the lofty pillar till he be near the roof beams④, that he may hang there and live for long, and suffer grievous torment.'

So he spake, and they gave good heed⑤ and hearkened⑥. So they went forth to the chamber, but the goatherd who was within knew not of their coming. Now he was seeking for the armour in the secret place of the chamber, but they twain stood in waiting on either side the doorposts. And when Melanthius, the goatherd, was crossing the threshold with a goodly helm in one hand, and in the other a wide shield and an old, stained with rust, the shield of the hero Laertes that he bare when he was young—but at that time it was laid by, and the seams⑦ of the straps were loosened—then the twain rushed on him and caught him, and dragged him in by the hair, and cast him on the floor in sorrowful plight, and bound him hand and foot in a bitter bond, tightly winding each limb behind his back, even as the son of Laertes bade them, the steadfast goodly Odysseus. And they made fast to his body a twisted rope, and dragged him up the lofty pillar till he came near the roof beams. Then didst thou speak to him and gird⑧ at him, swineherd Eumaeus:

'Now in good truth, Melanthius, shalt thou watch all night, lying in a soft bed as beseems⑨ thee, nor shall the early-born Dawn escape thy ken⑩, when she comes forth from the streams of Oceanus, on her golden throne, in the hour when thou art wont to drive the goats to make a meal for the wooers in the halls.'

So he was left there, stretched tight in the deadly bond. But they twain got into their harness⑪, and closed the shining door, and went to Odysseus, wise and crafty chief. There they stood breathing fury, four men by the threshold, while those others within the halls were many and good warriors. Then Athene, daughter of Zeus, drew nigh them, like Mentor⑫ in fashion⑬ and in

---

① device /dɪˈvaɪs/: 计谋,计策

② baleful /ˈbeɪlfl/: 邪恶的

③ twain: two

④ beam: 梁

⑤ heed: attention

⑥ hearken /ˈhɑːkən/: 听

⑦ seam: 接缝

⑧ gird /ɡɜːd/: 嘲笑

⑨ beseem /bɪˈsiːm/: 适合

⑩ ken: 视野

⑪ harness /ˈhɑːnɪs/: 铠甲

⑫ Mentor /ˈmentə/: An old friend of Ulysses, to whom Ulysses entrusted his house when he was fighting in Troy. Mentor was also the adviser of Telemachus during the absence of Ulysses.

⑬ fashion: 形状,外貌

voice, and Odysseus was glad when he saw her and spake, saying：

'Mentor, ward from us hurt, and remember me thy dear companion, that befriended thee often, and thou art of like age with me.'

So he spake, deeming the while that it was Athene, summoner① of the host②. But the wooers on the other side shouted in the halls, and first Agelaus son of Damastor③ rebuked Athene, saying：

'Mentor, let not the speech of Odysseus beguile thee to fight against the wooers, and to succour④ him. For methinks that on this wise we shall work our will. When we shall have slain these men, father and son, thereafter shalt thou perish with them, such deeds thou art set on doing in these halls；nay, with thine own head shalt thou pay the price. But when with the sword we shall have overcome your violence, we will mingle all thy possessions, all that thou hast at home or in the field, with the wealth of Odysseus, and we will not suffer⑤ thy sons nor thy daughters to dwell in the halls, nor thy good wife to gad⑥ about in the town of Ithaca.'

So spake he, and Athene was mightily angered at heart, and chid Odysseus in wrathful words：'Odysseus, thou hast no more steadfast might nor any prowess⑦, as when for nine whole years continually thou didst battle with the Trojans for high born Helen, of the white arms, and many men thou slewest in terrible warfare, and by thy device the wide-wayed city of Priam⑧ was taken. How then, now that thou art come to thy house and thine own possessions, dost thou bewail thee and art of feeble courage to stand before the wooers？ Nay, come hither, friend, and stand by me, and I will show thee a thing, that thou mayest know what manner of man is Mentor, son of Alcimus⑨, to repay good deeds in the ranks of foemen.'

She spake, and gave him not yet clear victory in full, but still for a while made trial of the might and prowess of Odysseus and his renowned son. As for her she flew up to the roof timber of the murky⑩ hall, in such fashion as a swallow flies, and there sat down.

Now Agelaus, son of Damastor, urged on the wooers, and likewise Eurynomus⑪ and Amphimedon⑫ and Demoptolemus⑬ and Peisandrus⑭ son of Polyctor⑮, and wise Polybus⑯, for

---

① summoner /ˈsʌmənə/：召集人
② host：军队
③ Damastor：/ˈdæməstə/
④ succour /ˈsʌkə/：帮助
⑤ suffer：允许
⑥ gad：走动
⑦ prowess /ˈprauɪs/：勇敢,勇气,胆量
⑧ the wide-wayed city of Priam：Troy, whose roads are wide
⑨ Alcimus：/əlˈsaɪməs/
⑩ murky /ˈmɜːki/：黑暗的
⑪ Eurynomus：/juəˈrɪnəməs/
⑫ Amphimedon：/ˌæmfɪˈmedən/
⑬ Demoptolemus：/ˌdeməpˈtɒləməs/
⑭ Peisandrus：/peɪˈsændrəs/
⑮ Polyctor：/ˈpɒlɪktə/
⑯ Polybus：/ˈpɒlɪbəs/

these were in valiancy① far the best men of the wooers, that still lived and fought for their lives; for the rest had fallen already beneath the bow and the thick rain of arrows. Then Agelaus spake among them, and made known his word to all:

'Friends, now at last will this man hold his unconquerable hands. Lo, now has Mentor left him and spoken but vain boasts, and these remain alone at the entrance of the doors. Wherefore now, throw not your long spears all together, but come, do ye six cast first, if perchance Zeus may grant us to smite Odysseus and win renown. Of the rest will we take no heed, so soon as that man shall have fallen.'

So he spake and they all cast their javelins, as he bade them, eagerly; but behold, Athene so wrought that they were all in vain. One man smote the doorpost of the stablished hall, and another the well-fastened door, and the ashen② spear of yet another wooer, heavy with bronze, stuck fast in the wall. So when they had avoided all the spears of the wooers, the steadfast goodly Odysseus began first to speak among them:

'Friends, now my word is that we too cast and hurl into the press③ of the wooers, that are mad to slay and strip us beyond the measure of their former iniquities④.'

So he spake, and they all took good aim and threw their sharp spears, and Odysseus smote Demoptolemus, and Telemachus Euryades⑤, and the swineherd slew Elatus⑥, and the neatherd Peisandrus. Thus they all bit the wide floor with their teeth, and the wooers fell back into the inmost part of the hall. But the others dashed upon them and drew forth the shafts from the bodies of the dead.

Then once more the wooers threw their sharp spears eagerly; but behold, Athene so wrought that many of them were in vain. One man smote the doorpost of the stablished hall, and another the well-fastened door, and the ashen spear of another wooer, heavy with bronze, struck in the wall. Yet Amphimedon hit Telemachus on the hand by the wrist lightly, and the shaft of bronze wounded the surface of the skin. And Ctesippus⑦ grazed⑧ the shoulder of Eumaeus with a long spear high above the shield, and the spear flew over and fell to the ground. Then again Odysseus, the wise and crafty, he and his men cast their swift spears into the press of the wooers, and now once more Odysseus, waster⑨ of cities, smote Eurydamas⑩, and Telemachus Amphimedon, and the swineherd slew Polybus, and last, the neatherd struck Ctesippus in the breast and boasted over him, saying:

---

① valiancy /'vælɪənsi/: 勇敢
② ashen /'æʃn/: (坚硬的)梣木制成的
③ press: 人群
④ iniquities /ɪ'nɪkwɪtɪz/: (复数)错误的行为,罪恶,伤害
⑤ Euryades: /juə'raɪədiːz/
⑥ Elatus: /ɪ'lætəs/
⑦ Ctesippus: /'tesɪpəs/
⑧ graze: 擦过
⑨ waster /'weɪstə/: 掠夺者,蹂躏者
⑩ Eurydamas: /juə'rɪdəməs/

'O son of Polytherses①, thou lover of jeering, never give place at all to folly to speak so big②, but leave thy case to the gods, since in truth they are far mightier than thou. This gift is thy recompense③ for the ox-foot④ that thou gavest of late to the divine Odysseus, when he went begging through the house.'

So spake the keeper of the shambling kine⑤. Next Odysseus wounded the son of Damastor in close fight with his long spear, and Telemachus wounded Leocritus⑥ son of Euenor⑦, right in the flank⑧ with his lance, and drave the bronze point clean through, that he fell prone and struck the ground full with his forehead. Then Athene held up her destroying aegis on high from the roof, and their minds were scared, and they fled through the hall, like a drove⑨ of kine that the flitting⑩ gadfly⑪ falls upon and scatters hither and thither in spring time, when the long days begin. But the others set on like vultures of crooked claws and curved beak, that come forth from the mountain and dash upon smaller birds, and these scour low in the plain, stooping in terror from the clouds, while the vultures pounce on them and slay them, and there is no help nor way of flight, and men are glad at the sport; even so did the company of Odysseus set upon the wooers and smite them right and left through the hall; and there rose a hideous moaning as their heads were smitten, and the floor all ran with blood.

Now Leiodes⑫ took hold of the knees of Odysseus eagerly, and besought him and spake winged words: 'I entreat thee by thy knees, Odysseus, and do thou show mercy on me and have pity. For never yet, I say, have I wronged a maiden in thy halls by froward⑬ word or deed, nay I bade the other wooers refrain, whoso of them wrought thus. But they hearkened not unto me to keep their hands from evil. Wherefore they have met a shameful death through their own infatuate deeds. Yet I, the soothsayer among them, that have wrought no evil, shall fall even as they, for no grace abides for good deeds done.'

Then Odysseus of many counsels looked askance⑭ at him, and said: 'If indeed thou dost avow thee to be the soothsayer of these men, thou art like to have often prayed in the halls that the issue of a glad return might be far from me, and that my dear wife should follow thee and bear thee children; wherefore thou shalt not escape the bitterness of death.'

---

① Polytherses: /ˌpɒlɪˈθɜːsiːz/

② big: 骄傲地，自大地

③ recompense /ˈrekəmpens/: 回报

④ the ox-foot: 在 The Odyssey 第 20 卷中，Odysseus 装成乞丐在自己的家中乞讨。为了侮辱 Odysseus，Ctesippus 从篮子中捡起一只牛脚，使劲地朝 Odysseus 扔过去，说是送给他的礼物。

⑤ the keeper of the shambling kine: Philoetius; shamble /ˈʃæmbl/: 笨拙地行走; kine: （古语）cow 的复数形式。

⑥ Leocritus: /lɪˈɒkrɪtəs/

⑦ Euenor: /juəˈiːnə/

⑧ flank: 肋

⑨ drove: 牛群

⑩ flit: 轻快地飞

⑪ gadfly /ˈɡædflaɪ/: 牛虻（méng）

⑫ Leiodes: /ˌliːɪˈəʊdiːz/

⑬ froward /ˈfrəʊəd/: 不恰当的

⑭ askance /əˈskæns/: 斜着眼睛地

Therewith he caught up a sword in his strong hand, that lay where Agelaus had let it fall to the ground when he was slain, and drave it clean through his neck, and as he yet spake his head fell even to the dust.

But the son of Terpes①, the minstrel, still sought how he might shun black fate, Phemius②, who sang among the wooers of necessity③. He stood with the loud lyre in his hand hard by the postern gate, and his heart was divided within him, whether he should slip forth from the hall and sit down by the well-wrought altar of great Zeus of the household court, whereon Laertes and Odysseus had burnt many pieces of the thighs of oxen, or should spring forward and beseech Odysseus by his knees. And as he thought thereupon this seemed to him the better way, to embrace the knees of Odysseus, son of Laertes. So he laid the hollow lyre on the ground between the mixing-bowl and the high seat inlaid④ with silver, and himself sprang forward and seized Odysseus by the knees, and besought him and spake winged words:

' I entreat thee by thy knees, Odysseus, and do thou show mercy on me and have pity. It will be a sorrow to thyself in the aftertime⑤ if thou slayest me who am a minstrel, and sing before gods and men. Yea none has taught me but myself, and the god has put into my heart all manner of lays⑥, and methinks I sing to thee as to a god, wherefore be not eager to cut off my head. And Telemachus will testify of this, thine own dear son, that not by mine own will or desire did I resort to thy house to sing to the wooers at their feasts; but being so many and stronger than I they led me by constraint. '

So he spake, and the mighty prince Telemachus heard him and quickly spake to his father at his side: ' Hold thy hand, and wound not this blameless man with the sword; and let us save also the henchman⑦ Medon⑧, that ever had charge of me in our house when I was a child, unless perchance Philoetius or the swineherd have already slain him, or he hath met thee in thy raging through the house. '

So he spake, and Medon, wise of heart, heard him. For he lay crouching beneath a high seat, clad about in the new-flayed⑨ hide of an ox and shunned black fate. So he rose up quickly from under the seat, and cast off the ox-hide, and sprang forth and caught Telemachus by the knees, and besought him and spake winged words:

' Friend, here am I; prithee⑩ stay thy hand and speak to thy father, lest he harm me with the sharp sword in the greatness of his strength, out of his anger for the wooers that wasted his

---

① Terpes: /'tɜːpiːz/
② Phemius: /'fiːmɪəs/
③ of necessity /nɪ'sesəti/: （因为受到胁迫）迫不得已
④ inlay /ɪn'leɪ/: 镶嵌
⑤ aftertime /'ɑːftətaɪm/: 未来
⑥ lay: 歌曲,旋律
⑦ henchman /'hentʃmən/: 值得信任的侍从
⑧ Medon: /'miːdn/
⑨ flay: 剥皮
⑩ prithee /'prɪðiː/: 请

possessions in the halls, and in their folly held thee in no honour.'

And Odysseus of many counsels smiled on him and said: 'Take courage, for lo, he has saved thee and delivered thee, that thou mayst know in thy heart, and tell it even to another, how far more excellent are good deeds than evil. But go forth from the halls and sit down in the court apart from the slaughter, thou and the full-voiced① minstrel, till I have accomplished all that I must needs do in the house.'

Therewith the two went forth and gat them from the hall. So they sat down by the altar of great Zeus, peering about on every side, still expecting death. And Odysseus peered all through the house, to see if any man was yet alive and hiding away to shun black fate. But he found all the sort of them fallen in their blood in the dust, like fishes that the fishermen have drawn forth in the meshes of the net into a hollow of the beach from out the grey sea, and all the fish, sore longing for the salt sea waves, are heaped upon the sand, and the sun shines forth and takes their life away; so now the wooers lay heaped upon each other. Then Odysseus of many counsels spake to Telemachus:

'Telemachus, go, call me the nurse Eurycleia②, that I may tell her a word that is on my mind.'

So he spake, and Telemachus obeyed his dear father, and smote at the door, and spake to the nurse Eurycleia: 'Up now, aged wife③, that overlookest all the women servants in our halls, come hither, my father calls thee and has somewhat to say to thee.'

Even so he spake, and wingless her speech remained④, and she opened the doors of the fair-lying halls, and came forth, and Telemachus led the way before her. So she found Odysseus among the bodies of the dead, stained with blood and soil of battle, like a lion that has eaten of an ox of the homestead and goes on his way, and all his breast and his cheeks on either side are flecked⑤ with blood, and he is terrible to behold; even so was Odysseus stained, both hands and feet. Now the nurse, when she saw the bodies of the dead and the great gore⑥ of blood, made ready to cry aloud for joy, beholding so great an adventure. But Odysseus checked and held her in her eagerness, and uttering his voice spake to her winged words:

'Within thine own heart rejoice, old nurse, and be still, and cry not aloud; for it is an unholy thing to boast over slain men. Now these hath the destiny of the gods overcome⑦, and their own cruel deeds, for they honoured none of earthly men, neither the bad nor yet the good, that came among them. Wherefore they have met a shameful death through their own infatuate deeds. But come, tell me the tale of the women in my halls, which of them dishonour me, and which be guiltless.'

Then the good nurse Eurycleia answered him: 'Yea now, my child, I will tell thee all the

---

① full-voiced: 声音洪亮的

② Eurycleia: /ˌjuərɪˈkliːɪə/

③ wife: 中年的或年老的女人

④ and wingless her speech remained: and she spoke no words.

⑤ fleck: 使有斑点

⑥ gore: 凝结的血

⑦ Now these hath the destiny of the gods overcome: Now the destiny of the gods hath overcome these.

truth. Thou hast fifty women-servants in thy halls, that we have taught the ways of housewifery, how to card wool and to bear bondage. Of these twelve in all have gone the way of shame, and honour not me, nor their lady Penelope. And Telemachus hath but newly come to his strength①, and his mother suffered him not to take command over the women in this house. But now, let me go aloft to the shining upper chamber, and tell all to thy wife, on whom some god hath sent a sleep.'

And Odysseus of many counsels answered her, saying: 'Wake her not yet, but bid the women come hither, who in time past behaved themselves unseemly.'

So he spake, and the old wife passed through the hall, to tell the women and to hasten their coming. Then Odysseus called to him Telemachus, and the neatherd, and the swineherd, and spake to them winged words:

'Begin ye now to carry out the dead, and bid the women help you, and thereafter cleanse② the fair high seats and the tables with water and porous③ sponges④. And when ye have set all the house in order, lead the maidens without⑤ the stablished hall, between the vaulted room and the goodly fence of the court, and there slay them with your long blades, till they shall have all given up the ghost and forgotten the love that of old⑥ they had at the bidding⑦ of the wooers, in secret dalliance⑧.'

Even so he spake, and the women came all in a crowd together, making a terrible lament and shedding big tears. So first they carried forth the bodies of the slain, and set them beneath the gallery of the fenced court, and propped them one on another; and Odysseus himself hasted the women and directed them, and they carried forth the dead perforce. Thereafter they cleansed the fair high seats and the tables with water and porous sponges. And Telemachus, and the neatherd, and the swineherd, scraped with spades the floor of the well-builded house, and, behold, the maidens carried all forth and laid it without the doors.

Now when they had made an end of setting the hall in order, they led the maidens forth from the stablished hall, and drove them up in a narrow space between the vaulted room and the goodly fence of the court, whence none might avoid⑨; and wise Telemachus began to speak to his fellows, saying: 'God forbid that I should take these women's lives by a clean death, these that have poured dishonour on my head and on my mother, and have lain with the wooers.'

With that word he tied the cable of a dark-prowed ship to a great pillar and flung it round the vaulted room, and fastened it aloft, that none might touch the ground with her feet. And even as

---

① And Telemachus hath but newly come to his strength: Telemachus 刚长大成人。
② cleanse /klenz/: 清洗
③ porous /'pɔːrəs/: 多空的
④ sponge /spʌndʒ/: 海绵
⑤ without: outside
⑥ of old: 过去,从前
⑦ bidding: 命令,邀请
⑧ dalliance /'dælɪəns/: 调情
⑨ avoid: 逃走

when thrushes①, long of wing, or doves fall into a net that is set in a thicket, as they seek to their roosting-place②, and a loathly③ bed harbours them, even so the women held their heads all in a row, and about all their necks nooses were cast, that they might die by the most pitiful death. And they writhed④ with their feet for a little space, but for no long while.

Then they led out Melanthius through the doorway and the court, and cut off his nostrils and his ears with the pitiless sword, and drew forth his vitals⑤ for the dogs to devour raw, and cut off his hands and feet in their cruel anger.

Thereafter they washed their hands and feet, and went into the house to Odysseus, and all the adventure was over. So Odysseus called to the good nurse Eurycleia: 'Bring sulphur⑥, old nurse, that cleanses all pollution and bring me fire, that I may purify the house with sulphur, and do thou bid Penelope come here with her handmaidens, and tell all the women to hasten into the hall.'

Then the good nurse Eurycleia made answer: 'Yea, my child, herein thou hast spoken aright. But go to, let me bring thee a mantle and a doublet⑦ for raiment, and stand not thus in the halls with thy broad shoulders wrapped in rags; it were blame in thee so to do.'

And Odysseus of many counsels answered her, saying: 'First let a fire now be made me in the hall.'

So he spake, and the good nurse Eurycleia was not slow to obey, but brought fire and brimstone⑧; and Odysseus thoroughly purged the women's chamber and the great hall and the court.

Then the old wife went through the fair halls of Odysseus to tell the women, and to hasten⑨ their coming. So they came forth from their chamber with torches in their hands, and fell about Odysseus, and embraced him and kissed and clasped⑩ his head and shoulders and his hands lovingly, and a sweet longing⑪ came on him to weep and moan, for he remembered them every one.

---

① thrush：鸫
② roosting-place：（鸟的）栖息处
③ loathly /ˈləʊðli/：让人反感的，让人厌恶的
④ writhe /raɪð/：蠕动
⑤ vitals：身体中的重要器官
⑥ sulphur /ˈsʌlfə/：硫磺
⑦ doublet /ˈdʌblɪt/：男式紧身上衣
⑧ brimstone /ˈbrɪmstən/：sulphur
⑨ hasten /ˈheɪsn/：催促
⑩ clasp /klɑːsp/：紧紧地拥抱
⑪ longing /ˈlɒŋɪŋ/：欲望，渴望

The Homeric Hymns

《荷马式的赞歌》（*The Homeric Hymns*）是一个包含 33 首赞歌的集子。这些赞歌多数歌颂希腊神话中的那些最重要的神并讲述与其相关的故事，创作于公元前 8 世纪至公元前 6 世纪之间。这些赞歌中使用的是荷马史诗中使用的那种六步格（hexameter），所以说它们是"荷马式的（Homeric）"。本读本从《荷马式的赞歌》中选取了两首，即"To Aphrodite"（第 6 首）和"To Dionysus"（第 7 首）。

To Aphrodite
Translated into English by Hugh G. Evelyn-White

Muse, tell me the deeds of golden Aphrodite the Cyprian[①], who stirs up sweet passion in the gods and subdues the tribes of mortal men and birds that fly in air and all the many creatures that the dry land rears, and all the sea: all these love the deeds of rich-crowned Cytherea[②].

Yet there are three hearts that she cannot bend nor yet ensnare[③]. First is the daughter of Zeus who holds the aegis, bright-eyed Athene; for she has no pleasure in the deeds of golden Aphrodite[④], but delights in wars and in the work of Ares[⑤], in strifes and battles and in preparing famous crafts. She first taught earthly craftsmen to make chariots of war and cars variously wrought with bronze, and she, too, teaches tender maidens in the house and puts knowledge of goodly arts in each one's mind. Nor does laughter-loving Aphrodite ever tame in love Artemis, the huntress

---

① the Cyprian /ˈsɪprɪən/：由于 Aphrodite 出生在 Cyprus 并在那里受崇拜，所以被称为 the Cyprian。参见 Hesiod 的 *Theogony* 选段"Offsping of Earth and Heaven"。

② Cytherea /ˌsɪθəˈriːə/：Aphrodite；参见 Hesiod 的 *Theogony* 选段"Offsping of Earth and Heaven"。

③ ensnare /ɪnˈsneə/：诱惑，使进入圈套

④ the deeds of golden Aphrodite：love and sex

⑤ Ares：参见 *The Age of Fable* 第 1 章关于 Mars 的叙述。

with shafts of gold; for she loves archery and the slaying of wild beasts in the mountains, the lyre also and dancing and thrilling cries and shady woods and the cities of upright men. Nor yet does the pure maiden Hestia love Aphrodite's works[①]. She was the first-born child of wily Cronos and youngest too[②], by will of Zeus who holds the aegis—a queenly maid whom both Poseidon and Apollo sought to wed. But she was wholly unwilling, nay, stubbornly refused; and touching the head of father Zeus[③] who holds the aegis, she, that fair goddess, sware[④] a great oath which has in truth been fulfilled, that she would be a maiden[⑤] all her days. So Zeus the Father gave her an high honour instead of marriage, and she has her place in the midst of the house and has the richest portion. In all the temples of the gods she has a share of honour, and among all mortal men she is chief of the goddesses.

Of these three Aphrodite cannot bend or ensnare the hearts. But of all others there is nothing among the blessed gods or among mortal men that has escaped Aphrodite. Even the heart of Zeus, who delights in thunder, is led astray by her; though he is greatest of all and has the lot of highest majesty, she beguiles even his wise heart whensoever she pleases, and mates[⑥] him with mortal women, unknown to Hera, his sister and his wife, the grandest far in beauty among the deathless goddesses—most glorious is she whom wily Cronos with her mother Rhea did beget: and Zeus, whose wisdom is everlasting, made her his chaste and careful wife.

But upon Aphrodite herself Zeus cast sweet desire to be joined in love with a mortal man, to the end[⑦] that, very soon, not even she should be innocent of a mortal's love; lest laughter-loving Aphrodite should one day softly smile and say mockingly among all the gods that she had joined the gods in love with mortal women who bare[⑧] sons of death[⑨] to the deathless gods, and had mated the goddesses with mortal men.

And so he put in her heart sweet desire for Anchises[⑩] who was tending cattle at that time among the steep hills of many-fountained Ida, and in shape was like the immortal gods. Therefore, when laughter-loving Aphrodite saw him, she loved him, and terribly desire seized her in her heart. She went to Cyprus, to Paphos, where her precinct[⑪] is and fragrant altar, and passed into her sweet-smelling temple. There she went in and put to[⑫] the glittering doors, and there the

---

① Aphrodite's works: love and sex
② Cronos 的孩子们出生时，他把他们吞到自己的肚子里，后来他又被迫把他们吐出来。Hestia 是 Cronos 的第一个孩子，是最先被他吞入肚子的，但又是最后一个被吐出来的，所以才会有这里这看似矛盾的表述。参见 Hesiod 的 *Theogony* 选段"Offspring of Cronos and Rhea"。
③ father Zeus: Zeus 是 Hestia 的弟弟，不是她的父亲，但 Zeus 被称为 the father of gods and men，所以这里才说 father Zeus，下一句才说 Zeus the Father。
④ sware /sweə/: swore
⑤ maiden /'meɪdn/: 处女
⑥ mate: 使交配
⑦ end: 目的
⑧ bare: bore
⑨ sons of death: 会死的儿子
⑩ Anchises: father of Aeneas; 参见 *The Age of Fable* 第 31 章、32 章。
⑪ precinct /'priːsɪŋkt/: 神庙四周的土地
⑫ put to: 关上

Graces bathed her with heavenly oil such as blooms① upon the bodies of the eternal gods—oil divinely sweet, which she had by her, filled with fragrance. And laughter-loving Aphrodite put on all her rich clothes, and when she had decked② herself with gold, she left sweet-smelling Cyprus and went in haste towards Troy, swiftly travelling high up among the clouds. So she came to many-fountained Ida, the mother of wild creatures and went straight to the homestead across the mountains. After her came grey wolves, fawning③ on her, and grim-eyed lions, and bears, and fleet leopards, ravenous for deer: and she was glad in heart to see them, and put desire in their breasts, so that they all mated, two together, about the shadowy coombes④.

But she herself came to the neat-built shelters, and him she found left quite alone in the homestead—the hero Anchises who was comely⑤ as the gods. All the others were following the herds over the grassy pastures, and he, left quite alone in the homestead, was roaming hither and thither and playing thrillingly upon the lyre. And Aphrodite, the daughter of Zeus stood before him, being like a pure maiden in height and mien⑥, that he should not be frightened when he took heed of her with his eyes. Now when Anchises saw her, he marked her well and wondered at her mien and height and shining garments. For she was clad in a robe out-shining the brightness of fire, a splendid robe of gold, enriched with all manner of needlework, which shimmered⑦ like the moon over her tender breasts, a marvel to see. Also she wore twisted brooches and shining earrings in the form of flowers; and round her soft throat were lovely necklaces.

And Anchises was seized with love, and said to her: "Hail, lady, whoever of the blessed ones you are that are come to this house, whether Artemis, or Leto, or golden Aphrodite, or high-born Themis, or bright-eyed Athene. Or, maybe, you are one of the Graces come hither, who bear the gods company and are called immortal, or else one of those who inhabit this lovely mountain and the springs of rivers and grassy meads⑧. I will make you an altar upon a high peak in a far seen place, and will sacrifice rich offerings to you at all seasons. And do you feel kindly towards me and grant that I may become a man very eminent among the Trojans, and give me strong offspring for the time to come. As for my own self, let me live long and happily, seeing the light of the sun, and come to the threshold of old age, a man prosperous among the people."

Thereupon Aphrodite the daughter of Zeus answered him: "Anchises, most glorious of all men born on earth, know that I am no goddess: why do you liken⑨ me to the deathless ones⑩?

---

① bloom：发光，发亮

② deck /dek/：装饰，打扮

③ fawn /fɔːn/：(狗等动物)摇着尾巴讨好

④ coombe /kuːm/：峡谷

⑤ comely /ˈkʌmli/：长得标致的

⑥ mien /miːn/：外表，外貌

⑦ shimmer /ˈʃɪmə/：闪烁，发出微光

⑧ those who inhabit this lovely mountain and the springs of rivers and grassy meads：the nymphs

⑨ liken /ˈlaɪkən/：把……比作

⑩ the deathless ones：the gods and goddesses, the immortals

Nay, I am but a mortal, and a woman was the mother that bare me. Otreus[1] of famous name is my father, if so be you have heard of him, and he reigns over all Phrygia rich in fortresses. But I know your speech[2] well beside my own, for a Trojan nurse brought me up at home: she took me from my dear mother and reared me thenceforth when I was a little child. So comes it, then, that I well know you tongue also. And now the Slayer of Argus[3] with the golden wand has caught me up from the dance of huntress Artemis, her with the golden arrows. For there were many of us, nymphs and marriageable[4] maidens, playing together; and an innumerable company encircled us: from these the Slayer of Argus with the golden wand rapt[5] me away. He carried me over many fields of mortal men and over much land untilled[6] and unpossessed[7], where savage wild-beasts roam through shady coombes, until I thought never again to touch the life-giving earth with my feet. And he said that I should be called the wedded wife of Anchises, and should bear you goodly children. But when he had told and advised me, he, the strong Slayer of Argus, went back to the families of the deathless gods, while I am now come to you: for unbending necessity is upon me. But I beseech you by Zeus and by your noble parents—for no base folk could get such a son as you—take me now, stainless[8] and unproved in love[9], and show me to your father and careful mother and to your brothers sprung from the same stock[10]. I shall be no ill-liking[11] daughter for them, but a likely[12]. Moreover, send a messenger quickly to the swift-horsed[13] Phrygians, to tell my father and my sorrowing mother; and they will send you gold in plenty and woven stuffs[14], many splendid gifts; take these as bride-piece[15]. So do, and then prepare the sweet marriage that is honourable in the eyes of men and deathless gods."

When she had so spoken, the goddess put sweet desire in his heart. And Anchises was seized with love, so that he opened his mouth and said:

"If you are a mortal and a woman was the mother who bare you, and Otreus of famous name is your father as you say, and if you are come here by the will of Hermes the immortal Guide[16], and are to be called my wife always, then neither god nor mortal man shall here restrain me till I

---

① Otreus: /ˈəʊtrɪəs/
② speech：语言，话
③ the Slayer of Argus：Hermes (Mercury)；参见 *The Age of Fable* 第 4 章。
④ marriageable /ˈmærɪdʒəbl/：已达到结婚年龄的
⑤ rapt /ræpt/：rap 的过去式；rap：抢走
⑥ untilled /ˌʌnˈtɪld/：没有耕种的，未开垦的
⑦ unpossessed /ˌʌnpəˈzest/：无主的，没被占有的
⑧ stainless /ˈsteɪnlɪs/：没有污点的，纯洁的
⑨ unproved in love：没有体验过爱情的，没有性经验的
⑩ stock /stɒk/：祖先，世系
⑪ ill-liking：不讨人喜欢的
⑫ likely /ˈlaɪkli/：适合的，合格的
⑬ swift-horsed：马跑得快的
⑭ woven stuffs：纺织品，织物
⑮ bride-piece：嫁妆
⑯ the immortal Guide：the Guide 是 Hermes 的称号之一。

have lain with you in love right now; no, not even if far-shooting Apollo himself should launch grievous shafts from his silver bow. Willingly would I go down into the house of Hades, O lady, beautiful as the goddesses, once I had gone up to your bed."

So speaking, he caught her by the hand. And laughter-loving Aphrodite, with face turned away and lovely eyes downcast①, crept to the well-spread couch which was already laid with soft coverings for the hero; and upon it lay skins of bears and deep-roaring lions which he himself had slain in the high mountains. And when they had gone up upon the well-fitted bed, first Anchises took off her bright jewelry of pins and twisted brooches and earrings and necklaces, and loosed her girdle and stripped off her bright garments and laid them down upon a silver-studded seat. Then by the will of the gods and destiny he lay with her, a mortal man with an immortal goddess, not clearly knowing what he did.

But at the time when the herdsmen drive their oxen and hardy② sheep back to the fold③ from the flowery pastures, even then Aphrodite poured soft sleep upon Anchises, but herself put on her rich raiment. And when the bright goddess had fully clothed herself, she stood by the couch, and her head reached to the well-hewn roof-tree④; from her cheeks shone unearthly beauty such as belongs to rich-crowned Cytherea. Then she aroused him from sleep and opened her mouth and said:

"Up, son of Dardanus⑤! —why sleep you so heavily? —and consider whether I look as I did when first you saw me with your eyes."

So she spake. And he awoke in a moment and obeyed her. But when he saw the neck and lovely eyes of Aphrodite, he was afraid and turned his eyes aside another way, hiding his comely face with his cloak. Then he uttered winged words and entreated her:

"So soon as ever I saw you with my eyes, goddess, I knew that you were divine; but you did not tell me truly. Yet by Zeus who holds the aegis I beseech you, leave me not to lead a palsied⑥ life among men, but have pity on me; for he who lies with a deathless goddess is no hale⑦ man afterwards."

Then Aphrodite the daughter of Zeus answered him: "Anchises, most glorious of mortal men, take courage and be not too fearful in your heart. You need fear no harm from me nor from the other blessed ones, for you are dear to the gods: and you shall have a dear son who shall reign among the Trojans, and children's children after him, springing up continually. His name shall be Aeneas, because I felt awful grief in that I laid me in the bed of mortal man: yet are those of your race always the most like to gods of all mortal men in beauty and in stature⑧.

---

① downcast /ˈdaʊnkɑːst/：（眼睛）朝下看的

② hardy /ˈhɑːdi/：强壮的

③ fold /fəʊld/：羊栏

④ roof-tree：栋梁

⑤ Dardanus：参见 *The Age of Fable* 第 26 章关于 Dardanus 的注释。

⑥ palsied /ˈpɔːlzɪd/：瘫痪的，被剥夺了行动能力的，步履蹒跚的

⑦ hale：强壮的，健康的

⑧ stature /ˈstætʃə/：身材，体型

"Verily wise Zeus carried off golden-haired Ganymedes[①] because of his beauty, to be amongst the Deathless Ones and pour drink for the gods in the house of Zeus—a wonder to see—honoured by all the immortals as he draws the red nectar from the golden bowl. But grief that could not be soothed filled the heart of Tros[②]; for he knew not whither the heaven-sent whirlwind[③] had caught up his dear son, so that he mourned him always, unceasingly, until Zeus pitied him and gave him high-stepping horses such as carry the immortals as recompense[④] for his son. These he gave him as a gift. And at the command of Zeus, the Guide, the slayer of Argus, told him all, and how his son would be deathless and unageing[⑤], even as the gods. So when Tros heard these tidings[⑥] from Zeus, he no longer kept mourning but rejoiced in his heart and rode joyfully with his storm-footed[⑦] horses.

"So also golden-throned Eos[⑧] rapt away Tithonus[⑨] who was of your race and like the deathless gods. And she went to ask the dark-clouded Son of Cronos[⑩] that he should be deathless and live eternally; and Zeus bowed his head to her prayer and fulfilled her desire. Too simple was queenly Eos: she thought not in her heart to ask youth for him and to strip him of the slough of deadly age. So while he enjoyed the sweet flower of life he lived rapturously[⑪] with golden-throned Eos, the early-born, by the streams of Ocean, at the ends of the earth; but when the first grey hairs began to ripple from his comely head and noble chin, queenly Eos kept away from his bed, though she cherished him in her house and nourished him with food and ambrosia and gave him rich clothing. But when loathsome old age pressed full upon him, and he could not move nor lift his limbs, this seemed to her in her heart the best counsel: she laid him in a room and put to the shining doors. There he babbles[⑫] endlessly, and no more has strength at all, such as once he had in his supple[⑬] limbs.

"I would not have you be deathless among the deathless gods and live continually after such sort. Yet if you could live on such as now you are in look and in form, and be called my husband, sorrow would not then enfold my careful heart. But, as it is, harsh old age will soon enshroud[⑭] you—ruthless age which stands someday at the side of every man, deadly, wearying, dreaded even by the gods.

---

① Ganymedes /ˌɡænɪ'miːdiːz/: 即 Ganymede, 参见 *The Age of Fable* 第 19 章。

② Tros /trɒs/: Tros is the son of Dardanus, the father of Ganymedes, and the king of Troy, which is named after him.

③ whirlwind /'wɜːlwɪnd/: 旋风

④ recompense /'rekəmpens/: 补偿

⑤ unageing /'ʌn'eɪdʒɪŋ/: 不会变老的

⑥ tiding /'taɪdɪŋ/: 消息, 信息

⑦ storm-footed: 跑起来脚步快如风暴的

⑧ Eos /'iːɒs/: 即罗马神话中的黎明女神 Aurora。

⑨ Tithonus: 参见 *The Age of Fable* 第 26 章。

⑩ the dark-clouded Son of Cronos: Zeus

⑪ rapturously /'ræptjʊərəsli/: 激动地, 欣喜地

⑫ babble /'bæbl/: 喋喋不休, 唠叨

⑬ supple /'sʌpl/: 灵活的

⑭ enshroud /ɪn'ʃraʊd/: 包裹住

"And now because of you I shall have great shame among the deathless gods henceforth[1], continually. For until now they feared my jibes[2] and the wiles by which, or soon or late, I mated all the immortals with mortal women, making them all subject to my will. But now my mouth shall no more have this power among the gods; for very great has been my madness, my miserable and dreadful madness, and I went astray out of my mind who have gotten a child beneath my girdle, mating with a mortal man. As for the child, as soon as he sees the light of the sun, the deep-breasted[3] mountain Nymphs who inhabit this great and holy mountain shall bring him up. They rank[4] neither with mortals nor with immortals: long indeed do they live, eating heavenly food and treading the lovely dance among the immortals, and with them the Sileni[5] and the sharp-eyed Slayer of Argus mate in the depths of pleasant caves; but at their birth pines or high-topped oaks spring up with them upon the fruitful earth, beautiful, flourishing trees, towering high upon the lofty mountains (and men call them holy places of the immortals, and never mortal lops them with the axe); but when the fate of death is near at hand, first those lovely trees wither where they stand, and the bark[6] shrivels[7] away about them, and the twigs fall down, and at last the life of the Nymph and of the tree leave the light of the sun together. These Nymphs shall keep my son with them and rear him, and as soon as he is come to lovely boyhood, the goddesses will bring him here to you and show you your child. But, that I may tell you all that I have in mind, I will come here again towards the fifth year and bring you my son. So soon as ever you have seen him—a scion[8] to delight the eyes—you will rejoice in beholding him; for he shall be most godlike: then bring him at once to windy Ilion[9]. And if any mortal man ask you who got your dear son beneath her girdle, remember to tell him as I bid you: say he is the offspring of one of the flower-like Nymphs who inhabit this forest-clad hill. But if you tell all and foolishly boast that you lay with rich-crowned Aphrodite, Zeus will smite you in his anger with a smoking thunderbolt. Now I have told you all. Take heed: refrain and name me not, but have regard to the anger of the gods."

When the goddess had so spoken, she soared up to windy heaven.

Hail, goddess, queen of well-builded Cyprus! With you have I begun; now I will turn me to another hymn.

---

① henceforth /'hensfɔ:θ/: 从现在起
② jibe /dʒaɪb/: 嘲笑的话语，嘲笑
③ deep-breasted: 丰乳的
④ rank: 属于特定行列或阶层
⑤ Sileni /saɪ'li:naɪ/: silenus 的复数形式；silenus /saɪ'li:nəs/: 森林之神，表现为留胡须、长着马尾巴和马腿的老人。
⑥ bark: 树皮
⑦ shrivel /'ʃrɪvl/: 皱缩，枯萎
⑧ scion /'saɪən/: 继承人，后裔，后代
⑨ Ilion: Troy

To Dionysus

Translated into English by Hugh G. Evelyn-White

I will tell of Dionysus①, the son of glorious Semele, how he appeared on a jutting② headland③ by the shore of the fruitless sea, seeming like a stripling④ in the first flush of manhood⑤: his rich, dark hair was waving about him, and on his strong shoulders he wore a purple robe. Presently there came swiftly over the sparkling sea Tyrsenian⑥ pirates on a well-decked ship—a miserable doom led them on. When they saw him they made signs to one another and sprang out quickly, and seizing him straightway, put him on board their ship exultingly⑦; for they thought him the son of heaven-nurtured kings. They sought to bind him with rude bonds, but the bonds would not hold him, and the withes⑧ fell far away from his hands and feet: and he sat with a smile in his dark eyes. Then the helmsman⑨ understood all and cried out at once to his fellows and said:

"Madmen! What god is this whom you have taken and bind, strong that he is? Not even the well-built ship can carry him. Surely this is either Zeus or Apollo who has the silver bow, or Poseidon, for he looks not like mortal men but like the gods who dwell on Olympus. Come, then, let us set him free upon the dark shore at once: do not lay hands on him, lest he grow angry and stir up dangerous winds and heavy squalls⑩."

So said he: but the master chid him with taunting words: "Madman, mark the wind and help hoist sail on the ship: catch all the sheets⑪. As for this fellow we men will see to him: I reckon he is bound for Egypt or for Cyprus or to the Hyperboreans or further still. But in the end he will speak out and tell us his friends and all his wealth and his brothers, now that providence⑫ has thrown him in our way."

When he had said this, he had mast and sail hoisted on the ship, and the wind filled the sail and the crew hauled taut⑬ the sheets on either side. But soon strange things were seen among

---

① Dionysus 即 Bacchus，参见 *The Age of Fable* 第 21 章。

② jut /dʒʌt/：突出，伸出

③ headland /ˈhedlənd/：突向海中的尖形陆地，海角，岬角

④ stripling /ˈstrɪplɪŋ/：年轻人，小伙子

⑤ in the first flush of manhood：洋溢着青春活力的

⑥ Tyrsenian /tɜːˈsiːnɪən/：Tyrrhenian, Etruscan；参见 *The Age of Fable* 第 21 章关于 Mæonia 的注释。

⑦ exultingly /ɪɡˈzʌltɪŋli/：欣喜地

⑧ withe /wɪθ/：（用于捆绑的）坚韧枝条

⑨ helmsman /ˈhelmzmən/：舵手

⑩ squall /skwɔːl/：伴有雨和雪的、突然的、持续时间短的强风

⑪ sheet /ʃiːt/：（诗歌用语）帆

⑫ providence /ˈprɒvɪdəns/：天意

⑬ taut /tɔːt/：（帆）拉得紧的

them. First of all sweet, fragrant wine ran streaming throughout all the black ship and a heavenly smell arose, so that all the seamen were seized with amazement when they saw it. And all at once a vine spread out both ways along the top of the sail with many clusters hanging down from it, and a dark ivy-plant twined① about the mast, blossoming with flowers, and with rich berries growing on it; and all the thole-pins② were covered with garlands. When the pirates saw all this, then at last they bade the helmsman to put the ship to land. But the god changed into a dreadful lion there on the ship, in the bows③, and roared loudly: amidships④ also he showed his wonders and created a shaggy⑤ bear which stood up ravening, while on the forepeak⑥ was the lion glaring fiercely with scowling brows. And so the sailors fled into the stern⑦ and crowded bemused⑧ about the right-minded⑨ helmsman, until suddenly the lion sprang upon the master and seized him; and when the sailors saw it they leapt out overboard one and all into the bright sea, escaping from a miserable fate, and were changed into dolphins. But on the helmsman Dionysus had mercy and held him back and made him altogether happy, saying to him: "Take courage, good …; you have found favour with my heart. I am loud-crying Dionysus whom Cadmus' daughter Semele bare of union with Zeus."

Hail, child of fair-faced Semele! He who forgets you can in no wise⑩ order sweet song.

---

① twine /twaɪn/: 缠绕
② thole-pin /ˈθəʊlpɪn/: 桨架,桨座
③ bow: (常用复数)船头
④ amidships /əˈmɪdʃɪps/: 在船的中央
⑤ shaggy /ˈʃægi/: 身上长满粗毛的
⑥ forepeak /ˈfɔːpiːk /: 船首舱
⑦ stern /stɜːn/: 船尾
⑧ bemused /bɪˈmjuːzd/: 困惑的,茫然的,迷糊的
⑨ right-minded /ˈraɪtˈmaɪndɪd/: 头脑正常的,有正义感的
⑩ wise /waɪz/: way

Hesiod

　　赫西奥德（Hesiod /ˈhiːsiəd /）是最早的希腊诗人之一，被称为"希腊教诲诗之父"。赫西奥德生卒年月不详，学者们普遍猜测他生活在公元前 700 年前后。赫西奥德有两部完整的诗作流传至今，一部是《工作与日子》（*Works and Days*），另一部是《神谱》（*Theogony*）。

　　《工作与日子》是赫西奥德写给弟弟佩尔塞斯（Perses）的一首教诲诗，全诗共 828 行。为了向弟弟解释人为什么必须努力工作，赫西奥德使用大约三分之一的篇幅讲述了普罗米修斯（Prometheus）和潘多拉（Pandora）的故事，以及五个时代更迭的故事。在剩余的三分之二的篇幅中，赫西奥德告诉弟弟怎样做个合格的农夫，具体到什么时候该干什么活。本读本从《工作与日子》中选取了两个选段：第一个选段"Prometheus，Epimetheus，and Pandora"对应希腊语原诗的第 42 行至第 105 行，第二个选段"The Five Races"对应希腊语原诗的第 106 行至第 201 行。

　　《神谱》全诗共 1 022 行，用六步格（hexameter）写成。《神谱》的独特之处在于它非常系统地叙述了希腊众神的谱系。本读本从《神谱》中选取了 3 个选段：第 1 个选段"Offspring of Earth and Heaven"对应希腊语原诗的第 116 行至第 206 行，第 2 个选段"Offspring of Cronos and Rhea"对应希腊语原诗的第 453 行至第 506 行，第 3 个选段"The Defeat of Cronos by Zeus"对应希腊语原诗的第 617 行至第 735 行。

Works and Days
Translated into English by Hugh G. Evelyn-White

Prometheus，Epimetheus，and Pandora

　　For the gods keep hidden from men the means① of life. Else you② would easily do work enough in a day to supply you for a full year even without working; soon would you put away your

---

① means：手段，方法
② you：Hesiod 的弟弟 Perses /ˈpɜːsiːz/

rudder over the smoke[1], and the fields worked by ox and sturdy[2] mule would run to waste. But Zeus in the anger of his heart hid it[3], because Prometheus the crafty[4] deceived him; therefore he planned sorrow and mischief against men. He hid fire; but that[5] the noble son of Iapetus[6] stole again for men from Zeus the counsellor in a hollow fennel-stalk[7], so that Zeus who delights in thunder did not see it. But afterwards Zeus who gathers the clouds said to him in anger:

"Son of Iapetus, surpassing all in cunning[8], you are glad that you have outwitted[9] me and stolen fire—a great plague to you yourself and to men that shall be. But I will give men as the price for fire an evil thing in which they may all be glad of heart while they embrace their own destruction."

So said the father of men and gods[10], and laughed aloud. And he bade famous Hephaestus[11] make haste and mix earth with water and to put in it the voice and strength of human kind, and fashion a sweet, lovely maiden-shape, like to the immortal goddesses in face; and Athene to teach her needlework and the weaving of the varied web; and golden Aphrodite to shed grace[12] upon her head and cruel longing and cares that weary[13] the limbs. And he charged[14] Hermes the guide, the Slayer of Argus[15], to put in her a shameless mind and a deceitful nature.

So he ordered. And they obeyed the lord Zeus the son of Cronos. Forthwith[16] the famous Lame God[17] moulded clay in the likeness of a modest maid, as the son of Cronos purposed. And the goddess bright-eyed Athene girded and clothed her, and the divine Graces and queenly Persuasion put necklaces of gold upon her, and the rich-haired Hours crowned her head with spring flowers. And Pallas Athene bedecked[18] her form with all manners of finery[19]. Also the Guide, the Slayer of Argus, contrived within her lies and crafty words and a deceitful nature at the will of loud thundering Zeus, and the Herald of the gods[20] put speech in her. And he called this woman Pandora[21], because all they who dwelt on Olympus gave each a gift, a plague to men who eat

---

① put away your rudder over the smoke：把船舵收藏起来不再使用，即不再出海谋生。

② sturdy /ˈstɜːdi/：强壮的，健壮的

③ it：the means of life

④ crafty /ˈkrɑːfti/：狡猾的，诡计多端的

⑤ that：the fire

⑥ Iapetus /aɪˈæpɪtəs/：巨人之一，Prometheus 的父亲。

⑦ fennel-stalk：茴香茎

⑧ cunning：欺骗技巧

⑨ outwit /aʊtˈwɪt/：（在智慧或知识方面）超过，骗过

⑩ the father of men and gods：Zeus

⑪ Hephaestus：即 Hephæstos；参见 *The Age of Fable* 第 1 章关于 Vulcan（Hephæstos）的叙述。

⑫ grace：优美，优雅

⑬ weary /ˈwɪəri/：使疲乏

⑭ charge：命令

⑮ the Slayer of Argus：参见 *The Age of Fable* 第 4 章 Io 的故事。

⑯ forthwith：立刻，马上

⑰ the famous Lame God：Hephaestus

⑱ bedeck /bɪˈdek/：装饰

⑲ finery /ˈfaɪnəri/：美貌，优雅，华丽的衣服

⑳ the Herald of the gods：Hermes

㉑ Pandora：This word in Greek means "all-gifted" or "all-endowed". In Greek, the word "Pandora (Πανδώρα)" contains two parts, "pan (παν)" meaning "all" and "dora (δ ωρα)" meaning "gifts", so Pandora is somebody who receives gifts from all gods.

bread.

But when he had finished the sheer, hopeless snare, the Father sent glorious Argus-Slayer, the swift messenger of the gods, to take it to Epimetheus as a gift. And Epimetheus did not think on what Prometheus had said to him, bidding him never take a gift of Olympian Zeus, but to send it back for fear it might prove to be something harmful to men. But he took the gift, and afterwards, when the evil thing was already his, he understood.

For ere① this the tribes of men lived on earth remote and free from ills and hard toil and heavy sickness which bring the Fates upon men; for in misery men grow old quickly. But the woman took off the great lid of the jar with her hands and scattered all these and her thought caused sorrow and mischief to men. Only Hope remained there in an unbreakable home within under the rim of the great jar, and did not fly out at the door; for ere that, the lid of the jar stopped her, by the will of Aegis-holding Zeus who gathers the clouds. But the rest, countless plagues, wander amongst men; for earth is full of evils and the sea is full. Of themselves diseases come upon men continually by day and by night, bringing mischief to mortals silently; for wise Zeus took away speech from them. So is there no way to escape the will of Zeus.

The Five Races

Or if you will, I will sum you up another tale well and skillfully—and do you lay it up in your heart,—how the gods and mortal men sprang from one source.

First of all the deathless gods who dwell on Olympus made a golden race of mortal men who lived in the time of Cronos when he was reigning in heaven. And they lived like gods without sorrow of heart, remote and free from toil and grief: miserable age② rested not on them; but with legs and arms never failing they made merry with feasting beyond the reach of all evils. When they died, it was as though they were overcome with sleep, and they had all good things; for the fruitful earth unforced bare③ them fruit abundantly and without stint④. They dwelt in ease and peace upon their lands with many good things, rich in flocks and loved by the blessed gods.

But after earth had covered this generation—they are called pure spirits dwelling on the earth, and are kindly, delivering from harm, and guardians of mortal men; for they roam everywhere over the earth, clothed in mist and keep watch on judgements and cruel deeds, givers of wealth; for this royal right also they received; —then they who dwell on Olympus made a second generation which was of silver and less noble by far. It was like the golden race neither in body nor in spirit. A child was brought up at his good mother's side an hundred years, an utter simpleton⑤, playing childishly in his own home. But when they were full grown and were come to the full measure of their prime⑥, they lived only a little time in sorrow because of their

---

① ere /eə/：before
② age：年老
③ bare：动词 bear 的过去式，即现代英语中的 bore。
④ without stint：不停地，不断地；stint：停顿
⑤ simpleton /ˈsɪmpəltən/：傻子
⑥ prime：人生中的青壮年时期

foolishness, for they could not keep from sinning and from wronging one another, nor would they serve the immortals, nor sacrifice on the holy altars of the blessed ones as it is right for men to do wherever they dwell. Then Zeus the son of Cronos was angry and put them away, because they would not give honour to the blessed gods who live on Olympus.

But when earth had covered this generation also—they are called blessed spirits of the underworld by men, and, though they are of second order, yet honour attends them also—Zeus the Father made a third generation of mortal men, a brazen race, sprung from ash-trees①; and it was in no way equal to the silver age, but was terrible and strong. They loved the lamentable works of Ares② and deeds of violence; they ate no bread, but were hard of heart like adamant, fearful men. Great was their strength and unconquerable the arms which grew from their shoulders on their strong limbs. Their armour was of bronze, and their houses of bronze, and of bronze were their implements③: there was no black iron. These were destroyed by their own hands and passed to the dank④ house of chill Hades⑤, and left no name: terrible though they were, black Death seized them, and they left the bright light of the sun.

But when earth had covered this generation also, Zeus the son of Cronos made yet another, the fourth, upon the fruitful earth, which was nobler and more righteous⑥, a god-like race of hero-men who are called demi-gods, the race before our own, throughout the boundless earth. Grim war and dread battle destroyed a part of them, some in the land of Cadmus at seven-gated Thebe⑦ when they fought for the flocks of Oedipus⑧, and some, when it had brought them in ships over the great sea gulf⑨ to Troy for rich-haired Helen's sake⑩: there death's end enshrouded a part of them. But to the others father Zeus the son of Cronos gave a living and an abode apart from men, and made them dwell at the ends of earth. And they live untouched by sorrow in the islands of the blessed along the shore of deep swirling Ocean⑪, happy heroes for whom the grain-giving earth bears honey-sweet fruit flourishing thrice a year, far from the deathless gods, and Cronos rules over them; for the father of men and gods released him⑫ from his bonds⑬. And these last equally have honour and glory.

And again far-seeing Zeus made yet another generation, the fifth, of men who are upon the bounteous earth.

---

① ash-tree：（木质坚硬的）梣树

② the lamentable works of Ares：wars；Ares：参见 *The Age of Fable* 第 1 章关于 Mars（Ares）的叙述。

③ implement /ˈɪmplɪmənt/：工具

④ dank /dæŋk/：潮湿而寒冷的

⑤ Hades /ˈheɪdiːz/：阴间

⑥ righteous /ˈraɪtʃəs/：正直的，高尚的

⑦ Thebe：Thebes

⑧ 参见 *The Age of Fable* 第 23 章 Antigone 的故事。

⑨ the great sea gulf：the Aegean Sea

⑩ 参见 *The Age of Fable* 第 27、28 章。

⑪ deep swirling Ocean：大西洋

⑫ him：Cronos；参见 *The Age of Fable* 第 1 章 Saturn（Cronos）被其子 Jupiter 推翻并囚禁的故事。

⑬ bond：监禁，囚禁

Thereafter, would① that I② were not among the men of the fifth generation, but either had died before or been born afterwards. For now truly is a race of iron, and men never rest from labour and sorrow by day, and from perishing by night; and the gods shall lay sore trouble upon them. But, notwithstanding, even these shall have some good mingled with their evils. And Zeus will destroy this race of mortal men also when they come to have grey hair on the temples at their birth. The father will not agree with his children, nor the children with their father, nor guest with his host, nor comrade with comrade; nor will brother be dear to brother as aforetime③. Men will dishonour their parents as they grow quickly old, and will carp④ at them, chiding them with bitter words, hard-hearted they, not knowing the fear of the gods. They will not repay their aged parents the cost their nurture⑤, for might shall be their right: and one man will sack another's city. There will be no favour for the man who keeps his oath or for the just or for the good; but rather men will praise the evil-doer and his violent dealing. Strength will be right and reverence will cease to be; and the wicked will hurt the worthy man, speaking false words against him, and will swear an oath upon them. Envy, foul-mouthed, delighting in evil, with scowling face, will go along with wretched men one and all. And then Aidos and Nemesis⑥, with their sweet forms wrapped in white robes, will go from the wide-pathed earth and forsake mankind to join the company of the deathless gods: and bitter sorrows will be left for mortal men, and there will be no help against evil.

Theogony
Translated into English by Hugh G. Evelyn-White

Offspring of Earth and Heaven

Verily at the first Chaos came to be⑦, but next wide-bosomed Earth, the ever-sure⑧ foundations of all the deathless ones⑨ who hold the peaks of snowy Olympus, and dim Tartarus in

---

① would：但愿
② I：Hesiod himself
③ aforetime /əˈfɔːtaɪm/：过去，从前
④ carp：挑剔，找岔
⑤ nurture /ˈnɜːtʃə/：养育，抚养
⑥ （译者注）Aidos, as a quality, is that feeling of reverence or shame which restrains men from wrong; Nemesis is the feeling of righteous indignation aroused especially by the sight of the wicked in undeserved prosperity.
⑦ be：存在
⑧ ever-sure：永远牢固的
⑨ the deathless ones：the gods and goddesses

the depth of the wide-pathed Earth, and Eros (Love), fairest among the deathless gods, who unnerves[1] the limbs and overcomes the mind and wise counsels[2] of all gods and all men within them. From Chaos came forth Erebus[3] and black Night; but of Night were born Aether[4] and Day, whom she conceived and bare[5] from union in love with Erebus. And Earth first bare starry Heaven, equal to herself, to cover her on every side, and to be an ever-sure abiding-place for the blessed gods. And she brought forth long Hills, graceful haunts of the goddess-Nymphs who dwell amongst the glens[6] of the hills. She bare also the fruitless deep[7] with his raging swell, Pontus[8], without sweet union of love. But afterwards she lay with Heaven and bare deep-swirling Oceanus[9], Coeus[10] and Crius[11] and Hyperion and Iapetus, Theia and Rhea, Themis[12] and Mnemosyne[13] and gold-crowned Phoebe[14] and lovely Tethys. After them was born Cronos the wily, youngest and most terrible of her children, and he hated his lusty[15] sire[16].

And again, she bare the Cyclopes, overbearing[17] in spirit, Brontes[18], and Steropes[19] and stubborn-hearted Arges[20], who gave Zeus the thunder and made the thunderbolt: in all else they were like the gods, but one eye only was set in the midst of their foreheads. And they were surnamed Cyclopes (Orb-eyed) because one orbed[21] eye was set in their foreheads. Strength and might and craft were in their works.

And again, three other sons were born of Earth and Heaven, great and doughty[22] beyond telling, Cottus[23] and Briareos[24] and Gyes[25], presumptuous children. From their shoulders sprang an hundred arms, not to be approached, and each had fifty heads upon his shoulders on their strong

---

① unnerve /ʌnˈnɜːv/：使丧失力气，使变得虚弱
② counsel：判断力，智慧
③ Erebus /ˈerɪbəs/：Darkness
④ Aether /ˈiːθə/：Sky
⑤ bare：生（bear 的过去式形式）
⑥ glen：峡谷，山谷
⑦ deep：大海
⑧ Pontus：/ˈpɒntəs/
⑨ Oceanus：/əʊˈsɪənəs/
⑩ Coeus：/ˈsiːəs/
⑪ Crius：/ˈkraɪəs/
⑫ Themis：/ˈθiːmɪs/
⑬ Mnemosyne：/niːˈmɒzɪniː/
⑭ Phoebe：/ˈfiːbi/
⑮ lusty /ˈlʌsti/：性欲强的
⑯ sire /ˈsaɪə/：父亲
⑰ overbearing /ˌəʊvəˈbeərɪŋ/：盛气凌人的，傲慢的
⑱ Brontes：/ˈbrɒntiːz/
⑲ Steropes：/ˈstɪərəpiːz/
⑳ Arges：/ˈɑːdʒiːz/
㉑ orbed /ɔːbd/：圆的
㉒ doughty /ˈdaʊti/：无所畏惧的
㉓ Cottus：/ˈkɒtəs/
㉔ Briareos：/braɪˈeərɪəs/
㉕ Gyes：/gaɪz/

limbs, and irresistible was the stubborn strength that was in their great forms. For of all the children that were born of Earth and Heaven, these were the most terrible, and they were hated by their own father from the first.

And he used to hide them all away in a secret place of Earth so soon as each was born, and would not suffer① them to come up into the light: and Heaven rejoiced in his evil doing. But vast Earth groaned within, being straitened, and she made the element of grey flint② and shaped a great sickle, and told her plan to her dear sons. And she spoke, cheering them, while she was vexed in her dear heart:

"My children, gotten③ of a sinful father, if you will obey me, we should punish the vile outrage of your father; for he first thought of doing shameful things."

So she said; but fear seized them all, and none of them uttered a word. But great Cronos the wily took courage and answered his dear mother:

"Mother, I will undertake to do this deed, for I reverence not our father of evil name, for he first thought of doing shameful things."

So he said: and vast Earth rejoiced greatly in spirit, and set and hid him in an ambush④, and put in his hands a jagged⑤ sickle, and revealed to him the whole plot.

And Heaven came, bringing on night and longing for love, and he lay about Earth spreading himself full upon her.

Then the son from his ambush stretched forth his left hand and in his right took the great long sickle with jagged teeth, and swiftly lopped⑥ off his own father's members⑦ and cast them away to fall behind him. And not vainly did they fall from his hand; for all the bloody drops that gushed forth Earth received, and as the seasons moved round she bare the strong Erinyes and the great Giants with gleaming armour, holding long spears in their hands and the Nymphs whom they call Meliae⑧ all over the boundless earth. And so soon as he had cut off the members with flint and cast them from the land into the surging sea, they were swept away over the main⑨ a long time: and a white foam⑩ spread around them from the immortal flesh, and in it there grew a maiden. First she drew near holy Cythera⑪, and from there, afterwards, she came to sea-girt⑫ Cyprus, and came forth an awful and lovely goddess, and grass grew up about her beneath her shapely feet. Her gods

---

① suffer: 允许
② flint: (坚硬的)燧石
③ gotten: begotten
④ ambush /'æmbʊʃ/: 埋伏地
⑤ jagged /'dʒæɡɪd/: 有锯齿的
⑥ lop: 砍掉
⑦ members: 器官
⑧ Meliae: /'miːliiː/
⑨ main: 大海
⑩ foam: 泡沫
⑪ Cythera /sɪ'θɪərə/: 希腊岛屿名,是伊奥尼亚群岛 (Ionian Islands)最南端和最东端的一个岛,现在属于阿提卡大区 (Attica)。
⑫ sea-girt: 被大海包围的

and men call Aphrodite[1], and the foam-born goddess and rich-crowned Cytherea[2], because she grew amid the foam, and Cytherea because she reached Cythera, and Cyprogenes[3] because she was born in billowy Cyprus, and Philommedes[4] because sprang from the members. And with her went Eros, and comely Desire followed her at her birth at the first and as she went into the assembly of the gods. This honour she has from the beginning, and this is the portion allotted to her amongst men and undying gods—the whisperings of maidens and smiles and deceits with sweet delight and love and graciousness.

Offspring of Cronos and Rhea

But Rhea was subject in love to Cronos and bare splendid children, Hestia[5], Demeter[6], and gold-shod[7] Hera and strong Hades, pitiless in heart, who dwells under the earth, and the loud-crashing Earth-Shaker[8], and wise Zeus, father of gods and men, by whose thunder the wide earth is shaken. These great Cronos swallowed[9] as each came forth from the womb to his mother's knees with this intent, that no other of the proud sons of Heaven should hold the kingly office amongst the deathless gods. For he learned from Earth and starry Heaven that he was destined to be overcome by his own son, strong though he was, through the contriving of great Zeus. Therefore he kept no blind outlook, but watched and swallowed down his children: and unceasing grief seized Rhea. But when she was about to bear Zeus, the father of gods and men, then she besought her own dear parents, Earth and starry Heaven, to devise some plan with her that the birth of her dear child might be concealed, and that retribution[10] might overtake great, crafty Cronos for his own father and also for the children whom he had swallowed down. And they readily heard and obeyed their dear daughter, and told her all that was destined to happen touching Cronos the king and his stout-hearted son. So they sent her to Lyctus[11], to the rich land of Crete, when she was ready to bear great Zeus, the youngest of her children. Him did vast Earth receive from Rhea in wide Crete to nourish and to bring up. Thither came Earth carrying him swiftly through the black night to Lyctus first, and took him in her arms and hid him in a remote cave beneath the secret places of the holy earth on thick-wooded Mount Aegeum[12]; but to the mightily ruling son of Heaven, the earlier king of the gods, she gave a great stone wrapped in swaddling clothes. Then he took it in his hands and thrust it down into his belly: wretch! He knew not in his heart that in place of the

---

① Her gods and men call Aphrodite: Gods and men call her Aphrodite.

② Cytherea: /ˌsɪθəˈriːə/

③ Cyprogenes /ˌsaɪprəˈdʒiːniːz/: 该词在希腊语中的意思是"诞生于塞浦路斯的"。

④ Philommedes /ˌfɪləˈmiːdiːz/: 该词在希腊语中的意思是"爱笑的"。"爱笑的"(laughter-loving)是 Aphrodite 称号之一。

⑤ Hestia /ˈhestɪə/: 参见 The Age of Fable 第 1 章关于 Vesta 的叙述。

⑥ Demeter /dɪˈmiːtə/: 参见 The Age of Fable 第 1 章关于 Ceres 的叙述。

⑦ gold-shod: 穿金鞋的

⑧ Earth-Shaker: 即海神 Poseidon。

⑨ These great Cronos swallowed: Great Cronos swallowed these.

⑩ retribution /ˌretrɪˈbjuːʃn/: 报复,惩罚

⑪ Lyctus /ˈlɪktəs/: 又叫 Lyttos,古代克里特岛最重要的城市之一。

⑫ Mount Aegeum /ˈiːdʒɪəm/: 即位于克里特岛的 Ida 山;参见 The Age of Fable 第 5 章关于 Ida 的注释。

stone his son was left behind, unconquered and untroubled, and that he was soon to overcome him by force and might and drive him from his honours, himself to reign over the deathless gods.

After that, the strength and glorious limbs of the prince increased quickly, and as the years rolled on, great Cronos the wily was beguiled by the deep suggestions of Earth, and brought up again his offspring, vanquished by the arts and might of his own son, and he vomited up first the stone which he had swallowed last. And Zeus set it fast in the wide-pathed earth at goodly Pytho① under the glens of Parnassus, to be a sign thenceforth and a marvel to mortal men. And he set free from their deadly bonds the brothers of his father, sons of Heaven whom his father in his foolishness had bound. And they remembered to be grateful to him for his kindness, and gave him thunder and the glowing thunderbolt and lightening: for before that, huge Earth had hidden these. In them he trusts and rules over mortals and immortals.

The Defeat of Cronos by Zeus

But when first their father② was vexed in his heart with Obriareus and Cottus and Gyes, he bound them in cruel bonds, because he was jealous of their exceeding manhood③ and comeliness and great size: and he made them live beneath the wide-pathed earth, where they were afflicted④, being set to dwell under the ground, at the end of the earth, at its great borders, in bitter anguish for a long time and with great grief at heart. But the son of Cronos⑤ and the other deathless gods whom rich-haired Rhea bare from union with Cronos, brought them up again to the light at Earth's advising. For she herself recounted all things to the gods fully, how that with these⑥ they would gain victory and a glorious cause to vaunt themselves. For the Titan gods⑦ and as many as sprang from Cronos⑧ had long been fighting together in stubborn war with heart-grieving toil, the lordly Titans from high Othrys⑨, but the gods, givers of good, whom rich-haired Rhea bare in union with Cronos, from Olympus. So they, with bitter wrath, were fighting continually with one another at that time for ten full years, and the hard strife had no close or end for either side, and the issue of the war hung evenly⑩ balanced. But when he⑪ had provided those three with all things fitting, nectar and ambrosia which the gods themselves eat, and when their proud spirit revived within them all after they had fed on nectar and delicious ambrosia, then it was that the father of men and gods spoke⑫ amongst them:

---

① Pytho /ˈpaɪθə/: 即 Delphi
② their father: Heaven
③ manhood /ˈmænhʊd/: 勇气
④ afflict /əˈflɪkt/: 折磨,是苦恼
⑤ the son of Cronos: Zeus
⑥ these: Obriareus, Cottus, and Gyes
⑦ the Titan gods: Cronos and the Titans
⑧ as many as sprang from Cronos: the numerous offsprings of Cronos
⑨ Othrys /ˈəʊθrɪs/: 希腊山名,位于 Thessaly 南部。
⑩ evenly /ˈiːvənli/: 对等地,均等地
⑪ he: Zeus
⑫ the father of men and gods: Zeus

"Hear me, bright children of Earth and Heaven, that I may say what my heart within me bids. A long while now have we, who are sprung from Cronos and the Titan gods, fought with each other every day to get victory and to prevail. But do you show your great might and unconquerable strength, and face the Titans in bitter strife; for remember our friendly kindness, and from what sufferings you are come back to the light from your cruel bondage under misty gloom through our counsels."

So he said. And blameless Cottus answered him again: "Divine one, you speak that which we know well: nay, even of ourselves we know that your wisdom and understanding is exceeding, and that you became a defender of the deathless ones from chill doom. And through your devising we are come back again from the murky gloom and from our merciless bonds, enjoying what we looked not for, O lord, son of Cronos. And so now with fixed purpose and deliberate counsel we will aid your power in dreadful strife and will fight against the Titans in hard battle."

So he said: and the gods, givers of good things, applauded when they heard his word, and their spirit longed for war even more than before, and they all, both male and female, stirred up hated battle that day, the Titan gods, and all that were born of Cronos together with those dread, mighty ones of overwhelming strength whom Zeus brought up to the light from Erebus beneath the earth. An hundred arms sprang from the shoulders of all alike, and each had fifty heads growing upon his shoulders upon stout limbs. These, then, stood against the Titans in grim strife, holding huge rocks in their strong hands. And on the other part the Titans eagerly strengthened their ranks, and both sides at one time showed the work of their hands and their might. The boundless sea rang terribly around, and the earth crashed loudly: wide Heaven was shaken and groaned, and high Olympus reeled from its foundation under the charge of the undying gods, and a heavy quaking reached dim Tartarus and the deep sound of their feet in the fearful onset and of their hard missiles. So, then, they launched their grievous shafts upon one another, and the cry of both armies as they shouted reached to starry heaven; and they met together with a great battle-cry.

Then Zeus no longer held back his might; but straight his heart was filled with fury and he showed forth all his strength. From Heaven and from Olympus he came forthwith, hurling his lightning: the bolts flew thick and fast from his strong hand together with thunder and lightning, whirling an awesome flame. The life-giving earth crashed around in burning, and the vast wood crackled loud with fire all about. All the land seethed①, and Ocean's streams and the unfruitful sea. The hot vapour lapped round the earthborn Titans: flame unspeakable rose to the bright upper air; the flashing glare of the thunder-stone and lightning blinded their eyes for all that there were strong. Astounding heat seized Chaos: and to see with eyes and to hear the sound with ears it seemed even as if Earth and wide Heaven above came together; for such a mighty crash would have arisen if Earth were being hurled to ruin, and Heaven from on high were hurling her down; so great a crash was there while the gods were meeting together in strife. Also the winds brought

---

① seethe /siːð/: 沸腾

rumbling earthquake and duststorm①, thunder and lightning and the lurid② thunderbolt, which are the shafts of great Zeus, and carried the clangour③ and the warcry into the midst of the two hosts. An horrible uproar of terrible strife arose: mighty deeds were shown and the battle inclined. But until then, they kept at one another and fought continually in cruel war.

And amongst the foremost Cottus and Briareos and Gyes insatiate④ for war raised fierce fighting: three hundred rocks, one upon another, they launched from their strong hands and overshadowed the Titans with their missiles, and buried them beneath the wide-pathed earth, and bound them in bitter chains when they had conquered them by their strength for all their great spirit, as far beneath the earth to Tartarus. For a brazen anvil falling down from heaven nine nights and days would reach the earth upon the tenth: and again, a brazen anvil falling from earth nine nights and days would reach Tartarus upon the tenth. Round it runs a fence of bronze, and night spreads in triple line all about it like a neck-circlet, while above grow the roots of the earth and unfruitful sea. There by the counsel of Zeus who drives the clouds the Titan gods are hidden under misty gloom, in a dank⑤ place where are the ends of the huge earth. And they may not go out; for Poseidon fixed gates of bronze upon it, and a wall runs all round it on every side. There Gyes and Cottus and great-souled Obriareus live, trusty warders⑥ of Zeus who holds the aegis.

---

① duststorm /ˈdʌststɔːm/：沙尘暴

② lurid /ˈljuərɪd/：闪着红光的

③ clangour /ˈklæŋɡə/：铿锵声

④ insatiate /ɪnˈseɪʃɪət/：永不满足的

⑤ dank /dæŋk/：潮湿而寒冷的

⑥ warder /ˈwɔːdə/：卫兵，哨兵

Apollonius

(c.295 B.C.—215 B.C.)

　　阿波罗尼奥斯（Apollonius /ˌæpəˈləʊnɪəs /）是古希腊诗人、文法学家。阿波罗尼奥斯出生于亚历山大（Alexandria），曾当过亚历山大图书馆的馆长，后移居罗德岛（Rhodes），所以被称为"罗德岛的阿波罗尼奥斯"（Apollonius Rhodius）。阿波罗尼奥斯的主要作品是史诗《阿尔戈船英雄纪》（*Argonautica*）。

　　《阿尔戈船英雄纪》共 4 卷，讲述希腊英雄们乘坐阿尔戈船寻找金羊毛的故事。这部史诗的非凡之处在其心理描写和对爱情的描写。本读本从《阿尔戈船英雄纪》选取了 5 个片段：第 1 选段"Phineus and the Harpies"和第 2 个选段"The Symplegades"选自史诗的第 2 卷，第 3 个选段"Medea's Love for Jason"、第 4 个选段"Interview of Jason and Medea"和第 5 个选段"The Contest"选自史诗的第 3 卷。

Argonautica

Translated into English by R. C. Seaton

Phineus and the Harpies

　　There Phineus①, son of Agenor, had his home by the sea, Phineus who above all men endured most bitter woes because of the gift of prophecy which Leto's son② had granted him aforetime③. And he reverenced④ not a whit⑤ even Zeus himself, for he foretold unerringly⑥ to men

---

① Phineus：/ˈfɪnjuːs/

② Leto's son：Apollo；Leto is the Greek name of Latona.

③ aforetime /əˈfɔːtaɪm/：之前，早先

④ reverence /ˈrevərəns/：尊敬

⑤ not a whit：一点都不

⑥ unerringly /ʌnˈɜːrɪŋli/：准确地，不会出错地

his① sacred will. Wherefore② Zeus sent upon him a lingering③ old age, and took from his eyes the pleasant light, and suffered④ him not to have joy of the dainties⑤ untold⑥ that the dwellers around ever brought to his house, when they came to enquire the will of heaven. But on a sudden, swooping through the clouds, the Harpies⑦ with their crooked beaks incessantly snatched the food away from his mouth and hands. And at times not a morsel of food was left, at others but a little, in order that he might live and be tormented. And they poured forth over all a loathsome stench⑧; and no one dared not merely to carry food to his mouth but even to stand at a distance; so foully reeked⑨ the remnants of the meal. But straightway when he heard the voice and the tramp⑩ of the band⑪ he knew that they were the men passing by, at whose coming Zeus' oracle had declared to him that he should have joy of his food. And he rose from his couch, like a lifeless dream, bowed over his staff, and crept to the door on his withered feet, feeling the walls; and as he moved, his limbs trembled for weakness and age; and his parched⑫ skin was caked⑬ with dirt, and naught but the skin held his bones together. And he came forth from the hall with wearied knees and sat on the threshold of the courtyard; and a dark stupor⑭ covered him, and it seemed that the earth reeled⑮ round beneath his feet, and he lay in a strengthless trance⑯, speechless. But when they⑰ saw him they gathered round and marvelled. And he at last drew laboured breath from the depths of his chest and spoke among them with prophetic utterance:

"Listen, bravest of all the Hellenes⑱, if it be truly ye, whom by a king's ruthless command⑲ Jason⑳ is leading on the ship Argo㉑ in quest of the fleece㉒. It is ye truly. Even yet my soul by its divination㉓ knows everything. Thanks I render to thee, O king, son of Leto, plunged in

---

① his：Zeus'

② wherefore：因此

③ lingering /ˈlɪŋɡərɪŋ/：漫长的,拖延的

④ suffer：允许

⑤ dainty /ˈdeɪnti/：美味佳肴

⑥ untold：数不清的,无数的

⑦ Harpies /ˈhɑːpɪz/：参见 *The Age of Fable* 第 31 章。

⑧ stench /stentʃ/：臭味

⑨ reek：发出臭味

⑩ tramp：脚步声

⑪ the band：the Argonauts

⑫ parched /pɑːtʃt/：干裂的

⑬ cake：(被一层变硬的东西)覆盖

⑭ stupor /ˈstjuːpə/：恍惚,麻木

⑮ reel：旋转

⑯ trance /trɑːns/：半睡半醒的状态

⑰ they：the Argonauts

⑱ Hellene /ˈheliːn/：希腊人

⑲ This king is Pelias, uncle of Jason.

⑳ Jason /ˈdʒeɪsn/：参见 *The Age of Fable* 第 17 章。

㉑ Argo：/ˈɑːɡəʊ/

㉒ the fleece：the Golden Fleece

㉓ divination /ˌdɪvɪˈneɪʃn/：占卜,预言,预测

bitter affliction though I be. I beseech you by Zeus the god of suppliants, the sternest foe to sinful men, and for the sake of Phoebus and Hera herself, under whose especial care ye have come hither, help me, save an ill-fated① man from misery, and depart not uncaring and leaving me thus as ye see. For not only has the Fury set her foot on my eyes and I drag on to the end a weary old age; but besides my other woes a woe hangs over me—the bitterest of all. The Harpies, swooping down from some unseen den② of destruction, ever③ snatch the food from my mouth. And I have no device to aid me. But it were easier, when I long for a meal, to escape my own thoughts than them, so swiftly do they fly through the air. But if haply they do leave me a morsel of food it reeks of decay and the stench is unendurable④, nor could any mortal bear to draw near even for a moment, no, not if his heart were wrought of adamant⑤. But necessity, bitter and insatiate⑥, compels me to abide and abiding to put food in my cursed belly. These pests⑦, the oracle declares, the sons of Boreas⑧ shall restrain. And no strangers are they that shall ward them off if indeed I am Phineus who was once renowned among men for wealth and the gift of prophecy, and if I am the son of my father Agenor; and, when I ruled among the Thracians, by my bridal gifts I brought home their sister Cleopatra⑨ to be my wife."

So spake⑩ Agenor's son; and deep sorrow seized each of the heroes, and especially the two sons of Boreas. And brushing away a tear they drew nigh, and Zetes spake as follows, taking in his own⑪ the hand of the grief-worn⑫ sire⑬:

"Unhappy one, none other of men is more wretched than thou, methinks. Why upon thee is laid the burden of so many sorrows? Hast thou with baneful⑭ folly sinned against the gods through thy skill in prophecy? For this are they greatly wroth⑮ with thee? Yet our spirit is dismayed within us for all our desire to aid thee, if indeed the god has granted this privilege to us two. For plain to discern to men of earth are the reproofs of the immortals. And we will never check the Harpies when they come, for all our desire, until thou hast sworn that for this we shall not lose the favour of heaven."

Thus he spake; and towards him the aged sire opened his sightless eyes, and lifted them up

---

① ill-fated：命不好的

② den：动物的巢穴

③ ever：总是

④ unendurable /ˌʌnɪnˈdjuərəbl/：不可忍受的

⑤ adamant /ˈædəmənt/：（金刚石等）硬石，坚硬无比的物质

⑥ insatiate /ɪnˈseɪʃɪət/：不能满足的，难以满足的

⑦ These pests：the Harpies

⑧ the sons of Boreas：Zetes /ˈziːtiːz/ and Calais /kəˈleɪɪs/, twin sons of Boreas, the North Wind, and Orithyia.

⑨ Cleopatra /klɪəˈpɑːtrə/：The daughter of Boreas and Orithyia, and therefore the sister of Zetes and Calais. This Cleopatra is not the famous queen of Egypt.

⑩ spake：spoke

⑪ his own：his own hand

⑫ grief-worn：悲痛欲绝的

⑬ sire：老人，长者

⑭ baneful：有害的

⑮ wroth /rəʊθ/：生气的

and replied with these words:

"Be silent, store not up such thoughts in thy heart, my child. Let the son of Leto be my witness, he who of his gracious will taught me the lore of prophecy, and be witness the ill-starred doom which possesses me and this dark cloud upon my eyes, and the gods of the underworld—and may their curse be upon me if I die perjured thus—no wrath from heaven will fall upon you two for your help to me."

Then were those two eager to help him because of the oath. And quickly the younger heroes prepared a feast for the aged man, a last prey for the Harpies; and both stood near him, to smite with the sword those pests when they swooped down. Scarcely had the aged man touched the food when they forthwith①, like bitter blasts or flashes of lightning, suddenly darted from the clouds, and swooped down with a yell, fiercely craving for food; and the heroes beheld them and shouted in the midst of their onrush②; but they at the cry devoured everything and sped away over the sea after; and an intolerable stench remained. And behind them the two sons of Boreas raising their swords rushed in pursuit. For Zeus imparted to them tireless strength; but without Zeus they could not have followed, for the Harpies used ever to outstrip③ the blasts of the west wind when they came to Phineus and when they left him. And as when, upon the mountain-side, hounds, cunning in the chase, run in the track of horned goats or deer, and as they strain a little behind gnash their teeth upon the edge of their jaws in vain; so Zetes and Calais rushing very near just grazed the Harpies in vain with their finger-tips. And assuredly they would have torn them to pieces, despite heaven's will, when they had overtaken them far off at the Floating Islands, had not swift Iris seen them and leapt down from the sky from heaven above, and cheeked④ them with these words:

"It is not lawful, O sons of Boreas, to strike with your swords the Harpies, the hounds of mighty Zeus; but I myself will give you a pledge, that hereafter⑤ they shall not draw near to Phineus."

With these words she took an oath by the waters of Styx, which to all the gods is most dread and most awful, that the Harpies would never thereafter again approach the home of Phineus, son of Agenor, for so it was fated. And the heroes yielding to the oath, turned back their flight to the ship. And on account of this men call them the Islands of Turning though aforetime they called them the Floating Islands. And the Harpies and Iris parted. They entered their den in Minoan Crete⑥; but she sped up to Olympus, soaring aloft on her swift wings.

The Symplegades

So the tale is told, but the chieftains⑦ stayed there by constraint, and every day the

---

① forthwith: 立刻,马上

② onrush /ˈɒnrʌʃ/: 袭击,攻击

③ outstrip /aʊtˈstrɪp/: 超于,超过

④ cheek: 无礼地对……说话

⑤ hereafter /hɪərˈɑːftə/: 从今以后

⑥ Minoan /mɪˈnəʊən/ Crete: Crete of King Minos

⑦ the chieftains: the Argonauts

Thynians①, doing pleasure to Phineus, sent them gifts beyond measure. And afterwards they raised an altar to the blessed twelve② on the sea-beach opposite and laid offerings thereon and then entered their swift ship to row, nor did they forget to bear with them a trembling dove; but Euphemus③ seized her and brought her all quivering with fear, and they loosed the twin hawsers④ from the land.

Nor did they start unmarked⑤ by Athena, but straightway swiftly she set her feet on a light cloud, which would waft her on, mighty though she was, and she swept on to the sea with friendly thoughts to the oarsmen. And as when one roveth⑥ far from his native land, as we men often wander with enduring heart, nor is any land too distant but all ways are clear to his view, and he sees in mind his own home, and at once the way over sea and land seems plain, and swiftly thinking, now this way, now that, he strains with eager eyes; so swiftly the daughter of Zeus⑦ darted down and set her foot on the cheerless shore of Thynia.

Now when they reached the narrow strait of the winding passage, hemmed in on both sides by rugged cliffs, while an eddying current from below was washing against the ship as she⑧ moved on, they went forward sorely in dread; and now the thud⑨ of the crashing rocks⑩ ceaselessly struck their ears, and the sea-washed shores resounded, and then Euphemus grasped the dove in his hand and started to mount the prow⑪; and they, at the bidding of Tiphys⑫, son of Hagnias⑬, rowed with good will to drive Argo between the rocks, trusting to their strength. And as they rounded a bend they saw the rocks opening for the last time of all. Their spirit melted within them; and Euphemus sent forth the dove to dart forward in flight; and they all together raised their heads to look; but she flew between them, and the rocks again rushed together and crashed as they met face to face. And the foam leapt up in a mass like a cloud; awful was the thunder of the sea; and all round them the mighty welkin⑭ roared.

The hollow caves beneath the rugged cliffs rumbled⑮ as the sea came surging in; and the white foam of the dashing wave spurted⑯ high above the cliff. Next the current whirled the ship

---

① the Thynians /'θaɪnɪənz/: inhabitants of Thynia /'θaɪnɪə /, an ancient district along the north coast of the Sea of Marmara

② the blessed twelve: 参见 *The Age of Fable* 第 14 章关于 Twelve of the heavenly powers 的注释。

③ Euphemus: /juː'fiːməs/

④ hawser /'hɔːzə/: 锚索

⑤ unmarked /ʌn'mɑːkt/: 不受关注的

⑥ roveth: roves

⑦ the daughter of Zeus: Athena

⑧ she: the ship Argo

⑨ thud /θʌd/: 物体撞击时发出的砰砰的声音

⑩ the crashing rocks: the Symplegades /sɪm'plegədiːz/

⑪ prow: 船头

⑫ Tiphys: /'tɪfɪs/

⑬ Hagnias: /'hægnɪəs/

⑭ welkin /'welkɪn/: 天空, 苍穹

⑮ rumble /'rʌmbl/: 发出轰隆声

⑯ spurt /spɜːt/: 喷射

round. And the rocks shore① away the end of the dove's tail-feathers; but away she flew unscathed②. And the rowers gave a loud cry; and Tiphys himself called to them to row with might and main③. For the rocks were again parting asunder. But as they rowed they trembled, until the tide returning drove them back within the rocks. Then most awful fear seized upon all; for over their head was destruction without escape. And now to right and left broad Pontus④ was seen, when suddenly a huge wave rose up before them, arched, like a steep rock; and at the sight they bowed with bended heads. For it seemed about to leap down upon the ship's whole length and to overwhelm⑤ them. But Tiphys was quick to ease the ship as she laboured with the oars; and in all its mass the wave rolled away beneath the keel, and at the stern⑥ it raised Argo herself and drew her far away from the rocks; and high in air was she borne. But Euphemus strode among all his comrades and cried to them to bend to their oars with all their might; and they with a shout smote the water. And as far as the ship yielded to the rowers, twice as far did she leap back, and the oars were bent like curved bows as the heroes used their strength.

Then a vaulted billow rushed upon them, and the ship like a cylinder⑦ ran on the furious wave plunging through the hollow sea. And the eddying current held her between the clashing rocks; and on each side they shook and thundered; and the ship's timbers were held fast. Then Athena with her left hand thrust back one mighty rock and with her right pushed the ship through; and she, like a winged arrow, sped through the air. Nevertheless the rocks, ceaselessly clashing, shore off as she passed the extreme end of the stern-ornament. But Athena soared up to Olympus, when they had escaped unscathed. And the rocks in one spot at that moment were rooted fast for ever to each other, which thing had been destined by the blessed gods, when a man in his ship should have passed between them alive. And the heroes breathed again after their chilling fear, beholding at the same time the sky and the expanse of sea spreading far and wide. For they deemed that they were saved from Hades; and Tiphys first of all began to speak:

"It is my hope that we have safely escaped this peril—we, and the ship; and none other is the cause so much as Athena, who breathed into Argo divine strength when Argus⑧ knitted her together with bolts; and she may not be caught. Son of Aeson⑨, no longer fear thou so much the hest⑩ of thy king, since a god hath granted us escape between the rocks; for Phineus, Agenor's son, said that our toils hereafter would be lightly accomplished."

He spake, and at once he sped the ship onward through the midst of the sea past the

---

① shore /ʃɔː/: shear 的过去式形式; shear /ʃɪə/: (用刀、剑等锋利武器)砍断,切断,斩断
② unscathed /ʌnˈskeɪðd/: 未受伤害的
③ with might and main: 竭尽全力地; main: 力量,体力
④ Pontus /ˈpɒntəs/: 古代小亚细亚北部地区名,临黑海。
⑤ overwhelm /ˌəʊvəˈwelm/: 打翻,掀翻
⑥ stern /stɜːn/: 船尾
⑦ cylinder /ˈsɪlɪndə/: 圆筒
⑧ Argus: Argo 的建造者
⑨ Son of Aeson: Jason
⑩ hest /hest/: 命令

Bithynian coast①. But Jason with gentle words addressed him in reply: "Tiphys, why dost thou comfort thus my grieving heart? I have erred and am distraught② in wretched and helpless ruin. For I ought, when Pelias③ gave the command, to have straightway refused this quest to his face, yea, though I were doomed to die pitilessly, torn limb from limb, but now I am wrapped in excessive fear and cares unbearable, dreading to sail through the chilling paths of the sea, and dreading when we shall set foot on the mainland. For on every side are unkindly④ men. And ever when day is done I pass a night of groans from the time when ye first gathered together for my sake, while I take thought for all things; but thou talkest at thine ease, eating only for thine own life; while for myself I am dismayed not a whit; but I fear for this man and for that equally, and for thee, and for my other comrades, if I shall not bring you back safe to the land of Hellas⑤."

Thus he spake, making trial of the chiefs; but they shouted loud with cheerful words. And his heart was warmed within him at their cry and again he spake outright⑥ among them:

"My friends, in your valour my courage is quickened. Wherefore now, even though I should take my way through the gulfs of Hades, no more shall I let fear seize upon me, since ye are steadfast⑦ amid cruel terrors. But now that we have sailed out from the striking rocks⑧, I trow⑨ that never hereafter will there be another such fearful thing, if indeed we go on our way following the counsel of Phineus."

Medea's Love for Jason

He⑩ spake outright; and Jason rose from his seat, and Augeias⑪ and Telamon⑫ at once; and Argus followed alone, for he signed⑬ to his brothers⑭ to stay there on the spot meantime; and so they went forth from the hall. And wonderfully among them all shone the son of Aeson for beauty and grace; and the maiden⑮ looked at him with stealthy glance, holding her bright veil aside, her heart smouldering with pain; and her soul creeping like a dream flitted in his track as he went. So they passed forth from the palace sorely troubled. And Chalciope⑯, shielding herself from the

---

① Bithynia /bɪˈθaɪnɪə/: 位于小亚细亚西北部,临马尔马拉海、博斯普鲁斯海峡、黑海,与 Thynia 隔海相望。

② distraught /dɪˈstrɔːt/: 心烦意乱的,非常烦恼的

③ Pelias: king of Iolcus /ˈaɪəlkəs/ in Thessaly and uncle of Jason

④ unkindly: 坏的,邪恶的

⑤ Hellas /ˈhelæs/: Greece

⑥ outright /ˈaʊtraɪt/: 立刻,马上

⑦ steadfast /ˈstedfɑːst/: 坚强的,坚定不移的

⑧ the striking rocks: the Symplegades

⑨ trow: 确信

⑩ He: Aeetes, king of Colchis

⑪ Augeias: /ɔːˈdʒiːɪəs/

⑫ Telamon: /ˈteləmən/

⑬ sign: 打手势

⑭ his brothers: 参见下面关于 Chalciope 的注释。

⑮ the maiden: Medea

⑯ Chalciope /ˌkælsɪˈəʊpɪ/: daughter of Aeetes, sister of Medea, and mother of Argus, Phrontis, Melas, and Cytissorus, the Argonauts

wrath of Aeetes, had gone quickly to her chamber with her sons. And Medea likewise followed, and much she brooded in her soul all the cares that the Loves awaken. And before her eyes the vision still appeared—himself what like he was, with what vesture① he was clad, what things he spake, how he sat on his seat, how he moved forth to the door—and as she pondered she deemed there never was such another man; and ever in her ears rung his voice and the honey-sweet words which he uttered. And she feared for him, lest the oxen or Aeetes with his own hand should slay him; and she mourned him as though already slain outright, and in her affliction② a round tear through very grievous pity coursed down her cheek; and gently weeping she lifted up her voice aloud:

"Why does this grief come upon me, poor wretch? Whether he be the best of heroes now about to perish, or the worst, let him go to his doom. Yet I would that he had escaped unharmed; yea, may this be so, revered③ goddess, daughter of Perses④, may he avoid death and return home; but if it be his lot to be o'ermastered⑤ by the oxen, may he first learn this, that I at least do not rejoice in his cruel calamity."

Interview of Jason and Medea

So she⑥ spake, and the crafty counsel pleased them⑦ all. And straightway Argus drew Aeson's son apart from his comrades as soon as he heard from his brothers that Medea had gone at daybreak to the holy shrine of Hecate, and led him over the plain; and with them went Mopsus⑧, son of Ampycus⑨, skilled to utter oracles from the appearance of birds⑩, and skilled to give good counsel to those who set out on a journey.

Never yet had there been such a man in the days of old, neither of all the heroes of the lineage of Zeus himself, nor of those who sprung from the blood of the other gods, as on that day the bride of Zeus⑪ made Jason, both to look upon and to hold converse⑫ with. Even his comrades wondered as they gazed upon him, radiant with manifold graces; and the son of Ampycus rejoiced in their journey, already foreboding how all would end.

Now by the path along the plain there stands near the shrine a poplar⑬ with its crown⑭ of

---

① vesture /ˈvestʃə/：衣服

② affliction：苦恼，折磨

③ revere /rɪˈvɪə/：尊敬，崇敬，敬畏

④ daughter of Perses：Hecate

⑤ overmaster /ˌəʊvəˈmɑːstə/：制伏，压倒

⑥ she：Medea

⑦ them：Medea's maidens

⑧ Mopsus：/ˈmɒpsəs/

⑨ Ampycus：/ˈæmpɪkəs/

⑩ utter oracles from the appearance of birds：通过鸟儿的外表来解读神谕；在古希腊和古罗马，通过观察鸟儿的飞行姿态和聆听鸟儿的鸣叫声音来进行占卜是非常常见的做法。

⑪ the bride of Zeus：Hera

⑫ converse /ˈkɒnvɜːs/：交流，对话

⑬ poplar /ˈpɒplə/：杨树

⑭ crown：树顶

countless leaves, whereon often chattering crows would roost①. One of them meantime as she clapped her wings aloft in the branches uttered the counsels of Hera:

"What a pitiful seer② is this, that has not the wit to conceive even what children know, how that no maiden will say a word of sweetness or love to a youth when strangers be near. Begone, sorry prophet, witless③ one; on thee neither Cypris④ nor the gentle Loves breathe in their kindness."

She spake chiding, and Mopsus smiled to hear the god-sent voice of the bird, and thus addressed them: "Do thou, son of Aeson, pass on to the temple, where thou wilt find the maiden⑤; and very kind will her greeting be to thee through the prompting⑥ of Cypris, who will be thy helpmate in the contest, even as Phineus, Agenor's son, foretold. But we two, Argus and I, will await thy return, apart in this very spot; do thou all alone be a suppliant and win her over with prudent words."

He spake wisely, and both at once gave approval. Nor was Medea's heart turned to other thoughts, for all her singing, and never a song that she essayed pleased her long in her sport. But in confusion she ever faltered, nor did she keep her eyes resting quietly upon the throng of her handmaids; but to the paths far off she strained her gaze, turning her face aside. Oft⑦ did her heart sink fainting within her bosom whenever she fancied she heard passing by the sound of a footfall or of the wind. But soon he appeared to her longing eyes, striding along loftily, like Sirius⑧ coming from ocean, which rises fair and clear to see, but brings unspeakable mischief to flocks; thus then did Aeson's son come to her, fair to see, but the sight of him brought love-sick care. Her heart fell from out her bosom, and a dark mist came over her eyes, and a hot blush covered her cheeks. And she had no strength to lift her knees backwards or forwards, but her feet beneath were rooted to the ground; and meantime all her handmaidens had drawn aside. So they two stood face to face without a word, without a sound, like oaks or lofty pines, which stand quietly side by side on the mountains when the wind is still; then again, when stirred by the breath of the wind, they murmur ceaselessly; so they two were destined to tell out all their tale, stirred by the breath of Love. And Aeson's son saw that she had fallen into some heaven-sent calamity, and with soothing words thus addressed her:

"Why, pray⑨, maiden, dost thou fear me so much, all alone as I am? Never was I one of these idle boasters⑩ such as other men are—not even aforetime, when I dwelt in my own country.

---

① roost：（鸟）栖息

② seer /sɪə/：预言者

③ witless /'wɪtləs/：没有智慧的,愚蠢的

④ Cypris /'saɪprɪs/：Aphrodite, worshipped in Cyprus

⑤ the maiden：Medea

⑥ prompting：敦促

⑦ oft：often

⑧ Sirius /'sɪrɪəs/：天狼星,七八月出现,夜空中最明亮的星星。天狼星出现的时间是北半球最酷热的季节。在酷热的季节里,无论是人还是牲畜都感到难受,所以接下来才会说 but brings unspeakable mischief to flocks。

⑨ pray：请问

⑩ boaster /'bəʊstə/：自夸之人,夸夸其谈者,危险之人

Wherefore, maiden, be not too much abashed[①] before me, either to enquire whatever thou wilt or to speak thy mind. But since we have met one another with friendly hearts, in a hallowed[②] spot, where it is wrong to sin, speak openly and ask questions, and beguile me not with pleasing words, for at the first thou didst promise thy sister[③] to give me the charms[④] my heart desires. I implore thee by Hecate herself, by thy parents, and by Zeus who holds his guardian hand over strangers and suppliants; I come here to thee both a suppliant and a stranger, bending the knee in my sore need. For without thee and thy sister never shall I prevail in the grievous contest. And to thee will I render thanks hereafter for thy aid, as is right and fitting for men who dwell far off, making glorious thy name and fame; and the rest of the heroes, returning to Hellas, will spread thy renown and so will the heroes' wives and mothers, who now perhaps are sitting on the shore and making moan for us; their painful affliction thou mightest scatter to the winds. In days past the maiden Ariadne[⑤], daughter of Minos, with kindly intent rescued Theseus from grim contests—the maiden whom Pasiphae[⑥] daughter of Helios bare. But she, when Minos had lulled his wrath to rest, went aboard the ship with him and left her fatherland; and her even the immortal gods loved, and, as a sign in mid-sky, a crown of stars, which men call Ariadne's crown[⑦], rolls along all night among the heavenly constellations. So to thee too shall be thanks from the gods, if thou wilt save so mighty an array of chieftains. For surely from thy lovely form thou art like[⑧] to excel in gentle courtesy."

Thus he spake, honouring her; and she cast her eyes down with a smile divinely sweet; and her soul melted within her, uplifted by his praise, and she gazed upon him face to face; nor did she know what word to utter first, but was eager to pour out everything at once. And forth from her fragrant girdle ungrudgingly[⑨] she brought out the charm; and he at once received it in his hands with joy. And she would even have drawn out all her soul from her breast and given it to him, exulting in his desire; so wonderfully did love flash forth a sweet flame from the golden head of Aeson's son; and he captivated her gleaming eyes; and her heart within grew warm, melting away as the dew melts away round roses when warmed by the morning's light. And now both were fixing their eyes on the ground abashed, and again were throwing glances at each other, smiling with the light of love beneath their radiant brows. And at last and scarcely then did the maiden greet him:

"Take heed now, that I may devise help for thee. When at thy coming my father has given thee the deadly teeth from the dragon's jaws for sowing, then watch for the time when the night is parted in twain, then bathe in the stream of the tireless[⑩] river, and alone, apart from others, clad

---

① abashed /əˈbæʃt/：不安的，害臊的

② hallowed /ˈhæləʊd/：神圣的

③ thy sister：Chalciope

④ charm：符咒

⑤ Ariadne：参见 *The Age of Fable* 第 20 章。

⑥ Pasiphae：/pəˈsɪfeɪiː/

⑦ Ariadne's crown：参见 *The Age of Fable* 第 21 章 Ariadne 的故事。

⑧ like：likely

⑨ ungrudgingly /ʌnˈɡrʌdʒɪŋli/：慷慨地，自愿地

⑩ tireless /ˈtaɪələs/：不会疲倦的

in dusky raiment, dig a rounded① pit; and therein slay a ewe, and sacrifice it whole, heaping high the pyre on the very edge of the pit. And propitiate only-begotten Hecate, daughter of Perses②, pouring from a goblet the hive-stored labour of bees③. And then, when thou hast heedfully sought the grace④ of the goddess, retreat from the pyre; and let neither the sound of feet drive thee to turn back, nor the baying⑤ of hounds, lest haply thou shouldst maim⑥ all the rites and thyself fail to return duly⑦ to thy comrades. And at dawn steep⑧ this charm in water, strip⑨, and anoint thy body therewith as with oil; and in it there will be boundless prowess and mighty strength, and thou wilt deem thyself a match not for men but for the immortal gods. And besides, let thy spear and shield and sword be sprinkled. Thereupon the spear-heads of the earthborn men shall not pierce thee, nor the flame of the deadly bulls as it rushes forth resistless. But such thou shalt be not for long, but for that one day; still never flinch⑩ from the contest. And I will tell thee besides of yet another help. As soon as thou hast yoked the strong oxen, and with thy might and thy prowess hast ploughed all the stubborn⑪ fallow⑫, and now along the furrows the Giants are springing up, when the serpent's teeth are sown on the dusky clods, if thou markest them uprising in throngs from the fallow, cast unseen among them a massy stone; and they over it, like ravening⑬ hounds over their food, will slay one another; and do thou thyself hasten to rush to the battle-strife, and the fleece thereupon thou shalt bear far away from Aea⑭; nevertheless, depart wherever thou wilt, or thy pleasure takes thee, when thou hast gone hence."

Thus she spake, and cast her eyes to her feet in silence, and her cheek, divinely fair, was wet with warm tears as she sorrowed for that he was about to wander far from her side over the wide sea: and once again she addressed him face to face with mournful words, and took his right hand; for now shame had left her eyes:

"Remember, if haply thou returnest to thy home, Medea's name; and so will I remember thine, though thou be far away. And of thy kindness tell me this, where is thy home, whither wilt thou sail hence in thy ship over the sea; wilt thou come near wealthy Orchomenus⑮, or near the

---

① rounded /ˈraʊndɪd/：圆形的
② only-begotten Hecate, daughter of Perses：Hecate, Perses 的独生女；only-begotten /ˈəʊnlɪbɪˈɡɒtən/：(子女)独生的
③ the hive-stored labour of bees：honey
④ grace：恩惠
⑤ baying /ˈbeɪɪŋ/：(猎犬的)吠声
⑥ maim：伤害
⑦ duly /ˈdjuːli/：准时地，按时地
⑧ steep：把……浸泡在水中
⑨ strip：脱掉衣服
⑩ flinch：退缩
⑪ stubborn /ˈstʌbən/：难对付的，棘手的
⑫ fallow /ˈfæləʊ/：休耕地
⑬ raven /ˈrævən/：狼吞虎咽
⑭ Aea /ˈiːə/：Colchis 的一个地区
⑮ Orchomenus /ɔːˈkɒmɪnəs/：古希腊有几个城市叫这个名字，一个在 Boeotia，一个在 Arcadia，一个在 Thessaly。此处指 Boeotia 的 Orchomenus。

Aeaean isle①? And tell me of the maiden, whosoever she be that thou hast named, the far-renowned daughter of Pasiphae, who is kinswoman to my father.②"

Thus she spake; and over him too, at the tears of the maiden, stole Love the destroyer, and he thus answered her:

"All too surely do I deem that never by night and never by day will I forget thee if I escape death and indeed make my way in safety to the Achaean land③, and Aeetes set not before us some other contest worse than this. And if it pleases thee to know about my fatherland, I will tell it out; for indeed my own heart bids me do that. There is a land encircled by lofty mountains, rich in sheep and in pasture, where Prometheus, son of Iapetus, begat④ goodly Deucalion, who first founded cities and reared temples to the immortal gods, and first ruled over men. This land the neighbours who dwell around call Haemonia⑤. And in it stands Ioleus⑥, my city, and in it many others, where they have not so much as heard the name of the Aeaean isle; yet there is a story that Minyas⑦ starting thence, Minyas son of Aeolus, built long ago the city of Orchomenus that borders on the Cadmeians⑧. But why do I tell thee all this vain talk, of our home and of Minos' daughter, far-famed Ariadne, by which glorious name they called that lovely maiden of whom thou askest me? Would that, as Minos then was well inclined to Theseus for her sake, so may thy father be joined to us in friendship!"

Thus he spake, soothing her with gentle converse. But pangs most bitter stirred her heart and in grief did she address him with vehement words:

"In Hellas, I ween⑨, this is fair—to pay heed to covenants⑩; but Aeetes is not such a man among men as thou sayest was Pasiphae's husband, Minos; nor can I liken myself to Ariadne; wherefore speak not of guest-love. But only do thou, when thou hast reached Iolcus, remember me, and thee even in my parents' despite, will I remember. And from far off may a rumour come to me or some messenger-bird, when thou forgettest me; or me, even me, may swift blasts catch up and bear over the sea hence to Iolcus, that so I may cast reproaches in thy face and remind thee that it was by my good will thou didst escape. May I then be seated in thy halls, an unexpected guest!"

Thus she spake with piteous tears falling down her cheeks, and to her Jason replied: "Let the empty blasts wander at will, lady, and the messenger-bird, for vain is thy talk. But if thou comest to those abodes and to the land of Hellas, honoured and reverenced shalt thou be by women

①　the Aeaean isle: 参见 *The Age of Fable* 第 29 章关于 the Ææan isle 的注释。

②　Aeetes, Medea's father, is the son of Helios, and Pasiphae is the daughter of Helios.

③　the Achaean land: Greece

④　begat: begot

⑤　The neighbours who dwell around call this land Haemonia. Haemonia /hiːˈməʊnɪə/: Thessaly

⑥　Ioleus: /ˈaɪəlɪəs/

⑦　Minyas /ˈmɪnɪæs/: 传说中 Thessaly 的国王

⑧　the Cadmeians: the Thebans; 参见 *The Age of Fable* 第 12 章 Cadmus 建立 Thebes 的故事。

⑨　ween /wiːn/: 认为, 相信

⑩　covenant /ˈkʌvənənt/: 契约, 协议

and men; and they shall worship thee even as a goddess, for that by thy counsel their sons came home again, their brothers and kinsmen and stalwart① husbands were saved from calamity. And in our bridal chamber shalt thou prepare our couch; and nothing shall come between our love till the doom of death fold us round."

Thus he spake; and her soul melted within her to hear his words; nevertheless she shuddered to behold the deeds of destruction to come. Poor wretch! Not long was she destined to refuse a home in Hellas. For thus Hera devised it, that Aeaean Medea might come to Ioleus for a bane② to Pelias, forsaking her native land.

And now her handmaids, glancing at them from a distance, were grieving in silence; and the time of day required that the maiden should return home to her mother's side. But she thought not yet of departing, for her soul delighted both in his beauty and in his winsome③ words, but Aeson's son took heed, and spake at last, though late: "It is time to depart, lest the sunlight sink before we know it, and some stranger notice all; but again will we come and meet here."

So did they two make trial of one another thus far with gentle words; and thereafter parted. Jason hastened to return in joyous mood to his comrades and the ship, she to her handmaids; and they all together came near to meet her, but she marked them not at all as they thronged around. For her soul had soared aloft amid the clouds. And her feet of their own accord mounted the swift chariot, and with one hand she took the reins, and with the other the whip of cunning workmanship, to drive the mules; and they rushed hasting to the city and the palace. And when she was come Chalciope in grief for her sons questioned her; but Medea, distraught by swiftly-changing thoughts, neither heard her words nor was eager to speak in answer to her questions. But she sat upon a low stool at the foot of her couch, bending down, her cheek leaning on her left hand, and her eyes were wet with tears as she pondered what an evil deed she had taken part in by her counsels.

The Contest

Now when Aeson's son had joined his comrades again in the spot where he had left them when he departed, he set out to go with them, telling them all the story, to the gathering of the heroes; and together they approached the ship. And when they saw Jason they embraced him and questioned him. And he told to all the counsels of the maiden and showed the dread charm; but Idas④ alone of his comrades sat apart biting down his wrath; and the rest joyous in heart, at the hour when the darkness of night stayed them, peacefully took thought for themselves. But at daybreak they sent two men to go to Aeetes and ask for the seed, first Telamon himself, dear to Ares, and with him Aethalides⑤, Hermes' famous son. So they went and made no vain journey;

---

① stalwart /ˈstɔːlwət/: 强壮的,勇敢的

② bane: 死亡,毁灭

③ winsome /ˈwɪnsəm/: 让人愉快的

④ Idas: /ˈaɪdæs/

⑤ Aethalides: /ˌiːθəˈlɪdiːz/

but when they came, lordly Aeetes gave them for the contest the fell① teeth of the Aonian② dragon which Cadmus found in Ogygian③ Thebes when he came seeking for Europa and there slew—the warder④ of the spring of Ares.⑤ There he settled by the guidance of the heifer whom Apollo by his prophetic word granted him to lead him on his way. But the teeth the Tritonian goddess⑥ tore away from the dragon's jaws and bestowed as a gift upon Aeetes and the slayer⑦. And Agenor's son, Cadmus, sowed them on the Aonian plains and founded an earthborn people of all who were left from the spear when Ares did the reaping; and the teeth Aeetes then readily gave to be borne⑧ to the ship⑨, for he deemed not that Jason would bring the contest to an end, even though he should cast the yoke upon the oxen.

Far away in the west the sun was sailing beneath the dark earth, beyond the furthest hills of the Aethiopians; and Night was laying the yoke upon her steeds; and the heroes were preparing their beds by the hawsers. But Jason, as soon as the stars of Helice⑩, the bright-gleaming bear, had set, and the air had all grown still under heaven, went to a desert⑪ spot, like some stealthy⑫ thief, with all that was needful; for beforehand⑬ in the daytime had he taken thought for everything; and Argus came bringing a ewe and milk from the flock; and them he took from the ship. But when the hero saw a place which was far away from the tread⑭ of men, in a clear meadow beneath the open sky, there first of all he bathed his tender body reverently in the sacred river; and round him he placed a dark robe, which Hypsipyle⑮ of Lemnos had given him aforetime, a memorial⑯ of many a loving embrace. Then he dug a pit in the ground of a cubit's depth and heaped up billets⑰ of wood, and over it he cut the throat of the sheep, and duly placed the carcase⑱ above; and he kindled the logs placing fire beneath, and poured over them mingled

---

① fell：凶猛的，可怕的，毁灭性的
② Aonian /eɪˈəʊnɪən/：Aonia 的；Aonia /eɪˈəʊnɪə/ 是古希腊的一个地区，是 Boeotia 的一个部分，著名的 Helicon 山在该地区境内。
③ Ogygian /əʊˈdʒɪdʒɪən/：Ogyges 的；Ogyges /əʊˈdʒɪdʒiːz/ 是传说中 Thebes 的创建者和国王。
④ warder /ˈwɔːdə/：守护者
⑤ 参见 The Age of Fable 第 12 章 Cadmus 的故事。
⑥ the Tritonian /trɪˈtəʊnɪən/ goddess：Minerva；Tritonis /trɪˈtəʊnɪs/ 是位于北非的一个湖泊，该湖被认为是神话中好几个神的诞生地。诞生在此湖的神中，最为显赫的是 Minerva，所以 the Tritonian goddess 就指 Minerva。
⑦ the slayer：Cadmus
⑧ borne：bear 的过去分词；bear：运送
⑨ the ship：Argo
⑩ Helice /ˈhelɪsiː/：（诗歌用语）大熊星座
⑪ desert /ˈdezət/：无人居住的，荒芜的
⑫ stealthy /ˈstelθi/：偷偷摸摸的
⑬ beforehand /bɪˈfɔːhænd/：提前，预先
⑭ tread /tred/：脚印，脚步声
⑮ Hypsipyle /hɪpˈsɪpɪli/：Lemnos 女王；Jason 和他的朋友们在前往 Colchis 途中路过 Lemnos 时，她热情地款待了他们，并为 Jason 生了两个儿子。
⑯ memorial /mɪˈmɔːrɪəl/：纪念品
⑰ billet /ˈbɪlɪt/：一截粗木头
⑱ carcase（carcass）/ˈkɑːkəs/：人或动物的尸体

libations, calling on Hecate Brimo① to aid him in the contests. And when he had called on her he drew back; and she heard him, the dread goddess, from the uttermost depths and came to the sacrifice of Aeson's son; and round her horrible serpents twined themselves among the oak boughs; and there was a gleam of countless torches; and sharply howled around her the hounds of hell. All the meadows trembled at her step; and the nymphs that haunt the marsh and the river shrieked, all who dance round that mead② of Amarantian Phasis③. And fear seized Aeson's son, but not even so did he turn round as his feet bore him forth, till he came back to his comrades; and now early dawn arose and shed her light above snowy Caucasus.

Then Aeetes arrayed his breast in the stiff corslet④ which Ares gave him when he had slain Phlegraean⑤ Mimas⑥ with his own hands; and upon his head he placed a golden helmet with four plumes⑦, gleaming like the sun's round light when he first rises from Ocean. And he wielded his shield of many hides, and his spear, terrible, resistless; none of the heroes could have withstood its shock⑧ now that they had left behind Heracles far away, who alone could have met it in battle. For the king his well-fashioned chariot of swift steeds was held near at hand by Phaëthon⑨, for him to mount; and he mounted, and held the reins in his hands. Then from the city he drove along the broad highway, that he might be present at the contest; and with him a countless multitude rushed forth. And as Poseidon rides, mounted in his chariot, to the Isthmian contest or to Taenarus⑩, or to Lerna's⑪ water, or through the grove of Hyantian⑫ Onchestus⑬, and thereafter passes even to Calaureia⑭ with his steeds, and the Haemonian⑮ rock, or well-wooded Geraestus⑯; even so was Aeetes, lord of the Colchians, to behold.

Meanwhile, prompted by Medea, Jason steeped the charm in water and sprinkled with it his shield and sturdy spear, and sword; and his comrades round him made proof of his weapons with might and main, but could not bend that spear even a little, but it remained firm in their stalwart hands unbroken as before. But in furious rage with them Idas, Aphareus' son, with his great

---

① Brimo /'braɪməʊ/：愤怒者；Brimo 是 Hecate 和 Proserpina 的称号。

② mead /miːd/：（诗歌用语）草坪

③ Amarantian Phasis /'fæsɪs/：Phasis 是 Colchis 的一条河流，注入黑海；Amarantian 的意思是"花永不凋谢的"。该河今天叫 the Rione River，在格鲁吉亚境内。在诗歌中，Phasis 可指 Colchis。

④ corslet /'kɔːslɪt/：护身盔甲

⑤ Phlegraean /'fliːɡriːən/：Phlegra 的；Phlegra /'fliːɡrə/ 是古代马其顿的一个地区，据说众神在此用闪电杀死反叛的巨人们。关于众神与巨人之间的战争，参见 The Age of Fable 第 16 章的相关叙述。

⑥ Mimas /'maɪməs/：反叛的巨人之一

⑦ plume /pluːm/：装饰用的大羽毛

⑧ shock：打击

⑨ Phaëthon：/'feɪθən/

⑩ Taenarus：参见 The Age of Fable 第 24 章关于 Tænarus 的注释。

⑪ Lerna /'lɜːnə/：沼泽名，位于伯罗奔尼撒半岛东海岸附近。

⑫ Hyantian /haɪ'eɪnʃən/：of Boeotia，Boeotian

⑬ Onchestus /ən'kiːstəs/：古希腊城镇名，位于 Boeotia 境内。

⑭ Calaureia /ˌkælə'riːɪə/：Trœzen 附近的一个岛屿；关于 Trœzen，参见 The Age of Fable 第 20 章的注释。

⑮ Haemonian /hiː'məʊnɪən/：Thessalian

⑯ Geraestus：/ɡə'riːstəs/

sword hewed at the spear near the butt, and the edge leapt back repelled by the shock, like a hammer from the anvil; and the heroes shouted with joy for their hope in the contest. And then he sprinkled his body, and terrible prowess entered into him, unspeakable, dauntless; and his hands on both sides thrilled vigorously as they swelled with strength. And as when a warlike steed eager for the fight neighs and beats the ground with his hoof, while rejoicing he lifts his neck on high with ears erect; in such wise① did Aeson's son rejoice in the strength of his limbs. And often hither and thither did he leap high in air tossing in his hands his shield of bronze and ashen spear. Thou wouldst say that wintry lightning flashing from the gloomy sky kept on darting forth from the clouds what time they bring with them their blackest rainstorm. Not long after that were the heroes to hold back from the contests; but sitting in rows on their benches they sped swiftly on to the plain of Ares. And it lay in front of them on the opposite side of the city, as far off as is the turning-post that a chariot must reach from the starting-point, when the kinsmen of a dead king appoint funeral games for footmen and horsemen. And they found Aeetes and the tribes of the Colchians; these were stationed on the Caucasian heights, but the king by the winding brink of the river.

Now Aeson's son, as soon as his comrades had made the hawsers fast, leapt from the ship, and with spear and shield came forth to the contest; and at the same time he took the gleaming helmet of bronze filled with sharp teeth, and his sword girt round his shoulders, his body stripped, in somewise② resembling Ares and in somewise Apollo of the golden sword. And gazing over the field he saw the bulls' yoke of bronze and near it the plough, all of one piece, of stubborn③ adamant④. Then he came near, and fixed his sturdy spear upright on its butt, and taking his helmet off leant it against the spear. And he went forward with shield alone to examine the countless tracks of the bulls, and they from some unseen lair⑤ beneath the earth, where was their strong steading, wrapt in murky smoke, both rushed out together, breathing forth flaming fire. And sore⑥ afraid were the heroes at the sight. But Jason, setting wide his feet, withstood their onset⑦, as in the sea a rocky reef withstands the waves tossed by the countless blasts. Then in front of him he held his shield; and both the bulls with loud bellowing attacked him with their mighty horns; nor did they stir⑧ him a jot⑨ by their onset. And as when through the holes of the furnace the armourers' bellows anon gleam brightly, kindling the ravening flame, and anon cease from blowing, and a terrible roar rises from the fire when it darts up from below; so the bulls roared, breathing forth swift flame from their mouths, while the consuming heat played round him, smiting

---

① wise：方式，方法

② in somewise：somehow

③ stubborn /ˈstʌbən/：坚硬的

④ adamant /ˈædəmənt/：金刚石等硬石

⑤ lair /leə/：动物的窝，动物的巢穴

⑥ sore：extremely

⑦ onset /ˈɒnset/：进攻，攻击

⑧ stir：使移动

⑨ jot /dʒɒt/：一点点

like lightning; but the maiden's charms protected him. Then grasping the tip of the horn of the right-hand bull, he dragged it mightily with all his strength to bring it near the yoke of bronze, and forced it down on to its knees, suddenly striking with his foot the foot of bronze. So also he threw the other bull on to its knees as it rushed upon him, and smote it down with one blow. And throwing to the ground his broad shield, he held them both down where they had fallen on their fore-knees, as he strode from side to side, now here, now there, and rushed swiftly through the flame. But Aeetes marvelled at the hero's might. And meantime the sons of Tyndareus①—for long since had it been thus ordained for them—near at hand gave him the yoke from the ground to cast round them. Then tightly did he bind their necks; and lifting the pole of bronze between them, he fastened it to the yoke by its golden tip. So the twin heroes② started back from the fire to the ship. But Jason took up again his shield and cast it on his back behind him, and grasped the strong helmet filled with sharp teeth, and his resistless spear, wherewith, like some ploughman with a Pelasgian③ goad④, he pricked the bulls beneath, striking their flanks; and very firmly did he guide the well fitted plough handle, fashioned of adamant.

The bulls meantime raged exceedingly, breathing forth furious flame of fire; and their breath rose up like the roar of blustering winds, in fear of which above all seafaring⑤ men furl⑥ their large sail. But not long after that they moved on at the bidding of the spear; and behind them the rugged fallow was broken up, cloven by the might of the bulls and the sturdy ploughman. Then terribly groaned the clods⑦ withal⑧ along the furrows of the plough as they were rent, each a man's burden⑨; and Jason followed, pressing down the cornfield with firm foot; and far from him he ever sowed the teeth along the clods as each was ploughed, turning his head back for fear lest the deadly crop of earthborn men should rise against him first; and the bulls toiled onwards treading with their hoofs of bronze.

But when the third part of the day was still left as it wanes from dawn, and wearied labourers call for the sweet hour of unyoking to come to them straightway, then the fallow was ploughed by the tireless ploughman, four plough-gates⑩ though it was; and he loosed the plough from the oxen. Them he scared in flight towards the plain; but he went back again to the ship, while he still saw the furrows free of the earthborn men. And all round his comrades heartened⑪ him with their shouts. And in the helmet he drew from the river's stream and quenched his thirst with the water.

---

① the sons of Tyndareus /tɪnˈdeərɪəs/: Castor and Pollux

② the twin heroes: Castor and Pollux

③ Pelasgian /pɪˈlæzɡɪən/: 佩拉斯吉人的;佩拉斯吉人是史前居住在希腊、小亚细亚和爱琴海诸岛的一个民族。

④ goad: 赶牛棒

⑤ seafaring /ˈsiːfeərɪŋ/: 在海上航行的,以航海为职业的

⑥ furl /fɜːl/: 卷起

⑦ clod: 犁地时翻起的土块

⑧ withal /wɪˈðɔːl/: at the same time

⑨ a man's burden: 一个人能搬动的重量

⑩ plough-gate /ˈplaʊɡeɪt/: 一块耕地

⑪ hearten /ˈhɑːtn/: 鼓励,鼓舞

Then he bent his knees till they grew supple①, and filled his mighty heart with courage, raging like a boar, when it sharpens its teeth against the hunters, while from its wrathful mouth plenteous foam drips to the ground. By now the earthborn men were springing up over all the field; and the plot of Ares, the death-dealer, bristled② with sturdy shields and double-pointed spears and shining helmets; and the gleam reached Olympus from beneath, flashing through the air. And as when abundant snow has fallen on the earth and the storm blasts have dispersed the wintry clouds under the murky night, and all the hosts of the stars appear shining through the gloom; so did those warriors shine springing up above the earth. But Jason bethought him of the counsels of Medea full of craft, and seized from the plain a huge round boulder③, a terrible quoit④ of Ares Enyalius⑤; four stalwart youths could not have raised it from the ground even a little. Taking it in his hands he threw it with a rush far away into their midst; and himself crouched unseen behind his shield, with full confidence. And the Colchians gave a loud cry, like the roar of the sea when it beats upon sharp crags; and speechless amazement seized Aeetes at the rush of the sturdy quoit. And the Earthborn, like fleet-footed⑥ hounds, leaped upon one another and slew with loud yells; and on earth their mother they fell beneath their own spears, like pines or oaks, which storms of wind beat down. And even as a fiery star leaps from heaven, trailing a furrow of light, a portent to men, whoever see it darting with a gleam through the dusky sky; in such wise did Aeson's son rush upon the earthborn men, and he drew from the sheath his bare sword, and smote here and there, mowing them down, many on the belly and side, half risen to the air—and some that had risen as far as the shoulders—and some just standing upright, and others even now rushing to battle. And as when a fight is stirred up concerning boundaries, and a husbandman, in fear lest they should ravage his fields, seizes in his hand a curved sickle, newly sharpened, and hastily cuts the unripe crop, and waits not for it to be parched in due season by the beams of the sun; so at that time did Jason cut down the crop of the Earthborn; and the furrows were filled with blood, as the channels of a spring with water. And they fell, some on their faces biting the rough clod of earth with their teeth, some on their backs, and others on their hands and sides, like to sea-monsters to behold. And many, smitten before raising their feet from the earth, bowed down as far to the ground as they had risen to the air, and rested there with the damp of death on their brows. Even so, I ween⑦, when Zeus has sent a measureless rain, new planted orchard-shoots droop to the ground, cut off by the root—the toil of gardening men; but heaviness of heart and deadly anguish come to the owner of the farm, who planted them; so at that time did bitter grief come upon the heart of King Aeetes. And he went back to the city among the Colchians, pondering how he might most quickly oppose the heroes. And the day died, and Jason's contest was ended.

---

① supple /'sʌpl/：灵活的

② bristle /'brɪsl/：布满（猪鬃之类的硬毛）

③ boulder /'bəʊldə/：巨石

④ quoit /kɔɪt；kwɔɪt/：石头飞盘

⑤ Enyalius /ɪ'naɪəlɪəs/：Enyalius（Eνυ αλιoς）是战神 Ares（Mars）的称号，意思是"好战的，尚武的，英勇的"。

⑥ fleet-footed：跑得快的

⑦ ween /wiːn/：认为，相信

Apollodorus

阿波罗多鲁斯（Apollodorus /əˌpɒləˈdɔːrəs /）是古希腊学者，生活在公元前 140 前后。阿波罗多鲁斯最著名的著作是《编年史》（*The Chronicle*），记载了特洛伊沦陷至公元前 144 年的希腊历史。希腊神话汇编《图书馆》（*The Library*）虽然归于阿波罗多鲁斯的名下，但学者们普遍认为这不是他的作品。

《图书馆》共有 3 卷，是一部希腊神话的汇编。作者在研究各种文献的基础上，以概要的形式将希腊神话故事汇编在一起，不做任何解释和评论。本读本从《图书馆》选取了 1 个片段：该选段"Hercules"选自第 2 卷。《图书馆》有多种英译本，这里采用的是弗雷泽（Sir James George Frazer）的译本。弗雷泽是苏格兰著名的人类学家、民俗学家、古典学者，著有《金枝》（*The Golden Bough*）。

The Library
Translated into English by Sir James George Frazer

Hercules

But before Amphitryon[①] reached Thebes, Zeus came by night and prolonging the one night threefold[②] he assumed the likeness of Amphitryon and bedded with Alcmena[③] and related what had happened concerning the Teleboans[④]. But when Amphitryon arrived and saw that he was not welcomed by his wife, he inquired the cause; and when she told him that he had come the night

---

① Amphitryon /æmˈfɪtrɪən/：king of Thebes

② threefold：三倍

③ Alcmena：/ælkˈmiːnə/

④ the Teleboans /ˈtelɪbəʊnz /：古希腊部落

before and slept with her, he learned from Tiresias how Zeus had enjoyed her. And Alcmena bore two sons, to wit①, Hercules②, whom she had by Zeus and who was the elder by one night, and Iphicles③, whom she had by Amphitryon. When the child was eight months old, Hera desired the destruction④ of the babe and sent two huge serpents to the bed. Alcmena called Amphitryon to her help, but Hercules arose and killed the serpents by strangling them with both his hands. However, Pherecydes⑤ says that it was Amphitryon who put the serpents in the bed, because he would know which of the two children was his, and that when Iphicles fled, and Hercules stood his ground, he knew that Iphicles was begotten of his body.

Hercules was taught to drive a chariot by Amphitryon, to wrestle by Autolycus⑥, to shoot with the bow by Eurytus, to fence⑦ by Castor, and to play the lyre by Linus. This Linus was a brother of Orpheus⑧; he came to Thebes and became a Theban⑨, but was killed by Hercules with a blow of the lyre; for being struck by him, Hercules flew into a rage and slew him. When he was tried for murder, Hercules quoted a law of Rhadamanthys⑩, who laid it down that whoever defends himself against a wrongful aggressor shall go free, and so he was acquitted⑪. But fearing he might do the like again, Amphitryon sent him to the cattle farm; and there he was nurtured and outdid⑫ all in stature⑬ and strength. Even by the look of him it was plain that he was a son of Zeus; for his body measured four cubits, and he flashed a gleam of fire from his eyes; and he did not miss, neither with the bow nor with the javelin.

While he was with the herds and had reached his eighteenth year he slew the lion of Cithaeron⑭, for that animal, sallying⑮ from Cithaeron, harried⑯ the kine⑰ of Amphitryon and of Thespius⑱. Now this Thespius was king of Thespiae⑲, and Hercules went to him when he wished to catch the lion. The king entertained him for fifty days, and each night, as Hercules went forth to the hunt, Thespius bedded one of his daughters with him (fifty daughters having been borne to

---

① to wit：that is to say
② Hercules：/ˈhɜːkjuliːz/
③ Iphicles：/ˈaɪfɪkliːz/
④ destruction：消灭
⑤ Pherecydes /ˌferɪˈsaɪdiːz/：公元前 5 世纪初期的希腊散文作家。
⑥ Autolycus：/ˌɔːtəˈlaɪkəs/
⑦ fence：击剑
⑧ 参见 The Age of Fable 第 24 章。
⑨ Theban /ˈθiːbn/：an inhabitant of Thebes
⑩ Rhadamanthys：即 Rhadamanthus,克里特岛的法律制定者,阴间的三个判官之一,另外两个是 Minos 和 Aeacus。
⑪ acquit /əˈkwɪt/：宣布……无罪
⑫ outdo：超过
⑬ stature /ˈstætʃə/：身高,体格
⑭ Cithaeron：参见 The Age of Fable 第 24 章关于 Cithæron 的注释。
⑮ sally /ˈsæli/：跑出来
⑯ harry /ˈhæri/：袭击
⑰ kine：cow 的复数形式
⑱ Thespius：/ˈθiːspɪəs/
⑲ Thespiae /ˈθiːspiiː/：古希腊城市名,位于 Helicon 山脚下。

him by Megamede①, daughter of Arneus②); for he was anxious that all of them should have children by Hercules. Thus Hercules, though he thought that his bed-fellow was always the same, had intercourse③ with them all. And having vanquished the lion, he dressed himself in the skin and wore the scalp④ as a helmet.

As he was returning from the hunt, there met him heralds sent by Erginus⑤ to receive the tribute⑥ from the Thebans. Now the Thebans paid tribute to Erginus for the following reason. Clymenus⑦, king of the Minyans⑧, was wounded with a cast of a stone by a charioteer of Menoeceus⑨, named Perieres⑩, in a precinct of Poseidon at Onchestus; and being carried dying to Orchomenus⑪, he with his last breath charged his son Erginus to avenge his death. So Erginus marched against Thebes, and after slaughtering not a few of the Thebans he concluded a treaty with them, confirmed by oaths, that they should send him tribute for twenty years, a hundred kine every year. Falling in with⑫ the heralds on their way to Thebes to demand this tribute, Hercules outraged them; for he cut off their ears and noses and hands, and having fastened them by ropes from their necks, he told them to carry that tribute to Erginus and the Minyans. Indignant at this outrage, Erginus marched against Thebes. But Hercules, having received weapons from Athena and taken the command, killed Erginus, put the Minyans to flight, and compelled them to pay double the tribute to the Thebans. And it chanced that in the fight Amphitryon fell fighting bravely. And Hercules received from Creon his eldest daughter Megara⑬ as a prize of valor, and by her he had three sons, Therimachus, Creontiades, and Deicoon. But Creon gave his younger daughter to Iphicles, who already had a son Iolaus by Automedusa, daughter of Alcathus. And Rhadamanthys, son of Zeus, married Alcmena after the death of Amphitryon, and dwelt as an exile at Ocaleae in Boeotia.

Having first learned from Eurytus the art of archery, Hercules received a sword from Hermes, a bow and arrows from Apollo, a golden breastplate⑭ from Hephaestus, and a robe from Athena; for he had himself cut a club at Nemea.

Now it came to pass that after the battle with the Minyans Hercules was driven mad through the jealousy of Hera and flung⑮ his own children, whom he had by Megara, and two children of

---

① Megamede：/mɪˈɡæmɪdi/

② Arneus：/ˈɑːnɪəs/

③ intercourse /ˈɪntəkɔːs/：性交

④ scalp /skælp/：头皮

⑤ Erginus：/ˈɜːdʒɪnəs/

⑥ tribute /ˈtrɪbjuːt/：贡

⑦ Clymenus：/ˈklaɪmɪnəs/

⑧ the Minyans /ˈmɪnɪənz/：古希腊部落名,居住在希腊中部地区。

⑨ Menoeceus /mɪˈniːsjuːs/：Thebes 国王 Creon 之子；关于 Creon,参见 *The Age of Fable* 第 23 章 Antigone 的故事。

⑩ Perieres：/pɪˈraɪəriːz/

⑪ Orchomenus：参见 *Argonautica* 选段"Interview of Jason and Medea"中关于 Orchomenus 的注释。

⑫ fall in with：碰巧遇到,偶然遇到

⑬ Megara：/ˈmeɡərə/

⑭ breastplate /ˈbreɪstpleɪt/：护胸铠甲

⑮ fling：扔

Iphicles into the fire; wherefore he condemned himself to exile, and was purified by Thespius, and repairing to Delphi he inquired of the god where he should dwell. The Pythian① priestess then first called him Hercules, for hitherto② he was called Alcides③. And she told him to dwell in Tiryns④, serving Eurystheus⑤ for twelve years and to perform the ten labours imposed on him, and so, she said, when the tasks were accomplished, he would be immortal.

When Hercules heard that, he went to Tiryns and did as he was bid by Eurystheus. First, Eurystheus ordered him to bring the skin of the Nemean lion; now that was an invulnerable beast begotten by Typhon. On his way to attack the lion he came to Cleonae⑥ and lodged⑦ at the house of a day-laborer⑧, Molorchus⑨; and when his host would have offered a victim⑩ in sacrifice, Hercules told him to wait for thirty days, and then, if he had returned safe from the hunt, to sacrifice to Saviour Zeus, but if he were dead, to sacrifice to him as to a hero. And having come to Nemea and tracked the lion, he first shot an arrow at him⑪, but when he perceived that the beast was invulnerable, he heaved up his club and made after⑫ him. And when the lion took refuge in a cave with two mouths, Hercules built up⑬ the one entrance and came in upon the beast through the other, and putting his arm round its neck held it tight till he had choked⑭ it; so laying it on his shoulders he carried it to Cleonae. And finding Molorchus on the last of the thirty days about to sacrifice the victim to him as to a dead man, he sacrificed to Saviour Zeus and brought the lion to Mycenae. Amazed at his manhood⑮, Eurystheus forbade him thenceforth⑯ to enter the city, but ordered him to exhibit the fruits of his labours before the gates. They say, too, that in his fear he had a bronze jar made for himself to hide in under the earth, and that he sent his commands for the labours through a herald, Copreus⑰, son of Pelops⑱ the Elean⑲. This Copreus had killed Iphitus⑳ and fled to Mycenae, where he was purified㉑ by Eurystheus and took up his abode.

---

① Pythian: of Delphi
② hitherto /ˈhɪðətuː/: 直到现在
③ Alcides: /ælˈsaɪdiːz/
④ Tiryns /ˈtɪrɪnz/: 古希腊城市,距离著名的 Mycenae 不远。
⑤ Eurystheus: /juəˈrɪsθiəs/
⑥ Cleonae /ˈkliːəniː/: 希腊古城名,位于 Nemea 以东不远处。关于 Nemea,参见 *The Age of Fable* 第 19 章的注释。
⑦ lodge /lɒdʒ/: 暂时居住
⑧ day-laborer: 按天计酬的打散工者
⑨ Molorchus: /ˈmɒləkəs/
⑩ victim: 杀死来供奉给神的动物,牺牲
⑪ him: the lion
⑫ make after: 追逐
⑬ build up: 堵塞
⑭ choke: 掐住脖子使窒息
⑮ manhood: 勇气
⑯ thenceforth /ˈðensfɔːθ/: 从那时起
⑰ Copreus: /ˈkɒprɪəs/
⑱ Pelops: /ˈpiːlɒps/
⑲ Elean /ˈiːlɪən/: an inhabitant of Elis; 关于 Elis,参见 *The Age of Fable* 第 7 章的注释。
⑳ Iphitus: /ˈɪfɪtəs/
㉑ purify /ˈpjuərɪfaɪ/: 洗清某人的罪过

As a second labour he ordered him to kill the Lernaean① hydra②. That creature, bred in the swamp of Lerna③, used to go forth into the plain and ravage④ both the cattle and the country. Now the hydra had a huge body, with nine heads, eight mortal, but the middle one immortal. So mounting a chariot driven by Iolaus⑤, he came to Lerna, and having halted his horses, he discovered the hydra on a hill beside the springs of the Amymone⑥, where was its den. By pelting⑦ it with fiery shafts he forced it to come out, and in the act of doing so he seized and held it fast. But the hydra wound⑧ itself about one of his feet and clung to him. Nor could he effect⑨ anything by smashing its heads with his club, for as fast as one head was smashed there grew up two. A huge crab also came to the help of the hydra by biting his foot. So he killed it, and in his turn called for help on Iolaus who, by setting fire to a piece of the neighboring wood and burning the roots of the heads with the brands, prevented them from sprouting. Having thus got the better of ⑩ the sprouting heads, he chopped off the immortal head, and buried it, and put a heavy rock on it, beside the road that leads through Lerna to Elaeus⑪. But the body of the hydra he slit up and dipped his arrows in the gall⑫. However, Eurystheus said that this labour should not be reckoned⑬ among the ten because he had not got the better of the hydra by himself, but with the help of Iolaus.

As a third labour he ordered him to bring the Cerynitian⑭ hind⑮ alive to Mycenae. Now the hind was at Oenoe⑯; it had golden horns and was sacred to Artemis; so wishing neither to kill nor wound it, Hercules hunted it a whole year. But when, weary with the chase, the beast took refuge on the mountain called Artemisius⑰, and thence passed to the river Ladon⑱, Hercules shot it just as it was about to cross the stream, and catching it put it on his shoulders and hastened through Arcadia. But Artemis with Apollo met him, and would have wrested⑲ the hind from him, and rebuked him for attempting to kill her sacred animal. Howbeit, by pleading necessity and laying the blame on Eurystheus, he appeased the anger of the goddess and carried the beast alive to Mycenae.

---

① Lernaean /lɜːˈniːən/: of Lerna

② hydra /ˈhaɪdrə/: 蛇, 水蛇

③ Lerna /ˈlɜːnə/: 沼泽名, 位于伯罗奔尼撒半岛东海岸附近。

④ ravage /ˈrævɪdʒ/: 破坏, 蹂躏

⑤ Iolaus: /ˌaɪəˈleɪəs/

⑥ the Amymone: 参见 *The Age of Fable* 第 19 章关于 Amymone 的叙述。

⑦ pelt: 不停地打击

⑧ wind /waɪnd/: 缠绕

⑨ effect /ɪˈfekt/: 实现, 完成

⑩ get the better of: 打败, 战胜

⑪ Elaeus /ɪˈliːəs/: 古希腊城市名

⑫ gall /ɡɔːl/: 胆汁

⑬ reckon /ˈrekən/: (在计算中)包括

⑭ Cerynitian /səˈrɪnɪtɪən/: of Cerynites /səˈrɪnɪtiːz/, a river starting in Arcadia

⑮ hind /haɪnd/: 3 岁或 3 岁以上的雌马鹿

⑯ Oenoe /ˈiːniː/: 古希腊城镇名, 位于 Marathon 附近。

⑰ Artemisius: /ˌɑːtɪˈmɪsɪəs/

⑱ Ladon /ˈlædn/: 发源于 Achaea, 流经 Arcadia 西部, 注入阿尔菲奥斯河 (Alpheus 或 Alphios)。

⑲ wrest /rest/: 强行夺取

As a fourth labour he ordered him to bring the Erymanthian① boar alive; now that animal ravaged Psophis②, sallying from a mountain which they call Erymanthus. So passing through Pholoe③ he was entertained by the centaur④ Pholus⑤, a son of Silenus by a Melian⑥ nymph. He set roast meat before Hercules, while he himself ate his meat raw. When Hercules called for wine, he said he feared to open the jar which belonged to the centaurs in common. But Hercules, bidding him be of good courage, opened it, and not long afterwards, scenting⑦ the smell, the centaurs arrived at the cave of Pholus, armed with rocks and firs. The first who dared to enter, Anchius and Agrius⑧, were repelled by Hercules with a shower of brands, and the rest of them he shot and pursued as far as Malea⑨. Thence they took refuge with Chiron⑩, who, driven by the Lapiths⑪ from Mount Pelion⑫, took up his abode at Malea. As the centaurs cowered about Chiron, Hercules shot an arrow at them, which, passing through the arm of Elatus, stuck in the knee of Chiron. Distressed at this, Hercules ran up to him, drew out the shaft, and applied a medicine which Chiron gave him. But the hurt proving incurable, Chiron retired to the cave and there he wished to die, but he could not, for he was immortal. However, Prometheus offered himself to Zeus to be immortal in his stead, and so Chiron died. The rest of the centaurs fled in different directions, and some came to Mount Malea, and Eurytion⑬ to Pholoe, and Nessus to the river Evenus⑭. The rest of them Poseidon received at Eleusis and hid them in a mountain. But Pholus, drawing the arrow from a corpse, wondered that so little a thing could kill such big fellows; howbeit, it slipped from his hand and lighting⑮ on his foot killed him on the spot. So when Hercules returned to Pholoe, he beheld Pholus dead; and he buried him and proceeded to the boar hunt. And when he had chased the boar with shouts from a certain thicket, he drove the exhausted animal into deep snow, trapped it, and brought it to Mycenae.

The fifth labour he laid on him was to carry out the dung⑯ of the cattle of Augeas in a single day. Now Augeas was king of Elis; some say that he was a son of the Sun, others that he was a son of Poseidon, and others that he was a son of Phorbas; and he had many herds of cattle. Hercules

---

① Erymanthian /ˌerɪˈmænθɪən/: of Erymanthus /ˌerɪˈmænθəs/, a mountain in Achaea
② Psophis /ˈsəʊfɪs/: 古希腊城市名，位于 Arcadia 西北角。
③ Pholoe /ˈfəʊliː/: a village in ancient Greece
④ centaur: 参见 *The Age of Fable* 第 16 章。
⑤ Pholus: /ˈfəʊləs/
⑥ Melian /ˈmiːlɪən/: of Melos /ˈmiːlɒs/; Melos 岛属于南爱琴大区基克拉泽斯州，是基克拉泽斯群岛中的一个岛屿。
⑦ scent: 闻到
⑧ Anchius: /ˈæŋkɪəs/; Agrius: /ˈægrɪəs/
⑨ Malea /ˈmæliə/: 即 Maleas 角，位于伯罗奔尼撒最东南角。
⑩ Chiron: 参见 *The Age of Fable* 第 16 章。
⑪ the Lapiths /ˈlæpɪθs/: 居住在 Thessaly 山区的野蛮部落，以其在 Pirithous 的婚礼上与马人（the Centaurs）的打斗而著名。参见 *The Age of Fable* 第 16 章。
⑫ Mount Pelion: 参见 *The Age of Fable* 第 16 章关于 Pelion 的注释。
⑬ Eurytion: /juəˈrɪtɪɒn/
⑭ Evenus /ˈiːvənəs/: 希腊河流名，流经西希腊大区埃托利亚—阿卡纳尼亚州（Aetolia-Acarnania）东部和南部。
⑮ light: 掉落
⑯ dung /dʌŋ/: 粪

accosted him, and without revealing the command of Eurystheus, said that he would carry out the dung in one day, if Augeas would give him the tithe① of the cattle. Augeas was incredulous②, but promised. Having taken Augeas's son Phyleus③ to witness, Hercules made a breach in the foundations of the cattle-yard, and then, diverting the courses of the Alpheus and Peneus④, which flowed near each other, he turned them into the yard, having first made an outlet for the water through another opening. When Augeas learned that this had been accomplished at the command of Eurystheus, he would not pay the reward; nay more, he denied that he had promised to pay it, and on that point he professed himself ready to submit to arbitration⑤. The arbitrators⑥ having taken their seats, Phyleus was called by Hercules and bore witness against his father, affirming that he had agreed to give him a reward. In a rage Augeas, before the voting took place, ordered both Phyleus and Hercules to pack⑦ out of Elis. So Phyleus went to Dulichium⑧ and dwelt there, and Hercules repaired to Dexamenus⑨ at Olenus⑩. He found Dexamenus on the point of betrothing⑪ perforce⑫ his daughter Mnesimache⑬ to the centaur Eurytion, and being called upon by him for help, he slew Eurytion when that centaur came to fetch his bride. But Eurystheus would not admit this labour either among the ten, alleging that it had been performed for hire.

The sixth labour he enjoined on him was to chase away the Stymphalian⑭ birds. Now at the city of Stymphalus⑮ in Arcadia was the lake called Stymphalian, embosomed in a deep wood. To it countless birds had flocked for refuge, fearing to be preyed upon by the wolves. So when Hercules was at a loss how to drive the birds from the wood, Athena gave him brazen castanets⑯, which she had received from Hephaestus. By clashing these on a certain mountain that overhung the lake, he scared the birds. They could not abide the sound, but fluttered up in a fright, and in that way Hercules shot them.

The seventh labour he enjoined on him was to bring the Cretan⑰ bull. Acusilaus⑱ says that this was the bull that ferried across Europa for Zeus;⑲ but some say it was the bull that Poseidon

---

① tithe /taɪð/：十分之一

② incredulous /ɪnˈkredjuləs/：不愿意相信的,怀疑的

③ Phyleus：/ˈfɪlɪəs/

④ Peneus：Thessaly 境内的主要河流

⑤ arbitration /ˌɑːbɪˈtreɪʃn/：仲裁

⑥ arbitrator /ˈɑːbɪtreɪtə/：仲裁人

⑦ pack：(拿着包裹)离开

⑧ Dulichium /dəˈlɪkɪəm/：伊奥尼亚海中的一个岛

⑨ Dexamenus：/dɪˈksæmɪnəs/

⑩ Olenus /ˈəʊlɪnəs/：古希腊城市名,位于 Aetolia 南部。

⑪ betroth /bɪˈtrəʊð/：使女子与……订婚

⑫ perforce：被迫,不得已

⑬ Mnesimache：/niːˈsɪməki/

⑭ Stymphalian：/stɪmˈfeɪlɪən/

⑮ Stymphalus：/stɪmˈfeɪləs/

⑯ castanets /ˌkæstəˈnets/：响板

⑰ Cretan /ˈkriːtn/：of Crete

⑱ Acusilaus /əˌkjuːsɪˈleɪəs/：公元前 6 世纪后半叶的希腊散文作家、神话作家。

⑲ 参见 The Age of Fable 第 12 章关于 Europa 的注释。

sent up from the sea when Minos promised to sacrifice to Poseidon what should appear out of the sea. And they say that when he saw the beauty of the bull he sent it away to the herds and sacrificed another to Poseidon; at which the god was angry and made the bull savage. To attack this bull Hercules came to Crete, and when, in reply to his request for aid, Minos told him to fight and catch the bull for himself, he caught it and brought it to Eurystheus, and having shown it to him he let it afterwards go free. But the bull roamed to Sparta and all Arcadia, and traversing the Isthmus arrived at Marathon① in Attica and harried② the inhabitants.

The eighth labour he enjoined on him was to bring the mares of Diomedes the Thracian③ to Mycenae. Now this Diomedes was a son of Ares and Cyrene, and he was king of the Bistones④, a very warlike Thracian people, and he owned man-eating mares. So Hercules sailed with a band of volunteers, and having overpowered⑤ the grooms⑥ who were in charge of the mangers⑦, he drove the mares to the sea. When the Bistones in arms came to the rescue, he committed the mares to the guardianship⑧ of Abderus⑨, who was a son of Hermes, a native of Opus⑩ in Locris⑪, and a minion⑫ of Hercules; but the mares killed him by dragging him after them. But Hercules fought against the Bistones, slew Diomedes and compelled the rest to flee. And he founded a city Abdera⑬ beside the grave of Abderus who had been done to death, and bringing the mares he gave them to Eurystheus. But Eurystheus let them go, and they came to Mount Olympus, as it is called, and there they were destroyed by the wild beasts.

The ninth labour he enjoined on Hercules was to bring the belt of Hippolyte⑭. She was queen of the Amazons, who dwelt about the river Thermodon⑮, a people great in war; for they cultivated the manly virtues, and if ever they gave birth to children through intercourse with the other sex, they reared the females; and they pinched off the right breasts that they might not be trammelled⑯ by them in throwing the javelin, but they kept the left breasts, that they might suckle.⑰ Now Hippolyte had the belt of Ares in token of her superiority to all the rest. Hercules was sent to fetch

①　Marathon /ˈmærəθən/：希腊地名，位于 Attica 东部海岸，公元前 490 年希腊人曾在此击败强大的波斯军队。
②　harry /ˈhæri/：骚扰，蹂躏
③　Thracian /ˈθreɪʃn/：色雷斯人；参见 *The Age of Fable* 第 17 章关于 Thrace 的注释。
④　the Bistones /bɪsˈtəʊniːz/：色雷斯的古代部落名，居住地在 Abdera（参见下面的注释）附近。
⑤　overpower：制伏
⑥　groom：马夫
⑦　manger /ˈmeɪndʒə/：马槽
⑧　guardianship：看管
⑨　Abderus：/ˈæbdərəs/
⑩　Opus：/ˈəʊpəs/
⑪　Locris /ˈləʊkrɪs/：古希腊地区名，大致相当于今希腊弗西奥蒂斯州（Phthiotis）南部的滨海地区。
⑫　minion：受宠爱的人
⑬　Abdera /æbˈdɪərə/：希腊古城名，位于今希腊的克桑西州（Xanthi），在奈斯托斯河（the Nestos River）河口东北方向的不远处。
⑭　Hippolyte /hɪˈpɒlɪti/：也可拼写为 Hippolyta
⑮　the river Thermodon /θəˈməʊdn/：在今土耳其境内，注入黑海。
⑯　trammel /ˈtræml/：妨碍
⑰　参见 *The Age of Fable* 第 19 章关于 Amazon 的注释。

this belt because Admete①, daughter of Eurystheus, desired to get it. So taking with him a band of volunteer comrades in a single ship he set sail and put in to the island of Paros②, which was inhabited by the sons of Minos, to wit, Eurymedon, Chryses, Nephalion, and Philolaus. But it chanced that two of those in the ship landed and were killed by the sons of Minos. Indignant at this, Hercules killed the sons of Minos on the spot and besieged the rest closely, till they sent envoys③ to request that in the room of④ the murdered men he would take two, whom he pleased. So he raised the siege⑤, and taking on board the sons of Androgeus⑥, son of Minos, to wit, Alcaeus and Sthenelus, he came to Mysia⑦, to the court of Lycus, son of Dascylus⑧, and was entertained by him; and in a battle between him and the king of the Bebryces⑨ Hercules sided with Lycus and slew many, amongst others King Mygdon⑩, brother of Amycus⑪. And he took much land from the Bebryces and gave it to Lycus, who called it all Heraclea⑫.

Having put in at the harbour of Themiscyra⑬, he received a visit from Hippolyte, who inquired why he was come, and promised to give him the belt. But Hera in the likeness of an Amazon went up and down the multitude saying that the strangers who had arrived were carrying off the queen. So the Amazons in arms charged⑭ on horseback down on the ship. But when Hercules saw them in arms, he suspected treachery, and killing Hippolyte stripped her of her belt. And after fighting the rest he sailed away and touched at Troy.

But it chanced⑮ that the city was then in distress consequently on the wrath of Apollo and Poseidon. For desiring to put the wantonness⑯ of Laomedon⑰ to the proof, Apollo and Poseidon assumed the likeness of men and undertook to fortify Pergamum⑱ for wages. But when they had fortified it, he would not pay them their wages. Therefore Apollo sent a pestilence, and Poseidon a sea monster, which, carried up by a flood, snatched away the people of the plain. But as oracles foretold deliverance from these calamities if Laomedon would expose his daughter Hesione⑲ to be

---

① Admete /əd'miːti/：也可拼写为 Admeta。
② Paros /'peərɒs/：希腊岛屿，是基克拉泽斯群岛（the Cyclades）中的一个岛，属于今希腊南爱琴大区基克拉泽斯州。
③ envoy /'envɔɪ/：使者
④ in the room of：接替某人，替代某人
⑤ raise the siege：停止包围，解除包围
⑥ Androgeus：/æn'drɒdʒɪəs/
⑦ Mysia /'mɪsɪə/：古代地区名，在今土耳其境内，北临马尔马拉海（the Sea of Marmara），西临爱琴海（the Aegean Sea）。
⑧ Dascylus：/'dæskɪləs/
⑨ the Bebryces /'bebrɪsiːz/：古代部落名，居住在 Bithynia；参见 *Argonautica* 选段 "The Symplegades" 中关于 Bithynia 的注释。
⑩ Mygdon：/'mɪgdn/
⑪ Amycus：/'æmɪkəs/
⑫ Heraclea /'herəklɪə/：the city of Heracles. Heracles is the Greek name of Hercules, which is his name in Latin.
⑬ Themiscyra /θɪ'mɪsɪrə/：the capital of the Amazons
⑭ charge：冲锋
⑮ it chanced：it happened
⑯ wantonness /'wɒntənnəs/：变化无常
⑰ Laomedon：king of Troy and father of Priam
⑱ Pergamum /'pɜːgəməm/：Troy
⑲ Hesione：/hɪ'saɪəni/

devoured by the sea monster, he exposed her by fastening her to the rocks near the sea. Seeing her exposed, Hercules promised to save her on condition of receiving from Laomedon the mares which Zeus had given in compensation for the rape① of Ganymede②. On Laomedon's saying that he would give them, Hercules killed the monster and saved Hesione. But when Laomedon would not give the stipulated③ reward, Hercules put to sea after threatening to make war on Troy.

And he touched at Aenus④, where he was entertained by Poltys⑤. And as he was sailing away he shot and killed on the Aenian beach a lewd fellow, Sarpedon, son of Poseidon and brother of Poltys. And having come to Thasos⑥ and subjugated the Thracians who dwelt in the island, he gave it to the sons of Androgeus to dwell in. From Thasos he proceeded to Torone⑦, and there, being challenged to wrestle by Polygonus and Telegonus⑧, sons of Proteus⑨, son of Poseidon, he killed them in the wrestling match. And having brought the belt to Mycenae he gave it to Eurystheus.

As a tenth labour he was ordered to fetch the kine of Geryon⑩ from Erythia⑪. Now Erythia was an island near the ocean⑫; it is now called Gadira⑬. This island was inhabited by Geryon, son of Chrysaor by Callirrhoe, daughter of Ocean. He had the body of three men grown together and joined in one at the waist, but parted in three from the flanks and thighs. He owned red kine, of which Eurytion was the herdsman and Orthus⑭, the two-headed hound, begotten by Typhon on Echidna, was the watchdog. So journeying through Europe to fetch the kine of Geryon he destroyed many wild beasts and set foot in Libya, and proceeding to Tartessus⑮ he erected as tokens of his journey two pillars over against each other at the boundaries of Europe and Libya.⑯ But being heated by the Sun on his journey, he bent his bow at the god, who in admiration of his hardihood⑰, gave him a golden goblet in which he crossed the ocean. And having reached Erythia he lodged on Mount Abas⑱. However the dog, perceiving him, rushed at him; but he smote it with his club, and when the herdsman Eurytion came to the help of the dog, Hercules killed him

---

① rape：抢走

② Ganymede：prince of Troy, known for his beauty. 关于 Zeus（Jupiter）抢走 Ganymede 的故事，参见 *The Age of Fable* 第 19 章。

③ stipulated /'stɪpjuleɪtɪd/：约定好的

④ Aenus /'iːnəs/：即今土耳其城市埃内兹（Enez），埃内兹位于土耳其与希腊的交界处，临爱琴海。

⑤ Poltys：/'pɒltɪs/

⑥ Thasos /'θeɪsɒs/：希腊岛屿名，位于爱琴海北部，属于今希腊东马其顿和色雷斯大区卡瓦拉州（Kavala）。

⑦ Torone /tə'rəuni/：希腊城市名，位于今希腊哈尔基季基州（Chalcidice）锡索尼亚（Sithonia）南部海岸。

⑧ Polygonus：/pə'lɪgənəs /；Telegonus：/tɪ'legənəs /

⑨ 参见 *The Age of Fable* 第 22 章关于 Proteus 的叙述。

⑩ Geryon：/'gerɪən/

⑪ Erythia /ɪ'rɪθɪə/：岛屿名，位于西班牙（Spain）南部城市加的斯（Cadiz）附近的大西洋上。

⑫ the ocean：大西洋

⑬ Gadira：/gə'daɪərə/

⑭ Orthus：/'ɔːθəs/

⑮ Tartessus /tɑː'tiːsəs/：古代地区名，位于西班牙南部。

⑯ 参见 *The Age of Fable* 第 19 章关于 the Pillars of Hercules 的叙述。

⑰ hardihood /'hɑːdɪhud /：胆大

⑱ Abas：/'æbəs/

also. But Menoetes①, who was there pasturing the kine of Hades, reported to Geryon what had occurred, and he②, coming up with③ Hercules beside the river Anthemus, as he was driving away the kine, joined battle with him and was shot dead. And Hercules, embarking the kine in the goblet and sailing across to Tartessus, gave back the goblet to the Sun.

And passing through Abderia④ he came to Liguria⑤, where Ialebion and Dercynus, sons of Poseidon, attempted to rob him of the kine, but he killed them and went on his way through Tyrrhenia⑥. But at Rhegium⑦ a bull broke away and hastily plunging into the sea swam across to Sicily, and having passed through the neighboring country since called Italy after it, for the Tyrrhenians called the bull "italus", came to the plain of Eryx⑧, who reigned over the Elymi⑨. Now Eryx was a son of Poseidon, and he mingled the bull with his own herds. So Hercules entrusted the kine to Hephaestus and hurried away in search of the bull. He found it in the herds of Eryx, and when the king refused to surrender it unless Hercules should beat him in a wrestling bout⑩, Hercules beat him thrice, killed him in the wrestling, and taking the bull drove it with the rest of the herd to the Ionian Sea. But when he came to the creeks⑪ of the sea, Hera afflicted the cows with a gadfly, and they dispersed among the skirts of the mountains of Thrace. Hercules went in pursuit, and having caught some, drove them to the Hellespont; but the remainder were thenceforth wild. Having with difficulty collected the cows, Hercules blamed the river Strymon⑫, and whereas it had been navigable⑬ before, he made it unnavigable by filling it with rocks; and he conveyed the kine and gave them to Eurystheus, who sacrificed them to Hera.

When the labours had been performed in eight years and a month, Eurystheus ordered Hercules, as an eleventh labour, to fetch golden apples from the Hesperides⑭, for he did not acknowledge the labour of the cattle of Augeas nor that of the hydra. These apples were not, as some have said, in Libya, but on Atlas among the Hyperboreans⑮. They were presented by Earth to Zeus after his marriage with Hera, and guarded by an immortal dragon with a hundred heads,

---

① Menoetes：/mɪˈniːtiːz/

② he：Geryon

③ come up with：追上，赶上

④ Abderia /æbˈdɪərɪə/：Abdera /æbˈdɪərə/ 是腓尼基人（the Phoenicians）在西班牙南部建立的一座城市，Abderia 指由 Abdera 管辖的土地。不要把这里的 Abdera 与位于色雷斯（Thrace）南部的 Abdera 混淆起来。

⑤ Liguria /lɪˈgjuːrɪə/：古代地区名，位于意大利西北部海岸。

⑥ Tyrrhenia /tɪˈriːnɪə/：即 Etruria，位于意大利西部。参见 *The Age of Fable* 第 21 章关于 Mæonia 的注释。

⑦ Rhegium /ˈriːdʒɪəm/：参见 *The Age of Fable* 第 25 章关于 Ibycus 的注释。

⑧ Eryx：/ˈerɪks/

⑨ the Elymi /ɪˈlɪmaɪ/（Elymians /ɪˈlɪmɪənz/）：古代部落名，居住在西西里岛西部。

⑩ bout /baʊt/：摔跤比赛，拳击比赛

⑪ creek：海岸边的水湾

⑫ Strymon /ˈstrɪmɒn/：该河在今希腊中马其顿大区塞雷州（Serres）境内，注入爱琴海。

⑬ navigable /ˈnævɪgəbl/：（河流或海洋）可通航的

⑭ the Hesperides：the daughters of Hesperus, the Evening Star

⑮ the Hyperboreans：参见 *The Age of Fable* 第 1 章关于 the Hyperboreans 的叙述。

offspring of Typhon and Echidna①, which spoke with many and divers② sorts of voices. With it the Hesperides also were on guard, to wit, Aegle, Erythia, Hesperia, and Arethusa③. So journeying he came to the river Echedorus④. And Cycnus⑤, son of Ares and Pyrene⑥, challenged him to single combat. Ares championed⑦ the cause of Cycnus and marshalled the combat, but a thunderbolt was hurled between the two and parted the combatants. And going on foot through Illyria⑧ and hastening to the river Eridanus⑨ he came to the nymphs, the daughters of Zeus and Themis. They revealed Nereus⑩ to him, and Hercules seized him while he slept, and though the god turned himself into all kinds of shapes, the hero bound him and did not release him till he had learned from him where were the apples and the Hesperides. Being informed, he traversed Libya. That country was then ruled by Antaeus, son of Poseidon, who used to kill strangers by forcing them to wrestle. Being forced to wrestle with him, Hercules hugged⑪ him, lifted him aloft, broke and killed him; for when he touched earth so it was that he waxed⑫ stronger, wherefore⑬ some said that he was a son of Earth.⑭

After Libya he traversed Egypt. That country was then ruled by Busiris⑮, a son of Poseidon by Lysianassa⑯, daughter of Epaphus⑰. This Busiris used to sacrifice strangers on an altar of Zeus in accordance with a certain oracle. For Egypt was visited with dearth⑱ for nine years, and Phrasius⑲, a learned seer⑳ who had come from Cyprus, said that the dearth would cease if they slaughtered a stranger man in honor of Zeus every year. Busiris began by slaughtering the seer himself and continued to slaughter the strangers who landed. So Hercules also was seized and haled to the altars, but he burst his bonds and slew both Busiris and his son Amphidamas㉑.

---

① Echidna /eˈkɪdnə/：怪物，一半是女人，一半是蛇。
② divers /ˈdaɪvəz/：各种各样的
③ These are names of the Hesperides.
④ Echedorus：/ˌiːkɪˈdɔːrəs/
⑤ Cycnus：/ˈsɪknəs/
⑥ Pyrene：/pɪˈriːni/
⑦ champion：支持
⑧ 参见 *The Age of Fable* 第 4 章 Illyria 的注释。
⑨ 参见 *The Age of Fable* 第 5 章 Eridanus 的注释。
⑩ Nereus /ˈnɪərɪuːs/：海神之一，年老，能预知未来，能随意变化自己的形状。参见 *The Age of Fable* 第 22 章关于 Nereus 的叙述。
⑪ hug：（在摔跤中）抱住
⑫ wax：逐渐变得
⑬ wherefore：因此
⑭ 关于 Hercules 与 Antaeus 的搏斗，参见 *The Age of Fable* 第 19 章中更详细的叙述。
⑮ Busiris：/buˈsɪərɪs/
⑯ Lysianassa：/ˌlɪsɪˈænəsə/
⑰ Epaphus：/ɪˈpæfəs/
⑱ dearth /dɜːθ/：饥荒，食物稀缺而昂贵
⑲ Phrasius：/ˈfreɪsɪəs/
⑳ seer：预言家
㉑ Amphidamas：/ˌæmfɪˈdæməs/

And traversing Asia① he put in to Thermydrae②, the harbor of the Lindians③. And having loosed one of the bullocks④ from the cart of a cowherd, he sacrificed it and feasted. But the cowherd, unable to protect himself, stood on a certain mountain and cursed. Wherefore to this day, when they sacrifice to Hercules, they do it with curses.

And passing by Arabia he slew Emathion, son of Tithonus⑤, and journeying through Libya to the outer sea he received the goblet from the Sun. And having crossed to the opposite mainland he shot on the Caucasus the eagle, offspring of Echidna and Typhon, that was devouring the liver of Prometheus, and he released Prometheus, after choosing for himself the bond⑥ of olive, and to Zeus he presented Chiron, who, though immortal, consented to die in his stead.

Now Prometheus had told Hercules not to go himself after the apples but to send Atlas, first relieving him of the burden of the sphere⑦; so when he was come to Atlas in the land of the Hyperboreans, he took the advice and relieved Atlas. But when Atlas had received three apples from the Hesperides, he came to Hercules, and not wishing to support the sphere he said that he would himself carry the apples to Eurystheus, and bade Hercules hold up the sky in his stead. Hercules promised to do so, but succeeded by craft⑧ in putting it on Atlas instead. For at the advice of Prometheus he begged Atlas to hold up the sky till he should put a pad⑨ on his head. When Atlas heard that, he laid the apples down on the ground and took the sphere from Hercules. And so Hercules picked up the apples and departed. But some say that he did not get them from Atlas, but that he plucked the apples himself after killing the guardian snake. And having brought the apples he gave them to Eurystheus. But he, on receiving them, bestowed them on Hercules, from whom Athena got them and conveyed them back again; for it was not lawful that they should be laid down anywhere.

A twelfth labour imposed on Hercules was to bring Cerberus from Hades. Now this Cerberus had three heads of dogs, the tail of a dragon, and on his back the heads of all sorts of snakes. When Hercules was about to depart to fetch him⑩, he went to Eumolpus⑪ at Eleusis⑫, wishing to be initiated⑬. However it was not then lawful for foreigners to be initiated: since he proposed to be initiated as the adoptive son of Pylius. But not being able to see the mysteries because he had

---

① Asia：小亚细亚半岛

② Thermydrae：/ˈθɜːmɪdriː/

③ The Lindians /ˈlɪndɪənz /are inhabitants of Lindus /ˈlɪndəs /, a city in Rhodes /rəʊdz /, a Greek island close to the western coast of Turkey.

④ bullock /ˈbʊlək/：阉割过的公牛

⑤ 关于 Tithonus 的故事，参见 *The Age of Fable* 第 26 章。

⑥ bond：镣铐

⑦ the sphere：the sky

⑧ craft：计谋，欺骗

⑨ pad：垫子

⑩ him：Cerebus

⑪ Eumolpus /juəˈmɒlpəs/：a Thracian who founded the Eleusinian mysteries

⑫ Eleusis /ɪˈljuːsɪs/：希腊 Attica 最重要的城市之一，位于雅典西北方向。

⑬ initiate /ɪˈnɪʃieɪt /：接纳……加入秘密宗教仪式

not been cleansed of the slaughter of the centaurs, he was cleansed by Eumolpus and then initiated. And having come to Taenarum① in Laconia②, where is the mouth of the descent to Hades, he descended through it. But when the souls saw him, they fled, save③ Meleager④ and the Gorgon Medusa⑤. And Hercules drew his sword against the Gorgon, as if she were alive, but he learned from Hermes that she was an empty phantom. And being come near to the gates of Hades he found Theseus⑥ and Pirithous, him who wooed Persephone in wedlock and was therefore bound fast. And when they beheld Hercules, they stretched out their hands as if they should be raised from the dead by his might. And Theseus, indeed, he took by the hand and raised up, but when he would have brought up Pirithous, the earth quaked and he let go. And he rolled away also the stone of Ascalaphus⑦. And wishing to provide the souls with blood, he slaughtered one of the kine of Hades. But Menoetes, son of Ceuthonymus, who tended the kine, challenged Hercules to wrestle, and, being seized round the middle, had his ribs broken; howbeit, he was let off at the request of Persephone⑧. When Hercules asked Pluto for Cerberus, Pluto ordered him to take the animal provided he mastered⑨ him without the use of the weapons which he carried. Hercules found him at the gates of Acheron⑩, and, cased in his cuirass⑪ and covered by the lion's skin, he flung his arms round the head of the brute, and though the dragon in its tail bit him, he never relaxed his grip and pressure till it yielded. So he carried it off and ascended through Troezen⑫. But Demeter turned Ascalaphus into a short-eared owl, and Hercules, after showing Cerberus to Eurystheus, carried him back to Hades.

After his labours Hercules went to Thebes and gave Megara to Iolaus⑬, and, wishing himself to wed, he ascertained that Eurytus⑭, prince of Oechalia⑮, had proposed the hand of his daughter Iole as a prize to him who should vanquish himself and his sons in archery. So he came to Oechalia, and though he proved himself better than them at archery, yet he did not get the bride; for while Iphitus, the elder of Eurytus's sons, said that Iole should be given to Hercules, Eurytus and the others refused, and said they feared that, if he got children, he would again kill his offspring. Not long after, some cattle were stolen from Euboea by Autolycus, and Eurytus supposed

---

① Taenarum /tiːˈneərəm/：位于希腊 Laconia 最南端的海角,也是欧洲大陆的最南端。

② Laconia /ləˈkəʊnɪə/：今天希腊的一个州,古代希腊的一个地区,Sparta 为其首府。

③ save：除……以外

④ 参见 *The Age of Fable* 第 18 章。

⑤ 参见 *The Age of Fable* 第 15 章。

⑥ 参见 *The Age of Fable* 第 20 章。

⑦ Ascalaphus /əˈskeɪləfəs/：因为告发 Proserpine 吃石榴,Ascalaphus 被 Ceres（Demeter）压在一块石头下。Hercules 在阴间把石头移开后,Ascalaphus 被变为一只猫头鹰。

⑧ Persephone：Proserpine

⑨ master：战胜,驯服

⑩ Acheron /ˈækərɒn/：阴间的河流之一,也指阴间。

⑪ cuirass /kwɪˈræs/：护胸铠甲

⑫ Troezen /ˈtriːzən/：参见 *The Age of Fable* 第 20 章关于 Trœzen 的注释。

⑬ He gave his wife Megara to Iolus who had helped him to kill the Lernaean hydra.

⑭ Eurytus：/juˈrɪtəs/

⑮ Oechalia /iːˈkeɪlɪə/：a town in Euboea /juːˈbiːə/, the second largest island of Greece

that it was done by Hercules; but Iphitus did not believe it and went to Hercules. And meeting him, as he came from Pherae① after saving the dead Alcestis for Admetus②, he invited him to seek the kine with him. Hercules promised to do so and entertained him; but going mad again he threw him from the walls of Tiryns. Wishing to be purified of the murder he repaired to Neleus③, who was prince of the Pylians④. And when Neleus rejected his request on the score of ⑤ his friendship with Eurytus, he went to Amyclae⑥ and was purified by Deiphobus, son of Hippolytus. But being afflicted with a dire disease on account of the murder of Iphitus he went to Delphi and inquired how he might be rid of the disease. As the Pythian priestess answered him not by oracles, he was fain to plunder the temple, and, carrying off the tripod, to institute an oracle of his own. But Apollo fought him, and Zeus threw a thunderbolt between them. When they had thus been parted, Hercules received an oracle, which declared that the remedy for his disease was for him to be sold, and to serve for three years, and to pay compensation for the murder to Eurytus. After the delivery of the oracle, Hermes sold Hercules, and he was bought by Omphale⑦, daughter of Iardanes⑧, queen of Lydia, to whom at his death her husband Tmolus had bequeathed the government. Eurytus did not accept the compensation when it was presented to him, but Hercules served Omphale as a slave, and in the course of his servitude he seized and bound the Cercopes⑨ at Ephesus⑩; and as for Syleus⑪ in Aulis, who compelled passing strangers to dig, Hercules killed him with his daughter Xenodoce, after burning the vines with the roots. And having put in to the island of Doliche⑫, he saw the body of Icarus washed ashore and buried it, and he called the island Icaria instead of Doliche.⑬ In return Daedalus made a portrait statue⑭ of Hercules at Pisa⑮, which Hercules mistook at night for living and threw a stone and hit it. And during the time of his servitude with Omphale it is said that the voyage to Colchis⑯ and the hunt of the Calydonian boar⑰

---

① Pherae /ˈfiːriː/：Thessaly 的一座城市，Admetus 居住的地方。
② 参见 The Age of Fable 第 23 章 Admetus 和 Alcestis 的故事。
③ Neleus：/ˈniːljuːs/
④ the Pylians /ˈpaɪlɪənz/：inhabitants of Pylus /ˈpaɪləs/，kingdom of Neleus in Peloponnese
⑤ on the score of：because of
⑥ Amyclae /əˈmɪkliː/：Laconia 城市名，位于 Sparta 以南不远处。
⑦ Omphale：/ˈɒmfəli/
⑧ Iardanes：/ˌaɪəˈdæniːz/
⑨ the Cercopes /səˈkəʊpiːz/：这兄弟俩是两个强盗，身材高大，力大无比，他们拦路抢劫过路人并处死他们。后来 Zeus 把他俩变成两只猴子。
⑩ Ephesus /ˈɪfiːsəs/：位于小亚细亚西海岸的一座城市，以用于 Diana 的神庙而著称。
⑪ Syleus：/ˈsɪlɪəs/
⑫ Doliche：/ˈdəʊlɪki/
⑬ 参见 The Age of Fable 第 20 章 Icarus 的故事以及关于 Icaria 的注释。
⑭ portrait statue：半身雕像
⑮ Pisa /ˈpiːzə/：古希腊城市名，位于 Elis，在 Alpheus 河畔，古希腊奥林匹克运动会的举办地。关于 Elis，参见 The Age of Fable 第 7 章的注释。不要把该城与因为斜塔而著名的意大利城市比萨（Pisa）混淆起来。
⑯ the voyage to Colchis：参见 The Age of Fable 第 17 章 The Golden Fleece 的故事。
⑰ the hunt of the Calydonian boar：参见 The Age of Fable 第 18 章 Meleager 的故事。

took place, and that Theseus① on his way from Troezen cleared the Isthmus of malefactors②.

After his servitude, being rid of his disease he mustered③ an army of noble volunteers and sailed for Ilium④ with eighteen ships of fifty oars each. And having come to port at Ilium, he left the guard⑤ of the ships to Oicles⑥ and himself with the rest of the champions set out to attack the city. Howbeit Laomedon marched against the ships with the multitude and slew Oicles in battle, but being repulsed⑦ by the troops of Hercules, he was besieged. The siege once laid, Telamon was the first to breach⑧ the wall and enter the city, and after him Hercules. But when he saw that Telamon had entered it first, he drew his sword and rushed at him, loath that anybody should be reputed a better man than himself. Perceiving that, Telamon collected stones that lay to hand, and when Hercules asked him what he did, he said he was building an altar to Hercules the Glorious Victor. Hercules thanked him, and when he had taken the city and shot down Laomedon and his sons, except Podarces⑨, he assigned Laomedon's daughter Hesione as a prize to Telamon and allowed her to take with her whomsoever of the captives she would. When she chose her brother Podarces, Hercules said that he must first be a slave and then be ransomed by her. So when he was being sold she took the veil from her head and gave it as a ransom; hence Podarces was called Priam⑩.

When Hercules was sailing from Troy, Hera sent grievous storms, which so vexed Zeus that he hung her from Olympus. Hercules sailed to Cos⑪, and the Coans⑫, thinking he was leading a piratical squadron, endeavored to prevent his approach by a shower of stones. But he forced his way in and took the city by night, and slew the king, Eurypylus⑬, son of Poseidon by Astypalaea. And Hercules was wounded in the battle by Chalcedon; but Zeus snatched him away, so that he took no harm. And having laid waste Cos, he came through Athena's agency⑭ to Phlegra⑮, and sided with the gods in their victorious war on the giants.

Not long afterwards he collected an Arcadian army, and being joined by volunteers from the

---

① 参见 *The Age of Fable* 第 20 章 Theseus 的故事。
② cleared the Isthmus of malefactors：铲除科林斯地峡的作恶者；the Isthmus：参见 *The Age of Fable* 第 20 章关于 the Corinthian isthmus 的注释；malefactor /ˈmælɪfæktə/：作恶者
③ muster /ˈmʌstə/：召集
④ Ilium：Troy；参见 *The Age of Fable* 第 27 章关于 Troy 的注释。
⑤ guard：守卫，保护
⑥ Oicles：/ˈɔɪkliːz/
⑦ repulse /rɪˈpʌls/：击退
⑧ breach：攻破
⑨ Podarces：/pəʊˈdɑːsiːz/
⑩ Priam：Priam 的名字在古希腊语中是 Πρίαμος（Priamos），源自古希腊语动词 πρίαμαι（priamai）。动词 πρίαμαι（priamai）的意思是"买，赎"，所以 Πρίαμος（Priamos）的本意是"买来的，赎来的"。
⑪ Cos /kɒs/：参见 *The Iliad* 选段"Deception of Jupiter by Juno"中关于 Cos 的注释。
⑫ the Coans /ˈkəʊənz/：inhabitants of Cos
⑬ Eurypylus：/jʊəˈrɪpɪləs/
⑭ agency /ˈeɪdʒənsi/：施加影响
⑮ Phlegra /ˈflegrə/：古代马其顿（Macedonia）地区名

first① men in Greece he marched against Augeas②. But Augeas, hearing of the war that Hercules was levying, appointed Eurytus and Cteatus③ generals of the Eleans④. They were two men joined in one, who surpassed all of that generation in strength and were sons of Actor by Molione⑤, though their father was said to be Poseidon; now Actor was a brother of Augeas. But it came to pass that on the expedition Hercules fell sick; hence he concluded a truce⑥ with the Molionides⑦. But afterwards, being apprized⑧ of his illness, they attacked the army and slew many. On that occasion, therefore, Hercules beat a retreat⑨; but afterwards at the celebration of the third Isthmian festival, when the Eleans sent the Molionides to take part in the sacrifices, Hercules waylaid and killed them at Cleonae⑩, and marching on Elis took the city. And having killed Augeas and his sons, he restored Phyleus and bestowed on him the kingdom. He also celebrated the Olympian games and founded an altar of Pelops, and built six altars of the twelve gods⑪.

After the capture of Elis he marched against Pylus, and having taken the city he slew Periclymenus⑫, the most valiant of the sons of Neleus, who used to change his shape in battle. And he slew Neleus and his sons, except Nestor⑬; for he was a youth and was being brought up among the Gerenians⑭. In the fight he also wounded Hades, who was siding with the Pylians.

Having taken Pylus he marched against Lacedaemon⑮, wishing to punish the sons of Hippocoon⑯, for he was angry with them, both because they fought for Neleus, and still angrier because they had killed the son of Licymnius⑰. For when he⑱ was looking at the palace of Hippocoon, a hound of the Molossian⑲ breed ran out and rushed at him, and he threw a stone and hit the dog, whereupon the Hippocoontids⑳ darted out and despatched㉑ him with blows of their

---

① first：第一流的，最杰出的，最优秀的
② 这个 Augeas 即本选段中前面已经提到过的那个 Augeas。
③ Cteatus：/ˈtiːətəs/
④ the Eleans /ˈiːlɪənz/：inhabitants of Elis
⑤ Molione：/məˈlaɪəni/
⑥ truce /truːs/：停战
⑦ the Molionides /ˌmɒlɪˈɒlɪdiːz/：Eurytus and Cteatus, sons of Molione
⑧ apprize /əˈpraɪz/：告知
⑨ beat a retreat：（击鼓让军队）撤退
⑩ Cleonae /ˈkliːəniː/：Argolis 的城市名，位于 Nemea 附近。
⑪ 希腊神话中最重要的神有 12 个，这个数字是固定的，关于这 12 个神是哪些，有几种差异不大的说法。
⑫ Periclymenus：/ˌperɪˈklaɪmɪnəs/
⑬ This Nestor is the young Nestor in the hunt of the Calydonian boar and "the oldest of the Grecian chiefs" in the Trojan War.
⑭ the Gerenians /gəˈriːnɪənz/：inhabitants of Gerena /gəˈriːnə /, an ancient Greek city not far from Pylus
⑮ Lacedaemon /ˌlæsɪˈdiːmən/：Sparta
⑯ Hippocoon：/ˌhɪpəˈkəʊɒn/
⑰ the son of Licymnius /lɪˈsɪmnɪəs/：Oeonos /ˈiːənəs /, whose father, Licymnius, is the uncle of Hercules.
⑱ he：Oeonos, the son of Licymnius
⑲ Molossian /məˈlɒsɪən/：of Molossia /məˈlɒsɪə /；Molossia 是希腊 Epirus 的一个地区，以产一种高大、健壮的狗而闻名，这种狗头大、耳垂。
⑳ the Hippocoontids /hɪˌpɒkəˈɒntɪdz/：the sons of Hippocoon
㉑ despatch：杀死

cudgels①. It was to avenge his death that Hercules mustered an army against the Lacedaemonians. And having come to Arcadia he begged Cepheus② to join him with his sons, of whom he had twenty. But fearing lest, if he quitted Tegea③, the Argives④ would march against it, Cepheus refused to join the expedition. But Hercules had received from Athena a lock of the Gorgon's hair in a bronze jar and gave it to Sterope⑤, daughter of Cepheus, saying that if an army advanced against the city, she was to hold up the lock of hair thrice from the walls, and that, provided she did not look before her, the enemy would be turned to flight. That being so, Cepheus and his sons took the field, and in the battle he and his sons perished, and besides them Iphicles, the brother of Hercules. Having killed Hippocoon and his sons and subjugated the city, Hercules restored Tyndareus⑥ and entrusted the kingdom to him.

Passing by Tegea, Hercules debauched Auge⑦, not knowing her to be a daughter of Aleus⑧. And she brought forth⑨ her babe secretly and deposited it in the precinct of Athena⑩. But the country being wasted by a pestilence, Aleus entered the precinct and on investigation discovered his daughter's motherhood. So he exposed the babe on Mount Parthenius⑪, and by the providence⑫ of the gods it was preserved: for a doe that had just cast⑬ her fawn⑭ gave it suck, and shepherds took up the babe and called it Telephus⑮. And her father gave Auge to Nauplius⑯, son of Poseidon, to sell far away in a foreign land; and Nauplius gave her to Teuthras⑰, the prince of Teuthrania⑱, who made her his wife.

And having come to Calydon, Hercules wooed Deianira, daughter of Oeneus⑲. He wrestled for her hand with Achelous⑳, who assumed the likeness of a bull; but Hercules broke off one of his horns. So Hercules married Deianira, but Achelous recovered the horn by giving the horn of

---

① cudgel /ˈkʌdʒəl/：短而粗的棍棒

② Cepheus：/ˈsiːfjuːs/

③ Tegea /ˈtiːdʒiə/：a city in Arcadia

④ the Argives /ˈɑːɡaɪvz/：the inhabitants of Argo, a city-state in ancient Greece

⑤ Sterope：/ˈstɪərəpi/

⑥ Tyndareus /tɪnˈdeəriəs/：husband of Leda and father of Castor, Pollux, Helen, and Clytemnestra

⑦ Auge：/ˈɔːdʒi/

⑧ Aleus /ˈælɪəs/：king of Tegea

⑨ bring forth：give birth to

⑩ the precinct /ˈpriːsɪŋkt /of Athena：Athena 神庙的四周

⑪ Mount Parthenius /ˈpɑːθɪnɪəs/：Arcadia 和 Argolis 之间的一座山

⑫ providence /ˈprɒvɪdəns/：神的旨意

⑬ cast：（动物）早产

⑭ fawn：幼鹿

⑮ Telephus /ˈtelɪfəs/：Telephus 后来成了 Mysia 的国王。关于 Mysia,参见 *The Age of Fable* 第 17 章的注释。

⑯ Nauplius：/ˈnɔːplɪəs/

⑰ Teuthras /ˈtjuːθrəs/：king of Mysia

⑱ Teuthrania /tjuːˈθreɪnɪə/：a town in Mysia

⑲ Oeneus：/ˈiːnɪəs/

⑳ 关于 Hercules 和 Achelous 的摔跤比赛,参见 *The Age of Fable* 第 23 章。

Amalthea① in its stead. Now Amalthea was a daughter of Haemonius②, and she had a bull's horn, which, according to Pherecydes, had the power of supplying meat or drink in abundance, whatever one might wish.

And Hercules marched with the Calydonians against the Thesprotians③, and having taken the city of Ephyra④, of which Phylas was king, he had intercourse with the king's daughter Astyoche⑤, and became the father of Tlepolemus⑥. While he stayed among them, he sent word to Thespius to keep seven of his sons, to send three to Thebes and to despatch the remaining forty to the island of Sardinia⑦ to plant⑧ a colony. After these events, as he was feasting with Oeneus, he killed with a blow of his knuckles⑨ Eunomus, son of Architeles, when the lad was pouring water on his hands; now the lad was a kinsman of Oeneus. Seeing that it was an accident, the lad's father pardoned Hercules; but Hercules wished, in accordance with the law, to suffer the penalty of exile, and resolved to depart to Ceyx⑩ at Trachis⑪. And taking Deianira with him, he came to the river Evenus, at which the centaur Nessus sat and ferried passengers across for hire⑫, alleging⑬ that he had received the ferry⑭ from the gods for his righteousness. So Hercules crossed the river by himself, but on being asked to pay the fare he entrusted Deianira to Nessus to carry over. But he, in ferrying her across, attempted to violate her. She cried out, Hercules heard her, and shot Nessus to the heart when he emerged from the river. Being at the point of death, Nessus called Deianira to him and said that if she would have a love charm to operate on Hercules she should mix the seed he had dropped on the ground with the blood that flowed from the wound inflicted by the barb⑮. She did so and kept it by her.

Going through the country of the Dryopes⑯ and being in lack of food, Hercules met Thiodamas⑰ driving a pair of bullocks⑱; so he unloosed and slaughtered one of the bullocks and feasted. And when he came to Ceyx at Trachis he was received by him and conquered the Dryopes.

---

① Amalthea /ˌæməlˈθiːə/: The horn of Amalthea is the cornucopia.

② Haemonius: /hiːˈməʊniəs/

③ the Thesprotians /θɪˈsprəʊtɪənz/: 古希腊部落,他们居住的地方叫 Thesprotis /θɪˈsprəʊtɪs/,位于 Epirus 西南海岸。

④ Ephyra: /ˈiːfɪrə/

⑤ Astyoche: /əˈstɪəki/

⑥ Tlepolemus: /ˌtliːpəˈliːməs/

⑦ Sardinia /sɑːˈdɪnɪə/: 地中海岛屿名,位于意大利以西,科西嘉岛以南。

⑧ plant: 建立(殖民地、城市、教堂等)

⑨ knuckle /nʌkl/: 手指关节,拳头

⑩ Ceyx /ˈsiːɪks/: 参见 *The Age of Fable* 第 9 章。

⑪ Trachis /ˈtrækɪs/: Thessaly 城市名,也叫 Trachin,位于 Oeta 山脚下。

⑫ hire: 报酬

⑬ allege /əˈledʒ/: 宣称

⑭ ferry /ˈferi/: 渡船

⑮ barb: (箭、鱼钩等的)倒钩

⑯ Dryopes /ˈdraɪəpiːz/: 古希腊部落名

⑰ Thiodamas: /θɪəˈdæməs/

⑱ bullock /ˈbʊlək/: 小公牛,阉割过的公牛

And afterwards setting out from there, he fought as an ally of Aegimius①, king of the Dorians②. For the Lapiths, commanded by Coronus③, made war on him in a dispute about the boundaries of the country; and being besieged he called in the help of Hercules, offering him a share of the country. So Hercules came to his help and slew Coronus and others, and handed the whole country over to Aegimius free. He slew also Laogoras④, king of the Dryopes, with his children, as he was banqueting in a precinct of Apollo; for the king was a wanton fellow and an ally of the Lapiths. And as he passed by Itonus⑤ he was challenged to single combat by Cycnus a son of Ares and Pelopia; and closing with him Hercules slew him also. But when he was come to Ormenium⑥, king Amyntor⑦ took arms and forbade him to march through; but when he would have hindered his passage, Hercules slew him also.

On his arrival at Trachis he mustered an army to attack Oechalia, wishing to punish Eurytus. Being joined by Arcadians⑧, Melians⑨ from Trachis, and Epicnemidian Locrians⑩, he slew Eurytus and his sons and took the city. After burying those of his own side who had fallen, to wit, Hippasus, son of Ceyx, and Argius and Melas, the sons of Licymnius, he pillaged the city and led Iole captive. And having put in at Cenaeum⑪, a headland⑫ of Euboea⑬, he built an altar of Cenaean⑭ Zeus. Intending to offer sacrifice, he sent the herald Lichas⑮ to Trachis to fetch fine raiment⑯. From him Deianira learned about Iole, and fearing that Hercules might love that damsel⑰ more than herself, she supposed that the spilt blood of Nessus was in truth a love-charm, and with it she smeared the tunic⑱. So Hercules put it on and proceeded to offer sacrifice. But no sooner was the tunic warmed than the poison of the hydra began to corrode⑲ his skin; and on that he lifted Lichas by the feet, hurled him down from the headland, and tore off the tunic, which

---

① Aegimius：/iːˈdʒɪmɪəs/

② the Dorians /ˈdɔːrɪənz/：inhabitants of Doris /ˈdɔːrɪs/；Doris 是古希腊的一个很小的山区地区,位于 Oeta 山和 Parnassus 山之间。

③ Coronus：/kəˈrəʊnəs/

④ Laogoras：/leɪˈɒɡərəs/

⑤ Itonus /ɪˈtəʊnəs/：古希腊城市名,在 Thessaly。

⑥ Ormenium：/ɔːˈmiːnɪəm/

⑦ Amyntor：/əˈmɪntə/

⑧ Arcadians /ɑːˈkeɪdɪənz/：inhabitants of Arcadia

⑨ Melians：/ˈmelɪənz/：古希腊部落名,居住在今中希腊大区弗西奥蒂斯州（Phthiotis 或 Fthiotis）斯派尔希奥斯河（Spercheios）河口处。Trachis 是该部落的主要城市。

⑩ Epicnemidian Locrians /ˈlɒkrɪənz/：the Locrians 是古希腊的一个部落,分为东西两支,东支居住在埃维亚岛（Euboea 或 Evvoia）对岸的希腊东部海岸,称为 Epicnemidian Locrians。

⑪ Cenaeum /sɪˈniːəm /：位于 Euboea 岛的最西北端的海角。

⑫ headland：海角

⑬ Euboea /juːˈbɪə/：希腊第二大岛

⑭ Cenaean：Cenaeum 的

⑮ Lichas：/ˈlaɪkəs/

⑯ raiment /ˈreɪmənt/：衣服

⑰ damsel /ˈdæmzəl/：出生高贵的年轻未婚女性

⑱ tunic /ˈtjuːnɪk/：古希腊人和古罗马人穿的一种短袖束腰外衣,下摆到膝盖,男女通用。

⑲ corrode /kəˈrəʊd/：逐渐损坏,腐蚀

clung to his body, so that his flesh was torn away with it. In such a sad plight he was carried on shipboard to Trachis: and Deianira, on learning what had happened, hanged herself. But Hercules, after charging Hyllus[①] his elder son by Deianira, to marry Iole when he came of age, proceeded to Mount Oeta, in the Trachinian territory, and there constructed a pyre, mounted it, and gave orders to kindle it. When no one would do so, Poeas[②], passing by to look for his flocks, set a light to it. On him Hercules bestowed his bow. While the pyre was burning, it is said that a cloud passed under Hercules and with a peal of thunder wafted him up to heaven. Thereafter he obtained immortality, and being reconciled to Hera he married her daughter Hebe, by whom he had sons, Alexiares and Anicetus.

---

① Hyllus: /'hɪləs/
② Poeas /'piːəs/: Philoctetes 的父亲

Virgil

(70 B.C.—19 B.C.)

维吉尔（Virgil /ˈvɜːdʒɪl/）是古罗马最伟大的诗人。《牧歌》（*The Eclogues*）是维吉尔的成名作。《农事诗》（*The Georgics*）创作于公元前 37 年至公元前 30 年，是一部关于农业的教诲诗。维吉尔最著名的诗作是英雄史诗《埃涅阿斯纪》（*The Aeneid*）。

《埃涅阿斯纪》共 12 卷，讲述特洛伊英雄埃涅阿斯（Aeneas）率领特洛伊人逃离被希腊人攻克的特洛伊城到意大利建立新国家的故事。本读本从《埃涅阿斯纪》中选取了 5 个片段：第 1 个选段"The Trojan Horse"选自史诗的第 2 卷，第 2 个选段"Dido's Love for Aeneas"和第 3 个选段"Dido's Death"选自史诗的第 4 卷，第 4 个选段"Camilla"选自史诗的第 7 卷，第 5 个选段"Death of Turnus"选自史诗的第 12 卷。《埃涅阿斯纪》有多种英语译本，此处采用的是德莱顿（John Dryden）的英雄双行体（heroic couplet）译本。德莱顿是英国 17 世纪著名的诗人、剧作家和文学评论家。

The Aeneid
Translated into English by John Dryden

The Trojan Horse

All were attentive to the godlike man①,

When from his lofty couch he thus began：

"Great queen②, what you command me to relate

Renews the sad remembrance of our fate：

---

① the godlike man：Æneas
② Great queen：Dido, queen of Carthage

An empire from its old foundations rent,

And ev'ry① woe the Trojans underwent；

A peopled② city made a desart③ place；

All that I saw, and part of which I was：

Not ev'n④ the hardest of our foes could hear,

Nor stern Ulysses tell without a tear.⑤

And now the latter watch of wasting night,

And setting stars, to kindly rest invite；

But, since you take such int'rest⑥ in our woe,

And Troy's disastrous end desire to know,

I will restrain my tears, and briefly tell

What in our last and fatal night befell.

"By destiny compell'd, and in despair,

The Greeks grew weary of the tedious⑦ war,

And by Minerva's aid a fabric rear'd,

Which like a steed of monstrous height appear'd：

The sides were plank'd with pine；they feign'd it made

For their return, and this the vow they paid.

Thus they pretend, but in the hollow side

Selected numbers of their soldiers hide：

With inward arms the dire machine⑧ they load,

And iron bowels stuff the dark abode.

In sight of Troy lies Tenedos⑨, an isle

(While Fortune did on Priam's empire⑩ smile)

Renown'd for wealth；but, since⑪, a faithless bay,

Where ships expos'd to wind and weather lay.⑫

---

① ev'ry：every；省掉字母 e 的目的是强调在本行中 every 读作两个音节。
② peopled /'piːpld/：住满人的
③ desart：desert（无人烟的,荒废的）
④ ev'n：even；读作一个音节。
⑤ 从特洛伊返回家乡的过程中，Ulysses 在 Scheria 停留了一段时间,受到国王 Alcinous 的款待。在 Alcinous 举办的宴会上,游吟诗人 Demodocus 吟唱了特洛伊沦陷的故事。在 *The Odyssey* 第 8 卷中,Homer 这样描写 Ulysses 在听到特洛伊沦陷的故事后的反应：These were the things the great bard (Demodocus) sang of. Odysseus (Ulysses) meanwhile was greatly moved, and down from his eyes came coursing over his cheeks.
⑥ int'rest：interest；读作两个音节。
⑦ tedious /'tiːdɪəs /：漫长的
⑧ the dire machine：the horse
⑨ Tenedos /'tenədɒs/：岛屿名,位于爱琴海北部,离 Troy 不远。该岛现在叫 Bozcaada,属于土耳其。
⑩ Priam's empire：Troy
⑪ since：从那时起
⑫ Where ships lay expos'd to wind and weather.

There was their fleet conceal'd. We thought, for Greece

Their sails were hoisted, and our fears release.

The Trojans, coop'd① within their walls so long,

Unbar their gates, and issue② in a throng,

Like swarming bees, and with delight survey

The camp deserted, where the Grecians lay:

The quarters of the sev'ral chiefs they show'd;

Here Phoenix③, here Achilles, made abode;

Here join'd the battles; there the navy rode.

Part on the pile④ their wond'ring eyes employ:

The pile by Pallas rais'd to ruin Troy.

Thymoetes⑤ first ('t⑥ is doubtful whether hir'd,

Or so the Trojan destiny requir'd)

Mov'd⑦ that the ramparts⑧ might be broken down,

To lodge the monster fabric in the town.

But Capys⑨, and the rest of sounder mind,

The fatal present to the flames designed,

Or to the wat'ry deep⑩; at least to bore⑪

The hollow sides, and hidden frauds explore.

The giddy⑫ vulgar⑬, as their fancies guide,

With noise say nothing, and in parts divide.

Laocoon, follow'd by a num'rous crowd,

Ran from the fort, and cried, from far, aloud:

'O wretched countrymen! what fury reigns?

What more than madness has possess'd your brains?

Think you the Grecians from your coasts are gone?

And are Ulysses' arts⑭ no better known?

---

① coop /kuːp／：关在笼子里,关在狭窄的地方

② issue：出来

③ Phoenix /ˈfiːnɪks／：Achilles 的军师

④ the pile：the huge wooden horse

⑤ Thymoetes：/θɪˈmiːtiːz/

⑥ 't：it

⑦ move：提议,建议

⑧ rampart /ˈræmpɑːt／：防御土墙

⑨ Capys：/ˈkæpɪs/

⑩ deep：大海

⑪ bore：在……上钻孔

⑫ giddy /ˈgɪdi／：疯狂的,愚蠢的

⑬ vulgar /ˈvʌlgə／：平民百姓

⑭ arts：诡计

This hollow fabric either must inclose①,

Within its blind② recess③, our secret foes;

Or 't is an engine rais'd above the town,

T' o'erlook④ the walls, and then to batter down.

Somewhat is sure design'd, by fraud or force:

Trust not their presents, nor admit⑤ the horse.'

Thus having said, against the steed he threw

His forceful spear, which, hissing as flew,

Pierc'd thro' the yielding planks of jointed wood,

And trembling in the hollow belly stood.

The sides, transpierc'd, return a rattling sound,

And groans of Greeks inclos'd come issuing thro' the wound.

And, had not Heav'n the fall of Troy design'd,

Or had not men been fated to be blind,

Enough was said and done t'inspire⑥ a better mind.

Then had our lances pierc'd the treach'rous wood,

And Ilian⑦ tow'rs and Priam's empire stood.

Meantime, with shouts, the Trojan shepherds bring

A captive Greek, in bands⑧, before the king⑨;

Taken to take; who made himself their prey,

T' impose on their belief, and Troy betray;

Fix'd on his aim, and obstinately bent

To die undaunted, or to circumvent⑩.

About the captive, tides of Trojans flow;

All press to see, and some insult the foe.

Now hear how well the Greeks their wiles disguis'd;

Behold a nation in a man compris'd.

Trembling the miscreant⑪ stood, unarm'd and bound;

He star'd, and roll'd his haggard⑫ eyes around,

---

① inclose：enclose

② blind：隐蔽的,秘密的

③ recess /rɪ'ses/：隐秘处,深处

④ T' o'erlook：to overlook

⑤ admit：允许进入

⑥ t'inspire：to inspire

⑦ Ilian /'ɪlɪən/：Trojan

⑧ band：带子

⑨ the king：Priam

⑩ circumvent /ˌsɜːkəm'vent/：欺骗

⑪ miscreant /'mɪskrɪənt/：恶棍,无赖

⑫ haggard /'hægəd/：憔悴的

Then said：'Alas！what earth remains, what sea
Is open to receive unhappy me?
What fate a wretched fugitive attends①,
Scorn'd by my foes, abandon'd by my friends?'
He said, and sigh'd, and cast a rueful② eye：
Our pity kindles③, and our passions④ die.
We cheer the youth to make his own defense,
And freely tell us what he was, and whence：
What news he could impart, we long to know,
And what to credit from a captive foe.

"His fear at length dismiss'd, he said：'Whate'er
My fate ordains, my words shall be sincere：
I neither can nor dare my birth disclaim⑤;
Greece is my country, Sinon⑥ is my name.
Tho' plung'd by Fortune's pow'r in misery,
'T is not in Fortune's pow'r to make me lie.
If any chance has hither brought the name
Of Palamedes⑦, not unknown to fame,
Who suffer'd from the malice of the times,
Accus'd and sentenc'd for pretended⑧ crimes,
Because these fatal wars he would prevent;
Whose death the wretched Greeks too late lament—
Me, then a boy, my father, poor and bare
Of other means, committed to his care,
His kinsman and companion in the war.
While Fortune favor'd, while his arms support
The cause, and rul'd the counsels, of the court,
I made some figure there⑨; nor was my name
Obscure⑩, nor I without my share of fame.

---

① attend /əˈtend /：等待
② rueful /ˈruːfl/：可怜的
③ kindle /ˈkɪndl /：被激发
④ passion：愤怒
⑤ disclaim /dɪsˈkleɪm/：否认
⑥ Sinon：/ˈsaɪnən/
⑦ 由于 Palamedes 戳穿了 Ulysses 装疯的诡计, Ulysses 不得不前往 Troy 参战, 所以 Ulysses 怀恨在心, 设计将 Palamedes 害死。关于 Palamedes 怎样戳穿了 Ulysses 装疯的诡计, 参见 *The Age of Fable* 第 27 章。
⑧ pretended /ˈprɪtendɪd/：虚假的, 虚构的
⑨ 我还算是个人物。
⑩ obscure /əbˈskjuə/：不知名的, 不为人所知的

But when Ulysses, with fallacious① arts,
Had made impression in the people's hearts,
And forg'd② a treason in my patron's name
(I speak of things too far divulg'd③ by fame),
My kinsman fell. Then I, without support,
In private mourn'd his loss, and left the court.
Mad as I was, I could not bear his fate
With silent grief, but loudly blam'd the state,
And curs'd the direful author of my woes.
'T was told again; and hence my ruin rose.
I threaten'd, if indulgent Heav'n once more
Would land me safely on my native shore,
His death with double vengeance to restore.
This mov'd the murderer's hate; and soon ensued
Th' effects of malice from a man so proud.
Ambiguous rumors thro' the camp he spread,
And sought, by treason, my devoted head;
New crimes invented; left unturn'd no stone,
To make my guilt appear, and hide his own;
Till Calchas was by force and threat'ning wrought—
But why—why dwell I on that anxious thought?
If on my nation just revenge you seek,
And 't is t' appear a foe, t' appear a Greek;
Already you my name and country know;
Assuage your thirst of blood, and strike the blow:
My death will both the kingly brothers④ please,
And set insatiate⑤ Ithacus⑥ at ease.'
This fair unfinish'd tale, these broken starts,
Rais'd expectations in our longing hearts:
Unknowing as we were in Grecian arts.
His former trembling once again renew'd,
With acted⑦ fear, the villain thus pursued:

---

① fallacious /fə'leɪʃəs/：欺骗的，误导人的
② forge /fɔːdʒ/：杜撰，编造
③ divulge /daɪ'vʌldʒ/：宣布，公布
④ the kingly brothers：Agamemnon and Menelaus
⑤ insatiate /ɪn'seɪʃɪət/：永不满足的
⑥ Ithacus /'ɪθəkəs/：Ulysses, who is from Ithaca
⑦ acted /'æktɪd /：假装的

"'Long had the Grecians (tir'd with fruitless care,
And wearied with an unsuccessful war)
Resolv'd to raise the siege①, and leave the town②;
And, had the gods permitted, they had gone;
But oft the wintry seas and southern winds
Withstood③ their passage④ home, and chang'd their minds.
Portents and prodigies their souls amaz'd;
But most, when this stupendous pile⑤ was rais'd:
Then flaming meteors⑥, hung in air, were seen,
And thunders rattled thro' a sky serene⑦.
Dismay'd, and fearful of some dire event,
Eurypylus t' enquire their fate was sent.
He from the gods this dreadful answer brought:
"O Grecians, when the Trojan shores you sought,
Your passage with a virgin's blood was bought⑧:
So must your safe return be bought again,
And Grecian blood once more atone⑨ the main⑩."
The spreading rumor round the people ran;
All fear'd, and each believ'd himself the man.
Ulysses took th' advantage of their fright;
Call'd Calchas, and produc'd in open sight:
Then bade him name the wretch, ordain'd by fate
The public victim, to redeem the state.
Already some presag'd⑪ the dire event,
And saw what sacrifice Ulysses meant.
For twice five days the good old seer⑫ withstood
Th' intended treason, and was dumb to blood,
Till, tir'd, with endless clamors and pursuit
Of Ithacus, he stood no longer mute;

① raise the siege：停止包围，解除包围
② the town：Troy
③ withstand：阻止，阻挡
④ passage：旅程
⑤ this stupendous pile：the wooden horse；stupendous /stjuːˈpendəs/：让人吃惊的，巨大的
⑥ meteor /ˈmiːtɪə/：流星
⑦ serene /sɪˈriːn/：晴朗的，无云的，宁静的
⑧ This virgin is Iphigenia, daughter of Agamemnon. 参见 *The Age of Fable* 第 27 章。
⑨ atone /əˈtəʊn/：抚慰，使息怒
⑩ main：大海
⑪ presage /ˈpresɪdʒ/：预言
⑫ the good old seer：Calchas

But, as it was agreed, pronounc'd that I
Was destin'd by the wrathful gods to die.
All prais'd the sentence, pleas'd the storm should fall
On one alone, whose fury threaten'd all.
The dismal day was come; the priests① prepare
Their leaven'd cakes, and fillets② for my hair.
I follow'd nature's laws, and must avow
I broke my bonds and fled the fatal blow.
Hid in a weedy lake all night I lay,
Secure of safety when they sail'd away.
But now what further hopes for me remain,
To see my friends, or native soil, again;
My tender③ infants, or my careful④ sire⑤,
Whom they returning will to death require;
Will perpetrate⑥ on them their first design⑦,
And take the forfeit⑧ of their heads for mine?
Which, O! if pity mortal minds can move,
If there be faith below⑨, or gods above,
If innocence and truth can claim desert⑩,
Ye Trojans, from an injur'd wretch avert.'

"False tears true pity move; the king commands
To loose his fetters, and unbind his hands:
Then adds these friendly words: 'Dismiss thy⑪ fears;
Forget the Greeks; be mine as thou wert⑫ theirs.
But truly tell, was it for force or guile,
Or some religious end, you rais'd the pile?'
Thus said the king. He, full of fraudful arts,
This well-invented tale for truth imparts:

---

① priest:(古希腊、罗马)祭司
② fillet:束发带
③ tender:年幼的
④ careful:悲伤的,忧心忡忡的
⑤ sire /ˈsaɪə/:父亲
⑥ perpetrate /ˈpeɪpɪtreɪt/:施行
⑦ design /dɪˈzaɪn/:意图,计划
⑧ forfeit /ˈfɔːfɪt/:丧失
⑨ below:在人世间
⑩ desert /dɪˈzɜːt/:应得的奖赏或回报
⑪ thy:your
⑫ thou wert:you were

'Ye lamps of heav'n!' he said, and lifted high
His hands now free, 'thou venerable sky!
Inviolable pow'rs, ador'd with dread!
Ye fatal fillets, that once bound this head!
Ye sacred altars, from whose flames I fled!
Be all of you adjur'd; and grant I may,
Without a crime, th' ungrateful Greeks betray,
Reveal the secrets of the guilty state,
And justly punish whom I justly hate!
But you, O king, preserve the faith you gave,
If I, to save myself, your empire save.
The Grecian hopes, and all th' attempts they made,
Were only founded on Minerva's aid.
But from the time when impious Diomede,
And false Ulysses, that inventive head,
Her fatal image① from the temple drew,
The sleeping guardians of the castle slew,
Her virgin statue with their bloody hands
Polluted, and profan'd her holy bands;
From thence the tide of fortune left their shore,
And ebb'd much faster than it flow'd before:
Their courage languish'd, as their hopes decay'd;
And Pallas, now averse, refus'd her aid.
Nor did the goddess doubtfully declare
Her alter'd mind and alienated care.
When first her fatal image touch'd the ground,
She sternly cast her glaring eyes around,
That sparkled as they roll'd, and seem'd to threat:
Her heav'nly limbs distill'd a briny sweat.
Thrice from the ground she leap'd, was seen to wield
Her brandish'd lance, and shake her horrid shield.
Then Calchas bade our host for flight
And hope no conquest from the tedious war,
Till first they sail'd for Greece; with pray'rs besought
Her injur'd pow'r, and better omens brought.
And now their navy plows the wat'ry main,
Yet soon expect it on your shores again,

---

① Her fatal image：the Palladium

With Pallas pleas'd; as Calchas did ordain.
But first, to reconcile the blue-ey'd maid①
For her stol'n statue and her tow'r betray'd,
Warn'd by the seer, to her offended name
We rais'd and dedicate this wondrous frame,
So lofty, lest thro' your forbidden gates
It pass, and intercept② our better fates:
For, once admitted there, our hopes are lost;
And Troy may then a new Palladium③ boast④;
For so religion and the gods ordain,
That, if you violate with hands profane
Minerva's gift, your town in flames shall burn,
(Which omen, O ye gods, on Graecia⑤ turn!)
But if it climb, with your assisting hands,
The Trojan walls, and in the city stands;
Then Troy shall Argos and Mycenae⑥ burn,
And the reverse of fate on us return.'

"With such deceits he gain'd their easy hearts,
Too prone to credit⑦ his perfidious⑧ arts.
What Diomede, nor Thetis' greater son⑨,
A thousand ships, nor ten years' siege, had done—
False tears and fawning⑩ words the city won.

"A greater omen, and of worse portent,
Did our unwary⑪ minds with fear torment,
Concurring⑫ to produce the dire event.

---

① the blue-ey'd maid: Minerva
② intercept /ˌɪntəˈsept/: 终止
③ Palladium /pəˈleɪdɪəm/: 女神 Pallas（Minerva）的木制雕像。据说该雕像是特洛伊（Troy）建立时 Jupiter 从天上扔下来的，只要它能安然无恙地留在特洛伊城里，特洛伊城就不可能被攻陷。为了攻陷特洛伊，希腊人 Ulysses 和 Diomede 从特洛伊城里的 Minerva 神庙偷走了该神像。
④ boast: 自豪地拥有
⑤ Graecia /ˈgriːsɪə/: Greece
⑥ Argos and Mycenae: Greek cities
⑦ credit /ˈkredɪt/: 相信
⑧ perfidious /pəˈfɪdɪəs/: 背信弃义的
⑨ Thetis' greater son: Achilles
⑩ fawning /ˈfɔːnɪŋ/: 奉承的
⑪ unwary /ʌnˈweəri/: 不小心的，没有意识到危险的
⑫ concur /kənˈkɜː/: 共同作用，合作

Laocoon①, Neptune's priest by lot that year,
With solemn pomp then sacrific'd a steer②;
When, dreadful to behold, from sea we spied
Two serpents, rank'd abreast, the seas divide,
And smoothly sweep along the swelling tide.
Their flaming crests above the waves they show;
Their bellies seem to burn the seas below;
Their speckled③ tails advance to steer their course,
And on the sounding shore the flying billows force.
And now the strand, and now the plain they held;
Their ardent eyes with bloody streaks were fill'd;
Their nimble tongues they brandish'd as they came,
And lick'd their hissing jaws, that sputter'd flame.
We fled amaz'd; their destin'd way they take,
And to Laocoon and his children make;
And first around the tender boys they wind,
Then with their sharpen'd fangs their limbs and bodies grind.
The wretched father, running to their aid
With pious haste, but vain, they next invade;
Twice round his waist their winding volumes roll'd;
And twice about his gasping throat they fold.
The priest thus doubly chok'd, their crests divide,
And tow'ring o'er his head in triumph ride.
With both his hands he labors at the knots;
His holy fillets the blue venom④ blots⑤;
His roaring fills the flitting air around.
Thus, when an ox receives a glancing wound,
He breaks his bands, the fatal altar flies,
And with loud bellowings breaks the yielding skies.
Their tasks perform'd, the serpents quit their prey,
And to the tow'r of Pallas make their way:
Couch'd at her feet, they lie protected there
By her large buckler⑥ and protended⑦ spear.

---

① Laocoon: /leɪˈɒkəʊɒn/
② steer /stɪə/: 小公牛
③ speckled /ˈspekəld/: 有斑点的
④ venom /ˈvenəm/: 蛇的毒液
⑤ blot: 弄脏
⑥ buckler /ˈbʌklə/: 盾牌
⑦ protend /prəʊˈtend/: 伸出

Amazement seizes all; the gen'ral cry

Proclaims Laocoon justly doom'd to die,

Whose hand the will of Pallas had withstood,

And dared to violate the sacred wood①.

All vote t' admit the steed, that vows be paid

And incense offer'd to th' offended maid.

A spacious breach is made; the town lies bare;

Some hoisting-levers, some the wheels prepare

And fasten to the horse's feet; the rest

With cables haul along th' unwieldly② beast.

Each on his fellow for assistance calls;

At length the fatal fabric mounts the walls,

Big with destruction. Boys with chaplets③ crown'd,

And choirs of virgins, sing and dance around.

Thus rais'd aloft, and then descending down,

It enters o'er our heads, and threats the town.

O sacred city, built by hands divine!

O valiant heroes of the Trojan line!

Four times he④ struck: as oft the clashing sound

Of arms was heard, and inward groans rebound.

Yet, mad with zeal, and blinded with our fate,

We haul along the horse in solemn state;

Then place the dire portent within the tow'r.

Cassandra⑤ cried, and curs'd th' unhappy hour;

Foretold our fate; but, by the god's decree,

All heard, and none believ'd the prophecy.

With branches we the fanes⑥ adorn, and waste,

In jollity⑦, the day ordain'd to be the last.

Meantime the rapid heav'ns roll'd down the light,

And on the shaded ocean rush'd the night;

Our men, secure, nor guards nor sentries held,

But easy sleep their weary limbs compell'd.

The Grecians had embark'd their naval pow'rs

---

① the sacred wood: the wooden horse

② unwieldly /ʌn'wiːldli/ (unwieldy /ʌn'wiːldi/): 身躯庞大而笨重的

③ chaplet /'tʃæplɪt/: 戴在头上的花环

④ he: the wooden horse

⑤ Cassandra /kə'sændrə/: 特洛伊国王 Priam 和王后 Hecuba 的女儿,能准确预知未来,但不被人相信。

⑥ fane: 神庙

⑦ jollity /'dʒɒləti/: 狂欢

From Tenedos, and sought our well-known shores,

Safe under covert of the silent night,

And guided by th' imperial galley's light;

When Sinon, favor'd by the partial gods,

Unlock'd the horse, and op'd① his dark abodes;

Restor'd to vital air our hidden foes,

Who joyful from their long confinement rose.

Tysander bold, and Sthenelus their guide,

And dire Ulysses down the cable slide:

Then Thoas, Athamas, and Pyrrhus haste;

Nor was the Podalirian hero② last,

Nor injur'd Menelaus, nor the fam'd

Epeus③, who the fatal engine④ fram'd⑤.

A nameless crowd succeed; their forces join

T' invade the town, oppress'd with sleep and wine.

Those few they find awake first meet their fate;

Then to their fellows they unbar the gate.

Dido's Love for Aeneas

But anxious cares already seiz'd the queen⑥:

She fed within her veins a flame unseen;

The hero's⑦ valor, acts, and birth inspire

Her soul with love, and fan the secret fire.

His words, his looks, imprinted in her heart,

Improve⑧ the passion, and increase the smart⑨.

Now, when the purple morn⑩ had chas'd away

The dewy shadows, and restor'd the day,

Her sister⑪ first with early care she sought,

---

① op'd: opened

② the Podalirian /ˌpɒʊdəˈlɪərɪən / hero: Machaon, a hero like Podalirius /ˌpɒʊdəˈlɪərɪəs /. Machaon and Podalirius, sons of Aesculapius, are both famous physicians.

③ Epeus /ˈiːpɪəs/: the builder of the Trojan Horse

④ the fatal engine: the wooden horse

⑤ frame: 制作, 建造

⑥ the queen: Dido, queen of Carthage

⑦ hero's: Aeneas's

⑧ improve: 增加, 加强

⑨ smart: 剧烈的心理上的痛苦

⑩ morn /mɔːn/: morning

⑪ Her sister: Anna

And thus in mournful accents① eas'd her thought：

"My dearest Anna, what new dreams affright②
My lab'ring③ soul! what visions of the night
Disturb my quiet, and distract my breast
With strange ideas of our Trojan guest④!
His worth, his actions, and majestic air,
A man descended from the gods declare⑤.
Fear ever argues⑥ a degenerate kind;
His birth is well asserted by his mind.
Then, what he suffer'd, when by Fate betray'd!
What brave attempts for falling Troy he made!
Such were his looks, so gracefully he spoke,
That, were I not resolv'd against the yoke
Of hapless marriage, never to be curst⑦
With second love, so fatal was my first,
To this one error I might yield again;
For, since Sichaeus⑧ was untimely slain,
This only man is able to subvert⑨
The fix'd foundations of my stubborn heart.
And, to confess my frailty, to my shame,
Somewhat I find within, if not the same,
Too like the sparkles of my former flame.
But first let yawning earth a passage rend,
And let me thro' the dark abyss descend;
First let avenging Jove, with flames from high,
Drive down this body to the nether sky⑩,
Condemn'd with ghosts in endless night to lie,
Before I break the plighted⑪ faith I gave!

---

① accents /ˈæksənts/：语言
② affright /əˈfraɪt/：惊吓
③ lab'ring（labouring）：受煎熬的,痛苦的
④ our Trojan guest：Aeneas
⑤ declare：显示,表明
⑥ argue：证明,显示
⑦ curst：cursed；be cursed with：受……所苦,因……遭殃
⑧ Sichaeus：参见 *The Age of Fable* 第 31 章"Dido"一节。
⑨ subvert /səbˈvɜːt/：颠覆
⑩ the nether sky：阴间,地狱；nether /ˈneðə/：下面的,位于地表之下的
⑪ plight /plaɪt/：保证,发誓

No! he who had my vows① shall ever have;
For, whom I lov'd on earth, I worship in the grave."

She said: the tears ran gushing② from her eyes,
And stopp'd her speech. Her sister thus replies:
"O dearer than the vital air I breathe③,
Will you to grief your blooming years④ bequeath,
Condemn'd to waste in woes your lonely life,
Without the joys of mother or of wife?
Think you these tears, this pompous train of woe,
Are known or valued by the ghosts below?
I grant that, while your sorrows yet were green⑤,
It well became a woman, and a queen,
The vows of Tyrian princes to neglect,
To scorn Hyarbas⑥, and his love reject,
With all the Libyan lords of mighty name;
But will you fight against a pleasing flame!
This little spot of land⑦, which Heav'n bestows,
On ev'ry side is hemm'd⑧ with warlike foes;
Gaetulian⑨ cities here are spread around,
And fierce Numidians⑩ there your frontiers bound;
Here lies a barren waste of thirsty land,
And there the Syrtes⑪ raise the moving sand;
Barcaean⑫ troops besiege the narrow shore,

---

① he who had my vows: Sichaeus, her husband killed by her brother Pygmalion
② gush: 涌出
③ O dearer than the vital air I breathe: Anna means that Dido, her sister, is dearer to her than the most important air that she breathes.
④ blooming years: 青春年华
⑤ green: (伤口、悲伤等)新的,刚产生的
⑥ Hyarbas /ˈhaɪəbəs/: 这个名字在其他译本里和神话词典里的拼写是 Iarbas /ˈaɪəbəs/。
⑦ This little spot of land: Carthage; 关于 Carthage 的建立,参见 *The Age of Fable* 第 31 章 Dido 的故事。
⑧ hem: 包围
⑨ Gaetulian /gɪˈtjuːlɪən/: the Gaetulians 是古代居住在 Numidia 以东和以南沙漠地区的柏柏尔人 (the Berbers /ˈbɜːbəz/)。 Numidia /njuːˈmɪdɪə/ 是北非古王国,位于撒哈拉沙漠 (the Sahara) 以北,大致相当于现在的阿尔及利亚 (Algeria) 北部地区。柏柏尔人是居住在的黎波里 (Tripoli) 以西的北非地区的各个民族的总称。
⑩ Numidians /njuːˈmɪdɪənz/: inhabitants of Numidia
⑪ the Syrtes /ˈsɜːtiːz/: 指 Syrtis Major 和 Syrtis Minor;Syrtis Major 即现在的 the Gulf of Sidra, 位于利比亚以北,米苏拉塔 (Misratah) 以东,班加西 (Benghazi) 以西;Syrtis Minor 即现在的 the Gulf of Gabes, 位于突尼斯以东。因为有流沙,这两个地方对于船只的航行是非常危险的。
⑫ Barcaean: Barca /ˈbɑːkə/ 是古希腊在北非的殖民地,位于今利比亚的海岸地区。

And from the sea Pygmalion① threatens more.

Propitious Heav'n, and gracious Juno, lead

This wand'ring navy to your needful aid:

How will your empire spread, your city rise,

From such a union, and with such allies?

Implore the favor of the pow'rs above②,

And leave the conduct of the rest to love.

Continue still your hospitable way,

And still invent occasions of their stay,

Till storms and winter winds shall cease to threat,

And planks and oars repair their shatter'd fleet."

These words, which from a friend and sister came,

With ease resolv'd③ the scruples④ of her fame,

And added fury⑤ to the kindled flame.

Inspir'd with hope, the project they pursue;

On ev'ry altar sacrifice renew:

A chosen ewe of two years old they pay

To Ceres, Bacchus, and the God of Day⑥;

Preferring Juno's pow'r, for Juno ties

The nuptial knot and makes the marriage joys.

The beauteous queen before her altar stands,

And holds the golden goblet in her hands.

A milk-white heifer she with flow'rs adorns,

And pours the ruddy⑦ wine betwixt⑧ her horns;

And, while the priests with pray'r the gods invoke,

She feeds their altars with Sabaean⑨ smoke,

With hourly care the sacrifice renews,

And anxiously the panting entrails⑩ views.

What priestly rites, alas! what pious art,

---

① Pygmalion: brother of Dido and murderer of her husband, Sichaeus. This Pygmalion is not the one who falls in love with his own ivory statue.

② the pow'rs above: the gods and goddesses in heaven

③ resolve /rɪˈzɒlv/: 消除,打消

④ scruple /ˈskruːpl/: 疑虑

⑤ fury: 猛烈

⑥ the God of Day: Apollo

⑦ ruddy /ˈrʌdi/: 红色的

⑧ betwixt /bɪˈtwɪkst/: between

⑨ Sabaean /səˈbiːən/: Saba /ˈsæbə/ 位于阿拉伯半岛西南部的一个王国,盛产香料和农产品。

⑩ entrails: 内脏;古人通过观看献祭动物的内脏来进行占卜,预知吉凶。

What vows avail to cure a bleeding heart!
A gentle fire she feeds within her veins,
Where the soft god secure in silence reigns.

Sick with desire, and seeking him she loves,
From street to street the raving① Dido roves.
So when the watchful shepherd, from the blind②,
Wounds with a random shaft the careless hind③,
Distracted④ with her pain she flies the woods,
Bounds o'er the lawn, and seeks the silent floods,
With fruitless care; for still the fatal dart
Sticks in her side, and rankles⑤ in her heart.
And now she leads the Trojan chief along
The lofty walls, amidst the busy throng;
Displays her Tyrian wealth, and rising town,
Which love, without his labor, makes his own.
This pomp she shows, to tempt her wand'ring guest;
Her falt'ring tongue forbids to speak the rest.
When day declines, and feasts renew the night,
Still on his face she feeds her famish'd sight;
She longs again to hear the prince relate
His own adventures and the Trojan fate.
He tells it o'er and o'er; but still in vain,
For still she begs to hear it once again.
The hearer on the speaker's mouth depends,
And thus the tragic story never ends.
Then, when they part, when Phoebe's⑥ paler light
Withdraws, and falling stars to sleep invite,
She last remains, when ev'ry guest is gone,
Sits on the bed he press'd, and sighs alone;
Absent, her absent hero sees and hears;
Or in her bosom young Ascanius⑦ bears,

---

① raving：疯狂的
② blind：(猎人的)埋伏处
③ hind /haɪnd/：(3 岁或 3 岁以上的)母鹿
④ distract /dɪ'strækt/：是困惑,使苦恼,使发狂
⑤ rankle /'ræŋkl/：疼痛不已
⑥ Phoebe /'fiːbi/：the moon；Phoebe (Φοίβη)是古希腊语 φοῖβος 一词的阴性形式,意思是"明亮的",是老一代月亮女神 Selene /sɪ'liːni /的称号。
⑦ Ascanius：son of Aeneas, also called Iulus

And seeks the father's image in the child,
If love by likeness might be so beguil'd.

Meantime the rising tow'rs are at a stand①;
No labors exercise the youthful band②,
Nor use of arts, nor toils of arms they know;
The mole③ is left unfinish'd to the foe;
The mounds④, the works⑤, the walls, neglected lie,
Short of their promis'd heighth⑥, that seem'd to threat the sky.

Dido's Death

His⑦ vows, in haughty terms, he⑧ thus preferr'd,
And held his altar's horns. The mighty Thund'rer⑨ heard;
Then cast his eyes on Carthage, where he found
The lustful pair⑩ in lawless pleasure drown'd,
Lost in their loves, insensible of shame,
And both forgetful of their better fame.
He calls Cyllenius⑪, and the god attends,
By whom his menacing command he sends:
"Go, mount the western winds, and cleave the sky;
Then, with a swift descent, to Carthage fly:
There find the Trojan chief⑫, who wastes his days
In slothful⑬ riot⑭ and inglorious⑮ ease,
Nor minds the future city, giv'n by fate.
To him this message from my mouth relate:
'Not so fair Venus hop'd, when twice she won

---

① at a stand：停止，停顿
② band：一群人
③ mole：有防波堤的港口
④ mound：防御工事
⑤ the works：防御工事
⑥ heighth：height
⑦ Iarbas's
⑧ he：即在选段"Dido's Love for Aeneas"中提到的向 Dido 求爱但被拒绝的 Iarbas。
⑨ The mighty Thund'rer：Jupiter
⑩ The lustful pair：Aeneas and Dido
⑪ Cyllenius /saɪˈliːnɪəs/：Cyllene /saɪˈliːni/ 是位于希腊 Arcadia 东北部的一座山，Hermes 在此出生和长大，所以被叫作 Cyllenius。
⑫ the Trojan chief：Aeneas
⑬ slothful /ˈsləʊθfl/：懒惰的
⑭ riot /ˈraɪət/：纵情声色
⑮ inglorious /ɪnˈɡlɔːrɪəs/：可耻的

Thy life with pray'rs, nor promis'd such a son①.

Hers② was a hero, destin'd to command

A martial③ race, and rule the Latian land④,

Who should his ancient line from Teucer⑤ draw,

And on the conquer'd world impose the law.'

If glory cannot move a mind so mean,

Nor future praise from fading pleasure wean,

Yet why should he defraud⑥ his son⑦ of fame,

And grudge⑧ the Romans their immortal name!

What are his vain designs! what hopes he more

From his long ling'ring on a hostile shore,

Regardless to redeem⑨ his honor lost,

And for his race to gain th' Ausonian⑩ coast!

Bid him with speed the Tyrian court⑪ forsake;

With this command the slumb'ring warrior wake."

...

Arriving there, he⑫ found the Trojan prince⑬

New ramparts⑭ raising for the town's defense.

A purple scarf, with gold embroider'd o'er⑮,

(Queen Dido's gift,) about his waist he wore;

A sword, with glitt'ring gems diversified,

For ornament, not use, hung idly by his side.

Then thus, with winged words, the god began,

Resuming his own shape："Degenerate⑯ man,

---

① Aeneas is the son of Venus.

② Hers：Her son, Aeneas

③ martial /ˈmɑːʃl/：好战的,尚武的

④ the Latian /ˈleɪʃən /land：Latium /ˈleɪʃɪəm /；Latium 是位于古意大利中部的一个地区,是罗马帝国的发源地。

⑤ 因为把自己的女儿嫁给了 Dardanus（Troy 的建立者）,所以 Teucer /ˈtjuːsə /是历代特洛伊王的祖先。

⑥ defraud /dɪˈfrɔːd/：骗取

⑦ 即在选段"Dido's Love for Aeneas"中提到的 Ascanius。

⑧ grudge：不愿意给予

⑨ redeem：重获,恢复

⑩ Ausonian /ɔːˈsəʊnɪən/：意大利的

⑪ the Tyrian court：the court of Dido, the Tyrian Queen

⑫ he：Hermes

⑬ the Trojan prince：Aeneas

⑭ rampart /ˈræmpɑːt/：防御土墙

⑮ o'er /ɔː/：over

⑯ degenerate /dɪˈdʒenərət/：堕落的

Thou① woman's property, what mak'st② thou here,

These foreign walls and Tyrian tow'rs to rear,

Forgetful of thy own? All-pow'rful③ Jove,

Who sways the world below and heav'n above,

Has sent me down with this severe command:

"What means thy ling'ring in the Libyan land?

If glory cannot move a mind so mean,

Nor future praise from flitting pleasure wean,

Regard the fortunes of thy④ rising heir:

The promis'd crown let young Ascanius wear,

To whom th' Ausonian scepter, and the state

Of Rome's imperial name is ow'd by fate."

So spoke the god; and, speaking, took his flight,

Involv'd in clouds, and vanish'd out of sight.

The pious prince was seiz'd with sudden fear;

Mute was his tongue, and upright stood his hair.

Revolving⑤ in his mind the stern command,

He longs to fly, and loathes the charming land.

What should he say? or how should he begin?

What course, alas! remains to steer between

Th' offended lover and the pow'rful queen?

This way and that he turns his anxious mind,

And all expedients⑥ tries, and none can find.

Fix'd on the deed, but doubtful of the means,

After long thought, to this advice he leans:

Three chiefs he calls, commands them to repair

The fleet, and ship their men with silent care;

Some plausible⑦ pretense⑧ he bids them find,

To color⑨ what in secret he design'd.

Himself, meantime, the softest hours would choose,

---

① thou：（主格、单数）you

② mak'st：当主语是 thou 时，谓语动词后需要加屈折变化词尾-est；-st 是-est 的变体。

③ all-powerful：全能的

④ thy：（单数）your，在以元音开头的名词前用 thine。

⑤ revolve /rɪ'vɒlv/：考虑，思考

⑥ expedient /ɪk'spiːdɪənt/：（为达到某种目的而采取的）方法

⑦ plausible /'plɔːzɪbl/：可被接受的，可信的

⑧ pretense /prɪ'tens/：借口

⑨ color：使可信

Before the love-sick lady heard the news；

And move her tender mind，by slow degrees，

To suffer① what the sov'reign pow'r② decrees：

Jove will inspire him，when，and what to say．

They hear with pleasure，and with haste obey．

But soon the queen perceives the thin disguise：

（What arts can blind a jealous woman's eyes！）

She was the first to find the secret fraud，

Before the fatal news was blaz'd③ abroad．

Love the first motions of the lover hears，

Quick to presage，and ev'n in safety fears．

Nor impious Fame④ was wanting to report

The ships repair'd，the Trojans' thick⑤ resort⑥，

And purpose to forsake the Tyrian court．

Frantic with fear，impatient of the wound，

And impotent of mind，she roves the city round．

Less wild the Bacchanalian dames⑦ appear，

When，from afar，their nightly god⑧ they hear，

And howl about the hills，and shake the wreathy spear．

At length she finds the dear perfidious⑨ man；

Prevents his form'd excuse，and thus began：

"Base and ungrateful！could you hope to fly⑩，

And undiscover'd scape⑪ a lover's eye？

Nor could my kindness your compassion move，

Nor plighted vows，nor dearer bands of love？

Or is the death of a despairing queen

Not worth preventing，tho'⑫ too well foreseen？

Ev'n when the wintry winds command your stay，

---

① suffer：允许

② the sov'reign pow'r：Jupiter

③ blaze：公开，宣布

④ Fame：传闻，谣言

⑤ thick：（人群）密集的

⑥ resort /rɪ'zɔːt /：（人群的）聚集

⑦ the Bacchanalian /ˌbækə'neɪlɪən /dames：酒神 Bacchus 的女信徒

⑧ their nightly god：Bacchus

⑨ perfidious /pə'fɪdɪəs/：背信弃义的

⑩ fly：逃离

⑪ scape：escape

⑫ tho'：though

You dare① the tempests, and defy the sea.

False as you are, suppose you were not bound

To lands unknown, and foreign coasts to sound②;

Were Troy restor'd, and Priam's happy reign,

Now durst you tempt, for Troy, the raging main③?

See whom you fly! am I the foe you shun?

Now, by those holy vows, so late begun,

By this right hand, (since I have nothing more

To challenge, but the faith you gave before;)

I beg you by these tears too truly shed,

By the new pleasures of our nuptial bed;

If ever Dido, when you most were kind,

Were pleasing in your eyes, or touch'd your mind;

By these my pray'rs, if pray'rs may yet have place,

Pity the fortunes of a falling race.

For you I have provok'd④ a tyrant's hate⑤,

Incens'd the Libyan and the Tyrian state;

For you alone I suffer in my fame,

Bereft of honor, and expos'd to shame.

Whom have I now to trust, ungrateful guest?

(That only name remains of all the rest!)

What have I left? or whither can I fly?

Must I attend⑥ Pygmalion's cruelty,

Or till Hyarba shall in triumph lead

A queen that proudly scorn'd his proffer'd bed?

Had you deferr'd, at least, your hasty flight,

And left behind some pledge of our delight,

Some babe to bless the mother's mournful sight,

Some young Aeneas, to supply your place,

Whose features might express his father's face;

I should not then complain to live bereft

Of all my husband, or be wholly left."

---

① dare：冒险面对

② sound：探测

③ main：大海

④ provoke /prə'vəuk /：激发

⑤ a tyrant's hate：the hate of Hyarbas

⑥ attend：等待

Here paus'd the queen. Unmov'd he holds his eyes,
By Jove's command; nor suffer'd① love to rise,
Tho' heaving in his heart; and thus at length replies:
"Fair queen, you never can enough repeat
Your boundless favors, or I own my debt;
Nor can my mind forget Eliza's name②,
While vital breath inspires this mortal frame③.
This only let me speak in my defense:
I never hop'd a secret flight from hence,
Much less pretended to the lawful claim
Of sacred nuptials, or a husband's name.
For, if indulgent Heav'n would leave me free,
And not submit my life to fate's decree,
My choice would lead me to the Trojan shore,
Those relics to review, their dust adore,
And Priam's ruin'd palace to restore.
But now the Delphian oracle commands,
And fate invites me to the Latian lands.
That is the promis'd place to which I steer,
And all my vows are terminated there.
If you, a Tyrian, and a stranger born,
With walls and tow'rs a Libyan town adorn,
Why may not we—like you, a foreign race—
Like you, seek shelter in a foreign place?
As often as the night obscures the skies
With humid shades, or twinkling stars arise,
Anchises' angry ghost in dreams appears,
Chides my delay, and fills my soul with fears;
And young Ascanius justly may complain
Of his defrauded and destin'd reign.
Ev'n now the herald of the gods④ appear'd:
Waking I saw him, and his message heard.
From Jove he came commission'd, heav'nly bright
With radiant beams, and manifest to sight

---

① suffer: 允许
② Eliza /ɪˈlaɪzə/ (or Elissa) is another name of Dido.
③ this mortal frame: his body
④ the herald of the gods: Hermes

(The sender① and the sent② I both attest③)

These walls he enter'd, and those words express'd.

Fair queen, oppose not what the gods command;

Forc'd by my fate, I leave your happy land."

Thus while he spoke, already she began,

With sparkling eyes, to view the guilty man;

From head to foot survey'd his person o'er,

Nor longer these outrageous④ threats forebore:

"False as thou art, and, more than false, forsworn⑤!

Not sprung from noble blood, nor goddess-born,

But hewn from harden'd entrails of a rock!

And rough Hyrcanian⑥ tigers gave thee suck!

Why should I fawn? what have I worse to fear?

Did he once look, or lent a list'ning ear,

Sigh'd when I sobb'd, or shed one kindly tear? —

All symptoms of a base ungrateful mind,

So foul, that, which is worse, 'tis hard to find.

Of man's injustice why should I complain?

The gods, and Jove himself, behold in vain

Triumphant treason; yet no thunder flies,

Nor Juno views my wrongs with equal eyes;

Faithless is earth, and faithless are the skies!

Justice is fled, and Truth is now no more!

I sav'd the shipwrack'd exile⑦ on my shore;

With needful food his hungry Trojans fed;

I took the traitor to my throne and bed:

Fool that I was—'t is little to repeat

The rest—I stor'd⑧ and rigg'd⑨ his ruin'd fleet.

I rave⑩, I rave! A god's command he pleads,

---

① The sender：Jupiter

② the sent：Hermes

③ attest：叫……作证

④ outrageous /aut'reidʒəs/：愤怒的

⑤ forsworn /fɔː'swɔːn/：发伪誓的，背弃誓言的，背信弃义的

⑥ Hyrcanian /hɜː'keiniən/：Hyrcania /hɜː'keiniə/是古代地区名,濒临里海（the Caspian Sea）,当时以荒凉、野蛮、未开化而著称。

⑦ the shipwrack'd exile：Aeneas; shipwrack'd: shipwrecked

⑧ store：修复

⑨ rig：给船提供装备

⑩ rave：疯狂,表现出疯狂的迹象

And makes Heav'n accessary① to his deeds.
Now Lycian② lots③, and now the Delian god④,
Now Hermes is employ'd from Jove's abode,
To warn him hence; as if the peaceful state
Of heav'nly pow'rs were touch'd with human fate!
But go! thy flight no longer I detain—
Go seek thy promis'd kingdom thro' the main!
Yet, if the heav'ns will hear my pious vow,
The faithless waves, not half so false as thou,
Or secret sands, shall sepulchers⑤ afford
To thy proud vessels, and their perjur'd lord.
Then shalt thou call on injur'd Dido's name:
Dido shall come in a black sulph'ry⑥ flame,
When death has once dissolv'd her mortal frame;
Shall smile to see the traitor vainly weep:
Her angry ghost, arising from the deep,
Shall haunt thee waking, and disturb thy sleep.
At least my shade thy punishment shall know,
And Fame shall spread the pleasing news below."

Abruptly here she stops; then turns away
Her loathing eyes, and shuns the sight of day.
Amaz'd he stood, revolving in his mind
What speech to frame, and what excuse to find.
Her fearful maids their fainting mistress led,
And softly laid her on her iv'ry⑦ bed.

But good Aeneas, tho' he much desir'd
To give that pity which her grief requir'd;
Tho' much he mourn'd, and labor'd with his love,
Resolv'd at length, obeys the will of Jove;
Reviews his forces: they with early care

---

① accessary (accessory) /ək'sesəri/: 同谋,帮凶
② Lycian /'lɪsɪən/: Lycia 境内有座城市叫 Patara /pə'teərə/,该城以拥有 Apollo 的神示所而著称,所以 Lycian 一词可表示"of Apollo"之意。关于 Lycia,参见 *The Age of Fable* 第 4 章的注释。
③ lot: 命运或神的安排
④ the Delian god: Apollo, born in Delos
⑤ sepulcher /'sepəlkə/: 坟墓
⑥ sulph'ry: sulphury
⑦ iv'ry: ivory

Unmoor their vessels, and for sea prepare.
The fleet is soon afloat, in all its pride,
And well-calk'd galleys in the harbor ride.
Then oaks for oars they fell'd; or, as they stood,
Of its green arms despoil'd the growing wood,
Studious of flight. The beach is cover'd o'er
With Trojan bands, that blacken all the shore:
On ev'ry side are seen, descending down,
Thick swarms of soldiers, loaden from the town.
Thus, in battalia①, march embodied② ants,
Fearful of winter, and of future wants③,
T' invade the corn, and to their cells convey
The plunder'd forage④ of their yellow prey⑤.
The sable troops⑥, along the narrow tracks,
Scarce bear the weighty burthen⑦ on their backs:
Some set their shoulders to the pond'rous⑧ grain;
Some guard the spoil; some lash the lagging train;
All ply their sev'ral⑨ tasks, and equal toil sustain.

What pangs the tender breast of Dido tore,
When, from the tow'r, she saw the cover'd shore,
And heard the shouts of sailors from afar,
Mix'd with the murmurs of the wat'ry war!
All-pow'rful Love! what changes canst thou cause
In human hearts, subjected to thy laws!
Once more her haughty soul the tyrant⑩ bends:
To pray'rs and mean submissions she descends.
No female arts or aids she left untried,
Nor counsels unexplor'd, before she died.
"Look, Anna! look! the Trojans crowd to sea;

---

① battalia /bəˈtɑːlɪə/：战斗队形
② embodied /emˈbɒdɪd/：形成战斗队形的
③ want：缺乏食物
④ forage /ˈfɒrɪdʒ/：(动物找的)食物
⑤ their yellow prey：the corn, which is yellow
⑥ The sable troops：the ants; sable /ˈseɪbl/：黑色的
⑦ burthen：burden
⑧ pond'rous：ponderous /ˈpɒndrəs/ (沉重的,巨大的)
⑨ sev'ral：各自的
⑩ the tyrant：Love

They spread their canvas①, and their anchors weigh②.
The shouting crew their ships with garlands bind,
Invoke the sea gods, and invite the wind.
Could I have thought this threat'ning blow so near,
My tender soul had been forewarn'd to bear.
But do not you my last request deny;
With yon perfidious man your int'rest try,
And bring me news, if I must live or die.
You are his fav'rite; you alone can find
The dark recesses③ of his inmost mind:
In all his trusted secrets you have part,
And know the soft approaches to his heart.
Haste then, and humbly seek my haughty foe;
Tell him, I did not with the Grecians go④,
Nor did my fleet against his friends employ⑤,
Nor swore the ruin of unhappy Troy,
Nor mov'd with hands profane his father's dust⑥:
Why should he then reject a suit so just!
Whom does he shun, and whither would he fly!
Can he this last, this only pray'r deny!
Let him at least his dang'rous flight delay,
Wait better winds, and hope a calmer sea.
The nuptials⑦ he disclaims⑧ I urge no more:
Let him pursue the promis'd Latian shore.
A short delay is all I ask him now;
A pause of grief, an interval from woe,
Till my soft soul be temper'd to sustain
Accustom'd sorrows, and inur'd to pain.
If you in pity grant this one request,
My death shall glut the hatred of his breast."
This mournful message pious Anna bears,

---

① canvas /ˈkænvəs/：帆
② weigh：起（锚）
③ recesses /rɪˈsesɪz/：深处
④ I did not with the Grecians go：我没有与希腊人为伍（攻打特洛伊）。
⑤ employ /ɪmˈplɔɪ/：使用，利用
⑥ dust：遗骸，尸骨
⑦ nuptial：婚姻
⑧ disclaim：拒绝承认

And seconds① with her own② her sister's tears:
But all her arts are still employ'd in vain;
Again she comes, and is refus'd again.
His harden'd heart nor pray'rs nor threat'nings move;
Fate, and the god, had stopp'd his ears to love.
…

The wretched queen, pursued by cruel fate,
Begins at length the light of heav'n to hate,
And loathes to live. Then dire portents③ she sees,
To hasten on the death her soul decrees:
Strange to relate! for when, before the shrine,
She pours in sacrifice the purple wine,
The purple wine is turn'd to putrid④ blood,
And the white offer'd milk converts to mud.
This dire presage⑤, to her alone reveal'd,
From all, and ev'n her sister, she conceal'd.
A marble temple stood within the grove,
Sacred to death, and to her murther'd love⑥;
That honor'd chapel she had hung around
With snowy fleeces, and with garlands crown'd:
Oft, when she visited this lonely dome,
Strange voices issued from her husband's tomb;
She thought she heard him summon her away,
Invite her to his grave, and chide her stay.
Hourly 't is heard, when with a boding note
The solitary screech owl⑦ strains⑧ her⑨ throat,
And, on a chimney's top, or turret's height⑩,
With songs obscene disturbs the silence of the night.
Besides, old prophecies augment her fears;

---

① second /'sekənd/：支持
② her own：her own tears
③ portent：凶兆
④ putrid /'pjuːtrɪd/：腐败的，腐烂的
⑤ presage /'presɪdʒ/：预兆
⑥ her murther'd love：her husband Sichaeus, murdered by her brother Pygmalion
⑦ screech owl：长耳鸮
⑧ strain：使劲地伸展
⑨ her：the screech owl's
⑩ height：顶端，顶部

And stern Aeneas in her dreams appears,

Disdainful as by day：she seems, alone,

To wander in her sleep, thro' ways unknown,

Guideless and dark；or, in a desart① plain,

To seek her subjects, and to seek in vain：

Like Pentheus②, when, distracted with his fear,

He saw two suns, and double Thebes, appear；

Or mad Orestes③, when his mother's ghost

Full in his face infernal torches toss'd,

And shook her snaky locks④：he shuns the sight,

Flies o'er the stage, surpris'd with mortal fright；

The Furies guard the door and intercept⑤ his flight.

Now, sinking underneath a load of grief,

From death alone she seeks her last relief；

The time and means resolv'd⑥ within her breast,

She to her mournful sister thus address'd

(Dissembling⑦ hope, her cloudy front she clears,

And a false vigor in her eyes appears)：

"Rejoice!" she said. "Instructed from above⑧,

My lover I shall gain, or lose my love⑨.

Nigh⑩ rising⑪ Atlas⑫, next⑬ the falling sun,⑭

Long tracts of Ethiopian climates⑮ run：

There a Massylian⑯ priestess I have found,

Honor'd for age, for magic arts renown'd：

Th' Hesperian⑰ temple was her trusted care；

---

① desart：desert（荒芜的, 无人居住的）

② 参见 *The Age of Fable* 第 21 章。

③ 参见 *The Age of Fable* 第 28 章。

④ lock：头发

⑤ intercept /ˌɪntəˈsept/：阻止

⑥ resolve：决定

⑦ dissemble /dɪˈsembl/：假装

⑧ from above：from the gods

⑨ lose my love：摆脱我对他的爱

⑩ nigh：在……附近

⑪ rising：高耸的

⑫ Atlas：Atlas 山脉, 位于非洲西北角, 西临大西洋, 北临直布罗陀海峡和地中海, 是巨人 Atlas 生活的地方。

⑬ next：在……附近

⑭ Atlas 山脉在 Carthage 以西, 所以 Dido 说 next the falling sun。

⑮ climate：地区

⑯ The Massylians are a people in Numidia.

⑰ Hesperian /hesˈpɪərɪən/：of the Hesperides, daughters of Atlas

'T was she supplied the wakeful dragon's fare①.

She poppy② seeds in honey taught to steep,

Reclaim'd③ his④ rage, and sooth'd him⑤ into sleep.

She watch'd the golden fruit; her charms unbind

The chains of love, or fix them on the mind:

She stops the torrents, leaves the channel dry,

Repels the stars, and backward bears the sky.

The yawning earth rebellows to her call,

Pale ghosts ascend, and mountain ashes fall.

Witness, ye gods, and thou my better part⑥,

How loth I am to try this impious art!

Within the secret court, with silent care,

Erect a lofty pile, expos'd in air:

Hang on the topmost part the Trojan vest,

Spoils, arms, and presents, of my faithless guest.

Next, under these, the bridal bed be plac'd,

Where I my ruin in his arms embrac'd:

All relics of the wretch⑦ are doom'd to fire;

For so the priestess and her charms require."

Thus far she said, and farther speech forbears;

A mortal paleness in her face appears:

Yet the mistrustless⑧ Anna could not find

The secret fun'ral in these rites design'd;

Nor thought so dire a rage possess'd her mind.

Unknowing of a train⑨ conceal'd so well,

She fear'd no worse than when Sichaeus fell;

Therefore obeys. The fatal pile they rear,

Within the secret court, expos'd in air.

The cloven holms and pines are heap'd on high,

And garlands on the hollow spaces lie.

---

① fare：食物

② poppy /ˈpɒpi/：罂粟

③ reclaim /rɪˈkleɪm/：降服

④ his：the dragon's

⑤ him：the dragon

⑥ my better part：my dear sister

⑦ All relics of the wretch：Aeneas 留下的所有东西

⑧ mistrustless /mɪsˈtrʌstləs /：毫不怀疑的

⑨ train：一连串的行动

Sad cypress, vervain, yew, compose the wreath,
And ev'ry baleful green denoting death.
The queen, determin'd to the fatal deed,
The spoils and sword he left, in order spread,
And the man's image on the nuptial bed.

And now (the sacred altars plac'd around)
The priestess enters, with her hair unbound,
And thrice invokes the pow'rs below the ground.
Night, Erebus, and Chaos she proclaims,
And threefold① Hecate②, with her hundred names,
And three Dianas③: next, she sprinkles round
With feign'd Avernian④ drops the hallow'd ground;
Culls hoary simples⑤, found by Phoebe's light,
With brazen sickles reap'd at noon of night⑥;
Then mixes baleful⑦ juices in the bowl,
And cuts the forehead of a newborn foal⑧,
Robbing the mother's love. The destin'd queen
Observes, assisting at the rites obscene;
A leaven'd cake in her devoted hands
She holds, and next the highest altar stands:
One tender foot was shod⑨, her other bare;
Girt was her gather'd gown, and loose her hair.
Thus dress'd, she summon'd, with her dying breath,
The heav'ns and planets conscious of her death,
And ev'ry pow'r, if any rules above,
Who minds, or who revenges, injur'd love.

'T was dead of night, when weary bodies close
Their eyes in balmy⑩ sleep and soft repose:

---

① threefold：由 3 个部分组成的
② Hecate /ˈhekəti/：希腊神话中主管魔术和巫术的女神,她的雕像通常有 3 个身躯或 3 个头,所以用 threefold 来形容她。
③ three Dianas：Diana 的雕像经常放置在 3 条路相遇的路口,其头部由面对 3 条路的 3 张脸构成,所有才有 three Dianas 这个说法。
④ Avernian /əˈvɜːnɪən/：地狱的
⑤ simple：有药用价值的植物
⑥ noon of night：午夜
⑦ baleful /ˈbeɪfl/：有害的,致命的
⑧ foal：刚出生的马
⑨ shod：穿着鞋的
⑩ balmy /ˈbɑːmi/：宜人的,温和的

The winds no longer whisper thro' the woods,

Nor murm'ring tides disturb the gentle floods.

The stars in silent order mov'd around;

And Peace, with downy wings, was brooding on the ground.

The flocks and herds, and party-color'd① fowl,

Which haunt the woods, or swim the weedy pool,

Stretch'd on the quiet earth, securely lay,

Forgetting the past labors of the day.

All else of nature's common gift partake:

Unhappy Dido was alone awake.

Nor sleep nor ease the furious queen can find;

Sleep fled her eyes, as quiet fled her mind.

Despair, and rage, and love divide her heart;

Despair and rage had some, but love the greater part.

Then thus she said within her secret mind:

"What shall I do? what succor② can I find?

Become a suppliant to Hyarbas' pride,

And take my turn, to court and be denied?

Shall I with this ungrateful Trojan go,

Forsake an empire, and attend③ a foe?

Himself I refug'd, and his train④ reliev'd—

'T is true—but am I sure to be receiv'd?

Can gratitude in Trojan souls have place?

Laomedon⑤ still lives in all his race?

Then, shall I seek alone the churlish crew,

Or with my fleet their flying sails pursue?

What force have I but those whom scarce before

I drew reluctant from their native shore?

Will they again embark at my desire,

Once more sustain the seas, and quit their second Tyre?

Rather with steel⑥ thy guilty breast invade,

And take the fortune thou thyself hast made.

Your pity, sister, first seduc'd my mind,

---

① party-color'd (parti-colored):杂色的

② succor /ˈsʌkə/：帮助

③ attend：侍奉

④ train：随行人员

⑤ Laomedon：特洛伊（Troy）国王，Priam 之父，以欺诈和背信弃义而臭名昭著。

⑥ steel：刀，剑

Or seconded too well what I design'd.

These dear-bought pleasures had I never known,

Had I continued free, and still my own;

Avoiding love, I had not found despair,

But shar'd with salvage① beasts the common air.

Like them, a lonely life I might have led,

Not mourn'd the living, nor disturb'd the dead."

These thoughts she brooded in her anxious breast.

On board, the Trojan found more easy rest.

Resolv'd to sail, in sleep he pass'd the night;

And order'd all things for his early flight.

To whom once more the winged god② appears;

His former youthful mien③ and shape he wears,

And with this new alarm invades his ears:

"Sleep'st thou, O goddess-born! and canst thou drown

Thy needful cares, so near a hostile town,

Beset with foes; nor hear'st the western gales

Invite thy passage, and inspire thy sails?

She harbors in her heart a furious hate,

And thou shalt find the dire effects too late;

Fix'd on revenge, and obstinate to die.

Haste swiftly hence, while thou hast pow'r to fly.

The sea with ships will soon be cover'd o'er,

And blazing firebrands kindle all the shore.

Prevent her rage, while night obscures the skies,

And sail before the purple morn arise.

Who knows what hazards thy delay may bring?

Woman's a various④ and a changeful thing."

Thus Hermes in the dream; then took his flight

Aloft in air unseen, and mix'd with night.

Twice warn'd by the celestial messenger,

The pious prince arose with hasty fear;

---

① salvage：savage
② the winged god：Hermes
③ mien /miːn/：外表，样子
④ various：易变的

Then rous'd his drowsy① train without delay:
"Haste to your banks; your crooked② anchors weigh③,
And spread your flying sails, and stand to sea.
A god commands: he stood before my sight,
And urg'd us once again to speedy flight.
O sacred pow'r, what pow'r soe'er thou art,
To thy blest④ orders I resign⑤ my heart.
Lead thou the way; protect thy Trojan bands,
And prosper⑥ the design thy will commands."
He said: and, drawing forth his flaming sword,
His thund'ring arm divides the many-twisted cord.
An emulating⑦ zeal inspires his train:
They run; they snatch; they rush into the main.
With headlong haste they leave the desert shores,
And brush the liquid seas with lab'ring oars.

Aurora⑧ now had left her saffron⑨ bed,
And beams of early light the heav'ns o'erspread,
When, from a tow'r, the queen, with wakeful eyes,
Saw day point upward from the rosy skies.
She look'd to seaward; but the sea was void⑩,
And scarce in ken⑪ the sailing ships descried.
Stung with despite⑫, and furious with despair,
She struck her trembling breast, and tore her hair.
"And shall th' ungrateful traitor go," she said,
"My land forsaken, and my love betray'd?
Shall we not arm? not rush from ev'ry street,
To follow, sink, and burn his perjur'd fleet?
Haste, haul my galleys out! pursue the foe!

① drowsy /ˈdraʊzi/: 瞌睡的
② crooked /ˈkrʊkɪd/: 弯的
③ weigh: 起（锚）
④ blest: blessed（神圣的,值得尊敬的）
⑤ resign /rɪˈzaɪn/: 把……交给
⑥ prosper /ˈprɒspə/: 使……成功或顺利
⑦ emulate /ˈemjuleɪt/: 竞争
⑧ Aurora: the dawn
⑨ saffron /ˈsæfrən/: 橙黄色的
⑩ void /vɔɪd/: 空的
⑪ ken: 视野
⑫ despite /dɪˈspaɪt/: 遭受蔑视

Bring flaming brands! set sail, and swiftly row!

What have I said? where am I? Fury turns

My brain; and my distemper'd bosom burns.

Then, when I gave my person and my throne,

This hate, this rage, had been more timely shown.

See now the promis'd faith, the vaunted name,

The pious man, who, rushing thro' the flame,

Preserv'd his gods, and to the Phrygian shore

The burthen① of his feeble father bore!

I should have torn him piecemeal②; strow'd③ in floods

His scatter'd limbs, or left expos'd in woods;

Destroy'd his friends and son; and, from the fire,

Have set the reeking④ boy before the sire.

Events are doubtful, which on battles wait:

Yet where's the doubt, to souls secure of fate?

My Tyrians, at their injur'd queen's command,

Had toss'd their fires amid the Trojan band;

At once extinguish'd all the faithless name;

And I myself, in vengeance of my shame,

Had fall'n upon the pile, to mend the fun'ral flame.

Thou Sun, who view'st at once the world below;

Thou Juno, guardian of the nuptial vow;

Thou Hecate hearken from thy dark abodes!

Ye Furies, fiends, and violated gods,

All pow'rs invok'd with Dido's dying breath,

Attend her curses and avenge her death!

If so the Fates ordain, Jove commands,

Th' ungrateful wretch should find the Latian lands,

Yet let a race untam'd, and haughty foes,

His peaceful entrance with dire arms oppose:

Oppress'd with numbers in th' unequal field,

His men discourag'd, and himself expell'd,

Let him for succor sue from place to place,

Torn from his subjects, and his son's embrace.

First, let him see his friends in battle slain,

---

① burthen: burden

② piecemeal /'piːsmiːl/: into pieces

③ strow: strew（撒）

④ reeking:（因为在火上烤而）冒着气和烟的

And their untimely fate lament in vain;

And when, at length, the cruel war shall cease,

On hard conditions may he buy his peace:

Nor let him then enjoy supreme command;

But fall, untimely, by some hostile hand,

And lie unburied on the barren sand!

These are my pray'rs, and this my dying will;

And you, my Tyrians, ev'ry curse fulfil.

Perpetual hate and mortal wars proclaim,

Against the prince, the people, and the name.

These grateful off'rings on my grave bestow;

Nor league, nor love, the hostile nations know!

Now, and from hence, in ev'ry future age,

When rage excites your arms, and strength supplies the rage,

Rise some avenger of our Libyan blood,

With fire and sword pursue the perjur'd brood[①];

Our arms, our seas, our shores, oppos'd to theirs;

And the same hate descend on all our heirs!"[②]

This said, within her anxious mind she weighs

The means of cutting short[③] her odious days.

Then to Sichaeus' nurse she briefly said

(For, when she left her country, hers was dead):

"Go, Barce, call my sister. Let her care

The solemn rites of sacrifice prepare;

The sheep, and all th' atoning off'rings bring,

Sprinkling her body from the crystal spring

With living drops; then let her come, and thou

With sacred fillets bind thy hoary[④] brow.

Thus will I pay my vows to Stygian Jove,

And end the cares of my disastrous love;

Then cast the Trojan image on the fire,

And, as that burns, my passions shall expire."

---

① brood：一群人
② 参见 *The Age of Fable* 第 31 章关于 Carthage 的注释。
③ cut short：中断,使停止
④ hoary /'hɔːri/：(头发)花白的

The nurse moves onward, with officious① care,
And all the speed her aged limbs can bear.
But furious Dido, with dark thoughts involv'd,
Shook at the mighty mischief she resolv'd.
With livid spots distinguish'd was her face;
Red were her rolling eyes, and discompos'd her pace;
Ghastly she gaz'd, with pain she drew her breath,
And nature shiver'd at approaching death.

Then swiftly to the fatal place she pass'd,
And mounts the fun'ral pile with furious haste;
Unsheathes② the sword the Trojan left behind
(Not for so dire an enterprise design'd).
But when she view'd the garments loosely spread,
Which once he wore, and saw the conscious bed,
She paus'd, and with a sigh the robes embrac'd;
Then on the couch her trembling body cast,
Repress'd the ready tears, and spoke her last:
"Dear pledges of my love, while Heav'n so pleas'd,
Receive a soul, of mortal anguish eas'd:
My fatal course is finish'd; and I go,
A glorious name, among the ghosts below.
A lofty city③ by my hands is rais'd,
Pygmalion punish'd, and my lord④ appeas'd.
What could my fortune have afforded more,
Had the false Trojan never touch'd my shore!"
Then kiss'd the couch; and, "Must I die," she said,
"And unreveng'd? 'T is doubly to be dead!
Yet ev'n this death with pleasure I receive:
On any terms, 't is better than to live.
These flames, from far, may the false Trojan view;
These boding omens his base flight pursue!"

She said, and struck; deep enter'd in her side

---

① officious /ə'fɪʃəs/：积极的
② unsheathe /ʌn'ʃiːð/：从剑鞘中拔出
③ A lofty city：Carthage
④ lord：husband

The piercing steel, with reeking purple① dyed:

Clogg'd in the wound the cruel weapon stands;

The spouting blood came streaming on her hands.

Her sad attendants saw the deadly stroke,

And with loud cries the sounding palace shook.

Distracted, from the fatal sight they fled,

And thro' the town the dismal rumor spread.

First from the frighted court the yell began;

Redoubled, thence from house to house it ran:

The groans of men, with shrieks, laments, and cries

Of mixing women, mount the vaulted skies.

Not less the clamor, than if—ancient Tyre,

Or the new Carthage, set by foes on fire—

The rolling ruin, with their lov'd abodes,

Involv'd the blazing temples of their gods.

Her sister hears; and, furious with despair,

She beats her breast, and rends her yellow hair,

And, calling on Eliza's name aloud,

Runs breathless to the place, and breaks the crowd.

"Was all that pomp of woe for this prepar'd;

These fires, this fun'ral pile, these altars rear'd?

Was all this train of plots contriv'd," said she,

"All only to deceive unhappy me?

Which is the worst? Didst thou in death pretend

To scorn thy sister, or delude thy friend?

Thy summon'd sister, and thy friend, had come;

One sword had serv'd us both, one common tomb:

Was I to raise the pile, the pow'rs invoke,

Not to be present at the fatal stroke?

At once thou hast destroy'd thyself and me,

Thy town, thy senate, and thy colony!

Bring water; bathe the wound; while I in death

Lay close my lips to hers, and catch the flying breath."

This said, she mounts the pile with eager haste,

And in her arms the gasping queen embrac'd;

Her temples② chaf'd③; and her own garments tore,

---

① purple：血液

② temple：太阳穴

③ chafe：搓，揉

To stanch the streaming blood, and cleanse the gore.

Thrice Dido tried to raise her drooping head,

And, fainting thrice, fell grov'ling on the bed;

Thrice op'd① her heavy eyes, and sought the light,

But, having found it, sicken'd at the sight,

And clos'd her lids② at last in endless night.

Then Juno, grieving that she should sustain

A death so ling'ring, and so full of pain,

Sent Iris③ down, to free her from the strife

Of lab'ring nature, and dissolve④ her life.

For since she died, not doom'd by Heav'n's decree,

Or her own crime, but human casualty⑤,

And rage of love, that plung'd her in despair,

The Sisters⑥ had not cut the topmost hair,

Which Proserpine and they can only know;

Nor made her sacred to the shades below.

Downward the various goddess⑦ took her flight,

And drew a thousand colors from the light;

Then stood above the dying lover's head,

And said："I thus devote thee to the dead.

This off'ring to th' infernal gods I bear."

Thus while she spoke, she cut the fatal hair：

The struggling soul was loos'd, and life dissolv'd in air.

Camilla

Last, from the Volscians⑧ fair Camilla⑨ came,

And led her warlike⑩ troops, a warrior dame⑪;

Unbred to spinning, in the loom unskill'd,

She chose the nobler Pallas of the field.

---

① ope：open
② lid：眼皮
③ Iris 是彩虹女神,诸神之使者。
④ dissolve /dɪ'zɒlv/：结束,终结
⑤ casualty /'kæʒjuəlti/：命运
⑥ The Sisters：the Fates
⑦ the various goddess：Iris；various：多种色彩的
⑧ the Volscians /'vɒlʃənz/：古代意大利中部的部落,英勇善战。公元前 4 世纪被罗马人征服。
⑨ Camilla：/kə'mɪlə/
⑩ warlike /'wɔːlaɪk/：英勇善战的
⑪ a warrior dame：女战士

Mix'd with the first, the fierce virago① fought,
Sustain'd the toils of arms, the danger sought,
Outstripp'd② the winds in speed upon the plain,
Flew o'er the fields, nor hurt the bearded③ grain:
She swept④ the seas, and, as she skimm'd⑤ along,
Her flying feet unbath'd⑥ on billows hung.
Men, boys, and women, stupid with surprise,
Where'er she passes, fix their wond'ring eyes:
Longing they look, and, gaping at the sight,
Devour her o'er and o'er with vast delight;
Her purple habit⑦ sits with such a grace
On her smooth shoulders, and so suits her face;
Her head with ringlets of her hair is crown'd,
And in a golden caul⑧ the curls are bound.
She shakes her myrtle jav'lin; and, behind,
Her Lycian quiver⑨ dances in the wind.

Death of Turnus

Now, in clos'd field, each other from afar
They⑩ view; and, rushing on, begin the war.
They launch⑪ their spears; then hand to hand they meet;
The trembling soil resounds⑫ beneath their feet:
Their bucklers⑬ clash; thick⑭ blows descend from high,
And flakes of fire⑮ from their hard helmets fly.
Courage conspires with chance, and both ingage⑯
With equal fortune yet, and mutual rage.

---

① virago /vɪˈrɑːgəʊ/：女战士
② outstrip /aʊtˈstrɪp/：超过，超越
③ bearded /ˈbɪədɪd/：（谷物）长芒的
④ sweep：在……的表面快速移动
⑤ skim：（在表面或空中）轻快地移动
⑥ unbathed /ˌʌnˈbeɪðd/：不湿的
⑦ habit：衣服
⑧ caul /kɔːl/：女性使用的头饰
⑨ quiver /ˈkwɪvə/：箭袋，箭筒
⑩ They：Aeneas and Turnus
⑪ launch /lɔːntʃ/：投掷
⑫ resound /rɪˈzaʊnd/：发出回声
⑬ buckler /ˈbʌklə/：小的圆盾牌
⑭ thick：密集的，众多的
⑮ flakes of fire：火花
⑯ ingage（engage）：交战，交手

As when two bulls for their fair female fight

In Sila's① shades, or on Taburnus's height②;

With horns adverse③ they meet; the keeper④ flies⑤;

Mute stands the herd; the heifers⑥ roll their eyes,

And wait th' event⑦; which victor⑧ they shall bear⑨,

And who shall be the lord, to rule the lusty year:

With rage of love the jealous rivals burn,

And push for push, and wound for wound return;

Their dewlaps⑩ gor'd⑪, their sides are lav'd in blood;

Loud cries and roaring sounds rebellow⑫ thro' the wood:

Such was the combat in the listed ground⑬;

So clash their swords, and so their shields resound.

Jove sets the beam⑭; in either scale⑮ he lays

The champions' fate, and each exactly weighs.

On this side, life and lucky chance ascends;

Loaded with death, that other scale descends.

Rais'd on the stretch⑯, young Turnus aims a blow

Full on the helm of his unguarded⑰ foe:

Shrill shouts and clamors ring on either side,

As hopes and fears their panting hearts divide.

But all in pieces flies the traitor sword,

And, in the middle stroke, deserts⑱ his lord⑲.

---

① Sila /ˈsaɪlə/：意大利地区名，位于意大利南部的卡拉布里亚区（Calabria），多山，林木茂密。

② Taburnus /ˈtæbənəs/：山名，位于意大利坎帕尼亚区（Campania）；height：山顶

③ adverse /ˈædvɜːs/：敌对的

④ keeper /ˈkiːpə/：牧牛人

⑤ fly：逃跑，逃离

⑥ heifer /ˈhefə/：小母牛

⑦ event：结果

⑧ victor /ˈvɪktə/：胜利者

⑨ bear：承受

⑩ dewlap /ˈdjuːlæp/：（牛颈部）下垂的皮

⑪ gore /gɔː/：（牛、羊等用角）抵破

⑫ rebellow /rɪˈbeləʊ/：发出响亮的回声

⑬ listed ground：竞技场

⑭ beam：天平，秤，天平的横杆

⑮ scale /skeɪl/：秤盘

⑯ stretch：四肢的伸展

⑰ unguarded /ˌʌnˈgɑːdɪd/：没有防备的

⑱ desert /dɪˈzɜːt/：放弃

⑲ his lord：Turnus；his：the sword's

Now 't is but death, or flight①; disarm'd he flies,
When in his hand an unknown hilt② he spies.
Fame says that Turnus, when his steeds he join'd,
Hurrying to war, disorder'd in his mind,
Snatch'd the first weapon which his haste could find.
'T was not the fated sword his father bore,
But that③ his charioteer④ Metiscus⑤ wore.
This, while the Trojans fled, the toughness⑥ held;
But, vain against the great Vulcanian shield⑦,
The mortal-temper'd⑧ steel⑨ deceiv'd his hand:
The shiver'd⑩ fragments shone amid the sand.

Surpris'd with fear, he fled along the field,
And now forthright⑪, and now in orbits wheel'd⑫;
For here the Trojan troops the list⑬ surround,
And there the pass is clos'd with pools and marshy ground.
Æneas hastens, tho' with heavier pace—
His wound, so newly knit, retards⑭ the chase,
And oft his trembling knees their aid refuse—
Yet, pressing foot by foot, his foe pursues.

Thus, when a fearful stag is clos'd around
With crimson toils⑮, or in a river found,
High on the bank the deep-mouth'd⑯ hound appears,
Still opening, following still, where'er he⑰ steers;

---

① flight：逃跑
② hilt /hɪlt /：剑柄
③ that：the sword
④ charioteer /ˌtʃærɪəˈtɪə/：战车或马车的驾驶人
⑤ Metiscus：/ˈmetɪskəs/
⑥ toughness /ˈtʌfnəs/：坚硬，坚韧
⑦ Vulcanian /vʌlˈkeɪnɪən /shield：a shield produced or made by Vulcan
⑧ mortal-temper'd：凡人锻炼的
⑨ steel：剑
⑩ shiver /ˈʃɪvə/：碎裂
⑪ forthright /ˈfɔːθraɪt/：径直往前地
⑫ wheel：转圈
⑬ list：竞技场
⑭ retard /rɪˈtɑːd/：妨碍
⑮ toil：网，罗网
⑯ deep-mouthed /ˈdiːpmaʊðd/：张着大嘴的
⑰ he：the stag

The persecuted creature①, to and fro,

Turns here and there, to scape② his Umbrian foe③:

Steep is th' ascent④, and, if he gains the land,

The purple death is pitch'd along the strand.

His eager foe, determin'd to the chase,

Stretch'd at his length, gains ground at ev'ry pace;

Now to his beamy⑤ head he⑥ makes his way,

And now he holds, or thinks he holds, his prey:

Just at the pinch⑦, the stag springs out with fear;

He bites the wind, and fills his sounding jaws with air:

The rocks, the lakes, the meadows ring with cries;

The mortal tumult⑧ mounts⑨, and thunders in the skies.

Thus flies the Daunian prince⑩, and, flying, blames

His tardy⑪ troops, and, calling by their names,

Demands his trusty sword. The Trojan threats

The realm with ruin, and their ancient seats

To lay in ashes, if they dare supply

With arms or aid his vanquish'd enemy:

Thus menacing, he still pursues the course,

With vigor, tho' diminish'd of his force.

Ten times already round the listed place

One chief had fled, and t'other giv'n the chase:

No trivial⑫ prize is play'd; for on the life

Or death of Turnus now depends the strife.

Within the space, an olive tree had stood,

A sacred shade, a venerable wood,

For vows to Faunus paid, the Latins' guardian god⑬.

---

① persecuted creature：the stag

② scape：escape

③ Umbrian /'ʌmbrɪən/foe：the hound；Umbrian：来自 Umbria 的；Umbria /'ʌmbrɪə/：意大利地区名,位于意大利中部。

④ ascent /ə'sent/：斜坡

⑤ beamy /'biːmi/：(鹿等)角已完全长好的

⑥ he：the hound

⑦ pinch /pɪntʃ/：危机时刻

⑧ tumult /'tjuːmʌlt/：吵闹,喧哗

⑨ mount /maʊnt/：变得大声

⑩ the Daunian prince：Turnus；Daunian /'dɔːnɪən/：Rutulian

⑪ tardy /'tɑːdi/：慢的,行动迟缓的

⑫ trivial /'trɪvɪəl/：普通的,微不足道的

⑬ guardian god：守护神

Here hung the vests, and tablets were ingrav'd,
Of sinking mariners from shipwrack sav'd.
With heedless hands the Trojans fell'd the tree,
To make the ground inclos'd for combat free.
Deep in the root, whether by fate, or chance,
Or erring haste, the Trojan drove his lance;
Then stoop'd, and tugg'd① with force immense, to free
Th' incumber'd② spear from the tenacious③ tree;
That, whom his fainting limbs pursued in vain,
His flying weapon might from far attain.

Confus'd with fear, bereft of human aid,
Then Turnus to the gods, and first to Faunus pray'd:
"O Faunus, pity! and thou Mother Earth,
Where I thy foster son receiv'd my birth,
Hold fast the steel! If my religious hand
Your plant has honor'd, which your foes profan'd,
Propitious hear my pious pray'r!" He said,
Nor with successless vows invok'd their aid.
Th' incumbent hero wrench'd④, and pull'd, and strain'd;
But still the stubborn earth the steel detain'd.
Juturna⑤ took her time; and, while in vain
He⑥ strove, assum'd Metiscus' form again,
And, in that imitated shape, restor'd
To the despairing prince⑦ his Daunian sword.
The Queen of Love⑧, who, with disdain and grief,
Saw the bold nymph afford this prompt relief,
T' assert her offspring⑨ with a greater deed,
From the tough root the ling'ring weapon freed.

---

① tug /tʌg/: 使劲地拔
② incumber (encumber) /ɪnˈkʌmbə/: 妨害,阻碍
③ tenacious /tɪˈneɪʃəs/: 坚韧的
④ wrench /rentʃ/: 使劲地拔
⑤ Juturna /dʒuˈtɜːnə/: Turnus 的妹妹
⑥ He: Aeneas
⑦ the despairing prince: Turnus
⑧ Queen of Love: Venus, mother of Aeneas
⑨ her offspring: Æneas

Once more erect①, the rival chiefs advance:
One trusts the sword, and one the pointed lance;
And both resolv'd alike to try their fatal chance.

Meantime imperial Jove to Juno spoke,
Who from a shining cloud beheld the shock②:
"What new arrest③, O Queen of Heav'n, is sent
To stop the Fates now lab'ring in th' event?
What farther hopes are left thee to pursue?
Divine Æneas, (and thou know'st it too,)
Foredoom'd④, to these celestial seats are due.
What more attempts for Turnus can be made,
That thus thou ling'rest in this lonely shade?
Is it becoming of the due respect
And awful honor of a god elect,
A wound unworthy of our state to feel,
Patient of human hands and earthly steel?
Or seems it just, the sister⑤ should restore
A second sword, when one was lost before,
And arm a conquer'd wretch against his conqueror?
For what, without thy knowledge and avow⑥,
Nay more, thy dictate⑦, durst Juturna do?
At last, in deference to⑧ my love, forbear
To lodge within thy soul this anxious care;
Reclin'd upon my breast, thy grief unload:
Who should relieve the goddess, but the god?
Now all things to their utmost⑨ issue⑩ tend,
Push'd by the Fates to their appointed end.
While leave⑪ was giv'n thee, and a lawful hour
For vengeance, wrath, and unresisted pow'r,

① erect /ɪˈrekt/：身体挺直的
② shock：敌对双方的交锋
③ arrest /əˈrest/：阻止
④ foredoomed /fɔːˈduːmd/：注定的
⑤ the sister：Juturna, the sister of Turnus
⑥ avow /əˈvaʊ/：（庄严的）承诺
⑦ dictate /ˈdɪkteɪt/：命令
⑧ in deference /ˈdefərəns /to：服从，遵从
⑨ utmost /ˈʌtməʊst/：最后的
⑩ issue：（行动的）终结
⑪ leave：允许

Toss'd on the seas, thou couldst thy foes distress①,
And, driv'n ashore, with hostile arms oppress;
Deform the royal house; and, from the side
Of the just bridegroom, tear the plighted bride:
Now cease at my command." The Thund'rer② said;
And, with dejected③ eyes, this answer Juno made:
"Because your dread decree too well I knew,
From Turnus and from earth unwilling I withdrew.
Else should you not behold me here, alone,
Involv'd in empty clouds, my friends bemoan,
But, girt with vengeful flames, in open sight
Engag'd against my foes in mortal fight.
'T is true, Juturna mingled in the strife
By my command, to save her brother's life—
At least to try; but, by the Stygian lake,
(The most religious oath the gods can take,)
With this restriction, not to bend the bow,
Or toss the spear, or trembling dart to throw.
And now, resign'd④ to your superior might,
And tir'd with fruitless toils, I loathe the fight.
This let me beg (and this no fates withstand⑤)
Both for myself and for your father's land⑥,
That, when the nuptial bed⑦ shall bind the peace,
(Which I, since you ordain, consent to bless,)
The laws of either nation be the same;
But let the Latins still retain their name,
Speak the same language which they spoke before,
Wear the same habits⑧ which their grandsires⑨ wore.
Call them not Trojans: perish the renown
And name of Troy, with that detested town⑩.

---

① distress /dɪ'stres/: 使苦恼,折磨
② The Thund'rer: Jupiter (Jove)
③ dejected /dɪ'dʒektɪd/: 沮丧的,情绪低落的
④ resign /rɪ'zaɪn/: 听从,服从
⑤ withstand: 反对
⑥ your father's land: Italy; Jupiter 推翻他的父亲 Saturn 后,Saturn 逃到了意大利。
⑦ the nuptial bed: marriage of Aeneas and Lavinia, daughter of Latinus
⑧ habit: 衣服
⑨ grandsire /'grændsaɪə/: 祖先
⑩ that detested town: Troy; detest /dɪ'test/: 恨,讨厌

Latium be Latium still; let Alba① reign

And Rome's immortal majesty remain."

Then thus the founder of mankind② replies

(Unruffled③ was his front④, serene⑤ his eyes):

"Can Saturn's issue, and heav'n's other heir⑥,

Such endless anger in her bosom bear?

Be mistress, and your full desires obtain;

But quench the choler⑦ you foment⑧ in vain.

From ancient blood th' Ausonian people⑨ sprung,

Shall keep their name, their habit, and their tongue.

The Trojans to their customs⑩ shall be tied:

I will, myself, their common rites provide;

The natives⑪ shall command, the foreigners subside⑫.

All shall be Latium; Troy without a name;

And her lost sons forget from whence they came.

From blood so mix'd, a pious race shall flow,

Equal to gods, excelling all below⑬.

No nation more respect to you shall pay,

Or greater off'rings on your altars lay."

Juno consents, well pleas'd that her desires

Had found success, and from the cloud retires.

The peace thus made, the Thund'rer next prepares

To force the wat'ry goddess⑭ from the wars.

Deep in the dismal regions void of light⑮,

---

① Alba /ˈælbə/：即 Alba Longa，意大利中部 Latium 地区的古城，位于罗马东南方向不远处。

② the founder of mankind：Jupiter (Jove)；founder /ˈfaʊndə/：创立者，缔造者

③ unruffled /ˈʌnˈrʌfld/：平静的，不受强烈感情影响的

④ front：面部，面部表情

⑤ serene /sɪˈriːn/：平静的

⑥ Saturn's issue 和 heav'n's other heir 都指 Juno；issue：孩子，后代

⑦ choler /ˈkɒlə/：愤怒

⑧ foment /fəˈment/：挑起，激起

⑨ th' Ausonian people：the Latins. Ausonia /ɔːˈsəʊnɪə/：意大利中部和南部古代被称作 Ausonia，Ausonia 也可指整个意大利。

⑩ their customs：the customs of the Ausonian people

⑪ The natives：the Ausonians

⑫ subside /səbˈsaɪd/：融入

⑬ all below：凡间的所有人

⑭ the wat'ry goddess：Juturna, a river nymph

⑮ the dismal regions void of light：阴间；dismal /ˈdɪzml/：阴沉的；void：缺乏的

Three daughters① at a birth were born to Night：

These② their brown mother, brooding on her care,

Indued③ with windy wings to flit in air,

With serpents girt alike, and crown'd with hissing hair.

In heav'n the Diræ④ call'd, and still at hand,

Before the throne of angry Jove they stand,

His ministers of wrath, and ready still

The minds of mortal men with fears to fill,

Whene'er the moody sire⑤, to wreak⑥ his hate

On realms or towns deserving of their fate,

Hurls down diseases, death and deadly care,

And terrifies the guilty world with war.

One sister plague of these⑦ from heav'n he sent,

To fright Juturna with a dire portent.

The pest⑧ comes whirling down：by far more slow

Springs the swift arrow from the Parthian⑨ bow,

Or Cydon⑩ yew⑪, when, traversing⑫ the skies,

And drench'd in pois'nous juice, the sure destruction⑬ flies.

With such a sudden and unseen a flight

Shot thro' the clouds the daughter of the night⑭.

Soon as the field inclos'd she had in view,

And from afar her destin'd quarry⑮ knew,

Contracted, to the boding bird⑯ she turns,

Which haunts the ruin'd piles⑰ and hallow'd urns⑱,

---

① Three daughters：即 Erinyes 或 Furies，参见 *The Age of Fable* 第 1 章关于 Erinyes 的叙述。

② These：these three daughters

③ indue（endue）/ɪnˈdjuː/：赋予

④ Diræ：/ˈdaɪriː/

⑤ the moody sire：Jupiter（Jove）；moody：愤怒的

⑥ wreak /riːk/：发泄（愤怒等）

⑦ One sister plague of these：one of the Erinyes

⑧ The pest：One sister plague of these

⑨ Parthian /ˈpɑːθɪən/：of Parthia；Parthia /ˈpɑːθɪə/：古国名，位于今伊朗东北部，士兵精于射箭。

⑩ Cydon /ˈsaɪdən/：（诗歌用语）克里特岛的；Cydonia /saɪˈdəʊnɪə/：古城名，位于希腊克里特岛北部海岸。

⑪ yew /juː/：a bow made of yew-wood

⑫ traverse /ˈtrævəs/：（锋利的物体或武器）刺穿，穿过

⑬ destruction /dɪˈstrʌkʃn/：the swift arrow from the Parthian bow or Cydon yew, which is destructive

⑭ the daughter of the night：one of the Erinyes

⑮ quarry /ˈkwɒrɪ/：（鸟、猎人、猎狗等）追逐或进攻的目标

⑯ the boding bird：猫头鹰

⑰ pile：用于火葬的柴堆

⑱ urn：装骨灰的罐子，（诗歌用语）坟墓

And beats about the tombs with nightly wings,
Where songs obscene on sepulchers she sings.
Thus lessen'd in her form, with frightful cries
The Fury round unhappy Turnus flies,
Flaps on his shield, and flutters o'er his eyes.

A lazy chillness crept along his blood;
Chok'd was his voice; his hair with horror stood.
Juturna from afar beheld her fly,
And knew th' ill omen, by her screaming cry
And stridor① of her wings. Amaz'd with fear,
Her beauteous breast she beat, and rent her flowing hair.

"Ah me!" she cries, "in this unequal strife
What can thy sister more to save thy life?
Weak as I am, can I, alas! contend
In arms with that inexorable② fiend?
Now, now, I quit the field! forbear to fright
My tender soul, ye baleful③ birds of night;
The lashing④ of your wings I know too well,
The sounding flight, and fun'ral screams of hell!
These are the gifts you bring from haughty Jove,
The worthy recompense of ravish'd love!
Did he for this exempt⑤ my life from fate?
O hard conditions of immortal state,
Tho' born to death, not privileg'd to die,
But forc'd to bear impos'd eternity!
Take back your envious bribes, and let me go
Companion to my brother's ghost below!
The joys are vanish'd: nothing now remains,
Of life immortal, but immortal pains.
What earth will open her devouring womb,
To rest a weary goddess in the tomb!"
She drew a length of sighs; nor more she said,

---

① stridor /ˈstraɪdə/：尖锐而刺耳的声音
② inexorable /ɪnˈeksərəbl/：无情的,不宽容的
③ baleful /ˈbeɪlfl/：不吉祥的
④ lashing /ˈlæʃɪŋ/：拍打
⑤ exempt /ɪɡˈzempt/：免除,豁免

But in her azure mantle wrapp'd her head,

Then plung'd into her stream, with deep despair,

And her last sobs came bubbling up in air.

Now stern Æneas waves his weighty spear

Against his foe, and thus upbraids① his fear:

"What farther subterfuge② can Turnus find?

What empty hopes are harbor'd in his mind?

'T is not thy swiftness can secure thy flight③;

Not with their feet, but hands, the valiant④ fight.

Vary thy shape in thousand forms, and dare

What skill and courage can attempt in war;

Wish for the wings of winds, to mount the sky;

Or hid, within the hollow earth to lie!"

The champion shook his head, and made this short reply:

"No threats of thine my manly mind can move;

'T is hostile heav'n I dread, and partial Jove."

He said no more, but, with a sigh, repress'd

The mighty sorrow in his swelling breast.

Then, as he roll'd his troubled eyes around,

An antique stone he saw, the common bound⑤

Of neighb'ring fields, and barrier of the ground;

So vast, that twelve strong men of modern days

Th' enormous weight from earth could hardly raise.

He heav'd⑥ it at a lift, and, pois'd on high,

Ran stagg'ring on against his enemy,

But so disorder'd, that he scarcely knew

His way, or what unwieldly⑦ weight he threw.

His knocking knees are bent beneath the load,

And shiv'ring cold congeals⑧ his vital blood.

---

① upbraid /ʌpˈbreɪd/：责备

② subterfuge /ˈsʌbtəfjuːdʒ/：逃跑方式

③ can secure thy flight：that can secure thy flight

④ valiant /ˈvælɪənt/：强壮而结实的，勇敢的

⑤ bound /baʊnd/：边界

⑥ heave /hiːv/：举起

⑦ unwieldly /ʌnˈwiːldɪ/：笨重的，庞大的

⑧ congeal /kənˈdʒiːl/：使冻结，使凝结

The stone drops from his arms, and, falling short①
For want of vigor②, mocks his vain effort.
And as, when heavy sleep has clos'd the sight,
The sickly fancy labors in the night;
We seem to run; and, destitute③ of force,
Our sinking limbs forsake us in the course:
In vain we heave for breath; in vain we cry;
The nerves, unbrac'd, their usual strength deny;
And on the tongue the falt'ring accents die:
So Turnus far'd; whatever means he tried,
All force of arms and points of art employ'd,
The Fury flew athwart, and made th' endeavor void.

A thousand various thoughts his soul confound;
He star'd about, nor aid nor issue④ found;
His own men stop the pass, and his own walls surround.
Once more he pauses, and looks out again,
And seeks the goddess charioteer⑤ in vain.
Trembling he views the thund'ring chief advance,
And brandishing aloft the deadly lance:
Amaz'd he cow'rs beneath his conqu'ring foe,
Forgets to ward⑥, and waits the coming blow.
Astonish'd while he stands, and fix'd with fear,
Aim'd at his shield he sees th' impending spear.

The hero measur'd first, with narrow view,
The destin'd mark; and, rising as he threw,
With its full swing the fatal weapon flew.
Not with less rage the rattling thunder falls,
Or stones from batt'ring-engines break the walls:
Swift as a whirlwind, from an arm so strong,
The lance drove on, and bore the death along.

---

① short：很快地，突然地
② vigor /ˈvɪgə/：力量，力气
③ destitute /ˈdestɪtjuːt/of：缺乏……的
④ issue：出口
⑤ the goddess charioteer：his sister, Juturna
⑥ ward /wɔːd/：防卫

Naught① could his sev'nfold② shield the prince avail,
Nor aught, beneath his arms, the coat of mail:
It pierc'd thro' all, and with a grisly③ wound
Transfix'd④ his thigh, and doubled⑤ him to ground.
With groans the Latins rend⑥ the vaulted⑦ sky:
Woods, hills, and valleys, to the voice reply.

Now low on earth the lofty chief is laid,
With eyes cast upward, and with arms display'd,
And, recreant⑧, thus to the proud victor pray'd:
"I know my death deserv'd, nor hope to live:
Use what the gods and thy good fortune give.
Yet think, O think, if mercy may be shown—
Thou hadst a father once, and hast a son—
Pity my sire, now sinking to the grave;
And for Anchises' sake old Daunus⑨ save!
Or, if thy vow'd revenge pursue my death,
Give to my friends my body void of breath!
The Latian chiefs have seen me beg my life;
Thine is the conquest, thine the royal wife⑩:
Against a yielded⑪ man, 't is mean⑫ ignoble strife."

In deep suspense⑬ the Trojan⑭ seem'd to stand,
And, just prepar'd to strike, repress'd⑮ his hand.
He roll'd his eyes, and ev'ry moment felt
His manly soul with more compassion melt;
When, casting down a casual glance, he spied

---

① Naught /nɔːt/：nothing
② sevenfold：七层的
③ grisly /ˈɡrɪzli/：引起恐惧的
④ transfix /trænsˈfɪks/：刺穿
⑤ double /ˈdʌbl/：使（身体）弯曲
⑥ rend /rend/：（声音等）刺破,划破
⑦ vaulted /ˈvɔːltɪd/：拱形的
⑧ recreant /ˈrekrɪənt/：向对手投降的,胆小的,怯懦的
⑨ Daunus /ˈdɔːnəs/：father of Turnus
⑩ the royal wife：Lavinia
⑪ yielded /ˈjiːldɪd/：投降的
⑫ mean /miːn/：不高尚的
⑬ suspense /səˈspens/：不确定
⑭ the Trojan：Æneas
⑮ repress /rɪˈpres/：抑制

The golden belt that glitter'd on his side,

The fatal spoils which haughty Turnus tore

From dying Pallas①, and in triumph wore.

Then, rous'd anew② to wrath③, he loudly cries

(Flames, while he spoke, came flashing from his eyes):

"Traitor, dost thou, dost thou to grace pretend④,

Clad, as thou art, in trophies of my friend?

To his sad soul a grateful off'ring go!

'T is Pallas, Pallas gives this deadly blow."

He rais'd his arm aloft, and, at the word,

Deep in his bosom drove the shining sword.

The streaming blood distain'd⑤ his arms around,

And the disdainful soul came rushing thro' the wound.

---

① Pallas：关于 Pallas 之死,参见 *The Age of Fable* 第33章。

② anew /əˈnjuː/：又一次

③ wrath /rɒθ/：愤怒

④ to grace pretend：pretend to grace；pretend to：妄求；grace：宽恕

⑤ distain：弄脏

Ovid

(43 B.C.—A.D. 17)

奥维德（Ovid /ˈɒvɪd /）是古罗马最著名的诗人之一，生于罗马以东大约 140 公里处的小城苏尔摩（Sulmo），死于流放地黑海西海岸的托米斯（Tomis）。奥维德是位多产的诗人，最著名的作品是《爱的艺术》（*Art of Love*）和《变形记》（*The Metamorphoses*）。

《变形记》共 15 卷，是奥维德最长的作品。《变形记》是一部神话故事集，以构思巧妙、语言机智而著称。本读本从《变形记》中选取了 5 个片段：第 1 个选段"Tiresias"和第 2 个选段"Echo and Narcissus"选自第 3 卷，第 3 个选段"Hermaphroditus"选自第 4 卷，第 4 个选段"Tereus, Procne, and Philomela"选自第 6 卷，第 5 个选段"Daedalus and Icarus"选自第 8 卷。《变形记》有多种英文译本，其中英国文艺复兴时期的翻译家阿瑟·戈尔丁（Arthur Golding）的诗译非常有名。本读本采用的是美国著名古典文学学者和翻译家 Frank Justus Miller 的散文译本。

The Metamorphoses
Translated into English by Frank Justus Miller

Tiresias

Now while these things were happening on the earth by the decrees of fate, when the cradle of Bacchus, twice born[1], was safe, it chanced that Jove (as the story goes), while warmed with wine, put care aside and bandied good-humoured jests with Juno in an idle hour. "I maintain,"

---

[1] twice born：Bacchus 是 Jupiter 和 Semele 的儿子。Semele 怀 Bacchus 时，嫉妒的 Juno 装成个凡间妇女，向 Semele 暗示说她的情人未必真是 Jupiter。为了证明这一点，Jupiter 来时，Semele 要求他以天神光彩夺目的本来面目来见她。Semele 被 Jupiter 的光彩化为灰烬，Jupiter 从灰烬中取出 Bacchus，把他放到自己的大腿里，等到 Bacchus 足月后才让他出生，所以 Bacchus"出生了两次"（twice born）。

said he, "that your pleasure in love① is greater than that which we enjoy." She held the opposite view. And so they decided to ask the judgment of wise Tiresias②. He knew both sides of love. For once, with a blow of his staff, he had outraged two huge serpents mating③ in the green forest; and, wonderful to relate, from man he was changed into a woman, and in that form spent seven years. In the eighth year, he saw the same serpents again and said: "Since striking you there is such magic power as to change the nature of the giver of the blow, now will I strike you once again." So saying, he struck the serpents and his former state was restored and he became as he had been born. He therefore, being asked to arbitrate④ the playful dispute of the gods, took side with Jove. Saturnia⑤, they say, grieved more deeply than she should and than the issue warranted, and condemned the arbitrator⑥ to perpetual blindness. But the Almighty Father⑦ (for no god may undo⑧ what another god has done) in return for his loss of sight gave Tiresias the power to know the future, lightening⑨ the penalty by the honour.

Echo and Narcissus

He⑩, famed⑪ far and near through all the Boeotian⑫ towns, gave answers that none could censure⑬ to those who sought his aid. The first to make trial of his truth and assured⑭ utterances was the nymph, Liriope⑮, whom once the river-god, Cephisus⑯, embraced in his winding stream and ravished, while imprisoned in his waters. When her time came the beauteous nymph brought forth⑰ a child, whom a nymph might love even as a child, and named him Narcissus. When asked whether this child would live to reach well-ripened age, the seer replied: "If he ne'er know himself." Long did the saying of the prophet seem but empty words. But what befell⑱ proved its truth—the event, the manner of his death, the strangeness of his infatuation⑲. For Narcissus had reached his sixteenth year and might seem either boy or man. Many youths and many maidens

---

① love: sex

② Tiresias: /taɪˈriːsɪæz/

③ mate: 交配

④ arbitrate /ˈɑːbɪtreɪt/: 关于……做出权威决定

⑤ Saturnia /səˈtɜːnɪə/: Juno, daughter of Saturn

⑥ arbitrator /ˈɑːbɪtreɪtə/: 仲裁人

⑦ the Almighty Father: Jupiter

⑧ undo /ʌnˈduː/: 恢复,取消

⑨ lighten: 减轻

⑩ He: Tiresias

⑪ famed /feɪmd/: 著名的,名气大的

⑫ Boeotian /bɪˈəʊʃn/: of Boeotia

⑬ censure /ˈsenʃə/: 挑错,指责

⑭ assured /əˈʃʊəd/: 确定的

⑮ Liriope: /lɪˈraɪəpi/

⑯ Cephisus: /səˈfɪsəs/

⑰ bring forth: 生

⑱ befall /bɪˈfɔːl/: 发生

⑲ infatuation /ɪnˌfætjuˈeɪʃn/: 迷恋

sought his love; but in that slender form was pride so cold that no youth, no maiden touched his heart. Once as he was driving the frightened deer into his nets, a certain nymph of strange speech beheld him, resounding Echo, who could neither hold her peace① when others spoke, nor yet begin to speak till others had addressed her.

Up to this time Echo had form and was not a voice alone; and yet, though talkative, she had no other use of speech than now—only the power out of many words to repeat the last she heard. Juno had made her thus; for often when she might have surprised② the nymphs in company with her lord③ upon the mountain-sides, Echo would cunningly hold the goddess in long talk until the nymphs were fled. When Saturnia realized this, she said to her: "That tongue of thine, by which I have been tricked④, shall have its power curtailed⑤ and enjoy the briefest use of speech." The event confirmed her threat. She merely repeats the concluding phrases of a speech and returns the words she hears. Now when she saw Narcissus wandering through the fields, she was inflamed with love and followed him by stealth; and the more she followed, the more she burned by a nearer flame; as when quick-burning sulphur⑥, smeared⑦ round the tops of torches, catches fire from another fire brought near. Oh, how often does she long to approach him with alluring⑧ words and make soft prayers to him! But her nature forbids this, nor does it permit her to begin; but as it allows, she is ready to await the sounds to which she may give back her own words. By chance the boy, separated from his faithful companions, had cried: "Is anyone here?" and "Here!" cried Echo back. Amazed, he looks around in all directions and with loud voice cries "Come!"; and "Come!" she calls him calling. He looks behind him and, seeing no one coming, calls again: "Why do you run from me?" and hears in answer his own words again. He stands still, deceived by the answering voice, and "Here let us meet," he cries. Echo, never to answer other sound more gladly, cries: "Let us meet"; and to help her own words she comes forth from the woods that she may throw her arms around the neck she longs to clasp. But he flees at her approach and, fleeing, says: "Hands off! embrace me not! May I die before I give you power o'er me!" "I give you power o'er me!" she says, and nothing more. Thus spurned⑨, she lurks⑩ in the woods, hides her shamed face among the foliage⑪, and lives from that time on in lonely caves. But still, though spurned, her love remains and grows on grief; her sleepless cares waste away her wretched form; she becomes gaunt⑫ and wrinkled and all moisture fades from her body into the air. Only her

---

① hold one's peace：保持沉默

② surprise /sə'praɪz/：当场捉住

③ lord：丈夫

④ trick：(用诡计)欺骗

⑤ curtail /kɜː'teɪl/：剥夺

⑥ sulphur /'sʌlfə/：硫磺

⑦ smear /smɪə/：涂抹（厚厚的一层）

⑧ alluring /ə'ljuərɪŋ/：引诱的，勾引的

⑨ spurn /spɜːn/：蔑视

⑩ lurk /lɜːk/：躲藏

⑪ foliage /'fəʊliɪdʒ/：树叶

⑫ gaunt /gɔːnt/：骨瘦如柴的

voice and her bones remain；then，only voice；for they say that her bones were turned to stone. She hides in woods and is seen no more upon the mountain-sides；but all may hear her，for voice，and voice alone，still lives in her.

Thus had Narcissus mocked her，thus had he mocked other nymphs of the waves or mountains；thus had he mocked the companies of men. At last one of these scorned youth，lifting up his hands to heaven，prayed："So may he himself love，and not gain the thing he loves！" The goddess，Nemesis①，heard his righteous② prayer. There was a clear pool with silvery bright water，to which no shepherds ever came，or she-goats feeding on the mountain-side，or any other cattle；whose smooth surface neither bird nor beast nor falling bough ever ruffled. Grass grew all around its edge，fed by the water near，and a coppice③ that would never suffer the sun to warm the spot. Here the youth，worn by the chase and the heat，lies down，attracted thither by the appearance of the place and by the spring. While he seeks to slake his thirst another thirst springs up，and while he drinks he is smitten④ by the sight of the beautiful form he sees. He loves an unsubstantial⑤ hope and thinks that substance which is only shadow. He looks in speechless wonder at himself and hangs there motionless in the same expression，like a statue carved from Parian⑥ marble. Prone⑦ on the ground，he gazes at his eyes，twin stars，and his locks，worthy of Bacchus，worthy of Apollo；on his smooth cheeks，his ivory neck，the glorious beauty of his face，the blush mingled with snowy white：all things，in short，he admires for which he is himself admired. Unwittingly⑧ he desires himself；he praises，and is himself what he praises；and while he seeks，is sought；equally he kindles love and burns with love. How often did he offer vain kisses on the elusive pool？How often did he plunge his arms into the water seeking to clasp the neck he sees there，but did not clasp himself in them！What he sees he knows not；but that which he sees he burns for，and the same delusion mocks and allures his eyes. O fondly foolish boy，why vainly seek to clasp a fleeting image？What you seek is nowhere；but turn yourself away，and the object of your love will be no more. That which you behold is but the shadow of a reflected form and has no substance of its own. With you it comes，with you it stays，and it will go with you—if you can go.

No thought of food or rest can draw him from the spot；but，stretched on the shaded grass，he gazes on that false image with eyes that cannot look their fill⑨ and through his own eyes perishes. Raising himself a little，and stretching his arms to the trees，he cries："Did anyone，O ye woods，ever love more cruelly than I？You know，for you have been the convenient haunts of many lovers.

---

① Nemesis /'nemɪsɪs/：希腊神话中的惩罚女神，她惩罚犯罪、傲慢等，同时抑制过分的好运。

② righteous /'raɪtʃəs/：正当的，正义的

③ coppice /'kɒpɪs/：小灌木林

④ smite：使迷恋，使神魂颠倒

⑤ unsubstantial /'ʌnsəb'stænʃl/：无实质的，虚幻的

⑥ Parian /'peərɪən/：of Paros；Paros /'peərɒs/：希腊岛屿，古时以盛产大理石而著称，现在是基克拉泽斯群岛（the Cyclades）中的一个岛，属于今希腊南爱琴大区基克拉泽斯州。

⑦ prone：俯卧的

⑧ unwittingly /ʌn'wɪtɪŋli/：毫不知情地

⑨ look their fill：看够

Do you in the ages past, for your life is one of centuries, remember anyone who has pined away like this? I am charmed, and I see; but what I see and what charms me I cannot find"—so serious is the lover's delusion—"and, to make me grieve the more, no mighty ocean separates us, no long road, no mountain ranges, no city walls with close-shut gates; by a thin barrier of water we are kept apart. He himself is eager to be embraced. For, often as I stretch my lips towards the lucent① wave, so often with upturned face he strives to lift his lips to mine. You would think he could be touched—so small a thing it is that separates our loving hearts. Whoever you are, come forth hither! Why, O peerless youth, do you elude me? or whither do you go when I strive to reach you? Surely my form and age are not such that you should shun them, and me too the nymphs have loved. Some ground for hope you offer with your friendly looks, and when I have stretched out my arms to you, you stretch yours too. When I have smiled, you smile back; and I have often seen tears, when I weep, on your cheeks. My becks② you answer with your nod; and, as I suspect from the movement of your sweet lips, you answer my words as well, but words which do not reach my ears.—Oh, I am he! I have felt it, I know now my own image. I burn with love of my own self; I both kindle the flames and suffer them. What shall I do? Shall I be wooed or woo? Why woo at all? What I desire, I have; the very abundance of my riches beggars③ me. Oh, that I might be parted from my own body! and, strange prayer for a lover, I would that what I love were absent from me! And now grief is sapping④ my strength; but a brief space of life remains to me and I am cut off in my life's prime. Death is nothing to me, for in death I shall leave my troubles; I would he that is loved might live longer; but as it is, we two shall die together in one breath."

He spoke and, half distraught⑤, turned again to the same image. His tears ruffled⑥ the water, and dimly the image came back from the troubled pool. As he saw it thus depart, he cried: "Oh, whither do you flee? Stay here, and desert⑦ not him who loves thee, cruel one! Still may it be mine to gaze on what I may not touch, and by that gaze feed my unhappy passion." While he thus grieves, he plucks away his tunic at its upper fold and beats his bare breast with pallid⑧ hands. His breast when it is struck takes on a delicate glow; just as apples sometimes, though white in part, flush red in other part, or as grapes hanging in clusters take on a purple hue when not yet ripe. As soon as he sees this, when the water has become clear again, he can bear no more; but, as the yellow wax melts before a gentle heat, as hoar frost melts before the warm morning sun, so does he, wasted with love, pine away, and is slowly consumed by its hidden fire. No longer has he that ruddy colour mingling with the white, no longer that strength and vigour, and all that lately was so pleasing to behold; scarce does his form remain which once Echo had

---

① lucent /ˈluːsənt/：透明的,清澈的
② beck /bek/：(用点头等表示的)召唤
③ beggar /ˈbegə/：使变穷,使变成乞丐
④ sap：削弱,破坏
⑤ distraught /dɪsˈtrɔːt/：发狂的,心神错乱的
⑥ ruffle /ˈrʌfl/：使泛起涟漪
⑦ desert /dɪˈzɜːt/：离开,抛弃
⑧ pallid /ˈpælɪd/：苍白的

loved so well. But when she saw it, though still angry and unforgetful, she felt pity; and as often as the poor boy says "Alas!" again with answering utterance she cries "Alas!" and as his hands beat his shoulders she gives back the same sounds of woe. His last words as he gazed into the familiar spring were these: "Alas, dear boy, vainly beloved!" and the place gave back his words. And when he said "Farewell!" "Farewell!" said Echo too. He drooped his weary head on the green grass and death sealed the eyes that marvelled at their master's beauty. And even when he had been received into the infernal abodes①, he kept on gazing on his image in the Stygian pool②. His naiad-sisters beat their breasts and shore their locks in sign of grief for their dear brother; the dryads, too, lamented, and Echo gave back their sounds of woe. And now they were preparing the funeral pile, the brandished torches and the bier; but his body was nowhere to be found. In place of his body they find a flower③, its yellow centre girt with white petals.

Hermaphroditus

"How the fountain of Salmacis④ is of ill-repute⑤, how it enervates⑥ with its enfeebling⑦ waters and renders soft and weak all men who bathe therein, you shall now hear. The cause is hidden; but the enfeebling power of the fountain is well known. A little son of Hermes and of the goddess of Cythera⑧ the naiads nursed within Ida's caves. In his fair face mother and father could be clearly seen; his name also he took from them⑨. When fifteen years had passed, he left his native mountains and abandoned his foster-mother, Ida⑩, delighting to wander in unknown lands and to see strange rivers, his eagerness making light of toil. He came even to the Lycian cities and to the Carians⑪, who dwell hard by⑫ the land of Lycia⑬. Here he saw a pool of water crystal clear to the very bottom. No marshy reeds grew there, no unfruitful swamp-grass, nor spiky⑭ rushes⑮; it is clear water. But the edges of the pool are bordered with fresh grass, and herbage ever green. A nymph⑯ dwells in the pool, one that loves not hunting, nor is wont to bend the bow or strive

---

① the infernal abodes: 阴间
② the Stygian pool: 即阴间的河流 Cocytus; 亡灵要进入阴间, 必须先坐船渡过该河。参见 *The Age of Fable* 第 32 章 "The Infernal Regions" 一节。pool: 河流水深且平静之处
③ a flower: narcissus
④ Salmacis: /ˈsælməsɪs/
⑤ ill-repute: 坏名声
⑥ enervate /ˈenəveɪt/: 使衰弱, 使失去活力
⑦ enfeeble /ɪnˈfiːbl/: 使衰弱
⑧ the goddess of Cythera: Aphrodite; 参见 *Theogony* 中的 "Offspring of Earth and Heaven" 选段。
⑨ 他的名字是 Hermaphroditus /hɜːˌmæfrəˈdaɪtəs/, 是 Hermes 和 Aphrodite 两个名字的组合。
⑩ 参见 *The Age of Fable* 第 5 章关于 Ida 的注释。
⑪ the Carians /ˈkeərɪənz/: 古代居住在安纳托利亚 (Anatolia) 西南部 Caria 这个地方的居民。
⑫ hard by: 在……旁边, 紧靠
⑬ 关于 Lycia, 参见 *The Age of Fable* 第 4 章的注释。
⑭ spiky /ˈspaɪki/: 尖的, 戳人的
⑮ rush /rʌʃ/: 灯芯草
⑯ A nymph: Salmacis

with speed of foot. She only of the naiads follows not in swift Diana's train. Often, 'tis[1] said, her sisters would chide her: 'Salmacis, take now either hunting-spear or painted quiver, and vary your ease with the hardships of the hunt.' But she takes no hunting-spear, no painted quiver, nor does she vary her ease with the hardships of the hunt; but at times she bathes her shapely[2] limbs in her own pool; often combs her hair with a boxwood comb, often looks in the mirror-like waters to see what best becomes her. Now, wrapped in a transparent robe, she lies down to rest on the soft grass or the soft herbage. Often she gathers flowers; and on this occasion, too, she chanced to be gathering flowers when she saw the boy[3] and longed to possess what she saw.

"Not yet, however, did she approach him, though she was eager to do so, until she had calmed herself, until she had arranged her robes and composed her countenance, and taken all pains to appear beautiful. Then did she speak: 'O youth, most worthy to be believed a god, if thou art indeed a god, thou must be Cupid; or if thou art mortal, happy are they who gave thee birth, blest[4] is thy brother, fortunate indeed any sister of thine and thy nurse who gave thee suck. But far, oh, far happier than they all is she, if any be thy promised bride, if thou shalt deem any worthy to be thy wife. If there be any such, let mine be stolen joy; if not, may I be thine, thy bride, and may we be joined in wedlock[5].' The maiden said no more. But the boy blushed rosy red; for he knew not what love is. But still the blush became him well. Such colour have apples hanging in sunny orchards, or painted ivory; such has the moon, eclipsed, red under white, when brazen vessels clash vainly for her relief.[6] When the nymph begged and prayed for at least a sister's kiss, and was in act to throw her arms round his snowy neck, he cried: 'Have done, or I must flee and leave this spot—and you.' Salmacis trembled at this threat and said: 'I yield the place to you, fair stranger,' and turning away, pretended to depart. But even so she often looked back, and deep in a neighbouring thicket she hid herself, crouching on bended knees. But the boy, freely as if unwatched and alone, walks up and down on the grass, dips his toes in the lapping waters, and his feet. Then quickly, charmed with the coolness of the soothing stream, he threw aside the thin garments from his slender form. Then did he truly attract her, and the nymph's love kindled as she gazed at the naked form. Her eyes shone bright as when the sun's dazzling face is reflected from the surface of a glass held opposite his rays. Scarce can she endure delay, scarce bear her joy postponed, so eager to hold him in her arms, so madly incontinent[7]. He, clapping his body with hollow palms, dives into the pool, and swimming with alternate strokes

---

① 'tis: it is
② shapely /ˈʃeɪpli/: 形状美观的，好看的
③ the boy: Hermaphroditus
④ blest: blessed
⑤ wedlock /ˈwedlɒk/: 婚姻
⑥ 发生月全食的时候，白色的月亮变为红色。古人不懂月食的原理，所以月食发生时，为了解救被遮住的月亮，他们会敲打一些金属器具，发出刺耳的响声。clash /klæʃ/: 发出刺耳的响声; her: 月亮的; relief /rɪˈliːf/: 解救
⑦ incontinent /ɪnˈkɒntɪnənt/: （在性欲方面）缺乏自制力的

flashes with gleaming body through the transparent flood①, as if one should encase② ivory figures or white lilies in translucent③ glass. 'I win, and he is mine!' cries the naiad, and casting off all her garments dives also into the waters: she holds him fast④ though he strives against her, steals reluctant kisses, fondles⑤ him, touches his unwilling breast, clings to him on this side and on that. At length, as he tries his best to break away from her, she wraps him round with her embrace, as a serpent, when the king of birds⑥ has caught her and is bearing her on high: which, hanging from his claws, wraps her folds around his head and feet and entangles his flapping wings with her tail; or as the ivy oft-times⑦ embraces great trunks of trees, or as the sea-polyp⑧ holds its enemy caught beneath the sea, its tentacles⑨ embracing him on every side. The son of Atlas⑩ resists as best he may and denies the nymph the joy she craves; but she holds on, and clings as if grown fast to him.'Strive as you may, wicked boy,'she cries,'still shall you not escape me. Grant me this, ye gods, and may no day ever come that shall separate him from me or me from him.'The gods heard her prayer. For their two bodies, joined together as they were, were merged in one, with one face and form for both. As when one grafts a twig on some tree, he sees the branches grow one, and with common life come to maturity, so were these two bodies knit in close embrace: they were no longer two, nor such as to be called, one, woman, and one, man. They seemed neither, and yet both.

"When now he saw that the waters into which he had plunged had made him but half-man, and that his limbs had become enfeebled there, stretching out his hands and speaking, though not with manly tones, Hermaphroditus cried: 'Oh, grant this boon, my father and my mother, to your son who bears the names of both: whoever comes into this pool as man may he go forth half-man, and may he weaken at touch of the water.' His parents heard the prayer of their two-formed son and charged the waters with that uncanny⑪ power."

Tereus, Procne, and Philomela

Now all the neighbouring princes assembled, and the near-by cities urged their kings to go and offer sympathy: Argos and Sparta and Peloponnesian Mycenae; Calydon, which had not yet incurred Diana's wrath; fertile Orchomenos and Corinth, famed for works of bronze; warlike Messene, Patrae, and low-lying Cleonae; Nelean Pylos and Troezen, not yet ruled by Pittheus;

---

① flood：河

② encase /ɪnˈkeɪs/：把……装入

③ translucent /trænˈsluːsənt/：透明的

④ fast：紧紧地

⑤ fondle /ˈfɒndl/：抚摸，爱抚

⑥ the king of birds：鹰

⑦ oft-times /ˈɒftaɪmz/：often

⑧ the sea-polyp /ˈpɒlɪp/：珊瑚虫

⑨ tentacle /ˈtentəkl/：（某些动物的）触手

⑩ The son of Atlas：即 Hermaphroditus；Hermaphroditus 是 Hermes 的儿子，Hermes 是 Zeus 和 Maia 的儿子，Maia 是 Atlas 的女儿，所以 Hermaphroditus 是 Atlas 的后裔。son：（男性）后裔或子孙。

⑪ uncanny /ʌnˈkæni/：奇怪的，奇特的

and all the other cities which are shut off by the Isthmus between its two seas, and those which are outside visible from the Isthmus between its two seas. But of all cities—who could believe it? — you, Athens, alone did nothing. War hindered this friendly service, and barbaric hordes from oversea held the walls of Mopsopia① in alarm.② Now Tereus③ of Thrace had put these④ to flight with his relieving troops⑤, and by the victory had a great name. And since he was strong in wealth and in men, and traced his descent⑥, as it happened, from Gradivus⑦, Pandion⑧, king of Athens, allied him to himself by wedding him to Procne⑨. But neither Juno, bridal⑩ goddess, nor Hymen, nor the Graces were present at that wedding. The Furies lighted⑪ them with torches stolen from a funeral; the Furies spread the couch, and the uncanny screech-owl brooded and sat on the roof of their chamber. Under this omen were Procne and Tereus wedded; under this omen was their child conceived. Thrace, indeed, rejoiced with them, and they themselves gave thanks to the gods; both the day on which Pandion's daughter was married to their illustrious king, and that day on which Itys⑫ was born, they made a festival: even so is our true advantage hidden.

Now Titan⑬ through five autumnal seasons had brought round the revolving years,⑭ when Procne coaxingly to her husband said: "If I have found any favour in your sight, either send me to visit my sister or let my sister come to me. You will promise my father that after a brief stay she shall return. If you give me a chance to see my sister you will confer on me a precious boon." Tereus accordingly bade them launch his ship, and plying oar and sail, he entered the Cecropian⑮ harbour and came to land on the shore of Piraeus⑯. As soon as he came into the presence of his father-in-law they joined right hands, and the talk began with good wishes for their health. He had begun to tell of his wife's request, which was the cause of his coming, and to promise a speedy return should the sister be sent home with him, when lo! Philomela⑰ entered, attired in rich apparel, but richer still in beauty; such as we are wont to hear the naiads described, and dryads when they move about in the deep woods, if only one should give to them refinement and apparel

---

① Mopsopia /mɒpˈsəʊpɪə/：即雅典（Athens）；Mopsopia 一词源于雅典国王 Mopsopius 的名字。
② Thebes 遭受了劫难，希腊各地的国王们纷纷表示同情，只有 Athens 没有任何表示，因为 Athens 正忙于应对野蛮人的入侵。关于 Thebes 遭受的劫难，参见 The Age of Fable 第 14 章"Niobe"一节。
③ Tereus：/ˈtɪərɪəs/
④ these: barbaric hordes from oversea
⑤ relieving troops：援军，救兵
⑥ descent /dɪˈsent/：血统，出生
⑦ Gradivus /grəˈdaɪvəs/：即战神 Mars；该拉丁语单词的意思是"在战斗中行走的人"。
⑧ Pandion：/pənˈdaɪən/
⑨ Procne：/ˈprɒkni/
⑩ bridal /ˈbraɪdl/：婚礼的
⑪ light：用光照着……走路
⑫ Itys /ˈɪtɪs/：son of Procne and Tereus
⑬ Titan：Helios, the Sun
⑭ Five years had passed.
⑮ Cecropian /sɪˈkrəʊpɪən/：雅典的；Cecrops /ˈsiːkrɒps/ 是雅典（Athens）的建立者和首任国王，据说他从泥土中诞生，腰部以上为人形，以下为蛇形。
⑯ Piraeus /paɪˈriːəs/：雅典的主要港口，位于雅典城西南方向。
⑰ Philomela：/ˌfɪləʊˈmiːnə/

like hers. The moment he saw the maiden Tereus was inflamed with love, quick as if one should set fire to ripe grain, or dry leaves, or hay stored away in the mow①. Her beauty, indeed, was worth it; but in his case his own passionate nature pricked② him on, and, besides, the men of his clime③ are quick to love: his own fire and his nation's burnt in him. His impulse was to corrupt her attendants' care and her nurse's faithfulness, and even by rich gifts to tempt the girl herself, even at the cost of all his kingdom; or else to ravish her and to defend his act by bloody war. There was nothing which he would not do or dare, smitten by this mad passion. His heart could scarce contain the fires that burnt in it. Now, impatient of delay, he eagerly repeated Procne's request, pleading his own cause under her name. Love made him eloquent, and as often as he asked more urgently than he should, he would say that Procne wished it so. He even added tears to his entreaties, as though she had bidden him to do this too. Ye gods, what blind night rules in the hearts of men! In the very act of pushing on his shameful plan Tereus gets credit for a kind heart and wins praise from wickedness. Ay, more—Philomela herself has the same wish; winding her arms about her father's neck, she coaxes him to let her visit her sister; by her own welfare (yes, and against it, too) she urges her prayer. Tereus gazes at her, and as he looks feels her already in his arms; as he sees her kisses and her arms about her father's neck, all this goads him on, food and fuel for his passion; and whenever she embraces her father he wishes that he were in the father's place—indeed, if he were, his intent would be no less impious. The father yields to the prayers of both. The girl is filled with joy; she thanks her father and, poor unhappy wretch, she deems that success for both sisters which is to prove a woeful happening for them both.

Now Phoebus' toils were almost done and his horses were pacing down the western sky.④ A royal feast was spread, wine in cups of gold. Then they surrender their sated⑤ bodies to peaceful slumber. But although the Thracian king retired, his heart seethes with thoughts of her. Recalling her look, her movement, her hands, he pictures at will what he has not yet seen, and feeds his own fires, his thoughts preventing sleep. Morning came; and Pandion, wringing his son-in-law's hand as he was departing, consigned⑥ his daughter to him with many tears and said: "Dear son, since a natural plea has won me, and both my daughters have wished it, and you also have wished it, my Tereus, I give her to your keeping; and by your honour and the ties that bind us, by the gods, I pray you guard her with a father's love, and as soon as possible—it will seem a long time in any case to me—send back to me this sweet solace of my tedious years⑦. And do you, my Philomela, if you love me, come back to me as soon as possible; it is enough that your sister is so far away." Thus he made his last requests and kissed his child good-bye, and gentle tears fell as he spoke the words; and he asked both their right hands as pledge of their promise, and joined

①　mow /maʊ/：草垛

②　prick /prɪk/：驱使

③　clime：按气候条件划分的地区

④　Now evening was coming.

⑤　sated /'seɪtɪd/：胃口、欲望等得到充分满足的

⑥　consign /kən'saɪn/：托付

⑦　this sweet solace of my tedious years：Philomela；solace /'sɒləs/：安慰，慰藉

them together and begged that they would remember to greet for him his daughter and her son①. His voice broke with sobs, he could hardly say farewell, as he feared the forebodings of his mind.

As soon as Philomela was safely embarked upon the painted ship and the sea was churned beneath the oars and the land was left behind, Tereus exclaimed: "I have won! in my ship I carry the fulfilment of my prayers!" The barbarous fellow triumphs, he can scarce postpone his joys, and never turns his eyes from her, as when the ravenous bird of Jove② has dropped in his high eyrie③ some hare caught in his hooked talons; the captive has no chance to escape, the captor gloats④ over his prize⑤.

And now they were at the end of their journey, now, leaving the travel-worn⑥ ship, they had landed on their own shores; when the king dragged off Pandion's daughter to a hut deep hidden in the ancient woods; and there, pale and trembling and all fear, begging with tears to know where her sister was, he shut her up. Then, openly confessing his horrid purpose, he violated her, just a weak girl and all alone, vainly calling, often on her father, often on her sister, but most of all upon the great gods. She trembled like a frightened lamb, which, torn and cast aside by a grey wolf, cannot yet believe that it is safe; and like a dove which, with its own blood all smeared over its plumage, still palpitates⑦ with fright, still fears those greedy claws that have pierced it. Soon, when her senses came back, she dragged at her loosened hair, and like one in mourning, beating and tearing her arms, with outstretched hands she cried: "Oh, what a horrible thing you have done, barbarous, cruel wretch! Do you care nothing for my father's injunctions⑧, his affectionate tears, my sister's love, my own virginity, the bonds of wedlock? You have confused all natural relations: I have become a concubine⑨, my sister's rival; you, a husband to both. Now Procne must be my enemy. Why do you not take my life, that no crime may be left undone, you traitor? Aye, would that you had killed me before you wronged me so. Then would my shade⑩ have been innocent and clean. If those who dwell on high⑪ see these things, nay, if there are any gods at all, if all things have not perished with me, sooner or later you shall pay dearly for this deed. I will myself cast shame aside and proclaim what you have done. If I should have the chance, I would go where people throng⑫ and tell it; if I am kept shut up in these woods, I will fill the woods with my story and move the very rocks to pity. The air of heaven shall hear it, and, if there is any god in heaven, he shall hear it too."

---

① his daughter and her son: Procne and Itys
② the ravenous bird of Jove: 鹰;ravenous /ˈrævənəs/: 掠夺成性的,饥饿的
③ eyrie /ˈaɪəri/: 鹰筑于高山或悬崖峭壁之上的巢
④ gloat /gləʊt/: (心怀歹意或贪婪地)看,色眯眯地看
⑤ prize /praɪz/: 奖品
⑥ travel-worn: 旅途劳顿的
⑦ palpitate /ˈpælpɪteɪt/: 颤抖
⑧ injunction /ɪnˈdʒʌŋkʃn/: 嘱咐
⑨ concubine /ˈkɒŋkjubaɪn/: 情妇,妾
⑩ shade: 鬼魂
⑪ those who dwell on high: the gods
⑫ throng /θrɒŋ/: (很多人)聚集

The savage tyrant's wrath was aroused by these words, and his fear no less. Pricked on by both these spurs, he drew his sword which was hanging by his side in its sheath, caught her by the hair, and twisting her arms behind her back, he bound them fast. At sight of the sword Philomela gladly offered her throat to the stroke, filled with the eager hope of death. But he seized her tongue with pincers①, as it protested against the outrage, calling ever on the name of her father and struggling to speak, and cut it off with his merciless blade. The mangled root② quivers, while the severed tongue lies palpitating on the dark earth, faintly murmuring; and, as the severed tail of a mangled snake is wont to writhe, it twitches convulsively, and with its last dying movement it seeks its mistress's feet. Even after this horrid deed—one would scarce believe it—the monarch is said to have worked his lustful will again and again upon the poor mangled form.

With such crimes upon his soul he had the face to return to Procne's presence. She on seeing him at once asked where her sister was. He groaned in pretended grief and told a made-up story of death; his tears gave credence③ to the tale. Then Procne tore from her shoulders the robe gloaming with a broad golden border and put on black weeds; she built also a cenotaph④ in honour of her sister, brought pious offerings to her imagined spirit⑤, and mourned her sister's fate, not meet⑥ so to be mourned.

Now through the twelve signs⑦, a whole year's journey, has the sun-god passed. And what shall Philomela do? A guard prevents her flight; stout walls of solid stone fence in the hut; speechless lips can give no token of her wrongs. But grief has sharp wits, and in trouble cunning comes. She hangs a Thracian web on her loom, and skilfully weaving purple signs on a white background, she thus tells the story of her wrongs. This web, when completed, she gives to her one attendant and begs her with gestures to carry it to the queen. The old woman, as she was bid, takes the web to Procne, not knowing what she bears in it. The savage tyrant's wife unrolls the cloth, reads the pitiable fate of her sister, and (a miracle that she could!) says not a word. Grief chokes the words that rise to her lips, and her questing tongue can find no words strong enough to express her outraged feelings. Here is no room for tears, but she hurries on to confound right and wrong, her whole soul bent on the thought of vengeance⑧.

It was the time when the Thracian matrons were wont to celebrate the biennial⑨ festival of Bacchus. Night was in their secret⑩; by night Mount Rhodope⑪ would resound with the shrill clash

---

① pincers /ˈpɪnsəz/：钳子
② root：舌根
③ credence /ˈkriːdəns/：信任，相信
④ cenotaph /ˈsenəʊtɑːf/：衣冠冢
⑤ spirit：鬼魂
⑥ meet：适合的
⑦ the twelve signs：黄道带的十二宫；参见 *The Age of Fable* 第 5 章关于 the twelve signs of the zodiac 的注释。
⑧ vengeance /ˈvendʒəns/：报复
⑨ biennial /baɪˈenɪəl/：两年一次的
⑩ 黑夜知晓她们的秘密。
⑪ Rhodope /ˈrɒdəpi/：山名，大部分位于今保加利亚境内，少部分位于希腊。

of brazen cymbals①; so by night the queen goes forth from her house, equips herself for the rites of the god and dons② the array of frenzy③; her head was wreathed with trailing vines, a deer-skin hung from her left side, a light spear rested on her shoulder. Swift she goes through the woods with an attendant throng of her companions, and driven on by the madness of grief, Procne, terrific in her rage, mimics④ thy madness, O Bacchus! She comes to the secluded⑤ lodge at last, shrieks aloud and cries "Euhoe!"⑥ breaks down the doors, seizes her sister, arrays her in the trappings⑦ of a Bacchante⑧, hides her face with ivy-leaves, and, dragging her along in amazement, leads her within her own walls.

When Philomela perceived that she had entered that accursed house the poor girl shook with horror and grew pale as death. Procne found a place, and took off the trappings of the Bacchic rites and, uncovering the shame-blanched face of her wretched sister, folded her in her arms. But Philomela could not lift her eyes to her sister, feeling herself to have wronged her. And, with her face turned to the ground, longing to swear and call all the gods to witness that that shame had been forced upon her, she made her hand serve for voice. But Procne was all on fire, could not contain her own wrath, and chiding her sister's weeping, she said: "This is no time for tears, but for the sword, for something stronger than the sword, if you have such a thing. I am prepared for any crime, my sister; either to fire this palace with a torch, and to cast Tereus, the author of our wrongs, into the flaming ruins, or to cut out his tongue and his eyes, to cut off the parts which brought shame to you, and drive his guilty soul out through a thousand wounds. I am prepared for some great deed; but what it shall be I am still in doubt."

While Procne was thus speaking Itys came into his mother's presence. His coming suggested what she could do, and regarding him with pitiless eyes, she said: "Ah, how like your father you are!" Saying no more, she began to plan a terrible deed and boiled with inward rage. But when the boy came up to her and greeted his mother, put his little arms around her neck and kissed her in his winsome⑨, boyish way, her mother-heart was touched, her wrath fell away, and her eyes, though all unwilling, were wet with tears that flowed in spite of her. But when she perceived that her purpose was wavering through excess of mother-love, she turned again from her son to her sister; and gazing at both in turn, she said: "Why is one able to make soft, pretty speeches, while her ravished tongue dooms the other to silence? Since he calls me mother, why does she not call me sister? See the kind of man you have married, daughter of Pandion! You are unworthy of your father! Faithfulness to such a husband as Tereus is a crime." Without more words she

---

① cymbal /'sɪmbl/: 一种打击乐器
② don /dɒn/: 穿上
③ frenzy /'frenzi/: 疯狂
④ mimic /'mɪmɪk/: 模仿
⑤ secluded /sɪ'kluːdɪd/: 隐蔽的
⑥ Euhoe: 酒神节 (festival of Bacchus) 中纵酒狂欢者发出的吼叫声
⑦ trappings /'træpɪŋz/: 服饰
⑧ Bacchante /'bækənt/: 酒神 Bacchus 的女信徒
⑨ winsome /'wɪnsəm/: 可爱的,迷人的

dragged Itys away, as a tigress drags a suckling fawn through the dark woods on Ganges' banks[1]. And when they reached a remote part of the great house, while the boy stretched out pleading hands as he saw his fate, and screamed, "Mother! mother!" and sought to throw his arms around her neck, Procne smote him with a knife between breast and side—and with no change of face. This one stroke sufficed to slay the lad; but Philomela cut the throat also, and they cut up the body still warm and quivering with life. Part[2] bubbles[3] in brazen kettles, part sputters[4] on spits[5]; while the whole room drips with gore.

　　This is the feast to which the wife invites Tereus, little knowing what it is. She pretends that it is a sacred feast after their ancestral fashion, of which only a husband may partake, and removes all attendants and slaves. So Tereus, sitting alone in his high ancestral banquet-chair, begins the feast and gorges himself with[6] flesh of his own flesh. And in the utter blindness of his understanding he cries: "Go, call me Itys hither!" Procne cannot hide her cruel joy, and eager to be the messenger of her bloody news, she says: "You have, within, him whom you want." He looks about and asks where the boy is. And then, as he asks and calls again for his son, just as she was, with streaming hair, and all stained with her mad deed of blood, Philomela springs forward and hurls the gory head of Itys straight into his father's face; nor was there ever any time when she longed more to be able to speak, and to express her joy in fitting words. Then the Thracian king overturns the table with a great cry and invokes the snaky sisters[7] from the Stygian pit[8]. Now, if he could, he would gladly lay open his breast and take thence the horrid feast and half-consumed flesh of his son; now he weeps bitterly and calls himself his son's most wretched tomb; then with drawn sword he pursues the two daughters of Pandion. As they fly from him you would think that the bodies of the two Athenians[9] were poised on wings; they were poised on wings! One flies to the woods, the other rises to the roof.[10] And even now their breasts have not lost the marks of their murderous deed, their feathers are stained with blood. Tereus, swift in pursuit because of his grief and eager desire for vengeance, is himself changed into a bird. Upon his head a stiff crest appears, and a huge beak stands forth instead of his long sword. He is the hoopoe[11], with the look of one armed for war.

---

[1]　Ganges's banks: 恒河的河岸; Ganges /ˈgændʒiːz/: 恒河, 发源于喜马拉雅山, 流经印度北部和孟加拉国, 注入孟加拉湾。

[2]　part: part of the boy's body

[3]　bubble: 冒着气泡（煮）

[4]　sputter: 发出劈劈啪啪的声音

[5]　spit: 烤肉叉

[6]　gorge oneself with: 大吃……

[7]　the snaky sisters: the Furies; 参见 The Age of Fable 第 1 章关于 the Erinyes 的叙述。

[8]　the Stygian pit: 阴间

[9]　the two Athenians: Procne and Philomela, who are from Athens

[10]　Philomela is changed into a nightingale that "flies to the woods," Procne a swallow that "rises to the roof."

[11]　hoopoe /ˈhuːpuː/: 戴胜鸟

Daedalus and Icarus

Minos① duly paid his vows to Jove, a hundred bulls, when he disembarked② upon the Cretan strand③; and he hung up his spoils of war to adorn his palace. But now his family's disgrace④ had grown big, and the queen's foul adultery⑤ was revealed to all by her strange hybrid monster-child⑥. Minos planned to remove this shame from his house and to hide it away in a labyrinthine enclosure⑦ with blind⑧ passages. Daedalus, a man famous for his skill in the builder's art, planned and performed the work. He confused the usual passages and deceived the eye by a conflicting maze of divers winding paths. Just as the watery Maeander⑨ plays in the Phrygian fields, flows back and forth in doubtful course and, turning back on itself, beholds its own waves coming on their way, and sends its uncertain waters now towards their source and now towards the open sea: so Daedalus made those innumerable winding passages, and was himself scarce able to find his way back to the place of entry, so deceptive was the enclosure he had built.

In this labyrinth Minos shut up the monster of the bull-man form and twice he fed him on Athenian blood⑩; but the third tribute⑪, demanded after each nine years, brought the creature's overthrow. And when, by the virgin Ariadne's help, the difficult entrance, which no former adventurer had ever reached again, was found by winding up the thread, straightway the son of Aegeus⑫, taking Minos' daughter, spread his sails for Dia; and on that shore he cruelly abandoned his companion. To her, deserted and bewailing bitterly, Bacchus brought love and help. And, that she might shine among the deathless stars, he sent the crown she wore up to the skies. Through the thin air it flew; and as it flew its gems were changed to gleaming fires and, still keeping the appearance of a crown, it took its place between the Kneeler⑬ and the Serpent-holder⑭.

Meanwhile Daedalus, hating Crete and his long exile, and longing to see his native land⑮,

---

① Minos 是克里特（Crete）国王。

② disembark /ˈdɪsɪmˈbɑːk /：下船

③ strand /strænd/：码头

④ family's disgrace：家丑

⑤ the queen's foul adultery：Minos 的王后叫 Pasiphae，她迷恋海神 Poseidon 送给她丈夫的一头公牛，所以她请著名工匠 Daedalus 制作了一头中空的、真牛大小木母牛。她爬入木母牛中，与公牛进行了交配，生下了牛身人头的（人身牛头的）怪物 Minotaur。Minotaur 一词在希腊语中是 Μινώταυρος，由 Μίνως（Minos）和 ταῦρος[tauros（公牛）] 两个部分构成，意思是"Minos 的公牛"。

⑥ her strange hybrid monster-child：Minotaur；hybrid /ˈhaɪbrɪd/：混合的，杂种的

⑦ labyrinthine enclosure：迷宫；labyrinthine /ˌlæbəˈrɪnθaɪn/：迷宫的

⑧ blind：堵死的，一端不通的

⑨ Maeander：参见 The Age of Fable 第 20 章关于"Mæander"的注释。

⑩ blood：活人

⑪ tribute /ˈtrɪbjuːt/：贡品

⑫ the son of Aegeus：Theseus；参见 The Age of Fable 第 20 章。

⑬ the Kneeler /ˈniːlə/：武仙星座（the Hercules）

⑭ the Serpent-holder：蛇夫星座（Ophiuchus /ɒˈfjuːkəs /）

⑮ His native land is Athens.

was shut in by the sea. "Though he may block① escape by land and water," he said, "yet the sky is open, and by that way will I go. Though Minos rules over all, he does not rule the air." So saying, he sets his mind at work upon unknown arts, and changes the laws of nature. For he lays feathers in order, beginning at the smallest, short next to long, so that you would think they had grown upon a slope. Just so the old-fashioned rustic pan-pipes with their unequal reeds rise one above another. Then he fastened the feathers together with twine② and wax at the middle and bottom; and, thus arranged, he bent them with a gentle curve, so that they looked like real birds' wings. His son, Icarus, was standing by and, little knowing that he was handling his own peril, with gleeful face would now catch at the feathers which some passing breeze had blown about, now mould the yellow wax with his thumb, and by his sport would hinder his father's wondrous task. When now the finishing touches had been put upon the work, the master③ workman himself balanced his body on two wings and hung poised on the beaten air. He taught his son also and said: "I warn you, Icarus, to fly in a middle course, lest, if you go too low, the water may weight④ your wings; if you go too high, the fire may burn them. Fly between the two. And I bid you not to shape your course by Boötes or Helice⑤ or the drawn sword of Orion⑥, but fly where I shall lead." At the same time he tells him the rules of flight and fits the strange wings on his boy's shoulders. While he works and talks the old man's cheeks are wet with tears, and his fatherly hands tremble. He kissed his son, which he was destined never again to do, and rising on his wings, he flew on ahead, fearing for his companion, just like a bird which has led forth her fledglings⑦ from the high nest into the unsubstantial air. He encourages the boy to follow, instructs him in the fatal art of flight, himself flapping his wings and looking back on his son. Now some fisherman spies them, angling⑧ for fish with his flexible rod, or a shepherd, leaning upon his crook, or a plowman, on his plow-handles—spies them and stands stupefied⑨, and believes them to be gods that they could fly through the air. And now Juno's sacred Samos had been passed on the left, and Delos and Paros; Lebinthos was on the right and Calymne⑩, rich in honey, when the boy began to rejoice in his bold flight and, deserting his leader⑪, led by a desire for the open sky, directed his course to a greater height. The scorching rays of the nearer sun softened the fragrant wax which held his wings. The wax melted; his arms were bare as he beat them up and down, but, lacking wings, they took no hold on the air. His lips, calling to the last upon his

---

① block /blɒk/：阻止

② twine /twaɪn/：（两股或多股搓成的）线

③ master：大师级的

④ weight：使变重

⑤ Helice /ˈhelɪsiː/：（诗歌用语）大熊星座

⑥ the drawn sword of Orion：猎户座（Orion）的外形是系着腰带、手持宝剑的猎人。

⑦ fledgling /ˈfledʒlɪŋ/：刚会飞的小鸟

⑧ angle /ˈæŋgl/：用鱼钩和诱饵钓鱼

⑨ stupefied /ˈstjuːpɪfaɪd/：惊呆的

⑩ Calymne /kəˈlɪmni/：即卡利姆诺斯岛（Kalymnos），位于爱琴海，离土耳其西海岸不远，现在属于希腊南爱琴大区。

⑪ leader /ˈliːdə/：带路的人

father's name, were drowned in the dark blue sea, which took its name from him.[①] But the unhappy father, now no longer father, called: "Icarus, Icarus, where are you? In what place shall I seek you? Icarus," he called again; and then he spied the wings floating on the deep, and cursed his skill. He buried the body in a tomb, and the land was called from the name of the buried boy.

---

① 参见 *The Age of Fable* 第 20 章"Dædalus"一节关于 the Icarian Sea 的注释。

附录 专有名词读音表

A

Abas /ˈæbəs/

Abdera /æbˈdɪərə/

Abderia /æbˈdɪərɪə/

Abderus /ˈæbdərəs/

Absyrtus /əbˈsɜːtəs/

Abydos /əˈbaɪdɒs/

Abyla /əˈbɪlə/

Acestes /əˈsestiːz/

Acetes /əˈsiːtiːz/

Achaean /əˈkiːən/

Achaia (Achaea) /əˈkɪə/

Achelous /ˌækɪˈləʊəs/

Acheron /ˈækərɒn/

Achilles /əˈkɪliːz/

Acis /ˈæsɪs/

Acrisius /əˈkrɪsɪəs/

Actæon /ækˈtiːɒn/

Acusilaus /əˌkjuːsɪˈleɪəs/

Admeta /ədˈmiːtə/

Admete /ədˈmiːti/

Admetus /ædˈmiːtəs/

Adonis /əˈdəʊnɪs/

Adrastus /əˈdræstəs/

Aea /ˈiːə/

Æacus /ˈiːəkəs/

Æa /iːˈiːə/

Æetes /iːˈiːtiːz/

Ægean /iːˈdʒiːən/

Aegeum /ˈiːdʒɪəm/

Ægeus /ˈiːdʒjuːs/

Aegimius /iːˈdʒɪmɪəs/

Ægina /ɪˈdʒaɪnə/

Ægis /ˈiːdʒɪs/

Ægisthus /iːˈdʒɪsθəs/

Æneas /ɪˈniːæs/

Aenus /ˈiːnəs/

Æolus /ˈiːəʊləs/

Æschylus /ˈiːskɪləs/

Æsculapius /ˌiːskjuːˈleɪpɪəs/

Æson /ˈiːsɒn/

Aethalides /iːˈθəˈlɪdiːz/

Aether /ˈiːθə/

Æthiopia /ˌiːθɪˈəʊpɪə/

Æthiopian /ˌiːθɪˈəʊpɪən/

Æthra /ˈiːθrə/

Ætna (Etna) /ˈetnə/

Agamemnon /ˌægəˈmemnən/

Agave /əˈgeɪvi/

Agelaus /ˌædʒɪˈleɪəs/

Agenor /əˈdʒiːnɔː/

Agrius /ˈægrɪəs/

Ajax /ˈeɪdʒæks/

Alba Longa /ˈælbə ˈlɒŋgə/

Alba /ˈælbə/

Alcestis /ælˈsestɪs/

Alcides /ælˈsaɪdiːz/

Alcimus /əlˈsaɪməs/

Alcinoüs /ˌælsɪˈnəʊəs/

Alcmena /ælkˈmiːnə/

Alecto /əˈlektəʊ/

Aleus /ˈælɪəs/

Alexandrus /ˌælɪgˈzɑːndrəs/

Alpheus /ælˈfiːəs/

Alps /ælps/

Altes /ˈæltiːz/

Althea /əlˈθiːə/

Amalthea /ˌæməlˈθiːə/

Amata /əˈmætə/

Amathos /əˈmæθəs/

Amazenus /ˌæməˈziːnəs/

Amazon /ˈæməzən/

Amphiaraus /ˌæmfɪəˈreɪəs/

Amphidamas /ˌæmfɪˈdæməs/

Amphimedon /ˌæmfɪˈmedən/

Amphinomus /ˌæmfɪˈnəʊməs/

Amphion /æmˈphaɪən/

Amphitrite /ˈæmfɪtraɪti/

Amphitryon /æmˈfɪtrɪən/

Amphrysos /æmˈfrɪsəs/

Ampycus /ˈæmpɪkəs/

Amyclae /əˈmɪkliː/

Amycus /ˈæmɪkəs/

Amymone /ˌæmɪˈməʊni/

Amyntor /əˈmɪntə/

Anatolia /ˌænəˈtəʊlɪə/

Anaxarete /ˌænəkˈsærɪti/

Anchises /æŋˈkaɪsiːz/

Anchius /ˈæŋkɪəs/

Andræmon /ænˈdriːmən/

Androgeus /ænˈdrɒdʒɪəs/

Andromache /ænˈdrɒməki/

Andromeda /ænˈdrɒmɪdə/

Antæus /ænˈtiːəs/

Antea /ænˈtiːə/

Anteros /ænˈtɪərɒs/

Anthor /ˈænθə/

Antigone /ænˈtɪgəni/

Antilochus /ənˈtɪləkəs/

Antinous /ænˈtɪnəʊəs/

Antiope /ænˈtaɪəpiː/

Aonia /eɪˈəʊnɪə/

Apennines /ˈæpənaɪnz/

Aphareus /ˈæfərɪəs/

Aphrodite /ˌæfrəˈdaɪti/

Apollo /əˈpɒləʊ/

Apollodorus /əˌpɒləˈdəʊrəs/

Apollonius /ˌæpəˈləʊnɪəs/

Aquarius /əˈkweərɪəs/

Aquilo /əˈkwɪləʊ/

Arachne /əˈrækni/

Arcadia /ɑːˈkeɪdɪə/

Arcadians /ɑːˈkeɪdɪənz/

Archer /ˈɑːtʃə/

Areopagus /ˌærɪˈɒpəgəs/

Ares /ˈeəriːz/

Arethusa /ˌærɪˈθjuːzə/

Arges /ˈɑːdʒiːz/

Argo /ˈɑːgəʊ/

Argolis /ˈɑːgəlɪs/

Argonaut /ˈɑːgənɔːt/

Argos /ˈɑːgɒs/

Argus /ˈɑːgəs/

Ariadne /ˌærɪˈædni/

Aries /ˈeəriːz/

Arimaspian /ˌærɪˈmæspɪənz/

Arion /əˈraɪən/

Aristæus /ˌærɪsˈtiːəs/

Arneus /ˈɑːnɪəs/

Artemis /ˈɑːtɪmɪs/

Artemisius /ˌɑːtɪˈmɪsɪəs/

Aruns /ˈærənz/

Ascalaphus /əˈskeɪləfəs/

Ascanius /æˈskeɪnɪəs/

Assyria /əˈsɪrɪə/

Asterius /əˈstɪrɪəs/

Astyoche /əˈstɪəki/

Atalanta /ˌætəˈlæntə/

Ate /ˈɑːtɪ/

Athamas /ˈæθəməs/

Athena /əˈθiːnə/

Athenæum /ˌæθɪˈniːəm/

Athene /əˈθiːni/

Athens /ˈæθɪnz/

Athos /ˈæθɒs/

Atlantis /ətˈlæntɪs/

Atlas /ˈætləs/

Attica /ˈætɪkə/

Auge /ˈɔːdʒɪ/

Augeas /ɔːˈdʒiːæs/

Augeias /ɔːˈdʒiːɪəs/

Augustus /ɔːˈgʌstəs/

Aulis /ˈɔːlɪs/

Aurora /ɔːˈrɔːrə/

Ausonia /ɔːˈsəʊnɪə/

Auster /ˈɔːstə/

Autolycus /ɔːˈtəˈlaɪkəs/

Autonoë /ɔːˈtəʊnəʊi/

B

Babylonia /ˌbænɪˈləʊnɪə/

Bacchanal /ˈbækənəl/

Bacchante /ˈbækənt/

Bacchus /ˈbækəs/

Barca /ˈbɑːkə/

Baucis /ˈbɔːsɪs/

Bebryces /ˈbebrɪsiːz/

Bellerophon /bəˈlerəfən/

Belus /ˈbeləs/

Berbers /ˈbəːbəz/

Bistones /bɪsˈtəʊniːz/

Bithynia /bɪˈθaɪnɪə/

Bœotia /biˈəʊʃɪə/

Boötes /bəʊˈəʊtiːz/

Boreas /ˈbɔːrɪəs/

Bosphorus /ˈbɒsfərəs/

Bosporus /ˈbɒspərəs/

Briareos /braɪˈeərɪəs/

Briareus /braɪˈeərɪəs/

Brimo /ˈbraɪməʊ/

Briseis /braɪˈsiːɪs/

Brontes /ˈbrɒntiːz/

Busiris /bʊˈsɪərɪs/

Byrsa /ˈbɜːsə/

C

Cacus /ˈkækəs/

Cadmus /ˈkædməs/

Calais /kəˈleɪɪs/

Calaureia /ˌkæləˈriːɪə/

Calchas /ˈkælkəs/

Calliope /kəˈlaɪəpi/

Callisto /kəˈlɪstəʊ/

Calpe /ˈkælpi/

Calydon /ˈkælɪdən/

Calymne /kəˈlɪmni/

Calypso /kəˈlɪpsəʊ/

Camenæ /kəˈmiːniː/

Camilla /kəˈmɪlə/

Cancer /ˈkænsə/

Capaneus /kəˈpænjuːs/

Capitol /ˈkæpɪtəl/

Capitolinus /ˌkæpɪtəʊˈlɪnəs/

Capricorn /ˈkæprɪkɔːn/

Capys /ˈkæpɪs/

Carians /ˈkeərɪənz/

Carthage /ˈkɑːθɪdʒ/

Cassandra /kəˈsændrə/

Cassiopeia /ˌkæsɪəʊˈpiːə/

Castalia /kæˈsteɪlɪə/

Castor /ˈkɑːstə/

Caucasus /ˈkɔːkəsəs/

Cayster /ˈkeɪstə/

Cebriones /ˌserɪˈəʊniːz/

Cecrops /ˈsiːkrɒps/

Celeus /ˈsiːlɪəs/

Cenaeum /sɪˈniːəm/

Centaur /ˈsentɔː/

Cephalus /ˈsefələs/

Cepheus /ˈsiːfjuːs/

Cephisus /sɪˈfɪsəs/

Cerberus /ˈsɜːbərəs/

Cercopes /səˈkəʊpiːz/

Ceres /ˈsɪəriːz/

Cerynites /səˈrɪnɪtiːz/

Cestus /ˈsestəs/

Ceyx /ˈsiːɪks/

Chalciope /ˌkælsɪˈəʊpi/

Chalcis /ˈkælsɪs/

Chaos /ˈkeɪɒs/

Charon /ˈkeərən/

Charybdis /kəˈrɪbdɪs/

Chimæra /kaɪˈmɪərə/

Chios /ˈkaɪɒs/

Chiron /ˈkaɪərən/

Chryseis /kraɪˈsiːɪs/

Chryses /ˈkraɪsiːz/

Ciconians /sɪˈkəʊnɪənz/

Cimon /ˈsaɪmən/

Circe /ˈsɜːsi/

Cithæron /sɪˈθiːrɒn/

Cleonae /ˈkliːəniː/

Cleopatra /ˌklɪə'pɑːtrə/

Clymene /'klɪmɪni/

Clymenus /'klaɪmɪnəs/

Clytemnestra /ˌklaɪtɪm'nestrə/

Clytie /'klɪtɪiː/

Cnidos /'naɪdəs/

Cnossus /'nɒsəs/

Coans /'kəʊənz/

Cocytus /kəʊ'saɪtəs/

Coeus /'siːəs/

Colchis /'kɒlkɪs/

Copreus /'kɒprɪəs/

Corinth /'kɒrɪnθ/

Cornucopia /ˌkɔːnju'kəʊpɪə/

Coronus /kə'rəʊnəs/

Corybantes /ˌkɒrɪ'bæntiːz/

Cos /kɒs/

Cottus /'kɒtəs/

Crawford /'krɔːfəd/

Creon /'kriːɒn/

Creusa /krɪ'uːzə/

Crius /'kraɪəs/

Cronion /'krəʊnɪən/

Cronos /'krəʊnəs/

Cteatus /'tiːətəs/

Ctesippus /'tesɪpəs/

Cumæ /'kjuːmiː/

Cupid /'kjuːpɪd/

Cyane /sɪ'æni/

Cybele /'sɪbəliː/

Cyclopes /saɪ'kləʊpiːz/

Cyclops /'saɪklɒpz/

Cycnus /'sɪknəs/

Cydonia /saɪ'dəʊnɪə/

Cyllene /saɪ'liːni/

Cyllenius /saɪ'liːnɪəs/

Cymindis /sɪ'mɪndɪs/

Cynthia /'sɪnθɪə/

Cynthius /'sɪnθɪəs/

Cynthus /'sɪnθəs/

Cyprian /'sɪprɪən/

Cypris /'saɪprɪs/

Cyprogenes /ˌsaɪprə'dʒiːniːz/

Cyprus /'saɪprəs/

Cyrene /saɪ'riːni/

Cythera /sɪ'θɪərə/

Cytherea /ˌsɪθə'riːə/

D

Dædalus /'diːdələs/

Damastor /'dæməstə/

Danaan /də'næən/

Danaë /'dæneɪiː/

Danaüs /'dæneɪəs/

Daphne /'dæfni/

Dardanelles /ˌdɑːdə'nelz/

Dardanus /'dɑːdənəs/

Dascylus /'dæskɪləs/

Daunus /'dɔːnəs/

Deianira /ˌdiːə'naɪərə/

Deiphobus /dɪ'ɪfəbəs/

Dejanira /ˌdedʒə'naɪərə/

Delos /'diːlɒs/

Delphi /'delfaɪ/

Delphos /'delfəs/

Demeter /dɪ'miːtə/

Demodocus /dɪ'mɒdəkəs/

Demoptolemus /ˌdemɒp'tɒləməs/

Deucalion /djuː'keɪlɪən/

Dexamenus /dɪ'ksæmɪnəs/

Dia /'daɪə/

Diana /daɪ'ænə/

Dido /'daɪdəʊ/

Diomed /'daɪəmed/

Diomede /'daɪəmiːd/

Diomedes /ˌdaɪə'miːdiːz/

Dione /daɪ'əʊnɪ/

Dionysus /ˌdaɪə'naɪsəs/

Dioscuri /ˌdaɪɒs'kjuəri/

Diræ /'daɪriː/

Dirce /'dɜːsi/

Dis /dɪs/

Doliche /'dəʊlɪki/

Dolius /'dəʊlɪəs/

Dorians /'dɔːrɪənz/

Doris /'dɔːrɪs/

Dryad /'draɪəd/

Dryope /'draɪəpi/

Dryopes /'draɪəpiːz/

Dulichium /də'lɪkɪəm/

E

Echedorus /ˌiːkɪ'dɔːrəs/

Echidna /e'kɪdnə/

Echo /'ekəʊ/

Egeria /ɪ'dʒɪərɪə/

Elaeus /ɪ'liːəs/

Elatus /ɪ'lætəs/

Elean /'iːlɪən/

Eleans /'iːlɪənz/

Electra /ɪ'lektrə/

Eleusis /ɪ'ljuːsɪs/

Elis /'iːlɪs/

Eliza /ɪ'laɪzə/

Ellas /'elæs/

Elymi /ɪ'lɪmaɪ/

Elymians /ɪ'lɪmɪənz/

Elysium /ɪ'lɪzɪəm/

Emathia /ɪ'mæθɪə/

Enceladus /en'selədəs/

Endymion /en'dɪmɪən/

Enna /'enə/

Enyalius /ɪ'naɪəlɪəs/

Epaphus /ɪ'pæfəs/

Epeus /'iːpɪəs/

Ephesus /ɪ'fiːsəs/

Ephyra /'iːfɪrə/

Epidaurus /ˌepi'dɔːrəs/

Epimetheus /ˌepɪ'miːθjuːs/

Epirus /ɪ'paɪrəs/

Erebus /'erɪbəs/

Erginus /'ɜːdʒɪnəs/

Eridanus /ɪ'rɪdənəs/

Erinyes /ɪ'rɪnɪiːz/

Eriphyle /ˌerɪ'fɪli/

Eris /'erɪs/

Erisichthon /ˌerɪ'sɪkθən/

Eros /'ɪərɒs/

Erymanthus /ˌerɪ'mænθəs/

Erytheia /ˌerɪ'θiːɪə/

Erythia /ɪ'rɪθɪə/

Eryx /ˈerɪks/

Eteocles /ɪˈtiːəkliːz/

Etruscans /ɪˈtrʌskənz/

Euboea /juːˈbiːə/

Euenor /juəˈiːnə/

Eumæus /juəˈmiːəs/

Eumenides /juːˈmenɪdiːz/

Eumolpus /juəˈmɒlpəs/

Euphemus /juːˈfiːməs/

Euphrates /juːˈfreɪtiːz/

Europa /juəˈrəʊpə/

Eurus /ˈjuərəs/

Euryades /juəˈraɪədiːz/

Euryalus /juəˈraɪələs/

Euryclea /juəˈrɪkliə/

Eurycleia /ˌjuərɪˈkliːɪə/

Eurydamas /juəˈrɪdəməs/

Eurydice /juəˈrɪdɪsi/

Eurylochus /juːˈrɪləkəs/

Eurymachus /juəˈrɪməkəs/

Eurynomus /juəˈrɪnəməs/

Eurypylus /juəˈrɪpɪləs/

Eurystheus /juəˈrɪsθɪəs/

Eurytion /juəˈrɪtɪɒn/

Eurytus /juˈrɪtəs/

Euxine /ˈjuːksaɪn/

Evadne /ɪˈvædni/

Evander /ɪˈvændə/

Evenus /ˈiːvənəs/

F

Faun /fɔːn/

Faunus /ˈfɔːnəs/

Favonius /fəˈvəʊnɪəs/

Forum /ˈfɔːrəm/

G

Gadira /gəˈdaɪərə/

Gaetulian /gɪˈtjuːlɪən/

Galatea /ˌgæləˈtiːə/

Ganges /ˈgændʒiːz/

Ganymede /ˈgænɪmiːd/

Ganymedes /ˌgænɪˈmiːdiːz/

Gargarus /ˈgɑːgərəs/

Gemini /ˈdʒemɪnaɪ/

Genius /ˈdʒiːnɪəs/

Geraestus /gəˈriːstəs/

Gerena /gəˈriːnə/

Gerenians /gəˈriːnɪənz/

Geryon /ˈgerɪən/

Gibraltar /dʒɪˈbrɔːltə/

Glaucus /ˈglɔːkəs/

Gordius /ˈgɔːdɪəs/

Gorgon /ˈgɔːgən/

Graces /ˈgreɪsɪz/

Gradivus /grəˈdaɪvəs/

Grææ /ˈgriːiː/

Graecia /ˈgriːsɪə/

Griffin /ˈgrɪfɪn/

Gyes /gaɪz/

H

Hades /ˈheɪdiːz/

Hæmon /ˈhiːmɒn/

Hæmonia /hiːˈməʊnɪə/

Haemonius /hiːˈməʊnɪəs/

Hæmus /ˈhiːməs/

Hagnias /ˈhægnɪəs/

Halcyone /hælˈsaɪəni/

Hamadryad /ˌhæməˈdraɪəd/

Harmonia /hɑːˈməʊnɪə/

Harpies /ˈhɑːpɪz/

Hebe /ˈhiːbɪ/

Hebrus /ˈhiːbrəs/

Hecate /ˈhekəti/

Hector /ˈhektə/

Hecuba /ˈhekjubə/

Helen /ˈhelɪn/

Helenus /ˈhelənəs/

Heliades /heˈlaɪədiːz/

Helice /ˈhelɪsiː/

Helicon /ˈhelɪkən/

Hellas /ˈhelæs/

Helle /ˈheli/

Hellene /ˈheliːn/

Hellespont /ˈhelɪspɒnt/

Hephæstos /hɪˈfiːstəs/

Hera /ˈhɪərə/

Heraclea /ˈherəkliə/

Hercules /ˈhɜːkjuliːz/

Hermaphroditus /hɜːˌmæfrəˈdaɪtəs/

Hermes /ˈhɜːmiːz/

Hermione /hɜːˈmaɪəni/

Hero /ˈhɪərəʊ/

Hesiod /ˈhesɪəd/

Hesione /hɪˈsaɪəni/

Hesperia /heˈspɪərɪə/

Hesperides /heˈsperɪdiːz/

Hesperus /ˈhespərəs/

Hestia /ˈhestɪə/

Hippocoon /ˌhɪpəˈkəʊɒn/

Hippocoontids /hɪˌpɔkəˈɒntɪdz/

Hippocrene /ˌhɪpəʊˈkriːni/

Hippodamia /ˌhɪpəʊdəˈmaɪə/

Hippolyta /hɪˈpɒlɪtə/

Hippolyte /hɪˈpɒlɪti/

Hippolytus /hɪˈpɒlɪtəs/

Hippomenes /hɪˈpɒməniːz/

Homer /ˈhəʊmə/

Hyacinthus /ˌhaɪəˈsɪnθəs/

Hyades /ˈhaɪədiːz/

Hyarbas /ˈhaɪəbəs/

Hydra /ˈhaɪdrə/

Hyllus /ˈhɪləs/

Hymen /ˈhaɪmən/

Hymettus /haɪˈmetəs/

Hyperborean /ˌhaɪpəːbɔːˈrɪən/

Hyperion /haɪˈpɪərɪən/

Hypsipyle /hɪpˈsɪpɪli/

Hyrcania /hɜːˈkeɪnɪə/

I

Iapetus /aɪˈæpɪtəs/

Iarbas /ˈaɪəbəs/

Iardanes /ˌaɪəˈdæniːz/

Iasius /ˈaɪəsɪəs/

Ibycus /ˈɪbɪkəs/

Icaria /aɪˈkeərɪə/

Icarius /aɪˈkeərɪəs/

Icarus /ˈaɪkərəs/

Ida /ˈaɪdə/

Idæus /ɪˈdiːəs/

Idas /ˈaɪdæs/

Iliad /ˈɪlɪæd/

Ilion /ˈɪlɪən/

Ilios /ˈɪlɪəs/

Ilium /ˈɪlɪəm/

Ilius /ˈɪlɪəs/

Illyria /ɪˈlɪrɪə/

Imbrus /ˈɪmbrəs/

Inachus /ˈaɪnəkəs/

Ino /ˈaɪnəu/

Io /ˈaɪəu/

Iobates /aɪəˈbæti:z/

Iolaus /ˌaɪəˈleɪəs/

Iolcus /ˈaɪəlkəs/

Iole /ˈaɪəlɪ/

Ioleus /ˈaɪəlɪəs/

Ionia /aɪˈəunɪə/

Iphicles /ˈaɪfɪkli:z/

Iphigenia /ɪˌfɪdʒɪˈnaɪə/

Iphis /ˈaɪfɪs/

Iphitus /ˈɪfɪtəs/

Iris /ˈaɪərɪs/

Ismarus /ɪsˈmærəs/

Ismene /ɪsˈmi:ni:/

Ithaca /ˈɪθəkə/

Ithacus /ˈɪθəkəs/

Itonus /ɪˈtəunəs/

Itys /ˈɪtɪs/

Iulus /aɪˈju:ləs/

Ixion /ɪkˈsaɪən/

J

Janiculum /dʒeɪˈnɪkələm/

Janus /ˈdʒeɪnəs/

Jason /ˈdʒeɪsn/

Jocasta /dʒəuˈkæstə/

Jove /dʒəuv/

Juno /ˈdʒu:nəu/

Jupiter /ˈdʒu:pɪtə/

Juturna /dʒuˈtɜ:nə/

K

Kedalion /kəˈdeɪlɪən/

L

Lacedaemon /ˌlæsɪˈdi:mən/

Laconia /ləˈkəunɪə/

Ladon /ˈlædn/

Laertes /leɪˈɜ:ti:z/

Læstrygonians /ˌli:strɪˈgəunɪənz/

Laius /ˈlaɪəs/

Lampetia /ləmˈpi:tɪə/

Laocoon /leɪˈɒkəuɒn/

Laocoön /leɪˈɒkəuɒn/

Laodamia /ˌleɪəudəˈmaɪə/

Laogoras /leɪˈɒgərəs/

Laomedon /leɪˈɒmɪdən/

Laothoe /ˌleɪəˈθəui/

Lapithæ /ˈlæpɪθi:/

Lapiths /ˈlæpɪθs/

Lares /ˈlɑ:ri:z/

Larva /ˈlɑ:və/

Latinus /ləˈtɪnəs/

Latium /ˈleɪʃɪəm/

Latmos /ˈlætməs/

Latona /ləˈtəunə/

Lausus /ˈlɔ:səs/

Lavinia /ləˈvɪnɪə/

Lavinium /ləˈvɪnɪəm/

Leander /lɪˈændə/

Lebynthos /ˈlebɪnθəs/

Lectum /ˈlektəm/

Leda /ˈli:də/

Lefkada /lefˈkædə/

Lefkas /ˈlefkəs/

Leiodes: /ˌli:ɪˈəudi:z/

Lemnos /ˈlemnɒs/

Lemur /ˈli:mə/

Leo /ˈli:əu/

Leocritus /lɪˈɒkrɪtəs/

Lerna /ˈlɜ:nə/

Lethe /ˈli:θi/

Leto /ˈli:təu/

Leucadia /ljuˈkeɪdɪə/

Leucothea /ljuˈkɔθɪə/

Levitha /ləˈvɪθə/

Libethra /lɪˈbeθrə/

Libra /ˈlaɪbrə/

Libya /ˈlɪbɪə/

Lichas /ˈlaɪkəs/

Licymnius /lɪˈsɪmnɪəs/

Liguria /lɪˈguːrɪə/

Lindians /ˈlɪndɪənz/

Lindus /ˈlɪndəs/

Linus /ˈlaɪnəs/

Liriope /lɪˈraɪəpi/

Locrians /ˈlɒkrɪənz/

Locris /ˈləukrɪs/

Lotis /ˈləutɪs/

Lycaon /laɪˈkeɪɒn/

Lycia /ˈlɪsɪə/

Lycomedes /ˌlaɪkəˈmi:di:z/

Lyctus /ˈlɪktəs/

Lycus /ˈlaɪkəs/

Lydia /ˈlɪdɪə/

Lynceus /ˈlɪŋkɪəs/

Lyra /ˈlaɪərə/

Lysianassa /ˌlɪsɪˈænəsə/

M

Macedonia /ˌmæsɪˈdəunɪə/

Machaon /məˈkeɪɒn/

Mæander /mɪˈændə/

Mæonia /mi:ˈəunɪə/

Malea /ˈmælɪə/

Marathon /ˈmærəθən/

Mars /mɑ:z/

Marsyas/ˈmɑ:saɪəs/

Medea /mɪˈdɪə/

Media /ˈmi:dɪə/

Mediterranean /ˌmedɪtəˈreɪnɪən/

Medon /ˈmi:dn/

Medusa /mɪˈdju:zə/

Megamede /mɪˈgæmɪdi/

Megara /ˈmegərə/

Melampus /mɪˈlæmpəs/

Melanthius /mɪˈlænθɪəs/

Meleager /ˌmelɪˈeɪgə/

Meliae /ˈmi:lɪi:/

Melians /ˈmelɪənz/

Melicertes /ˌmelɪˈsɜ:ti:z/

Melisseus /mɪˈlɪsɪəs/

Melos /ˈmi:lɒs/

Memnon /ˈmemnɒn/

Menelaus /ˌmenɪˈleɪəs/

Menœceus /mɪˈniːsjuːs/

Menoetes /mɪˈniːtiːz/

Mentor /ˈmentə/

Mercury /ˈmɜːkjuri/

Merope /ˈmerəpɪ/

Metabus /mɪˈtæbəs/

Metanim /mɪˈtænɪm/

Metiscus /meˈtɪskəs/

Mezentius /mɪˈzentɪəs/

Midas /ˈmaɪdəs/

Mimas /ˈmaɪməs/

Minerva /mɪˈnɜːvə/

Minos /ˈmaɪnɒs/

Minotaur /ˈmɪnətɔː/

Minyans /ˈmɪnɪənz/

Minyas /ˈmɪnɪæs/

Mnemosyne /niːˈmɒzɪniː/

Mnesimache /niːˈsɪməki/

Molione /məˈlaɪəni/

Molionides /ˌmɒlɪˈɒlɪdiːz/

Molorchus /ˈmɒləkəs/

Molossia /məˈlɒsɪə/

Momus /ˈməʊməs/

Mopsopia /mɒpˈsəʊpɪə/

Mopsus /ˈmɒpsəs/

Morpheus /ˈmɔːfjuːs/

Musæus /mjuˈsiːəs/

Muses /ˈmjuːzɪz/

Mycenæ /maɪˈsiːni/

Mygdon /ˈmɪgdn/

Myrmidon /ˈmɜːmɪdən/

Mysia /ˈmɪsɪə/

N

Naiad /ˈnaɪæd/

Narcissus /nɑːˈsɪsəs/

Nauplius /ˈnɔːplɪəs/

Nausicaa /nɔːˈsɪkɪə/

Nausithoüs /ˌnɔːsɪˈθəʊəs/

Naxos /ˈnæksɒs/

Neleus /ˈniːljuːs/

Nemea /nɪˈmiːə/

Nemesis /ˈnemɪsɪs/

Neoptolemus /ˌniːɒpˈtɒləməs/

Nephele /ˈnefɪli/

Neptune /ˈneptjuːn/

Nereid /ˈnɪərɪːɪd/

Nereus /ˈnɪərɪuːs/

Nessus /ˈnesəs/

Nestor /ˈnestɔː/

Nile /naɪl/

Niobe /ˈnaɪəʊbi/

Nisus /ˈnaɪsəs/

Notus /ˈnəʊtəs/

Numa /ˈnjuːmə/

Numidia /njuːˈmɪdɪə/

Numidians /njuːˈmɪdɪənz/

Nysa /ˈnɪsə/

O

Oceanus /əʊˈsɪənəs/

Odysseus /əˈdɪsjuːs/

Odyssey /ˈɒdɪsi/

Oechalia /iːˈkeɪlɪə/

Œdipus /ˈiːdɪpəs/

Oeager /ˈiːəgə/

Oeneus /ˈiːnɪəs/

Œneus /ˈiːnjuːs/

Oenoe /ˈiːniː/

Œnone /iːˈnəʊni/

Œnopion /iːˈnəʊpɪən/

Oeonos /ˈiːənəs/

Oeta /ˈiːtə/

Œta /ˈiːtə/

Ogyges /əʊˈdʒɪdʒiːz/

Oicles /ˈɔɪkliːz/

Olympia /əˈlɪmpɪə/

Olympiad /əˈlɪmpɪæd/

Olympus /əˈlɪmpəs/

Omphale /ˈɒmfəli/

Onchestus /ɒnˈkiːstəs/

Ophiuchus /ɒˈfjuːkəs/

Ops /ɒps/

Opus /ˈəʊpəs/

Orchomenus /ɔːˈkɒmɪnəs/

Oread /ˈɔːrɪæd/

Orestes /ɒˈrestiːz/

Orion /əˈraɪən/

Orithyia /ˌɒrɪˈθɪɪə/

Ormenium /ɔːˈmiːnɪəm/

Orpheus /ˈɔːfjuːs/

Orthus /ˈɔːθəs/

Ossa /ˈɒsə/

Othrys /ˈəʊθrɪs/

Otreus /ˈəʊtrɪəs/

Ovid /ˈɒvɪd/

P

Pactolus /pækˈtəʊləs/

Palæmon /pəˈliːmɒn/

Palamedes /ˌpæləˈmiːdiːz/

Palinurus /ˌpælɪˈnʌrəs/

Palladium /pəˈleɪdɪəm/

Pallas /ˈpæləs/

Pan /pæn/

Pandion /pənˈdaɪən/

Pandora /pænˈdɔːrə/

Paphlagonia /ˌpæfləˈgəʊnɪə/

Paphos /ˈpeɪfɒs/

Paris /ˈpærɪs/

Parnassus /pɑːˈnæsəs/

Paros /ˈpeərɒs/

Parthenius /ˈpɑːθɪnɪəs/

Parthia /ˈpɑːθɪə/

Pasiphae /pəˈsɪfeɪɪ/

Pasithea /ˌpæsɪˈθɪə/

Patara /pəˈteərə/

Patroclus /pəˈtrɒkləs/

Pegasus /ˈpegəsəs/

Peisandrus /peɪˈsændrəs/

Peleus /ˈpiːljuːs/

Pelias /ˈpiːlɪæs/

Pelion /ˈpiːlɪən/

Pelops /ˈpiːlɒps/

Penates /pɪˈnɑːtiːz/

Penelope /pəˈneləpi/

Peneus /ˈpiːnjuːs/

Penthesilea /ˌpenθesɪˈliːə/

Pentheus /ˈpenθjuːs/

Perdix /ˈpɜːdɪks/

Pergamum /ˈpɜːgəməm/

Periander /ˌperɪˈændə/

Periclymenus /ˌperɪˈklaɪmɪnəs/

Perieres /pɪˈraɪərɪːz/

Periphetes /ˌperɪˈfiːtiːz/

Persephone /pɜːˈsefəni/

Perses /ˈpɜːsiːz/

Perseus /ˈpɜːsjuːs/

Phæacian /fɪˈeɪʃn/

Phædra /ˈfiːdrə/

Phaëthon /ˈfeɪθən/

Phaëthusa /ˌfeɪɪˈθjuːzə/

Phaëton /ˈfeɪtn/

Phaon /ˈfeɪɒn/

Phasis /ˈfæsɪs/

Phemius /ˈfiːmɪəs/

Pherae /ˈfiːriː/

Pherecydes /ˌferɪˈsaɪdiːz/

Philemon /fɪˈliːmɒn/

Philoctetes /ˌfɪləkˈtiːtiːz/

Philoetius /fɪləˈiːtɪəs/

Philomela /ˌfɪləʊˈmiːnə/

Philommedes /ˌfɪləˈmiːdiːz/

Phineus /ˈfɪnjuːs/

Phlegethon /ˈfledʒɪθən/

Phlegra /ˈflegrə/

Phocis /ˈfəʊsɪs/

Phoebe /ˈfiːbi/

Phœbus /ˈfiːbəs/

Phœnicia /fəˈnɪʃə/

Phoenicia /fəˈnɪʃə/

Phoenix /ˈfiːnɪks/

Pholoe /ˈfəʊliː/

Pholus /ˈfəʊləs/

Phorbas /ˈfɔːbəs/

Phosphoros /ˈfɒsfərəs/

Phrasius /ˈfreɪsɪəs/

Phrygia /ˈfrɪdʒɪə/

Phryxus /ˈfrɪksəs/

Phyleus /ˈfɪlɪəs/

Pieria /paɪˈɪərɪə/

Pindar /ˈpɪndə/

Pindus /ˈpɪndəs/

Piraeus /paɪˈriːəs/

Pirene /pɪˈriːnə/

Pirithous /paɪˈrɪθəʊəs/

Pisa /ˈpiːzə/

Pisces /ˈpaɪsiːz/

Pleiads /ˈplaɪədz/

Plexippus /ˈpleksɪpəs/

Pluto /ˈpluːtəʊ/

Plutus /ˈpluːtəs/

Po /pəʊ/

Podalirius /ˌpəʊdəˈlɪərɪəs/

Podarces /pəʊˈdɑːsiːz/

Poeas /ˈpiːəs/

Polites /pəˈlɪtiːz/

Pollux /ˈpɒləks/

Poltys /ˈpɒtlɪs/

Polybus /ˈpɒlɪbəs/

Polyctor /ˈpɒlɪktə/

Polydamas /ˌpɒlɪˈdæməs/

Polydectes /ˌpɒlɪˈdektiːs/

Polydore /ˌpɒlɪˈdɔːri/

Polydorus /ˌpɒlɪˈdɔːrəs/

Polygonus /pəˈlɪgənəs/

Polynices /ˌpɒlɪˈnaɪsiːz/

Polyphemus /ˌpɒlɪˈfiːməs/

Polytherses /ˌpɒlɪˈθɜːsiːz/

Polyxena /pɒˈlɪksɪnə/

Pomona /pəˈməʊnə/

Pontus /ˈpɒntəs/

Portunus /ˈpɔːtənəs/

Poseidon /pɒˈsaɪdən/

Priam /ˈpraɪəm/

Procne /ˈprɒkni/

Procris /ˈprɒkrɪs/

Procrustes /prəʊˈkrʌstiːz/

Prœtus /ˈpriːtəs/

Prometheus /prəˈmiːθjuːs/

Proserpina /prəˈsɜːpɪnə/

Proserpine /ˈprɒsəpaɪn/

Protesilaus /prəˌtesɪˈleɪəs/

Proteus /ˈprəʊtɪəs/

Psophis /ˈsəʊfɪs/

Psyche /ˈsaɪki/

Punjab /pʌnˈdʒɑːb/

Pygmalion /pɪgˈmeɪlɪən/

Pygmy /ˈpɪgmi/

Pylades /ˈpɪlədiːz/

Pylians /ˈpaɪlɪənz/

Pylus /ˈpaɪləs/

Pyramus /ˈpɪrəməs/

Pyrene /pɪˈriːni/

Pyrrha /ˈpɪrə/

Pyrrhus /ˈpɪrəs/

Pytho /ˈpaɪθə/

Python /ˈpaɪθən/

R

Remus /ˈriːməs/

Rhadamanthus /ˌrædəˈmænθəs/

Rhea /ˈriːə/

Rhegium /ˈriːdʒɪəm/

Rhodes /rəʊdz/

Rhodope /ˈrɒdəpi/

Rhœcus /ˈriːkəs/

Romulus /ˈrɒmjuləs/

Rutulians /ruˈtuːlɪənz/

S

Saba /ˈsæbə/

Sagittarius /ˌsædʒɪˈteərɪəs/

Salamis /ˈsæləmɪs/

Salmoneus /səlˈməʊnjuːs/

Samos /ˈseɪmɒs/

Samothrace /ˌsæməˈθreɪs/

Sappho /ˈsæfəʊ/

Sardinia /sɑːˈdɪnɪə/

Sarpedon /sɑːˈpiːdən/

Saturn /ˈsætɜːn/

Saturnalia /ˌsætəˈneɪlɪə/

Saturnia /səˈtɜːnɪə/

Satyr /ˈsætə/

Scamander /ˈskæməndə/

Scheria /ˈskiːrɪə/

Scopas /ˈskəʊpəs/

Scorpio /ˈskɔːpɪəʊ/

Scylla /ˈsɪlə/

Scyros /ˈskɪrɒs/

Scythia /ˈsɪðɪə/

Semele /ˈsemɪli/

Semiramis /seˈmɪrəmɪs/

Selene /sɪˈliːni/

Seriphus /ˈserɪfəs/

Sestos /ˈsestɒs/

Sibyl /ˈsɪbɪl/

Sichæus /ˈsɪkiːəs/

Sicily /ˈsɪsɪli/

Sila /ˈsaɪlə/
Sileni /saɪˈliːnaɪ/
Silenus /saɪˈliːnəs/
Silvia /ˈsɪlvɪə/
Simonides /saɪˈmɒnɪdiːz/
Sinon /ˈsaɪnən/
Sintians /ˈsɪnʃənz/
Siren /ˈsaɪərən/
Sirius /ˈsɪrɪəs/
Sisyphus /ˈsɪsɪfəs/
Skyros /ˈskaɪrəs/
Somnus /ˈsɒmnəs/
Sparta /ˈspɑːtə/
Sphinx /sfɪŋks/
Sterope /ˈsterəpi/
Steropes /ˈstɪərəpiːz/
Strophius /ˈstrəʊfɪəs/
Strymon /ˈstrɪmɒn/
Stymphalus /stɪmˈfeɪləs/
Styx /stɪks/
Syleus /ˈsɪlɪəs/
Sylvanus /sɪlˈvænəs/
Symplegades /sɪmˈplegədiːz/
Syrinx /ˈsɪrɪŋks/
Syrtes /ˈsɜːtiːz/

T

Taburnus /ˈtæbənəs/
Taenarum /tiːˈneərəm/
Tænarus /tiːˈneərəs/
Tagus /ˈteɪgəs/
Tantalus /ˈtæntələs/
Tarchon /ˈtɑːkən/
Tarentum /təˈrentəm/
Tarquin /ˈtɑːkwɪn/
Tartarus /ˈtɑːtərəs/
Tartessus /tɑːˈtiːsəs/
Tauris /ˈtɔːrɪs/
Taurus /ˈtɔːrəs/
Tegea /ˈtiːdʒɪə/
Telamon /ˈteləmən/
Teleboans /ˈtelɪməʊnz/
Telegonus /tɪˈlegənəs/
Telemachus /tɪˈleməkəs/

Tellus /ˈteləs/
Tenedos /ˈtenədɒs/
Tereus /ˈtɪərɪəs/
Terpes /ˈtɜːpiːz/
Terra /ˈterə/
Tethys /ˈteθɪs/
Teucer /ˈtjuːsə/
Teuthrania /tjuːˈθreɪnɪə/
Teuthras /ˈtjuːθrəs/
Thamyris /ˈθæmərɪs/
Thasos /ˈθeɪsɒs/
Thebes /θiːbz/
Themis /ˈθiːmɪs/
Themiscyra /θɪˈmɪsɪrə/
Thermodon /θəˈməʊdn/
Thermydrae /ˈθəːmɪdriː/
Thersites /θɜːˈsaɪtiːz/
Theseum /θɪˈsiːəm/
Theseus /ˈθiːsjuːs/
Thespiae /ˈθiːspɪiː/
Thespius /ˈθiːspɪəs/
Thesprotians /θɪˈsprəʊtɪənz/
Thesprotis /θɪˈsprəʊtɪs/
Thessaly /ˈθesəli/
Thestius /ˈθiːstɪəs/
Thetis /ˈθetɪs/
Thiodamas /θɪəˈdæməs/
Thisbe /ˈθɪzbi/
Thoas /ˈθəʊəs/
Thrace /θreɪs/
Thracian /ˈθreɪʃn/
Thrasymedes /ˌθræsɪˈmiːdiːz/
Thrinakia /θrɪˈneɪkɪə/
Thymoetes /θɪˈmiːtiːz/
Thynia /ˈθaɪnɪə/
Thynians /ˈθaɪnɪənz/
Tiber /ˈtaɪbə/
Tiphys /ˈtɪfɪs/
Tiresias /taɪˈriːsɪæz/
Tiryns /ˈtɪrɪnz/
Tisiphone /tɪˈsɪfəni/
Titan /ˈtaɪtən/

Tithonus /tɪˈθəʊnəs/
Tityus /ˈtaɪtɪəs/
Tlepolemus /ˌtliːpəˈliːməs/
Tmolus /ˈtmɒləs/
Torone /təˈrəʊni/
Toxeus /ˈtɒksəs/
Trachin /ˈtrætʃɪn/
Trachis /ˈtrækɪs/
Triptolemus /trɪpˈtɒlɪməs/
Triton /ˈtraɪtn/
Tritonis /trɪˈtəʊnɪs/
Trœzen /ˈtriːzən/
Tros /trɒs/
Troy /trɔɪ/
Turnus /ˈtɜːnəs/
Tyana /ˈtaɪənə/
Tyndareus /tɪnˈdeərɪəs/
Typhon /ˈtaɪfɒn/
Tyre /ˈtaɪə/
Tyrrhenia /tɪˈriːnɪə/
Tyrrheus /ˈtɪrjuːs/

U

Ulysses /juːˈlɪsiːz/
Umbria /ˈʌmbrɪə/

V

Venus /ˈviːnəs/
Vertumnus /vɜːˈtʌmnəs/
Vestal /ˈvestl/
Vesuvius /vɪˈsuːvɪəs/
Virgil /ˈvɜːdʒɪl/
Virgo /ˈvɜːgəʊ/
Volscens /ˈvɒlsəns/
Volscians /ˈvɒlʃənz/
Vulcan /ˈvʌlkən/

W

Wain /weɪn/

Z

Zephyr /ˈzefə/
Zephyrus /ˈzefərəs/
Zetes /ˈziːtiːz/
Zethus /ˈzeθəs/
Zeus /zjuːs/

主要参考书目

Apollodorus. *The Library*. Trans. Sir James Frazer. Cambridge, Massachusetts: Harvard University Press; London: William Heinemann Ltd., 1976.

Apollodorus. *The Library of Greek Mythology*. Trans. Robin Hard. Oxford: Oxford University Press, 1997.

Apollonius. *The Argonautica*. Trans. R. C. Seaton. Cambridge, Massachusetts: Harvard University Press; London: William Heinemann Ltd., 1988.

Bulfinch, Thomas. *Bulfinch's Mythology*. New York: The Modern Library, n. d.

Glare, P. G. W. *Oxford Latin Dictionary*. Oxford: Oxford University Press, 1968.

Graves, Robert. *The Greek Myths*. London: Penguin Books, 1960.

Grimal, Pierre. *The Penguin Dictionary of Classical Mythology*. Ed. Stephen Kershaw. London: Penguin Books, 1991.

Grimal, Pierre. *Dictionaire de la Mythologie Grecque et Romaine*. Paris: Presses Universitaires de France, 1951.

Hamilton, Edith. *Mythology*. New York: Mentor Books-The New American Library, 1942.

Hesiod. *The Homeric Hymns and Homerica*. Trans. Hugh G. Evelyn-White. Cambridge, Massachusetts: Harvard University Press; London: William Heinemann Ltd., 1982.

Homer. *The Iliad*. New York: Pocket Books, 2006.

Homer. *The Iliad*. Trans. Robert Fitzgerald. Beijing: Foreign Language Teaching and Research Press; Oxford: Oxford University Press, 1995.

Homer. *The Odyssey*. Trans. Walter Shewring. Beijing: Foreign Language Teaching and Research Press; Oxford: Oxford University Press, 1995.

Homer. *The Odyssey of Homer*. Trans. S. H. Butcher and A. Lang. The Harvard Classics. 22. New York: P. F. Collier & Son Company, 1909.

Howatson, M. C., and Ian Chilvers. *Oxford Dictionary of Classical Literature*. Shanghai: Shanghai Foreign Language Education Press, 2000.

Jones, Daniel. *Everyman's English Pronouncing Dictionary*. 12th ed. London: J. M. Dent & Sons Ltd; New York: E. P. Dutton & CO. INC., 1963.

Liddell, Henry George, and Robert Scott, comps. *A Greek-English Lexicon*. Oxford: Clarendon Press, 1996.

Morford, Mark P. O., and Robert J. Lenardon. *Classical Mythology*. 7th ed. New York and Oxford: Oxford University Press, 2003.

Ovid. *The Metamorphoses*. Trans. Horace Gregory. New York: Signet Classics, 2001.

Ovid. *Metamorphoses*. Trans. Frank Justus Miller. Cambridge, Massachusetts: Harvard University Press; London: William Heinemann Ltd., 1984.

Room, Adrian. *Who's Who in Classical Mythology*. Beijing: Foreign Language Teaching and Research Press. 2007.

Simpson, D. P. *Cassell's Latin Dictionary*. Hoboken, New Jersey: Wiley Publishing, Inc., 1997.

Virgil. *The Aeneid*. Ware: Wordsworth Classics, 1995.

Virgil. *Virgil's Aeneid*. Trans. John Dryden. The Harvard Classics. 13. New York: P. F. Collier & Son Company, 1909.

Virgil. *Virgil's Works*. Trans. J. W. Mackail. New York: The Modern Library, 1950.

Upton, Clive，William A. Kretzschmar, Jr.，and Rafal Konopka, Eds. *Oxford Dictionary of Pronunciation for Current English*. Beijing：Foreign Language Teaching and Research Press，2003.

鲍特文尼克,等. 神话词典[M]. 北京：商务印书馆,1985.

鲁刚,郑述谱. 希腊罗马神话词典[M].北京：中国社会科学出版社,1984.

雒玉玲. 希腊地图册[M]. 北京：中国地图出版社, 2010.

星球地图出版社. 世界地图册[M]. 北京：星球地图出版社,1998.

中国地图出版社. 意大利地图册[M]. 北京：中国地图出版社, 2008.